D1498347
DISC

Forecasting Non-stationary Economic Time Series

Zeuthen Lecture Book Series
Karl Gunnar Persson, editor

Modeling Bounded Rationality, Ariel Rubinstein

Forecasting Non-stationary Economic Time Series, Michael P. Clements and David F. Hendry

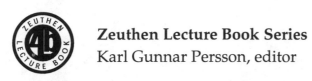

© 1999 Massachusetts Institute of Technology

All rights reserved. No part of this book may be reproduced in any form by any electronic or mechanical means (including photocopying, recording, or information storage and retrieval) without permission in writing from the publisher.

Library of Congress Cataloging-in-Publication Data

Clements, Michael P.
Forecasting non-stationary economic time series / Michael P. Clements and David F. Hendry.
p. cm.—(Zeuthen lecture book series)
Includes bibliographical references and index.
ISBN 0-262-03272-4 (hc.: alk. paper)
1. Time-series analysis. 2. Economic forecasting—Statistical methods.
I. Hendry, David F. II. Title. III. Series
HA30.3.C55 1999
330′.01′51955-dc21 99-22998

CIP

This book was set in Palatino and printed and bound in the United States of America.

[redacted]

Forecasting Non-stationary Economic Time Series

Michael P. Clements
and
David F. Hendry

The MIT Press
Cambridge, Massachusetts
London, England

[redacted]

To the Leverhulme Trust and the ESRC

"Because of the things we don't know we don't know, the future is largely unpredictable. But some developments can be anticipated, or at least imagined, on the basis of existing knowledge."

Maxine Singer, "Thoughts of a Nonmillenarian", *Bulletin of the American Academy of Arts and Sciences*, 1997 (**51**), 2, p39.

"The purpose of economics is, to a great extent, a practical one: to enable people to **forecast** or influence economic activity."

Frederik Zeuthen, *Economic Theory*, 1955, p5.

Contents

Figures

Tables

Series Foreword

The Zeuthen Lectures offer a forum for leading scholars to develop and synthesize novel results in theoretical and applied economics. They aim to present advances in knowledge in a form accessible to a wide audience of economists and advanced students of economics. The choice of topics will range from abstract theorizing to economic history. Regardless of the topic, the emphasis in the lecture series will be on originality and relevance. The Zeuthen Lectures are organized by the Institute of Economics, University of Copenhagen.

The lecture series is named after Frederik Zeuthen, a former professor at the Institute of Economics.

Karl Gunnar Persson

Foreword

Most people would agree that good forecasts are indispensable to influencing future activity. When it comes to defining a good forecast, views tend to be more diverse. Evidence of this is the large discrepancy between the way forecasting is treated in textbooks and the way it is practiced by professional forecasters.

Given its importance, it seems odd that forecasting has not always received the full attention it deserves among econometricians. We were therefore delighted when David Hendry of Nuffield College, Oxford University, agreed to lecture on the topic of forecasting for the 1997 Zeuthen lectures delivered at the Institute of Economics, University of Copenhagen. He is not only one of the world's leading econometricians with a wide experience of macroeconometric modeling, but in recent years has worked extensively with Michael Clements on the econometrics of forecasting.

In the previous book by the same authors, *Forecasting Economic Time Series*, the foundations for forecasting economic time series in a stationary world with no structural breaks were laid out. The present book brings the subject a huge step forward by addressing forecasting in a non-stationary world with structural breaks. Since the daily activities of professional forecasters take place in such a world, the book's practical relevance is likely to be high.

From the outset the authors make the important distinction between forecasting and predictability. The former is the process of making statements about the future, whereas the latter is the property that the conditional distribution of future values given the past depends on the past. This distinction is useful, since it facilitates the distinction between "extraordinary" future events which violate the probability formulation of the sample model, and "ordinary" future events, which are consistent with the probability formulation.

There are, however, many possible sources of forecast errors. A great merit of this book is the systematic treatment of these errors and the careful investigation of their importance in practical situations. A major finding is that forecast failure in the presence of structural breaks is crucially related to shifts in the deterministic terms in the model, in particular to shifts in the equilibrium mean. This finding is fundamental for understanding why intercept corrections and over-differencing have worked so well in practice when time series have been subject to structural shifts. It has also been crucial for the finding of new solutions, such as co-breaking and modeling intercept shifts.

I am convinced that econometricians will benefit greatly from the detailed theoretical framework of this book that allows important forecasting problems to be addressed and further developed. I am also convinced that professional forecasters will appreciate the practical orientation of this book in the sense that the theoretical arguments all through the text are underpinned by economic examples and Monte Carlo simulations.

In addition to the formalization of forecasting under structural nonstationarity, this book contains a multitude of surprising research results which make it a highly stimulating read. The reader realizes quickly that many conventional beliefs have to be reversed when structural shifts are introduced. For example: well-specified models do not necessarily outperform badly-specified models; causal models do not always outperform non-causal models; the practice of intercept corrections favored by practitioners, and often despised by theorists, is shown to have certain optimality properties. Finally, many results in the book have implications far beyond the topic of forecasting. For example: using forecasting performance as a criterion for policy model choice can be very misleading; and using model-based rational expectations in the presence of structural breaks can be theoretically flawed.

To conclude, Michael Clements and David Hendry have written a book that takes a huge step forward towards making economic forecasting both a useful, practical and relevant theoretical activity, in the spirit of Frederik Zeuthen.

Katarina Juselius
Institute of Economics
University of Copenhagen

Preface

This book is the second of our two volumes on macroeconomic forecasting. Their common objective is to provide a formal analysis of the models, procedures, and measures of economic forecasting with a view to improving forecasting practice. To reduce the present discrepancy between theory and practice (a problem also noted by statistical forecasters such as Fildes and Makridakis, 1995) it is necessary to develop a theory of economic forecasting under relatively weak assumptions. The first volume – the outcome of presenting the Marshall Lectures at Cambridge University in 1992 – set the scene for forecasting economic time series which could be described by (difference) stationary representations. This companion volume – the fruits of delivering the Zeuthen Lectures at Copenhagen University in 1997 – discusses forecasting in the presence of structural breaks and emphasizes the role of deterministic non-stationarities. Together, they seek to explain the occurrence of systematic mis-forecasting in economics. A third volume, analyzing open models (with "exogenous" variables), is in progress.

To help understand such recurrent episodes of forecast failure, the two volumes address the main issues facing a theory of macroeconomic forecasting based on empirical econometric models. Economies evolve and are subject to sudden shifts, precipitated by changes in legislation, economic policy, major discoveries, and political turmoil. Further, forecasting *models* are just that, and empirically, the extent of mis-specification of the model for the process generating the data is unknown, but probably large. The data series used may be inaccurate, prone to revision, and are often provided after a non-negligible delay. Since an imperfect tool is being used to forecast a complicated and changing process, we explore the implications of this state of affairs for the practice of economic forecasting. As noted in our first volume, conclusions which can be established formally for constant-parameter stationary processes forecast by correctly specified models often do not hold when such assumptions are relaxed: here we investigate what can be shown when models are mis-specified in unknown ways for non-stationary processes that are subject to structural breaks. Many of the predictions of the resulting theory have been examined both in specific empirical settings and via Monte Carlo simulations. The close concordance we generally obtained both confirms the feasibility of a theory of forecasting that allows for structural breaks in an economic mechanism for which the econometric model is mis-specified and shows that such a theory can provide a useful basis for interpreting, and potentially circumventing, systematic forecast failure in economics.

Although recent well-publicized debacles are transforming "economic forecasting" into a phrase akin to "military intelligence", our results are not in fact highly critical of current practices. Rather, we seek to understand and explain why some of those activities seem to work empirically despite receiving little formal support from "textbook" forecasting theory. This understanding leads us to suggest how improvements can be made. Our general criticism remains one of the dearth of formal research into the nature of macroeconomic forecasting, to rationalize both forecasting practices (such as intercept corrections) and outcomes (such as major forecast failures).

Initially, model specification and estimation held center stage: "good models, well estimated, and well tested" were expected to forecast well, whereas "poor" ones (e.g., failing residual diagnostic tests) should forecast badly. Such notions fell at the first hurdle: causal models could not be shown to dominate non-casual, even before any consideration of the adequacy of specification and estimation. Thus, "good" models may fail, while "poor" models need not. In the forecasting context, one may even question our epithets, but their importance is that the degree of data congruence or non-congruence of a model is neither necessary nor sufficient for forecasting success or failure. Our taxonomies of forecast errors highlighted the roles that changes in deterministic factors played in systematic forecast-error biases, and closer inspection revealed that the key role lay with shifts in "equilibrium means": their specification and estimation; modeling movements in them; the consequences of unanticipated changes in their values; corrections and updates to offset any such changes; and formulating models to avoid their impact – these are the topics that dominate the results in this book. We present experiments where all the parameters of a model change, but this is rarely detected when the equilibrium mean stays constant. Conversely, other changes of the same magnitude, which shift equilibrium means, are easily detected. We show stochastic mis-specifications that have little impact on forecast accuracy, whereas the corresponding deterministic mis-specifications have a pernicious effect. We find that intercept corrections and over-differencing can help attenuate the impacts of shifts in equilibrium means – hence their efficacy in forecasting. Congruent models that experience an equilibrium-mean shift may fail badly, but non-congruent models that track outcomes with a lag, and have no equilibrium mean, need not fail. Further illustrations are provided below.

It has been difficult to overcome the intuition that the goodness of specification and estimation of a model's (zero-mean) stochastic components is less important for forecasting than that of its deterministic elements, but the weight of theory and empirical evidence, strongly corroborated by some surprising Monte Carlo simulation findings, eventually convinced us. To draw on an analogy from Kuhn (1962), both aspects clearly matter in "normal forecasting", but the latter is dramatically more important during "forecasting debacles", and those come all too frequently in economics. Consequently, to explain the empirical evidence on economic forecasting performance, we focus on the deterministic elements of the story.

Our results on forecasting also have wider implications for the conduct of empirical econometric research, the formulation of models, testing economic hypotheses, and undertaking model-based policy analysis. For example, model simplification that narrows uncertainty about deterministic terms can improve forecasts. Further, forecast performance may be a misleading criterion for model choice – unless the sole objective is short-term forecasting – so model selection for other purposes should not be based on a consideration of forecast performance. For example, selecting the best forecasting model for economic-policy analysis may be inappropriate. We also establish that testing economic theories by whole-sample goodness of fit, say, could be misleading, for the same reason that "good" models may exhibit forecast failure. Since forecast failure may be occasioned by forecast-period events alone, there need be no possible within-sample tests indicative of later failure. Thus, comparisons between models in the forecasting arena may have little merit outside of it.

We have drawn extensively on our published papers: chapter 1 reviews material in Clements and Hendry (1998b); chapter 2 draws on Hendry and Doornik (1997); chapter 3 on Clements and Hendry (1997, 1998d) and Hendry and Clements (1998); chapter 5 on Clements and Hendry (1996b, 1998d) and Hendry and Clements (1998); chapter 6 on Clements and Hendry (1996b); chapter 7 on Clements and Hendry (1998a); chapter 8 on Clements and Hendry (1998d); chapter 10 on Clements and Krolzig (1998); and chapter 11 extends Clements and Hendry (1996b).

We are grateful to the following publishers for permission to draw on the material listed below.

Clements and Hendry (1996b), "Intercept Corrections and Structural Change", *Journal of Applied Econometrics*, **11**, 475–94, is used with permission of John Wiley and Sons Limited.

Permission to reproduce parts of Clements and Hendry (1997), "An Empirical Study of Seasonal Unit Roots in Forecasting", *International Journal of Forecasting*, **13**, 341–56, and Clements and Hendry (1998a), "Forecasting Economic Processes", *International Journal of Forecasting*, **14**, 111–31 was granted by Elsevier Science.

Permission was granted by the Scottish Economic Society to use material in Hendry and Doornik (1997), "The Implications for Econometric Modelling of Forecast Failure", *Scottish Journal of Political Economy*, **44**, 437–61.

Permission to reproduce parts of Clements and Krolzig (1998), "A Comparison of the Forecast Performance of Markov-switching and Threshold Autoregressive models of US GNP", *Econometrics Journal*, **1**, C44–75, was granted by Blackwell Publishers.

The National Institute for Economic and Social Research granted permission to draw on Hendry and Clements (1998), "Economic Forecasting in the Face of Structural Breaks", forthcoming in Holly, S. and Weale, M. (eds), *Econometric Modelling: Techniques and Applications*, Cambridge University Press.

Permission to use material from Clements and Hendry (1998d), "On Winning Forecasting Competitions in Economics" was granted by the *Spanish Economic Review.*

We are indebted to many colleagues and friends for their comments, discussions and criticisms of our ideas, and the various drafts of this book. In particular, we wish to thank: Sule Akkoyunlu, Manuel Arellano, Anindya Banerjee, Olympia Bover, Gunnar Bårdsen, Julia Campos, Jurgen Doornik, Rob Engle, Rebecca Emerson, Neil Ericsson, Tony Espasa, Clive Granger, Eilev Jansen, Søren Johansen, Katarina Juselius, Hans-Martin Krolzig, Massimiliano Marcellino, Grayham Mizon, John Muellbauer, Bent Nielsen, Jean-François Richard, Paul Ruud, Marianne Sensier, Neil Shephard, Timo Teräsvirta and Ken Wallis. We are also very grateful to Jurgen Doornik for his immense help in organizing the styles and computing background for the camera-ready production, especially the use of his excellent OxEdit and indexing programs. Also, Jurgen Doornik and Hans-Martin Krolzig kindly allowed us to draw extensively from Hendry and Doornik (1997) and Clements and Krolzig (1998).

The research reported in the book was generously financed by the United Kingdom Economic and Social Research Council, and we are delighted to acknowledge our gratitude for their sustained level of support over the last seven years, through the funding of *The Econometrics of Economic Policy* (R000233447), and *The Econometrics of Macroeconomic Forecasting* (L116251015). MPC records his gratitude to the Department of Economics, University of Warwick, for his appointment as a Research Fellow in Economics, and DFH is greatly indebted to Nuffield College, Oxford, as well as to the Leverhulme Trustees for the award of a Personal Research Professorship: together, these allowed us the time to undertake the research and write the book. We are also grateful to Cambridge and Copenhagen Universities for their stimulus to integrate the research resulting from their lecture-series invitations into monographs.

All the computations and graphics reported in this book were performed in the PcGive Professional suite of programs (see Doornik and Hendry, 1996, 1997 and Hendry and Doornik, 1996) or using the Gauss Programming Language 3.2., Aptech Systems, Washington. A demonstration version of GiveWin and PcGive can be found on the Web page:

http://www.nuff.ox.ac.uk/users/hendry/

Information on corrections will also be placed there.

Scientific Word (TCI Software Research, New Mexico) in combination with MikTEX and DVIPS eased the writing of the book in LaTEX.

Michael P. Clements and David F. Hendry, December 1998

Common Acronyms

AIC	Akaike information criterion
AR	autoregressive process
ARCH	autoregressive conditional heteroscedasticity
ARIMA	autoregressive integrated moving average
ARMA	autoregressive-moving average
BVAR	Bayesian vector autoregression
CE	conditional efficiency
CLI	composite leading indicator
CMC	contemporaneous mean co-breaking
DE	dynamic estimator (multi-step criterion minimization)
DF	Dickey–Fuller (distribution or statistic)
DGP	data-generation process
DHSY	Davidson, Hendry, Srba and Yeo (1978)
DS	difference stationary
DV	vector autoregression in first differences
DDV	vector autoregression in second differences
DW	Durbin–Watson statistic
EqCM	equilibrium-correction mechanism or model
EM	expectation maximization algorithm
ErCM	error-correction mechanism or model
FIML	full-information maximum likelihood
GARCH	generalized ARCH
GFESM	generalized forecast-error second-moment criterion
GNP	gross national product
I(0)	integrated of order 0
I(1)	integrated of order 1
IID	independent, identically distributed
IMA	integrated moving average
IV	instrumental variables
LM	Lagrange-multiplier test
LR	likelihood-ratio test
M1	narrow money (transactions)
MA	moving-average process
MAE	mean absolute error
MCSD	Monte Carlo standard deviation
MCSE	Monte Carlo standard error
MDS	martingale difference sequence

ML	maximum likelihood
MLE	maximum likelihood estimator
MSE	mean-square error
MMSFE	minimum mean-square forecast error
MSFE	mean-square forecast error
MS-AR	Markov-switching autoregressive model
RMSE	root mean-square forecast error
OLS	ordinary least squares
SC	Schwarz criterion
SETAR	self-exciting threshold autoregression
TMSFE	trace mean-square forecast error
TS	trend stationary
URF	unrestricted reduced form
VAR	vector autoregressive representation
VARMA	vector autoregressive moving-average representation
VEqCM	vector equilibrium correction mechanism or model

1 Economic Forecasting

Summary

This book addresses the problems confronting forecasting in economies subject to structural breaks. When an econometric model coincides with the mechanism generating the data in an unchanging world, the theory of economic forecasting is reasonably well developed. However, less is known about forecasting when model and mechanism differ in a non-stationary and changing world. Here, we review the results in Clements and Hendry (1998b) for economic time series that can be transformed to stationarity by differencing and cointegration, to set the scene for a more general development that allows for structural breaks. Thus, we consider the basic concepts, models, and measures that will underpin such an analysis of forecasting. Finally, we investigate the role of causal information in forecasting and demonstrate that its efficacy cannot be established, so non-causal variables may sometimes generate superior forecasts.

1.1 Introduction

A theory of economic forecasting applicable to time series which can be transformed to stationarity by differencing and cointegration is presented in Clements and Hendry (1998b). That theory allowed the econometric model to be mis-specified for the mechanism generating the data, with parameters estimated from data evidence. In such a setting, many useful results can be established about the statistical properties of forecasting procedures. However, a general theory of macroeconomic forecasting must also allow for other forms of non-stationarity, including processes that are subject to intermittent structural breaks. That crucial generalization was only discussed tangentially in our earlier book. This volume extends the analysis to address the problems confronting forecasting in economies which are subject to structural breaks, and thereby reveals many important differences from the results that obtain when there are no structural breaks.

The analysis commences in §1.2 by reviewing the situation where the econometric model in use coincides with the process that generated the data. The optimality of forecasting based on conditional expectations (in terms of bias and mean-square forecast error) is discussed, and important practical difficulties are noted. Section 1.3 summarizes the main results from Clements and Hendry (1998b).[1] Since much of the formal background remains pertinent, the rest of the chapter expands on the topics summarized: this also serves to introduce our notation. Thus, §1.4 reconsiders the basic concepts needed to develop the analysis of forecasting when the model and data generation process (DGP) differ. The notions of (un)predictable and forecastable are discussed: despite their close usage, these concepts differ substantively since the former is a property of random variables relative to available information, whereas forecasting is a procedure in which statements are made about future events.

Section 1.5 describes a framework for forecasting integrated-cointegrated variables using vector autoregressions. The measurement of forecast accuracy is considered in §1.6, highlighting that evaluation may be dependent on the transformations examined for vector processes, or when forecasting more than 1-step ahead; that section focuses on the invariance, or otherwise, of putative accuracy measures to isomorphic representations of the model. In §1.7, we deduce the implications for causal information when forecasting, and the marked changes that occur in provable results if there are structural breaks. Specifically, non-causal variables may outperform in forecasting when

[1] This reviewed and extended research reported in Clements and Hendry (1993, 1994, 1995a, 1995b, 1996a) and Hendry and Clements (1994a, 1994b)

the model and mechanism differ in a world subject to structural breaks. An example shows the potential importance in forecasting of excluding irrelevant, but changing, effects, a precursor to clarifying the role of parsimony in modeling.

Given this background, the book then analyses in detail the potential sources of forecast failure, and discusses some possible solutions.

1.2 Background

The theory of economic forecasting is reasonably well developed under the assumption that the econometric model coincides with the mechanism generating the data in a (difference) stationary world: see, for example, Klein (1971) and Granger and Newbold (1986). We focus on closed systems, that is, ones which endogenize all the variables needed for forecasting (other than deterministic terms). Thus, we do not address policy issues (see, e.g., Banerjee, Hendry and Mizon, 1996, and Hendry and Mizon, 1998c).

Consider an n-dimensional stochastic process $\mathbf{x}_t$, which is a function of past information $\mathbf{X}_{t-1} = (\ldots \mathbf{x}_1 \ldots \mathbf{x}_{t-1})$, with density $\mathsf{D}_{\mathbf{x}_t}(\mathbf{x}_t|\mathbf{X}_{t-1}, \boldsymbol{\theta})$ for $\boldsymbol{\theta} \in \boldsymbol{\Theta} \subseteq \mathbb{R}^k$. A statistical forecast $\widetilde{\mathbf{x}}_{T+h}$ for horizon $T+h$, conditional on information up to period T is given by $\widetilde{\mathbf{x}}_{T+h} = \mathbf{f}_T(\mathbf{X}_T)$, where $\mathbf{f}_T(\cdot)$ reflects that an estimate of $\boldsymbol{\theta}$ may be needed, using data prior to forecasting. There are many possible choices for $\mathbf{f}_T(\cdot)$. Forecasts calculated as the conditional expectation:

$$\widehat{\mathbf{x}}_{T+h} = \mathsf{E}[\mathbf{x}_{T+h} \mid \mathbf{X}_T], \tag{1.1}$$

are conditionally unbiased:

$$\mathsf{E}\left[\mathbf{x}_{T+h} - \widehat{\mathbf{x}}_{T+h} \mid \mathbf{X}_T\right] = \mathsf{E}\left[\mathbf{x}_{T+h} \mid \mathbf{X}_T\right] - \mathsf{E}\left[\mathbf{x}_{T+h} \mid \mathbf{X}_T\right] = \mathbf{0}, \tag{1.2}$$

and no other predictor conditional on only $\mathbf{X}_T$ has a smaller mean-square forecast error (MSFE) matrix:

$$\mathsf{M}\left[\widehat{\mathbf{x}}_{T+h} \mid \mathbf{X}_T\right] = \mathsf{E}\left[\left(\mathbf{x}_{T+h} - \widehat{\mathbf{x}}_{T+h}\right)\left(\mathbf{x}_{T+h} - \widehat{\mathbf{x}}_{T+h}\right)' \mid \mathbf{X}_T\right]. \tag{1.3}$$

Moreover, both (1.2) and (1.3) hold for all h. In that sense, selecting the conditional expectation for $\widetilde{\mathbf{x}}_{T+h}$ is optimal.

However, the practical application of this result faces considerable difficulty. First, such a formulation ignores the need to choose which variables are included in $\mathbf{x}_t$, although this is a key determinant of the accuracy and precision of the resulting forecasts – even supposing the conditional expectation of the selection could be calculated. This is an issue of forecast-error dominance – one choice of the components in $\mathbf{x}_t$ delivering a "smaller" MSFE matrix than another – not of forecast failure, namely the forecast errors being systematically biased and having a forecast-period MSFE matrix greatly in excess of the in-sample equivalent. Further, in economics, all models are mis-specified for the mechanism in unknown ways. For example, inappropriate data transformations may have been used, incorrect parameter restrictions imposed, and invalid conditioning assumptions made, among many other possible problems. In such a setting, the mean forecast from the model is not the conditional expectation, and may prove a poor approximation thereto. Next, the estimation of unknown parameters increases the uncertainty inherent in forecasts due to the vagaries of sampling. Indeed, empirical econometric models are invariably constructed in the light of data evidence, which introduces potential selection biases. Further, the available data are measured with error, and subject to revision, so $\mathbf{X}_T$ is not even known when the forecasts are to be calculated. Together, these problems can be summarized in terms of (1.1) as not knowing what $\mathbf{X}_T$ comprises, nor how it influences the conditional expectations operator.

An even more serious problem is that economies are manifestly non-stationary for many reasons, and in particular, are subject to unanticipated structural breaks: the mechanism to be forecast is changing. At an anecdotal level, this is apparent from recurrent episodes of forecast failure, and has been documented more formally. For example, Stock and Watson (1996) find that structural instability pervades the 76 representative Post War US macroeconomic time series they consider, and the 5,700 bivariate forecasting relations that exist between those series.[2] Thus it would appear to be extremely difficult to correctly model the underlying processes when there are breaks, and the costs of failing to do so can be large. In terms of (1.1), $\mathsf{E}[\cdot|\cdot]$ itself is time dependent, and we do not know the operator applicable to the time periods we wish to forecast. Finally, depending on the objectives of forecasting, MSFE may or may not be a sensible criterion.

[2] As Hendry (1988) proves, and Stock and Watson (1996, p. 22-3) note, instability in bivariate VARs implies instability in larger VARs.

Consequently, the results in (1.1)–(1.3) do not provide a basis for a relevant theory of forecasting. Rather little is known about forecasting in non-stationary economies subject to structural breaks. A detailed treatment of forecasting in such a setting required further development than was possible in Clements and Hendry (1998b), and is presented in a unified framework in this volume. Despite the lack of strong and specific assumptions about the relation between the forecasting model and the evolving mechanism, many useful insights can be derived, albeit that these are usually articulated in special cases below.

There are many ways to make economic forecasts, including guessing; informal models; extrapolation; leading indicators; surveys; time-series models; and econometric systems. To focus on statistical forecasting, we will not consider the first three. Leading indicators were discussed in Clements and Hendry (1998b, ch. 9), based on Emerson and Hendry (1996). Scalar time-series models include Kalman (1960) and Box and Jenkins (1976), with the latter's autoregressive integrated moving-average models (ARIMAs) being a dominant class, based on the Wold decomposition theorem (see Wold, 1938: any purely non-deterministic stationary time series can be expressed as an infinite moving average; Cox and Miller, 1965, p.286–8, provide a lucid discussion). Also see Harvey (1989) and Harvey and Shephard (1992) for a related model class. The most common multivariate time-series class is the vector autoregression (VAR): see e.g., Doan, Litterman and Sims (1984). Although originally formulated for stationary processes, Johansen (1988) provides the generalization to integrated-cointegrated data.

The final class comprises econometric models of multivariate time-series. These serve a number of related goals besides providing forecasts, such as: consolidating empirical and theoretical knowledge of how economies function; providing a framework for a progressive research strategy; helping to explain their own failures; and providing a consistent framework for policy analysis and the interpretation of data measurements at the forecast origin. It is, therefore, natural to consider how well econometric models may be expected to forecast. While such systems form the focus of the book, it will soon become apparent that our understanding of how well econometric-model forecasts can be expected to fare is enhanced by also analyzing the forecast performance of time-series models.

The success of model-based forecasts depends upon:

(a) there being regularities to be captured;
(b) such regularities being informative about the future;
(c) the proposed method capturing those regularities; and:
(d) excluding non-regularities that swamp the regularities.

The first two are characteristics of the economic system; the last two of the forecasting method. The history of economic forecasting in the UK suggests that there are some regularities informative about future events, but also major irregularities as well (see e.g., Burns, 1986, Wallis, 1989, Pain and Britton, 1992, and Cook, 1995). The dynamic integrated systems with intermittent structural breaks that are formalized below seem consistent with such evidence. However, in such an environment, achieving (c) without suffering from (d) is difficult, and motivates the conceptual structure proposed below, as well as the emphasis on issues such as parsimony and collinearity (ch. 4), and the re-examination of the role of causal information when forecasting models are mis-specified.

Several results that can be established for correctly-specified models of stationary processes transpire to be misleading once model mis-specification interacts with non-stationary data (denoting thereby the general sense of processes whose first two moments are not constant over time). Conversely, it becomes feasible to account for the empirical success of procedures that difference data (see, e.g., Eitrheim, Husebø and Nymoen, 1997), or use intercept corrections (see e.g., Theil, 1961, Klein, 1971, Wallis and Whitley, 1991, and ch. 5), although these methods have no rationale when models are correctly specified. Potential improvements also merit investigation, so co-breaking is considered (ch. 9), and shown to clarify some of the problems experienced with leading indicators. Chapter 10 investigates attempts to model structural changes.

There are several related lines of research. Fildes and Makridakis (1995) and others have noted anomalies between the outcomes of empirical-accuracy studies of univariate time-series forecasting methods, and a statistical paradigm of theoretical time-series analysis (see, e.g., Box and Jenkins, 1976, and compare Fildes and Makridakis, 1995). Essentially, the forecasting methods that appear to work empirically in forecasting competitions are not those which would have been predicted by statistical theory, and Fildes and Makridakis (1995) suggest that the most serious culprit is the assumption of constancy which underpins that paradigm: this matches the importance we attribute to structural breaks. Next, the "dynamic linear models" of West and Harrison (1989) (see Pole, West and Harrison, 1994, for applications) put parameter non-constancy centre stage. Conceptually the difference in approach does not seem to lie in their allowing the parameters of the observation (measurement) equation to evolve according to a system (transition) equation, since the latter becomes the constant-parameter basis, but in interventions based on continuous monitoring of forecast performance: the adequacy of the model is questioned when the latest observations lie in a tail of the forecast distribution, possibly leading to a subjective intervention. In practice, "time-varying parameter" (TVP) models based on Kalman filtering could prove either a useful complement to, or even substitute for, the methods of robustifying forecasts to structural change that we propose, and more work needs to be done in this area.

Finally, allowing for an unknown mis-match between the model and the intermittently-changing process to be forecast derives from the need to develop an empirically-relevant forecasting theory. As noted, we wish to explain the success in forecasting of practices, such as intercept-corrections and double-differenced predictors, whose rationale is far from obvious given (1.1)–(1.3). Most importantly, we want to explain why forecast failure is prevalent in economics. This issue has profound methodological implications for the econometric enterprise, related to historical concerns about the autonomy or invariance of econometric equations (see, *inter alia*, Frisch, 1934, Keynes, 1939, Haavelmo, 1944, Wold and Juréen, 1953, Lucas, 1976, and Hendry, 1995b). If in-sample model mis-specification *per se*, or data-based model-selection, are the culprits, then designing congruent data representations could be questioned. Alternatively, if poor estimation strategies, or incorrect calculation of prediction intervals explained the observed failures, then improved technique could pay dividends. Should the parameters of macro-econometric systems transpire to depend critically on policy-regime changes, then different types of model class may be required, perhaps centered on so called "rational expectations" (see Muth, 1961). However, if the causes lie in structural breaks due to unanticipated changes in legislation, discoveries, financial innovations, and so on, the existing classes of models may be useful, but require modification in how they are used for generating forecasts. Our framework allows these issues to be studied, and suggests that the last is the main explanation for systematic forecast failure. Thus, congruent models continue to provide useful in-sample tools, despite the abundant evidence of changes in economies; forecast failure becomes an indicator of such changes, not grounds for dismissing models; new approaches to using models in forecasting need to be developed to mitigate the potential consequences of structural breaks; and a progressive research strategy, learning from past mistakes, becomes imperative.

1.3 Forecasting Economic Time Series

Since we both draw on, and extend, the analysis in our earlier book, *Forecasting Economic Time Series*, (Clements and Hendry, 1998b), its contents are now outlined under sub-headings that roughly coincide with our earlier treatment. The review summarizes results when forecasting in processes that are reducible to stationarity by differencing and cointegration, although it cannot substitute for a careful reading of the book. Aspects essential to forecasting in non-stationary time series are developed later.

1.3.1 Predictability and forecastability

We distinguished between (un)predictability and (un)forecastability, recognizing that the two concepts are commonly used interchangeably (§1.4 provides formal definitions). Unpredictability refers to the relationship between a random variable and an information set – a variable is unpredictable if the conditional distribution (given that information set) coincides with the unconditional distribution. Predictability is necessary but not sufficient for forecastability: latter requires both a systematic relationship, and knowledge of the form of the conditional density, namely, how the information set enters the data-generation process (DGP). Thus, although the conditional expectation delivers the minimum mean-square forecast error (MSFE), its optimality properties are not a useful basis for forecasting when the form of the conditional expectation is both unknown and changing over time. Indeed, we also established that non-causal variables may outperform in forecasting relative to (previously) causally-relevant variables when the model is mis-specified for the DGP, and the DGP undergoes structural breaks. We review that result below, given its importance in explaining the roles of practical procedures that would otherwise seem unjustifiable. Since a mis-specified model of a non-constant DGP is undoubtedly common in economics, we see that forecasting with an empirical model is fundamentally different from forecasting using the DGP.

While it may seem obvious that we cannot forecast the unpredictable, nevertheless that theme permeates this volume: more aspects of reality are unpredictable than just the stochastic errors on postulated equations and their estimated parameters, which is all that forecast-error variance formulae usually reflect. Rather, the regular occurrence of forecast failure reveals that other unanticipated changes do occur over the forecast horizon.

1.3.2 Assessing forecast accuracy

Forecast-accuracy assessment requires an agreed metric. In any given context, the costs of making various forecast errors may be well defined (e.g., profits foregone), but the multi-purpose nature of macroeconomic forecasting has led to MSFE-based measures being the dominant criteria for assessing accuracy. However, for multi-step forecasts or multivariate models, such measures are not invariant to non-singular, scale-preserving, linear transforms, even though linear models are. Further, unpredictability is not invariant under intertemporal transforms, so uniquely acceptable measures of predictability do not exist. Consequently, different rankings across models or methods can be obtained from various measures by choosing alternative, yet isomorphic, representations of a given model. Thus, MSFE rankings can be an artefact of the transformation selected. A generalized forecast-error second moment criterion (denoted GFESM) is invariant, but cannot resolve all problems relating to model choice across different forecast horizons, especially since the objectives of forecasters differ. Although it is desirable that forecasts be unbiased and efficient, in practice, performance relative to rival forecasts determines the worth of any forecasting procedure.

1.3.3 *Time-series properties of the variables*

Both stationary and non-stationary (integrated of order one – I(1)) processes were considered, where the latter could be made stationary by differencing, and the former were stationary around a deterministic polynomial of time. We defined forecasts, forecast errors, forecast-error variances, and prediction intervals (often called forecast-confidence intervals), and made explicit the distinction between conditional and unconditional forecasts. The impact of parameter estimation uncertainty was also analyzed.

We found that forecasts and prediction intervals derived from linear autoregressive models depended crucially on the time-series properties of the variables. In practice, it may be difficult to discriminate between a trend-stationary and difference-stationary DGP in-sample, although their implications for how accurately the process can be forecast are different. For UK Net National Income (denoted Y) over 1870–1993 (data from Friedman and Schwartz, 1982, and Attfield, Demery and Duck, 1995), we compare a random-walk model for $y = \log Y$:

$$y_t = \gamma + y_{t-1} + e_t, \tag{1.4}$$

where γ is the average growth rate, with the linear trend model:

$$y_t = \alpha + \gamma t + v_t, \quad \text{where } v_t = \rho v_{t-1} + \varepsilon_t \tag{1.5}$$

so $\{v_t\}$ is "corrected" for first-order residual serial correlation. The whole-sample residual standard deviations ($\widehat{\sigma}$) of 3.4% and 3.3% are close, and the reduction of (1.5) to (1.4) is insignificant at conventional levels, with $\chi^2(2) = 5.3$.

Figure 1.1 illustrates the forecasts.[3] Panels a and b are based on (1.4), whereas c and d are for (1.5); the columns show forecasts over 1889–1993 and 1899–1993 respectively, based only on information prior to the forecast origin. Using the conventionally-calculated formulae (assuming white-noise errors and efficiently-estimated, constant, parameters: see §4.3.1), "95% prediction intervals" are shown as bands around these multi-step forecasts.

Whilst the two models are statistically indistinguishable – parametric restrictions implied in going from (1.5) to (1.4) are not rejected –

---

[3] 2×2 panels of graphs are labelled $\begin{bmatrix} a & b \\ c & d \end{bmatrix}$.

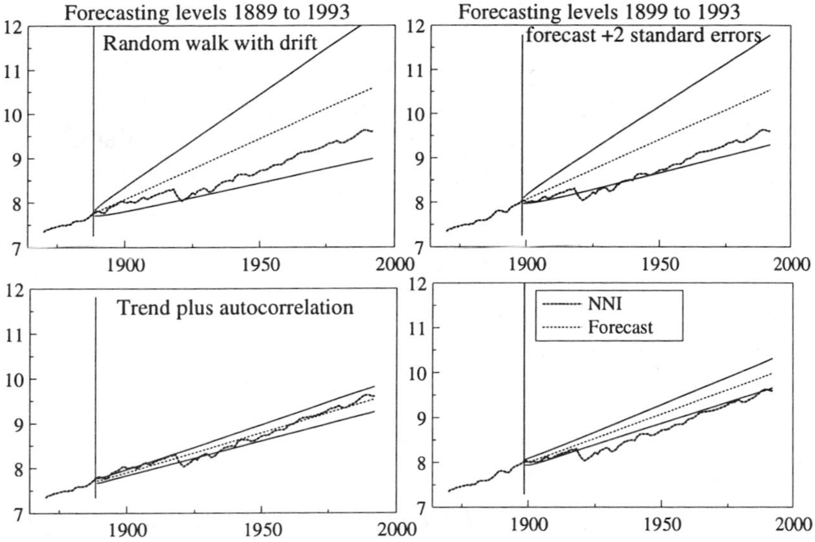

Figure 1.1
Long-horizon forecasts of UK Net National Income.

comparisons in fig. 1.1 between rows show the much larger prediction uncertainties calculated from (1.4), as well as its absolutely lower accuracy; but comparisons across columns show that those from (1.5) seriously overstate precision, since the second-column forecasts systematically lie outside its "95% prediction intervals". Thus, panel d reveals forecast failure , despite dominating b.[4] We therefore reconsidered the notion of "the limit to forecastability" namely, the horizon up to which forecasts are informative. Section 1.6 will compare these two models in terms of forecasting growth rates, rather than levels.

1.3.4 ARCH, asymmetric loss, and non-linearity

Next, we discussed the impact of autoregressive-conditional heteroscedasticity (ARCH) on prediction intervals, and point predictions for asymmetric loss functions. False rejection of forecasting models can occur when the former is ignored, and the latter reveals that biased forecasts need not be "irrational".

[4] Such long-horizon forecasts are merely illustrative: e.g., Stock (1996) demonstrates the technical difficulties – even ignoring the two (unpredicted) world wars.

We also considered forecasting in non-linear models, focusing on two classes of non-linear model, SETAR (self-exciting threshold autoregression) and MS-AR (Markov-switching autoregression), which have been used to model (univariate) economic time series. The SETAR model is an example of a piece-wise linear model, in that the model is linear within a regime but moves between regimes depending upon the realized value of the process a number of periods previously. The MS-AR model is also linear conditional upon the regime that the process is in, but now the regime-determining variable is an unobservable, assumed to follow a Markov chain. While such models possess some attractive features in terms of characterizing the history of the process, their forecast performance was not clearly superior.

1.3.5 *Simulation methods*

Since stochastic simulation and Monte Carlo are used extensively in econometrics, we discussed their applications to forecasting. Examples included obtaining small-sample distributions of estimators and tests, deriving approximations to finite-sample biases, and obtaining empirical distributions of tests statistics under both null and alternative hypotheses. We reviewed "sophisticated" Monte Carlo techniques such as control variables and antithetic variates, and thereby showed that when error distributions are symmetric, unbiased forecasts may result even when the parameter estimates are biased in the models from which forecasts are generated.

1.3.6 *Forecasting in cointegrated systems*

Forecasting with systems of integrated variables is a non-trivial extension of the univariate analysis of forecasting with an integrated variable because of cointegration, whereby a linear combination of individually-integrated variables may be non-integrated (I(0)). We established representations of integrated-cointegrated systems relevant for forecasting, derived asymptotic forecast-error variances for multi-step forecasts (which transpired to be useful guides to the finite-sample outcomes even in cointegrated I(1) systems), and addressed the implications for forecast accuracy of small-sample parameter estimation uncertainty. In bivariate systems, imposing too few cointegration vectors seemed to impose greater costs in forecast accuracy than including levels terms which did not cointegrate. Why this might be the case can be seen once we abstract from parameter estimation uncertainty, and compare forecasts from a correctly-specified model with those from a model specified solely in differences (denoted the DV model).

Figure 1.2 (reproduced from Clements and Hendry, 1998b) plots the ratio of the trace MSFE (TMSFE) for the DV to that for the correctly-specified model (vertical axis), over a 1 to 20-step ahead forecast horizon (horizontal axis). The models are compared in terms of their ability to predict the levels of the variables, their first-differences, and a cointegrating combination. It is apparent that forecast gains to imposing cointegration depend on the transformation selected, and moreover, for levels and differences evaluation, gains to imposing cointegration are greater at short, rather than long, horizons. In fact, whether cointegration is imposed or not makes no difference to the rate at which the MSFEs (or prediction intervals) increase in the forecast horizon. For the levels of the variables, these rates are $O(h)$ in the horizon, h, and for the differences and cointegrating combination, they are $O(1)$, for both models.

The GFESM unambiguously indicates gains to imposing cointegration. However, when breaks occur, differencing may play a robustifying role, potentially reversing the empirical implications in favor of retaining too few cointegration vectors.

1.3.7 Intercept corrections

Forecasts from large-scale macro-econometric models often embody adjustments by their proprietors. The value-added of such adjustments has long been recognized. We outlined a general framework for analyzing adjustments typically made to model-based forecasts, based on the relationships between the DGP, the estimated econometric model, the mechanics of the forecasting technique, the data accuracy, and any information about future events known at the beginning of the forecast period. This suggested various rationales for intercept corrections. Intercept corrections were shown to offer some protection against structural breaks, an issue of importance in the present book.

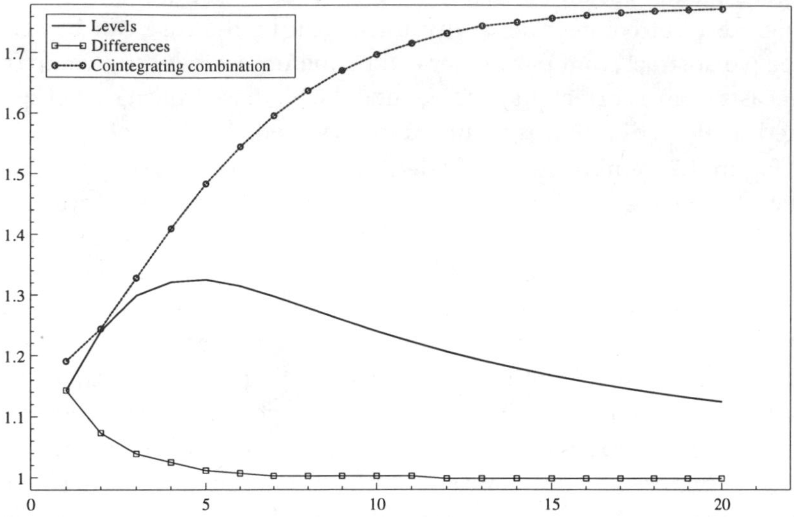

Figure 1.2
Ratio of TMSFEof the DV model to the correctly specified case.

1.3.8 *A taxonomy of forecast errors*

The framework for analyzing forecasts from large-scale macro-econometric models suggested an extended taxonomy of forecast errors, where forecast errors were decomposed into five major categories: parameter non-constancy, model mis-specification, sampling variability, variable mis-measurement, and error uncertainty. The sources of forecast error from this taxonomy dovetailed withseveral rationales for intercept corrections. The body of evidence we amassed flagged parameter change as the prime culprit for most of the more dramatic episodes of forecast failure, and that issue forms the focus of this book. Other sources of forecast error, such as model mis-specification, and parameter estimation uncertainty in an unchanged environment, seem unable to account for the observed extent of forecast failure.

1.3.9 *Leading indicators*

Leading-indicator systems are altered sufficiently frequently to suggest they do not systematically lead for long. A framework was proposed for index analysis, and applied to the UK longer-leading indicator. The effects of adding composite leading indicators (CLIs) to macro models were considered theoretically and empirically, and our evidence confirmed that CLIs are at best an adjunct to, and not a substitute for, econometric modeling. Indeed, since economic relationships alter, and it seems unlikely that non-causal relations will systematically exhibit co-breaking (whereby breaks in individual series cancel using appropriate linear combinations), we believe econometric modeling is the dominant strategy. We extend the results on co-breaking in this volume. Although it is impossible to prove that causal information is superior to non-causal information when the model is mis-specified for the DGP and the DGP is non-constant, a case can be made for causal information on the grounds of capturing persistent relationships between variables: co-breaking on a systematic basis must depend on such causal links.

1.3.10 *Forecast combination*

A combination of forecasts may be superior (on MSFE) to each of the constituents. However, forecast combination runs counter to encompassing: a test for forecast encompassing is the same as that for whether there is any benefit to combination. When models do not draw on a common information pool, so are of an essentially different type, or are differentially susceptible to structural breaks, then a case can be made for combination. Nevertheless, if the aim of an econometric modeling exercise is discovering forecasting models that can be reliably used to forecast on an ongoing basis, then combination is only a stop-gap measure. We return to combination ideas below, but in the context of systems with structural breaks, where the weights to be used for any proposed combination may differ from those conventionally proposed.

1.3.11 *Multi-step estimation*

We also evaluated multi-step (or dynamic) estimation (DE) strategies. When a model is mis-specified, minimization of 1-step in-sample errors may be reasonable for forecasting 1-step ahead, but there is no guarantee that it will deliver reliable forecasts at longer lead times. One-step error minimization can only be shown to be optimal for multi-step ahead forecasting in general when the model coincides with the

DGP. Otherwise estimation by minimizing the in-sample counterpart of the desired step-ahead horizon may be advantageous. We showed that although model mis-specification is necessary, it is not sufficient to justify DE. Moreover, DE can alter the implicit model class across horizons. Conversely, any change in the preferred model as the forecast horizon alters entails mis-specification of all the models under consideration. Thus, DE may accommodate incorrectly-specified models as the forecast lead alters, improving forecast performance for some mis-specifications, but in stationary processes, the gains typically fade rapidly in the forecast horizon. When the process contains unit roots, then unmodeled MA errors, with large negative correlations, will tend to exacerbate the downward bias of OLS, and a Monte Carlo showed somewhat improved forecast accuracy from DE in this instance. However, solutions other than DE exist for this problem. The Monte Carlo indicated a relatively small impact of parameter-estimation uncertainty on forecast-error distributions. A drawback of DE is its lack of invariance to linear transformations, so different decisions could result for levels versus first differences.

1.3.12 Parsimony

Many forecasters believe that parsimony is important for multi-step forecast accuracy, despite the lack of a general theory other than model-selection criteria. We considered the decision as to whether to retain a variable in a forecasting model for forecasts at each horizon, and related this decision to the value of a t-test for the coefficient on that variable being zero, thereby clarifing the non-monotonic forecast-confidence intervals reported by Chong and Hendry (1986). However, that result did not generalize usefully to vector processes, since powers of a matrix can greatly affect the importance of individual elements. We also established that collinearity between regressors could not justify parsimony in stationary processes, but here we will emphasize its role in systems which are subject to structural breaks, as well as reconsider the theory of parsimony in such processes. For example, Box–Jenkins methods might outperform econometric models in forecasting, even when the latter are the DGP within sample, by imposing differences so that unknown shifts in means become blips, and robustness is thereby achieved (see Clements and Hendry, 1996b). Such results suggest a "forecasting *versus* policy" dilemma: the econometric model provides the better guide to policy, but may not forecast as well as a "robustified" extrapolative predictor.

1.3.13 *Testing predictive failure*

Finally, we discussed tests of predictive failure based on 1-step forecast errors, which, as a consequence, are invariant to linear transformations, in contrast to multi-period forecast accuracy comparisons based on MSFE-measures. Such "structural stability" was tested by checking whether a model was constant across different sub-samples, or whether estimates over one period provided adequate ex post forecasts over a subsequent period. We also considered tests of equal forecast accuracy between rival sequences of forecasts.

Thus, the previous book discussed many aspects of economic forecasting in processes that were reducible to stationarity after differencing or cointegration transforms. It explicitly allowed for the forecasting model to be a mis-specified representation of the data-generation process, and for the evaluation of forecast accuracy by MSFEs to depend on which isomorphic form of the model was used. In this book, we extend the analyses to processes that are subject to structural breaks, where many results change radically. First, we review some of the essential background elements more formally.

1.4 Concepts

In this section, we formally define the predictability of a stochastic process relative to the available information, and the resulting forecastability of the series, then draw some implications.

1.4.1 *Unpredictability*

$\{\nu_t\}$ is an unpredictable process with respect to an information set $\mathcal{I}_{t-1}$ if:

$$\mathsf{D}_{\nu_t}(\nu_t \mid \mathcal{I}_{t-1}) = \mathsf{D}_{\nu_t}(\nu_t), \tag{1.6}$$

so the conditional and unconditional distributions coincide.[5] Unpredictability is invariant under non-singular contemporaneous transforms: for example, if $\boldsymbol{\nu}_t$ is unpredictable, so is $\mathbf{B}\boldsymbol{\nu}_t$ where $|\mathbf{B}| \neq 0$. However, unpredictability is not invariant under intertemporal transforms since if $\mathbf{u}_t = \boldsymbol{\nu}_t + \mathbf{Ah}(\mathcal{I}_{t-1})$:

$$\mathsf{D}_{\mathbf{u}_t}(\mathbf{u}_t \mid \mathcal{I}_{t-1}) \neq \mathsf{D}_{\mathbf{u}_t}(\mathbf{u}_t),$$

when $\mathbf{Ah}(\cdot) \neq \mathbf{0}$. The concept resolves the apparent "paradox" that (e.g.) although the change in the log of real equity prices may be unpredictable, the level is predictable: since $x_t = \Delta x_t + x_{t-1}$, the "prediction" of the current level is merely its immediate past value. Below, we assume that when the time series $\mathbf{x}_t$ is of interest, the information set $\mathcal{I}_{t-1}$ includes at least the history of $\mathbf{x}_t$. When $\mathbf{x}_t = \boldsymbol{\nu}_t$, therefore, $\mathbf{x}_t$ must be an innovation, and (weak) white noise when its second moment exists.

Unpredictability is relative to the information set used, since it can happen that when $\mathcal{J}_{t-1} \subset \mathcal{I}_{t-1}$:

$$\mathsf{D}_{\mathbf{u}_t}(\mathbf{u}_t \mid \mathcal{J}_{t-1}) = \mathsf{D}_{\mathbf{u}_t}(\mathbf{u}_t) \quad \text{whereas} \quad \mathsf{D}_{\mathbf{u}_t}(\mathbf{u}_t \mid \mathcal{I}_{t-1}) \neq \mathsf{D}_{\mathbf{u}_t}(\mathbf{u}_t).$$

However, $\mathcal{J}_{t-1} \subset \mathcal{I}_{t-1}$ does not preclude predictability. Unpredictability may also be relative to the time period, since it is possible to have:

$$\mathsf{D}_{\mathbf{u}_t}(\mathbf{u}_t \mid \mathcal{I}_{t-1}) = \mathsf{D}_{\mathbf{u}_t}(\mathbf{u}_t) \quad \text{for} \quad t = 1, \ldots, T \tag{1.7}$$

whereas:

$$\mathsf{D}_{\mathbf{u}_t}(\mathbf{u}_t \mid \mathcal{I}_{t-1}) \neq \mathsf{D}_{\mathbf{u}_t}(\mathbf{u}_t) \quad \text{for} \quad t = T+1, \ldots, T+H, \tag{1.8}$$

or vice versa. Finally, unpredictability may be relative to the horizon considered in that:

$$\mathsf{D}_{\mathbf{u}_t}(\mathbf{u}_t \mid \mathcal{I}_{t-2}) = \mathsf{D}_{\mathbf{u}_t}(\mathbf{u}_t) \quad \text{whereas} \quad \mathsf{D}_{\mathbf{u}_t}(\mathbf{u}_t \mid \mathcal{I}_{t-1}) \neq \mathsf{D}_{\mathbf{u}_t}(\mathbf{u}_t). \tag{1.9}$$

The converse, that:

$$\mathsf{D}_{\mathbf{u}_t}(\mathbf{u}_t \mid \mathcal{I}_{t-1}) = \mathsf{D}_{\mathbf{u}_t}(\mathbf{u}_t) \quad \text{whereas} \quad \mathsf{D}_{\mathbf{u}_t}(\mathbf{u}_t \mid \mathcal{I}_{t-2}) \neq \mathsf{D}_{\mathbf{u}_t}(\mathbf{u}_t), \tag{1.10}$$

is not possible because $\mathcal{I}_{t-2} \subseteq \mathcal{I}_{t-1}$ by definition.

[5]This definition is equivalent to the statistical independence of $\boldsymbol{\nu}_t$ from $\mathcal{I}_{t-1}$ and does not connote "wild": indeed, knowing $\mathsf{D}_{\nu_t}(\boldsymbol{\nu}_t)$ may be highly informative relative to not knowing it.

Sequential factorization of the joint density of $\mathbf{X}_T^1$ yields the prediction representation:

$$\mathsf{D}_{\mathsf{X}}\left(\mathbf{X}_T^1 \mid \mathcal{I}_0, \cdot\right) = \prod_{t=1}^{T} \mathsf{D}_{\mathsf{x}_t}\left(\mathbf{x}_t \mid \mathcal{I}_{t-1}, \cdot\right). \tag{1.11}$$

The deviation ϵ_t from the conditional mean of (1.11):

$$\epsilon_t = \mathbf{x}_t - \mathsf{E}\left[\mathbf{x}_t \mid \mathcal{I}_{t-1}\right],$$

is unpredictable in mean (see §1.4.2). Consequently, predictability requires combinations with $\mathcal{I}_{t-1}$: the "causes" must be in train. Such causes need not be direct, and could be very indirect: for example, a variable's own lags may "capture" actual past causes. Thus, when the relevant $\mathcal{I}_{t-1}$ is known, structure is not necessary for forecasting, even under changed conditions. Unfortunately, that $\mathcal{I}_{t-1}$ is known is most unlikely in economics, with important implications for understanding why *ad hoc* methods can work well, as seen below.

1.4.2 Moments

Forecasting tends to focus on first and second moments, assuming these exist. Then, $\boldsymbol{\nu}_t$ is unpredictable in mean at t if:

$$\mathsf{E}\left[\boldsymbol{\nu}_t \mid \mathcal{I}_{t-1}\right] = \mathsf{E}\left[\boldsymbol{\nu}_t\right].$$

Similarly, $\boldsymbol{\nu}_t$ is unpredictable in variance at t if:

$$\mathsf{V}\left[\boldsymbol{\nu}_t \mid \mathcal{I}_{t-1}\right] = \mathsf{V}\left[\boldsymbol{\nu}_t\right].$$

The converse of the latter includes (e.g.) autoregressive conditional heteroscedastic processes (ARCH, or its generalization, GARCH: see Engle, 1982, Bollerslev, Chou and Kroner, 1992, and Bollerslev, Engle and Nelson, 1994), or stochastic volatility schemes (see Shephard, 1996). Consequently, unpredictability in mean is not invariant under non-linear contemporaneous transforms, as in the weak white-noise ARCH process:

$$\mathsf{E}\left[\boldsymbol{\nu}_t \mid \mathcal{I}_{t-1}\right] = \mathsf{E}\left[\boldsymbol{\nu}_t\right] \text{ but } \mathsf{E}\left[\boldsymbol{\nu}_t\boldsymbol{\nu}_t' \mid \mathcal{I}_{t-1}\right] \neq \mathsf{E}\left[\boldsymbol{\nu}_t\boldsymbol{\nu}_t'\right].$$

1.4.3 Forecastability

A forecasting rule is any systematic operational procedure for making statements about future events. We will focus on statistical forecasting using formal estimated econometric models. Whereas predictability is a property (of a stochastic process in relation to an information set), forecasting is a process. Moreover, forecasting is undertaken for a purpose, so its evaluation depends on how well it achieves that intent. Consequently, it is extremely difficult to define "forecastability". One could perhaps define events as forecastable relative to a loss measure if the relevant procedure produced a lower expected loss than (say) the historical mean. This would be consistent with the change in the log of real equity prices being unforecastable, but the level forecastable using a random walk, on the criteria of bias or MSFE. Unfortunately, as shown in §1.6 below, MSFE rankings for multivariate, multi-step forecasts depend on the transformations used (e.g., levels versus first differences). Consequently, relative "accuracy" depends on the transformation that is evaluated, rendering most definitions ambiguous.

1.4.4 Implications

These concepts have a number of important implications applicable to most statistical forecasting methods. First, from (1.6), since the conditional mean of an unpredictable process is its unconditional mean, predictability is necessary for forecastability. However, it is not sufficient, since the relevant information set may be unknown in practice. Further, there is a potential ambiguity in the use of the phrase "information set" in the contexts of predictability and forecasting: $\mathcal{I}_{t-1}$ denotes the conditioning set generated by the relevant events, whereas forecastability also requires knowledge of how $\mathcal{I}_{t-1}$ enters the conditional density in (1.6). For example, $\mathbf{v}_{t-1}$ may matter, but in an awkward non-linear and time-dependent way that eludes empirical modeling.

Secondly, translating "regularity" as a systematic relation between the entity to be forecast and the available information, then conditions (a)–(d) above are sufficient for forecastability. They may not be necessary in principle (e.g., inspired guessing or precognition suffice), but for statistical forecasting, they seem close to necessary, as can be seen by considering the removal of any one of them (e.g., if no regularities exist to be captured; or the captured regularities are swamped by irregularities).

Thirdly, if the occurrence of large *ex ante* unpredictable shocks (such as earthquakes, or oil crises), induces their inclusion in later information sets (moving from (1.7) to (1.8) above), the past will seem more explicable than the future is forecastable. In a sense, the model "overfits" historically relative to its average forecast performance. Consequently, when the "true" $\mathcal{I}_{t-1}$ is unknown, to prevent the baseline innovation error variance being an underestimate, forecast-accuracy evaluation may require "unconditioning" from within-sample rare events that have been modeled *post hoc*.

Fourthly, from (1.11), intertemporal transforms affect predictability, so no unique measure of predictability, and hence of forecast accuracy, exists. Linear dynamic econometric systems are invariant under non-singular, scale-preserving, linear transforms – in that they retain the same error processes and associated likelihood functions – and transformed estimates of the original parameters are usually the direct estimates of the transformed parameters: such transforms are used regularly in empirical research. But by definition, the predictability of the transformed variables is altered by any transforms that are intertemporal (e.g., switching from modeling y_t by y_{t-1} to Δy_t by y_{t-1}).[6] This precludes unique rankings of methods, adding to the difficulty of both theoretical analysis and practical appraisal.

Since new unpredictable components enter in each period, forecast-error variances could increase or decrease for increasing horizons from any given T, as a consequence of (1.7) versus (1.8). For integrated processes, $\mathsf{V}[x_{T+h}|\mathcal{I}_T]$ is non-decreasing in h when the innovation distribution is homoscedastic. Otherwise, although Chong and Hendry (1986) show that prediction intervals may be non-monotonic in h when parameters are estimated, since the forecast origin T increases in real time, forecast uncertainty will be non-decreasing in h unless the innovation variance is ever decreasing (since h-steps ahead from T becomes $h-1$ from $T+1$).

Finally (see §1.7), when the "true" $\mathcal{I}_{t-1}$ is unknown, one cannot prove that 'genuinely' relevant information must always dominate

[6]While 1-step MSFE s are invariant to that particular transform, measures such as R^2 are not.

non-causal variables in forecasting. Rather, examples reveal that non-causal variables can provide the "best available" forecasting devices on some measures when the model is not the DGP. First, however, we describe the class of processes and models under analysis, and consider how to meaasure forecast accuracy.

1.5 Theoretical Framework

For an econometric theory of forecasting to deliver relevant conclusions about empirical forecasting, it must be based on assumptions that adequately capture the appropriate aspects of the real world to be forecast. Consequently, we consider a non-stationary (evolutionary) world subject to structural breaks, where the model differs from the mechanism, and requires estimation from available data. The present analysis considers integrated-cointegrated mechanisms which are linear in $\mathbf{x}_t$, but are also subject to shifts in the deterministic factors. Generalizations to longer lags, non-linear relations, and sample selection of models all seem feasible, but await formal development.

1.5.1 *The data generation process*

For exposition, the data-generation process (DGP) is defined over the period $t = 1, \ldots, T$ by a first-order vector autoregressive process (VAR) in the n variables $\mathbf{x}_t$:

$$\mathbf{x}_t = \boldsymbol{\tau} + \boldsymbol{\Upsilon}\mathbf{x}_{t-1} + \boldsymbol{\nu}_t \text{ where } \boldsymbol{\nu}_t \sim \mathsf{IN}_n\left[\mathbf{0}, \boldsymbol{\Omega}_\nu\right], \tag{1.12}$$

denoting an independent normal error with expectation $\mathsf{E}[\boldsymbol{\nu}_t] = \mathbf{0}$ and variance matrix $\mathsf{V}[\boldsymbol{\nu}_t] = \boldsymbol{\Omega}_\nu$. The DGP is integrated of order unity ($\mathsf{I}(1)$), and satisfies $r < n$ cointegration relations such that:[7]

$$\boldsymbol{\Upsilon} = \mathbf{I}_n + \boldsymbol{\alpha}\boldsymbol{\beta}', \tag{1.13}$$

[7]In (1.12), we assume none of the roots of $|\mathbf{I} - \boldsymbol{\Upsilon}L| = 0$ lies inside the unit circle (where L is the lag operator, so $L^s x_t = x_{t-s}$), and $\boldsymbol{\alpha}'_\perp \boldsymbol{\Phi}\boldsymbol{\beta}_\perp$ is rank $(n-r)$, where $\boldsymbol{\Phi}$ is the mean-lag matrix (here $\boldsymbol{\Upsilon}$), when $\boldsymbol{\alpha}_\perp$ and $\boldsymbol{\beta}_\perp$ are $n \times (n-r)$ matrices of rank $(n-r)$ such that $\boldsymbol{\alpha}'\boldsymbol{\alpha}_\perp = \boldsymbol{\beta}'\boldsymbol{\beta}_\perp = \mathbf{0}$.

where $\boldsymbol{\alpha}$ and $\boldsymbol{\beta}$ are $n \times r$ matrices of rank r. Then (1.12) can be reparameterized as the vector equilibrium-correction model (VEqCM):

$$\Delta \mathbf{x}_t = \boldsymbol{\tau} + \boldsymbol{\alpha}\boldsymbol{\beta}'\mathbf{x}_{t-1} + \boldsymbol{\nu}_t, \tag{1.14}$$

where $\Delta \mathbf{x}_t$ and $\boldsymbol{\beta}'\mathbf{x}_t$ are $\mathsf{I}(0)$. This is a standard formulation popularized by, e.g., Johansen (1988, 1995b), though the first-order assumption means that there are no lagged $\Delta \mathbf{x}_{t-i}$ $(i > 0)$ terms. Let:

$$\boldsymbol{\tau} = \boldsymbol{\gamma} - \boldsymbol{\alpha}\boldsymbol{\mu}, \tag{1.15}$$

where $\boldsymbol{\mu}$ is $r \times 1$ and $\boldsymbol{\beta}'\boldsymbol{\gamma} = \mathbf{0}$ so in deviations about means:[8]

$$(\Delta \mathbf{x}_t - \boldsymbol{\gamma}) = \boldsymbol{\alpha}\left(\boldsymbol{\beta}'\mathbf{x}_{t-1} - \boldsymbol{\mu}\right) + \boldsymbol{\nu}_t \tag{1.16}$$

where the system grows at the unconditional rate $\mathsf{E}[\Delta \mathbf{x}_t] = \boldsymbol{\gamma}$ with long-run solution $\mathsf{E}\left[\boldsymbol{\beta}'\mathbf{x}_t\right] = \boldsymbol{\mu}$. We assume that $\text{rank}(\boldsymbol{\beta}'\boldsymbol{\alpha}) = r$. Since $\boldsymbol{\beta}$ is $n \times r$ and of full column rank r, $\boldsymbol{\beta}'\boldsymbol{\gamma} = \mathbf{0}$ implies that there are r restrictions on the n parameters in $\boldsymbol{\gamma}$, so that the n parameters in $\boldsymbol{\tau}$ divide up in to r in $\boldsymbol{\mu}$ and $n - r$ in $\boldsymbol{\gamma}$.

1.5.2 I(0) representation

The notation $\mathbf{x}_t$ denotes an $\mathsf{I}(1)$ vector. However, we can always write this in terms of $\mathsf{I}(0)$ variables. Consider the case of no cointegration, so that $r = 0$ and $\boldsymbol{\Upsilon} = \mathbf{I}_n$. Then (1.14) becomes:

$$\mathbf{y}_t \equiv \Delta \mathbf{x}_t = \boldsymbol{\tau} + \boldsymbol{\nu}_t, \tag{1.17}$$

with $\boldsymbol{\tau} = \boldsymbol{\gamma}$. Here all the n $\mathbf{y}_t$variables are $\mathsf{I}(0)$ by virtue of first-differencing the $\mathsf{I}(1)$ $\mathbf{x}_t$ variables. More interestingly, a representation in terms of $\mathsf{I}(0)$ variables is also possible when there is cointegration. The r cointegrating combinations of the $\mathbf{x}_t$ are $\mathsf{I}(0)$ by construction. To maintain the dimension of the system, the remaining $(n - r)$ combinations need to be linearly independent of the cointegrating combinations. But these combinations will necessarily be $\mathsf{I}(1)$ and require differencing. This suggests a natural choice of $\mathbf{y}_t$ might be $\mathbf{y}_t' = (\mathbf{x}_t'\boldsymbol{\beta} : \Delta \mathbf{x}_t'\boldsymbol{\beta}_\perp)$, and the n-dimensional $\mathsf{I}(0)$ representation can then be expressed as:

$$\mathbf{y}_t = \boldsymbol{\phi} + \boldsymbol{\Pi}\mathbf{y}_{t-1} + \boldsymbol{\epsilon}_t \tag{1.18}$$

[8]In (1.16), $\boldsymbol{\gamma} = \boldsymbol{\beta}_\perp(\boldsymbol{\alpha}_\perp'\boldsymbol{\beta}_\perp)^{-1}\boldsymbol{\alpha}_\perp'\boldsymbol{\tau}$. The decomposition using $\boldsymbol{\tau} = \boldsymbol{\gamma} - \boldsymbol{\alpha}\boldsymbol{\mu}$ is not orthogonal since $\boldsymbol{\gamma}'\boldsymbol{\alpha}\boldsymbol{\mu} \neq \mathbf{0}$, but as a DGP, (1.16) is isomorphic to (1.14).

where:

$$\boldsymbol{\phi} = \begin{pmatrix} -\boldsymbol{\beta}'\boldsymbol{\alpha}\boldsymbol{\mu} \\ \boldsymbol{\beta}'_{\perp}(\boldsymbol{\gamma} - \boldsymbol{\alpha}\boldsymbol{\mu}) \end{pmatrix} \text{ and } \boldsymbol{\Pi} = \begin{pmatrix} \boldsymbol{\Lambda} & \mathbf{0} \\ \boldsymbol{\beta}'_{\perp}\boldsymbol{\alpha} & \mathbf{0} \end{pmatrix}, \tag{1.19}$$

as:

$$\boldsymbol{\beta}'\mathbf{x}_t = -\boldsymbol{\beta}'\boldsymbol{\alpha}\boldsymbol{\mu} + \boldsymbol{\Lambda}\boldsymbol{\beta}'\mathbf{x}_{t-1} + \boldsymbol{\beta}'\boldsymbol{\nu}_t,$$

where $\boldsymbol{\Lambda} = \mathbf{I}_r + \boldsymbol{\beta}'\boldsymbol{\alpha}$ denotes the dynamic matrix of the cointegration vectors, with all its eigenvalues inside the unit circle. Thus:

$$\mathbf{y}_t = \begin{pmatrix} -\boldsymbol{\beta}'\boldsymbol{\alpha}\boldsymbol{\mu} \\ \boldsymbol{\beta}'_{\perp}(\boldsymbol{\gamma} - \boldsymbol{\alpha}\boldsymbol{\mu}) \end{pmatrix} + \begin{pmatrix} \boldsymbol{\Lambda} \\ \boldsymbol{\beta}'_{\perp}\boldsymbol{\alpha} \end{pmatrix} \boldsymbol{\beta}'\mathbf{x}_{t-1} + \begin{pmatrix} \boldsymbol{\beta}' \\ \boldsymbol{\beta}'_{\perp} \end{pmatrix} \boldsymbol{\nu}_t. \tag{1.20}$$

While it is clearly restrictive to exclude any dynamics from $\Delta\mathbf{x}_{t-1}$, the resulting algebra is much simpler, and we doubt if the analysis is seriously misled by doing so. For stationary processes, the restrictions in (1.19) can be ignored subject to the eigenvalues of $\boldsymbol{\Pi}$ remaining inside the unit circle. As this formulation is obtained by pre-multiplying (1.12) by the non-singular matrix $(\boldsymbol{\beta} : \boldsymbol{\beta}_{\perp})'$, it is isomorphic to the original.

1.5.3 *The model class*

The form of the model coincides with (1.12) as a linear representation of $\mathbf{x}_t$, but is potentially mis-specified:

$$\mathbf{x}_t = \boldsymbol{\tau}_p + \boldsymbol{\Upsilon}_p\mathbf{x}_{t-1} + \mathbf{u}_t, \tag{1.21}$$

where the parameter estimates $(\hat{\boldsymbol{\tau}} : \hat{\boldsymbol{\Upsilon}} : \hat{\boldsymbol{\Omega}}_{\nu})$ are possibly inconsistent, with $\boldsymbol{\tau}_p \neq \boldsymbol{\tau}$ and $\boldsymbol{\Upsilon}_p \neq \boldsymbol{\Upsilon}$. Empirical econometric models like (1.21) are not numerically calibrated theoretical models, but have error processes which are derived, and so are not autonomous: see Gilbert (1986), Hendry (1995a), and Spanos (1986) inter alia. The theory of reduction explains the origin and status of such empirical models in terms of the implied information reductions relative to the process that generated the data. Some reductions, such as invalid marginalization, affect forecast accuracy directly, whereas others, such as aggregation, may primarily serve to define the object of interest.

Three specific models used below in analytic derivations are defined by $(\boldsymbol{\tau}_p = \boldsymbol{\tau}, \boldsymbol{\Upsilon}_p = \boldsymbol{\Upsilon})$ (the DGP in-sample); $(\boldsymbol{\tau}_p = \boldsymbol{\gamma}, \boldsymbol{\Upsilon}_p = \mathbf{I}_n)$, so that

$$\Delta \mathbf{x}_t = \boldsymbol{\gamma} + \boldsymbol{\xi}_t; \tag{1.22}$$

and:

$$\Delta^2 \mathbf{x}_t = \mathbf{u}_t. \tag{1.23}$$

Although empirical econometric models are invariably not facsimiles of the DGP, they could match the data evidence in all measurable respects – and so be congruent prior to forecasting – but since we allow for forecast-period structural change, the model will not coincide with the DGP in the forecast period. The forecast-error taxonomies also allow for in-sample mis-specification, and its consequences are investigated in chapter 4. The second model (1.22) is a VAR in the differences of the variables (denoted DV), but is correctly specified when $\boldsymbol{\alpha} = \mathbf{0}$ in (1.16), in which case $\boldsymbol{\xi}_t = \boldsymbol{\nu}_t$. Thus, its mis-specification in-sample is owing to omitting the cointegrating vectors, not differencing the data. The third model (denoted DDV) does difference the variables in (1.22), and is based on the assumption that economic variables do not accelerate or decelerate continually, namely $\mathsf{E}[\Delta^2 \mathbf{x}_t] = \mathbf{0}$, leading to forecasts of "same change".

1.6 Measuring Forecast Accuracy

Although an econometric analysis could begin by specifying a loss function from which the optimal predictor is derived, a well-defined mapping between forecast errors and their costs is not typical in macroeconomics. Consequently, measures of forecast accuracy are often based on the MSFE matrix:

$$\mathbf{V}_h \equiv \mathsf{E}\left[\mathbf{e}_{T+h}\mathbf{e}'_{T+h}\right] = \mathsf{V}\left[\mathbf{e}_{T+h}\right] + \mathsf{E}\left[\mathbf{e}_{T+h}\right]\mathsf{E}\left[\mathbf{e}'_{T+h}\right] \tag{1.24}$$

where $\mathbf{e}_{T+h}$ is a vector of h-step ahead forecast errors. Such measures may lack invariance to non-singular, scale-preserving, linear transformations for which the associated model class is invariant, so MSFE comparisons may yield inconsistent rankings between forecasting models on multi-step ahead forecasts depending on the particular transformations of variables examined (e.g., levels or differences). Clements and

Hendry (1993) show analytically that for multi-step forecasts, the trace, determinant, and the whole matrix $\mathbf{V}_h$ lack invariance.

Denote the linear forecasting system in (1.12) by:

$$\mathbf{\Gamma s}_t = \mathbf{u}_t \text{ with } \mathbf{u}_t \sim \mathsf{IN}_{2n+1}\left[\mathbf{0}, \mathbf{\Sigma}_u\right] \tag{1.25}$$

where $\mathbf{s}'_t = (\mathbf{x}'_t, 1, \mathbf{x}'_{t-1})$, $\mathbf{\Sigma}_u$ is symmetric, positive semi-definite and $\mathbf{\Gamma} = (\mathbf{I}_n : -\boldsymbol{\tau} : -\mathbf{\Upsilon})$. Then the likelihood and generalized variance of the system in (1.25) are invariant under scale-preserving, non-singular transformations of the form:

$$\mathbf{M\Gamma P}^{-1}\mathbf{Ps}_t = \mathbf{Mu}_t$$

so:

$$\mathbf{\Gamma}^* \mathbf{s}^*_t = \mathbf{u}^*_t \quad \text{with} \quad \mathbf{u}^*_t \sim \mathsf{IN}_{2n+1}\left[\mathbf{0}, \mathbf{M\Sigma}_u\mathbf{M}'\right]. \tag{1.26}$$

In (1.26), $\mathbf{s}^*_t = \mathbf{Ps}_t$, $\mathbf{M}$ and $\mathbf{P}$ are respectively $n \times n$ and $(2n+1) \times (2n+1)$ known non-singular matrices, where $|\mathbf{M}| = 1$, and $\mathbf{P}$ is the upper block-triangular matrix:

$$\mathbf{P} = \begin{pmatrix} \mathbf{I}_n & \mathbf{P}_{12} \\ \mathbf{0} & \mathbf{P}_{22} \end{pmatrix},$$

with $|\mathbf{P}_{22}| \neq 0$. Then:

$$|\mathbf{M\Sigma}_u\mathbf{M}'| = |\mathbf{\Sigma}_u|, \tag{1.27}$$

so the systems (1.25) and (1.26) are isomorphic. Forecasts and prediction intervals made in the original system and transformed after the event to $\mathbf{x}^*_t$, or made directly from the transformed system, are identical; and this remains true when parameters are estimated by any method that is equivariant (e.g., maximum likelihood). For example, if a system is estimated for $\mathbf{x}_t$ on $\mathbf{x}_{t-1}$ by full-information maximum likelihood with $\widehat{\Delta\mathbf{x}}_t$ obtained by an identity, then the forecasts $\widehat{\Delta\mathbf{x}}_{T+h}$ of $\Delta\mathbf{x}_{T+h}$ are identical to those obtained from modeling $\Delta\mathbf{x}_t$ on $\mathbf{x}_{t-1}$ with $\hat{\mathbf{x}}_t$ obtained by identity.

For transformations involving $\mathbf{M}$ only (i.e., $\mathbf{P} = \mathbf{I}_{2n+1}$), the matrix measure $\mathbf{V}_h$ and the determinant are invariant, but the trace is not: see e.g., Granger and Newbold (1986). When $\mathbf{M} = \mathbf{I}_n$, for transformations using $\mathbf{P}$, neither the determinant nor the MSFE matrix are invariant for

$h > 1$, even though the distribution of the $\mathbf{u}_t$ is unaffected by (1.26): see Clements and Hendry (1997).

Invariance to $\mathbf{P}$ transformations in a measure requires accounting for covariances between different step-ahead errors, leading to a generalized forecast-error second-moment matrix (GFESM, which is close to predictive likelihood: see Bjørnstad, 1990):

$$\mathbf{\Phi}_h = \mathsf{E}\left[\mathbf{E}_h \mathbf{E}_h'\right],$$

where $\mathbf{E}_h$ stacks the forecast errors up to and including h-steps ahead:

$$\mathbf{E}_h' = \left[\mathbf{e}_{T+1}', \mathbf{e}_{T+2}', \ldots, \mathbf{e}_{T+h-1}', \mathbf{e}_{T+h}'\right].$$

Then, $|\mathbf{\Phi}_h|$ is also unaffected by $\mathbf{M}$ transforms, since denoting the vector of stacked forecast errors from the transformed model by $\tilde{\mathbf{E}}_h'$:

$$\tilde{\mathbf{E}}_h' = \left[\mathbf{e}_{T+1}'\mathbf{M}', \mathbf{e}_{T+2}'\mathbf{M}', \ldots, \mathbf{e}_{T+h-1}'\mathbf{M}', \mathbf{e}_{T+h}'\mathbf{M}'\right],$$

we have:

$$\left|\tilde{\mathbf{\Phi}}_h\right| = \left|\mathsf{E}\left[\tilde{\mathbf{E}}_h \tilde{\mathbf{E}}_h'\right]\right| = \left|\mathsf{E}\left[\mathbf{E}_h \mathbf{E}_h'\right]\right|,$$

since $|\mathbf{I}_n \otimes \mathbf{M}| = 1$. Although invariance is useful to determine a unique measure for a fixed model independently of its representation, it is not compelling, and often several forecast-accuracy indices are reported.

Figure 1.3 illustrates, using (1.4) and (1.5) to forecast growth rates (Δy_t). The four panels look much more similar than those for the levels, although the systematic over-prediction of the growth rate by (1.4) can be discerned. Table 1.1 reports the forecast-error biases and standard deviations. Although we do not in fact see a reversal of rankings between these models on either horizon, the very large differences in performance apparent for levels become trivial for differences.

1.7 Causal Information in Economic Forecasting

We now consider the role of causal information in economic forecasting when the model and mechanism coincide, and when they do not, letting the mechanism be potentially non-constant over time.

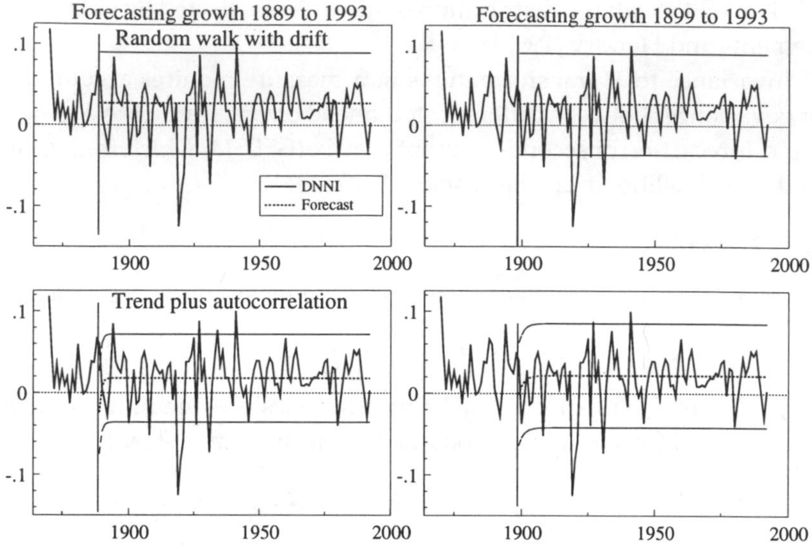

Figure 1.3
Long-horizon forecasts of growth in UK NNI.

When the model coincides with a constant mechanism, causal information is always useful, and produces better forecasts than non-causal: adding further variables produces no improvement. Providing the mechanism generates stationary data, causally-relevant information generally improves forecasts even when the model is mis-specified. Such a result cannot be shown for a mis-specified model of a non-constant mechanism: non-causal additional variables potentially can be more useful than causally-relevant ones so long as the model remains mis-specified. Because differenced-data models often fare better than apparently well-specified models, this result is one of the two major reasons we focus on structural breaks as a key to explaining empirical forecasting performance; the other is the dominant effect on systematic forecast biases of deterministic shifts in the taxonomy in §2.2.

As a counter example suffices to disprove the proposition that causal variables always dominate, we establish our claims using (1.12). We assume all parameters are known: estimation uncertainty would reinforce the main conclusions. While sufficiently-poor estimates would weaken any conclusions from the first case (that of a constant DGP),

Table 1.1
Multi-step forecast-error biases and SDs.

Horizon	1889–1993	1899–1993	1889–1993	1899–1993
equation	(1.4)	(1.4)	(1.5)	(1.5)
		biases		
levels	-0.62	-0.59	-0.01	-0.29
differences	-0.01	-0.01	-0.00	-0.00
		standard deviations		
levels	0.26	0.25	0.10	0.13
differences	0.034	0.034	0.034	0.034

our concern here is to establish that causally-relevant variables cannot be relied upon to produce the "best" forecasts when the model is mis-specified for a non-constant mechanism – parameter uncertainty would strengthen that finding.

1.7.1 *Model coincides with the mechanism*

Consider the DGP in (1.12) for the n variables $\mathbf{x}_t$, written in the lower-dimensional parameter space of the I(0) transformations $\mathbf{y}_t$ as in (1.20). The notation is simplest when the mechanism is constant, so we first prove the results in that setting, for 1-step forecasts.

From (1.18), the conditional expectation of $\mathbf{y}_{T+1}$ given $\mathbf{y}_T$ is:

$$\mathsf{E}\left[\mathbf{y}_{T+1} \mid \mathbf{y}_T\right] = \boldsymbol{\phi} + \boldsymbol{\Pi}\mathbf{y}_T,$$

and this delivers the (matrix) minimum MSFE. Under the present assumptions, the resulting forecast error is a homoscedastic innovation against all further information:

$$\mathsf{E}\left[\boldsymbol{\epsilon}_{T+1} \mid \mathbf{y}_T\right] = \mathbf{0} \text{ and } \mathsf{V}\left[\boldsymbol{\epsilon}_{T+1} \mid \mathbf{y}_T\right] = \boldsymbol{\Omega}_{\epsilon}. \tag{1.28}$$

Consequently, adding any further variables $\mathbf{z}_{t-1}$ to (1.18) will not improve the forecast accuracy in terms of mean or variance.

Conversely, replacing $y_{i,t-1}$ by any or all elements from a set of non-causal variables $\mathbf{z}_{t-1}$ will lead to inefficient forecasts unless there is perfect correlation between $y_{i,t}$ and $\mathbf{z}_t$. Denote the resulting regressor vector by $\overline{\mathbf{y}}_{t-1}$, then, forecasting from:

$$\mathbf{y}_t = \overline{\boldsymbol{\phi}} + \overline{\boldsymbol{\Pi}}\overline{\mathbf{y}}_{t-1} + \mathbf{e}_t,$$

where $\mathsf{E}[\mathbf{e}_t|\overline{\mathbf{y}}_{t-1}] = \mathbf{0}$ using:

$$\widetilde{\mathbf{y}}_{T+1} = \overline{\boldsymbol{\phi}} + \overline{\boldsymbol{\Pi}}\overline{\mathbf{y}}_T,$$

the forecast error is:

$$\mathbf{e}_{T+1} = \mathbf{y}_{T+1} - \widetilde{\mathbf{y}}_{T+1} = \left(\boldsymbol{\phi} - \overline{\boldsymbol{\phi}}\right) + \boldsymbol{\Pi}\mathbf{y}_T - \overline{\boldsymbol{\Pi}}\overline{\mathbf{y}}_T + \boldsymbol{\epsilon}_{T+1}.$$

Let $\mathbf{y}_t = \boldsymbol{\zeta} + \boldsymbol{\Psi}\overline{\mathbf{y}}_t + \mathbf{w}_t$ (say) with $\mathsf{E}\left[\mathbf{w}_t|\overline{\mathbf{y}}_t\right] = \mathbf{0}$ and $\mathsf{V}\left[\mathbf{w}_t|\overline{\mathbf{y}}_t\right] = \boldsymbol{\Phi}$, so:

$$\mathbf{e}_{T+1} = \left(\boldsymbol{\phi} - \overline{\boldsymbol{\phi}} + \boldsymbol{\Pi}\boldsymbol{\zeta}\right) + \left(\boldsymbol{\Pi}\boldsymbol{\Psi} - \overline{\boldsymbol{\Pi}}\right)\overline{\mathbf{y}}_T + \boldsymbol{\Pi}\mathbf{w}_T + \boldsymbol{\epsilon}_{T+1}$$

with mean:

$$\mathsf{E}\left[\mathbf{e}_{T+1} \mid \overline{\mathbf{y}}_T\right] = \left(\boldsymbol{\phi} - \overline{\boldsymbol{\phi}} + \boldsymbol{\Pi}\boldsymbol{\zeta}\right) + \left(\boldsymbol{\Pi}\boldsymbol{\Psi} - \overline{\boldsymbol{\Pi}}\right)\overline{\mathbf{y}}_T = \mathbf{0} \qquad (1.29)$$

by construction, so that $\overline{\boldsymbol{\phi}} = \boldsymbol{\phi} + \boldsymbol{\Pi}\boldsymbol{\zeta}$ and $\boldsymbol{\Pi}\boldsymbol{\Psi} = \overline{\boldsymbol{\Pi}}$; and variance:

$$\mathsf{V}\left[\mathbf{e}_{T+1} \mid \overline{\mathbf{y}}_T\right] = \boldsymbol{\Omega}_{\epsilon} + \boldsymbol{\Pi}\boldsymbol{\Phi}\boldsymbol{\Pi}'. \qquad (1.30)$$

Thus, (1.29) shows the forecasts are conditionally unbiased, but (1.30) entails they are inefficient.

Next, in a non-constant DGP, §2.2 shows that the main non-constancies of interest concern direct or indirect changes in the deterministic components of (1.12). Either $\boldsymbol{\tau}$ can change, or if $\boldsymbol{\Upsilon}$ changes, the unconditional means of the I(0) components alter. We only consider the former. Let $\boldsymbol{\tau}$ change to $\boldsymbol{\tau}^*$, so the DGP in the forecast period becomes:

$$\mathbf{x}_{T+1} = \boldsymbol{\tau}^* + \boldsymbol{\Upsilon}\mathbf{x}_T + \boldsymbol{\nu}_T \qquad (1.31)$$

Since the model also switches to (1.31) by being the mechanism, the forecast errors have the same properties as in (1.28), and the previous result is unchanged. Its converse, that (1.31) will dominate incorrect models, is more tedious to show, but follows from a generalization of the argument in (1.29) and (1.30).

Such powerful results are not surprising; but the assumption that the model coincides with the mechanism is extremely strong, and not empirically relevant.

1.7.2 *Model does not coincide with the mechanism*

First, we show that if the process is stationary, predictive failure is unconditionally unlikely, irrespective of how badly the model is specified (see e.g., Miller, 1978, and Hendry, 1979b), but that causal information still dominates non-causal. Even so, non-causal variables might help, if they act as proxies for the omitted causal variables. Then we provide an example where causal information does not help once structural breaks are introduced.

Reconsider the system in (1.18):

$$\mathbf{y}_t = \boldsymbol{\phi} + \mathbf{\Pi}\mathbf{y}_{t-1} + \boldsymbol{\epsilon}_t. \tag{1.32}$$

There are many ways in which a model could be mis-specified for the mechanism in (1.32), but we only consider the omission of some I (0) cointegrating components. Denote the resulting model by:

$$\mathbf{y}_t = \boldsymbol{\phi}_p + \mathbf{\Pi}_p\mathbf{y}_{t-1} + \boldsymbol{\eta}_t \tag{1.33}$$

where $\mathbf{\Pi}_p$ retains only a subset of the r cointegrating vectors in (1.32). Then, as:

$$\mathsf{E}[\mathbf{y}_t] = (\mathbf{I}_n - \mathbf{\Pi})^{-1}\boldsymbol{\phi} = \boldsymbol{\varphi} \ \text{(say)},$$

taking expectations in (1.33) under stationarity:

$$\mathsf{E}[\mathbf{y}_t] = \boldsymbol{\varphi} = \boldsymbol{\phi}_p + \mathbf{\Pi}_p\boldsymbol{\varphi},$$

so $\boldsymbol{\phi}_p = (\mathbf{I}_n - \mathbf{\Pi}_p)\boldsymbol{\varphi}$. For known parameters in (1.33), forccast $\widehat{\mathbf{y}}_{T+1}$ by $\boldsymbol{\phi}_p + \mathbf{\Pi}_p\mathbf{y}_T$, so that

$$\mathsf{E}\left[\widehat{\mathbf{y}}_{T+1}\right] = \boldsymbol{\phi}_p + \mathbf{\Pi}_p\boldsymbol{\varphi} = \boldsymbol{\varphi},$$

and hence the resulting forecasts are unconditionally unbiased, though inefficient. Adding any omitted $\mathbf{y}_{t-1}$ will improve forecasts if they act as a proxy for omitted $\boldsymbol{\beta}'\mathbf{x}_{t-1}$.

Thus, the notion of basing forecasting on "causal models" still has substance, perhaps qualified by the need to estimate parameters from small samples of badly-measured data. However, once the model is not the mechanism and the mechanism is non-constant, the dominance of causal information over non-causal cannot be shown. A counter example where non-causal information dominates causal on at least one forecast criterion, unless omniscience is assumed, is suggested in Hendry (1997). Such a result may help explain some of the apparent success of the approach in Box and Jenkins (1976). We now develop that analysis.

Partition the I(0) DGP in (1.18) into two blocks of dimensions n_1 and n_2, where $n_1 + n_2 = n$:

$$\begin{pmatrix} \mathbf{y}_{1,t} \\ \mathbf{y}_{2,t} \end{pmatrix} = \begin{pmatrix} \boldsymbol{\phi}_1 \\ \boldsymbol{\phi}_2 \end{pmatrix} + \begin{pmatrix} \boldsymbol{\Pi}_{1,2}\mathbf{y}_{2,t-1} \\ \boldsymbol{\Pi}_{2,2}\mathbf{y}_{2,t-1} \end{pmatrix} + \begin{pmatrix} \boldsymbol{\epsilon}_{1,t} \\ \boldsymbol{\epsilon}_{2,t} \end{pmatrix} \tag{1.34}$$

which holds till time T, then for $\tau \geq T$ changes to:

$$\begin{pmatrix} \mathbf{y}_{1,\tau} \\ \mathbf{y}_{2,\tau} \end{pmatrix} = \begin{pmatrix} \boldsymbol{\phi}_1 \\ \boldsymbol{\phi}_2 \end{pmatrix} + \begin{pmatrix} \boldsymbol{\Pi}^*_{1,2}\mathbf{y}_{2,\tau-1} \\ \boldsymbol{\Pi}_{2,2}\mathbf{y}_{2,\tau-1} \end{pmatrix} + \begin{pmatrix} \boldsymbol{\epsilon}_{1,\tau} \\ \boldsymbol{\epsilon}_{2,\tau} \end{pmatrix}. \tag{1.35}$$

Only the first block in (1.34) is modeled, with forecasts generated by the correct in-sample system:

$$\widehat{\mathbf{y}}_{1,\tau} = \boldsymbol{\phi}_1 + \boldsymbol{\Pi}_{1,2}\mathbf{y}_{2,\tau-1}, \tag{1.36}$$

so that after the break, the conditional forecast error is:

$$\mathsf{E}\left[\mathbf{y}_{1,\tau} - \widehat{\mathbf{y}}_{1,\tau} \mid \mathbf{y}_{2,\tau-1}\right] = \left(\boldsymbol{\Pi}^*_{1,2} - \boldsymbol{\Pi}_{1,2}\right)\mathbf{y}_{2,\tau-1}.$$

Since $\mathsf{E}[\mathbf{y}_{2,t}] = \left(\mathbf{I}_{n_2} - \boldsymbol{\Pi}_{2,2}\right)^{-1}\boldsymbol{\phi}_2 \neq \mathbf{0}\ \forall t$, $\mathbf{y}_{2,\tau-1}$ will almost always be non-zero, so the forecast error could be large as well as persistent. Unconditionally:

$$\mathsf{E}\left[\mathbf{y}_{1,\tau} - \widehat{\mathbf{y}}_{1,\tau}\right] = \left(\boldsymbol{\Pi}^*_{1,2} - \boldsymbol{\Pi}_{1,2}\right)\left(\mathbf{I}_{n_2} - \boldsymbol{\Pi}_{2,2}\right)^{-1}\boldsymbol{\phi}_2.$$

By way of contrast, consider the following forecasting rule:

$$\widetilde{\mathbf{y}}_{1,\tau} = \mathbf{y}_{1,\tau-1}. \tag{1.37}$$

This is a purely extrapolative method, but "error corrects" to the previous level of the variable being forecast. However, as $\mathbf{y}_{1,t-1}$ is absent from the DGP both pre and post break, it is a non-causal variable. At time T:

$$\begin{aligned} \Delta\mathbf{y}_{1,T} &= \boldsymbol{\phi}_1 + \boldsymbol{\Pi}^*_{1,2}\mathbf{y}_{2,T-1} + \boldsymbol{\epsilon}_{1,T} - \mathbf{y}_{1,T-1} \\ &= \left(\boldsymbol{\Pi}^*_{1,2} - \boldsymbol{\Pi}_{1,2}\right)\mathbf{y}_{2,T-1} + \boldsymbol{\Pi}_{1,2}\Delta\mathbf{y}_{2,T-1} + \Delta\boldsymbol{\epsilon}_{1,T}, \end{aligned}$$

whereas, at $T+1$:

$$\begin{aligned} \Delta\mathbf{y}_{1,T+1} &= \boldsymbol{\phi}_1 + \boldsymbol{\Pi}^*_{1,2}\mathbf{y}_{2,T} + \boldsymbol{\epsilon}_{1,T+1} - \mathbf{y}_{1,T} \\ &= \boldsymbol{\Pi}^*_{1,2}\Delta\mathbf{y}_{2,T-1} + \Delta\boldsymbol{\epsilon}_{1,T+1}, \end{aligned}$$

since the unconditional growth rate, $\mathsf{E}[\Delta \mathbf{y}_{2,\tau-1}]$, is zero throughout:

$$\begin{aligned} \mathsf{E}\left[\mathbf{y}_{1,\tau} - \widetilde{\mathbf{y}}_{1,\tau}\right] &= \mathsf{E}\left[\Delta \mathbf{y}_{1,\tau}\right] \\ &= \begin{cases} \left(\mathbf{\Pi}^{*}_{1,2} - \mathbf{\Pi}_{1,2}\right)\left(\mathbf{I}_{n_2} - \mathbf{\Pi}_{2,2}\right)^{-1} \phi_2 & \text{for } \tau = T \\ \mathbf{0} & \text{for } \tau > T. \end{cases} \end{aligned}$$

By construction, the lagged $\mathbf{y}_1$ is non-causal, yet forecasts based on it are less biased than from the "causal model" (1.36) after $T+1$. There exist changes in parameter values which would dominate any variance losses, so (1.37) could win on MSFE.

The inability to prove that causally-relevant variables will dominate for mis-specified models has important implications. First, there exist methods of robustifying forecasts against structural breaks which have already occurred: the differencing in (1.37) is one example, and there are others such as intercept corrections. We can now understand why such methods might outperform formal models: for large enough unmodeled breaks, "causal" models will lose on MSFE (and related criteria) to models that are robustified against breaks. Secondly, the differenced process in (1.37) is close to an ARIMA with a negative moving-average error and an outlier at the break point, although that is not the DGP (see the analysis of multi-step estimators in Clements and Hendry, 1996c). Finally, while the example is specifically constructed to demonstrate the possibility of dominating causal information , there are general classes of problems for which this may occur, based on the distinction between "error-correction" and "equilibrium-correction" mechanisms. These issues are discussed more formally in chapter 5. Although, the result has positive implications, and is far from being an attempt to down play the value of econometric systems, it suggests models for forecasting may need different design criteria than those for (say) testing theories or conducting policy analyses.

1.8 Conclusion

We have reviewed in summary form much of the main material from our earlier book as a basis for extending the analysis of economic forecasting to closed integrated-cointegrated systems that suffer structural breaks around a forecasting origin. The next chapter investigates the sources of forecast failure, and develops a taxonomy in table 2.1, which will be a core reference below: later chapters will explore in detail the importance of its components. Once the implications are established, we can consider potential solutions, several of which were hinted at above. The framework we adopt – which allows any form of model mis-specification, parameter break, estimation method, and data accuracy – incorporates sufficiently-realistic assumptions to account for the outcomes observed when economic forecasts are evaluated, both in absolute terms and relative to other methods. Nevertheless, despite its generality it seems able to deliver many conclusions of practical relevance.

The remainder of the book will develop these implications in the context of an integrated-cointegrated, first-order VAR, as that is a widely-used model, and sits at our margin of analytic tractability and empirical utility. Thus, following the exploration of the sources of forecast failure in chapter 2, which highlights the role of deterministic shifts, chapter 3 investigates their impacts on forecast-error biases and variances in a VEqCM. The other possible sources of forecast failure are analyzed in chapter 4. Together, these three chapters confirm the primacy of shifts in equilibrium means as the source of forecast failure. That suggests studying the usefulness of various strategies to offset such shifts, so chapters 5 and 6 consider differencing and intercept corrections respectively. To check the practical value of the theory, chapters 7 and 8 in turn evaluate scalar and multivariate empirical applications to consumers' expenditure, then a small monetary model of the UK. However, the book does not consider in detail the associated empirical modeling issues, such as estimation and testing theory, or data-based selection procedures. Phillips (1994) proposes an adaptive estimation and model-selection approach to developing forecasting models based on the PIC criterion, in which parameter estimates, lag length and deterministic factors are all determined sequentially. Since the focus is forecasting, we also generally use one-off critical values for (e.g.) constancy tests, since the forecast origin is always known, and that is the time at which the relevant tests will be undertaken. This contrasts with (say) the appropriate critical values for unknown break points that apply to in-sample inference (see e.g., Bai, Lumsdaine and Stock, 1998).

Next, chapters 9 and 10 develop approaches that might mitigate deterministic shifts, namely co-breaking (removing breaks across linear combinations of variables, analogous to cointegration) and regime-shift models respectively. A final empirical application in chapter 11 tries out various solutions to forecast failure, in the context of a small model of wages, prices and unemployment in the UK. Chapter 12 overviews the main findings of the book, including its implications for econometric methodology, and considers the way ahead. A set of exercises is provided at the end of the book, with a glossary of the main symbols.

2 Forecast Failure

Summary

This chapter discusses the sources of forecast failure and some of their main implications. We present taxonomies of forecast errors in both I(0) and I(1) systems, which suggest that structural breaks are the main culprit for systematic forecast failure. We distinguish between *ex ante* and *ex post* prediction, and between equilibrium correction (from cointegration) and error correction (offsetting past mistakes). While forecast failure is clearly damaging, it does not warrant jettisoning the strategy of building congruent empirical models to foster a deeper understanding of the economy, and it can serve as a catalyst in a progressive research strategy. This dual role of forecast failure is applied to both congruent and non-congruent models. A notion of extended parameter constancy is introduced to explain why *ex-ante* non-constancy is not a fatal flaw.

2.1 Introduction

That economic forecasting has suffered from bouts of serious predictive failure many times this century is beyond doubt. Examples include the ABC curves based on Persons (1924) apparently missing the onset of the Great Depression in 1929; the post-war mis-prediction of consumers' expenditure (see e.g. Duesenberry, 1949); the Korean War jump in inflation; the demise of Keynesian-style macro-econometric systems during the oil-crises of the 1970s (see e.g., Cooper and Nelson, 1975); and the under-predictions of consumers' expenditure in the UK in the mid 1980s followed by over-predictions in the early 1990s (see Muellbauer, 1994, and Cook, 1995, who reviews UK Treasury forecasts of consumers' expenditure). Despite advances in economic theory, in econometric techniques and methodology, in computing, in data availability, and especially in accumulated empirical knowledge, forecast failures and parameter non-constancies still abound. The problems of economic forecasting have been matched by professional scepticism, although that aspect dates from the early claims in (say) Morgenstern (1928) that the notion of economic forecasting is flawed in principle (but see Marget, 1929, reprinted with discussion in Hendry and Morgan, 1995).

Forecast failure is defined as significant mis-forecasting relative to the previous record (in-sample, or earlier forecasts), whereas poor forecasting is judged relative to some standard, either absolute (perhaps because of a policy requirement for accuracy), or relative to a rival model. Of course, forecast failure will induce poor forecasts relative to prior expectations, but forecasts may be poor simply because no device could do better (e.g., the series in question is unpredictable). We also distinguish between precision and accuracy: a forecast is precise if it has a small uncertainty attached to it, and is accurate if it is close to the outcome on average. Thus, both attributes are desirable in practice, and either alone may be useless (e.g., an exact point forecast that is 100% out, or an unbiased forecast with 100% standard errors).

A further useful distinction is between *ex-ante* forecast failure and *ex-post* predictive failure. The *ex ante* notion relates to incorrect statements about as yet unobserved events, and could be due to many causes, including data errors or false assumptions about non-modeled variables which are corrected later, so the relevant model remains constant when updated (see §2.7). Thus *ex-ante* forecast failure is primarily a function of forecast-period events, which chapter 3 shows are often caused by unmodeled shifts in equilibrium means. *Ex-post* predictive failure is rejection on a valid parameter-constancy test against the observed outcomes, and occurs when a model is non-constant on the whole available information set, and is a well-established notion.

Forecast failure may be predictable *ex ante*: for example, anticipation of the effects of the 1984 legal change permitting interest payments on retail sight deposits could have avoided mis-forecasting by a model of the transactions-demand for money which excluded that variable. However, because of ambiguities in the concept of a constant model, it transpires that predictive failure is not in general determinable purely from the in-sample information used in modeling (see Hendry, 1996, Ericsson, Hendry and Prestwich, 1998b, and §2.7 below).

In §2.2 (in particular, table 2.1) we enumerate the possible sources of forecast error in I(0) systems, and suggest that in practice, unmodeled shifts in deterministic factors may play an important role in forecast failure. We will illustrate this source with Monte Carlo simulation and empirical models as we proceed. Chapter 3 considers in more detail the central role in forecast failure of deterministic shifts, and chapter 4 the other potential sources of failure, such as model mis-specification and estimation uncertainty.

Our focus is on multivariate equilibrium-correction models (VEqCMs: see §1.5) given the widespread use of this model class in macroeconomic forecasting, and the belief that the economy can best be approximated as an integrated-cointegrated system. The taxonomy in §2.4 reveals the potential problems inherent in using VEqCMs when there are shifts in deterministic factors, and the extent to which such models can be "patched-up" for forecasting purposes is explored in chapters 5 and 6. Thus, equilibrium-correction models may perform poorly in certain states of nature, even though they characterize the data reasonably well in-sample. As chapter 1 showed that "non-causal models" can dominate models with "causal variables" when the latter are mis-specified and there are breaks in deterministic factors (see §1.7), other classes of model are worth considering when forecasting is the objective. The roles of non-deterministic model mis-specification, parameter uncertainty, and forecast-origin mis-measurement considered in chapter 4 are shown not to account for major systematic mis-forecasting *per se*, albeit that interacting with breaks, they can induce serious forecast errors.

The structure of this chapter is as follows. To determine the potential sources of forecast error, we formulate taxonomies of forecast errors for both integrated and non-integrated data. These taxonomies suggest that forecast biases may primarily result from unmodeled shifts in deterministic factors, the theme explored in detail in chapter 3. The I(0) taxonomy of forecast errors in §2.2 allows for structural change in the forecast period, the model and DGP to differ over the sample period, the parameters of the model to be estimated from the data, and the forecasts to commence from incorrect initial conditions. Thus, all the potential sources are included. The results re-emphasize the possible role of non-causal variables in forecasting, and hence warn of the potential dangers of selecting policy models by forecast-accuracy criteria. Section 2.3 evaluates the impact of the sources of predictive failure in congruent models of cointegrated processes. Section 2.4 considers I(1) systems, but focuses on structural breaks (the §2.10 derivation is inclusive). Section 1.7 discussed the role of causal variables: a DGP with an unmodeled switch in regime demonstrated the impossibility of establishing the primacy of causal variables without omniscience. Here the same result is established for equilibrium-correction models in §2.5 when there is a shift in the equilibrium mean. We also introduce the obverse issue of why non-congruent (e.g., differenced-data) models need not fail when forecasting, as a forerunner to a more formal treatment in chapter 5. Finally, §2.7 considers the possibility of obtaining parameter constancy despite *ex ante* forecast failure . By careful analysis of the non-constancy, it may be possible to obtain a fuller understanding of the economic phenomena – if so, this would constitute an increase in knowledge. The notion of what it means for a model to be constant is shown to be less than obvious, and a number of interesting cases can be distinguished. Returning to forecast mode, we investigate whether *ex ante* non-constancy is a fatal weakness in a model, and argue that, outside the forecasting context, it is not. Section 2.8 concludes.

2.2 An I(0) Taxonomy of Forecast Errors

To clarify the impact of structural breaks on forecasting, we reconsider the taxonomy of forecast errors in Clements and Hendry (1994) as adapted by Hendry (1997). Useful results can be established despite allowing general structural change in the forecast period, the model to differ from the DGP in unknown ways over the sample period, the parameters of the model to be estimated (perhaps inconsistently) from the data, and the forecasts to commence from values which may differ from the "true" forecast origin. The present analysis highlights the role of changes in deterministic terms. We focus on closed systems, because for multi-step forecasts, future values are needed for all the variables in the system, although autoregressive schemes may only poorly reflect the way in which future values of key policy variables are calculated in practice.

It is convenient to consider the first-order VAR (1.12) in I (0) space:[1]

$$\mathbf{y}_t = \boldsymbol{\phi} + \boldsymbol{\Pi}\mathbf{y}_{t-1} + \boldsymbol{\epsilon}_t \text{ with } \boldsymbol{\epsilon}_t \sim \mathsf{IN}_n\left[\mathbf{0}, \boldsymbol{\Omega}_\epsilon\right], \tag{2.1}$$

where the eigenvalues of $\boldsymbol{\Pi}$ lie inside the unit circle, and the unconditional mean of $\mathbf{y}_t$ is:

$$\mathsf{E}\left[\mathbf{y}_t\right] = \left(\mathbf{I}_n - \boldsymbol{\Pi}\right)^{-1}\boldsymbol{\phi} = \boldsymbol{\varphi} \tag{2.2}$$

so:

$$\mathbf{y}_t - \boldsymbol{\varphi} = \boldsymbol{\Pi}\left(\mathbf{y}_{t-1} - \boldsymbol{\varphi}\right) + \boldsymbol{\epsilon}_t. \tag{2.3}$$

This formulation is convenient for distinguishing between changes that induce biased forecasts, and those that do not. Section 2.4 develops a forecast-error taxonomy for I(1) systems. From (2.3), it can be seen that the system is an equilibrium-correction one, where (2.2) defines that equilibrium.

Given the information set $\{\mathbf{y}_t\}$, and the knowledge that the system is linear with one lag, using estimated parameters ("∧"s on parameters denote estimates, and on random variables, forecasts), the h-step ahead forecasts at forecast-origin T for $h = 1, \ldots, H$ are:

$$\hat{\mathbf{y}}_{T+h|T} - \hat{\boldsymbol{\varphi}} = \hat{\boldsymbol{\Pi}}\left(\hat{\mathbf{y}}_{T+h-1|T} - \hat{\boldsymbol{\varphi}}\right) = \hat{\boldsymbol{\Pi}}^h\left(\hat{\mathbf{y}}_T - \hat{\boldsymbol{\varphi}}\right), \tag{2.4}$$

where $\hat{\boldsymbol{\varphi}} = (\mathbf{I}_n - \hat{\boldsymbol{\Pi}})^{-1}\hat{\boldsymbol{\phi}}$. In this simple system, the h-step ahead forecast equals the estimated equilibrium mean, plus the deviation therefrom at the estimated forecast origin, scaled by the hth power of the dynamic matrix. Although the forecast origin $\hat{\mathbf{y}}_T$ is uncertain, we assume $\mathsf{E}[\hat{\mathbf{y}}_T] = \boldsymbol{\varphi}$, so on average $\hat{\mathbf{y}}_T$ is unbiased (otherwise, an additional term arises in the taxonomy from that bias). By using (2.4), we do not assume that the forecaster knows the DGP (2.1), since the taxonomy allows for the possibility that all the parameter estimates are inconsistent, reflecting any extent of model mis-specification. For example, $\hat{\boldsymbol{\Pi}}$

[1]The analysis assumes the transformed system remains I(0) after any structural change.

might be restricted to zero (dynamic mis-specification); the wrong variables used in the various equations, or the intercepts suppressed despite $\boldsymbol{\phi} \neq \mathbf{0}$. A subscript p on a parameter denotes the $\text{plim}_{T\to\infty}$ (under constant parameters) of the corresponding estimate.

Because the system is dynamic, the impacts of breaks differ with the time-lapse since the break. Thus, after a structural break, the system becomes non-stationary in that its first and second moments are not constant. Consequently, every moment has to be calculated explicitly, depending on the timing of the break. We consider the case when a single permanent break occurs at the forecast announcement: unknown to the forecaster, at time T, the parameters $(\boldsymbol{\phi} : \boldsymbol{\Pi})$ change to $(\boldsymbol{\phi}^* : \boldsymbol{\Pi}^*)$ where $\boldsymbol{\Pi}^*$ still has all its eigenvalues inside the unit circle. Thus, from $T+1$ onwards, the data are generated by:

$$\mathbf{y}_{T+h} = \boldsymbol{\phi}^* + \boldsymbol{\Pi}^*\mathbf{y}_{T+h-1} + \boldsymbol{\epsilon}_{T+h}, \quad h = 1, \ldots \tag{2.5}$$

Many factors could induce serious forecast errors, such as large blips (e.g., 1968:1 and 1968:2 for consumers' expenditure in the UK), but we construe the first blip to be the above change in the intercept, followed by a second shift superimposed thereon. While the properties of $\{\boldsymbol{\epsilon}_{T+h}\}$ are not explicitly altered, we do not preclude changes in their distribution, serial correlation, or variance. Letting $\boldsymbol{\phi}^* = (\mathbf{I}_n - \boldsymbol{\Pi}^*)\,\boldsymbol{\varphi}^*$:

$$\begin{aligned}\mathbf{y}_{T+h} - \boldsymbol{\varphi}^* &= \boldsymbol{\Pi}^*\left(\mathbf{y}_{T+h-1} - \boldsymbol{\varphi}^*\right) + \boldsymbol{\epsilon}_{T+h} \\ &= \left(\boldsymbol{\Pi}^*\right)^h\left(\mathbf{y}_T - \boldsymbol{\varphi}^*\right) + \sum_{i=0}^{h-1}\left(\boldsymbol{\Pi}^*\right)^i \boldsymbol{\epsilon}_{T+h-i}.\end{aligned} \tag{2.6}$$

The future outcomes, as a deviation from the new equilibrium, are the appropriate power of the new dynamic matrix, times the deviation at the forecast origin, but measured from the *new* equilibrium, plus the accumulated "discounted" future errors.

From (2.4) and (2.6), the h-step ahead forecast errors $\hat{\boldsymbol{\epsilon}}_{T+h|T} = \mathbf{y}_{T+h} - \hat{\mathbf{y}}_{T+h|T}$ are (letting $\mathbf{u}_t = \sum_{i=0}^{h-1}\left(\boldsymbol{\Pi}^*\right)^i \boldsymbol{\epsilon}_{T+h-i}$):

$$\hat{\boldsymbol{\epsilon}}_{T+h|T} = \boldsymbol{\varphi}^* - \hat{\boldsymbol{\varphi}} + \left(\boldsymbol{\Pi}^*\right)^h\left(\mathbf{y}_T - \boldsymbol{\varphi}^*\right) - \hat{\boldsymbol{\Pi}}^h\left(\hat{\mathbf{y}}_T - \hat{\boldsymbol{\varphi}}\right) + \mathbf{u}_t. \tag{2.7}$$

We can arrange (2.7) into interpretable factors, which can be analyzed separately without great loss, despite ignoring some interaction terms. Deviations between sample estimates and population parameters are denoted by $\boldsymbol{\delta}_{\varphi} = \hat{\varphi} - \varphi_p$, where $\varphi_p = (\mathbf{I}_n - \boldsymbol{\Pi}_p)^{-1}\boldsymbol{\phi}_p$, and $\boldsymbol{\delta}_{\Pi} = \hat{\boldsymbol{\Pi}} - \boldsymbol{\Pi}_p$, with $(\hat{\mathbf{y}}_T - \mathbf{y}_T) = \boldsymbol{\delta}_y$. To obtain a clearer interpretation of the various sources of forecast errors, we ignore all powers and cross-products in the $\boldsymbol{\delta}$s for parameters (these are generally of a smaller order of magnitude than the terms retained), but retain terms involving parameters interacting with the forecast origin. Appendix 2.9 details the derivation, and defines $\mathbf{C}_h$ and $\mathbf{F}_h$ matrices used in the taxonomy.

There are no entries for finite-sample estimation biases, because of the approximate unbiasedness of forecasts based on estimates of $\boldsymbol{\Pi}$ in (2.1) when the model is correctly specified, even though $\mathsf{E}[\boldsymbol{\delta}_{\Pi}^{\nu}] \neq \mathbf{0}$. To illustrate this result, we use an antithetic-variate argument based on normality (or more generally, any symmetric error distribution: see e.g., Hendry and Trivedi, 1972) when $\boldsymbol{\phi} = \mathbf{0}$. In zero-mean VARs, $\mathbf{y}_t(\boldsymbol{\epsilon}_t) = -\mathbf{y}_t(-\boldsymbol{\epsilon}_t)$, whereas $\widehat{\boldsymbol{\Pi}}$ is an even function of $\boldsymbol{\epsilon}_t$, so $\widehat{\boldsymbol{\Pi}}(\{\boldsymbol{\epsilon}_t\}) = \widehat{\boldsymbol{\Pi}}(\{-\boldsymbol{\epsilon}_t\})$. Denoting forecast errors by "$\widehat{\ }$" ("$\widetilde{\ }$"), when the generating process is $\{\boldsymbol{\epsilon}_t\}$ ($\{-\boldsymbol{\epsilon}_t\}$), the 1-step ahead forecast errors are:

$$\begin{aligned} \widehat{\boldsymbol{\epsilon}}_{T+1|T} &= \left(\boldsymbol{\Pi} - \widehat{\boldsymbol{\Pi}}(\{\boldsymbol{\epsilon}_t\})\right)\mathbf{y}_T + \boldsymbol{\epsilon}_{T+1}, \\ \widetilde{\boldsymbol{\epsilon}}_{T+1|T} &= -\left(\boldsymbol{\Pi} - \widehat{\boldsymbol{\Pi}}(\{-\boldsymbol{\epsilon}_t\})\right)\mathbf{y}_T - \boldsymbol{\epsilon}_{T+1}. \end{aligned} \tag{2.8}$$

Since $\mathsf{P}(\boldsymbol{\epsilon}_t) = \mathsf{P}(-\boldsymbol{\epsilon}_t)$ (from $\boldsymbol{\epsilon}_t \sim \mathsf{IN}_n[\mathbf{0}, \boldsymbol{\Omega}_\epsilon]$), by suitably matching the order of drawing equi-probable errors, $(\widehat{\boldsymbol{\epsilon}}_{T+1|T} + \widetilde{\boldsymbol{\epsilon}}_{T+1|T})$ averages to zero for every possible error-process drawing. Although the system is dynamic, parameter estimation bias does not necessarily bias the forecasts. When $\mathsf{E}[\boldsymbol{\delta}_{\phi}] \neq \mathbf{0}$, for multi-step forecasts, or in more complicated processes, the result is not exact, but suggests that finite-sample forecast error biases are unlikely to be the most serious problem. Hence we omit them from the taxonomy. We also omit terms that might arise from asymmetric error processes or loss-functions, where biases inadvertently or deliberately enter; it could be extended as needed for such cases. Selection biases are also omitted. Many of these issues were addressed separately in Clements and Hendry (1998b).

Table 2.1 combines the possible sources of forecast errors that arise from the decompositions. Five main sources are distinguished, but because of their central role below, we also separate elements involving shifts in deterministic terms from those involving changing dynamics.

Table 2.1
I(0) forecast-error taxonomy.

$\widehat{\epsilon}_{T+h\|T} \simeq$	$\left((\mathbf{\Pi}^*)^h - \mathbf{\Pi}^h\right)(\mathbf{y}_T - \boldsymbol{\varphi})$	(*ia*) slope change
	$+\left(\mathbf{I}_n - (\mathbf{\Pi}^*)^h\right)(\boldsymbol{\varphi}^* - \boldsymbol{\varphi})$	(*ib*) equilibrium-mean change
	$+\left(\mathbf{\Pi}^h - \mathbf{\Pi}_p^h\right)(\mathbf{y}_T - \boldsymbol{\varphi})$	(*iia*) slope mis-specification
	$+\left(\mathbf{I}_n - \mathbf{\Pi}_p^h\right)(\boldsymbol{\varphi} - \boldsymbol{\varphi}_p)$	(*iib*) equil.-mean mis-specification
	$-\mathbf{F}_h \boldsymbol{\delta}_{\Pi}^{\nu}$	(*iiia*) slope estimation
	$-\left(\mathbf{I}_n - \mathbf{\Pi}_p^h\right)\boldsymbol{\delta}_{\varphi}$	(*iiib*) equilibrium-mean estimation
	$-\left(\mathbf{\Pi}_p^h + \mathbf{C}_h\right)\boldsymbol{\delta}_y$	(*iv*) forecast origin uncertainty
	$+\sum_{i=0}^{h-1}(\mathbf{\Pi}^*)^i \epsilon_{T+h-i}$	(*v*) error accumulation.

Much of this book is a detailed study of the taxonomy sources, particularly the consequences of breaks: here, we overview the main results. The role of econometrics in reducing each source is discussed in Clements and Hendry (1994) and Hendry and Clements (1994a).

An alternative interpretation of the taxonomy in table 2.1 may be helpful. Forecasting models have three distinct components: deterministic terms (such as intercepts and trends; $\boldsymbol{\varphi}$ denotes the coefficients on the intercepts above) with known future values; observed stochastic variables (the $\mathbf{y}_t$) with unknown future values, and whose evolution is modeled by $\mathbf{\Pi}$; and unobserved errors with unknown values (ϵ_t). Each element is in principle susceptible to three types of mistake: they could be mis-specified, incorrectly estimated, or change in unanticipated ways. Thus, $3 \times 3 = 9$ types of mistake could be made, so our taxonomy is selective: before proceeding, we note those sources of error that are not being considered. We do not directly address forecast errors emanating from the effects on ϵ_t: a change in their mean is equivalent to a change in $\boldsymbol{\varphi}$; a change in their variance could induce forecast failure since prediction intervals calculated from the past fit of the model would be incorrect; and the model errors could be predictable (e.g., serially correlated) as a result of mis-specification of $\mathbf{\Pi}$. Consequently, some of these sources of forecast error will be picked up elsewhere in our taxonomy. We consider every potential effect of the deterministic and stochastic components, φ and $\mathbf{\Pi}$: change, mis-specification, and estimation uncertainty. Finally, the contribution of forecast origin uncertainty is also noted in the table: this can be viewed as mis-measurement of $\mathbf{y}_T$, an additional notion inapplicable to the unobserved disturbances or parameters.

In the present formulation, the second and fourth rows alone induce biases, whereas the remainder only affect forecast-error variances. Taking unconditional expectations in table 2.1, assuming finite-sample estimation biases are indeed negligible:

$$\mathsf{E}\left[\hat{\epsilon}_{T+h|T}\right] = \left(\mathbf{I}_n - (\mathbf{\Pi}^*)^h\right)(\varphi^* - \varphi) + \left(\mathbf{I}_n - \mathbf{\Pi}_p^h\right)(\varphi - \varphi_p). \tag{2.9}$$

Systematic forecast-error biases will result when (2.9) is non-zero. Deviations from this unconditional expectation induce unconditional forecast-error variance effects. As an alternative, consider taking expectations conditional on the forecast origin$\mathbf{y}_T$. Then $\mathsf{E}[\hat{\epsilon}_{T+h|T}|\mathbf{y}_T]$ equals $\mathsf{E}[\hat{\epsilon}_{T+h|T}]$ plus the following terms:

$$\left[\left((\mathbf{\Pi}^*)^h - \mathbf{\Pi}^h\right) + \left(\mathbf{\Pi}^h - \mathbf{\Pi}_p^h\right)\right](\mathbf{y}_T - \varphi) - \mathbf{\Pi}_p^h(\mathsf{E}\left[\hat{\mathbf{y}}_T \mid \mathbf{y}_T\right] - \mathbf{y}_T) \tag{2.10}$$

using $\mathsf{E}\left[\mathbf{C}_h\right] = \mathbf{0}$. Now deviations from this conditional expectation induce conditional forecast-error variance effects, so a different decomposition of the MSFE results, though the overall effect is the same. We will discuss the unconditional biases first, then comment on (2.10).

First consider the term involving $(\varphi - \varphi_p)$ in (2.9). Almost all estimation methods ensure that residuals have zero means in-sample, so provided φ has remained constant in-sample, this term is zero by construction. However, if φ has previously altered, and that earlier shift has not been modeled, then φ_p will be a weighted average of the in-sample values, and hence will not equal the end-of-sample value φ. One advantage of developing models that are congruent in-sample, even when the objective is forecasting, is to minimize such effects. When $\varphi = \varphi_p$, forecasts will be biased only to the extent that the long-run mean shifts from the in-sample population value.

Next, consider the case when $\varphi^* \neq \varphi$. A systematic bias results: since $(\mathbf{\Pi}^*)^h \to \mathbf{0}$ as $h \to \infty$, this is increasing in h, and eventually rises to the full effect of $(\varphi^* - \varphi)$. Consequently, a sequence of same-signed, increasing magnitude, forecast errors should result from a deterministic shift (here, in the equilibrium mean). However, the forecast-error bias is zero for processes that are, and remain, mean zero ($\varphi_p = \varphi = \varphi^* = \mathbf{0}$). More surprisingly, when $\varphi = \varphi_p$, no biases result if shifts in ϕ^* offset those in $\mathbf{\Pi}^*$ to leave φ unaffected (so $\varphi^* = \varphi$): see Hendry and Doornik (1997). Consequently, direct or induced shifts in the model's equilibrium means relative to those of the data lead to serious forecast biases. Moreover, such effects do not die out as the horizon increases, but converge to the full impact of the shift. There are variance effects as well in table 2.1, which are detrimental on a MSFE basis; and the *ex ante* forecast-error variance estimates will mis-estimate those ruling *ex post*, but these problems are likely to be of secondary importance when mean-shift structural breaks occur. Although non-linearities, asymmetric errors, or roots moving onto the unit circle could generate more complicated outcomes, this basic finding points up the requirement for eliminating systematic forecast-error biases. We explore that issue in detail in chapter 3.

By way of contrast, changes in the dynamics, and dynamic parameter mis-specifications, are both multiplied by mean-zero terms, so vanish on average: indeed, they would have no effect whatever on the forecast errors if the forecast origin equalled the equilibrium mean. Conversely, the larger the disequilibrium at the time of a shift in the dynamics, the larger the resulting impact. This is clearer in the conditional expectation (2.10), but as $\mathbf{\Pi}^*$, $\mathbf{\Pi}$ and $\mathbf{\Pi}_p$ (by assumption) have all their roots inside the unit circle, these effects die out as the horizon expands (the taxonomy would again need extending to allow for changes in the numbers of unit roots, and hence cointegrating vectors). Note that the forecasts are conditionally biased under constant parameters if inconsistent estimates are used. Similarly, when $\mathsf{E}[\hat{\mathbf{y}}_T|\mathbf{y}_T] \neq \mathbf{y}_T$, conditionally-biased forecasts result.

Next, consider the variance effects resulting from the taxonomy. The first four rows are accounted for by using (2.10), and analyzing conditional variances. That leaves the conditional variances of the powered-up estimated slope matrix coefficients $\widehat{\mathbf{\Pi}}$, the components from estimating the equilibrium means, the variances of $\hat{\mathbf{y}}_T - \mathsf{E}[\hat{\mathbf{y}}_T|\mathbf{y}_T]$, which also interact with the estimated dynamics through $\mathbf{C}_h$, and the variances of the cumulated errors (assumed independent over time):

$$\mathsf{V}\left[\epsilon_{T+h}\right] = \sum_{i=0}^{h-1} \left(\mathbf{\Pi}^{*}\right)^{i} \mathbf{\Omega}_{\epsilon} \left(\mathbf{\Pi}^{*}\right)^{i\prime}. \tag{2.11}$$

The first two are of order T^{-1} relative to (2.11), and for correct specifications have been derived by Schmidt (1974) and Baillie (1979b) (also see Chong and Hendry, 1986, and Doornik and Hendry, 1997); Clements and Hendry (1996c) derive the distributions when there are only unit roots in the dynamics. Our empirical experience from computing forecast-error variances from (2.11) and then adding the component from parameter estimation is that the latter is small in comparison. However, Marquez and Ericsson (1993) report large increases when simulating the effects of parameter uncertainty by Monte Carlo: chapter 4 examines the effects of parameter estimation (see §4.3.8 in particular).

2.2.1 *Attempts to offset structural breaks*

When a parameter change occurs, previously-announced forecasts will be incorrect from almost any procedure. Since most forecasters produce sequences of forecasts over time, consider the outcomes they might experience in the period following the break, where the new forecast origin is $T+1$. Forecasting $T+2$ from $T+1$ using (2.4) will generate the same bias as $T+1$, given by (2.9) for $h=1$. Thus, the in-sample congruent system will perform as badly sequentially as initially.

However, some robustness to regime shifts which would otherwise bias forecasts can be obtained. Two possibilities are intercept corrections (ICs) that carry forward the shift from time $T+1$; or by suitable differencing to eliminate the changed deterministic term in later periods. An IC can difference the forecast errors that would otherwise have been made, but at a cost in terms of increased forecast-error variance for larger values of h. Alternatively, first differencing the $\mathsf{I}(0)$ data produces the naive forecast $\Delta\widetilde{\mathbf{y}}_{T+2|T+1} = \mathbf{0}$, or $\widetilde{\mathbf{y}}_{T+2|T+1} = \mathbf{y}_{T+1}$, and as $\mathsf{E}[\mathbf{y}_{T+h}] = \boldsymbol{\varphi}^{*} + (\mathbf{\Pi}^{*})^{h}(\boldsymbol{\varphi} - \boldsymbol{\varphi}^{*})$, the mean forecast error is:

$$\begin{aligned}
\mathsf{E}\left[\widetilde{\epsilon}_{T+2|T+1}\right] &= \mathsf{E}\left[\mathbf{y}_{T+2} - \widetilde{\mathbf{y}}_{T+2|T+1}\right] \\
&= \left(\mathbf{\Pi}^{*}\right)^{2}\left(\boldsymbol{\varphi} - \boldsymbol{\varphi}^{*}\right) - \mathbf{\Pi}^{*}\left(\boldsymbol{\varphi} - \boldsymbol{\varphi}^{*}\right) \\
&= \mathbf{\Pi}^{*}\left(\mathbf{I}_{n} - \mathbf{\Pi}^{*}\right)\left(\boldsymbol{\varphi}^{*} - \boldsymbol{\varphi}\right).
\end{aligned}$$

The bias vanishes at $\mathbf{\Pi}^* = \mathbf{0}$ (or $\mathbf{\Pi}^* = \mathbf{I}_n$), and is smaller than (2.9) in general. Thus, once again, a non-causal variable ($\mathbf{y}_{t-1}$) can dominate on some forecast-accuracy measure; and over-differencing need not be disadvantageous in some circumstances (note that some of the $\Delta\mathbf{y}_t$ are second-differenced $\mathbf{x}_t$).

In chapter 5 we show that a VEqCM and DV for (1.12) have identical forecast-error biases when a forecast is made before a break occurs for a horizon that includes the break. This is so despite the former including, and the latter excluding, all the cointegration information; however, their forecast-error variances will differ. The biases for the VEqCM do not depend on whether the forecast starts pre or post the break: thus, there is no "error correction" after the break. However, the DV has different biases pre and post for breaks in $\boldsymbol{\alpha}$ and $\boldsymbol{\mu}$, and these are usually smaller than the corresponding biases from the VEqCM. A forecasting model like $\Delta^2\widetilde{\mathbf{x}}_{T+1|T} = \Delta^2\mathbf{x}_T$ is robust to some shifts, but may "over-insure" by not predicting any developments of interest, merely "tracking" by never being badly wrong.

Although such devices can improve forecast accuracy, especially on bias measures, they entail nothing about the usefulness for other purposes of the forecasting model. Even if the resulting (intercept corrected or differenced) forecast is more accurate than that from (2.4), this does not imply choosing the "robustified" model for policy, or later modeling exercises. If any policy changes were implemented on the basis of mechanistic forecasts, the latter would have the odd property of continuing to predict the same outcome however large the policy response. Thus, there may be benefits to combining robust predictors with forecasts from econometric systems in the policy context, and this is a hypothesis to consider if encompassing fails: see Hendry and Mizon (1998c).

2.3 Forecast Failure in Congruent Models

We now apply the closed-system forecast-error taxonomy set out in table 2.1 to interpret forecast failure in congruent models. The DGP is a cointegrated VAR, which coincides with the model in-sample, reduced to the I(0) representation in terms of $\mathbf{y}_t$. We reproduce the relevant elements from table 2.1 in table 2.2 for convenience. The possible causes of forecast failure in such a setting are post-estimation breaks (*ia*) and

Table 2.2
Partial I(0) forecast-error taxonomy.

$\widehat{\epsilon}_{T+h\|T}$	$\simeq$	$\left((\boldsymbol{\Pi}^*)^h - \boldsymbol{\Pi}^h\right)(\mathbf{y}_T - \boldsymbol{\varphi})$	(*ia*) slope change
		$+\left(\mathbf{I}_n - (\boldsymbol{\Pi}^*)^h\right)(\boldsymbol{\varphi}^* - \boldsymbol{\varphi})$	(*ib*) equilibrium-mean change
		$-\mathbf{F}_h \boldsymbol{\delta}_{\Pi}^{\nu}$	(*iiia*) slope estimation
		$-\left(\mathbf{I}_n - \boldsymbol{\Pi}^h\right)\boldsymbol{\delta}_{\varphi}$	(*iiib*) equilibrium-mean estimation
		$-\left(\boldsymbol{\Pi}^h + \mathbf{C}_h\right)\boldsymbol{\delta}_y$	(*iv*) forecast origin uncertainty
		$+\sum_{i=0}^{h-1} (\boldsymbol{\Pi}^*)^i \boldsymbol{\epsilon}_{T+h-i}$	(*v*) error accumulation.

(*ib*); poor parameter estimates (*iiia*) and (*iiib*); an inappropriate forecast origin (*iv*); or incorrectly-calculated prediction intervals used in evaluation. This section highlights how the sources can be discriminated *ex post* by the consequences of updating .

By analysis, and a Monte Carlo illustration in §3.3.1, equilibrium-mean shifts are shown to be a dominant cause of predictive failure , both *ex ante* and *ex post*. Indeed, chapter 3 considers a Monte Carlo example where both the intercept and the dynamics change, but the equilibrium mean remains constant, and no forecast failure is detected. Further, shifts in dynamics when the equilibrium mean remains zero also prove hard to detect relative to their inducing a shift in $\boldsymbol{\varphi}$. UK M1 provides one potential example of equilibrium-mean shifts following the introduction in 1984 of interest-bearing retail sight deposits: these sharply lowered the opportunity costs of holding M1, shifting the long-run equilibrium mean, which — when not modeled appropriately — induced substantial forecast errors: see Hendry (1996). We analyze this data set in chapter 8, but illustrate with a graph below. This example leads into the discussion in §2.5 of VEqCMs and differenced models.

Poor parameter estimates and an inappropriate forecast origin can be distinguished from other sources *ex post* in congruent models, as the extended sample size and more accurate revised data will reveal that no failure actually occurred. Chapter 4 discusses the former in detail, focusing on two possible sources, namely collinearity and a lack of parsimony. It demonstrates that by themselves, neither is able to account for forecast failure, although in the presence of structural breaks, they can exacerbate failure: *ex post*, moreover, predictive failure will not be found. In "open" models, that is, systems with non-modeled explanatory variables $\mathbf{z}_t$ whose future values are calculated outside of the forecasting model for $\mathbf{x}_t$, inaccurate values of $\mathbf{z}_t$ can also induce *ex ante* forecast failure that disappears *ex post* when the correct $\mathbf{z}_t$ are used (see the various forecast-error decompositions in e.g., Wallis, Andrews, Bell, Fisher and Whitley, 1984, 1985, Wallis, Andrews, Fisher, Longbottom and Whitley, 1986, Wallis, Fisher, Longbottom, Turner and Whitley, 1987, and Wallis and Whitley, 1991). Section 2.7 discusses the general issue of "model constancy".

Prediction intervals could be calculated incorrectly for many reasons in general, but in congruent models, a possible source is "overfitting" by retaining too many apparently significant estimated parameters, so underestimating the innovation variance. This is distinct from a pure lack of parsimony, which may entail retaining variables whose coefficients are small, but non-zero, without any testing having occurred. Nevertheless, parameter-estimation variances are of a smaller order of magnitude than the other terms, so even underestimating their contribution should not be overly detrimental. Underestimating the innovation variance is potentially more serious, as it is an $O(1)$ effect, but again, longer samples would reveal the "real" insignificance of the over-fitted variables, and lead to a less biased estimate of $\mathbf{\Omega}_\epsilon$. Breaks can induce residual serial correlation, but so can a changed error process that has become autocorrelated out of sample, so these effects can be separated only if the break is modeled.

We discuss the implications of forecast failure in congruent models in chapter 3. Section 2.6 addresses the converse issue of non-congruent models successfully forecasting when congruent models fail.

2.4 A VEqCM Forecast-error Taxonomy

It is possible to transform the I(0) forecast-error taxonomy in table 2.1, expressed in terms of $\mathbf{y}_t$, back to the original VEqCM parameters $\boldsymbol{\gamma}$, $\boldsymbol{\mu}$, $\boldsymbol{\alpha}$, and $\boldsymbol{\beta}$. This is somewhat involved, so here we focus on the elements likely to induce forecast failure, namely the structural breaks, although we keep $\boldsymbol{\beta}$ constant. The in-sample DGP was given in (1.20), namely:

$$\begin{pmatrix} \boldsymbol{\beta}'\mathbf{x}_t \\ \boldsymbol{\beta}'_{\perp}\Delta\mathbf{x}_t \end{pmatrix} = \begin{pmatrix} -\boldsymbol{\beta}'\boldsymbol{\alpha}\boldsymbol{\mu} \\ \boldsymbol{\beta}'_{\perp}(\boldsymbol{\gamma}-\boldsymbol{\alpha}\boldsymbol{\mu}) \end{pmatrix} + \begin{pmatrix} \boldsymbol{\Lambda} \\ \boldsymbol{\beta}'_{\perp}\boldsymbol{\alpha} \end{pmatrix}\boldsymbol{\beta}'\mathbf{x}_{t-1} + \begin{pmatrix} \boldsymbol{\beta}' \\ \boldsymbol{\beta}'_{\perp} \end{pmatrix}\boldsymbol{\nu}_t \tag{2.12}$$

where $\boldsymbol{\Lambda} = \mathbf{I}_r + \boldsymbol{\beta}'\boldsymbol{\alpha}$. Often, the mapping from I(1) VARs to I(0) VEqCMs selects $\boldsymbol{\alpha}'_{\perp}\Delta\mathbf{x}_t$ rather than $\boldsymbol{\beta}'_{\perp}\Delta\mathbf{x}_t$ to augment the cointegration relations, but the former is inconvenient here as we wish to allow for changes in $\boldsymbol{\alpha}$. Section 2.10 details the calculations. In this section, all terms involving parameter inconsistencies, estimation, forecast origin, and error accumulation have been omitted. However, since the impacts of breaks on growth rates and cointegrating combinations are very different, these terms are distinguished.

Since we are ignoring estimation issues, the forecasting model is effectively:

$$\begin{pmatrix} \boldsymbol{\beta}'\widehat{\mathbf{x}}_{T+h|T} \\ \boldsymbol{\beta}'_{\perp}\widehat{\Delta\mathbf{x}}_{T+h|T} \end{pmatrix} = \begin{pmatrix} \boldsymbol{\mu} \\ \boldsymbol{\beta}'_{\perp}\boldsymbol{\gamma} \end{pmatrix} + \begin{pmatrix} \boldsymbol{\Lambda} \\ \boldsymbol{\beta}'_{\perp}\boldsymbol{\alpha} \end{pmatrix}\boldsymbol{\Lambda}^{h-1}(\boldsymbol{\beta}'\mathbf{x}_T - \boldsymbol{\mu}),$$

for $h = 1, \ldots, H$. However, $(\boldsymbol{\gamma}, \boldsymbol{\mu}, \boldsymbol{\alpha})$ in (2.12) change after forecasting at time T to $(\boldsymbol{\gamma}^*, \boldsymbol{\mu}^*, \boldsymbol{\alpha})$. Let $\boldsymbol{\Lambda}^* = \mathbf{I}_r + \boldsymbol{\beta}'\boldsymbol{\alpha}^*$ (still with all its eigenvalues less than unity in absolute value) and define the forecast errors by:

$$\begin{pmatrix} \boldsymbol{\beta}'\hat{\mathbf{e}}_{T+h} \\ \boldsymbol{\beta}'_{\perp}\hat{\mathbf{e}}_{T+h} \end{pmatrix} = \begin{pmatrix} \boldsymbol{\beta}'\mathbf{x}_{T+h} - \boldsymbol{\beta}'\widehat{\mathbf{x}}_{T+h|T} \\ \boldsymbol{\beta}'_{\perp}\Delta\mathbf{x}_{T+h} - \boldsymbol{\beta}'_{\perp}\widehat{\Delta\mathbf{x}}_{T+h|T} \end{pmatrix}.$$

Then the partition of the forecast errors after structural breaks is shown in table 2.3, where the lettering *a, b* denotes effects for $\boldsymbol{\beta}'\mathbf{x}_{T+h}$ and $\boldsymbol{\beta}'_{\perp}\Delta\mathbf{x}_{T+h}$ respectively. Elements in rows are designed to be precisely zero if the associated parameter does not change.

It is simplest to commence from the bottom of the table, namely case (*3b*), and consider that in relation to (*3a*). This reveals that changes in equilibrium growth rates induce persistent equal-magnitude biases on the actual growth forecasts, since we are forecasting $\boldsymbol{\beta}'_{\perp}\Delta\mathbf{x}_{T+h}$. However, they are shown here as having no effect on the cointegration forecasts. That occurs because we have imposed $\boldsymbol{\beta}'\boldsymbol{\gamma} = \boldsymbol{\beta}'\boldsymbol{\gamma}^* = \mathbf{0}$, to ensure that the cointegration relations do not trend after the growth-rate

Table 2.3
VEqCM forecast-biases taxonomy.

$\boldsymbol{\beta}'\hat{\mathbf{e}}_{T+h\|T}$	$\simeq$	$\left((\boldsymbol{\Lambda}^*)^h - \boldsymbol{\Lambda}^h\right)(\boldsymbol{\beta}'\mathbf{x}_T - \boldsymbol{\mu})$	(*1a*) slope
		$+\left(\mathbf{I}_r - (\boldsymbol{\Lambda}^*)^h\right)(\boldsymbol{\mu}^* - \boldsymbol{\mu})$	(*2a*) mean
		$+0$	(*3a*) growth
$\boldsymbol{\beta}'_{\perp}\hat{\mathbf{e}}_{T+h\|T}$	$\simeq$	$\boldsymbol{\beta}'_{\perp}\left(\boldsymbol{\alpha}^*(\boldsymbol{\Lambda}^*)^{h-1} - \boldsymbol{\alpha}\boldsymbol{\Lambda}^{h-1}\right)(\boldsymbol{\beta}'\mathbf{x}_T - \boldsymbol{\mu})$	(*1b*) slope
		$-\boldsymbol{\beta}'_{\perp}\boldsymbol{\alpha}^*(\boldsymbol{\Lambda}^*)^{h-1}(\boldsymbol{\mu}^* - \boldsymbol{\mu})$	(*2b*) mean
		$+\boldsymbol{\beta}'_{\perp}(\boldsymbol{\gamma}^* - \boldsymbol{\gamma})$	(*3b*) growth

shift. If they trended either before or after (or both, as in the Total Final Expenditure equation in the UK M1 model in Hendry and Doornik, 1994), growth-rate changes would distort cointegration forecasts.

Next, cases (*2a*) and (*2b*) show the impacts of shifts in the equilibrium means, both of which are non-zero and persistent. Since $\boldsymbol{\Lambda}^h \to \mathbf{0}$ as $h \to \infty$, the latter is decreasing in h, and eventually vanishes, whereas the former increase to the full effect of $(\boldsymbol{\mu}^* - \boldsymbol{\mu})$.

Finally, slope changes in cases (*1a*) and (*1b*) remain mean-zero terms, so have no impact on forecast-error biases. As with the corresponding terms in table 2.1, a slope change has a greater effect, the more the economy is in disequilibrium at the forecast origin, now as measured by $(\boldsymbol{\beta}'\mathbf{x}_T - \boldsymbol{\mu})$. Further, providing both $\boldsymbol{\Lambda}$ and $\boldsymbol{\Lambda}^*$ have all their eigenvalues inside the unit circle, slope-change effects are decreasing in h.

2.5 Equilibrium Correction and Error Correction

The preceding analysis has important implications for the use in forecasting of equilibrium-correction mechanisms embodying cointegration relations. The formulation in (1.16), replicated as:

$$\Delta\mathbf{x}_t = \boldsymbol{\gamma} + \boldsymbol{\alpha}\left(\boldsymbol{\beta}'\mathbf{x}_{t-1} - \boldsymbol{\mu}\right) + \boldsymbol{\nu}_t \qquad (2.13)$$

clarifies that once the EqCMs are expressed as deviations from their means, the remaining intercepts are the growth rates. Providing the parameters remain constant, the term $(\boldsymbol{\beta}'\mathbf{x}_{t-1} - \boldsymbol{\mu})$ acts to correct past "mistakes", and induces the system to converge to $\mathsf{E}[\boldsymbol{\beta}'\mathbf{x}_t] = \boldsymbol{\mu}$ on average. An early paper investigating such corrections (Davidson, Hendry, Srba and Yeo, 1978, building on Phillips, 1957, and Sargan, 1964b) therefore called them "error-correction" mechanisms. For unchanged equilibria, this is an appropriate name – unfortunately, when equilibria change, such mechanisms completely fail to correct to the new values, as we now show.

Growth rates are small numbers ($0 - 0.02$ for quarterly real variables in most developed economies), even relative to residual standard deviations. Moreover, since in practice they do not change rapidly or by large amounts (with exceptions such as China since 1930, and some South-East Asian economies recently), the main problems from deterministic breaks concern shifts in the equilibrium means. However, both forms of shift can induce large shifts in levels, which will appear in practice as sustained unidirectional changes in some endogenous variables. Because estimated EqCMs drive relations back to the previous equilibrium means, they will take on large values – of precisely the wrong sign. This follows because the changed levels are viewed by the estimated model as disequilibria; the higher those levels, the more it seeks to "correct" them back to the old equilibrium, and hence the worse the forecast. Indeed, graphs similar to fig. 2.1 may be observed (also see, e.g., fig. 2 in Hendry, 1996), which shows the forecast failure for UK M1 noted above when using a model that omits the own rate of interest on M1 following the 1984 legislation change. Despite in-sample congruency, well-determined estimates, and theoretically-supported cointegration in an equation that had remained constant for almost a decade, the forecasts are for systematic falls in real M1 during the most rapid rise that has occurred historically ($D(m-p)$ in the graph denotes $\Delta \log(M/P)$). Almost all the forecast-horizon data lie outside the *ex ante* 95% prediction intervals.[2] Such an outcome is far from "error correction", and prompted the renaming of cointegration combinations to equilibrium correction (see Hendry, 1995a). We now investigate this problem analytically.

[2] A 4-variable system was modeled, and the forecasts shown are a sequence of 1-step ahead, using the pre-break estimated parameter values, and available lagged information.

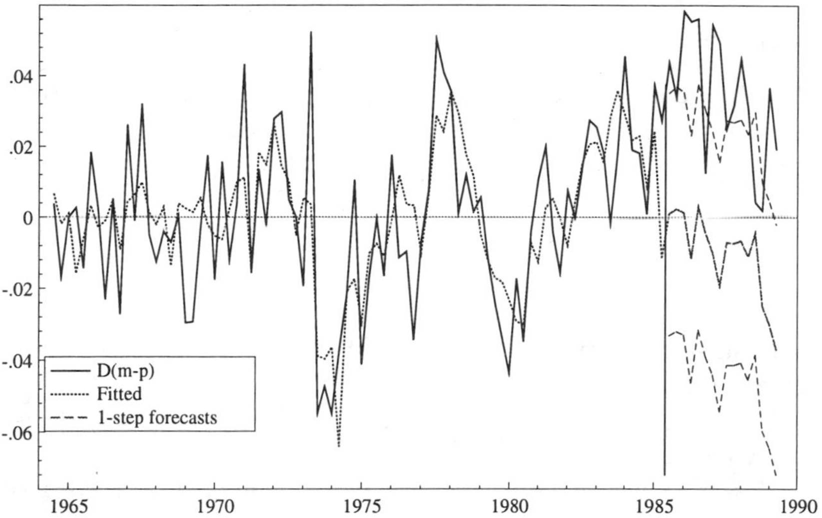

Figure 2.1
Sequence of 1-step forecasts for UK M1 growth, $\Delta(m-p)$.

Using (2.13) for the cointegrated VAR, the expected deviation from the outcome of a forecast for $\Delta \mathbf{x}_{T+1}$ based on an existing equilibrium mean $\boldsymbol{\mu}$ after a shift to $\boldsymbol{\mu}^*$ is:

$$\mathsf{E}\left[\Delta \mathbf{x}_{T+1} - \boldsymbol{\gamma} - \boldsymbol{\alpha}\left(\boldsymbol{\beta}'\mathbf{x}_T - \boldsymbol{\mu}\right)\right] = -\boldsymbol{\alpha}\left(\boldsymbol{\mu}^* - \boldsymbol{\mu}\right). \quad (2.14)$$

Thus, the growth in $\mathbf{x}_{T+1}$ is mis-predicted by $\boldsymbol{\alpha}(\boldsymbol{\mu} - \boldsymbol{\mu}^*)$, which could be large. In terms of predictive failure, later 1-step forecast-error biases are given by:

$$\mathsf{E}\left[\Delta \mathbf{x}_{T+h} - \boldsymbol{\gamma} - \boldsymbol{\alpha}\left(\boldsymbol{\beta}'\mathbf{x}_{T+h-1} - \boldsymbol{\mu}\right)\right] = -\boldsymbol{\alpha}\left(\mathbf{I}_r - \boldsymbol{\Lambda}^{h-1}\right)\left(\boldsymbol{\mu}^* - \boldsymbol{\mu}\right). \quad (2.15)$$

Since $\boldsymbol{\Lambda}^h \rightarrow \mathbf{0}$ as $h \rightarrow \infty$, the biases first fall one period after the shift, then steadily converge back to the value in (2.14). Since they all have the same sign, the failure is systematic, and matches the outcome in fig. 2.1, where most of the forecast errors have a similar magnitude. The biases in (2.14) and (2.15) are invariant to the transformation to levels. However, since:

$$\mathbf{x}_{T+h} = \boldsymbol{\gamma} - \boldsymbol{\alpha}\boldsymbol{\mu}^* + \left(\mathbf{I}_n + \boldsymbol{\alpha}\boldsymbol{\beta}'\right)\mathbf{x}_{T+h-1},$$

and:

$$\widehat{\mathbf{x}}_{T+h|T} = \boldsymbol{\gamma} - \boldsymbol{\alpha\mu} + \boldsymbol{\Upsilon}\widehat{\mathbf{x}}_{T+h-1|T},$$

where $\mathbf{I}_n + \boldsymbol{\alpha\beta}' = \boldsymbol{\Upsilon}$, letting $\mathbf{x}_{T+h} - \widehat{\mathbf{x}}_{T+h|T} = \mathbf{e}_{T+h|T}$, as $\boldsymbol{\Upsilon}^i\boldsymbol{\alpha} = \boldsymbol{\alpha\Lambda}^i$:

$$\begin{aligned}
\mathsf{E}\left[\mathbf{e}_{T+h|T}\right] &= -\sum_{i=0}^{h-1} \boldsymbol{\Upsilon}^i \boldsymbol{\alpha} \left(\boldsymbol{\mu}^* - \boldsymbol{\mu}\right) = -\boldsymbol{\alpha} \sum_{i=0}^{h-1} \boldsymbol{\Lambda}^i \left(\boldsymbol{\mu}^* - \boldsymbol{\mu}\right) \\
&= -\boldsymbol{\alpha} \left(\mathbf{I}_r - \boldsymbol{\Lambda}\right)^{-1} \left(\mathbf{I}_r - \boldsymbol{\Lambda}^h\right) \left(\boldsymbol{\mu}^* - \boldsymbol{\mu}\right) \\
&= \boldsymbol{\alpha} \left(\boldsymbol{\beta}'\boldsymbol{\alpha}\right)^{-1} \left(\mathbf{I}_r - \boldsymbol{\Lambda}^h\right) \left(\boldsymbol{\mu}^* - \boldsymbol{\mu}\right),
\end{aligned}$$

the multi-step forecast-error biases for the levels are cumulative, but convergent.

Consequently, VEqCMs will be reliable in forecasting only if they contain all the variables needed to track changed states of nature. Nevertheless, in policy analyses, EqCMs will frequently play a central role, so a method of retaining their economic importance and statistical efficacy without losing forecast robustness is highly desirable. Hendry and Mizon (1998b) consider some approaches to obtaining error correction for non-stationary processes, but conclude that common factors of unity are required, entailing differencing , and hence the elimination of the EqCM. Thus, forecast robustness ideas, such as intercept corrections (see ch. 6), and forecast-period corrections along the lines of exponentially-weighted moving averages, merit consideration.

2.6 Non-congruent Devices Need Not Fail

In §2.5, we indicated that EqCMs are particularly prone to forecast failure when the equilibrium mean shifts. It may be possible to avoid systematic mis-forecasting by "robustifying" the model to structural breaks. To the extent that such can be achieved, the resulting model need not fail, but need not be congruent either, as in the following differencing example.

Since step shifts in intercepts are reduced to blips by differencing, we might anticipate less failure for first-differenced models. To illustrate this, we use a Monte Carlo simulation consisting of six experiments, implemented in Ox by PcNaive for Windows (see Doornik, 1996, and Doornik and Hendry, 1998). The first three (denoted A, C, and D

Table 2.4
Design parameter values for I(0) process.

Case	A		C		D	
regime	1	2	1	2	1	2
β_1	0.85	0.85	0.85	0.70	0.85	0.85
α_1	1.5	1.5	1.5	1.5	1.5	0.375
α_2	5.0	5.0	5.0	5.0	5.0	5.0

for consistency with a later more extensive analysis) are for an I(0) VAR, the last three (F, H, I) for an I(1) process. First, in the I(0) process, the experiments are:

(A) a constant-parameter equation;
(C) a break in the dynamics when there is a non-zero mean;
(D) a break in the intercept, inducing φ^* equal to that in (C).

The baseline DGP for (A)–(D) is the VAR:

$$y_{1,t} = \alpha_1 + 0.3y_{2,t} + \beta_1 y_{1,t-1} - 0.15y_{2,t-1} + \epsilon_{1,t} \quad (2.16)$$

$$y_{2,t} = \alpha_2 - 0.5y_{1,t-1} + 0.75y_{2,t-1} + \epsilon_{2,t}. \quad (2.17)$$

The mutually independent $\epsilon_{i,t} \sim \mathsf{IN}[0, \sigma_{ii}]$ with variances of 0.1, and 0.5 respectively. All breaks occur at $T = 100$, reverting to the original value at $T = 150$ with the full-sample size of $T = 200$. We used $M = 1000$ replications, with common random numbers across all experiments. Three models are investigated: the first coincides with (2.16) in levels; the second expresses (2.16) isomorphically as (where $\kappa = 0.15/(1 - \beta_1)$):

$$\Delta y_{1,t} = \alpha_1 + 0.3\Delta y_{2,t} + (\beta_1 - 1)(y_{1,t-1} - \kappa y_{2,t-1}) + \epsilon_{1,t}; \quad (2.18)$$

and the third is (2.18) without the EqCM. Both *ex post* forecast tests over $T = 90, \ldots, 104$ and break-point Chow (1960) tests over $T = 50, \ldots, 104$ are reported. The break-point Chow test performs an F-test on the current residual sum of squares (RSS) versus the final RSS, so uses RSS_t versus RSS_{105} in fig. 2.2, and RSS_t versus RSS_{201} in fig. 2.3 for $t = 50, \ldots$. The forecast Chow test in fig. 2.2 uses RSS_t versus RSS_{49}. One-off critical values are used for a known break point, since the issue is the relative power to detect various shifts in different models, not to develop appropriate modeling procedures. The relevant experimental

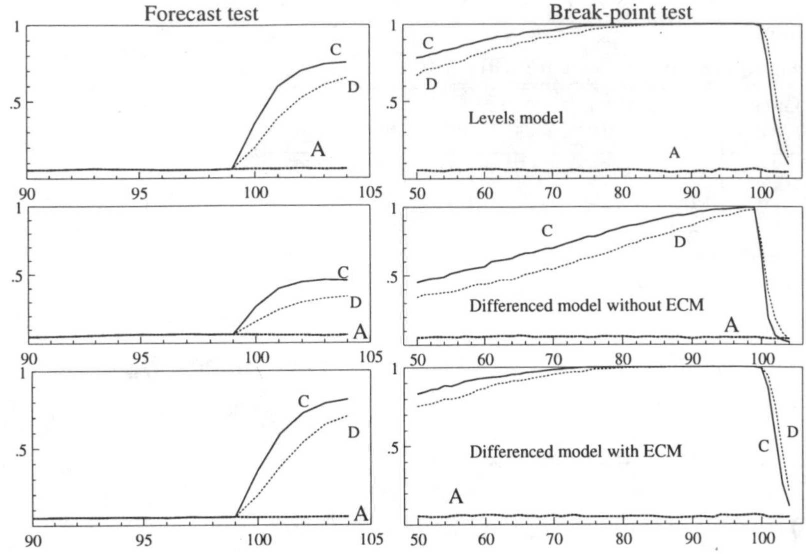

Figure 2.2
Constancy-test rejection frequencies for the I(0) process.

design parameter values for $(\alpha_1, \beta_1, \alpha_2)$ are recorded in table 2.4, where the pre- and post-break regimes are denoted by 1 and 2.

In the second set of experiments, we consider an I(1) DGP given by:

$$\begin{aligned} \Delta y_{1,t} &= \gamma_1 + 0.3\Delta y_{2,t} + \pi_1 (y_{1,t-1} - y_{2,t-1} - \mu_1) + \epsilon_{1,t} \\ \Delta y_{2,t} &= 0.025 + \epsilon_{2,t}, \end{aligned} \tag{2.19}$$

where $\epsilon_{i,t} \sim \mathsf{IN}[0, \sigma_{ii}]$, with $\sqrt{\sigma_{ii}}$ of 0.025, 0.036. The timing of the breaks was the same. The experiments were:

(F) a constant-parameter equation, with $\pi_1 = -0.15$;
(H) a break in the equilibrium mean from $\mu_1 = 1$ to 1.33;
(I) a break in the growth rate from $\gamma_1 = 0.025$ to 0.05.

A fuller motivation for this formulation is given in chapter 3, where we analyze the effects of deterministic shifts in cointegrated processes, and present further Monte Carlo evidence. For now we compare the forecast performance of two models to bring out the possible benefits of differencing. The first model is the first equation in (2.19), and the

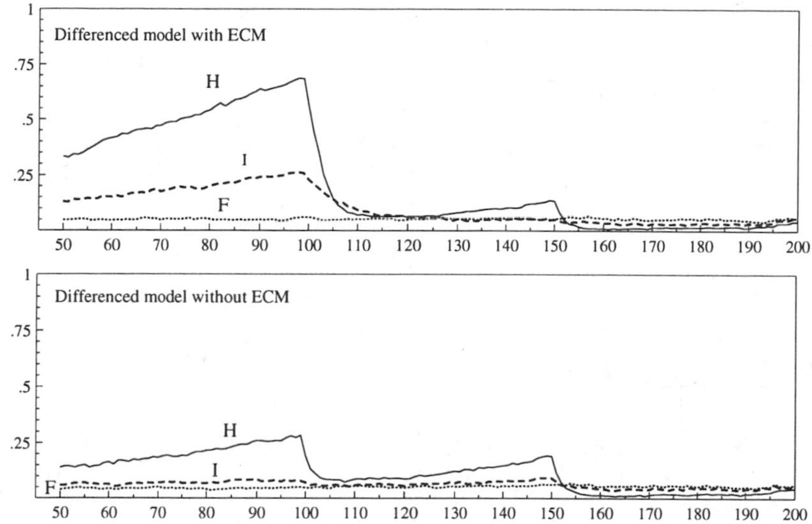

Figure 2.3
Constancy-test rejection frequencies for the I(1) process.

second is an equation in differences (i.e., omitting the EqCM). Here, we only report break-point Chow tests, but over most of the estimation sample $T = 50, \ldots, 200$.

Figures 2.2 and 2.3 show the outcomes for the I(0) and I(1) DGPs respectively. For the I(0) DGP, the size of the tests is close to the 5% nominal level used, even for the mis-specified models. The break-point tests are somewhat more powerful at detecting the shifts. The equilibrium-mean shifts are easily detected for all three models, whether due to the dynamics or the intercept changing. In particular, there is little benefit to using the differenced model. However, that is not so clearly the case for (2.19) when the system is I (1). The test sizes are again close to their nominal levels for both models. There is reasonable power to detect the equilibrium-mean shift, as the upper panel in fig. 2.3 shows, less so for the growth-rate change. However, the lower panel records a sharp drop in power for the model in differences in the I(1) case relative to the loss in power in the I(0) case. This changed outcome between I(0) and I(1) DGPs can be explained as follows. Since there is no natural scale

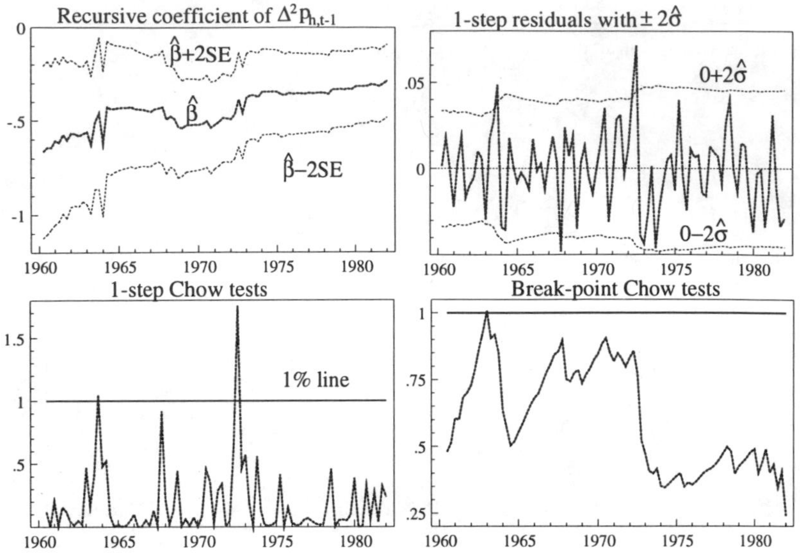

Figure 2.4
UK house price autoregression for $\Delta^2 p_{h,t}$.

for the intercept, a step break in the intercept can "swamp" other terms even after becoming a blip on differencing, leading to substantial — and easily detected — non-constancy in an I(0) system. That is unlike the outcome for a cointegrated DGP, where intercepts are growth rates (as in (1.16) above): only small changes in γ are likely, and changes in μ have less relevance to models in differences (although experiment (H) reveals that some non-constancy results). The empirical finding that differencing is effective in reducing predictive failure becomes indirect evidence that there are unit roots in economic processes. The implication most relevant to this section is that the non-congruent differenced model can experience much less forecast failure than the in-sample congruent model when faced with deterministic shifts. We return to the other important implications of these Monte Carlos in the next chapter.

As a possible empirical illustration of the advantages of over-differencing when structural breaks occur, consider forecasting UK house-prices over the turbulent period 1955–82. We begin by estimating a first-order autoregression in the second difference of the log of UK

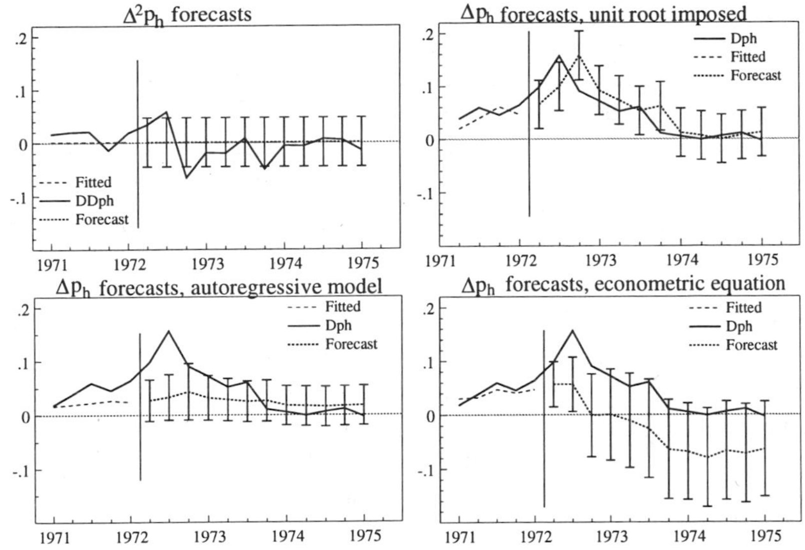

Figure 2.5
UK house price forecasts for $\Delta p_{h,t}$ and $\Delta^2 p_{h,t}$.

house prices, $\Delta^2 p_{h,t}$. Figure 2.4a–d shows the recursively-estimated coefficient (denoted $\widehat{\beta}$) with bands at $\widehat{\beta} \pm 2$SE; 1-step ahead forecast errors (with bands at $0 \pm 2\widehat{\sigma}$); and 1-step and break-point Chow tests computed recursively (scaled by their 1% critical values, so an outcome in excess of unity is significant as a "one-off" test). Despite the many known institutional changes, and the lack of any economic explanatory variables, no break-point test is significant at a (one-off) 1% level, and only one outlier is seen (in 1972 quarter 3).

A comparison across models of the forecasts and outcomes over the house-price boom of 1972(1)–1975(1) is reported in the four panels of fig. 2.5a–d, using a common scale. Here, the first row shows the results for forecasting $\Delta^2 p_{h,t}$ and $\Delta p_{h,t}$ using the simpler model $\Delta^2 \widehat{p}_{h,t} = 0$, rather than the first-order AR in the second differences. As we will establish, mopping up the autocorrelation in the residual by specifying lags (as in the AR in the second differences) may lose some of the benefit of "over-differencing". The second row records the results for forecasting $\Delta p_{h,t}$ from autoregressive and econometric equations respectively (taken from Hendry and Wallis, 1984). Two significant forecast errors are apparent for $\Delta^2 \widehat{p}_{h,t} = 0$, leading to systematic over-prediction of the first differences. However, these forecasts seem respectable in comparison to the second row, where large forecast errors result and (in the last panel) where the forecast-confidence bars also mushroom from the third forecast onwards, after the jump in house prices. Indeed, the econometric equation forecasts large falls in house prices during the largest ever boom: notwithstanding that apparently awful outcome, we show in §4.3.3 that the underlying equation has constant parameters. Conversely, despite the relatively impressive performance of the autoregressive equation in $\Delta^2 p_{h,t}$, it fails a constancy test over the house-price boom of 1972(2)–75(1): $\mathsf{F_{Ch}}(12, 57) = 3.1^{**}$ ($\mathsf{p} = 0.002$). Also, its residual standard deviation is 50% larger than that of the econometric model used in §4.3.5 ($\widehat{\sigma} = 2.3\%$ as against $\widehat{\sigma} = 1.5\%$). Finally, we note that the simpler model of $\Delta^2 p_{h,t} = 0$ outperforms its autoregressive counterpart, and again seek to explain that outcome in chapter 5.

2.7 Extended Model Constancy

Given the occurrence of non-constancy in practice, we now consider possible responses. We begin with the notion of *ex post* predictive failure, and the consequences for modeling practice. If a predictive failure is due to model mis-specification revealed by a change in the omitted variables' behavior (as investigated in §4.2 below), a re-specification is essential, and could recreate a full-sample constant representation. This situation corresponds to non-constancy in the pre-existing model, but is distinct progress, rather than failure, as it represents a genuine increase in understanding. Since several breaks could be attributable to a single omitted influence, small extensions to the model could in principle account for many forecast failures. Of course, discovering the culprit may require considerable ingenuity as well as improved theoretical analyses and (possibly) new measurements. Should the outcome necessitate new values for the in-sample parameters, then it confirms a structural break relative to the previous model.

However, an important possibility is that although an extended model is needed to accommodate the predictive failure, that does not entail non-constant parameters in the initial model. This may seem paradoxical, but can be explained as follows: the definitions here are from Hendry (1995a), and the following analysis builds on Hendry (1996). A parameter $\boldsymbol{\theta} \in \Theta \subseteq \mathbb{R}^k$ must be constant across realizations of the stochastic process it indexes, but need not be constant over time. It is constant over a time interval $\mathcal{T} = \{\ldots, -1, 0, 1, 2, \ldots\}$ if $\boldsymbol{\theta}$ takes the same value for all $t \in \mathcal{T}$. A model is constant if all its parameters are. Even so, it is well known that constant models can have time-varying coefficients, which are, in effect, latent variables that depend on more basic parameters, where these in turn are constant: the models in Harvey and Shephard (1992) are an example. Similarly, "random coefficient" models have underlying constant parameters characterizing their distributions (now conditionally heteroscedastic), so the notion of "constant parameter" requires a precise specification of what entities are treated as parameters.

Since $1-1$ transforms of parameters are valid, and essential since most models have many isomorphic representations, zero can become the population value of a parameter ψ_i in $\boldsymbol{\psi} = \mathbf{h}(\boldsymbol{\theta}) \in \Psi \subseteq \mathbb{R}^k$. Let the original parameters for a conditional density $\mathsf{D}_{\mathsf{y}|\mathsf{z}}(\mathbf{y}_t|\mathbf{z}_t; \boldsymbol{\theta})$ of $\mathbf{y}_t$ over T_1 be $\boldsymbol{\theta}$ given a conditioning vector $\mathbf{z}_t$, where sequential factorization of the T_1-sample joint density yields:

$$\prod_{t=1}^{T_1} \mathsf{D}_{\mathsf{y}|\mathsf{z}}\left(\mathbf{y}_t \mid \mathbf{z}_t; \boldsymbol{\theta}\right). \tag{2.20}$$

Consider a setting where (2.20) fails a constancy test over a horizon (T_1+1) to T, so to characterize the whole T-sample, an extended model with parameters $\boldsymbol{\rho} \subseteq \mathbb{R}^K$ (for $K > k$) given K variables $\mathbf{x}_t$ is needed, delivering:

$$\prod_{t=1}^{T} \mathsf{D}_{\mathsf{y}|\mathsf{z}}\left(\mathbf{y}_t \mid \mathbf{x}_t; \boldsymbol{\rho}\right). \tag{2.21}$$

In (2.21), we assume that $\boldsymbol{\rho}$ is constant. *Prima facie*, the model in (2.20) seems non-constant, since there are $K-k$ additional parameters in $\boldsymbol{\rho}$ compared to the T_1-sample parameters $\boldsymbol{\theta}$. However, consider a $1-1$ mapping from $\boldsymbol{\rho}$ to $\boldsymbol{\delta}$ (say), such that $\boldsymbol{\delta} = \mathbf{g}(\boldsymbol{\rho})$. Then if:

$$\boldsymbol{\delta}' = \left(\boldsymbol{\theta}', \mathbf{0}'\right), \tag{2.22}$$

the model is constant despite the apparent expansion.

For example, let $\mathbf{x}_t$ coincide with $\mathbf{z}_t$ over the T_1-sample, but be an alternative measure for the same theoretical construct over the forecast period. Consequently, (2.20) is:

$$\prod_{t=1}^{T_1} \mathsf{D}_{\mathsf{y}|\mathsf{z}}\left(\mathbf{y}_t \mid \mathbf{z}_t; \boldsymbol{\theta}\right) = \prod_{t=1}^{T_1} \mathsf{D}_{\mathsf{y}|\mathsf{z}}\left(\mathbf{y}_t \mid \mathbf{x}_t; \boldsymbol{\theta}\right). \tag{2.23}$$

When (2.22) holds, an appropriate transform of (2.21) is:

$$\prod_{t=1}^{T} \mathsf{D}_{\mathsf{y}|\mathsf{z}}\left(\mathbf{y}_t \mid \mathbf{x}_t; \boldsymbol{\delta}\right) = \prod_{t=1}^{T} \mathsf{D}_{\mathsf{y}|\mathsf{z}}\left(\mathbf{y}_t \mid \mathbf{x}_t; \boldsymbol{\theta}\right). \tag{2.24}$$

From (2.23), the parameter $\boldsymbol{\theta}$ characterizes both the T_1-sample models (2.20) and (2.21), as well as the T-sample model (from (2.24)), but not (2.20) over the T-sample. Thus, $\mathbf{z}_t$ happens to be an appropriate measure till T_1, but not thereafter, whereas $\mathbf{x}_t$ is appropriate throughout.

An empirical illustration of this situation is presented in §9.8. When the own rate of interest on money (R_o) is zero, a competitive interest rate R is a reasonable measure of the opportunity cost. The introduction of a non-zero own rate, however, will induce forecast failure. Countering this failure by adding R_o expands the model, and hence demonstrates *ex post* non-constancy. But if the two variables R and R_o can be replaced by the differential $R - R_o$ alone (the correct measure of opportunity cost), with all the model's coefficients remaining unaltered, then the model reverts back to the original dimensionality with unchanged parameters. Using R rather than $R - R_o$ explains the poor forecast performance manifest in fig. 2.1: see chapter 8 for a detailed empirical analysis.

Constancy has not lost its operational content because of the possibility that extended models may transpire to be the old model in disguise. Equation (2.20) is not constant in the space of $(\mathbf{y}_t : \mathbf{z}_t)$ for all T. Moreover, there may exist no $\mathbf{g}(\cdot)$ which reproduces the original parameters augmented by zeroes, allowing a reduction to the previous parameterization. However, the result does imply that there are no viable in-sample tests (that is test based only on data up to time T_1) for later forecast failure, since the observation of failure depends on how the model is extended, not on its within-sample properties. Thus, a test that correctly predicted that (2.20) would fail, delivers the incorrect outcome when the same model happens to use $\mathbf{x}_t$ rather than $\mathbf{z}_t$, noting that these variables are identical in-sample. Such a result also suggests that forecast failure is primarily a function of forecast-period events: when the forecast-horizon data manifest similar behavior to the in-sample, failure will not occur, whereas different behavior by the forecast-horizon data will induce failure. We will return to this issue on several occasions to clarify its importance for the role of forecast evaluation in econometric modeling.

2.7.1 *Is ex-ante non-constancy a fatal flaw?*

A critic might doubt the value of empirical models that are congruent within sample when there is a non-negligible probability that they will fail out of sample. We must emphasize that empirical research is part of a progressive strategy, in which knowledge gradually accumulates. This includes knowledge about general causes of structural changes, such that later models incorporate measures accounting for previous events, and hence are more robust (e.g., to wars, changes in credit rationing, financial innovations, etc.). For example, dummies for purchase tax changes in Davidson *et al.* (1978) later successfully accommodated the introduction of VAT and its near doubling in 1979.

Conversely, that some breaks can be attributed to a scenario of a constant, congruent model confronted with post-sample change does not entail that all are: for example, models may already have broken down in-sample, and later analysis of their predictive failure just reveals that they are not useful even as data descriptions.

A hypothetical analogy for why forecast failure need not be fatal is Halley's prediction of the return of the comet now named after him. Several planets were then unknown, and had one of them slightly perturbed that comet's trajectory, such that it then collided in the Oort cloud with another object, it would never have returned – and become a classic case of forecast failure: we note with interest the recent fate of comet Shoemaker–Levy in colliding with Jupiter. However, a Mystic Meg might have claimed in Halley's time that his comet would never reappear, and then have been correct. Nevertheless, Newtonian gravitation theory is not refuted by such forecast failure, nor are Meg's claims to mystic sources validated. Progressive understanding would have uncovered the explanation in due course, and been justly regarded as a success.

2.8 Conclusion

The main conclusions are that equilibrium-mean shifts are the primary determinant of systematic forecast failure; and that while there is no essential conflict between the existence of structural breaks and congruent modeling, there is no guarantee that the forecast performance of well-specified congruent models will be superior to that of models eschewing causal factors. In terms of a progressive research strategy, structural breaks highlight weaknesses in models, which a congruent modeling strategy can exploit, thereby leading to advances in empirical knowledge. The best available models would gradually incorporate all the main shift factors stimulated through time, and thereafter be more robust. However, for *ex ante* forecasting, models other than congruent econometric models may be worthy of consideration. Even with the "best available models" one could still be caught out when forecasting: e.g., by the sudden and unanticipated outbreak of a major war for which no effect was included in the forecast. Here we risk a second astronomical analogy: consider a spacecraft that is forecast to reach the moon at a specific time; unfortunately, prior to doing so, it is hit by a meteor and knocked badly off course. Forecast failure manifestly occurs, and here is purely a function of the forecast-period events. No implications arise for the physical principles on which inter-planetary trajectories are calculated: Newton's laws are certainly not rejected just because they were the basis of a model which produced forecasts that went badly awry. There may not even be implications for the forecasting algorithms in use at NASA – except if they do not rapidly adapt to the altered trajectory. The same logic applies to economic forecasting: forecast failure does not, though it could, entail an invalid model; it does reveal data behavior that is different from that in-sample; and speedy adaptation is important if, after breaks, sequences of large forecast errors of the same sign are to be avoided.

Because it is possible to design "non-causal" forecasting devices that are robust to important classes of structural breaks, any claim that the "best forecasting" model should be selected for policy cannot be substantiated. However, the concept of co-breaking (see ch. 9) – namely the possibility of eliminating structural breaks in deterministic factors in systems of equations by taking linear combinations of variables, analogous to cointegration removing unit roots – suggests a continued role for congruent modeling and causal information, since to be sustainable, co-breaking combinations seem to require causal relations.

By *post-hoc* modeling of unpredicted changes, equations may be "overfitted" relative to their likely forecast performance. If future unanticipated breaks occur, the average forecast mean-square error will exceed that found on fitting the past. This raises the issue as to whether we should measure innovation variances with or without modeling previous structural breaks. The latter may be a better guide to likely forecast errors, but the former may be more useful in a policy context by enabling less imprecise parameter estimates. In terms of modeling strategy, we also favor the former (e.g., including dummies for externally-identified breaks – not just observed outliers), perhaps computing prediction intervals from the model with no dummies.

Finally, there are several empirical examples of "extended constancy", whereby, despite initial forecast failure, a model may be found to provide a constant *ex post* explanation with unchanged parameters. In both cases, inappropriate measurement of some of the explanatory variables over the forecast horizon accounted for the initial misforecasting, which vanished when more reasonable measures were adopted. En route, expanded models were proposed which included additional variables thought necessary to achieve a constant fit, but in the event, re-parameterizations existed that reduced such models to the originals, thereby confirming parameter constancy.

2.9 Appendix A: Taxonomy Derivations for Table 2.1

First, we use the approximation:

$$\hat{\mathbf{\Pi}}^h = (\mathbf{\Pi}_p + \boldsymbol{\delta}_\Pi)^h \simeq \mathbf{\Pi}_p^h + \sum_{i=0}^{h-1} \mathbf{\Pi}_p^i \boldsymbol{\delta}_\Pi \mathbf{\Pi}_p^{h-i-1} = \mathbf{\Pi}_p^h + \mathbf{C}_h. \tag{2.25}$$

Let $(\cdot)^\nu$ denote a vectorizing operator which stacks the columns of an $m \times n$ matrix $\mathbf{A}$ in an $mn \times 1$ vector $\mathbf{a}$, after which $(\mathbf{a})^\nu = \mathbf{a}$. Also, let $\otimes$ be the associated Kronecker product, so that when $\mathbf{B}$ is $p \times q$, then $\mathbf{A} \otimes \mathbf{B}$ is an $mp \times nq$ matrix of the form $\{b_{ij}\mathbf{A}\}$. Consequently, when $\mathbf{ABC}$ is defined:

$$(\mathbf{ABC})^\nu = (\mathbf{A} \otimes \mathbf{C}')\mathbf{B}^\nu.$$

Using these, from (2.25):

$$\begin{aligned} \mathbf{C}_h (\mathbf{y}_T - \boldsymbol{\varphi}_p) &= (\mathbf{C}_h (\mathbf{y}_T - \boldsymbol{\varphi}_p))^\nu \\ &= \left(\sum_{i=0}^{h-1} \mathbf{\Pi}_p^i \otimes (\mathbf{y}_T - \boldsymbol{\varphi}_p)' \mathbf{\Pi}_p^{h-i-1\prime} \right) \boldsymbol{\delta}_\Pi^\nu \\ &= \mathbf{F}_h \boldsymbol{\delta}_\Pi^\nu. \end{aligned} \tag{2.26}$$

To highlight components due to different effects (parameter change, estimation inconsistency, and estimation uncertainty), we decompose the term $(\mathbf{\Pi}^*)^h (\mathbf{y}_T - \boldsymbol{\varphi}^*)$ in (2.7) into:

$$(\mathbf{\Pi}^*)^h (\mathbf{y}_T - \boldsymbol{\varphi}^*) = (\mathbf{\Pi}^*)^h (\mathbf{y}_T - \boldsymbol{\varphi}) + (\mathbf{\Pi}^*)^h (\boldsymbol{\varphi} - \boldsymbol{\varphi}^*),$$

whereas $\widehat{\mathbf{\Pi}}^h(\hat{\mathbf{y}}_T - \hat{\boldsymbol{\varphi}})$ equals:

$$\begin{aligned} &(\mathbf{\Pi}_p^h + \mathbf{C}_h) (\boldsymbol{\delta}_y - (\hat{\boldsymbol{\varphi}} - \boldsymbol{\varphi}_p) + (\mathbf{y}_T - \boldsymbol{\varphi}) - (\boldsymbol{\varphi}_p - \boldsymbol{\varphi})) \\ &= (\mathbf{\Pi}_p^h + \mathbf{C}_h) \boldsymbol{\delta}_y - (\mathbf{\Pi}_p^h + \mathbf{C}_h) \boldsymbol{\delta}_\varphi + (\mathbf{\Pi}_p^h + \mathbf{C}_h) (\mathbf{y}_T - \boldsymbol{\varphi}_p) \\ &= (\mathbf{\Pi}_p^h + \mathbf{C}_h) \boldsymbol{\delta}_y - (\mathbf{\Pi}_p^h + \mathbf{C}_h) \boldsymbol{\delta}_\varphi \\ &\quad + \mathbf{F}_h \boldsymbol{\delta}_\Pi^\nu + \mathbf{\Pi}_p^h (\mathbf{y}_T - \boldsymbol{\varphi}) - \mathbf{\Pi}_p^h (\boldsymbol{\varphi}_p - \boldsymbol{\varphi}). \end{aligned}$$

Thus, $(\mathbf{\Pi}^*)^h (\mathbf{y}_T - \boldsymbol{\varphi}^*) - \widehat{\mathbf{\Pi}}^h(\hat{\mathbf{y}}_T - \hat{\boldsymbol{\varphi}})$ yields:

$$\begin{aligned} &\left((\mathbf{\Pi}^*)^h - \mathbf{\Pi}_p^h\right) (\mathbf{y}_T - \boldsymbol{\varphi}) - \mathbf{F}_h \boldsymbol{\delta}_\Pi^\nu - (\mathbf{\Pi}_p^h + \mathbf{C}_h) \boldsymbol{\delta}_y \\ &\quad - (\mathbf{\Pi}^*)^h (\boldsymbol{\varphi}^* - \boldsymbol{\varphi}) + \mathbf{\Pi}_p^h (\boldsymbol{\varphi}_p - \boldsymbol{\varphi}) + (\mathbf{\Pi}_p^h + \mathbf{C}_h) \boldsymbol{\delta}_\varphi. \end{aligned} \tag{2.27}$$

The interaction $\mathbf{C}_h \boldsymbol{\delta}_\varphi$ is like a "covariance", but is omitted from the table. Hence (2.27) becomes:

$$\begin{aligned} &\left((\mathbf{\Pi}^*)^h - \mathbf{\Pi}^h\right) (\mathbf{y}_T - \boldsymbol{\varphi}) + (\mathbf{\Pi}^h - \mathbf{\Pi}_p^h) (\mathbf{y}_T - \boldsymbol{\varphi}) \\ &\quad - (\mathbf{\Pi}^*)^h (\boldsymbol{\varphi}^* - \boldsymbol{\varphi}) + \mathbf{\Pi}_p^h (\boldsymbol{\varphi}_p - \boldsymbol{\varphi}) \\ &\quad - (\mathbf{\Pi}_p^h + \mathbf{C}_h) \boldsymbol{\delta}_y - \mathbf{F}_h \boldsymbol{\delta}_\Pi^\nu + \mathbf{\Pi}_p^h \boldsymbol{\delta}_\varphi. \end{aligned}$$

The first and third rows have expectations of zero, so the second row collects the "non-central" terms.

Finally, for the term $\boldsymbol{\varphi}^* - \hat{\boldsymbol{\varphi}}$ in (2.7), we have (on the same principle):

$$(\boldsymbol{\varphi}^* - \boldsymbol{\varphi}) + (\boldsymbol{\varphi} - \boldsymbol{\varphi}_p) - \boldsymbol{\delta}_\varphi.$$

2.10 Appendix B: VEqCM Taxonomy Derivations

The underlying system in its explicit I(0) representation is:

$$\begin{pmatrix} (\boldsymbol{\beta}'\mathbf{x}_t - \boldsymbol{\mu}) \\ \boldsymbol{\beta}'_\perp (\Delta\mathbf{x}_t - \boldsymbol{\gamma}) \end{pmatrix} = \begin{pmatrix} \boldsymbol{\Lambda} \\ \boldsymbol{\beta}'_\perp \boldsymbol{\alpha} \end{pmatrix} (\boldsymbol{\beta}'\mathbf{x}_{t-1} - \boldsymbol{\mu}) + \begin{pmatrix} \boldsymbol{\beta}' \\ \boldsymbol{\beta}'_\perp \end{pmatrix} \boldsymbol{\nu}_t.$$

We allow for changes in $(\boldsymbol{\alpha}, \boldsymbol{\gamma}, \boldsymbol{\mu})$ but keep $(\boldsymbol{\beta} : \boldsymbol{\beta}_\perp)$ constant. Thus, after time T, the data are generated by:

$$\begin{pmatrix} (\boldsymbol{\beta}'\mathbf{x}_{T+h} - \boldsymbol{\mu}^*) \\ \boldsymbol{\beta}'_\perp (\Delta\mathbf{x}_{T+h} - \boldsymbol{\gamma}^*) \end{pmatrix} = \begin{pmatrix} \boldsymbol{\Lambda}^* \\ \boldsymbol{\beta}'_\perp \boldsymbol{\alpha}^* \end{pmatrix} (\boldsymbol{\beta}'\mathbf{x}_{T+h-1} - \boldsymbol{\mu}^*) + \mathbf{v}_{T+h} \qquad (2.28)$$

where:

$$\mathbf{v}_t = \begin{pmatrix} \boldsymbol{\beta}' \\ \boldsymbol{\beta}'_\perp \end{pmatrix} \boldsymbol{\nu}_t.$$

Consequently, iterating (2.28) back to the forecast origin:

$$\begin{aligned} \begin{pmatrix} \boldsymbol{\beta}'\mathbf{x}_{T+h} \\ \boldsymbol{\beta}'_\perp \Delta\mathbf{x}_{T+h} \end{pmatrix} &= \begin{pmatrix} \boldsymbol{\mu}^* - (\boldsymbol{\Lambda}^*)^h (\boldsymbol{\mu}^* - \boldsymbol{\mu}) \\ \boldsymbol{\beta}'_\perp \left[\boldsymbol{\gamma}^* - \boldsymbol{\alpha}^* (\boldsymbol{\Lambda}^*)^{h-1} (\boldsymbol{\mu}^* - \boldsymbol{\mu})\right] \end{pmatrix} \\ &\quad + \begin{pmatrix} \boldsymbol{\Lambda}^* \\ \boldsymbol{\beta}'_\perp \boldsymbol{\alpha}^* \end{pmatrix} (\boldsymbol{\Lambda}^*)^{h-1} (\boldsymbol{\beta}'\mathbf{x}_T - \boldsymbol{\mu}) \\ &\quad + \begin{pmatrix} \boldsymbol{\Lambda}^* \\ \boldsymbol{\beta}'_\perp \boldsymbol{\alpha}^* \end{pmatrix} \sum_{i=0}^{h-1} (\boldsymbol{\Lambda}^*)^i \mathbf{v}_{T+i} + \mathbf{v}_{T+h}. \end{aligned} \qquad (2.29)$$

However, the multi-step forecasts are calculated from:

$$\begin{pmatrix} \boldsymbol{\beta}'\widehat{\mathbf{x}}_{T+h|T} \\ \boldsymbol{\beta}'_\perp \widehat{\Delta\mathbf{x}}_{T+h|T} \end{pmatrix} = \begin{pmatrix} \widehat{\boldsymbol{\mu}} \\ \boldsymbol{\beta}'_\perp \widehat{\boldsymbol{\gamma}} \end{pmatrix} + \begin{pmatrix} \widehat{\boldsymbol{\Lambda}} \\ \boldsymbol{\beta}'_\perp \widehat{\boldsymbol{\alpha}} \end{pmatrix} \widehat{\boldsymbol{\Lambda}}^{h-1} (\boldsymbol{\beta}'\mathbf{x}_T - \widehat{\boldsymbol{\mu}}) \qquad (2.30)$$

so the forecast errors are the difference between the sequences in (2.29) and (2.30).

To simplify the notation, let:

$$\mathbf{D}^* = \begin{pmatrix} \boldsymbol{\Lambda}^* \\ \boldsymbol{\beta}'_\perp \boldsymbol{\alpha}^* \end{pmatrix}, \quad \widehat{\mathbf{D}} = \begin{pmatrix} \widehat{\boldsymbol{\Lambda}} \\ \boldsymbol{\beta}'_\perp \widehat{\boldsymbol{\alpha}} \end{pmatrix}, \quad \text{and } \widehat{\boldsymbol{\Lambda}} = (\mathbf{I}_r + \boldsymbol{\beta}'\widehat{\boldsymbol{\alpha}}).$$

Using the same approach as in §2.9, let:

$$\hat{\mathbf{u}}_{T+h|T} = \begin{pmatrix} \boldsymbol{\beta}'\mathbf{x}_{T+h} - \boldsymbol{\beta}'\widehat{\mathbf{x}}_{T+h|T} \\ \boldsymbol{\beta}'_{\perp}\Delta\mathbf{x}_{T+h} - \boldsymbol{\beta}'_{\perp}\widehat{\Delta\mathbf{x}}_{T+h|T} \end{pmatrix},$$

then an expression for $\hat{\mathbf{u}}_{T+h|T}$ is:

$$\begin{aligned}
&\begin{pmatrix} \left(\mathbf{I}_r - (\boldsymbol{\Lambda}^*)^h\right)(\boldsymbol{\mu}^* - \boldsymbol{\mu}) \\ \boldsymbol{\beta}'_{\perp}\left[(\boldsymbol{\gamma}^* - \boldsymbol{\gamma}) - \boldsymbol{\alpha}^*(\boldsymbol{\Lambda}^*)^{h-1}(\boldsymbol{\mu}^* - \boldsymbol{\mu})\right] \end{pmatrix} \\
&\quad + \left(\begin{pmatrix} \mathbf{I}_r + \boldsymbol{\beta}'\boldsymbol{\alpha}^* \\ \boldsymbol{\beta}'_{\perp}\boldsymbol{\alpha}^* \end{pmatrix}(\boldsymbol{\Lambda}^*)^{h-1} - \begin{pmatrix} \mathbf{I}_r + \boldsymbol{\beta}'\boldsymbol{\alpha} \\ \boldsymbol{\beta}'_{\perp}\boldsymbol{\alpha} \end{pmatrix}\boldsymbol{\Lambda}^{h-1}\right)(\boldsymbol{\beta}'\mathbf{x}_T - \boldsymbol{\mu}) \\
&\quad + \begin{pmatrix} \left(\mathbf{I}_r - \boldsymbol{\Lambda}^h\right)(\boldsymbol{\mu} - \boldsymbol{\mu}_p) \\ \boldsymbol{\beta}'_{\perp}\left[(\boldsymbol{\gamma} - \boldsymbol{\gamma}_p) - \boldsymbol{\alpha}\boldsymbol{\Lambda}^{h-1}(\boldsymbol{\mu} - \boldsymbol{\mu}_p)\right] \end{pmatrix} \\
&\quad + \left(\begin{pmatrix} \mathbf{I}_r + \boldsymbol{\beta}'\boldsymbol{\alpha} \\ \boldsymbol{\beta}'_{\perp}\boldsymbol{\alpha} \end{pmatrix}\boldsymbol{\Lambda}^{h-1} - \begin{pmatrix} \mathbf{I}_r + \boldsymbol{\beta}'\boldsymbol{\alpha}_p \\ \boldsymbol{\beta}'_{\perp}\boldsymbol{\alpha}_p \end{pmatrix}\boldsymbol{\Lambda}_p^{h-1}\right)(\boldsymbol{\beta}'\mathbf{x}_T - \boldsymbol{\mu}) \\
&\quad - \begin{pmatrix} \left(\mathbf{I}_r - \boldsymbol{\Lambda}^h\right)(\widehat{\boldsymbol{\mu}} - \boldsymbol{\mu}_p) \\ \boldsymbol{\beta}'_{\perp}\left[(\widehat{\boldsymbol{\gamma}} - \boldsymbol{\gamma}_p) - \boldsymbol{\alpha}\boldsymbol{\Lambda}^{h-1}(\widehat{\boldsymbol{\mu}} - \boldsymbol{\mu}_p)\right] \end{pmatrix} \\
&\quad - \left(\begin{pmatrix} \mathbf{I}_r + \boldsymbol{\beta}'\widehat{\boldsymbol{\alpha}} \\ \boldsymbol{\beta}'_{\perp}\widehat{\boldsymbol{\alpha}} \end{pmatrix}\widehat{\boldsymbol{\Lambda}}^{h-1} - \begin{pmatrix} \mathbf{I}_r + \boldsymbol{\beta}'\boldsymbol{\alpha}_p \\ \boldsymbol{\beta}'_{\perp}\boldsymbol{\alpha}_p \end{pmatrix}\boldsymbol{\Lambda}_p^{h-1}\right)(\boldsymbol{\beta}'\mathbf{x}_T - \boldsymbol{\mu}) \\
&\quad + \mathbf{v}_{T+h} + \begin{pmatrix} \mathbf{I}_r + \boldsymbol{\beta}'\boldsymbol{\alpha}^* \\ \boldsymbol{\beta}'_{\perp}\boldsymbol{\alpha}^* \end{pmatrix}\sum_{i=0}^{h-1}(\boldsymbol{\Lambda}^*)^i\,\mathbf{v}_{T+i}. \qquad (2.31)
\end{aligned}$$

This representation drops the cross-product estimation effect:

$$\left(\widehat{\mathbf{D}}\widehat{\boldsymbol{\Lambda}}^{h-1} - \mathbf{D}\boldsymbol{\Lambda}^{h-1}\right)(\widehat{\boldsymbol{\mu}} - \boldsymbol{\mu}),$$

although one may need to retain the term associated with $(\boldsymbol{\mu}_p - \boldsymbol{\mu})$ in some circumstances.

3 Deterministic Shifts

Summary

Given the sources of mis-prediction formalized in the taxonomy developed in §2.2, we now explore the roles of unmodeled shifts in parameters. It transpires that deterministic shifts (changes in equilibrium means and steady-state trends) in the model relative to the DGP are a dominant source of forecast failure. This chapter investigates the issue of structural breaks, and chapter 4 considers other potential sources, such as model mis-specification and estimation uncertainty. We first develop the analysis in a static context, extend it to I(0) process, and finally consider breaks in I(1) systems. Monte Carlo simulations and empirical models illustrate the analysis. Breaks in deterministic seasonal patterns are also discussed.

3.1 Introduction

Modern economies are often subject to major institutional, political, financial, and technological changes which manifest themselves as structural breaks in econometric models relative to the underlying data-generation process. Clements and Hendry (1995a) obtained formulae for unconditional forecast-error biases and asymptotic variances for a vector equilibrium-correction model (VEqCM), and for a vector autoregression in differences (DV), assuming constant parameters. Hendry and Clements (1998) derived unconditional forecast-error biases for systems with breaks. Here, we investigate conditional and unconditional biases, and unconditional variances for 1- and 2-step ahead forecasts for a VEqCM, both before and after deterministic breaks, to allow a better appraisal of likely mean-squared forecast errors. The formulae presented below are only for the levels of the variables, but specialize to previous results when no breaks occur. We use the shorthand "deterministic shifts" to refer to any changes in equilibrium means and steady-state trends in the model relative to the DGP. As shown in chapter 2, such shifts could be precipitated by changes in intercepts or dynamics (indirectly), or in equilibrium means and growth rates directly.

When a break has occurred a number of periods before forecasts are made, so that unconditional expectations (e.g., of growth rates of variables) at the forecast origin equal their post-break values, uncontaminated by pre-break values or the period of transition, then the analysis simplifies considerably. We consider this case in §5.8, and contrast the outcomes to those from using a DV. We digress in chapter 4 to show that model mis-specification, parameter uncertainty, and forecast-origin mis-measurement cannot account for major systematic mis-forecasting *per se*, albeit that interacting with breaks, they can induce serious forecast errors. Chapter 5 then extends the more general analysis to the DV, and also to a second-differenced system (DDV), and chapter 8 illustrates both analyses by a 4-variable monetary model of the UK.

The structure of the chapter is as follows. Section 3.2 highlights the role of deterministic shifts in forecast failure in a scalar static model. Section 3.3 then extends the analysis to I(0) dynamic systems, and reports a Monte Carlo study of its implications in §3.3.1. Section 3.4 describes the I(1) DGP used as the basis for the remaining analytic calculations, and analyzes the impacts of mean shifts in I(1) vector equilibrium-correction systems, following the evidence in Hendry and Doornik (1997) of their role in forecast failure in dynamic, cointegrated, systems. Next, §3.5 derives the unconditional and conditional biases in a VEqCM, in each case both before and after structural breaks in the deterministic terms, and §3.7 extends the analysis to obtain the (asymptotic) variances. In §3.8 , we also evaluate the impact of structural breaks in seasonals to gauge the differences that might arise when using seasonal data. Section 3.9 concludes.

3.2 Deterministic Shifts in a Static Regression

Any sufficiently large and prolonged change in the data properties over a forecast horizon relative to those entailed by a model will induce forecast failure. The source may be any deterministic mis-specification that changes over time, such as omitting a trend, or any deterministic shift. Many tests of parameter constancy are based on comparisons between in-sample and post-sample residual sums of squares, and events that greatly increase the latter should be detectable. However, we focus on deterministic shifts because the mean value of a variable experiencing a parameter change is a major determinant of the detectability of a break, for parameter shifts of a size that seem likely in economics. This claim is illustrated in this section by a scalar regression example, where analytic calculations are fairly straightforward. Later sections extend the analysis to I(0) and then I(1) processes.[1]

Consider the bivariate regression model:

$$y_t = \phi_0 + \phi_1 z_t + \epsilon_t \text{ where } \epsilon_t \sim \mathsf{IN}\left[0, \sigma_\epsilon^2\right], \tag{3.1}$$

when the explanatory variable $z_t \sim \mathsf{IN}[\eta, \sigma_z^2]$, independently of $\{\epsilon_t\}$. From (3.1), $\mathsf{E}[y_t] = \phi_0 + \phi_1\eta$. The sample size is $T = 60$, with the following fixed parameter values: $\sigma_z^2 = 1$ and $\sigma_\epsilon^2 = 1$. We consider two types of structural break at time $T_1 = 55$: first, when ϕ_1 shifts to $(1+\rho)\phi_1$ from a baseline of $\phi_1 = 1$, with $\phi_0 = 0$; then when ϕ_0 shifts to $(1+\rho)\,\phi_1\eta$ with ϕ_1 fixed at unity. In both types, therefore, $\mathsf{E}[y_t]$ shifts by $\rho\phi_1\eta$, when $\eta \neq 0$. We set $\rho = 0.25$, 0.50 and 1.00, and the parameter $\eta = \mathsf{E}[z]$ takes the values 0, 1, 2, and 4, creating twenty-one different experiments (when $\eta = 0$, ϕ_0 is unaffected by changing ρ, so the equation is unaltered over the forecast period).

To detect predictive failure, we consider the Chow (1960) test (denoted C here) for a known break point at time T_1 after fitting (3.1). This is representative of the type of test that can be used, and is calculated by:

$$C = \frac{RSS_T - RSS_{T_1}}{RSS_{T_1}} \times \frac{T_1 - 1}{T_2 + 1}.$$

[1]One-off critical values are again used for tests here, since the issue is the low power to detect mean-zero shifts, even when the break point is known.

Under the null hypothesis of no parameter change, $C \sim \mathsf{F}^{T_2+1}_{T_1-1}$ with $\mathsf{E}[\mathsf{F}^{T_2+1}_{T_1-1}] = (T_2+1)/(T_2-1)$. Based on the derivations in the appendix, when $\rho \neq 0$, the expectation of the Chow test is (setting $k = T^{-1}T_2$ where $T_2 = T - T_1$):

$$\mathsf{E}[C] \simeq \frac{\left[\sigma_\epsilon^2 + \rho^2\phi_1^2\left(\sigma_z^2 + \eta^2\right)(1-k)\right] T_2}{(T_2+1)\,\sigma_\epsilon^2}.$$

Hence, for the parameter values considered here, the non-centrality is approximately $\rho^2\left(1+\eta^2\right)(1-k)$, and so depends on the squared mean of z as well as on the squared size of the break, both relative to the equation standard error. Figure 3.1 records Monte Carlo rejection frequencies of sequences of break-point Chow tests (200 replications were used).[2] The outcomes for both one-off 5% and 1% test sizes are recorded (denoted in the figure by 0.05 and 0.01 respectively for shifts in ϕ_1, and by 0.05m and 0.01m respectively for shifts in ϕ_0). While the complete sequence of rejections is shown, we envisage an investigator conducting a test at a known point only: the comparisons within and between panels are the feature of interest.

First, we consider shifts in ϕ_1. Data means are often arbitrary for economic time series, since many variables are indices, or nominal magnitudes subject to a choice of units (e.g., £millions or \$billions), yet fig. 3.1 clearly reveals that the detectability of breaks depends on the scaling of the variables. Rejection frequencies at any potential break-point selection are substantially higher for a given break magnitude as η increases. This marked impact of increasing η on rejection frequencies for a given shift in ϕ_1 is clear from reading down the columns. Sufficiently large changes in zero-mean processes can be detected (see the first row), but at a doubling of the regression parameter value, the magnitude of the required change seems large relative to that likely to be encountered in practice.

We turn now to the rejection frequencies for shifts in $\mathsf{E}[y_t]$ equal to $\rho\phi_1\eta$, with ϕ_1 held constant. There is a close correspondence between rejections for shifts in ϕ_1 (indirectly altering $\mathsf{E}[y_t]$) and direct shifts in $\mathsf{E}[y_t]$ alone: changes in parameters (ϕ_1) and changes in deterministic components (ϕ_0) that have a similar effect on the equilibrium mean

[2] 3×3 panels of graphs are notionally labelled reading along rows as *a, b, c; d, e, f; g, h, i*.

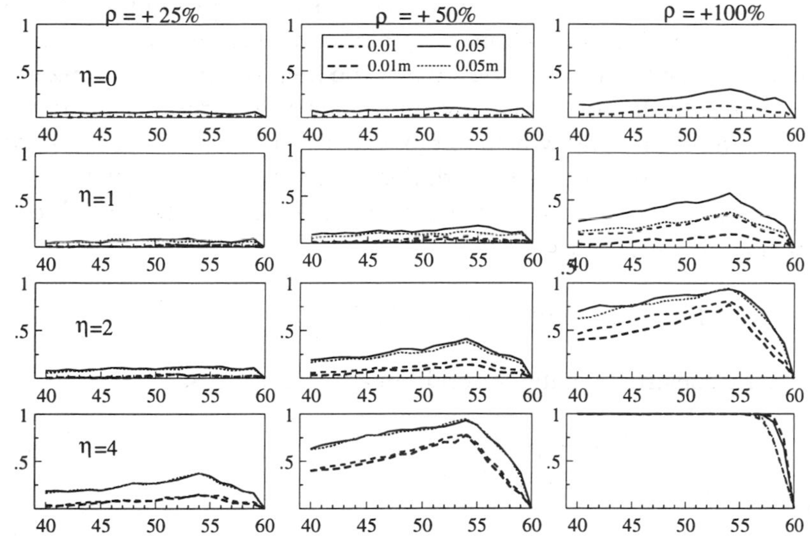

Figure 3.1
Sequentially-computed Chow test rejection frequencies.

have similar rejection rates. This is surprising as there are both slope and mean changes when ϕ_1 alters, and only mean changes when ϕ_0 shifts. Thus, we conclude that the main component in forecast failure of slope changes is the induced change in the equilibrium mean, albeit that a sufficiently-large slope change can be detected. However, we expect changes in economic parameters to be small relative to base-parameter values, making the first two columns of the figure most relevant. Consequently, we will focus on the impact of breaks in equilibrium means. The remaining sections of this chapter work through similar analyses with dynamic models, and again find that shifts in long-run means are responsible for forecast failure.

3.3 Deterministic Shifts in I(0) Processes

We extend the analysis of the previous section to show that intercept shifts (either from direct changes in deterministic factors, or induced by changes in dynamic adjustments) are a dominant cause of predictive failure in linear dynamic systems. Other breaks can cause forecast failures, but their ease of detection depends on the magnitudes of the long-run means (of the stationary combinations) relative to their error standard deviations. Intuitively, when the long-run mean is non-zero, breaks shift the location of the data, inducing a short-run "trend" to the new equilibrium mean which is more easily detected than a variance change around the origin. Indeed, this result was presaged by the taxonomy of forecast errors in table 2.1 for the DGP in (2.1), reproduced here for convenience as:

$$\mathbf{y}_t = \boldsymbol{\phi} + \boldsymbol{\Pi}\mathbf{y}_{t-1} + \boldsymbol{\epsilon}_t \text{ with } \boldsymbol{\epsilon}_t \sim \mathsf{IN}_n\left[\mathbf{0}, \boldsymbol{\Omega}_\epsilon\right], \tag{3.2}$$

where by construction, the unconditional mean of $\mathbf{y}_t$ is:

$$\mathsf{E}\left[\mathbf{y}_t\right] = \left(\mathbf{I}_n - \boldsymbol{\Pi}\right)^{-1} \boldsymbol{\phi} = \boldsymbol{\varphi} \tag{3.3}$$

so:

$$\mathbf{y}_t - \boldsymbol{\varphi} = \boldsymbol{\Pi}\left(\mathbf{y}_{t-1} - \boldsymbol{\varphi}\right) + \boldsymbol{\epsilon}_t. \tag{3.4}$$

Under the assumption of correct specification, negligible finite-sample biases, and correct initial conditions, then the unconditional expectation (2.9) was:

$$\mathsf{E}\left[\widehat{\boldsymbol{\epsilon}}_{T+h}\right] = \left(\mathbf{I}_n - \left(\boldsymbol{\Pi}^*\right)^h\right)\left(\boldsymbol{\varphi}^* - \boldsymbol{\varphi}\right). \tag{3.5}$$

First, the forecast bias is zero in mean-zero processes, $\boldsymbol{\varphi}^* = \boldsymbol{\varphi} = \mathbf{0}$. Secondly, the forecast bias is also zero when the long-run mean is constant: if $\boldsymbol{\varphi}^* = \boldsymbol{\varphi}$ changes in the dynamics ($\boldsymbol{\Pi}^*$) vanished on average in table 2.1. Further, and much less obvious *a priori*, $\mathsf{E}[\widehat{\boldsymbol{\epsilon}}_{T+1}]$ is zero when shifts in $\boldsymbol{\phi}^*$ offset those in $\boldsymbol{\Pi}^*$ to leave $\boldsymbol{\varphi}$ in (3.3) unaffected: the finding below that such changes are hard to detect supports our claim that changes in deterministic factors matter most for predictive failure. Finally from (3.5), a given differential ($\boldsymbol{\varphi}^* - \boldsymbol{\varphi}$), deriving from changes in $\boldsymbol{\Pi}$ only or $\boldsymbol{\phi}$ only, will induce a larger (smaller) forecast bias as ($\mathbf{I}_n - \boldsymbol{\Pi}^*$) becomes "larger" (nearer zero). In all cases, the detectability of failure is dependent on the magnitudes of the shifts relative to the error standard deviations. We now illustrate the implications of these analytical forecast results by simulating the power of some tests of parameter constancy to detect these various breaks.

Table 3.1
Design parameter values for I(0) process.

Case	A		B		C		D		E	
	1	2	1	2	1	2	1	2	1	2
β_1	0.85	0.85	0.85	0.70	0.85	0.70	0.85	0.85	0.85	0.70
α_1	1.5	1.5	0.0	0.0	1.5	1.5	1.5	0.375	0.375	1.5
α_2	5.0	5.0	0.0	0.0	5.0	5.0	5.0	5.0	5.0	5.0

3.3.1 *An I(0) Monte Carlo illustration*

The Monte Carlo simulation considers five experiments, of which three were discussed in §2.6: all five are reproduced here for convenience.

(A) a constant-parameter equation;
(B) a break in the dynamics when there is a zero mean;
(C) a break in the dynamics when there is a non-zero mean;
(D) a break in the intercept, inducing φ^* equal to that in (C);
(E) the break in (C) offset by the break in (D) to leave φ unaltered.

The DGP is again the I(0) VAR:

$$y_{1,t} = \alpha_1 + 0.3y_{2,t} + \beta_1 y_{1,t-1} - 0.15y_{2,t-1} + \epsilon_{1,t} \qquad (3.6)$$
$$y_{2,t} = \alpha_2 - 0.5y_{1,t-1} + 0.75y_{2,t-1} + \epsilon_{2,t}, \qquad (3.7)$$

for a full-sample size of $T = 200$. The $\{\epsilon_{i,t}\}$ and the structure of the breaks are as before: the regime over $T = 100$ (break on) to $T = 150$ (break off) is denoted 2, the remaining regime is 1. The forecasting model is the first equation in (3.6), estimated consistently by OLS.[3]

The complete set of experimental design parameter values is recorded in table 3.1, where it is apparent that the intercept change in the first equation is about four error standard deviations.

Since the process in (3.6) can be written as:

$$\begin{pmatrix} 1-\beta_1 L & -0.3+0.15L \\ 0.5L & 1-0.75L \end{pmatrix}\begin{pmatrix} y_{1,t} \\ y_{2,t} \end{pmatrix} = \begin{pmatrix} \alpha_1 \\ \alpha_2 \end{pmatrix} + \begin{pmatrix} \epsilon_{1,t} \\ \epsilon_{2,t} \end{pmatrix}, \qquad (3.8)$$

[3]Depending on the test statistic selected for analysis, as in the previous section, non-centrality parameters could be calculated in this scalar I (0) process to reveal the factors determining test power (see e.g., Hendry, 1995a).

Table 3.2
Outcomes for the equilibria corresponding to φ^*.

Case	A		B		C		D		E	
φ_1	10	10	0	0	10	7.5	10	7.5	7.5	7.5
φ_2	0	0	0	0	0	5	0	5	5	5

where L is the lag operator, the long-run solution is:

$$\begin{pmatrix} \varphi_1 \\ \varphi_2 \end{pmatrix} = \frac{1}{(1.3 - \beta_1)} \begin{pmatrix} \alpha_1 + 0.6\alpha_2 \\ 4(1 - \beta_1)\alpha_2 - 2\alpha_1 \end{pmatrix}.$$

This generates the equilibria corresponding to φ^* given in table 3.2.

Figure 3.2 shows the rejection frequencies from $T = 50$ to 200 of the break-point Chow tests for parameter constancy. Case (A) shows that the actual size of the test is close to the nominal 5%. As predicted by the absence of forecast biases, the power in the zero-mean process (B) is nearly equal to the size, so the change in the dynamics here is essentially undetectable. However, it is easily detected in case (C). Next, (D) does indeed generate nearly equal "powers" to (C), with the latter somewhat higher as anticipated since the dynamics were reduced. Further, in (C) and (D), on reversion to the state prior to the first break (increasing the dynamics), the power is higher for (D) than (C), although both tests become biased immediately after: this matches our empirical experience with macroeconomic data.

The key implications of the above analysis of forecast-error biases from equilibrium-mean shifts are that case (B) would not be readily detectable on such tests (as no shifts occur), and that (E) would be similar to (B). Both are manifest in fig. 3.2. In fact, the outcome in (E) is *identical* to (B): a shift in both intercept and dynamics with φ constant is no more detectable than just the dynamics changing in a zero-mean process. To understand why, consider the reduced forms of the first equations of their DGPs, expressed in deviations about means, denoted $\widetilde{y}$, where in (B), $\widetilde{y}_{1,t} = y_{1,t}$ with $\widetilde{y}_{2,t} = y_{2,t}$, whereas in (E), $\widetilde{y}_{1,t} = y_{1,t} - 7.5$ and $\widetilde{y}_{2,t} = y_{2,t} - 5$. Then, in the two regimes we have:

$$\begin{aligned} &(\text{B1}) \quad : \quad \widetilde{y}_{1,t} = 0.70\widetilde{y}_{1,t-1} + 0.075\widetilde{y}_{2,t-1} + (\epsilon_{1,t} + 0.3\epsilon_{2,t}) \\ &(\text{B2}) \quad : \quad \widetilde{y}_{1,t} = 0.55\widetilde{y}_{1,t-1} + 0.075\widetilde{y}_{2,t-1} + (\epsilon_{1,t} + 0.3\epsilon_{2,t}), \end{aligned} \tag{3.9}$$

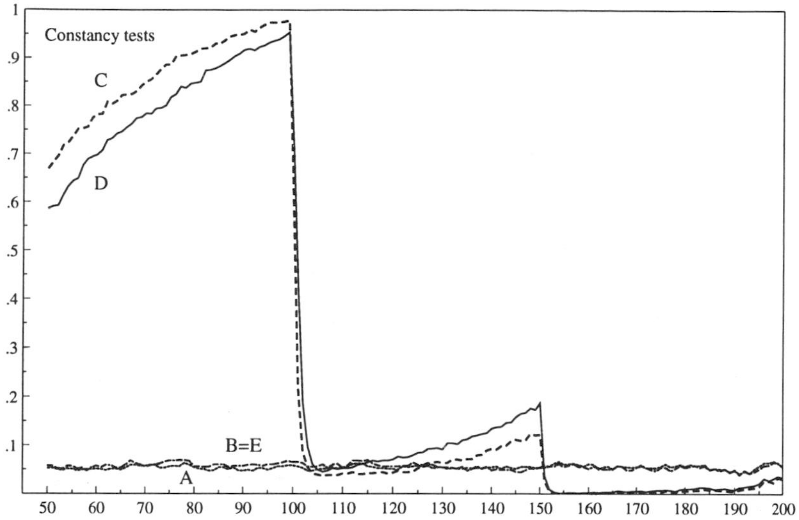

Figure 3.2
Rejection frequencies of the parameter constancy test.

$$
\begin{aligned}
\text{(E1)} \quad &: \quad \widetilde{y}_{1,t} = 0.70\widetilde{y}_{1,t-1} + 0.075\widetilde{y}_{2,t-1} + (\epsilon_{1,t} + 0.3\epsilon_{2,t}) \\
\text{(E2)} \quad &: \quad \widetilde{y}_{1,t} = 0.55\widetilde{y}_{1,t-1} + 0.075\widetilde{y}_{2,t-1} + (\epsilon_{1,t} + 0.3\epsilon_{2,t}) \,. \qquad (3.10)
\end{aligned}
$$

Thus, in mean-deviation form, their DGPs are identical both pre and post break, even at the break point. This outcome confirms the analytic calculations for the single forecast at $T+1$. The main message is that direct or induced deterministic shifts are more important for predictive failure than changes in parameters such as reaction speeds, feedbacks or latencies. Below, we note the impact of that conclusion on the formulation of forecasting models.

Since break-point tests are not optimal for long post-break samples, and their power depends on the date against which tests are conducted, we ran the same experiments with only 4 post-break observations to mimic a forecasting, as against a modeling, context: this delivers fig. 3.3 , where the upper graph is the forecast test. The rejection frequencies are higher than for the full-sample, but the pattern of results is unchanged: shifts in zero-mean processes remain a minor problem compared to non-zero means.

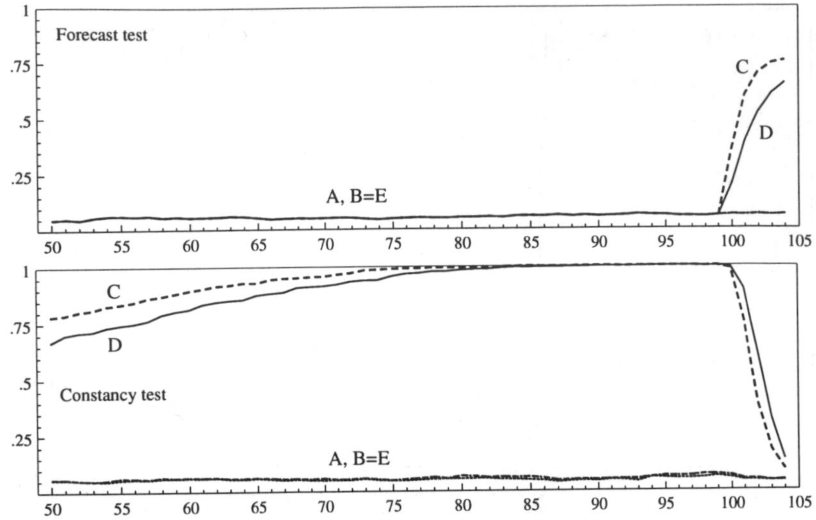

Figure 3.3
Rejections of forecast and constancy tests for four forecasts.

3.4 Deterministic Shifts in VEqCMs

As in (1.12), $\mathbf{x}_t$ is the $\mathsf{I}(1)$ vector of n time-series variables, satisfying r cointegration relations with the in-sample DGP (see Johansen and Juselius, 1990):

$$\Delta \mathbf{x}_t = \boldsymbol{\gamma} + \boldsymbol{\alpha}\left(\boldsymbol{\beta}'\mathbf{x}_{t-1} - \boldsymbol{\mu}\right) + \boldsymbol{\nu}_t \tag{3.11}$$

where $\boldsymbol{\nu}_t \sim \mathsf{IN}_n[\mathbf{0}, \boldsymbol{\Omega}_\nu]$. The forecasting model is the VEqCM matching (3.11) in-sample, but it will not coincide with the DGP in the forecast period when there is structural change. We note that:

$$\mathsf{E}\left[\boldsymbol{\beta}'\mathbf{x}_t\right] = \boldsymbol{\Lambda}\mathsf{E}\left[\boldsymbol{\beta}'\mathbf{x}_{t-1}\right] + \boldsymbol{\beta}'\boldsymbol{\tau} = \boldsymbol{\mu},$$

so that $\boldsymbol{\mu} = -\left(\boldsymbol{\beta}'\boldsymbol{\alpha}\right)^{-1}\boldsymbol{\beta}'\boldsymbol{\tau}$, where $\boldsymbol{\Lambda} = \left(\mathbf{I}_r + \boldsymbol{\beta}'\boldsymbol{\alpha}\right)$ has all its eigenvalues inside the unit circle, and as $\boldsymbol{\tau} = \boldsymbol{\gamma} - \boldsymbol{\alpha\mu}$, that:

$$\begin{aligned} \mathsf{E}\left[\Delta \mathbf{x}_t\right] &= \mathsf{E}\left[\boldsymbol{\alpha\beta}'\mathbf{x}_{t-1} + \boldsymbol{\tau} + \boldsymbol{\nu}_t\right] = \boldsymbol{\alpha}\mathsf{E}\left[\boldsymbol{\beta}'\mathbf{x}_{t-1}\right] + \boldsymbol{\tau} \\ &= \left[\mathbf{I}_n - \boldsymbol{\alpha}\left(\boldsymbol{\beta}'\boldsymbol{\alpha}\right)^{-1}\boldsymbol{\beta}'\right]\boldsymbol{\tau} = \mathbf{K}\boldsymbol{\tau} = \boldsymbol{\gamma}. \end{aligned} \tag{3.12}$$

The matrix $\mathbf{K}$ is non-symmetric but idempotent with $\boldsymbol{\beta}'\mathbf{K} = \mathbf{0}'$ and $\mathbf{K}\boldsymbol{\alpha} = \mathbf{0}$, so $\boldsymbol{\Upsilon}\mathbf{K} = \mathbf{K}$ and $\boldsymbol{\beta}'\boldsymbol{\gamma} = \mathbf{0}$.

We presented a taxonomy of forecast errors in VEqCMS under structural breaks (see table 2.3), and showed in §2.5 that VEqCMs will not "error correct" when the equilibrium mean shifts. Section 3.4.1 illustrates the susceptibility of VEqCMs to forecast failure for various types on non-constancies by Monte Carlo. Subsequent sections provide analytical treatments of the impacts of breaks on the properties of VEqCM forecasts.

3.4.1 *An* I(1) *Monte Carlo illustration*

We illustrate the analysis using the I(1) cointegrated DGP for which §2.6 reported the results in differences. Here, the model is estimated in levels, and breaks in dynamics are also considered, for comparison with the I(0) setting. Thus, the data are generated by the bivariate VAR:

$$\begin{aligned}\Delta y_{1,t} &= \gamma_1 + 0.3\Delta y_{2,t} + \pi_1 \left(y_{1,t-1} - y_{2,t-1} - \mu_1\right) + \epsilon_{1,t} \\ \Delta y_{2,t} &= 0.025 + \epsilon_{2,t}.\end{aligned} \tag{3.13}$$

As before, $\epsilon_{i,t} \sim \mathsf{IN}[0, \sigma_{ii}]$, with $\sqrt{\sigma_{ii}}$ of $0.025, 0.036$, and breaks occur at $T = 100$, reverting to the original parameter values at $T = 150$ with the full-sample size of $T = 200$. In these experiments, the first equation is estimated unrestrictedly in levels:

$$y_{1,t} = \beta_0 + \beta_1 y_{2,t} + \beta_2 y_{1,t-1} + \beta_3 y_{2,t-1} + \epsilon_{1,t} \tag{3.14}$$

We now consider the 4 experiments:

(F) a constant-parameter equation;
(G) a break in the EqCM parameter π_1 from -0.15 to -0.3;
(H) a break in the equilibrium mean from $\mu_1 = 1$ to 1.33;
(I) a break in the growth rate from $\gamma_1 = 0.025$ to 0.05.

The changes to the drift (γ_1) and intercept ($\tau_1 = \gamma_1 - \pi_1\mu_1$) are one and two error standard deviations respectively (see Hylleberg and Mizon, 1989, for an analysis of the role of $\gamma_1/\sqrt{\sigma_{11}}$). The formulation is invariant to what induces changes in τ_1, but large growth-rate changes are unlikely in OECD countries, whereas a shift in (say) the ratio of money

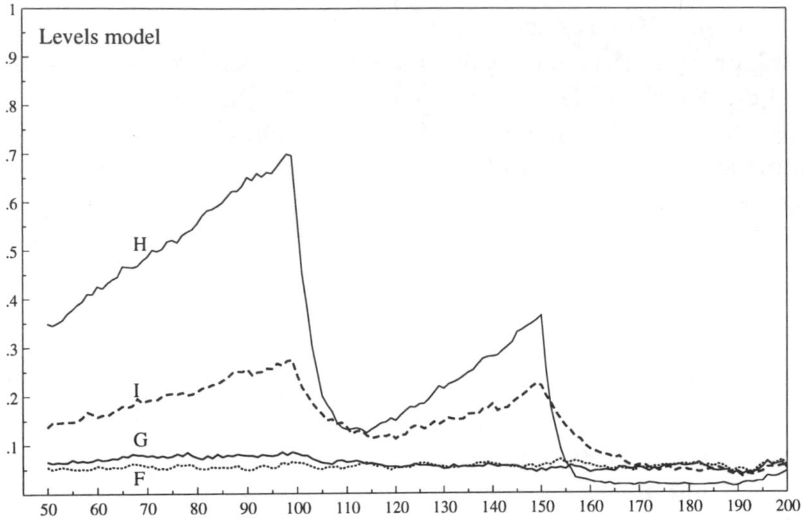

Figure 3.4
Constancy-test rejection frequencies in a cointegrated process.

to income from 25% to 10% (i.e., 0.15) is within the observed range empirically.

Experiment (F) checks the size of the constancy test in an I(1), cointegrated, setting; (G) demonstrates that a substantial change in the strength of reaction to a zero-mean disequilibrium is barely detectable (as it multiplies a zero-mean variable), and mimics (B) and (E) above; whereas (H) mimics the break effects found in case (D) above; finally, (I) examines a doubling of the growth rate. Figure 3.4 confirms the anticipated outcomes: the break-point test rejection frequencies under the null are close to their nominal size of 5%; the break in the equilibrium mean is easily detected; but that in the dynamics alone is not detectable. Case (I) is a large change in real growth, but is equivalent to only half the change in (H), and at about 25% rejection, is far less perceptible on these tests. As in §3.3.1, a more directed test would undoubtedly raise the actual powers, but not alter the basic conclusions.

On the basis that for all three general forms of DGP (static, I(0) and I(1) cointegrated), the findings are consistent and match the theoretical analyses, we now focus on shifts in equilibrium means, and derive the unconditional and conditional biases in a VEqCM from changes in its deterministic parameters, then obtain the unconditional (asymptotic) variances, when the dynamic coefficients alter.

3.5 Unconditional and Conditional Forecast-error Biases

The timing of a break relative to the forecast origin matters greatly, so to mimic the real-time nature of economic forecasting (where a forecast will eventually be made after any break), we consider forecasts made both pre and post breaks. Throughout, we assume the parameter values are known; estimation would add sampling uncertainty, and model selection could introduce additional biases. We also ignore model revision in the light of forecast failure: to the extent that such occurs correctly, it will bring the model back to the DGP and hence its forecasts to those made when no change occurs. There could be changes in any or all of the parameters of (3.11), namely $\boldsymbol{\alpha}$, $\boldsymbol{\beta}$, $\boldsymbol{\gamma}$, or $\boldsymbol{\mu}$, but here $\boldsymbol{\beta}$ will be held constant. We consider the effects of changes in all the other parameter on the VEqCM, both 1-step and 2-periods ahead.

The 1-step forecasts of the levels at forecast origin time $T+h$ ($h=0,1$) from the VEqCM (3.11) are obtained from:

$$\Delta\widehat{\mathbf{x}}_{T+h+1|T+h} = \boldsymbol{\gamma} + \boldsymbol{\alpha}\left(\boldsymbol{\beta}'\mathbf{x}_{T+h} - \boldsymbol{\mu}\right), \tag{3.15}$$

using $\widehat{\mathbf{x}}_{T+h+1|T+h} = \Delta\widehat{\mathbf{x}}_{T+h+1|T+h} + \mathbf{x}_{T+h}$. The 1-step forecast errors in levels are denoted by $\widehat{\mathbf{e}}_{T+h+1|T+h} = \mathbf{x}_{T+h+1} - \widehat{\mathbf{x}}_{T+h+1|T+h}$. The corresponding 2-step forecasts are:

$$\begin{aligned}\widehat{\mathbf{x}}_{T+h+2|T+h} &= \boldsymbol{\Upsilon}\widehat{\mathbf{x}}_{T+h+1|T+h} + \boldsymbol{\gamma} - \boldsymbol{\alpha\mu} \\ &= \boldsymbol{\Upsilon}^2\mathbf{x}_{T+h} + \left(\mathbf{I}_n + \boldsymbol{\Upsilon}\right)\left(\boldsymbol{\gamma} - \boldsymbol{\alpha\mu}\right) \end{aligned} \tag{3.16}$$

and similar expressions hold for their forecast errors.

After time T, the data are in fact generated by:

$$\Delta\mathbf{x}_{T+1} = \boldsymbol{\gamma}^* + \boldsymbol{\alpha}^*\left(\boldsymbol{\beta}'\mathbf{x}_T - \boldsymbol{\mu}^*\right) + \boldsymbol{\nu}_{T+1} \tag{3.17}$$

so we consider forecasting $\mathbf{x}$ from T to $T+1$; T to $T+2$; $T+1$ to $T+2$; and $T+1$ to $T+3$: the last two are forecasts prepared after the break, but still with no knowledge of the break having occurred. Changes in the feedback parameters are retained to clarify their role in affecting forecast variances. The detailed calculations are shown in Appendix B (§3.11):

here we focus on the final bias formulae. We distinguish unconditional and conditional forecast biases, and asymptotic variance formulae.

3.5.1 Forecasting levels from T to $T+1$

Let $\boldsymbol{\beta}'\mathbf{x}_T - \boldsymbol{\mu} = \boldsymbol{\kappa}_T$, then since $\mathsf{E}[\boldsymbol{\kappa}_T] = \mathbf{0}$ and $\mathsf{E}[\Delta\mathbf{x}_T] = \boldsymbol{\gamma}$:

$$\mathsf{E}\left[\widehat{\mathbf{e}}_{T+1|T} \mid I_T\right] = (\boldsymbol{\gamma}^* - \boldsymbol{\gamma}) - \boldsymbol{\alpha}^*(\boldsymbol{\mu}^* - \boldsymbol{\mu}) + (\boldsymbol{\alpha}^* - \boldsymbol{\alpha})\boldsymbol{\kappa}_T, \tag{3.18}$$

and:

$$\mathsf{E}\left[\widehat{\mathbf{e}}_{T+1|T}\right] = (\boldsymbol{\gamma}^* - \boldsymbol{\gamma}) - \boldsymbol{\alpha}^*(\boldsymbol{\mu}^* - \boldsymbol{\mu}). \tag{3.19}$$

The conditional and unconditional biases only differ to the extent that $\boldsymbol{\beta}'\mathbf{x}_T \neq \boldsymbol{\mu}$ and $\Delta\mathbf{x}_T \neq \boldsymbol{\gamma}$, noting that $\Delta\mathbf{x}_T = \boldsymbol{\gamma} + \boldsymbol{\alpha}\boldsymbol{\kappa}_{T-1} + \boldsymbol{\nu}_T$. When no deterministic breaks occur, (3.18) and (3.19) are zero.

3.5.2 Forecasting levels from $T+1$ to $T+2$

Having reached time $T+1$, data at $T+1$ is assumed available. As the unconditional expectations of the levels are altering along the adjustment path, and must be time dated due to the non-stationarity induced by the breaks, all terms have to be tracked. First, and assuming that no additional changes occur at time $T+1$, the DGP produces:

$$\Delta\mathbf{x}_{T+2} = \boldsymbol{\gamma}^* + \boldsymbol{\alpha}^*\left(\boldsymbol{\beta}'\mathbf{x}_{T+1} - \boldsymbol{\mu}^*\right) + \boldsymbol{\nu}_{T+2} \tag{3.20}$$

and as:

$$\mathbf{x}_{T+1} = \mathbf{x}_T + \boldsymbol{\gamma}^* + \boldsymbol{\alpha}^*\left(\boldsymbol{\beta}'\mathbf{x}_T - \boldsymbol{\mu}^*\right) + \boldsymbol{\nu}_{T+1},$$

then:

$$\boldsymbol{\beta}'\mathbf{x}_{T+1} - \boldsymbol{\mu}^* = \boldsymbol{\Lambda}^*\left(\boldsymbol{\beta}'\mathbf{x}_T - \boldsymbol{\mu}^*\right) + \boldsymbol{\beta}'\boldsymbol{\nu}_{T+1}, \tag{3.21}$$

where $\boldsymbol{\Lambda}^* = \left(\mathbf{I}_r + \boldsymbol{\beta}'\boldsymbol{\alpha}^*\right)$ has all its eigenvalues inside the unit circle. Let $\boldsymbol{\Upsilon}^* = \left(\mathbf{I}_n + \boldsymbol{\alpha}^*\boldsymbol{\beta}'\right)$, and note that $\boldsymbol{\alpha}^*\boldsymbol{\Lambda}^* = \boldsymbol{\Upsilon}^*\boldsymbol{\alpha}^*$. To avoid dependence of the new growth rate on the changed parameters, we maintain $\boldsymbol{\beta}'\boldsymbol{\gamma}^* = \mathbf{0}$ and set $\boldsymbol{\beta}'\mathbf{x}_{T+1} - \boldsymbol{\mu}^* = \boldsymbol{\kappa}^*_{T+1}$ so from (3.21):

$$\boldsymbol{\kappa}^*_{T+1} = \boldsymbol{\Lambda}^*\left(\boldsymbol{\kappa}_T - [\boldsymbol{\mu}^* - \boldsymbol{\mu}]\right) + \boldsymbol{\beta}'\boldsymbol{\nu}_{T+1}.$$

Finally:

$$\mathsf{E}\left[\Delta \mathbf{x}_{T+h}\right] = \boldsymbol{\gamma}^* - \boldsymbol{\alpha}^* \left(\boldsymbol{\Lambda}^*\right)^{h-1} \left(\boldsymbol{\mu}^* - \boldsymbol{\mu}\right) \overset{h\rightarrow\infty}{\rightarrow} \boldsymbol{\gamma}^*.$$

Since:

$$\mathsf{E}\left[\Delta \mathbf{x}_{T+1}\right] = \boldsymbol{\gamma}^* - \boldsymbol{\alpha}^* \left(\boldsymbol{\mu}^* - \boldsymbol{\mu}\right),$$

the conditional and unconditional biases of the 1-step forecast error are:

$$\mathsf{E}\left[\widehat{\mathbf{e}}_{T+2|T+1} \mid I_{T+1}\right] = \left(\boldsymbol{\gamma}^* - \boldsymbol{\gamma}\right) - \boldsymbol{\alpha}\left(\boldsymbol{\mu}^* - \boldsymbol{\mu}\right) + \left(\boldsymbol{\alpha}^* - \boldsymbol{\alpha}\right)\boldsymbol{\kappa}^*_{T+1} \tag{3.22}$$

and as:

$$\mathsf{E}\left[\boldsymbol{\kappa}^*_{T+1}\right] = -\boldsymbol{\Lambda}^*\left(\boldsymbol{\mu}^* - \boldsymbol{\mu}\right),$$

then:

$$\mathsf{E}\left[\widehat{\mathbf{e}}_{T+2|T+1}\right] = \left(\boldsymbol{\gamma}^* - \boldsymbol{\gamma}\right) - \left[\boldsymbol{\alpha} + \left(\boldsymbol{\alpha}^* - \boldsymbol{\alpha}\right)\boldsymbol{\Lambda}^*\right]\left(\boldsymbol{\mu}^* - \boldsymbol{\mu}\right). \tag{3.23}$$

In particular, when $\boldsymbol{\alpha}^* = \boldsymbol{\alpha}$, so only the deterministic terms change, then:

$$\mathsf{E}\left[\widehat{\mathbf{e}}_{T+2|T+1} \mid I_{T+1}\right] = \left(\boldsymbol{\gamma}^* - \boldsymbol{\gamma}\right) - \boldsymbol{\alpha}\left(\boldsymbol{\mu}^* - \boldsymbol{\mu}\right) = \mathsf{E}\left[\widehat{\mathbf{e}}_{T+2|T+1}\right].$$

These expressions highlight that the effects of breaks on the VEqCM persist even when information from after the break is used. Note that $\boldsymbol{\kappa}^*_{T+1}$ on average is "smaller than" $(\boldsymbol{\mu}^* - \boldsymbol{\mu})$ and so induces a smaller bias, as $\boldsymbol{\beta}'\boldsymbol{\alpha}$ corresponds to the roots inside the unit circle, and so dampens the effect of shifts in the equilibrium mean. Nevertheless, in general complicated effects result when all the parameters change.

3.5.3 *Forecasting levels from T to $T+2$*

This comprises 2-steps ahead forecasts made prior to the break using (3.16), to illustrate how the results change for multi-step forecasts. Now the corresponding 2-step ahead forecast-error biases are:

$$\mathsf{E}\left[\widehat{\mathbf{e}}_{T+2|T} \mid I_T\right] = \mathsf{E}\left[\widehat{\mathbf{e}}_{T+2|T}\right] + \left(\boldsymbol{\alpha}^*\left[\mathbf{I}_r + \boldsymbol{\Lambda}^*\right] - \boldsymbol{\alpha}\left[\mathbf{I}_r + \boldsymbol{\Lambda}\right]\right)\boldsymbol{\kappa}_T \tag{3.24}$$

where:

$$\mathsf{E}\left[\widehat{\mathbf{e}}_{T+2|T}\right] = 2\left(\boldsymbol{\gamma}^* - \boldsymbol{\gamma}\right) - \boldsymbol{\alpha}^*\left(\mathbf{I}_r + \boldsymbol{\Lambda}^*\right)\left(\boldsymbol{\mu}^* - \boldsymbol{\mu}\right). \tag{3.25}$$

Thus, the unconditional bias of the level suffers increasingly from the impact of a change in the equilibrium mean or the growth rate. If $\boldsymbol{\alpha}$ is constant (so $\boldsymbol{\Lambda}^* = \boldsymbol{\Lambda}$ also), (3.24) simplifies to $\mathsf{E}\left[\widehat{\mathbf{e}}_{T+2|T}\right]$ which illustrates the lack of impact on a VEqCM of the disequilibrium state of the economy when the break has constant dynamics. Otherwise, the conditional bias deviates from the unconditional by an amount that depends on the immediate past disequilibrium.

3.5.4 *Forecasting levels from $T+1$ to $T+3$*

The forecasting rule here is just a time-shifted version of (3.16). Again, the expectations are changing as adjustments to the new parameters continue, and the feature of practical importance lies in the changed expectations of the variables, $\boldsymbol{\beta}'\mathbf{x}_{T+1}$ and $\Delta\mathbf{x}_{T+1}$. Thus $\mathsf{E}[\widehat{\mathbf{e}}_{T+3|T+1}|I_{T+1}]$ equals:

$$\begin{aligned} & 2\left(\boldsymbol{\gamma}^* - \boldsymbol{\gamma}\right) - \boldsymbol{\alpha}\left(\mathbf{I}_r + \boldsymbol{\Lambda}\right)\left(\boldsymbol{\mu}^* - \boldsymbol{\mu}\right) + \left[\boldsymbol{\alpha}^*\left(\mathbf{I}_r + \boldsymbol{\Lambda}^*\right) - \boldsymbol{\alpha}\left(\mathbf{I}_r + \boldsymbol{\Lambda}\right)\right]\boldsymbol{\kappa}^*_{T+1} \\ = \; & \mathsf{E}\left[\widehat{\mathbf{e}}_{T+3|T+1}\right] + \left[\boldsymbol{\alpha}^*\left(\mathbf{I}_r + \boldsymbol{\Lambda}^*\right) - \boldsymbol{\alpha}\left(\mathbf{I}_r + \boldsymbol{\Lambda}\right)\right]\left(\boldsymbol{\kappa}^*_{T+1} - \mathsf{E}\left[\boldsymbol{\kappa}^*_{T+1}\right]\right) \end{aligned}$$

where:

$$\begin{aligned} \mathsf{E}\left[\widehat{\mathbf{e}}_{T+3|T+1}\right] = \; & 2\left(\boldsymbol{\gamma}^* - \boldsymbol{\gamma}\right) \\ & - \left[\boldsymbol{\alpha}^*\left(\mathbf{I}_r + \boldsymbol{\Lambda}^*\right)\boldsymbol{\Lambda}^* - \boldsymbol{\alpha}\left(\mathbf{I}_r + \boldsymbol{\Lambda}\right)\boldsymbol{\beta}'\boldsymbol{\alpha}^*\right]\left(\boldsymbol{\mu}^* - \boldsymbol{\mu}\right). \end{aligned}$$

In the special case that $\boldsymbol{\alpha}$ is constant:

$$\begin{aligned} \mathsf{E}\left[\widehat{\mathbf{e}}_{T+3|T+1} \mid I_{T+1}\right] & = \mathsf{E}\left[\widehat{\mathbf{e}}_{T+3|T+1}\right] \\ & = 2\left(\boldsymbol{\gamma}^* - \boldsymbol{\gamma}\right) - \boldsymbol{\alpha}\left(\mathbf{I}_r + \boldsymbol{\Lambda}\right)\left(\boldsymbol{\mu}^* - \boldsymbol{\mu}\right). \qquad (3.26) \end{aligned}$$

When $\boldsymbol{\alpha}$ is constant, (3.26) coincides with (3.25), so again the VEqCM has failed to benefit from forecasting after the break, as against before its occurrence.

3.5.5 *Overview*

The unconditional forecast-error bias calculations for levels are summarized in table 3.3 for each change in turn to highlight its specific effects, letting $\mathbf{R} = \mathbf{I}_r + \boldsymbol{\Lambda}$, $\boldsymbol{\delta}_{\mu} = \boldsymbol{\mu}^* - \boldsymbol{\mu}$ and $\boldsymbol{\delta}_{\gamma} = \boldsymbol{\gamma}^* - \boldsymbol{\gamma}$. When a parameter change occurs, forecasts will be incorrect from almost any statistical procedure, so a key question is how quickly a model adapts to

Table 3.3
Forecast biases at 1 & 2-steps pre & post break.

	Before break	Post break
	1-step forecasts	
$\mu \to \mu^*$	$-\alpha\delta_\mu$	$-\alpha\delta_\mu$
$\gamma \to \gamma^*$	δ_γ	δ_γ
$\alpha \to \alpha^*$	0	0
	2-step forecasts	
$\mu \to \mu^*$	$-\alpha\mathbf{R}\delta_\mu$	$-\alpha\mathbf{R}\delta_\mu$
$\gamma \to \gamma^*$	$2\delta_\gamma$	$2\delta_\gamma$
$\alpha \to \alpha^*$	0	0

the changed environment. The results of the previous analysis allow us to answer this question for the VEqCM: it has essentially the same pre and post break biases for changes in μ and γ, and so completely fails to adapt. However, because the VEqCM biases are almost the same pre and post break, a constant adjustment (i.e., an intercept correction) to its forecasts would dramatically reduce the bias when forecasting after the break.

3.6 Forecasting Levels and Growth Rates

When there is a shift in the equilibrium mean, the bias in forecasts from the VEqCM can either increase of decrease as the horizon increases, relative to 1-step forecasts. This result applies both to forecasts of levels and differences. First consider forecasts of the differences, when an equilibrium-mean shift occurs (μ shifts to μ^*), so for T to $T+1$, the 1-step forecasts of $\Delta\mathbf{x}_t$ are given by:

$$\widehat{\Delta\mathbf{x}}_{T+1|T} = \gamma + \alpha\left(\beta'\mathbf{x}_T - \mu\right)$$

with:

$$\begin{aligned} & \mathsf{E}\left[\Delta\mathbf{x}_{T+1} - \widehat{\Delta\mathbf{x}}_{T+1|T}\right] \\ &= \mathsf{E}\left[\Delta\mathbf{x}_{T+1} - \gamma - \alpha\left(\beta'\mathbf{x}_T - \mu\right)\right] = -\alpha\left(\mu^* - \mu\right). \end{aligned} \quad (3.27)$$

Next period, for $T+1$ to $T+2$, the 1-step bias remains:

$$\mathsf{E}\left[\Delta \mathbf{x}_{T+2} - \boldsymbol{\gamma} - \boldsymbol{\alpha}\left(\boldsymbol{\beta}'\mathbf{x}_{T+1} - \boldsymbol{\mu}\right)\right] = -\boldsymbol{\alpha}\left(\boldsymbol{\mu}^* - \boldsymbol{\mu}\right) \tag{3.28}$$

which continues as h increases.

For multi-step growth forecasts from T:

$$\widehat{\Delta \mathbf{x}}_{T+h|T} = \boldsymbol{\gamma} + \boldsymbol{\alpha}\left(\boldsymbol{\beta}'\widehat{\mathbf{x}}_{T+h-1} - \boldsymbol{\mu}\right) = \boldsymbol{\gamma} + \boldsymbol{\alpha}\boldsymbol{\Lambda}^{h-1}\left(\boldsymbol{\beta}'\mathbf{x}_T - \boldsymbol{\mu}\right),$$

whereas:

$$\Delta \mathbf{x}_{T+h} = \boldsymbol{\gamma} + \boldsymbol{\alpha}\boldsymbol{\Lambda}^{h-1}\left(\boldsymbol{\beta}'\mathbf{x}_T - \boldsymbol{\mu}^*\right) + \boldsymbol{\nu}_{T+h} + \boldsymbol{\alpha}\sum_{i=0}^{h-2}\boldsymbol{\Lambda}^i\boldsymbol{\beta}'\boldsymbol{\nu}_{T+h-1-i},$$

so:

$$\mathsf{E}\left[\Delta \mathbf{x}_{T+2} - \widehat{\Delta \mathbf{x}}_{T+2|T}\right] = -\boldsymbol{\alpha}\boldsymbol{\Lambda}\left(\boldsymbol{\mu}^* - \boldsymbol{\mu}\right), \tag{3.29}$$

followed by:

$$\mathsf{E}\left[\Delta \mathbf{x}_{T+h} - \widehat{\Delta \mathbf{x}}_{T+h|T}\right] = -\boldsymbol{\alpha}\boldsymbol{\Lambda}^{h-1}\left(\boldsymbol{\mu}^* - \boldsymbol{\mu}\right), \tag{3.30}$$

for all $h \geq 1$. Since $\boldsymbol{\Lambda}^h$ tends to zero as h increases, the forecast bias in (3.30) declines to zero. Consequently, the 1-step forecast-error biases for $\Delta\mathbf{x}$ extending (3.28) will exceed the multi-step in this setting. Intuitively, as $\boldsymbol{\gamma}$ has not altered, and the in-sample model has $\boldsymbol{\gamma}$ as its unconditional growth rate, its multi-step forecasts converge on $\boldsymbol{\gamma}$, and hence cease to be biased. The 1-step forecasts, however, keep discovering large values for the EqCM, and hence continue to mis-forecast.

Such a finding fits the empirical example in chapter 8, where the 1-step growth forecasts are worse than the multi-step after the break: when underlying growth is constant, the data and model both converge to that growth as h increases. Thus, a discrepancy where multi-step forecasts are less biased than 1-step may be a diagnostic index that an equilibrium shift is the source of the forecast failure.

Perhaps more surprisingly, multi-step forecasts of levels can also be less biased than 1-step forecasts. Since $\widehat{\mathbf{x}}_{T+h|T+h-1} = \mathbf{x}_{T+h-1} + \Delta\widehat{\mathbf{x}}_{T+h|T+h-1}$ with:

$$\mathsf{E}\left[\mathbf{x}_{T+h} - \widehat{\mathbf{x}}_{T+h|T+h-1}\right] = -\boldsymbol{\alpha}\left(\boldsymbol{\mu}^* - \boldsymbol{\mu}\right), \tag{3.31}$$

whereas:

$$\widehat{\mathbf{x}}_{T+h|T} = \mathbf{x}_T + \sum_{i=1}^{h} \widehat{\Delta \mathbf{x}}_{T+i|T},$$

then:

$$\mathsf{E}\left[\mathbf{x}_{T+h} - \widehat{\mathbf{x}}_{T+h|T}\right] = \boldsymbol{\alpha}\left(\boldsymbol{\beta}'\boldsymbol{\alpha}\right)^{-1}\left(\mathbf{I}_r - \boldsymbol{\Lambda}^h\right)\left(\boldsymbol{\mu}^* - \boldsymbol{\mu}\right). \tag{3.32}$$

The multi-step bias (3.32) can be less than the 1-step (3.31) for some parameter values: consider $n = 2$ where $\boldsymbol{\beta} = (1 \quad -1)'$ and $\boldsymbol{\alpha} = (-0.8\ 0.8)$, then for $h = 2$, $(\boldsymbol{\beta}'\boldsymbol{\alpha})^{-1}\left(\mathbf{I}_r - \boldsymbol{\Lambda}^h\right) \simeq -0.4$, and tends to -0.63 as $h \to \infty$.

3.7 Variance Effects after Structural Breaks

Forecast-error biases must be evaluated along side the forecast-error variances that a model introduces, and this section analyzes these. These formulae take account of the information that is averaged over when unconditional biases are computed: such terms now appear here as variance effects (e.g., the variance of the difference between $\boldsymbol{\beta}'\mathbf{x}_T$ and $\boldsymbol{\mu}$). Formulae for the h-step ahead asymptotic variances of the VEqCM in levels, differences and I(0) transformations, when there are no breaks, are provided in Clements and Hendry (1995a); here we focus on the results for levels when breaks occur. First, as:

$$\left(\boldsymbol{\beta}'\mathbf{x}_T - \boldsymbol{\mu}\right) = \boldsymbol{\Lambda}\left(\boldsymbol{\beta}'\mathbf{x}_{T-1} - \boldsymbol{\mu}\right) + \boldsymbol{\beta}'\boldsymbol{\nu}_T,$$

then:

$$\mathsf{V}\left[\boldsymbol{\beta}'\mathbf{x}_T\right] - \boldsymbol{\Lambda}\mathsf{V}\left[\boldsymbol{\beta}'\mathbf{x}_T\right]\boldsymbol{\Lambda}' = \boldsymbol{\beta}'\boldsymbol{\Omega}_\nu\boldsymbol{\beta}, \tag{3.33}$$

or:

$$\begin{aligned}\left[\left(\mathsf{V}\left[\boldsymbol{\beta}'\mathbf{x}_T\right]\right)^v\right]^{sm} &= \mathsf{V}\left[\boldsymbol{\beta}'\mathbf{x}_T\right] \\ &= \left[\left(\mathbf{I}_r - \boldsymbol{\Lambda}\otimes\boldsymbol{\Lambda}\right)^{-1}\left(\boldsymbol{\beta}'\boldsymbol{\Omega}_\nu\boldsymbol{\beta}\right)^v\right]^{sm} = \mathbf{V},\end{aligned} \tag{3.34}$$

where $[\mathbf{A}(\mathbf{B})^v]^{sm}$ denotes the symmetric matrix formed from a column created by vectoring, denoted $(\cdot)^v$. Also:

$$\mathsf{V}\left[\Delta\mathbf{x}_T\right] = \boldsymbol{\alpha}\mathbf{V}\boldsymbol{\alpha}' + \boldsymbol{\Omega}_\nu.$$

Table 3.4
1- & 2-step VEqCM unconditional variances.

	$T \to T+1$	$T \to T+2$
$\alpha = 0$	Ω	2Ω
$\alpha = \alpha^*$	Ω	$\Omega + \Upsilon\Omega\Upsilon'$
$\alpha \neq \alpha^*$	$\Omega + \delta_\alpha \mathbf{V} \delta_\alpha'$	$\Omega + \Upsilon^*\Omega\Upsilon^{*\prime} + \mathbf{D}^*\mathbf{V}\mathbf{D}^{*\prime}$
	$T+1 \to T+2$	$T+1 \to T+3$
$\alpha = 0$	Ω	2Ω
$\alpha = \alpha^*$	Ω	$\Omega + \Upsilon\Omega\Upsilon'$
$\alpha \neq \alpha^*$	$\Omega + \delta_\alpha \mathbf{V}^* \delta_\alpha'$	$\Omega + \Upsilon^*\Omega\Upsilon^{*\prime} + \mathbf{D}^*\mathbf{V}^*\mathbf{D}^{*\prime}$

Here and in the text $\alpha = \mathbf{0}$ implicitly implies $\alpha^* = \mathbf{0}$.

Analogous expressions hold for the variance matrices after the break. Appendix 3.12 reports the derivations for each of the four different combinations of forecast origins and horizons. Here we focus on the summary results, reported in table 3.4. The second and third columns show the variances for various values of α, the parameter change that most affects the variances, where $\delta_\alpha = \alpha^* - \alpha$, with $\mathbf{D}^* = \mathbf{C}^* - \mathbf{C}$, and $\mathbf{C}^* = \alpha^* (\mathbf{I}_r + \Lambda^*)$. The unstarred matrices replace any starred parameter with its unstarred value, so $\mathbf{D} = \mathbf{0}$, and following (3.33), $\mathbf{V}^* = \Lambda^*\mathbf{V}\Lambda^{*\prime} + \beta'\Omega\beta$.

Overall, the shift of the forecast origin does not greatly alter the results, beyond replacing $\mathbf{V}$ by $\mathbf{V}^*$. The 2-step pattern is similar to the 1-step outcomes, although the values are larger, and the formulae more complicated. The parameter changes would need to be very large to occasion major variance changes.

3.7.1 *Overview*

The formulae for the unconditional biases have already proved useful in explaining the outcomes of the various Monte Carlo studies of the determinants of forecast failure. Such studies average over complete replications of the in-sample and forecast-period data, which mimics what the analysis calculates. The practical problem is that only one data sample is ever produced over any historical epoch, and the value of the conditioning variables at the forecast origin can be vital to the success or failure of the forecast. The conditional expectations formulae come closer to capturing that aspect, and accordingly are much harder to interpret. And a Monte Carlo study of them would need to draw sequences that had the same forecast origins, which is harder still.

The unconditional variance formulae above throw some light on the impacts of breaks in dynamics, but at the cost of abstracting from estimation variances, and all mis-specification problems. They will prove of most value in chapter 5 when we compare the properties of VEqCM forecasts with those from DVs and DDVs, balancing the benefits of robustness to breaks against the costs of larger variances. Conditional variance formulae to complement the conditional expectations are feasible, but have not proved useful in interpreting empirical evidence.

3.8 Higher Frequency Data: Breaks in Seasonals

Shifts in deterministic components can be equally problematic for seasonal data, in principle and in practice. As indicated by the following analysis, based on Clements and Hendry (1997), differencing may once again offer at least a partial remedy.

Consider a quarterly logarithmic-transformed time series described by fixed, trending and shifting deterministic seasonals generalizing:

$$y_t = \sum_{i=1}^{4} \left(\alpha_i + \alpha_i^* \mathrm{I}_T^\tau + \beta_i t + \beta_i^* \mathrm{I}_T^\tau \left(t - \tau + 1\right)\right) Q_{i,t} + \epsilon_t. \tag{3.35}$$

In (3.35), $\epsilon_t \sim \mathsf{IN}[0, \sigma_\epsilon^2]$ for $t = 1, \ldots, T$, where the indicator variable $\mathrm{I}_{\tau+j}^\tau = 1$ for $t \in (\tau, \tau + j)$ and is zero otherwise. The $Q_{i,t}$ are seasonal dummies. Also, y_t is scalar, and we neglect additional sources of dynamics to focus on a change in the seasonal pattern at time τ (note that this usage of τ is restricted to the present section). The issue we wish to address here concerns conditions under which $\Delta_4 y_t$ has a constant, non-zero seasonal pattern or a changing seasonal pattern. We show that it may pay to impose unit and/or seasonal roots for forecasting even when it is statistically invalid to do so.

From (3.35), in terms of annual changes, the expression for $\Delta_4 y_t$ is:

$$\sum_{i=1}^{4} \Delta_4 \left(\alpha_i Q_{i,t} + \alpha_i^* \mathrm{I}_T^\tau Q_{i,t} + \beta_i t Q_{i,t} + \beta_i^* \mathrm{I}_T^\tau \left(t - \tau + 1\right) Q_{i,t} + \epsilon_t\right)$$

or:

$$\sum_{i=1}^{4}\left(\left(\alpha_i^* + \beta_i^*\left(t-\tau+1\right)\right)\mathrm{I}_{\tau+3}^{\tau}Q_{i,t} + 4\left(\beta_i + \beta_i^*\mathrm{I}_T^{\tau+4}\right)Q_{i,t}\right) + \Delta_4\epsilon_t \quad (3.36)$$

since $Q_{i,t} \equiv L^4 Q_{i,t}$:

$$\begin{aligned}
\Delta_4 Q_{i,t} &= 0\ \forall i,t; \\
\Delta_4 t Q_{i,t} &= \left(tQ_{i,t} - L^4 tQ_{i,t}\right) = 4Q_{i,t}; \\
\Delta_4 \mathrm{I}_T^{\tau} Q_{i,t} &= \mathrm{I}_{\tau+3}^{\tau} Q_{i,t};
\end{aligned}$$

and

$$\Delta_4 \mathrm{I}_T^{\tau}(t-\tau+1)Q_{i,t} = \begin{cases} (t-\tau+1)\mathrm{I}_{\tau+3}^{\tau}Q_{i,t} & \text{for } t-\tau = 0,3 \\ 4\mathrm{I}_T^{\tau+4}Q_{i,t} & \text{for } t-\tau > 3. \end{cases}$$

When the existence and timing of shifts in seasonality are unknown, all the terms involving products with the indicator variable will add to the residual, so over the sample as a whole, there will not be a redundant common factor of $(1-L^4)$. The residuals on (3.36) are likely to be negatively autocorrelated in the absence of any dynamic modeling, offset by any original positive autocorrelation in the $\{\epsilon_t\}$.

The evolving seasonal patterns of y_t and $\Delta_4 y_t$ are recorded in table 3.5 in the neighborhood of time τ. First, consider the pattern in y_t. The initially steady, if trending, seasonality is disturbed at τ, with a jump in the level when $\alpha_i^* \neq 0$ and in the trend when $\beta_i^* \neq 0$. The new level in each quarter becomes $\alpha_i + \alpha_i^* + \beta_i\tau$ and the new trend is $(\beta_i + \beta_i^*)$, so forecasts based on assuming $\alpha_i^* = \beta_i^* = 0$ will quickly become poor.

Next, consider $\Delta_4 y_t$. When there are no trending seasonals ($\beta_i = \beta_i^* = 0$), the break just produces a jump in the quarterly change in the annual growth rate equal to α_i^* for the four quarters from τ to $\tau + 3$. When there are no structural breaks, $\Delta_4 y_t$ has a constant seasonal pattern equal to $4\beta_i$, and so systematically changes more in some quarters than others. Also, there are complicated movements in the seasonal pattern of $\Delta_4 y_t$ whenever the coefficients α_i^* and β_i^* differ from zero (i.e., $\mathrm{I}_T^{\tau} = 1$). Finally, there is a permanent shift in the seasonal pattern when $\beta_i^* \neq 0$. Analogous to differencing a non-seasonal process, the Δ_4 filter reduces the impact of the effect of α_i^* to a transient "blip" for four quarters, and that of β_i^* from a trend to a level shift.

Table 3.5
Patterns in y_t and $\Delta_4 y_t$ for a shift in seasonal means.

t	$\mathsf{E}[y_t]$	$\mathsf{E}[\Delta_4 y_t]$
$\vdots$	$\vdots$	$\vdots$
$\tau-1$	$\sum_{i=1}^{4}(\alpha_i+\beta_i(\tau-1))Q_{i,\tau-1}$	$4\sum_{i=1}^{4}\beta_i Q_{i,\tau-1}$
τ	$\sum_{i=1}^{4}(\alpha_i+\alpha_i^*+\beta_i\tau+\beta_i^*)Q_{i,\tau}$	$\sum_{i=1}^{4}(4\beta_i+\alpha_i^*+\beta_i^*)Q_{i,\tau}$
$\tau+1$	$\sum_{i=1}^{4}(\alpha_i+\alpha_i^*+\beta_i(\tau+1)+2\beta_i^*)Q_{i,\tau+1}$	$\sum_{i=1}^{4}(4\beta_i+\alpha_i^*+2\beta_i^*)Q_{i,\tau+1}$
$\tau+2$	$\sum_{i=1}^{4}(\alpha_i+\alpha_i^*+\beta_i(\tau+2)+3\beta_i^*)Q_{i,\tau+2}$	$\sum_{i=1}^{4}(4\beta_i+\alpha_i^*+3\beta_i^*)Q_{i,\tau+2}$
$\tau+3$	$\sum_{i=1}^{4}(\alpha_i+\alpha_i^*+\beta_i(\tau+3)+4\beta_i^*)Q_{i,\tau+3}$	$\sum_{i=1}^{4}(4\beta_i+\alpha_i^*+4\beta_i^*)Q_{i,\tau+3}$
$\tau+4$	$\sum_{i=1}^{4}(\alpha_i+\alpha_i^*+\beta_i(\tau+4)+5\beta_i^*)Q_{i,\tau+4}$	$4\sum_{i=1}^{4}(\beta_i+\beta_i^*)Q_{i,\tau+4}$
$\tau+5$	$\sum_{i=1}^{4}(\alpha_i+\alpha_i^*+\beta_i(\tau+5)+6\beta_i^*)Q_{i,\tau+5}$	$4\sum_{i=1}^{4}(\beta_i+\beta_i^*)Q_{i,\tau+5}$
$\vdots$	$\vdots$	$\vdots$

Given the above patterns induced by changes in deterministic seasonals, we can show that imposing unit roots in the forecast model may improve the accuracy of rolling forecasts when the DGP is (3.35) and the shifts are not modeled. The advantages to using, say, fourth-differencing, arise for the same reason that zero-frequency differencing works in the nonseasonal case when there are structural breaks or regime shifts. Essentially, differencing sets the forecasts "back on track" after the break has occurred. The "full value" of the break is incorporated in future forecasts since differencing effectively projects only the present and gives no weight to the pre-break history of the process.

As an example, consider forecasting using (3.35) with the α_i^*, β_i^* terms absent (i.e., the shifts are not modeled). Forecasts of y_{T+j}, $j \geq 0$ made pre-break at time $\tau - 1$ rapidly become poor as described above. The outcome is moderated a little if the forecast origin is moved forward to τ, or $\tau + 1$, $\tau + 2, \ldots$ with the model estimates updated on the extended sample, but the impact of the post-break observations on the estimated model parameters (say, $\hat{\alpha}_i$, $\hat{\beta}_i$) will initially be slight. By way of contrast, consider forecasting with a model that imposes fourth-differencing, and for simplicity suppose the seasonality is not trending either pre- or post-break. Forecasts made at $\tau - 1, \tau, \ldots, \tau + 3$ will go awry, but thereafter, as suggested by the pattern for $\mathsf{E}[\Delta_4 y_t]$ above, the new pattern of deterministic seasonals ($\alpha_i + \alpha_i^*$) will be forecast for y_t.

The model based on (3.35) will continue to forecast the pattern based on the α_i, subject to the small adjustments referred to above from updating.

These findings suggest that imposing unit roots at both seasonal and zero frequencies may improve forecast accuracy when structural breaks occur in seasonals over the forecast period, even though such restrictions may not appear to be warranted on the basis of unit-root tests. While seasonal breaks may be less common than mean shifts, since seasonality probably changes relatively smoothly over time with slowly changing technology and institutions (see e.g., Harvey and Scott, 1994), even mean shifts have more complicated effects in seasonally-varying data.

3.9 Conclusion

The primary factor precipitating forecast failure is a shift in the equilibrium mean: all the Monte Carlo simulations illustrate various facets of this analysis for static, I(0) and I(1) processes. The empirical illustration in chapter 8 confirms the value of these results for interpreting forecast errors in a small monetary model of the UK. Chapters 5 and 6 will investigate potential remedies.

When breaks are not (in some loose sense) "exogenous" to the system under study, but are internally generated, then a more satisfactory solution than the use of dummy variables may be to attempt to model the structural change as an integral part of the DGP. This approach is explored in chapter 10 using regime-switching models. There, we sketch the non-linear model classes that appear promising, discuss the specification, estimation and calculation of forecasts, and the available empirical evidence on their forecast performance.

3.10 Appendix A: Chow-test Derivation

Imposing an intercept of zero, simplifying the notation to $\phi = \phi_1$ and defining the $T \times T$ matrix $\mathbf{D}$:

$$\mathbf{D} = \begin{pmatrix} \mathbf{0}_{T_1} & \mathbf{0} \\ \mathbf{0} & \mathbf{I}_{T_2} \end{pmatrix} \quad \text{so } \mathbf{Dz} = \begin{pmatrix} \mathbf{0} \\ \mathbf{z}_{T_2} \end{pmatrix},$$

as $T_1 + T_2 = T$, the DGP with the break parameterized becomes ($\delta = \rho\phi$):

$$\mathbf{y} = \mathbf{z}\phi + \mathbf{D}\mathbf{z}\delta + \boldsymbol{\epsilon},$$

whereas the estimate of ϕ from (3.1) (again without an intercept) is:

$$\widehat{\phi} = \left(\mathbf{z}'\mathbf{z}\right)^{-1}\mathbf{z}'\mathbf{y} = \phi + \left(\mathbf{z}'\mathbf{z}\right)^{-1}\mathbf{z}'\boldsymbol{\epsilon} + \delta\left(\mathbf{z}'\mathbf{z}\right)^{-1}\left(\mathbf{z}'_{T_2}\mathbf{z}_{T_2}\right)$$

so:

$$\mathsf{E}\left[\widehat{\phi}\right] = \phi + \delta k.$$

Next, using:

$$\widehat{\boldsymbol{\epsilon}} = \mathbf{y} - \widehat{\mathbf{y}} = \boldsymbol{\epsilon} + \mathbf{D}\mathbf{z}\delta - \mathbf{z}\left(\widehat{\phi} - \phi\right) = \mathbf{Q}_z\boldsymbol{\epsilon} + \delta\left[\mathbf{D} - \left(\mathbf{z}'\mathbf{z}\right)^{-1}\left(\mathbf{z}'_{T_2}\mathbf{z}_{T_2}\right)\right]\mathbf{z}$$

with $\mathbf{Q}_z = (\mathbf{I}_T - \mathbf{z}\left(\mathbf{z}'\mathbf{z}\right)^{-1}\mathbf{z}')$, then:

$$\mathsf{E}\left[\widehat{\boldsymbol{\epsilon}}\right] = \delta\eta\left(\mathbf{D} - k\mathbf{I}_T\right)$$

and hence:

$$\mathsf{E}\left[\widehat{\boldsymbol{\epsilon}}'\widehat{\boldsymbol{\epsilon}}\right] \simeq (T-1)\,\sigma_\epsilon^2 + \delta^2\left(\sigma_z^2 + \eta^2\right)(1-k)\,T_2.$$

Sub-sample values can be obtained by specialization. Analogous results can be derived for a shift in the intercept when a constant term is included in the regression.

3.11 Appendix B: Conditional Forecast-error Biases

3.11.1 From T to $T+1$

From (3.15):

$$\widehat{\mathbf{e}}_{T+1|T} = \boldsymbol{\gamma}^* + \boldsymbol{\alpha}^*\left(\boldsymbol{\beta}'\mathbf{x}_T - \boldsymbol{\mu}^*\right) + \boldsymbol{\nu}_{T+1} - \left[\boldsymbol{\gamma} + \boldsymbol{\alpha}\left(\boldsymbol{\beta}'\mathbf{x}_T - \boldsymbol{\mu}\right)\right]. \quad (3.37)$$

Let $\boldsymbol{\beta}'\mathbf{x}_T - \boldsymbol{\mu} = \boldsymbol{\kappa}_T$, then the conditional bias is:

$$\mathsf{E}\left[\widehat{\mathbf{e}}_{T+1|T} \mid I_T\right] = \left(\boldsymbol{\gamma}^* - \boldsymbol{\gamma}\right) - \boldsymbol{\alpha}^*\left(\boldsymbol{\mu}^* - \boldsymbol{\mu}\right) + \left(\boldsymbol{\alpha}^* - \boldsymbol{\alpha}\right)\boldsymbol{\kappa}_T \quad (3.38)$$

and unconditionally:

$$\mathsf{E}\left[\widehat{\mathbf{e}}_{T+1|T}\right] = \left(\boldsymbol{\gamma}^* - \boldsymbol{\gamma}\right) - \boldsymbol{\alpha}^*\left(\boldsymbol{\mu}^* - \boldsymbol{\mu}\right). \quad (3.39)$$

3.11.2 From $T+1$ to $T+2$

The 1-step forecast becomes:

$$\widehat{\mathbf{x}}_{T+2|T+1} = \mathbf{x}_{T+1} + \boldsymbol{\gamma} + \boldsymbol{\alpha}\left(\boldsymbol{\beta}'\mathbf{x}_{T+1} - \boldsymbol{\mu}\right) \tag{3.40}$$

with corresponding levels 1-step forecast error:

$$\widehat{\mathbf{e}}_{T+2|T+1} = \boldsymbol{\gamma}^* + \boldsymbol{\alpha}^*\left(\boldsymbol{\beta}'\mathbf{x}_{T+1} - \boldsymbol{\mu}^*\right) + \boldsymbol{\nu}_{T+2} - \left[\boldsymbol{\gamma} + \boldsymbol{\alpha}\left(\boldsymbol{\beta}'\mathbf{x}_{T+1} - \boldsymbol{\mu}\right)\right] \tag{3.41}$$

from which the conditional bias follows as cited in the text.

3.11.3 From T to $T+2$

The data are actually generated by:

$$\mathbf{x}_{T+2} = \left(\boldsymbol{\Upsilon}^*\right)^2 \mathbf{x}_T + \left(\mathbf{I}_n + \boldsymbol{\Upsilon}^*\right)\left(\boldsymbol{\gamma}^* - \boldsymbol{\alpha}^*\boldsymbol{\mu}^*\right) + \boldsymbol{\Upsilon}^*\boldsymbol{\nu}_{T+1} + \boldsymbol{\nu}_{T+2} \tag{3.42}$$

since ($\boldsymbol{\Upsilon}^* = \mathbf{I}_n + \boldsymbol{\alpha}^*\boldsymbol{\beta}'$):

$$\mathbf{x}_{T+1} = \boldsymbol{\Upsilon}^*\mathbf{x}_T + \left(\boldsymbol{\gamma}^* - \boldsymbol{\alpha}^*\boldsymbol{\mu}^*\right) + \boldsymbol{\nu}_{T+1}, \tag{3.43}$$

whereas:

$$\widehat{\mathbf{x}}_{T+2|T} = \boldsymbol{\Upsilon}\widehat{\mathbf{x}}_{T+1|T} + \boldsymbol{\gamma} - \boldsymbol{\alpha}\boldsymbol{\mu} = \boldsymbol{\Upsilon}^2\mathbf{x}_T + \left(\mathbf{I}_n + \boldsymbol{\Upsilon}\right)\left(\boldsymbol{\gamma} - \boldsymbol{\alpha}\boldsymbol{\mu}\right); \tag{3.44}$$

After some simplification, using:

$$\begin{aligned}\left(\boldsymbol{\Upsilon}^*\right)^2 - \boldsymbol{\Upsilon}^2 &= \left[\left(\mathbf{I}_n + \boldsymbol{\Upsilon}^*\right)\boldsymbol{\alpha}^* - \left(\mathbf{I}_n + \boldsymbol{\Upsilon}\right)\boldsymbol{\alpha}\right]\boldsymbol{\beta}' \\ &= \left[\boldsymbol{\alpha}^*\left(\mathbf{I}_r + \boldsymbol{\Lambda}^*\right) - \boldsymbol{\alpha}\left(\mathbf{I}_r + \boldsymbol{\Lambda}\right)\right]\boldsymbol{\beta}' \end{aligned} \tag{3.45}$$

as $\boldsymbol{\Upsilon}\boldsymbol{\gamma} = \boldsymbol{\gamma}$ and $\boldsymbol{\Upsilon}^*\boldsymbol{\gamma}^* = \boldsymbol{\gamma}^*$, the corresponding 2-step ahead forecast error $\widehat{\mathbf{e}}_{T+2|T} = \mathbf{x}_{T+2} - \widehat{\mathbf{x}}_{T+2|T}$ is:

$$\begin{aligned}&\left(\left(\boldsymbol{\Upsilon}^*\right)^2 - \boldsymbol{\Upsilon}^2\right)\mathbf{x}_T + 2\left(\boldsymbol{\gamma}^* - \boldsymbol{\gamma}\right) - \left(\mathbf{I}_n + \boldsymbol{\Upsilon}^*\right)\boldsymbol{\alpha}^*\boldsymbol{\mu}^* \\ &\qquad - \left(\mathbf{I}_n + \boldsymbol{\Upsilon}\right)\boldsymbol{\alpha}\boldsymbol{\mu} + \boldsymbol{\Upsilon}^*\boldsymbol{\nu}_{T+1} + \boldsymbol{\nu}_{T+2} \\ &= \left[\boldsymbol{\alpha}^*\left(\mathbf{I}_r + \boldsymbol{\Lambda}^*\right) - \boldsymbol{\alpha}\left(\mathbf{I}_r + \boldsymbol{\Lambda}\right)\right]\boldsymbol{\kappa}_T \qquad (3.46) \\ &\qquad + \mathsf{E}\left[\widehat{\mathbf{e}}_{T+2|T}\right] + \boldsymbol{\Upsilon}^*\boldsymbol{\nu}_{T+1} + \boldsymbol{\nu}_{T+2} \qquad (3.47)\end{aligned}$$

where $\mathsf{E}\left[\boldsymbol{\kappa}_T\right] = \mathbf{0}$, and unconditionally:

$$\mathsf{E}\left[\widehat{\mathbf{e}}_{T+2|T}\right] = 2\left(\boldsymbol{\gamma}^* - \boldsymbol{\gamma}\right) - \boldsymbol{\alpha}^*\left(\mathbf{I}_r + \boldsymbol{\Lambda}^*\right)\left(\boldsymbol{\mu}^* - \boldsymbol{\mu}\right).$$

3.11.4 From $T+1$ to $T+3$

The two-step derivations closely match those from T to $T+2$, shifted forward one period:

$$\mathbf{x}_{T+3} = (\boldsymbol{\Upsilon}^*)^2 \mathbf{x}_{T+1} + (\mathbf{I}_n + \boldsymbol{\Upsilon}^*)(\boldsymbol{\gamma}^* - \boldsymbol{\alpha}^*\boldsymbol{\mu}^*) + \boldsymbol{\Upsilon}^*\boldsymbol{\nu}_{T+2} + \boldsymbol{\nu}_{T+3} \quad (3.48)$$

so that:

$$\begin{aligned} \boldsymbol{\beta}'\mathbf{x}_{T+3} &= (\mathbf{I}_r + 2\boldsymbol{\beta}'\boldsymbol{\alpha}^* + \boldsymbol{\beta}'\boldsymbol{\alpha}^*\boldsymbol{\beta}'\boldsymbol{\alpha}^*)\boldsymbol{\beta}'\mathbf{x}_{T+1} && (3.49)\\ &\quad + \boldsymbol{\beta}'(\mathbf{I}_n + \boldsymbol{\Upsilon}^*)(\boldsymbol{\gamma}^* - \boldsymbol{\alpha}^*\boldsymbol{\mu}^*) && (3.50) \end{aligned}$$

with:

$$\begin{aligned} \boldsymbol{\beta}'\mathbf{x}_{T+2} &= (\mathbf{I}_r + 2\boldsymbol{\beta}'\boldsymbol{\alpha}^* + \boldsymbol{\beta}'\boldsymbol{\alpha}^*\boldsymbol{\beta}'\boldsymbol{\alpha}^*)\boldsymbol{\beta}'\mathbf{x}_{T} && (3.51)\\ &\quad + \boldsymbol{\beta}'(\mathbf{I}_n + \boldsymbol{\Upsilon}^*)(\boldsymbol{\gamma}^* - \boldsymbol{\alpha}^*\boldsymbol{\mu}^*). && (3.52) \end{aligned}$$

Here:

$$\widehat{\mathbf{x}}_{T+3} = \boldsymbol{\Upsilon}^2\mathbf{x}_{T+1} + (\mathbf{I}_n + \boldsymbol{\Upsilon})(\boldsymbol{\gamma} - \boldsymbol{\alpha}\boldsymbol{\mu}) \quad (3.53)$$

so using (3.45), $\widehat{\mathbf{e}}_{T+3|T+1}$ is:

$$\begin{aligned} & \left[(\boldsymbol{\Upsilon}^*)^2 - \boldsymbol{\Upsilon}^2\right]\mathbf{x}_{T+1} + (\mathbf{I}_n + \boldsymbol{\Upsilon}^*)(\boldsymbol{\gamma}^* - \boldsymbol{\alpha}^*\boldsymbol{\mu}^*) \\ & \qquad - (\mathbf{I}_n + \boldsymbol{\Upsilon})(\boldsymbol{\gamma} - \boldsymbol{\alpha}\boldsymbol{\mu}) + \boldsymbol{\Upsilon}^*\boldsymbol{\nu}_{T+2} + \boldsymbol{\nu}_{T+3} \\ &= [\boldsymbol{\alpha}^*(\mathbf{I}_r + \boldsymbol{\Lambda}^*) - \boldsymbol{\alpha}(\mathbf{I}_r + \boldsymbol{\Lambda})]\boldsymbol{\beta}'\mathbf{x}_{T+1} + 2(\boldsymbol{\gamma}^* - \boldsymbol{\gamma}) \\ & \qquad - \boldsymbol{\alpha}^*(\mathbf{I}_r + \boldsymbol{\Lambda}^*)\boldsymbol{\mu}^* + \boldsymbol{\alpha}(\mathbf{I}_r + \boldsymbol{\Lambda})\boldsymbol{\mu} + \boldsymbol{\Upsilon}^*\boldsymbol{\nu}_{T+2} + \boldsymbol{\nu}_{T+3} \\ &= 2(\boldsymbol{\gamma}^* - \boldsymbol{\gamma}) - \boldsymbol{\alpha}(\mathbf{I}_r + \boldsymbol{\Lambda})(\boldsymbol{\mu}^* - \boldsymbol{\mu}) + \\ & \qquad [\boldsymbol{\alpha}^*(\mathbf{I}_r + \boldsymbol{\Lambda}^*) - \boldsymbol{\alpha}(\mathbf{I}_r + \boldsymbol{\Lambda})]\boldsymbol{\kappa}^*_{T+1} + \boldsymbol{\Upsilon}^*\boldsymbol{\nu}_{T+2} + \boldsymbol{\nu}_{T+3} \\ &= \mathsf{E}\left[\widehat{\mathbf{e}}_{T+3|T+1}\right] + [\boldsymbol{\alpha}^*(\mathbf{I}_r + \boldsymbol{\Lambda}^*) - \boldsymbol{\alpha}(\mathbf{I}_r + \boldsymbol{\Lambda})] \\ & \qquad \times \left(\boldsymbol{\kappa}^*_{T+1} - \mathsf{E}\left[\boldsymbol{\kappa}^*_{T+1}\right]\right) + \boldsymbol{\Upsilon}^*\boldsymbol{\nu}_{T+2} + \boldsymbol{\nu}_{T+3}, \end{aligned}$$

as:

$$\mathsf{E}\left[\boldsymbol{\kappa}^*_{T+1}\right] = -\boldsymbol{\Lambda}^*(\boldsymbol{\mu}^* - \boldsymbol{\mu}),$$

where:

$$\begin{aligned} \mathsf{E}\left[\widehat{\mathbf{e}}_{T+3|T+1}\right] &= 2(\boldsymbol{\gamma}^* - \boldsymbol{\gamma}) \\ &\quad - \left[\boldsymbol{\alpha}^*(\mathbf{I}_r + \boldsymbol{\Lambda}^*)\boldsymbol{\Lambda}^* - \boldsymbol{\alpha}(\mathbf{I}_r + \boldsymbol{\Lambda})\boldsymbol{\beta}'\boldsymbol{\alpha}^*\right](\boldsymbol{\mu}^* - \boldsymbol{\mu}). \end{aligned}$$

3.12 Appendix C: Unconditional Forecast-error Variances

3.12.1 *Variances of levels from T to $T+1$*

When the parameters are known, a setting that favors the VEqCM relative to models we consider in chapter 5, the 1-step forecast errors can be written as:

$$\widehat{\mathbf{e}}_{T+1|T} - \mathsf{E}\left[\widehat{\mathbf{e}}_{T+1|T}\right] = \left(\boldsymbol{\alpha}^* - \boldsymbol{\alpha}\right)\left(\boldsymbol{\beta}'\mathbf{x}_T - \boldsymbol{\mu}\right) + \boldsymbol{\nu}_{T+1}. \tag{3.54}$$

Given the earlier analyses, and to help interpret the empirical forecast-error variances used later, we record the unconditional variance:

$$\mathsf{V}\left[\widehat{\mathbf{e}}_{T+1|T}\right] = \boldsymbol{\Omega}_{\nu} + \left(\boldsymbol{\alpha}^* - \boldsymbol{\alpha}\right)\mathbf{V}\left(\boldsymbol{\alpha}^* - \boldsymbol{\alpha}\right)'. \tag{3.55}$$

In the special case that $\boldsymbol{\alpha}^* = \boldsymbol{\alpha}$:

$$\mathsf{V}\left[\widehat{\mathbf{e}}_{T+1|T}\right] = \boldsymbol{\Omega}_{\nu},$$

though in practice, parameter estimation uncertainty will augment $\boldsymbol{\Omega}_{\nu}$.

3.12.2 *Variances of levels from $T+1$ to $T+2$*

At time $T+1$, the DGP produces (3.20) and since:

$$\boldsymbol{\beta}'\mathbf{x}_{T+1} - \boldsymbol{\mu}^* + \boldsymbol{\Lambda}^*\left(\boldsymbol{\mu}^* - \boldsymbol{\mu}\right) = \boldsymbol{\Lambda}^*\left(\boldsymbol{\beta}'\mathbf{x}_T - \boldsymbol{\mu}\right) + \boldsymbol{\beta}'\boldsymbol{\nu}_{T+1}, \tag{3.56}$$

then:

$$\mathsf{V}\left[\boldsymbol{\beta}'\mathbf{x}_{T+1}\right] = \boldsymbol{\Lambda}^*\mathbf{V}\boldsymbol{\Lambda}^{*\prime} + \boldsymbol{\beta}'\boldsymbol{\Omega}_{\nu}\boldsymbol{\beta} = \mathbf{V}^*,$$

and:

$$\mathsf{V}\left[\Delta\mathbf{x}_{T+1}\right] = \boldsymbol{\alpha}^*\mathbf{V}\boldsymbol{\alpha}^{*\prime} + \boldsymbol{\Omega}_{\nu},$$

with:

$$\mathsf{V}\left[\Delta\mathbf{x}_{T+2}\right] = \boldsymbol{\alpha}^*\mathsf{V}\left[\boldsymbol{\beta}'\mathbf{x}_{T+1}\right]\boldsymbol{\alpha}^{*\prime} + \boldsymbol{\Omega}_{\nu} = \boldsymbol{\alpha}^*\mathbf{V}^*\boldsymbol{\alpha}^{*\prime} + \boldsymbol{\Omega}_{\nu}.$$

Consequently:

$$\widehat{\mathbf{e}}_{T+2|T+1} - \mathsf{E}\left[\widehat{\mathbf{e}}_{T+2|T+1}\right] = \left(\boldsymbol{\alpha}^* - \boldsymbol{\alpha}\right)\left(\boldsymbol{\beta}'\mathbf{x}_{T+1} - \mathsf{E}\left[\boldsymbol{\beta}'\mathbf{x}_{T+1}\right]\right) + \boldsymbol{\nu}_{T+2},$$

so:

$$\mathsf{V}\left[\widehat{\mathbf{e}}_{T+2|T+1}\right] = \left(\boldsymbol{\alpha}^* - \boldsymbol{\alpha}\right)\mathbf{V}^*\left(\boldsymbol{\alpha}^* - \boldsymbol{\alpha}\right)' + \boldsymbol{\Omega}_{\nu}. \tag{3.57}$$

This is larger than (3.55) if there is any change in the feedback coefficient matrix, $\boldsymbol{\alpha}$, but otherwise is the same, confirming that changes in dynamics mainly induce variance effects.

3.12.3 *Variances of levels from T to $T+2$*

This comprises 2-steps ahead forecasts made prior to the break, to illustrate how the results change for multi-step forecasts. From before:

$$\widehat{\mathbf{e}}_{T+2|T} - \mathsf{E}\left[\widehat{\mathbf{e}}_{T+2|T}\right] = \left(\boldsymbol{\alpha}^*\left(\mathbf{I}_r + \boldsymbol{\Lambda}^*\right) - \boldsymbol{\alpha}\left(\mathbf{I}_r + \boldsymbol{\Lambda}\right)\right) \tag{3.58}$$

$$\times\left(\boldsymbol{\beta}'\mathbf{x}_T - \boldsymbol{\mu}\right) + \boldsymbol{\Upsilon}^*\boldsymbol{\nu}_{T+1} + \boldsymbol{\nu}_{T+2} \tag{3.59}$$

so, letting $\left(\boldsymbol{\alpha}^*\left(\mathbf{I}_r + \boldsymbol{\Lambda}^*\right) - \boldsymbol{\alpha}\left(\mathbf{I}_r + \boldsymbol{\Lambda}\right)\right) = \mathbf{D}^*$:

$$\mathsf{V}\left[\widehat{\mathbf{e}}_{T+2|T}\right] = \mathbf{D}^*\mathbf{V}\mathbf{D}^{*\prime} + \boldsymbol{\Upsilon}^*\boldsymbol{\Omega}_\nu\boldsymbol{\Upsilon}^{*\prime} + \boldsymbol{\Omega}_\nu. \tag{3.60}$$

When $\boldsymbol{\alpha}$ is constant, $\mathbf{D} = \mathbf{0}$ so:

$$\mathsf{V}\left[\widehat{\mathbf{e}}_{T+2|T}\right] = \boldsymbol{\Omega}_\nu + \boldsymbol{\Upsilon}\boldsymbol{\Omega}_\nu\boldsymbol{\Upsilon}',$$

which is the usual result, and if $\boldsymbol{\alpha} = \mathbf{0}$:

$$\mathsf{V}\left[\widehat{\mathbf{e}}_{T+2|T}\right] = 2\boldsymbol{\Omega}_\nu \tag{3.61}$$

revealing that a doubling in error variance results as the horizon grows.

3.12.4 *Variances of levels from $T+1$ to $T+3$*

Now:

$$\widehat{\mathbf{x}}_{T+3} = \boldsymbol{\Upsilon}^2\mathbf{x}_{T+1} + \left(\mathbf{I}_n + \boldsymbol{\Upsilon}\right)\left(\boldsymbol{\gamma} - \boldsymbol{\alpha}\boldsymbol{\mu}\right), \tag{3.62}$$

so $\left(\widehat{\mathbf{e}}_{T+3|T+1} - \mathsf{E}\left[\widehat{\mathbf{e}}_{T+3|T+1}\right]\right)$ equals:

$$\left[\boldsymbol{\alpha}^*\left(\mathbf{I}_r + \boldsymbol{\Lambda}^*\right) - \boldsymbol{\alpha}\left(\mathbf{I}_r + \boldsymbol{\Lambda}\right)\right]\left(\boldsymbol{\kappa}^*_{T+1} - \mathsf{E}\left[\boldsymbol{\kappa}^*_{T+1}\right]\right) + \boldsymbol{\Upsilon}^*\boldsymbol{\nu}_{T+2} + \boldsymbol{\nu}_{T+3},$$

(compare (3.58)) so that:

$$\mathsf{V}\left[\widehat{\mathbf{e}}_{T+3|T+1}\right] = \mathbf{D}^*\mathbf{V}^*\mathbf{D}^{*\prime} + \boldsymbol{\Upsilon}^*\boldsymbol{\Omega}_\nu\boldsymbol{\Upsilon}^{*\prime} + \boldsymbol{\Omega}_\nu.$$

Apart from the changed variance of $\boldsymbol{\kappa}^*_{T+1}$ over $\boldsymbol{\kappa}_T$, the formula has the same structure as (3.60) above, so new features appear for $T+1$ to $T+3$ (forecasting after the break) than we found for T to $T+1$.

4 Other Sources

Summary

We now analyze the remaining sources of mis-prediction formalized in the taxonomy developed in §2.2. The potential causes other than unmodeled shifts in parameters, are model mis-specification; parameter estimation uncertainty, possibly induced by collinearity, a lack of parsimony and model selection; and forecast origin mis-measurement. In this chapter we establish their likely effects, and investigate these via Monte Carlo simulation and empirical examples. The analysis suggests that mis-specification of stochastic elements of models, collinearity, and lack of parsimony *per se* are not the primary cause of forecast failure, although they may exacerbate problems of deterministic shifts.

4.1 Introduction

Our focus remains on explaining forecast failure in multivariate equilibrium-correction models (see §1.5). We first consider the role of model mis-specification in forecast failure (§4.2), investigate estimation uncertainty in §4.3, particularly the two potential problems of collinearity (§4.3.3), and a lack of parsimony (§4.3.5). As these problems were analyzed in detail in Clements and Hendry (1998b), they are treated more briefly here, with an emphasis on empirical and simulation results. They are shown not to account for systematic mis-forecasting *per se*; however, in conjunction with breaks in regressors, serious forecast errors may result. We explain how these interaction effects can be differentiated *post hoc* from the mean-shift problem. The results suggest that to get "forecast failure out, needs changed conditions in": that is, if the economic system was a stationary stochastic process after suitable differencing and cointegration, we would not observe much forecast failure. We also address the issue of "overfitting", which may induce forecast error deterioration. In §4.4, we briefly discuss the efficacy of multi-step estimation when models are mis-specified. We suggest that model mis-specification and estimation uncertainty do not in general interact adversely as far as forecast accuracy is concerned, in that OLS is often little worse than methods aimed at optimizing the model parameters for forecasting at particular horizons. Finally, forecast origin mis-measurement is discussed in §4.5. Section 4.6 concludes.

4.2 Model Mis-specification

In the absence of parameter non-constancies, model mis-specification always reduces forecast accuracy and may affect forecast failure, but in some surprising ways. The forecast-error taxonomy reveals non-negligible effects from both stochastic and deterministic mis-specification, so we first consider both forms of inadvertent mis-specification in stationary processes, then extend the analysis to non-stationary time series. Because shifts in the equilibrium means of models proved the most pernicious influence on forecast failure, we distinguish between mis-specifications of stochastic components that do not affect the estimation of the equilibrium mean (i.e., mean-zero variables and error terms), and of deterministic components which will. Next, the impact of structural breaks in mis-specified "causal" models is examined. In chapter 5 we will consider deliberate mis-specifications adopted to robustify forecasts against structural breaks. We also recall that chapter 2 established that the converse can occur, namely mis-specified models can out forecast models that were congruent in sample when deterministic shifts occur.

4.2.1 Mis-specification of stochastic components

In a stationary world, least-squares estimated models are consistent for their associated conditional expectations (when second moments exist), so forecasts on average attain their expected accuracy unconditionally (see, e.g., Miller, 1978, and Hendry, 1979a). Reconsider the I(0) VAR in (4.1), where before the break:

$$\mathbf{y}_t - \boldsymbol{\varphi} = \boldsymbol{\Pi}\left(\mathbf{y}_{t-1} - \boldsymbol{\varphi}\right) + \boldsymbol{\epsilon}_t \text{ with } \boldsymbol{\epsilon}_t \sim \mathsf{IN}_n\left[\mathbf{0}, \boldsymbol{\Omega}_\epsilon\right]. \tag{4.1}$$

Providing $\{\mathbf{y}_t\}$ is, and remains, stationary, then (4.1) is isomorphic to the mean-zero representation:

$$\mathbf{w}_t = \boldsymbol{\psi} + \boldsymbol{\Pi}\mathbf{w}_{t-1} + \boldsymbol{\epsilon}_t, \tag{4.2}$$

where $\mathbf{w}_t = \mathbf{y}_t - \boldsymbol{\varphi}$, and $\boldsymbol{\psi} = \mathbf{0}$. Omitting any set of $\{w_{j,t-1}\}$ in any equations will not bias the equilibrium mean, and although the fit will be inferior to the correctly-specified representation, the resulting model will on average forecast according to its in-sample operating characteristics. Whether the forecasts of a mis-specified model are better than, or inferior to, those from the estimated DGP (4.2) depends on the measures of forecast accuracy used, the precision with which parameters are estimated (since invalid zero restrictions on tiny coefficients can improve some measures of forecast accuracy: see Clements and Hendry, 1998b, ch.12), and on the horizon (see Clements and Hendry, 1998b, ch.11).

The same logic holds for the initial formulation in (4.1), despite the equilibrium mean being unknown. The unconditional moments of $\{\mathbf{y}_t\}$ are given by:

$$\begin{aligned}
\mathsf{E}\left[\mathbf{y}_t\right] &= \boldsymbol{\varphi} = \left(\mathbf{I}_n - \boldsymbol{\Pi}\right)^{-1}\boldsymbol{\phi} \\
\mathsf{E}\left[\left(\mathbf{y}_t - \boldsymbol{\varphi}\right)\left(\mathbf{y}_t - \boldsymbol{\varphi}\right)'\right] &= \mathbf{M} = \boldsymbol{\Omega}_\epsilon + \boldsymbol{\Pi}\mathbf{M}\boldsymbol{\Pi}' \\
\mathsf{E}\left[\left(\mathbf{y}_t - \boldsymbol{\varphi}\right)\left(\mathbf{y}_{t-1} - \boldsymbol{\varphi}\right)'\right] &= \boldsymbol{\Pi}\mathbf{M}.
\end{aligned} \tag{4.3}$$

To examine model mis-specification in more detail, let the DGP comprise two blocks:

$$\begin{pmatrix} \mathbf{y}_{1,t} \\ \mathbf{y}_{2,t} \end{pmatrix} = \begin{pmatrix} \boldsymbol{\phi}_1 \\ \boldsymbol{\phi}_2 \end{pmatrix} + \begin{pmatrix} \boldsymbol{\Pi}_{11} & \boldsymbol{\Pi}_{12} \\ \mathbf{0} & \boldsymbol{\Pi}_{22} \end{pmatrix} \begin{pmatrix} \mathbf{y}_{1,t-1} \\ \mathbf{y}_{2,t-1} \end{pmatrix} + \begin{pmatrix} \boldsymbol{\epsilon}_{1,t} \\ \boldsymbol{\epsilon}_{2,t} \end{pmatrix}. \tag{4.4}$$

Only the first block is modeled, with the model of $\mathbf{y}_{1,t}$ mis-specified by omitting $\mathbf{y}_{2,t-1}$. Setting $\boldsymbol{\Pi}_{21} = \mathbf{0}$ is to simplify the algebra, and is inconsequential for the 1-step analysis below. However, it could be a crucial restriction in other settings, such as conditional multi-step forecasts. Thus, from (4.4), the model in use is obtained by reduction as:

$$\begin{aligned}\mathbf{y}_{1,t} &= \boldsymbol{\phi}_1 + \boldsymbol{\Pi}_{11}\mathbf{y}_{1,t-1} + \boldsymbol{\Pi}_{12}\mathbf{y}_{2,t-1} + \boldsymbol{\epsilon}_{1,t} \\ &= (\boldsymbol{\phi}_1 + \boldsymbol{\Pi}_{12}\boldsymbol{\rho}) + (\boldsymbol{\Pi}_{11} + \boldsymbol{\Pi}_{12}\boldsymbol{\Psi}_{11})\,\mathbf{y}_{1,t-1} + (\boldsymbol{\Pi}_{12}\mathbf{u}_{2,t-1} + \boldsymbol{\epsilon}_{1,t}) \\ &= \boldsymbol{\delta}_1 + \boldsymbol{\Gamma}_{11}\mathbf{y}_{1,t-1} + \mathbf{v}_{1,t}, \end{aligned} \tag{4.5}$$

and letting $\boldsymbol{\Psi}_{11} = \mathbf{M}_{21}\mathbf{M}_{11}^{-1}$:

$$\mathbf{y}_{2,t} = \boldsymbol{\rho} + \boldsymbol{\Psi}_{11}\mathbf{y}_{1,t} + \mathbf{u}_{2,t}, \tag{4.6}$$

on enforcing $\mathsf{E}[\mathbf{y}_{1,t}\mathbf{u}_{2,t}'] = \mathbf{0}$, so that:

$$\boldsymbol{\rho} = \mathsf{E}\left[\mathbf{y}_{2,t} - \boldsymbol{\Psi}_{11}\mathbf{y}_{1,t}\right] = \boldsymbol{\varphi}_2 - \boldsymbol{\Psi}_{11}\boldsymbol{\varphi}_1 = (-\boldsymbol{\Psi}_{11} : \mathbf{I}_{n_2})\,(\mathbf{I}_n - \boldsymbol{\Pi})^{-1}\,\boldsymbol{\phi}. \tag{4.7}$$

Despite the mis-specification, the model given by the last row of (4.5) is well defined, and its error variance in any forecast period will on average match that in-sample. Importantly, the entailed equilibrium mean from:

$$\mathbf{y}_{1,t} = \boldsymbol{\delta}_1 + \boldsymbol{\Gamma}_{11}\mathbf{y}_{1,t-1} + \mathbf{v}_{1,t}, \tag{4.8}$$

remains $\boldsymbol{\varphi}_1$. From (4.5) and the middle expression in (4.7):

$$\boldsymbol{\delta}_1 = \boldsymbol{\phi}_1 + \boldsymbol{\Pi}_{12}\boldsymbol{\rho} = \boldsymbol{\phi}_1 - \boldsymbol{\Pi}_{12}\boldsymbol{\Psi}_{11}\boldsymbol{\varphi}_1 + \boldsymbol{\Pi}_{12}\boldsymbol{\varphi}_2.$$

From the first line of (4.3), $\boldsymbol{\phi}$ is given by:

$$\begin{pmatrix} \mathbf{I}_{n_1} - \boldsymbol{\Pi}_{11} & -\boldsymbol{\Pi}_{12} \\ \mathbf{0} & \mathbf{I}_{n_2} - \boldsymbol{\Pi}_{22} \end{pmatrix} \begin{pmatrix} \boldsymbol{\varphi}_1 \\ \boldsymbol{\varphi}_2 \end{pmatrix} = \begin{pmatrix} (\mathbf{I}_{n_1} - \boldsymbol{\Pi}_{11})\,\boldsymbol{\varphi}_1 - \boldsymbol{\Pi}_{12}\boldsymbol{\varphi}_2 \\ (\mathbf{I}_{n_2} - \boldsymbol{\Pi}_{22})\,\boldsymbol{\varphi}_2 \end{pmatrix},$$

and hence:

$$\begin{aligned}\boldsymbol{\delta}_1 &= (\mathbf{I}_{n_1} - \boldsymbol{\Pi}_{11})\,\boldsymbol{\varphi}_1 - \boldsymbol{\Pi}_{12}\boldsymbol{\varphi}_2 - \boldsymbol{\Pi}_{12}\boldsymbol{\Psi}_{11}\boldsymbol{\varphi}_1 + \boldsymbol{\Pi}_{12}\boldsymbol{\varphi}_2 \\ &= (\mathbf{I}_{n_1} - \boldsymbol{\Pi}_{11} - \boldsymbol{\Pi}_{12}\boldsymbol{\Psi}_{11})\,\boldsymbol{\varphi}_1 \\ &= (\mathbf{I}_{n_1} - \boldsymbol{\Gamma}_{11})\,\boldsymbol{\varphi}_1. \end{aligned} \tag{4.9}$$

Substituting (4.9) into (4.8):

$$\mathbf{y}_{1,t} - \boldsymbol{\varphi}_1 = \boldsymbol{\Gamma}_{11}\left(\mathbf{y}_{1,t-1} - \boldsymbol{\varphi}_1\right) + \mathbf{v}_{1,t},$$

as required: the mean-zero case implications still hold.

Thus, model mis-specification *per se* cannot account for forecast failure, because the model's out-of-sample forecast performance will be consistent with what would have been expected based on how well the model fits the historical data. However, an exception arises to the extent that inconsistent standard errors are used to judge forecast accuracy, as we now discuss.

Corsi, Pollock and Prakken (1982) find that residual autocorrelation, perhaps induced by other mis-specifications, leads to excess rejection on parameter-constancy tests. For example, untreated positive residual autocorrelation can downward bias estimated standard errors which thereby induces excess rejections on constancy tests. In practice, an investigator is likely to add extra lags of $\mathbf{y}_1$ to remove this residual autocorrelation. Although congruent models remain false in general, by having innovation residuals they are not prone to this problem.

4.2.2 *Deterministic mis-specification*

In a stationary context, the only possible deterministic mis-specification is having an incorrect long-run mean, which can lead to systematic forecast errors. This problem was discussed in chapter 2 for the unconditional forecast-error biases arising from table 2.1, namely the term $(\varphi - \varphi_p)$ in (2.9). Otherwise, if unrestricted intercepts are included in every equation, that possibility cannot occur on average, so we doubt the prevalence of such a source.

However, if the data being modeled are non-stationary, then systematic forecast errors and forecast failure are both possible. For example, if the equilibrium mean has changed earlier in the estimation sample, the intercept estimated on the whole sample will be a weighted average of the shifting means, and hence will be inconsistent – except by a fluke of cancellation – for the forecast-horizon value. Another possibility is omitting a deterministic trend, where the DGP is, say:

$$y_t = \gamma_0 + \gamma_1 t + u_t \tag{4.10}$$

when the forecasting model is:

$$\widehat{y}_{T+h} = \widehat{\rho}_0. \tag{4.11}$$

The moments in (4.10) change over time, and in particular, the unconditional mean is:

$$\mathsf{E}\left[y_t\right] = \gamma_0 + \gamma_1 t,$$

whereas (4.11) forecasts an unchanged mean, and hence experiences continuous changes in its "equilibrium mean". Whilst the in-sample OLS errors of the model will sum to zero by construction, they will be positively autocorrelated. This will become manifest in the forecast errors:

$$e_{T+h} = y_{T+h} - \widehat{y}_{T+h} = \gamma_0 - \widehat{\rho}_0 + \gamma_1 t + u_{T+h}$$

which have a trending mean, inducing serious forecast failure.[1] In both these cases, rigorous in-sample testing for congruency might reveal the latent problem and hence avoid forecast failure. Nevertheless, the key problem again appears to be correct specification of the deterministic components.

4.2.3 *Mis-specification in non-stationary processes*

Non-stationarity can take a wide variety of forms, and this section focuses on the presence of unit roots in the DGP, whereas the next analyses structural breaks. By reinterpreting the $\mathbf{y}_t$ in §4.2.1 in terms of reductions to stationarity of I(1) variables, we believe the results of that section – that model mis-specification *per se* cannot account for forecast failure – extends to congruent models of systems that are stationary after suitable cointegration and differencing. Thus we look elsewhere for the main causes of forecast failure. However, deterministic mis-specifications can become more serious, since the intercepts in part represent drift, and hence the effects noted in §4.2.2 may apply. Further, if the model is specified in levels, then because I(1) variables rarely have sample averages near zero, stochastic mis-specification may also involve deterministic mis-specification: omitting an I(1) variable may lose cointegration, and hence the associated equilibrium mean. As chapter 5 shows, however, in a world of deterministic shifts , such an unintended consequence may often be beneficial.

4.2.4 *Breaks in mis-specified "causal" models*

The case that we consider to be of greatest practical relevance is the interaction between model mis-specification and structural breaks. Let

[1] We are grateful to Søren Johansen for suggesting this example.

the $n_2 \times 1$ intercept ϕ_2 of the second block in (4.4) change at T_1 to ϕ_2^*, so that after T_1:

$$\mathsf{E}\left[\mathbf{y}_t \mid T > T_1\right] = \left(\mathbf{I}_n - \mathbf{\Pi}\right)^{-1} \phi^* = \varphi^*,$$

the second moments around φ^* remaining constant. Letting $\rho^* = (-\mathbf{\Psi}_{11} : \mathbf{I}_{n_2})(\mathbf{I}_n - \mathbf{\Pi})^{-1}\phi$, the analogous equation to (4.6) becomes:

$$\mathbf{y}_{2,t} = \rho^* + \mathbf{\Psi}_{11}\mathbf{y}_{1,t} + \mathbf{u}_{2,t}.$$

Thus, after T_1, as in (4.5):

$$\mathbf{y}_{1,t} = \delta_1^* + \mathbf{\Gamma}_{11}\mathbf{y}_{1,t-1} + \mathbf{v}_{1,t}. \tag{4.12}$$

Now rejection should match that in §3.3.1; and when the sample spans the break, severe residual autocorrelation will ensue, analogous to the creation of apparent unit roots (see e.g., Hendry and Neale, 1991). Thus, the under-specified $\mathbf{y}_{1,t}$ equation will mis-forecast, although the correctly-specified version would not. Consequently, if there is a source of forecast failure in the system (here, the change in ϕ_2), mis-specified equations will suffer indirect failure, even when correctly-specified ones would not. This is an example of our general maxim "forecast failure out needs changed conditions in". Of course, if the entire system was used to generate multi-step forecasts, but the change in ϕ_2 was not known, it would manifest direct failure.

4.2.5 *Monte Carlo evidence in an* I*(0) process*

A Monte Carlo study of the impact of model mis-specification and its interaction with deterministic shifts corroborates the analytical results. We used the bivariate DGP:

$$\begin{aligned} y_{1,t} &= 3 + 0.85y_{1,t-1} - 0.50y_{2,t-1} + \epsilon_{1,t} \\ y_{2,t} &= \alpha_2 + 0.80y_{2,t-1} + \epsilon_{2,t}. \end{aligned} \tag{4.13}$$

There were five experiments, all with $\epsilon_{i,t} \sim \mathsf{IN}[0, \sigma_{ii}]$, using $\sigma_{11} = 0.25$, $\sigma_{22} = 0.36$. In the first three, α_2 was changed from 5 to 4 at $T = 100$, reverting at $T = 150$; in the last two, α_2 remained constant. In the first experiment, the correctly-specified equation for $y_{1,t}$ was estimated, with α_2 changed. In the other four, $y_{2,t-1}$ was omitted causing the model to be mis-specified, and a scalar autoregression in $y_{1,t}$ (denoted AR(·)) was

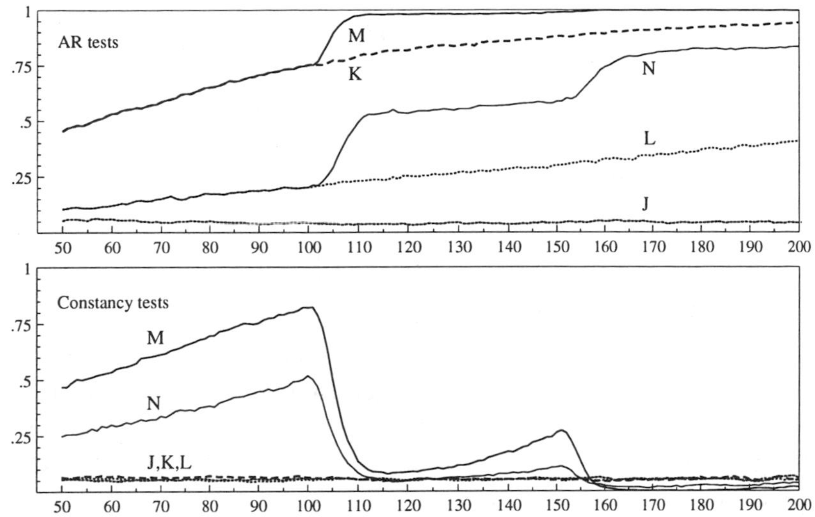

Figure 4.1
Autocorrelation and constancy test rejection frequencies when an omitted variable is subject to a mean shift.

estimated; in the first two, α_2 remained unchanged, but was changed in the last two. The experiments are labelled as:

(J) first equation of (4.13), α_2 changed;
(K) AR(1) in $y_{1,t}$, α_2 constant;
(L) AR(2) in $y_{1,t}$, α_2 constant;
(M) AR(1) in $y_{1,t}$, α_2 changed;
(N) AR(2) in $y_{1,t}$, α_2 changed.

Figure 4.1 shows the resulting rejection frequencies of the Chow constancy test and a residual autocorrelation test.[2] The autocorrelation is marked for the first-order model, but greatly attenuated for the second-order model, when there is no break. In both these cases, the Chow test rejects somewhat more than its nominal size of 5%. However, in the cases with a break, the constancy rejections are high for both lag specifications. Thus, an entailed mean shift is the culprit

[2]The autocorrelation test is the F-version of the Lagrange multiplier test of Breusch (1978) and Godfrey (1978), testing for first-order autocorrelation , following Kiviet (1986).

once more. Adding further lags of y_1 eliminates the remaining residual autocorrelation (little more than 5% rejection with 5 lags), thereby reducing the power of this constancy test to about 30% at the break point.

4.3 Estimation Uncertainty

The forecast-error taxonomy (table 2.1) also revealed that parameter estimation uncertainty enters both through intercepts and slopes, and could potentially be an important source of forecast error. However, it seems unlikely to be a source of forecast failure by itself, since the in-sample and out-of-sample fits will be similar in the absence of any changes in the underlying DGP. We seek to establish that result in a range of cases, particularly when estimation uncertainty derives from collinearity between explanatory variables, and from a lack of parsimony, and illustrate the analyses both empirically and via Monte Carlo simulations. We also address the issue of "overfitting", which may be thought to induce forecast error deterioration: see, e.g., Todd (1990). In §4.3.8, we conjecture why estimation uncertainty may be perceived to be more important than it actually is.

First, we illustrate by an empirical example the impact on computed prediction intervals of adding parameter variances to the variances arising from the innovation errors. The 4-dimensional system is a variant of that studied in detail in chapter 8, modeling nominal M1 (M), total final expenditure (I), its implicit deflator (P), and the opportunity cost of holding money (R_n): lower case denotes logs, and $\Delta = (1 - L)$ is the first difference, when L is the lag operator. We consider multi-step forecasts over 1985(3)–1986(2) from an estimation sample of 1978(3)–1985(2) (both periods deliberately shortened to allow some discrimination), for $(m - p,\ \Delta p,\ i,\ R_n)$ using the VAR and VEqCM developed in Hendry and Doornik (1994). Figures 4.2 and 4.3 show the resulting forecasts with the bars based on the innovation errors only, and bands showing the overall 95% prediction intervals once parameter estimation variances are included. There are distinct differences between the bands and bars for the VAR (which has 12 parameters in every equation for $T = 28$), but virtually none in the VEqCM, which was obtained as a valid reduction of the VAR. Extending the estimation sample back to 1964(3) noticeably reduces the bands for the VAR.

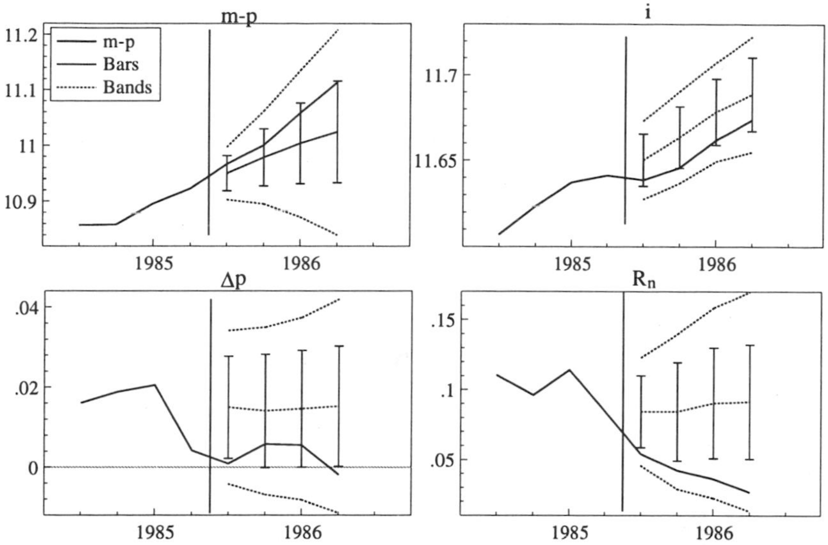

Figure 4.2
Forecasts and 95% prediction bars and bands for the monetary VAR.

4.3.1 Scalar autoregressive processes

To demonstrate the impact of estimation uncertainty on forecast uncertainty, we begin by considering simple scalar models for stationary, I(1), and trend-stationary processes. This allows us to contrast settings where parameters are known and where they have to be estimated, for a correctly specified model.

4.3.1.1 I(0) processes

Consider the AR(1) process:

$$y_t = \mu + \rho y_{t-1} + \epsilon_t, \tag{4.14}$$

which is weakly stationary when $|\rho| < 1$ (for appropriate initial conditions), and $\epsilon_t \sim \mathsf{IN}[0, \sigma_\epsilon^2]$. The process is strictly stationary when the disturbance term $\{\epsilon_t\}$ is IID, even without the normality of the disturbances (McCabe and Tremayne, 1993, p.221), but assuming normality facilitates the calculation of forecast confidence intervals. Similar results hold under weaker conditions on the $\{\epsilon_t\}$, and for more general stationary dynamic models.

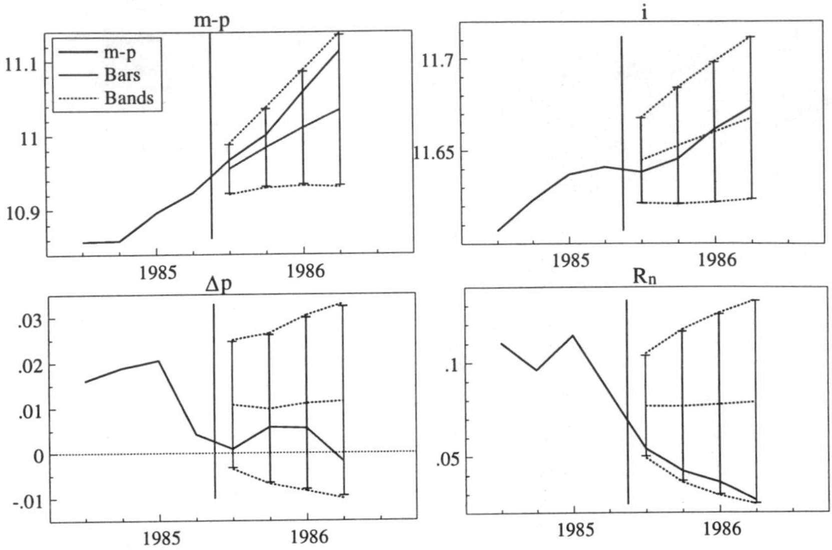

Figure 4.3
Forecasts and 95% prediction bars and bands for the monetary model.

When the values of the parameters μ and ρ are estimated, the 1-step ahead forecast $\widehat{y}_{T+1}$ is:

$$\widehat{y}_{T+1} = \widehat{\mu} + \widehat{\rho} y_T,$$

with forecast error $\widehat{e}_{T+1} = y_{T+1} - \widehat{y}_{T+1}$:

$$\widehat{e}_{T+1} = \epsilon_{T+1} + (\mu - \widehat{\mu}) + (\rho - \widehat{\rho})\, y_T = \epsilon_{T+1} + \left(\boldsymbol{\theta} - \widehat{\boldsymbol{\theta}}\right)' \mathbf{x}_T, \tag{4.15}$$

where $\mathbf{x}_t = [1\ y_t]'$ and $\boldsymbol{\theta} = [\mu\ \rho]'$. The forecast error variance (ignoring the slight dependence of $\widehat{\boldsymbol{\theta}}$ on $\mathbf{x}_T$) is:

$$\mathsf{V}\left[\widehat{e}_{T+1} \mid y_T\right] = \sigma_\epsilon^2 + \mathbf{x}_T' \mathsf{V}\left[\widehat{\boldsymbol{\theta}}\right] \mathbf{x}_T. \tag{4.16}$$

This depends upon the variance σ_ϵ^2 of the innovation process, irrespective of whether the parameters are estimated or known; and on the variances of the estimated parameters $\mathsf{V}[\widehat{\boldsymbol{\theta}}]$ and the forecast origin when the parameters are unknown. This second term is $O\left(T^{-1}\right)$ since:

$$\begin{aligned}
\mathsf{V}\left[\widehat{\boldsymbol{\theta}}\right] &= \sigma_{\epsilon}^{2}\mathsf{E}\left[\begin{array}{cc} T & \sum_{t=1}^{T} y_{t-1} \\ \sum_{t=1}^{T} y_{t-1} & \sum_{t=1}^{T} y_{t-1}^{2} \end{array}\right]^{-1} \\
&\simeq T^{-1}\left(\begin{array}{cc} \sigma_{\epsilon}^{2}+\mu^{2}\left(1+\rho\right)\left(1-\rho\right)^{-1} & -\mu\left(1+\rho\right) \\ -\mu\left(1+\rho\right) & \left(1-\rho^{2}\right) \end{array}\right).
\end{aligned} \tag{4.17}$$

The last approximation is valid asymptotically and is used below. When (4.16) uses the asymptotic variance of the estimated parameters, as in (4.17), it is known as the approximate forecast-error variance (or MSFE, more generally), as distinct from the asymptotic MSFE (no parameter estimation uncertainty). The order T^{-1} correction to MSFE s for parameter estimation uncertainty holds more generally (see, e.g., Chatfield, 1993, pp.123–4, for a discussion of the impact of parameter uncertainty on forecasts).

For h-step ahead forecasts from period T, straightforward calculations yield a forecast-error variance of:

$$\mathsf{V}\left[\epsilon_{T+h}\right] = \mathsf{V}[y_{T+h} \mid y_{T}] = \sigma_{\epsilon}^{2}\frac{\left(1-\rho^{2h}\right)}{\left(1-\rho^{2}\right)}. \tag{4.18}$$

in the known parameter case, which converges to the unconditional variance of the process as $h \to \infty$. When parameters but have to be estimated, a more complicated approximate formula results:

$$\mathsf{V}\left[\widehat{\epsilon}_{T+h} \mid y_{T}\right] = \sigma_{\epsilon}^{2}\frac{\left(1-\rho^{2h}\right)}{\left(1-\rho^{2}\right)} + \mathbf{d}'\mathsf{V}\left[\widehat{\boldsymbol{\theta}}\right]\mathbf{d}, \tag{4.19}$$

where:

$$\mathbf{d}' = \left(\frac{\left(1-\rho^{h}\right)}{\left(1-\rho\right)} : \left\{\mu\frac{\left[1-h\rho^{h-1}\left(1-\rho\right)-\rho^{h}\right]}{\left(1-\rho\right)^{2}} + h\rho^{h-1}y_{T}\right\}\right),$$

(see §4.7 for the detailed calculations). Again, however, the contribution to forecast uncertainty from $\mathbf{d}'\mathsf{V}\left[\widehat{\boldsymbol{\theta}}\right]\mathbf{d}$ remains $O\left(T^{-1}\right)$. As $h \to \infty$, $\mathbf{d}$ converges to:

$$\mathbf{d}' = \frac{1}{1-\rho}\left(1 : \frac{\mu}{1-\rho}\right),$$

and so:

$$\mathbf{d}'\mathsf{V}\left[\widehat{\boldsymbol{\theta}}\right]\mathbf{d} \to T^{-1}\frac{\sigma_\epsilon^2}{(1-\rho)^2} \text{ as } h \to \infty,$$

which is the long-run variance, and equals the variance of the equilibrium mean. Hence, for long-horizon forecasts in stationary processes, the estimation uncertainty is not dependent on the forecast origin, and only reflects the uncertainty attaching to estimating the equilibrium mean. Again, the deterministic term takes centre stage.

Another interesting implication of parameter estimation uncertainty evident from (4.19) is that conditional forecast-error variances may exceed their unconditional counterparts for some forecast horizons, due to the non-monotonicity of the second term in **d**. Nevertheless, that term is of order T^{-1}, so the effect is small.

4.3.1.2 I(1) processes

We now consider the impact of estimation uncertainty for forecasts from processes integrated of order one. The simplest example arises when $\rho = 1$ in (4.14):

$$y_t = y_{t-1} + \mu + \epsilon_t, \tag{4.20}$$

where again $\epsilon_t \sim \mathsf{IN}[0, \sigma_\epsilon^2]$. The h-step ahead forecast for known parameters, conditional on information available at time T is:

$$\widetilde{y}_{T+h} = \mu + y_{T+h-1} = \mu h + y_T. \tag{4.21}$$

Thus, the forecast is of a change in the variable from the forecast origin with a local trend, or slope, function. The conditional multi-period forecast error, $e_{T+h} = y_{T+h} - \widetilde{y}_{T+h}$, is:

$$e_{T+h} = \mu h + y_T + \sum_{i=0}^{h-1} v_{T+h-i} - (\mu h + y_T) = \sum_{i=0}^{h-1} \epsilon_{T+h-i}. \tag{4.22}$$

As is well known, the cumulative error has a variance that increases at $O(h)$ in the horizon h:

$$\mathsf{V}\left[e_{T+h}\right] = h\sigma_\epsilon^2, \tag{4.23}$$

in contrast to the $O(1)$ stationary forecast-error variance in (4.18). The h-step forecast error for levels using estimated parameter values is:

$$\begin{aligned}\widehat{e}_{T+h} = y_{T+h} - \widehat{y}_{T+h} &= \mu h + y_T + \sum_{i=0}^{h-1} v_{T+h-i} - \left(\widehat{\mu} h + \widehat{\rho}^h y_T\right) \\ &= \left(\mu - \widehat{\mu}\right) h + \left(1 - \widehat{\rho}^h\right) y_T + \sum_{i=0}^{h-1} \epsilon_{T+h-i}.\end{aligned} \tag{4.24}$$

We neglect the coefficient biases, treating such conditional forecasts as unbiased. Note in general, though, that the drift term μ in the $\mathsf{I}(1)$ process becomes the slope of a linear trend, and for any given realization of the process, $\mu \neq \widehat{\mu}$ induces an error which is increasing in the forecast horizon. The case of a local-to-unity root (e.g., $\rho = 1 - k/T$ for small k) when making long-horizon forecasts is analyzed in Stock (1996) who shows that considerable forecast uncertainty will result.

Generally, for estimated parameters in $\mathsf{I}(1)$ processes, the variance of the forecast error is hard to derive due to the non-standard nature of the distribution. However, the limiting distribution is normal when the unit-root model is estimated unrestrictedly for non-zero μ (see West, 1988): the estimate of ρ converges at a rate of $T^{\frac{3}{2}}$, so its variance can be neglected), whereas $\mathsf{V}[\widehat{\mu}] = \sigma_\epsilon^2 T^{-1}$ emphasizing the importance of accurately estimating the local trend.

We concentrate on the case in which ρ is correctly imposed at unity – a discussion of estimating unit roots is given in §4.4. Then, the forecast-error variance increases quadratically in the forecast horizon, h, for fixed T:

$$\mathsf{V}\left[\widehat{e}_{T+h}\right] = h\left(\sigma_\epsilon^2 + h\mathsf{V}\left[\widehat{\mu}\right]\right) \simeq h\sigma_\epsilon^2\left(1 + \frac{h}{T}\right). \tag{4.25}$$

If we control the rate at which T and h go to infinity by (see Sampson, 1991):

$$T = Ah^\kappa \tag{4.26}$$

where $\kappa \geq 0$, then:

$$\mathsf{V}\left[\widehat{e}_{T+h}\right] \simeq h\sigma_\epsilon^2\left(1 + A^{-1}h^{1-\kappa}\right) = \mathsf{V}_{\mathsf{ds}} \tag{4.27}$$

which is $O(h^2)$ for $\kappa = 0$, $O(h^{2-\kappa})$ for $0 < \kappa < 1$ and $O(h)$ for $\kappa \geq 1$ (see Sampson, 1991, eqn. 12). We now compare V_{ds} with that resulting when the DGP is trend stationary.

4.3.1.3 Deterministic non-stationarity

The trend-stationary DGP is given by:

$$y_t = \phi + \gamma t + u_t \tag{4.28}$$

where we maintain the assumption that $u_t \sim \mathsf{IN}[0, \sigma_u^2]$. The h-step ahead forecast for known parameters from (4.28), conditional on information available at time T is:

$$\widetilde{y}_{T+h} = \phi + \gamma (T + h), \tag{4.29}$$

with multi-period forecast error:

$$e_{T+h} = y_{T+h} - \widetilde{y}_{T+h} = u_{T+h}. \tag{4.30}$$

The conditional forecast-error variance is the variance of the disturbance term:

$$\mathsf{V}[e_{T+h}] = \sigma_u^2. \tag{4.31}$$

When parameters have to be estimated, (4.29) becomes:

$$\widehat{y}_{T+h} = \widehat{\phi} + \widehat{\gamma} (T + h), \tag{4.32}$$

and the multi-period forecast error and error variance are given respectively by:

$$\widehat{e}_{T+h} = \left(\phi - \widehat{\phi}\right) + (\gamma - \widehat{\gamma})(T + h) + u_{T+h}, \tag{4.33}$$

with:

$$\mathsf{V}[\widehat{e}_{T+h}] = \mathsf{V}\left[\widehat{\phi}\right] + (T+h)^2 \mathsf{V}[\widehat{\gamma}] + 2(T+h)\,\mathsf{C}\left[\widehat{\phi}, \widehat{\gamma}\right] + \sigma_u^2. \tag{4.34}$$

Thus, we need to evaluate $\mathsf{V}[\widehat{\boldsymbol{\theta}}]$, where $\widehat{\boldsymbol{\theta}} = [\widehat{\phi} : \widehat{\gamma}]'$:

$$\begin{aligned} \mathsf{V}\left[\widehat{\boldsymbol{\theta}}\right] &= \sigma_u^2 \left[\begin{pmatrix} T & \frac{1}{2}T(T+1) \\ \frac{1}{2}T(T+1) & \frac{1}{6}T(T+1)(2T+1) \end{pmatrix}^{-1} \right] \\ &= \sigma_u^2 T^{-1}(T-1)^{-1} \begin{pmatrix} 2(2T+1) & -6 \\ -6 & 12(T+1)^{-1} \end{pmatrix}. \end{aligned} \tag{4.35}$$

Substituting from (4.35) into (4.34), and simplifying by approximating $(T+1) \simeq T$ gives $\mathsf{V}[\widehat{e}_{T+h}]$ as:

$$\begin{aligned} &\simeq 4\sigma_u^2 T^{-1} - 12\,(T+h)\,\sigma_u^2 T^{-2} + 12\,(T+h)^2\,\sigma_u^2 T^{-3} + \sigma_u^2 \\ &= \sigma_u^2\left(1 + 4T^{-1} + 12hT^{-2} + 12h^2T^{-3}\right). \end{aligned} \tag{4.36}$$

From (4.36), the forecast-error variance grows with the square of the forecast horizon, for fixed T. We can again use (4.26) to determine the behavior of (4.36) as h and T go to infinity:

$$\mathsf{V}\left[\widehat{e}_{T+h}\right] \simeq \sigma_u^2\left(1 + 4A^{-1}h^{-\kappa} + 12A^{-2}h^{1-2\kappa} + 12A^{-3}h^{2-3\kappa}\right) = \mathsf{V}_{\mathsf{ts}}. \tag{4.37}$$

Thus, we find that (4.37) is $O(h^2)$ for $\kappa = 0$, $O(h^{2-3\kappa})$ for $0 < \kappa < \frac{2}{3}$, and $O(1)$ for $\kappa \geq \frac{2}{3}$ (see Sampson, 1991, eqn. 18).

To more easily compare (4.36) for the trend-stationary model (TS) with (4.25) for the difference-stationary model (DS), when T is not assumed fixed, we calculate the ratio of the two, and eliminate T using (4.26):

$$\frac{\mathsf{V}_{\mathsf{ds}}}{\mathsf{V}_{\mathsf{ts}}} = \frac{h + A^{-1}h^{2-\kappa}}{1 + 4A^{-1}h^{-\kappa} + 12A^{-2}h^{1-2\kappa} + 12A^{-3}h^{2-3\kappa}}. \tag{4.38}$$

From examination of (4.38), it is apparent that $\mathsf{V}_{\mathsf{ds}}/\mathsf{V}_{\mathsf{ts}} \to \infty$ as $h \to \infty$ (so T approaches ∞ at the rate determined by (4.26)) for all values of κ other than $\kappa = 0$. In fact, $\kappa = 0$ corresponds to a fixed T, and in that case $\mathsf{V}_{\mathsf{ds}}/\mathsf{V}_{\mathsf{ts}} \to A^2/12$ as $h \to \infty$. When we allow T to grow as h increases, no matter how slowly (κ close to but not equal to zero), then $\mathsf{V}_{\mathsf{ds}}/\mathsf{V}_{\mathsf{ts}} \to \infty$ and the forecast-error variance of the DS model swamps that of the TS model in the limit: see fig. 1.1. Thus, only when T is fixed will the DS and TS models be asymptotically indistinguishable, even allowing for parameter uncertainty.

Sampson (1991) argues that allowing for parameter uncertainty leads to forecast-error variances which grow with the square of the forecast horizon for both the DS and TS models, so that asymptotically the two are indistinguishable in terms of their implications for forecastability. As shown, this result requires that the estimation sample T remains fixed while the forecast horizon h goes to infinity.

Care is required in using such comparative findings to interpret empirical evidence, since the DGP is at best one of the two models DS or TS, whereas we have examined the forecast-error variances derived for each under its own DGP. There are two consequences. First, the computer reported error-variance formulae must be incorrect for one of the two models as these correspond to V_{ds} and V_{ts} above. Secondly, the actual forecast-error variance ratio of relevance will depend on which process generated the data. To illustrate, we derive the forecast-error variance ratios of the two models assuming each is the DGP in turn, but to keep the algebra simple we abstract from parameter estimation uncertainty. The more general analysis can be found in Clements and Hendry (1998c). For simplicity, assume $\phi = 0$ in the TS model, and that $y_0 = 0$ in the DS model.

When the TS model is the DGP, its forecast-error variance remains unchanged as (4.31). Using the incorrect DS predictor, $\mu h + y_T$, yields a forecast error:

$$e_{ds,T+h} = y_{T+h} - \widetilde{y}_{ds,T+h} = \gamma(T+h) + u_{T+h} - (\mu h + y_T) \tag{4.39}$$

and:

$$\mathsf{V}_{ds|ts} = \sigma_u^2 + \gamma^2(T+h)^2 + (\mu h + y_T)^2 - 2\gamma(T+h)(\mu h + y_T), \tag{4.40}$$

so that the relative loss to using the DS, $(\mathsf{V}_{ts|ts} - \mathsf{V}_{ds|ts})/\sigma_u^2$, is:

$$\sigma_u^{-2}\left[-\gamma^2(T+h)^2 + 2\gamma(T+h)(\mu h + y_T) - (\mu h + y_T)^2\right]. \tag{4.41}$$

The value of the parameter μ in the DS predictor that minimizes in-sample expected squared error loss is $\mu = \gamma$. Treating γ as known, substituting into (4.41) gives:

$$\frac{\mathsf{V}_{ts|ts} - \mathsf{V}_{ds|ts}}{\sigma_u^2} = -\sigma_u^{-2}(\gamma T - y_T)^2 = \frac{-u_T^2}{\sigma_u^2} \tag{4.42}$$

so that despite their radically different behavior when each is simultaneously assumed to be the DGP, they differ only by the period-T squared disturbance when the TS model is the DGP, independently of h. Specifically, the DS model forecast-error variance, when the TS model is the DGP, is of the same order as the TS model variance.

Suppose now that the DS model is the DGP, so that the DS model MSFE is given by (4.23). The value of γ that minimizes the in-sample prediction error for the TS predictor is $\gamma = \mu$, and the resulting forecast error is:

$$e_{ts,T+h} = \mu h + y_T + \sum_{i=0}^{h-1} \epsilon_{T+h-i} - \mu(T+h) = y_T - \mu T + \sum_{i=0}^{h-1} \epsilon_{T+h-i} \quad (4.43)$$

so:

$$\mathsf{V}_{ts|ds} = h\sigma_\epsilon^2 + (y_T - \mu T)^2 \quad (4.44)$$

and:

$$\frac{\mathsf{V}_{ds|ds} - \mathsf{V}_{ts|ds}}{\sigma_\epsilon^2} = -\frac{\left(\sum_{i=1}^T \epsilon_i\right)^2}{\sigma_\epsilon^2} \quad (4.45)$$

which has an expected value of $-T$, but nevertheless, does not depend on h, so that the forecast-error variances are of the same order in h.

4.3.2 *Non-modeled regressors*

In I(0) processes, parameter uncertainty can be a major cause of uncertainty when forecasting far from the sample means. This result is illustrated by the conventional diagram in econometrics textbooks on the divergence of forecast confidence intervals when regressor values are far from their sample outcomes (see e.g., Kennedy, 1985, fig. 15.1). In the linear model $y_t = \boldsymbol{\beta}'\mathbf{z}_t + \nu_t$ with n regressors $\mathbf{z}_t$, the usual formula for the conditional 1-step ahead forecast error is:

$$\mathsf{E}\left[\widehat{\nu}_{T+1}^2 \mid \mathbf{z}_{T+1}\right] = \sigma_v^2 \left(1 + \mathbf{z}_{T+1}' \left(\mathbf{Z}'\mathbf{Z}\right)^{-1} \mathbf{z}_{T+1}\right) \quad (4.46)$$

where $\mathbf{Z}' = (\mathbf{z}_1, \ldots, \mathbf{z}_T)$. When $\mathbf{z}_t$ comprises just an intercept ($z_{1,t} = 1$) and a single zero-mean regressor $z_{2,t}$ (so $\overline{z}_2 = 0$):

$$\mathbf{z}_{T+1}' \left(\mathbf{Z}'\mathbf{Z}\right)^{-1} \mathbf{z}_{T+1} = T^{-1} \left(1 + \frac{z_{2,T+1}^2}{T^{-1}\sum_{t=1}^T z_{2,t}^2}\right). \quad (4.47)$$

Thus, values of $z_{2,T+1}^2$ that are very large relative to the in-sample average will induce considerable forecast uncertainty. This problem is closely related to the impact of shifts in regressors when they have considerable collinearity, as we now discuss.

4.3.3 *Collinearity in conditional equations*

It may be thought that severe "collinearity" might help account for forecast failure, since very imprecise parameter estimates could be far from the correct values, and hence produce misleading forecasts. However, in a linear model, collinearity cannot do so by itself, because forecasts from linear models are invariant under non-singular, scale-preserving, linear transformations, and hence are identical to those delivered for orthogonal variables. Nevertheless, as discussed in Clements and Hendry (1998b), poor *ex-ante* forecasts can result from a constant conditional model when there is a break in the process generating the regressors.

Since it is difficult to investigate collinearity and its changes in a VEqCM, where all variables are endogenous, we consider the single conditional equation in §4.3.2. Denote by $\lambda_1 \leq \lambda_2 \ldots \leq \lambda_n$ the eigenvalues of the second-moment matrix $\mathbf{Z}'\mathbf{Z}$ of the n regressors $\mathbf{z}_t$ in the linear model $y_t = \boldsymbol{\beta}'\mathbf{z}_t + \nu_t$, where the ratio λ_n/λ_1 is large. Let the impact of the forecast-period observations change the λ_i to λ_i^*. Then, from (4.46), $\widehat{\nu}_{T+1}$ has an expected squared value of:

$$\mathsf{E}\left[\widehat{\nu}_{T+1}^2\right] \simeq \sigma_v^2\left(1 + T^{-1}\sum_{i=1}^{n}\frac{\lambda_i^*}{\lambda_i}\right),$$

which can be large if λ_1 changes markedly (e.g., from 0.0001 to 0.1, say, so a factor of $1000/T$ is involved). Consequently, variance effects interacting with breaks in "exogenous" processes can produce poor forecasts. This result is related to that in (4.47), and reduces to it for an intercept and single regressor, in that "unusual" drawings for the regressors may entail values with relatively large squared values, but it also applies when their correlations alter. In practice, such a situation would be signalled by a large increase in forecast confidence intervals, but as these are not always calculated, we first proceed as if no confidence intervals were reported.

The problem discussed in §2.6, forecasting UK house prices over 1972–75, provides a possible empirical example: see fig. 2.5d. We postulate that the "forecast failure" was induced by the many changes in financial markets following the Competition and Credit Control regulations introduced in late 1971. This would have altered any previous

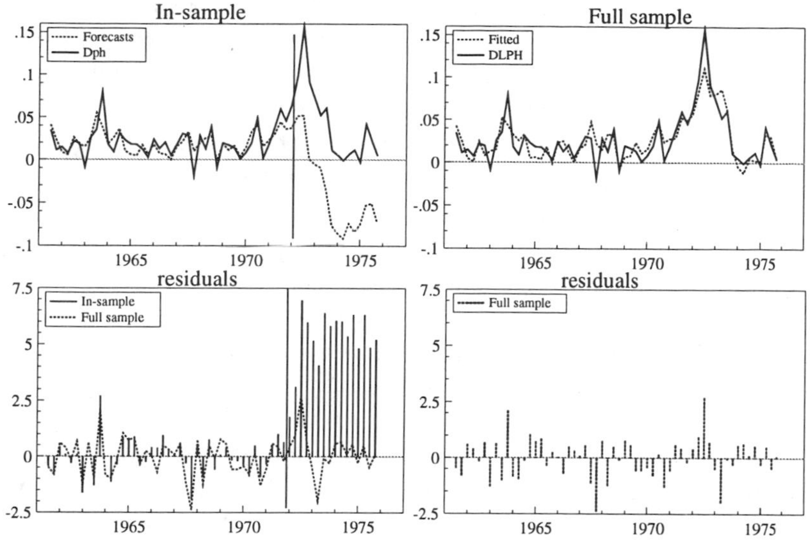

Figure 4.4
UK house price inflation: fitted values, forecasts and errors over 1972(1)–1975(4).

collinearity between the many regressors in the econometric model in Hendry (1984) (his equation (17), but replacing $(\Delta p_{h,t-1})^3$ by $\Delta p_{h,t-1}$) thereby producing poor *ex-ante* forecasts for the resultant price leap. Of course, a mis-specified model with a break in an omitted variable, or an equilibrium shift in the equation would also have precipitated failure. We now try empirically to illustrate the different implications of these rival explanations.

As the first column of fig. 4.4 confirms, using the in-sample parameter estimates, the sequence of 1-step forecasts is very poor, and the forecast-period residuals are large, and all of the same sign.

Similar episodes of *ex-ante* forecast failure in conditional models have often occurred in the history of econometrics: parochial examples include consumers' expenditure in the mid-1970s and early 1990s (see Davidson, Hendry, Srba and Yeo, 1978, Hendry, 1994, and ch. 7 for a follow up based on Clements and Hendry, 1998a), and UK M1 (see Hendry and Mizon, 1993, and Hendry, 1996). The first of these seems due to omitting the loss on liquid assets induced by the rapid increase in inflation, and a model including inflation became constant; the next (consumers' expenditure in the 1990s) remains a puzzle to some extent (see Muellbauer, 1994), but appears to be associated with the consequences of credit deregulation and negative equity in housing; and the last (UK M1) reflects the introduction of interest-bearing checking accounts which greatly reduced the opportunity cost of holding money, and was rectified by re-measuring that notion. Thus, all three examples seem to be breaks within the pre-existing relation relative to the relevant information set. How can one differentiate those outcomes (which deliver similar graphs for forecast residuals to fig. 4.4) from the present case where we believe a break in the regressor set induced apparent failure in what is in fact a constant relation?

Fortunately, the discrimination is direct from the postulated source: the collinear situation is detectable either from forecast confidence intervals widening markedly (as we saw in fig. 2.5d), or by the *ex-post* fit being similar to the in-sample fit. For the house-price equation, both are the case. The second column in fig. 4.4 shows the *ex-post* results on the same scaling: the equation does not fit significantly worse to the *ex-post* data. Panel c plots both *ex-ante* and *ex-post* residuals to confirm that the later fit is not at the expense of a deterioration earlier on. Formally, over the last 16 observations, a Chow test delivers $\mathsf{F_{Ch}}(16, 28) = 1.75$, $\mathsf{p} = 0.094$, despite the large change in the data. Updating the consumers' expenditure, or M1 equations, without the required modifications, produces significantly worse fits. Here, the contrast in fig. 4.4 between the *ex-ante* forecasts and forecast errors (first column) and the *ex-post* fit (second column), computed with the model specification unchanged, confirms no break in the house-price equation under analysis.

A related explanation is provided by Richard and Zhang (1996), who use the underlying economic theory of Hendry's model to show that considerable heteroscedasticity will result from its non-linear adjustment equation. Measuring the misprediction relative to an assumed constant error variance will then lead to a mistaken inference, in so far as using the correct heteroscedastic variance would entail an insignificant constancy-test outcome. This is similar in spirit to the implications of changes in collinearity.

4.3.4 *Changing collinearity in a VEqCM*

We return to the system in (4.1) using the block formulation in (4.4), but impose zero means for simplicity:

$$\begin{pmatrix} \mathbf{y}_{1,t} \\ \mathbf{y}_{2,t} \end{pmatrix} = \begin{pmatrix} \mathbf{\Pi}_{11} & \mathbf{\Pi}_{12} \\ \mathbf{0} & \mathbf{\Pi}_{22} \end{pmatrix} \begin{pmatrix} \mathbf{y}_{1,t-1} \\ \mathbf{y}_{2,t-1} \end{pmatrix} + \begin{pmatrix} \epsilon_{1,t} \\ \epsilon_{2,t} \end{pmatrix}. \tag{4.48}$$

Since $\mathbf{y}_1$ does not Granger cause $\mathbf{y}_2$, the results in (4.3) apply to $\mathbf{y}_2$:

$$\mathsf{E}\left[\mathbf{y}_{2,t}\mathbf{y}_{2,t}'\right] = \mathbf{M}_{22} = \mathbf{\Omega}_{\epsilon_2} + \mathbf{\Pi}_{22}\mathbf{M}_{22}\mathbf{\Pi}_{22}'. \tag{4.49}$$

Let the eigenvalues of $\mathbf{M}_{22}$ be $\lambda_1 \leq \lambda_2 \ldots \leq \lambda_{n_2}$ where as before, the ratio λ_{n_2}/λ_1 is very large. Changes in $\mathbf{\Omega}_{\epsilon_2}$ will alter $\mathbf{M}_{22}$ even when the slope parameters remain constant. The $\mathbf{y}_{1,t}$ equation block will experience a collinearity shift at the same time, and (as in §4.3.3) potentially produce a sequence of poor 1-step forecasts. *Ex post*, no deterioration in its fit will be discovered. However, although the $\mathbf{\Pi}$ matrix is constant, the second equation will have heteroscedastic residuals, which might suggest predictive failure on a Chow test (but as in Ericsson, Hendry and Prestwich, 1998b, a covariance test should not reject).

4.3.5 *Lack of parsimony*

Another potential source of forecast uncertainty is a lack of parsimony in model specification. This notion is taken to mean both incorrectly including irrelevant variables, and correctly including those that have small partial effects (conditional on the remaining specification), the elimination of which could improve forecast performance on some measures. Our main results on parsimony in stationary processes (when including variables of minor importance) were presented in Clements and Hendry (1998b, Ch. 12). Since the consequence of the second form of lack of parsimony is imprecise parameter estimates, it could at best explain "excess forecast variance", so that somewhat inaccurate forecasts are produced. However, systematic forecast failure (the main problem of concern here) could occur in the first case, if a change in data properties occurred somewhere in the associated economic system. Thus, falsely including regressors that alter substantially in a forecast period can induce forecast failure. An analytic example is the following.

Consider a DGP given by the variant of (4.4) where $\mathbf{\Pi}_{12} = \mathbf{0}$, but the forecaster uses the unrestrictedly-estimated forecasting model:

$$\widetilde{\mathbf{y}}_{T+1} = \widetilde{\boldsymbol{\phi}} + \widetilde{\mathbf{\Pi}}\mathbf{y}_T. \tag{4.50}$$

Although the resulting forecasts will be inefficient, in a constant-parameter world, they will be (essentially) unbiased:

$$\mathsf{E}[\mathbf{y}_{T+1} - \widetilde{\mathbf{y}}_{T+1}] = \boldsymbol{\varphi} - \mathsf{E}[\widetilde{\boldsymbol{\phi}} + \widetilde{\mathbf{\Pi}}\mathbf{y}_T] \simeq \boldsymbol{\varphi} - \boldsymbol{\phi} - \mathbf{\Pi}\boldsymbol{\varphi} = \mathbf{0}.$$

When the intercept $\boldsymbol{\phi}_2$ of the second block in (4.4) changes at T_1 to $\boldsymbol{\phi}_2^*$, the correctly-specified model for $\mathbf{y}_1$, using restricted estimates:

$$\widehat{\mathbf{y}}_{1,T+1} = \widehat{\boldsymbol{\phi}}_1 + \widehat{\mathbf{\Pi}}_{11}\mathbf{y}_{1,T}$$

will forecast as anticipated. However, for T somewhat larger than T_1, using (4.50):

$$\begin{aligned}\widetilde{\mathbf{y}}_{1,T+1} &= \widetilde{\boldsymbol{\phi}}_1 + \widetilde{\mathbf{\Pi}}_{11}\mathbf{y}_{1,T} + \widetilde{\mathbf{\Pi}}_{12}\mathbf{y}_{2,T} \\ &= \widetilde{\boldsymbol{\varphi}}_1 + \widetilde{\mathbf{\Pi}}_{11}\left(\mathbf{y}_{1,T} - \boldsymbol{\varphi}_1\right) + \widetilde{\mathbf{\Pi}}_{12}\left(\mathbf{y}_{2,T} - \boldsymbol{\varphi}_2\right),\end{aligned}$$

where:

$$\widetilde{\boldsymbol{\varphi}}_1 = \widetilde{\boldsymbol{\phi}}_1 + \widetilde{\mathbf{\Pi}}_{11}\boldsymbol{\varphi}_1 + \widetilde{\mathbf{\Pi}}_{12}\boldsymbol{\varphi}_2$$

could be poor as $\mathsf{E}[\mathbf{y}_{2,T}] \neq \boldsymbol{\varphi}_2$.

4.3.6 *An* I(0) *Monte Carlo illustration*

To mimic this case of over-inclusion in a Monte Carlo is not easy, as the falsely-included variable needs to play a substantive role. A proxy for an omitted relevant variable would play such a role, but conjointly entails a mis-specified model. Consequently, we let $y_{2,t}$ depend on $y_{1,t}$ directly (i.e., contemporaneously) with cross-correlated errors, and then incorrectly include $y_{2,t}$ as a regressor in the model of $y_{1,t}$. The equation determining $y_{2,t}$ then undergoes a structural break in its equilibrium mean. This example, therefore, embodies invalid weak exogeneity, and is an illustration of testing for it by a change in a marginal process (see Engle and Hendry, 1993, and Favero and Hendry, 1992). Thus, we end up with a mis-specified equation of a different form, but one which neatly illustrates the consequences of including irrelevant, but changing, variables that swamp the predictability correctly captured by the rest of the model, albeit in an open system.

The resulting DGP has the form:

$$\begin{aligned} y_{1,t} &= 1 + 0.85 y_{1,t-1} + \epsilon_{1,t} \\ y_{2,t} &= \alpha_2 + 1.95 y_{1,t} + 0.80 y_{2,t-1} + \epsilon_{2,t}, \end{aligned} \tag{4.51}$$

where:

$$\begin{pmatrix} \epsilon_{1,t} \\ \epsilon_{2,t} \end{pmatrix} \sim \mathsf{IN}_2 \left[\begin{pmatrix} 0 \\ 0 \end{pmatrix}, \begin{pmatrix} (0.25)^2 & (0.28)^2 \\ (0.28)^2 & (0.36)^2 \end{pmatrix} \right].$$

We formulated four experiments: in the first pair, there is no break, whereas in the second pair, the intercept (α_2) shifts in the $y_{2,t}$ equation:

(O) no break, correctly specified $y_{1,t}$ model (4.51);
(P) no break, $y_{2,t}$ falsely included in the $y_{1,t}$ model;
(Q) intercept shifts in the $y_{2,t}$ equation, correctly specified $y_{1,t}$ model;
(R) intercept shifts in the $y_{2,t}$ equation, $y_{2,t}$ falsely included in the $y_{1,t}$ model.

We set high inter-equation correlations and a large change from 7 to 0 for the shift in α_2 to emphasize that important non-constancies can derive from falsely including variables that change. The break occurs at $T_1 = 50$ for a full sample size of $T = 54$.

The upper row of fig. 4.5 shows the rejection frequencies for both the break-point and forecast tests. Panels a and b show that there is slight over-rejection in case (P) due to the "simultaneity", although both (O) and (Q) deliver the correct size. The rejection frequency in (R) exceeds 75% just prior to the break, using the break-point test, but is much lower on the forecast test. If that outcome empirically led to deleting $y_{2,t}$, then the full-sample fit of the reduced model would again be constant. Indeed, the main diagnosis of this case is the reduced significance of wrongly-included variables after re-estimation over the enlarged sample, and the increased constancy that should result when they are deleted from the model. Panels 4.5c,d show the recursively-computed mean values of the coefficients of $y_{1,t}$ and $y_{2,t}$. Although four post-break observations are rather few to be definitive, in case (R) the coefficient of $y_{2,t}$ dives almost immediately to zero, and that of $y_{1,t}$ rises to the DGP value: their respective standard errors lay between

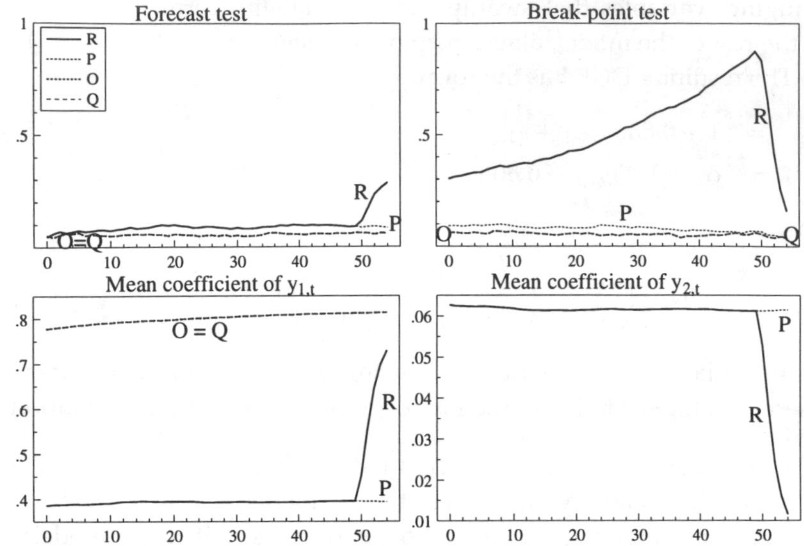

Figure 4.5
Constancy test rejection frequencies and recursive coefficients.

(0.02) – (0.005) and (0.15) – (0.05). This suggests estimation updating may be beneficial for such a mis-specification. There was no evidence of coefficient non-constancy in the other cases, as their graphs demonstrate.

There would be a failure of variance dominance here, in that the whole-sample constant model would fit less well than the non-constant over the period before the break, requiring care in evaluating between non-congruent models. Unfortunately, such an analysis would also apply in an I(1) process when the forecast failure is induced by a shift in the equilibrium mean, since dropping the EqCM could produce a more constant model in differences (see §2.5). Thus, diagnosing this problem is harder.

4.3.7 *Overfitting*

"Overfitting" is used to a refer to a variety of activities. In the time-series literature, ARIMA models are sometimes "overfit" when model identification, based on the ACF (autocorrelation function) and partial

ACF, is not conclusive – an additional AR or MA term is added to the preferred specification to assess the impact on model forecasts. For our purposes, the notion of overfitting in Todd (1990, p.217) is perhaps the most relevant, although it seems close to "lack of parsimony": see §4.3.5. Todd refers to overfitting as: fitting "not only the most salient features of the historical data, which are often the stable, enduring relationships" but also "features which often reflect merely accidental or random relationships that will not recur" Todd (1990, p.217). The latter is called sample dependence in Hendry (1995b).

It is useful to distinguish two cases: simply having a "generously parameterized model", and using the in-sample data evidence to select the variables to be retained. The first is a transient problem in a progressive research strategy, in that an extended data sample will reveal the accidental nature of the irrelevant effects by their becoming less significant. Moreover, although the resulting forecasts may be inaccurate, as argued in §4.3.5, systematic forecast failure will only occur if the data properties of the incorrectly included variables change during the forecast period. The second in turn raises two issues: model simplification by general-to-simple approaches, and "data mining". Despite commencing with an "over-parameterized representation", general-to-simple modeling need not lead to overfitting: simplification could either attenuate or exacerbate sample dependence. The former could occur if genuinely irrelevant factors were eliminated, whereas the latter could happen if the influences of accidental aspects were captured more "significantly" by being retained in a smaller parameterization (also a transient problem). The Monte Carlo results in Hoover and Perez (1996) suggest that general-to-simple procedures, extended as they suggest, often deliver a final equation that is close to the one which generated their data, supporting their efficacy in achieving the former.

The final issue relates to the impact on forecasting of the approach known as "data mining" – a prejudiced search for supportive evidence (see e.g., Leamer, 1978) – which may lead to either over or under fitting depending on the objective of the study. Gilbert (1986) distinguishes weak data mining – corroborating a prior belief – from strong data mining – ignoring or even hiding conflicting evidence. Since the apparent success/failure in forecasting of a model depends primarily on what happens over the forecast horizon relative to the in-sample model, and we have already shown that the degree of congruence/non-congruence of a model in-sample is neither necessary nor sufficient for forecasting success or failure, few general results seem likely on the implications of having data mined. In terms of developing congruent models, Hendry (1995b) argues that data-mining criticisms are avoided once all the available empirical evidence is explained: strong cannot occur as it entails conflicting evidence, nor can weak when all other models are encompassed. Even so, because unanticipated deterministic shifts can happen over any forecast period in economics, we are unable to establish the primacy for forecasting of in-sample congruent models (see §4.3.6).

4.3.8 Macro-econometric models and simulation

There appears to be a belief that parameter-estimation uncertainty is a significant source of forecast-error uncertainty in large-scale macro-econometric models, based on studies such as Fair (1980, 1984). These studies attempt, via simulation of the model, to assess the quantitative importance of factors such as the equation disturbances, and uncertainty surrounding the exogenous variables, as well as that due to estimating the model parameters. Ericsson and Marquez (1996) also explore this issue in a large practical forecasting system. However, there are at least three reasons why the impact of estimation uncertainty may be over-stated.

First, Sargan (1964a) shows that while full-information maximum likelihood (FIML) estimates of simultaneous systems have finite second-moments of reduced-form parameter estimates, methods which directly estimate the "structural" coefficients (e.g., three-stage least squares: 3SLS) may not, with a consequential impact on forecast second moments. Hoque, Magnus and Pesaran (1988) show that high-order forecast-error moments need not exist in autoregressive processes. Simulation studies that used estimation methods with no moments, but reported (say) mean forecast biases or MSFE s, could suggest that parameter estimation was a major contributor to forecast uncertainty (see Sargan, 1982, on the properties of Monte Carlo studies when moments do not exist, and Maasoumi, 1978, for a method of ensuring finite moments in estimates of parameters derived from simultaneous equations).

Secondly, measuring estimation and disturbance uncertainty by independent drawings of the parameters and errors from their own (estimated) distributions may be misleading – a more accurate picture of the role of estimation uncertainty should be obtained by re-estimating the model on each set of simulated data. Consider basing a simulation experiment on drawing independent values for an estimated parameter $\widehat{\theta}$ by:

$$\theta_j \sim \mathsf{IN}_k\left[\widehat{\theta}, \mathsf{V}\left[\widehat{\theta}\right]\right]. \tag{4.52}$$

In dynamic or simultaneous systems, drawings from (4.52) may yield (a) eigenvalues very close to, on, or occasionally outside, the unit circle; or (b) near singular outcomes for the matrix of endogenous variables, which when inverted lead to "wild" forecasts; whereas re-generating the data from the system and re-estimating the associated parameters by maximum likelihood could ensure neither problem occurred.

The final reason relates to the integrated nature of economic data, and the formulation of equations in macromodels. Often, these are open simultaneous systems of a form which can be expressed schematically in the closed case as:

$$\Delta \mathbf{x}_t = \boldsymbol{\tau} + \boldsymbol{\alpha}\boldsymbol{\beta}'\mathbf{x}_{t-1} + \boldsymbol{\Gamma}\Delta\mathbf{x}_{t-1} + \boldsymbol{\nu}_t. \tag{4.53}$$

However, $\boldsymbol{\tau}$ is rarely partitioned into the net growth rate ($\boldsymbol{\gamma}$) and the mean of the EqCM ($\boldsymbol{\mu}$). Consider the marginal distribution of $\boldsymbol{\tau}$:

$$\widehat{\boldsymbol{\tau}} \sim \mathsf{N}_n\left[\boldsymbol{\tau}, \mathsf{V}\left[\widehat{\boldsymbol{\tau}}\right]\right]. \tag{4.54}$$

In a system such as (4.53), $\mathsf{V}\left[\widehat{\boldsymbol{\tau}}\right]$ can be surprisingly large. For quarterly data, $\boldsymbol{\gamma}$ is a number of the order of 0.005 (approximately 2% p.a.), so deviations in $\widehat{\boldsymbol{\tau}}$ from $\boldsymbol{\tau}$ that are small relative to $\boldsymbol{\tau}$ can dramatically alter $\widehat{\boldsymbol{\gamma}}$ compared to $\boldsymbol{\gamma}$.

A simple Monte Carlo illustrates for estimating a bivariate VAR for cointegrated I(1) data. The DGP for a sample of size $T = 50$ is:

$$\begin{pmatrix} y_{1,t} \\ y_{2,t} \end{pmatrix} = \begin{pmatrix} 1.005 \\ 0.010 \end{pmatrix} + \begin{pmatrix} 0.8 & 0.2 \\ 0 & 1.0 \end{pmatrix} \begin{pmatrix} y_{1,t-1} \\ y_{2,t-1} \end{pmatrix} + \begin{pmatrix} \epsilon_{1,t} \\ \epsilon_{2,t} \end{pmatrix} \tag{4.55}$$

Table 4.1
VAR Monte Carlo estimates for an I(1) process.

	mean	MCSE	MCSD
$y_{1,t-1}$	0.794	0.023	0.026
$y_{2,t-1}$	0.205	0.021	0.022
1	1.0373	0.121	0.133
$y_{1,t-1}$	0.032	0.115	0.141
$y_{2,t-1}$	0.893	0.101	0.110
1	−0.093	0.594	0.750

where:

$$\begin{pmatrix} \epsilon_{1,t} \\ \epsilon_{2,t} \end{pmatrix} \sim \mathsf{IN}_2 \left[\begin{pmatrix} 0 \\ 0 \end{pmatrix}, \begin{pmatrix} 0.01^2 & 0 \\ 0 & 0.05^2 \end{pmatrix} \right].$$

There is one cointegrating vector, $(y_{1,t-1} - y_{2,t-1})$ with a feedback coefficient of -0.2, and a mean of -5.0; and the system exhibits growth of:

$$\begin{pmatrix} \gamma_1 \\ \gamma_2 \end{pmatrix} = \begin{pmatrix} 0.005 \\ 0.010 \end{pmatrix}.$$

The model was an unrestricted VAR(1) with intercepts; the Johansen (1988) trace test for cointegration rejected the null of no cointegration in every replication, and the hypothesis of more than one 10% of the time for a nominal size of 5% (see Doornik, Hendry and Nielsen, 1999, on the problems of determining cointegration rank). Table 4.1 shows the simulation means, MCSEs and MCSDs from 1000 replications: the first (second) three sets of numbers are for the $y_{1,t}$ ($y_{2,t}$) equation. Figure 4.6 records the histograms of the estimated intercepts and of their estimated standard errors.[3]

It is apparent that the intercepts are imprecisely estimated relative to the underlying growth rates, and have a large dispersion. Moreover, so do their estimated standard errors. Thus, (4.54) could generate wild outcomes, thereby suggesting that parameter estimation uncertainty is crucial. In one sense, that is a correct interpretation. However, when the cointegration vector is imposed, and centered on its sample mean, the

[3] We are grateful to Sule Akkyonlyu for bringing this issue to our attention.

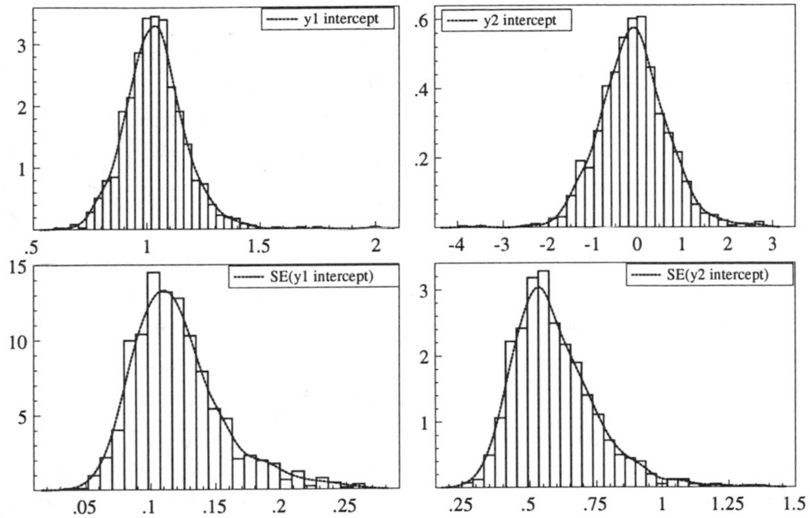

Figure 4.6
Histograms of estimated intercepts and standard errors in an I(1) VAR.

Table 4.2
VEqCM Monte Carlo estimates.

	mean	MCSE	MCSD
1	0.0049	0.0016	0.0016
c_{t-1}	0.2034	0.0194	0.0199
1	0.0113	0.0081	0.0105
c_{t-1}	−0.069	0.0962	0.0974

growth rate is often estimated rather precisely, so such poor behavior is avoidable. Table 4.2 reports the outcomes when the VAR is expressed as a VEqCM, using the population equilibrium mean correction:

$$c_t = y_{1,t} - y_{2,t} - 5.$$

The growth rates are now estimated accurately and quite precisely. While imposing the true μ may overstate the gains, our practical experience suggests γ is more precisely estimated after this transform: see Hendry and Doornik (1994) (the comparison between bands and bars in fig. 4.3 above was based on a VEqCM with that parameterization).

4.4 Model Mis-specification and Estimation Uncertainty

While in isolation neither model mis-specification nor estimation uncertainty appear likely to lead to serious forecast failure, the conjunction of the two may have an effect greater than the sum of the parts. The success of dynamic (or multi-step) estimation, whereby parameters are estimated by minimizing a sum of squared multi-step in-sample errors (see, e.g., Klein, 1971, Findley, 1983, Weiss, 1991, and Clements and Hendry, 1996c among others) would be indicative of important interactions between (1-step) estimation and mis-specification. The intuition is that when a model is not well specified, minimization of 1-step errors need not deliver reliable forecasts at longer lead times, and estimation by minimizing the in-sample counterpart of the desired step-ahead horizon may yield better forecasts.

Clements and Hendry (1996c) show that model mis-specification, while necessary to justify multi-step estimation, is not sufficient. Any gains that do accrue are likely to be greater for $\mathsf{I}(1)$ processes, when forecast success depends upon how accurately the unit roots are estimated. Estimating unit roots in the presence of unmodeled negative moving-average terms will exacerbate the downward bias of OLS, and this can be partly attenuated by multi-step estimation, leading to improved forecast accuracy. However, few economic time series seem likely to exhibit negative moving-average error autocorrelation of the size liable to cause serious problems for OLS when a model builder strives to develop congruent representations.

4.5 Forecast Origin Mis-measurement

A poor assessment of the state of the economy at the time a forecast is made may impart an important source of error. The frequency with which preliminary data are subsequently revised suggests that forecasts may often be conditioned on data measured with a substantial degree of error. Survey information would appear to have a useful role in providing estimates of forecast initial values, and in practice, forecasts will be conditioned on information of varying degrees of reliability, spanning several periods (see e.g., Wallis, Andrews, Fisher, Longbottom and Whitley, 1986). Typically, several "estimates" are released (such as the preliminary, or provisional, followed by revised figures), before the "final" data are made available. Gallo (1996) describes an approach which eschews all but the final data as "purist", compared to the "naive" approach which treats all published data as if it were "true". He treats the estimates that become available as forecasts of the "true" value based on different information sets. If later estimates do not fully encapsulate all the information in earlier ones, then the potential for pooling arises to extract a better "signal", from the noisy observations, of the initial state of the economy. Howrey (1978) considered predicting final values from preliminary ones, then using those updates where final values were not available: see Harvey, McKenzie, Blake and Desai (1983) and Boucelham and Teräsvirta (1990) for applications. Rahiala and Teräsvirta (1993) used a similar idea to extract a first estimate of quarterly industrial production from business survey data and forecast the next quarter. Clements and Hendry (1998b, Ch.8) considered pooling preliminary estimates and model predictions of the initial state. Nevertheless, unless the forecast origin values are systematically biased for the underlying state of the economy, "on average" this putative source of forecast failure will only have variance effects.

However, incorrect provisional data estimates may have distinctly adverse impacts on intercept correction (IC) strategies. If the usual procedure of "setting the model back on track" is used prior to forecasting, then the correction carried forward will embody all the data measurement errors. Thus, considerable value-added can result from a correct appraisal of current conditions before calculating forecasts. *Ex post*, changes in data values confound attempts at model evaluation, and even raise the awkward question as to what vintage of data forecasters are trying to forecast.

4.6 Conclusion

Chapter 3 established that shifts in deterministic terms were a primary source of forecast failure. We have now examined the roles of model mis-specification, collinearity, and lack of parsimony. We conclude that, by themselves, they are not the primary cause of forecast failure, albeit that they may exacerbate that problem. An implication is that modeling methods seem unlikely to account for forecast failure either, a conclusion reinforced by the results in Hoover and Perez (1996).

Deterministic factors again proved to be important in accounting for difficulties in forecasting. Deterministic mis-specification and deterministic shifts in omitted or falsely-included variables all could induce forecast failure. Even for parameter-estimation uncertainty, the variance of the equilibrium mean influenced long-horizon forecasts, and in conditional models large squared values of regressors (which are bound to have non-zero means) relative to the mean-square in-sample induced large forecast-error variances. The Monte Carlo illustration in §4.3.8 suggested that confounding growth rates with (numerically) much larger equilibrium means led to substantial increases in uncertainty, matching fig. 4.2. Consequently, the next chapter focuses on the impacts of shifts in equilibrium means of cointegration vectors and growth rates on models in first and second differences that seek robustness to such breaks, by having few, or no, deterministic terms. Conversely, chapter 6 conducts the analysis for intercept-correcting strategies that also seek to offset deterministic shifts. Chapters 7 and 8 provide scalar and vector empirical illustrations of some of these theoretical developments. Chapter 9 then proposes the concept of co-breaking to eliminate deterministic shifts in linear systems.

4.7 Appendix: Approximating Powers of Estimates

We use a number of approximations to obtain tractable expressions for variances of powers of estimated parameters, following Schmidt (1977), Baillie (1979b, 1979a) and Chong and Hendry (1986). Ericsson and Marquez (1989, 1996) and Campos (1992) provide good expositions and unifying treatments. We consider the stationary AR(1) model in (4.14):

$$y_t = \mu + \rho y_{t-1} + v_t \quad v_t \sim \mathsf{IN}\left[0, \sigma_v^2\right],$$

where estimation is by OLS. Let:

$$\widehat{\rho} = \rho + \delta, \tag{4.56}$$

where δ is $O_p(1/\sqrt{T})$, so that powers of δ are asymptotically negligible. Then the first approximation is:

$$\widehat{\rho}^h = (\rho + \delta)^h \simeq \rho^h + h\delta\rho^{h-1} = \rho^h + h\rho^{h-1}(\widehat{\rho} - \rho). \tag{4.57}$$

Consequently:

$$\mathsf{E}\left[\widehat{\rho}^{h}\right] \simeq \rho^{h} + h\rho^{h-1}\mathsf{E}\left[\widehat{\rho}-\rho\right] \simeq \rho^{h}$$

by the approximation that $\mathsf{E}[\widehat{\rho}-\rho]=0$ (see §2.2). Higher-order approximations can be calculated if needed. Next:

$$\mathsf{V}\left[\left(\widehat{\rho}^{h}-\rho^{h}\right)\right] \simeq \mathsf{V}\left[h\rho^{h-1}\left(\widehat{\rho}-\rho\right)\right] = h^{2}\rho^{2(h-1)}\mathsf{V}\left[\widehat{\rho}\right]. \tag{4.58}$$

This result also follows from the usual formula for a non-linear estimation function:

$$\mathsf{V}\left[\widehat{\rho}^{h}\right] \simeq \frac{\partial\rho^{h}}{\partial\rho}\mathsf{V}\left[\widehat{\rho}\right]\frac{\partial\rho^{h}}{\partial\rho}. \tag{4.59}$$

Further:

$$\mu\rho^{j} - \widehat{\mu}\widehat{\rho}^{j} = \rho^{j}\left(\mu-\widehat{\mu}\right) + \mu\left(\rho^{j}-\widehat{\rho}^{j}\right) - \left(\mu-\widehat{\mu}\right)\left(\rho^{j}-\widehat{\rho}^{j}\right), \tag{4.60}$$

where the final term is negligible relative to the first two as $T \to \infty$. The second main approximation comes in ignoring that term, so that from (4.57):

$$\begin{aligned}\sum_{j=0}^{h-1}\left(\mu\rho^{j}-\widehat{\mu}\widehat{\rho}^{j}\right) &\simeq \left(\mu-\widehat{\mu}\right)\sum_{j=0}^{h-1}\rho^{j} + \mu\left(\rho-\widehat{\rho}\right)\sum_{j=1}^{h-1} j\rho^{j-1} \\ &= \begin{array}{l}\left(\mu-\widehat{\mu}\right)\dfrac{\left(1-\rho^{h}\right)}{\left(1-\rho\right)} \\ +\left(\rho-\widehat{\rho}\right)\mu\dfrac{\left(1-h\rho^{h-1}(1-\rho)-\rho^{h}\right)}{\left(1-\rho\right)^{2}}\end{array} \\ &= \left(\boldsymbol{\theta}-\widehat{\boldsymbol{\theta}}\right)'\mathbf{d},\end{aligned} \tag{4.61}$$

say, where:

$$\mathbf{b}' = \left[\frac{\left(1-\rho^{h}\right)}{\left(1-\rho\right)} : \mu\frac{\left(1-h\rho^{h-1}(1-\rho)-\rho^{h}\right)}{(1-\rho)^{2}}\right].$$

Then:

$$\mathsf{E}\left[\left\{\sum_{j=0}^{h-1}\left(\mu\rho^{j}-\widehat{\mu}\widehat{\rho}^{j}\right)\right\}^{2}\right] = \mathbf{b}'\mathsf{V}\left[\widehat{\boldsymbol{\theta}}\right]\mathbf{b}. \tag{4.62}$$

Finally, using (4.57) and (4.61):

$$\begin{aligned}
&\mathsf{E}\left[\left\{\sum_{j=0}^{h-1}\left(\mu\rho^{j}-\widehat{\mu}\widehat{\rho}^{j}\right)\right\}\left(\rho^{h}-\widehat{\rho}^{h}\right)\right]y_T \\
&=h\rho^{h-1}\mathbf{b}'\mathsf{E}\left[\left(\boldsymbol{\theta}-\widehat{\boldsymbol{\theta}}\right)\left(\rho-\widehat{\rho}\right)\right]y_T \\
&=h\rho^{h-1}\mathbf{b}'\mathsf{V}\left[\widehat{\boldsymbol{\theta}}\right]\mathbf{s}y_T,
\end{aligned} \tag{4.63}$$

where $\mathbf{s}' = (0:1)$. Letting $h\rho^{h-1}y_T\mathbf{s} = \mathbf{c}$ and $\mathbf{d} = \mathbf{b} + \mathbf{c}$, then:

$$\mathsf{V}\left[\widehat{e}_{T+h} \mid y_T\right] = \sigma_v^2 \frac{1-\rho^{2h}}{1-\rho^2} + \mathbf{d}'\mathsf{V}\left[\widehat{\boldsymbol{\theta}}\right]\mathbf{d}, \tag{4.64}$$

where:

$$\mathsf{V}\left[\widehat{\boldsymbol{\theta}}\right] = T^{-1}\begin{bmatrix} \sigma_v^2 + \mu^2\frac{(1+\rho)}{(1-\rho)} & -\mu(1+\rho) \\ -\mu(1+\rho) & (1-\rho^2) \end{bmatrix} \tag{4.65}$$

from which our analytical approximations in the text are calculated.

5 Differencing

Summary

Some models offer greater protection against unforeseen structural breaks than others. In particular, models in first and second differences might robustify forecasts against breaks. We derive forecast-error biases and variances for vector autoregressions in these differences of the variables to demonstrate that when forecasting after structural breaks, they can outperform vector equilibrium-correction mechanisms. Deterministic shifts again induce forecast-error biases, whereas changes in the dynamics affect the variances. Since the differenced-data representations studied are non-congruent, we investigate the biases in their conventionally-calculated variances. We also examine trend shifts in post-transition forecasts.

5.1 Introduction

In chapter 3, we argued that shifts in deterministic components are one of the primary sources of mis-prediction, and that unforeseen structural breaks and regime shifts seem responsible for many of the more dramatic historical episodes of macroeconomic forecast failure. In this chapter, we establish a general framework for analyzing the impact of structural breaks on the performance of two non-congruent forecasting models, based on over-differencing, to evaluate their worth as counter measures to breaks. We focus on forecasts from vector autoregressions in first and second differences (denoted DVs and DDVs), in the spirit of Box and Jenkins (1976) time-series modeling. The former omits any EqCMs; the latter differences once more. We show that DVs and DDVs may be more robust than VEqCMs (i.e., models that include cointegrated combinations of levels) in the face of some forms of structural change. Chapter 6 evaluates the practice of "intercept corrections", and shows that these may help VEqCMs match the performance of differenced representations, at least in terms of lack of bias.

An empirical example of the possible benefits for forecasting of ignoring long-run information is Mizon (1995), who shows that only a DV forecasts UK wages and prices reasonably over the 1980s. Models such as VEqCMs, which include long-run information, tend to fail badly. The models are estimated on data up to Mrs. Thatcher coming to power (1979:2), then used to forecast the behavior of wages, prices, and unemployment during the 1980s. There is anecdotal evidence of structural change in the UK labor market during the 1980s in response to the dislocating effect of the 1979–81 recession, and government economic policies may have altered the long-run relationships between these three aggregates. Models which included long-run information tended to "correct" on the basis of an out-dated structure, and so deliver significant forecast errors, while models that eschewed such information performed reasonably well. More recently, Eitrheim, Husebø and Nymoen (1997) have re-estimated a variant of the Norges Bank macroeconomic model, specifying equations solely in differences, in some instances to good effect in terms of forecasting performance. Moreover, for the shortest-horizon evaluations they consider, DDVs perform well. We explain such results below.

We investigate analytically whether time-series models in differences can outperform econometric models, conditional on a structural break having occurred by the time of forecasting. We first consider forecasts made shortly before and after a break has occurred, when the economy is in a period of transition, characterized by unconditional expectations of $\mathsf{I}(0)$ transformations of the variables (i.e., differences and cointegrating combinations) equalling neither their pre- nor post-break steady-state values. As the formulae are relatively complex, we consider a DGP where the highest-order deterministic term is a constant. Later, to allow a linear trend in the DGP, we simplify by assuming that, at the time of forecasting, I(0) transformations of the variables equal their post-break expected values. The empirical illustrations in chapters 7 and 11 conform to the theory predictions derived below on the efficacy of differencing, and its costs as the horizon increases.

Section 5.2 describes the DV and DDV models, §5.3 their forecast-error biases (which §5.4 summarizes), and §5.5–§5.6 their forecast-error variances, around the break time. In §5.7, we evaluate the extent to which prediction intervals based on conventional formulae provide a misleading picture of the forecast uncertainty for such models, owing to their residual serial correlation. Section 5.8 describes the integrated-cointegrated DGP augmented by a linear time trend, which forms the basis for the analysis of VEqCM and DV errors made some time after the break has occurred. Section 5.9 provides concluding remarks. Detailed calculations are provided in §5.10 and §5.11.

5.2 Forecasting Models

The DGP is again an integrated-cointegrated linear dynamic system, given by (1.12), and reproduced here for convenience as:

$$\mathbf{x}_t = \boldsymbol{\tau} + \boldsymbol{\Upsilon}\mathbf{x}_{t-1} + \boldsymbol{\nu}_t \tag{5.1}$$

where $\boldsymbol{\nu}_t \sim \mathsf{IN}_n[\mathbf{0}, \boldsymbol{\Omega}_\nu]$ which we reparameterize as the VEqCM:

$$\Delta\mathbf{x}_t = \boldsymbol{\gamma} + \boldsymbol{\alpha}\left(\boldsymbol{\beta}'\mathbf{x}_{t-1} - \boldsymbol{\mu}\right) + \boldsymbol{\nu}_t. \tag{5.2}$$

The VAR in differences (DV) is defined here by:

$$\Delta\mathbf{x}_t = \boldsymbol{\gamma} + \boldsymbol{\xi}_t, \tag{5.3}$$

which is mis-specified unless the cointegrating rank r is zero, i.e., $\boldsymbol{\alpha} = \mathbf{0}$ in (5.2). When $r \neq 0$, the DV omits the causal information contained in the cointegrating vectors. In practice, lagged $\Delta\mathbf{x}_t$ may be used to approximate the omitted cointegrating vectors, but we do not consider such a model here as its behavior under structural breaks is rather complicated: Appendix §5.10 notes its derivation.

The second "model" we examine is a DV in the differences of the variables (the DDV), defined by:

$$\Delta^2\mathbf{x}_t = \boldsymbol{\zeta}_t \quad \text{or} \quad \mathbf{x}_t = \mathbf{x}_{t-1} + \Delta\mathbf{x}_{t-1} + \boldsymbol{\zeta}_t. \tag{5.4}$$

These models are convenient for the analytic calculations, and can be generalized in an obvious manner to allow for longer lag structures in empirical work, although the derivations become complicated.

Given (5.2), the error terms on (5.3) and (5.4) will be autocorrelated. It is important not to model the residual autocorrelation of DDV methods if their robustification properties are to be preserved: it may matter less for DVs. In (5.3), using (5.2):

$$\begin{aligned}\mathsf{E}\left[\boldsymbol{\xi}_t\boldsymbol{\xi}_{t-1}'\right] &= \boldsymbol{\alpha}\mathsf{E}\left[\left(\boldsymbol{\beta}'\mathbf{x}_{t-1}-\boldsymbol{\mu}\right)\left(\boldsymbol{\beta}'\mathbf{x}_{t-2}-\boldsymbol{\mu}\right)'\right]\boldsymbol{\alpha}'+\boldsymbol{\alpha}\boldsymbol{\beta}'\mathsf{E}\left[\mathbf{x}_{t-1}\boldsymbol{\nu}_{t-1}'\right]\\ &= \boldsymbol{\alpha}\boldsymbol{\Lambda}\mathsf{E}\left[\left(\boldsymbol{\beta}'\mathbf{x}_{t-2}-\boldsymbol{\mu}\right)\left(\boldsymbol{\beta}'\mathbf{x}_{t-2}-\boldsymbol{\mu}\right)'\right]\boldsymbol{\alpha}'+\boldsymbol{\alpha}\boldsymbol{\beta}'\boldsymbol{\Omega}_{\nu}\\ &= \boldsymbol{\alpha}\boldsymbol{\Lambda}\mathbf{V}\boldsymbol{\alpha}'+\boldsymbol{\alpha}\boldsymbol{\beta}'\boldsymbol{\Omega}_{\nu},\end{aligned}$$

whereas:

$$\mathsf{E}\left[\boldsymbol{\xi}_t\boldsymbol{\xi}_t'\right]=\boldsymbol{\alpha}\mathbf{V}\boldsymbol{\alpha}'+\boldsymbol{\Omega}_{\nu},$$

where from (3.34):

$$\mathbf{V}=\mathsf{E}\left[\left(\boldsymbol{\beta}'\mathbf{x}_t-\boldsymbol{\mu}\right)\left(\boldsymbol{\beta}'\mathbf{x}_t-\boldsymbol{\mu}\right)'\right].$$

For small values of $\boldsymbol{\alpha}$, therefore, "mopping up" $\mathsf{E}\left[\boldsymbol{\xi}_t\boldsymbol{\xi}_{t-1}'\right]$ by serial-correlation corrections or lagged differences, is unlikely to matter greatly, and may be reasonably successful as the covariance of $\boldsymbol{\beta}'\mathbf{x}_{t-1}$ with $\Delta\mathbf{x}_{t-1}$ is :

$$\begin{aligned}&\mathsf{E}\left[\left(\boldsymbol{\Lambda}\left(\boldsymbol{\beta}'\mathbf{x}_{t-2}-\boldsymbol{\mu}\right)+\boldsymbol{\beta}'\boldsymbol{\nu}_{t-1}\right)\left(\left(\boldsymbol{\beta}'\mathbf{x}_{t-2}-\boldsymbol{\mu}\right)'\boldsymbol{\alpha}'+\boldsymbol{\nu}_{t-1}'\right)\right]\\ &\quad= \boldsymbol{\Lambda}\mathbf{V}\boldsymbol{\alpha}'+\boldsymbol{\beta}'\boldsymbol{\Omega}_{\nu}.\end{aligned}$$

Adding lagged $\Delta\mathbf{x}_t$, therefore, is not an unreasonable strategy. Higher-order serial covariances are described by (for $s>0$):

$$\mathsf{E}\left[\boldsymbol{\xi}_t\boldsymbol{\xi}_{t-s}'\right]=\boldsymbol{\alpha}\boldsymbol{\Lambda}^{s}\mathbf{V}\boldsymbol{\alpha}'+\boldsymbol{\alpha}\boldsymbol{\Lambda}^{s-1}\boldsymbol{\beta}'\boldsymbol{\Omega}_{\nu}. \tag{5.5}$$

Similarly, for (5.4):

$$\begin{aligned}\mathsf{E}\left[\boldsymbol{\zeta}_t\boldsymbol{\zeta}_{t-1}'\right] &= \mathsf{E}\left[\left(\boldsymbol{\alpha}\boldsymbol{\beta}'\Delta\mathbf{x}_{t-1}+\Delta\boldsymbol{\nu}_t\right)\left(\Delta\mathbf{x}_{t-2}'\boldsymbol{\beta}\boldsymbol{\alpha}'+\Delta\boldsymbol{\nu}_{t-1}'\right)\right]\\ &= \boldsymbol{\alpha}\boldsymbol{\beta}'\mathsf{E}\left[\Delta\mathbf{x}_{t-1}\Delta\mathbf{x}_{t-2}'\right]\boldsymbol{\beta}\boldsymbol{\alpha}'+\mathsf{E}\left[\Delta\boldsymbol{\nu}_t\Delta\boldsymbol{\nu}_{t-1}'\right]\\ &= \boldsymbol{\alpha}\boldsymbol{\beta}'\left[\boldsymbol{\alpha}\boldsymbol{\Lambda}\mathbf{V}\boldsymbol{\alpha}'+\boldsymbol{\alpha}\boldsymbol{\beta}'\boldsymbol{\Omega}_{\nu}\right]\boldsymbol{\beta}\boldsymbol{\alpha}'-\boldsymbol{\Omega}_{\nu},\end{aligned}$$

where:

$$\begin{aligned}\mathsf{E}\left[\zeta_t\zeta_t'\right] &= \mathsf{E}\left[\left(\alpha\beta'\Delta\mathbf{x}_{t-1}+\Delta\boldsymbol{\nu}_t\right)\left(\Delta\mathbf{x}_{t-1}'\beta\alpha'+\Delta\boldsymbol{\nu}_t'\right)\right] \\ &= \boldsymbol{\Omega}_\nu+\left(\mathbf{I}_n-\alpha\beta'\right)\boldsymbol{\Omega}_\nu\left(\mathbf{I}_n-\beta\alpha'\right)+\alpha\beta'\alpha\mathbf{V}\alpha'\beta\alpha'.\end{aligned}$$

Consequently, for small α, on average the serial correlation will be close to:

$$\mathbf{S}=\mathsf{E}\left[\zeta_t\zeta_{t-1}'\right]\left(\mathsf{E}\left[\zeta_{t-1}\zeta_{t-1}'\right]\right)^{-1}\simeq-\boldsymbol{\Omega}_\nu\left(2\boldsymbol{\Omega}_\nu\right)^{-1}=-\tfrac{1}{2}\mathbf{I}_n.$$

This corresponds to a moving-average coefficient of -1 in each equation, which will "undo" the differencing (indeed, could pose problems, being a redundant common factor of unity), and hence "re-integrate" the equations, thereby losing any robustness that the over-differencing might deliver.

5.3 Forecast-error Biases in DVs and DDVs

As in chapter 3, there could be changes in any or all of the parameters, namely α, β, γ, or μ, but again β will be held constant. We consider the effects of changes in all the other parameter on the DV and DDV, both 1-step and 2-periods ahead. In this section, results are obtained for forecasts made immediately prior to the breaks occurring, and one period after the break.

The 1-step forecasts of the levels at forecast origin time $T+i$ $(i=0,1)$ from the DV (5.3) are:

$$\Delta\widetilde{\mathbf{x}}_{T+i+1|T+i}=\gamma, \tag{5.6}$$

and the DDV (5.4):

$$\Delta\overline{\mathbf{x}}_{T+i+1|T+i}=\Delta\mathbf{x}_{T+i}. \tag{5.7}$$

The 1-step forecast errors of the two models in terms of the levels are denoted by $\widetilde{\mathbf{e}}_{T+i+1|T+i}=\mathbf{x}_{T+i+1}-\widetilde{\mathbf{x}}_{T+i+1|T+i}$, and $\overline{\mathbf{e}}_{T+i+1|T+i}=\mathbf{x}_{T+i+1}-\overline{\mathbf{x}}_{T+i+1|T+i}$. The corresponding 2-step forecasts are:

$$\widetilde{\mathbf{x}}_{T+i+2|T+i}=\mathbf{x}_{T+i}+2\gamma; \tag{5.8}$$

and:

$$\overline{\mathbf{x}}_{T+i+2|T+i}=\overline{\mathbf{x}}_{T+i+1|T+i}+\Delta\overline{\mathbf{x}}_{T+i+1|T+i}=\mathbf{x}_{T+i}+2\Delta\mathbf{x}_{T+i}, \tag{5.9}$$

from (5.7). Similar expressions hold for their forecast errors. It is important that the DV does not difference the data *per se*, but merely excludes the EqCMs, whereas the DDV does difference: this helps account for their distinct behavior below.

After time T, the data are in fact generated by:

$$\Delta \mathbf{x}_{T+1} = \boldsymbol{\gamma}^* + \boldsymbol{\alpha}^* \left(\boldsymbol{\beta}' \mathbf{x}_T - \boldsymbol{\mu}^*\right) + \boldsymbol{\nu}_{T+1} \quad (5.10)$$

so we consider forecasting from T to $T+1$; T to $T+2$; $T+1$ to $T+2$; and $T+1$ to $T+3$: the last two are forecasts prepared after the break, but still with no knowledge of the break having occurred. Changes in the feedback parameters are included to clarify their role in affecting forecast variances. The detailed calculations are shown in Appendix §5.11; here we focus on the resulting formulae. The underlying algebra is similar to that used in §3.5.

5.3.1 *Forecasting levels from T to $T+1$*

Let $\boldsymbol{\beta}' \mathbf{x}_T - \boldsymbol{\mu} = \boldsymbol{\kappa}_T$, then:

$$\mathsf{E}\left[\widetilde{\mathbf{e}}_{T+1|T} \mid I_T\right] = \left(\boldsymbol{\gamma}^* - \boldsymbol{\gamma}\right) - \boldsymbol{\alpha}^* \left(\boldsymbol{\mu}^* - \boldsymbol{\mu}\right) + \boldsymbol{\alpha}^* \boldsymbol{\kappa}_T, \quad (5.11)$$

and:

$$\mathsf{E}\left[\overline{\mathbf{e}}_{T+1|T} \mid I_T\right] = \left(\boldsymbol{\gamma}^* - \Delta \mathbf{x}_T\right) - \boldsymbol{\alpha}^* \left(\boldsymbol{\mu}^* - \boldsymbol{\mu}\right) + \boldsymbol{\alpha}^* \boldsymbol{\kappa}_T. \quad (5.12)$$

Since $\mathsf{E}[\boldsymbol{\kappa}_T] = \mathbf{0}$ and $\mathsf{E}[\Delta \mathbf{x}_T] = \boldsymbol{\gamma}$, the two forecasting procedures deliver identical unconditional biases for forecasting from T to $T+1$ when an unknown break occurs at T after the forecast is made:

$$\mathsf{E}\left[\widetilde{\mathbf{e}}_{T+1|T}\right] = \mathsf{E}\left[\overline{\mathbf{e}}_{T+1|T}\right] = \left(\boldsymbol{\gamma}^* - \boldsymbol{\gamma}\right) - \boldsymbol{\alpha}^* \left(\boldsymbol{\mu}^* - \boldsymbol{\mu}\right).$$

Moreover, this is the same formula as for the VEqCM in §3.5. Thus, despite the VEqCM including, and the DV and DDV excluding, the in-sample equilibrium mean, they suffer identically from a shift in $\boldsymbol{\mu}$ after forecasting. Similarly, the DV and DDV suffer the same from growth-rate changes despite the latter excluding $\boldsymbol{\gamma}$. The conditional biases only differ to the extent that $\boldsymbol{\beta}' \mathbf{x}_T \neq \boldsymbol{\mu}$ and $\Delta \mathbf{x}_T \neq \boldsymbol{\gamma}$, noting that $\Delta \mathbf{x}_T = \boldsymbol{\gamma} + \boldsymbol{\alpha} \boldsymbol{\kappa}_{T-1} + \boldsymbol{\nu}_T$. When no break occurs, the corresponding result for the VEqCM, equation (3.18) above, is zero, whereas both (5.11) and (5.12) remain non-zero. Thus, here the VEqCM will always dominate in a constant-parameter environment, as then it coincides with the DGP.

5.3.2 *Forecasting levels from $T+1$ to $T+2$*

Having reached time $T+1$, with data at $T+1$ assumed available, the outcomes are remarkably different: the various predictors now deliver distinct outcomes. As the unconditional expectations of the levels are altering along the adjustment path, they must be time dated due to the non-stationarity induced by the breaks. First, and assuming that no additional changes occur at time $T+1$, the DGP produces:

$$\Delta \mathbf{x}_{T+2} = \boldsymbol{\gamma}^* + \boldsymbol{\alpha}^* \left(\boldsymbol{\beta}' \mathbf{x}_{T+1} - \boldsymbol{\mu}^*\right) + \boldsymbol{\nu}_{T+2} \tag{5.13}$$

and as:

$$\mathbf{x}_{T+1} = \mathbf{x}_T + \boldsymbol{\gamma}^* + \boldsymbol{\alpha}^* \left(\boldsymbol{\beta}' \mathbf{x}_T - \boldsymbol{\mu}^*\right) + \boldsymbol{\nu}_{T+1},$$

then:

$$\boldsymbol{\beta}' \mathbf{x}_{T+1} - \boldsymbol{\mu}^* = \boldsymbol{\Lambda}^* \left(\boldsymbol{\beta}' \mathbf{x}_T - \boldsymbol{\mu}^*\right) + \boldsymbol{\beta}' \boldsymbol{\nu}_{T+1}, \tag{5.14}$$

where $\boldsymbol{\Lambda}^* = \left(\mathbf{I}_r + \boldsymbol{\beta}'\boldsymbol{\alpha}^*\right)$ has all its eigenvalues inside the unit circle. Let $\boldsymbol{\Upsilon}^* = \left(\mathbf{I}_n + \boldsymbol{\alpha}^*\boldsymbol{\beta}'\right)$, and note that $\boldsymbol{\alpha}^*\boldsymbol{\Lambda}^* = \boldsymbol{\Upsilon}^*\boldsymbol{\alpha}^*$. To avoid dependence of the new growth rate on the changed parameters, we maintain $\boldsymbol{\beta}'\boldsymbol{\gamma}^* = \mathbf{0}$ and set $\boldsymbol{\beta}'\mathbf{x}_{T+1} - \boldsymbol{\mu}^* = \boldsymbol{\kappa}^*_{T+1}$ using:

$$\mathsf{E}\left[\Delta \mathbf{x}_{T+2}\right] = \boldsymbol{\gamma}^* - \boldsymbol{\alpha}^* \left(\boldsymbol{\Lambda}^*\right) \left(\boldsymbol{\mu}^* - \boldsymbol{\mu}\right).$$

The conditional biases of the two 1-step forecast errors are therefore:

$$\mathsf{E}\left[\widetilde{\mathbf{e}}_{T+2|T+1} \mid I_{T+1}\right] = \left(\boldsymbol{\gamma}^* - \boldsymbol{\gamma}\right) + \boldsymbol{\alpha}^* \boldsymbol{\kappa}^*_{T+1} \tag{5.15}$$

and:

$$\mathsf{E}\left[\overline{\mathbf{e}}_{T+2|T+1} \mid I_{T+1}\right] = \left(\boldsymbol{\gamma}^* - \Delta \mathbf{x}_{T+1}\right) + \boldsymbol{\alpha}^* \boldsymbol{\kappa}^*_{T+1}. \tag{5.16}$$

Consequently, these show considerable "error-correction" behavior at this post-break 1-step ahead horizon, completely removing the effect of $\mathsf{E}\left[\overline{\mathbf{e}}_{T+1|T}\right]$. In particular, when $\boldsymbol{\alpha}^* = \boldsymbol{\alpha}$, so only deterministic terms change, then:

$$\mathsf{E}\left[\widetilde{\mathbf{e}}_{T+2|T+1} \mid I_{T+1}\right] \quad = \quad \left(\boldsymbol{\gamma}^* - \boldsymbol{\gamma}\right) + \boldsymbol{\alpha} \boldsymbol{\kappa}^*_{T+1}$$

$$\mathsf{E}\left[\overline{\mathbf{e}}_{T+2|T+1} \mid I_{T+1}\right] = (\gamma^* - \Delta \mathbf{x}_{T+1}) + \boldsymbol{\alpha}\boldsymbol{\kappa}^*_{T+1}. \tag{5.17}$$

Relative to (3.22) for the VEqCM, the direct impact of $-\boldsymbol{\alpha}(\boldsymbol{\mu}^* - \boldsymbol{\mu})$ has been removed from (5.15) and (5.16), and the effect of $\boldsymbol{\kappa}^*_{T+1}$ differs depending on the relative size of $(\boldsymbol{\alpha}^* - \boldsymbol{\alpha})$ compared to $\boldsymbol{\alpha}^*$.

These expressions highlight the effects of first and second differencing relative to the VEqCM, since $\boldsymbol{\kappa}^*_{T+1}$ on average is "smaller than" $(\boldsymbol{\mu}^* - \boldsymbol{\mu})$ and so induces less bias. From (5.14):

$$\mathsf{E}\left[\boldsymbol{\kappa}^*_{T+1}\right] = -\boldsymbol{\Lambda}^* (\boldsymbol{\mu}^* - \boldsymbol{\mu}),$$

and as $\mathsf{E}[\Delta \mathbf{x}_{T+1}] = \gamma^* - \boldsymbol{\alpha}^* (\boldsymbol{\mu}^* - \boldsymbol{\mu})$, letting $\boldsymbol{\delta}_\mu = (\boldsymbol{\mu}^* - \boldsymbol{\mu})$, $\boldsymbol{\delta}_\gamma = (\gamma^* - \gamma)$, the unconditional forecast-error biases are:

$$\begin{aligned}
\mathsf{E}\left[\widehat{\mathbf{e}}_{T+2|T+1}\right] &= \boldsymbol{\delta}_\gamma - (\boldsymbol{\alpha} + (\boldsymbol{\alpha}^* - \boldsymbol{\alpha})\boldsymbol{\Lambda}^*)\boldsymbol{\delta}_\mu \\
\mathsf{E}\left[\widetilde{\mathbf{e}}_{T+2|T+1}\right] &= \boldsymbol{\delta}_\gamma - \boldsymbol{\alpha}^*\boldsymbol{\Lambda}^*\boldsymbol{\delta}_\mu \\
\mathsf{E}\left[\overline{\mathbf{e}}_{T+2|T+1}\right] &= -\boldsymbol{\alpha}^* (\boldsymbol{\beta}'\boldsymbol{\alpha}^*)\boldsymbol{\delta}_\mu.
\end{aligned} \tag{5.18}$$

Second differencing completely removes the impact of the changing growth rate, and as $\boldsymbol{\beta}'\boldsymbol{\alpha}^*$ corresponds to the roots inside the unit circle, it also dampens the effect of shifts in the equilibrium mean. The DV has not avoided the impact of changes in growth, but does attenuate the effect of shifts in $\boldsymbol{\mu}$. When the DGP is a VEqCM the DV arises by dropping equilibrium-correction terms, and not by first differencing all the terms in the equation. Even if $\boldsymbol{\alpha}$ does not change, the VEqCM is more biased than the DV.

5.3.3 *Forecasting levels from T to $T + 2$*

This comprises 2-steps ahead forecasts made prior to the break using (5.8), and (5.9), to illustrate how the results change for multi-step forecasts. Now the corresponding 2-step ahead unconditional forecast-error biases are the same, using $\breve{\mathbf{e}} = \widetilde{\mathbf{e}}$, and $\overline{\mathbf{e}}$:

$$\mathsf{E}\left[\breve{\mathbf{e}}_{T+2|T}\right] = 2(\gamma^* - \gamma) - \boldsymbol{\alpha}^* (\mathbf{I}_r + \boldsymbol{\Lambda}^*)(\boldsymbol{\mu}^* - \boldsymbol{\mu}). \tag{5.19}$$

The conditional forecast-error biases are:

$$\mathsf{E}\left[\widetilde{\mathbf{e}}_{T+2|T} \mid I_T\right] = \mathsf{E}\left[\widetilde{\mathbf{e}}_{T+2|T}\right] + \boldsymbol{\alpha}^* (\mathbf{I}_r + \boldsymbol{\Lambda}^*)\boldsymbol{\kappa}_T \tag{5.20}$$

and:

$$\mathsf{E}\left[\overline{\mathbf{e}}_{T+2|T} \mid I_T\right] = \mathsf{E}\left[\overline{\mathbf{e}}_{T+2|T}\right] + \boldsymbol{\alpha}^* \left(\mathbf{I}_r + \boldsymbol{\Lambda}^*\right) \boldsymbol{\kappa}_T - 2\boldsymbol{\alpha}\boldsymbol{\kappa}_{T-1}. \tag{5.21}$$

Thus, the unconditional biases suffer from the same impact after a change in the equilibrium mean or the growth rate, and again coincide with that from the VEqCM. If $\boldsymbol{\alpha}$ is constant (so $\boldsymbol{\Lambda}^* = \boldsymbol{\Lambda}$ also), (3.24) from earlier simplifies to $\mathsf{E}\left[\widehat{\mathbf{e}}_{T+2|T}\right]$ which appears to favor VEqCM over DV and DDV when the economy is in considerable disequilibrium. Otherwise, the conditional biases deviate from the unconditional by amounts that depend on past disequilibria.

5.3.4 *Forecasting levels from $T+1$ to $T+3$*

As earlier, the forecasting rules are just time-index shifted versions of (5.8) and (5.9), allowing for the expectations changing. Thus, for the DV, $\mathsf{E}[\widetilde{\mathbf{e}}_{T+3|T+1} \mid I_{T+1}]$ is given by

$$\begin{aligned} & 2\left(\boldsymbol{\gamma}^* - \boldsymbol{\gamma}\right) + \boldsymbol{\alpha}^* \left(\mathbf{I}_r + \boldsymbol{\Lambda}^*\right) \boldsymbol{\kappa}^*_{T+1} \\ = \quad & \mathsf{E}\left[\widetilde{\mathbf{e}}_{T+3|T+1}\right] + \boldsymbol{\alpha}^* \left(\mathbf{I}_r + \boldsymbol{\Lambda}^*\right) \left(\boldsymbol{\kappa}^*_{T+1} - \mathsf{E}\left[\boldsymbol{\kappa}^*_{T+1}\right]\right), \end{aligned}$$

where:

$$\mathsf{E}\left[\widetilde{\mathbf{e}}_{T+3|T+1}\right] = 2\left(\boldsymbol{\gamma}^* - \boldsymbol{\gamma}\right) - \boldsymbol{\alpha}^* \boldsymbol{\Lambda}^* \left(\mathbf{I}_r + \boldsymbol{\Lambda}^*\right) \left(\boldsymbol{\mu}^* - \boldsymbol{\mu}\right).$$

If $\boldsymbol{\alpha}$ is constant:

$$\mathsf{E}\left[\widetilde{\mathbf{e}}_{T+3|T+1} \mid I_{T+1}\right] = 2\left(\boldsymbol{\gamma}^* - \boldsymbol{\gamma}\right) + \boldsymbol{\alpha}\left(\mathbf{I}_r + \boldsymbol{\Lambda}\right) \boldsymbol{\kappa}^*_{T+1}. \tag{5.22}$$

This differs from the VEqCM bias, but is "smaller" on average, as:

$$\mathsf{E}\left[\boldsymbol{\kappa}^*_{T+1}\right] = -\boldsymbol{\Lambda}^* \left(\boldsymbol{\mu}^* - \boldsymbol{\mu}\right).$$

The DDV unconditional forecast-error bias is:

$$\mathsf{E}\left[\overline{\mathbf{e}}_{T+3|T+1}\right] = -\boldsymbol{\alpha}^* \left(2\mathbf{I}_r + \boldsymbol{\Lambda}^*\right) \boldsymbol{\beta}' \boldsymbol{\alpha}^* \left(\boldsymbol{\mu}^* - \boldsymbol{\mu}\right),$$

and $\mathsf{E}[\overline{\mathbf{e}}_{T+3|T+1} | I_{T+1}]$ becomes:

$$\begin{aligned} & 2\left(\boldsymbol{\gamma}^* - \Delta\mathbf{x}_{T+1}\right) + \boldsymbol{\alpha}^* \left(\mathbf{I}_r + \boldsymbol{\Lambda}^*\right) \boldsymbol{\kappa}^*_{T+1} \\ = \quad & 2\boldsymbol{\alpha}^* \left(\boldsymbol{\mu}^* - \boldsymbol{\mu}\right) + 2\left(\mathsf{E}\left[\Delta\mathbf{x}_{T+1}\right] - \Delta\mathbf{x}_{T+1}\right) + \boldsymbol{\alpha}^* \left(\mathbf{I}_r + \boldsymbol{\Lambda}^*\right) \boldsymbol{\kappa}^*_{T+1} \\ = \quad & \mathsf{E}\left[\mathbf{e}_{T+3|T+1}\right] + 2\left(\mathsf{E}\left[\Delta\mathbf{x}_{T+1}\right] - \Delta\mathbf{x}_{T+1}\right) \\ & + \boldsymbol{\alpha}^* \left(\mathbf{I}_r + \boldsymbol{\Lambda}^*\right) \left(\boldsymbol{\kappa}^*_{T+1} - \mathsf{E}\left[\boldsymbol{\kappa}^*_{T+1}\right]\right), \end{aligned}$$

Table 5.1
Unconditional biases at 1 & 2-steps, pre & post break.

	VEqCM	DV	DDV	VEqCM	DV	DDV
	Forecasting before break			Forecasting after break		
1-step forecasts						
$\boldsymbol{\mu}$	$-\boldsymbol{\alpha}\boldsymbol{\delta}_{\mu}$	$-\boldsymbol{\alpha}\boldsymbol{\delta}_{\mu}$	$-\boldsymbol{\alpha}\boldsymbol{\delta}_{\mu}$	$-\boldsymbol{\alpha}\boldsymbol{\delta}_{\mu}$	$-\boldsymbol{\alpha}\boldsymbol{\Lambda}\boldsymbol{\delta}_{\mu}$	$-\boldsymbol{\alpha}\boldsymbol{\beta}'\boldsymbol{\alpha}\boldsymbol{\delta}_{\mu}$
$\boldsymbol{\gamma}$	$\boldsymbol{\delta}_{\gamma}$	$\boldsymbol{\delta}_{\gamma}$	$\boldsymbol{\delta}_{\gamma}$	$\boldsymbol{\delta}_{\gamma}$	$\boldsymbol{\delta}_{\gamma}$	$\mathbf{0}$
$\boldsymbol{\alpha}$	$\mathbf{0}$	$\mathbf{0}$	$\mathbf{0}$	$\mathbf{0}$	$\mathbf{0}$	$\mathbf{0}$
2-step forecasts						
$\boldsymbol{\mu}$	$-\boldsymbol{\alpha}\mathbf{R}\boldsymbol{\delta}_{\mu}$	$-\boldsymbol{\alpha}\mathbf{R}\boldsymbol{\delta}_{\mu}$	$-\boldsymbol{\alpha}\mathbf{R}\boldsymbol{\delta}_{\mu}$	$-\boldsymbol{\alpha}\mathbf{R}\boldsymbol{\delta}_{\mu}$	$-\boldsymbol{\alpha}\boldsymbol{\Lambda}\mathbf{R}\boldsymbol{\delta}_{\mu}$	$-\boldsymbol{\alpha}\left(\mathbf{I}_r+\mathbf{R}\right)\boldsymbol{\beta}'\boldsymbol{\alpha}\boldsymbol{\delta}_{\mu}$
$\boldsymbol{\gamma}$	$2\boldsymbol{\delta}_{\gamma}$	$2\boldsymbol{\delta}_{\gamma}$	$2\boldsymbol{\delta}_{\gamma}$	$2\boldsymbol{\delta}_{\gamma}$	$2\boldsymbol{\delta}_{\gamma}$	$\mathbf{0}$
$\boldsymbol{\alpha}$	$\mathbf{0}$	$\mathbf{0}$	$\mathbf{0}$	$\mathbf{0}$	$\mathbf{0}$	$\mathbf{0}$

noting $\boldsymbol{\kappa}^*_{T+1}$ is "smaller" than $(\boldsymbol{\mu}^* - \boldsymbol{\mu})$ on average. Consequently, if $\boldsymbol{\alpha}$ is constant:

$$\mathsf{E}\left[\overline{\mathbf{e}}_{T+3|T+1}\right] = -\boldsymbol{\alpha}\left(2\mathbf{I}_r + \boldsymbol{\Lambda}\right)\boldsymbol{\beta}'\boldsymbol{\alpha}\left(\boldsymbol{\mu}^* - \boldsymbol{\mu}\right). \tag{5.23}$$

Hence the DDV avoids breaks in $\boldsymbol{\gamma}$, and differs in its reaction to changes in $\boldsymbol{\mu}$.

5.4 Comparing Unconditional Forecast-error Biases

To aid inter-method comparisons, the unconditional bias calculations for the VEqCM, DV and DDV are summarized in table 5.1, where $\mathbf{R} = \mathbf{I}_r + \boldsymbol{\Lambda}$. The outcomes are shown separately for each of the main break terms, for forecasts made both before a break occurs (first 3 columns) and after (last 3).

The DV, and particularly the DDV model, are "non-causal" in comparison to the "causal" VEqCM, and serve as an illustration of the proposition that non-causal information can dominate causal on some forecast-accuracy measures (here, bias). All the methods fare equally badly when forecasting before a break across a period when a break occurs. In the setting of structural shifts in deterministic terms that have occurred before a forecast is made, but the break is not modeled by the forecaster, the VEqCM invariably does worst or equal worst: clearly, such breaks are pernicious for a specification that embodies the wrong equilibrium mean or growth rate, and nevertheless continues to correct towards that. Dropping the EqCMs is beneficial, so that the DV has smaller biases than the VEqCM for shifts in $\boldsymbol{\mu}$ that have already occurred. The DDV shows distinctly smaller biases in several situations. We conclude that differencing does help alleviate the impact of deterministic shifts on forecast biases. However, there are forecast-error variance costs attached to such a strategy, and we now consider these.

5.5 Variance Effects after Structural Breaks

Forecast-error biases must be evaluated against the additional forecast-error variances that the non-congruent models introduce, and this section analyzes these. The formulae take account of the information that is averaged over when unconditional biases are computed, as in table 5.1: such terms appear here as variance effects (e.g., the difference between $\boldsymbol{\beta}'\mathbf{x}_T$ and $\boldsymbol{\mu}$). The unconditional forecast-error variance formulae derived in this section foreshadow the findings of the empirical forecast-accuracy comparison in §8.8. The variances and biases recorded there are unconditional in that they are formed by averaging over sixteen 1-step or thirteen 4-step ahead forecasts. Formulae for the h-step ahead asymptotic variances of VEqCM and DV in levels, differences and I(0) transformations, when there are no breaks, are provided in Clements and Hendry (1995a); here we focus on the results for levels.

5.5.1 *Variances of levels from T to $T+1$*

When the parameters are known, the 1-step forecast errors of the two models can be written as:

$$\widetilde{\mathbf{e}}_{T+1|T} - \mathsf{E}\left[\widetilde{\mathbf{e}}_{T+1|T}\right] = \boldsymbol{\alpha}^*\left(\boldsymbol{\beta}'\mathbf{x}_T - \boldsymbol{\mu}\right) + \boldsymbol{\nu}_{T+1}, \tag{5.24}$$

and :

$$\overline{\mathbf{e}}_{T+1|T} - \mathsf{E}\left[\overline{\mathbf{e}}_{T+1|T}\right] = \boldsymbol{\alpha}^*\left(\boldsymbol{\beta}'\mathbf{x}_T - \boldsymbol{\mu}\right) + \boldsymbol{\nu}_{T+1} - \left(\Delta\mathbf{x}_T - \boldsymbol{\gamma}\right). \tag{5.25}$$

Conditionally, these have the same variance components:

$$\mathsf{V}\left[\widetilde{\mathbf{e}}_{T+1|T} \mid \mathcal{I}_T\right] = \mathsf{V}\left[\overline{\mathbf{e}}_{T+1|T} \mid \mathcal{I}_T\right]$$

Given earlier analyses, and to help interpret the empirical forecast-error variances, we record the unconditional variances:

$$\mathsf{V}\left[\widetilde{\mathbf{e}}_{T+1|T}\right] = \boldsymbol{\Omega}_{\nu} + \boldsymbol{\alpha}^*\mathbf{V}\boldsymbol{\alpha}^{*\prime}, \tag{5.26}$$

where $\mathbf{V}$ (the variance matrix of the cointegration relations) is defined in (3.34); and:

$$\begin{aligned}\mathsf{V}\left[\overline{\mathbf{e}}_{T+1|T}\right] &= \left(\boldsymbol{\alpha}^{*}\boldsymbol{\Lambda}-\boldsymbol{\alpha}\right)\mathbf{V}\left(\boldsymbol{\alpha}^{*}\boldsymbol{\Lambda}-\boldsymbol{\alpha}\right)'+\boldsymbol{\Omega}_{\nu} \\ &\quad+\left(\mathbf{I}_{n}-\boldsymbol{\alpha}^{*}\boldsymbol{\beta}'\right)\boldsymbol{\Omega}_{\nu}\left(\mathbf{I}_{n}-\boldsymbol{\alpha}^{*}\boldsymbol{\beta}'\right)'. \end{aligned} \tag{5.27}$$

In the special case that $\boldsymbol{\alpha}^{*}=\boldsymbol{\alpha}$:

$$\mathsf{V}\left[\overline{\mathbf{e}}_{T+1|T}\right]=\boldsymbol{\alpha}\left(\boldsymbol{\beta}'\boldsymbol{\alpha}\right)\mathbf{V}\left(\boldsymbol{\alpha}'\boldsymbol{\beta}\right)\boldsymbol{\alpha}'+\boldsymbol{\Omega}_{\nu}+\left(\mathbf{I}_{n}-\boldsymbol{\alpha}\boldsymbol{\beta}'\right)\boldsymbol{\Omega}_{\nu}\left(\mathbf{I}_{n}-\boldsymbol{\alpha}\boldsymbol{\beta}'\right)'.$$

There are clear, and well known, variance costs to differencing or double differencing which need to be offset against the benefits of robustness to deterministic shifts. Even if $\boldsymbol{\alpha}$ does not change, (5.27) will generally not be less than (5.26), and will be more than double (3.55) in general. Thus, when there are no structural breaks, the three methods have the opposite variance ranking to their robustness, namely VEqCM is best, DV next and DDV third, as anticipated.

5.5.2 *Variances of levels from $T+1$ to $T+2$*

At time $T+1$:

$$\mathsf{V}\left[\widetilde{\mathbf{e}}_{T+2|T+1}\right]=\boldsymbol{\alpha}^{*}\mathbf{V}^{*}\boldsymbol{\alpha}^{*\prime}+\boldsymbol{\Omega}_{\nu}, \tag{5.28}$$

which coincides with (5.26), and the Clements and Hendry (1995a) result when $\boldsymbol{\alpha}$ remains constant. Finally:

$$\mathsf{V}\left[\overline{\mathbf{e}}_{T+2|T+1}\right]=\boldsymbol{\alpha}^{*}\left(\boldsymbol{\beta}'\boldsymbol{\alpha}^{*}\right)\mathbf{V}\left(\boldsymbol{\alpha}^{*\prime}\boldsymbol{\beta}\right)\boldsymbol{\alpha}^{*\prime}+\boldsymbol{\Omega}_{\nu}+\mathbf{B}^{*}\boldsymbol{\Omega}_{\nu}\mathbf{B}^{*\prime} \tag{5.29}$$

where $\mathbf{B}^{*}=\mathbf{I}_{n}-\boldsymbol{\alpha}^{*}\boldsymbol{\beta}'$, which is generally less than the double of (5.28) that might have been anticipated from the extra differencing. Even when no parameters change, (5.29) remains:

$$\mathsf{V}\left[\overline{\mathbf{e}}_{T+2|T+1}\right]=\boldsymbol{\alpha}\left(\boldsymbol{\beta}'\boldsymbol{\alpha}\right)\mathbf{V}\left(\boldsymbol{\alpha}'\boldsymbol{\beta}\right)\boldsymbol{\alpha}'+\boldsymbol{\Omega}_{\nu}+\mathbf{B}\boldsymbol{\Omega}\mathbf{B}' \tag{5.30}$$

so no useful simplifications result.

5.5.3 *Variances of levels from T to $T+2$*

This comprises 2-steps ahead forecasts made prior to the break, again to illustrate how the results change for multi-step forecasts:

$$\widetilde{\mathbf{e}}_{T+2|T}-\mathsf{E}\left[\widetilde{\mathbf{e}}_{T+2|T}\right]=\boldsymbol{\alpha}^{*}\left(\mathbf{I}_{r}+\boldsymbol{\Lambda}^{*}\right)\left(\boldsymbol{\beta}'\mathbf{x}_{T}-\boldsymbol{\mu}\right)+\boldsymbol{\Upsilon}^{*}\boldsymbol{\nu}_{T+1}+\boldsymbol{\nu}_{T+2},$$

so:

$$\mathsf{V}\left[\widetilde{\mathbf{e}}_{T+2|T}\right] = \boldsymbol{\alpha}^*\left(\mathbf{I}_r + \boldsymbol{\Lambda}^*\right)\mathbf{V}\left(\mathbf{I}_r + \boldsymbol{\Lambda}^{*\prime}\right)\boldsymbol{\alpha}^{*\prime} + \boldsymbol{\Upsilon}^*\boldsymbol{\Omega}_\nu\boldsymbol{\Upsilon}^{*\prime} + \boldsymbol{\Omega}_\nu. \tag{5.31}$$

For the DDV, $\overline{\mathbf{e}}_{T+2|T} - \mathsf{E}[\overline{\mathbf{e}}_{T+2|T}]$ is given by:

$$\begin{aligned}
&\boldsymbol{\alpha}^*\left(\mathbf{I}_r + \boldsymbol{\Lambda}^*\right)\left(\boldsymbol{\beta}'\mathbf{x}_T - \boldsymbol{\mu}\right) + \boldsymbol{\Upsilon}^*\boldsymbol{\nu}_{T+1} + \boldsymbol{\nu}_{T+2} - 2\left(\Delta\mathbf{x}_T - \boldsymbol{\gamma}\right) \\
&\quad = \left[\boldsymbol{\alpha}^*\left(\mathbf{I}_r + \boldsymbol{\Lambda}^*\right)\boldsymbol{\Lambda} - 2\boldsymbol{\alpha}\right]\left(\boldsymbol{\beta}'\mathbf{x}_{T-1} - \boldsymbol{\mu}\right) \\
&\qquad + \boldsymbol{\Upsilon}^*\boldsymbol{\nu}_{T+1} + \boldsymbol{\nu}_{T+2} + \left[\boldsymbol{\alpha}^*\left(\mathbf{I}_r + \boldsymbol{\Lambda}^*\right)\boldsymbol{\beta}' - 2\mathbf{I}_n\right]\boldsymbol{\nu}_T.
\end{aligned}$$

Letting $\left(\boldsymbol{\alpha}^*\left(\mathbf{I}_r + \boldsymbol{\Lambda}^*\right)\boldsymbol{\Lambda} - 2\boldsymbol{\alpha}\right) = \mathbf{F}^*$ and $\left(\boldsymbol{\alpha}^*\left(\mathbf{I}_r + \boldsymbol{\Lambda}^*\right)\boldsymbol{\beta}' - 2\mathbf{I}_n\right) = \mathbf{G}^*$:

$$\mathsf{V}\left[\overline{\mathbf{e}}_{T+2|T}\right] = \mathbf{F}^*\mathbf{V}\mathbf{F}^{*\prime} + \boldsymbol{\Upsilon}^*\boldsymbol{\Omega}_\nu\boldsymbol{\Upsilon}^{*\prime} + \boldsymbol{\Omega}_\nu + \mathbf{G}^*\boldsymbol{\Omega}_\nu\mathbf{G}^{*\prime}. \tag{5.32}$$

Even when $\boldsymbol{\alpha}$ is constant, so:

$$\mathbf{F}^* = \boldsymbol{\alpha}\left[\left(\mathbf{I}_r + \boldsymbol{\Lambda}\right)\boldsymbol{\Lambda} - 2\mathbf{I}_r\right] \quad \mathbf{G}^* = \left[\boldsymbol{\alpha}\left(\mathbf{I}_r + \boldsymbol{\Lambda}\right)\boldsymbol{\beta}' - 2\mathbf{I}_n\right],$$

no simplification is obtained. However, if $\boldsymbol{\alpha} = \mathbf{0}$, we have:

$$\mathsf{V}\left[\overline{\mathbf{e}}_{T+2|T}\right] = 6\boldsymbol{\Omega}_\nu, \tag{5.33}$$

revealing that a large increase in error variance results as the horizon grows. Over longer horizons, the rate of increase suggested by comparing (5.27) and (5.33) (approximately threefold) would restrict DDV to being useful at short horizons.

5.5.4 *Variances of levels from $T+1$ to $T+3$*

Again the forecast rules are shifted forward one period:

$$\widetilde{\mathbf{x}}_{T+3} = \mathbf{x}_{T+1} + 2\boldsymbol{\gamma}, \tag{5.34}$$

and:

$$\overline{\mathbf{x}}_{T+3} = \mathbf{x}_{T+1} + 2\Delta\mathbf{x}_{T+1}. \tag{5.35}$$

Then:

$$\begin{aligned}
\widetilde{\mathbf{e}}_{T+3|T+1} - \mathsf{E}\left[\widetilde{\mathbf{e}}_{T+3|T+1}\right] &= \boldsymbol{\alpha}^*\left(\mathbf{I}_r + \boldsymbol{\Lambda}^*\right)\left(\boldsymbol{\kappa}^*_{T+1} - \mathsf{E}\left[\boldsymbol{\kappa}^*_{T+1}\right]\right) \\
&\quad + \boldsymbol{\Upsilon}^*\boldsymbol{\nu}_{T+2} + \boldsymbol{\nu}_{T+3},
\end{aligned}$$

so that:

$$\mathsf{V}\left[\widetilde{\mathbf{e}}_{T+3|T+1}\right] = \boldsymbol{\alpha}^*\left(\mathbf{I}_r + \boldsymbol{\Lambda}^*\right)\mathbf{V}^*\left(\mathbf{I}_r + \boldsymbol{\Lambda}^{*\prime}\right)\boldsymbol{\alpha}^{*\prime} + \boldsymbol{\Upsilon}^*\boldsymbol{\Omega}_\nu\boldsymbol{\Upsilon}^{*\prime} + \boldsymbol{\Omega}_\nu,$$

Table 5.2
1-step unconditional variances.

$T \to T+1$	VEqCM	DV	DDV
$\boldsymbol{\alpha} = \mathbf{0}$	$\mathbf{0}$	$\mathbf{0}$	$\boldsymbol{\Omega}_\nu$
$\boldsymbol{\alpha} = \boldsymbol{\alpha}^*$	$\mathbf{0}$	$\boldsymbol{\alpha}\mathbf{V}\boldsymbol{\alpha}'$	$\mathbf{B}\boldsymbol{\Omega}_\nu\mathbf{B}' + \mathbf{AVA}'$
$\boldsymbol{\alpha} \neq \boldsymbol{\alpha}^*$	$\boldsymbol{\delta}_\alpha\mathbf{V}\boldsymbol{\delta}_\alpha'$	$\boldsymbol{\alpha}^*\mathbf{V}\boldsymbol{\alpha}^{*\prime}$	$\mathbf{B}^*\boldsymbol{\Omega}_\nu\mathbf{B}^{*\prime} + \mathbf{A}^*\mathbf{V}\mathbf{A}^{*\prime}$
$T+1 \to T+2$	VEqCM	DV	DDV
$\boldsymbol{\alpha} = \mathbf{0}$	$\mathbf{0}$	$\mathbf{0}$	$\boldsymbol{\Omega}_\nu$
$\boldsymbol{\alpha} = \boldsymbol{\alpha}^*$	$\mathbf{0}$	$\boldsymbol{\alpha}\mathbf{V}\boldsymbol{\alpha}'$	$\mathbf{B}\boldsymbol{\Omega}_\nu\mathbf{B}' + \mathbf{AVA}'$
$\boldsymbol{\alpha} \neq \boldsymbol{\alpha}^*$	$\boldsymbol{\delta}_\alpha\mathbf{V}^*\boldsymbol{\delta}_\alpha'$	$\boldsymbol{\alpha}^*\mathbf{V}^*\boldsymbol{\alpha}^{*\prime}$	$\mathbf{B}^*\boldsymbol{\Omega}_\nu\mathbf{B}^{*\prime} + \boldsymbol{\alpha}^*\boldsymbol{\beta}'\boldsymbol{\alpha}^*\mathbf{V}\boldsymbol{\alpha}^{*\prime}\boldsymbol{\beta}\boldsymbol{\alpha}^{*\prime}$

Here and in the text $\boldsymbol{\alpha} = \mathbf{0}$ implicitly implies $\boldsymbol{\alpha}^* = \mathbf{0}$.

matching (5.31). Finally $\overline{\mathbf{e}}_{T+3|T+1} - \mathsf{E}\left[\overline{\mathbf{e}}_{T+3|T+1}\right]$ equals:

$$\begin{aligned}
&\boldsymbol{\alpha}^*\left(\mathbf{I}_r + \boldsymbol{\Lambda}^*\right)\left(\boldsymbol{\kappa}^*_{T+1} - \mathsf{E}\left[\boldsymbol{\kappa}^*_{T+1}\right]\right) + \boldsymbol{\Upsilon}^*\boldsymbol{\nu}_{T+2} + \boldsymbol{\nu}_{T+3} \\
&\qquad -2\left(\Delta\mathbf{x}_{T+1} - \mathsf{E}\left[\Delta\mathbf{x}_{T+1}\right]\right) \\
&= \boldsymbol{\alpha}^*\left(\left(\mathbf{I}_r + \boldsymbol{\Lambda}^*\right)\boldsymbol{\Lambda}^* - 2\mathbf{I}_r\right)\boldsymbol{\kappa}_T \\
&\qquad + \boldsymbol{\Upsilon}^*\boldsymbol{\nu}_{T+2} + \boldsymbol{\nu}_{T+3} + \left(\boldsymbol{\alpha}^*\left(\mathbf{I}_r + \boldsymbol{\Lambda}^*\right)\boldsymbol{\beta}' - 2\mathbf{I}_n\right)\boldsymbol{\nu}_{T+1} \\
&= \mathbf{F}^{**}\boldsymbol{\kappa}_T + \boldsymbol{\Upsilon}^*\boldsymbol{\nu}_{T+2} + \boldsymbol{\nu}_{T+3} + \mathbf{G}^*\boldsymbol{\nu}_{T+1}
\end{aligned}$$

where $\boldsymbol{\alpha}^*\left(\left(\mathbf{I}_r + \boldsymbol{\Lambda}^*\right)\boldsymbol{\Lambda}^* - 2\mathbf{I}_r\right) = \mathbf{F}^{**}$ and $\mathbf{G}^*$ is as in (5.32), so that:

$$\mathsf{V}\left[\overline{\mathbf{e}}_{T+3|T+1}\right] = \mathbf{F}^{**}\mathbf{V}\mathbf{F}^{**\prime} + \boldsymbol{\Upsilon}^*\boldsymbol{\Omega}_\nu\boldsymbol{\Upsilon}^{*\prime} + \boldsymbol{\Omega}_\nu + \mathbf{G}^*\boldsymbol{\Omega}_\nu\mathbf{G}^{*\prime}. \tag{5.36}$$

These have become rather complicated expressions, so to review their implications, the next section evaluates them in some special cases.

5.6 Comparing Unconditional Forecast-error Variances

Table 5.2 shows the excess in the 1-step variances over $\boldsymbol{\Omega}_\nu$, for various values of $\boldsymbol{\alpha}$, the parameter change that most affects the variances, where $\boldsymbol{\delta}_\alpha = \boldsymbol{\alpha}^* - \boldsymbol{\alpha}$, $\mathbf{A}^* = \boldsymbol{\alpha}^*\boldsymbol{\Lambda} - \boldsymbol{\alpha}$ and $\mathbf{B}^* = \mathbf{I}_n - \boldsymbol{\alpha}^*\boldsymbol{\beta}'$.

The unstarred matrices replace any starred parameter with its unstarred value: thus, $\mathbf{A} = \boldsymbol{\alpha}\boldsymbol{\Lambda} - \boldsymbol{\alpha} = \boldsymbol{\alpha}\left(\boldsymbol{\beta}'\boldsymbol{\alpha}\right)$. The pattern is clear, and the only exception is the DDV when $\boldsymbol{\alpha} \neq \boldsymbol{\alpha}^*$, although the fact that $\mathbf{V}^* = \boldsymbol{\Lambda}^*\mathbf{V}\boldsymbol{\Lambda}^{*\prime} + \boldsymbol{\beta}'\boldsymbol{\Omega}_\nu\boldsymbol{\beta}$ allows considerable rearrangement without altering the substance.

Table 5.3
2-step unconditional variances.

$T \to T+2$	VEqCM	DV	DDV
$\boldsymbol{\alpha} = \mathbf{0}$	$\boldsymbol{\Omega}_{\nu}$	$\boldsymbol{\Omega}_{\nu}$	$5\boldsymbol{\Omega}_{\nu}$
$\boldsymbol{\alpha} = \boldsymbol{\alpha}^*$	$\boldsymbol{\Upsilon\Omega}_{\nu}\boldsymbol{\Upsilon}'$	$\boldsymbol{\Upsilon\Omega}_{\nu}\boldsymbol{\Upsilon}' + \mathbf{CVC}'$	$\mathbf{H}_{\alpha}$
$\boldsymbol{\alpha} \neq \boldsymbol{\alpha}^*$	$\boldsymbol{\Upsilon}^*\boldsymbol{\Omega}_{\nu}\boldsymbol{\Upsilon}^{*\prime} + \mathbf{D}^*\mathbf{V}\mathbf{D}^{*\prime}$	$\boldsymbol{\Upsilon}^*\boldsymbol{\Omega}_{\nu}\boldsymbol{\Upsilon}^{*\prime} + \mathbf{C}^*\mathbf{V}\mathbf{C}^{*\prime}$	$\mathbf{H}_{\alpha^*}$
$T+1 \to T+3$	VEqCM	DV	DDV
$\boldsymbol{\alpha} = \mathbf{0}$	$\boldsymbol{\Omega}_{\nu}$	$\boldsymbol{\Omega}_{\nu}$	$5\boldsymbol{\Omega}_{\nu}$
$\boldsymbol{\alpha} = \boldsymbol{\alpha}^*$	$\boldsymbol{\Upsilon\Omega}_{\nu}\boldsymbol{\Upsilon}'$	$\boldsymbol{\Upsilon\Omega}_{\nu}\boldsymbol{\Upsilon}' + \mathbf{CVC}'$	$\mathbf{H}_{\alpha}$
$\boldsymbol{\alpha} \neq \boldsymbol{\alpha}^*$	$\boldsymbol{\Upsilon}^*\boldsymbol{\Omega}_{\nu}\boldsymbol{\Upsilon}^{*\prime} + \mathbf{D}^*\mathbf{V}^*\mathbf{D}^{*\prime}$	$\boldsymbol{\Upsilon}^*\boldsymbol{\Omega}_{\nu}\boldsymbol{\Upsilon}^{*\prime} + \mathbf{C}^*\mathbf{V}^*\mathbf{C}^{*\prime}$	$\mathbf{H}_{\alpha^{**}}$

Next, table 5.3 records the excess in the 2-step variances over $\boldsymbol{\Omega}_{\nu}$, where:

$$\mathbf{C}^* = \boldsymbol{\alpha}^* \left(\mathbf{I}_r + \boldsymbol{\Lambda}^*\right), \quad \mathbf{D}^* = \mathbf{C}^* - \mathbf{C}, \quad \mathbf{F}^* = \mathbf{C}^*\boldsymbol{\Lambda} - 2\boldsymbol{\alpha},$$

and $\mathbf{G}^* = \mathbf{C}^*\boldsymbol{\beta}' - 2\mathbf{I}_n$. As before:

$$\mathbf{C} = \boldsymbol{\alpha}\left(\mathbf{I}_r + \boldsymbol{\Lambda}\right), \quad \mathbf{D} = \mathbf{0}, \quad \mathbf{F} = \boldsymbol{\alpha}(\boldsymbol{\beta}'\boldsymbol{\alpha})\left(2\mathbf{I}_r + \boldsymbol{\Lambda}\right),$$

and $\mathbf{G} = \boldsymbol{\alpha\beta}'(2\mathbf{I}_n + \boldsymbol{\alpha\beta}') - 2\mathbf{I}_n$. Also, $\mathbf{F}^{**} = \mathbf{C}^*\boldsymbol{\Lambda}^* - 2\boldsymbol{\alpha}^*$. These matrices again could be given different parameterizations, since (e.g.):

$$\mathbf{D}^* = 2\boldsymbol{\delta}_{\alpha} + \left[\boldsymbol{\alpha}^*(\boldsymbol{\beta}'\boldsymbol{\alpha}^*) - \boldsymbol{\alpha}(\boldsymbol{\beta}'\boldsymbol{\alpha})\right].$$

In the table, we have set:

$$\begin{aligned} \mathbf{H}_{\alpha} &= \boldsymbol{\Upsilon\Omega}_{\nu}\boldsymbol{\Upsilon}' + \mathbf{G}\boldsymbol{\Omega}_{\nu}\mathbf{G}' + \mathbf{FVF}'; \\ \mathbf{H}_{\alpha^*} &= \boldsymbol{\Upsilon}^*\boldsymbol{\Omega}_{\nu}\boldsymbol{\Upsilon}^{*\prime} + \mathbf{G}^*\boldsymbol{\Omega}_{\nu}\mathbf{G}^{*\prime} + \mathbf{F}^*\mathbf{V}\mathbf{F}^{*\prime}; \end{aligned}$$

and:

$$\mathbf{H}_{\alpha^{**}} = \boldsymbol{\Upsilon}^*\boldsymbol{\Omega}_{\nu}\boldsymbol{\Upsilon}^{*\prime} + \mathbf{G}^*\boldsymbol{\Omega}_{\nu}\mathbf{G}^{*\prime} + \mathbf{F}^{**}\mathbf{V}\mathbf{F}^{**\prime}.$$

The pattern is similar to the 1-step outcomes, although the values are larger, and the formulae more complicated: the rapid increase in the DDV variance is especially noticeable for $\boldsymbol{\alpha} = \mathbf{0}$; that component is present in the $\mathbf{H}$ matrices, but is less obvious. This effect probably explains the inability of the DDV to perform well over the 12-period horizon in Eitrheim *et al.* (1997), despite its outperformance in two of the three 4-period evaluations.

5.6.1 *Implications*

When forecasting before a break, all three models (VEqCM, DV and DDV) are susceptible to forecast failure, and there is little to choose between them, although the VEqCM has the smallest variance component when it is correctly specified in-sample. When forecasting after a break, the DDV has the greatest robustness to a deterministic shift, but the largest and most rapidly-increasing forecast-error variances in general. The DV lies between, depending on what deterministic terms change.

Nevertheless, the longer the multi-step evaluation horizon, the less well the DDV, and probably the DV will perform, partly from their variance terms, and partly because most breaks will be after forecasting, a case in which these models offer no gains. Conversely, the shorter the horizon, for a sequence of horizons, the more likely some breaks will precede forecasting, and consequently, DDV and DV may outperform the VEqCM, even when it is correctly-specified in-sample.

This behavior is precisely what was observed by Eitrheim *et al.* (1997) in their study of the forecasting performance of the Norges Bank model. Over the longest (12 quarter) evaluation horizon, the Bank's model performed well, followed by a DV (specifically modeled to be congruent), then the DV obtained by omitting the EqCMs: the equivalent of the DDV did worst. But, as we remarked, over a sequence of three 4-period divisions of the same evaluation data, the DDV did best more often than any other method. The empirical illustration in chapter 8 produces similar results using a 4-equation monetary model of the UK. We conclude that the robustness obtained against recent deterministic shifts by over-differencing is valuable only over fairly short horizons. We also conclude that forecast performance in a world of deterministic shifts is not a good guide to model choice beyond the objective of short-term forecasting. The VEqCM we analyze is the DGP in-sample, and only differs from it by failing to model the equilibrium-mean shifts in the forecast period. Its policy implications would be correct if calculated as a differential between two runs (scenarios) of the model, even though its forecasts of the outturns could be badly wrong (see Hendry and Mizon, 1998c). Similarly, testing economic theories of data behavior by whole-sample goodness of fit could be seriously misled by such breaks: the DV could well outperform, suggesting the irrelevance of lagged information from other variables, and the absence of cointegration. Indeed, this is an example of our earlier theorem (see §1.7.2) that non-causal information can out-forecast causal once breaks are allowed. Further, Hendry and Mizon (1999) show that an empirical finding of Granger causality (see Granger, 1969) does not necessarily entail actual causality if structural breaks occur, so the reverse problem also occurs. These are important methodological implications, and point to the need to test carefully for equilibrium-mean shifts before drawing conclusions about empirical relations whatever the aims of the study.

5.7 Correct Empirical Variances

For the DV and DDV models, the conventionally-programmed formulae for the forecast-error variances assume that the errors are serially uncorrelated. This can be misleading when the DGP is a VEqCM. In this section, we discuss the potential impact of the residual autocorrelation on the error bands shown in their forecast graphs. These are calculated assuming constant parameters, so there are no forecast-error biases. As discussed in §5.2, it is important not to model the residual autocorrelation of the DDV if its robustification properties are to be preserved.

Consider the DV model first. The programmed variance formulae (denoted $\mathbf{V}_{DV,p}$) assume it is the DGP, so its "error" $\boldsymbol{\xi}_t$ is treated as being serially uncorrelated, leading to the computation of:

$$\mathbf{V}_{DV,p}\left[\widetilde{\mathbf{e}}_{x,T+h}\right] = \mathsf{E}\left[\sum_{j=0}^{h-1}\sum_{i=0}^{h-1}\mathbf{I}^{i}\boldsymbol{\xi}_{T+h-i}\boldsymbol{\xi}'_{T+h-j}\mathbf{I}^{j\prime}\right] = h\boldsymbol{\Omega}_{\boldsymbol{\xi}} \sim O\left(h\right) \quad (5.37)$$

when $\boldsymbol{\Omega}_{\boldsymbol{\xi}}$ is replaced by an estimate of the in-sample error-covariance matrix. It is possible to obtain an "autocorrelation-corrected" formula for the DV, denoted $\mathbf{V}_{DV,c}$, which is also $O\left(h\right)$, based on the correct value for the term in square brackets in (5.37), allowing for the serial correlation in the $\{\boldsymbol{\xi}_t\}$ (see (5.5) above). The actual MSFE (denoted $\mathbf{V}_{DV,a}$) is:

$$\mathbf{V}_{DV,a}\left[\widetilde{\mathbf{e}}_{x,T+h}\right] = \sum_{i=0}^{h-1}\sum_{j=0}^{h-1}\boldsymbol{\alpha}\boldsymbol{\Lambda}^{i}\mathbf{V}\boldsymbol{\Lambda}^{j\prime}\boldsymbol{\alpha}' + \sum_{s=0}^{h-1}\boldsymbol{\Upsilon}^{s}\boldsymbol{\Omega}_{\nu}\boldsymbol{\Upsilon}^{s\prime} \sim O\left(h\right). \quad (5.38)$$

Similar problems afflict the DDV model forecasts, where the actual forecast-error uncertainty $\mathbf{V}_{DDV,a}$ is:

$$\sum_{i=0}^{h-1} \mathbf{\Upsilon}^i \mathbf{\Omega} \mathbf{\Upsilon}^{i\prime} + h^2 \mathbf{\Omega}_\xi + \boldsymbol{\alpha} \mathbf{\Lambda}_h \mathbf{V} \mathbf{\Lambda}_h' \boldsymbol{\alpha}'$$
$$-h \boldsymbol{\alpha} \mathbf{\Lambda}_h \mathbf{C}_{\beta x_T, \Delta x_T} - h \mathbf{C}'_{\beta x_T, \Delta x_T} \mathbf{\Lambda}_h' \boldsymbol{\alpha}',$$

where $\mathbf{\Lambda}_h = \sum_{i=0}^{h-1} \mathbf{\Lambda}^i$and $\mathbf{C}_{\beta x_T, \Delta x_T} = \mathbf{\Lambda} \mathbf{V} \boldsymbol{\alpha}' + \boldsymbol{\beta}' \mathbf{\Omega}$. This is $O\left(h^2\right)$. However, the programmed formula is:

$$\mathbf{V}_{DDV,p} = \left(\sum_{i=0}^{h} i^2 \right) \mathbf{\Omega}_\zeta = \frac{1}{6} h \left(h+1\right) \left(2h+1\right) \mathbf{\Omega}_\zeta \sim O\left(h^3\right) \qquad (5.39)$$

where:

$$\mathbf{\Omega}_\zeta = \mathbf{\Omega}_\nu + \left(\mathbf{I}_n - \boldsymbol{\alpha}\boldsymbol{\beta}'\right) \mathbf{\Omega}_\nu \left(\mathbf{I}_n - \boldsymbol{\beta}\boldsymbol{\alpha}'\right) + \mathbf{AVA}'.$$

Thus, a serious overestimation of the uncertainty results from using (5.39). An expression for $\mathbf{V}_{DDV,c}$ is also obtainable, but for simplicity, we will only report a numerical illustration.

5.7.0.1 Bivariate illustration

We now quantify the extent to which the formula in (5.37), calculated without allowing for the in-sample errors to be autocorrelated, is a misleading guide to the actual forecast-error uncertainty associated with the DV model forecasts, given by (5.38).

When $n = 2$, then $\mathbf{\Lambda} = 1 + \boldsymbol{\beta}'\boldsymbol{\alpha} = \lambda$ is a scalar. The formulae for the DV model simplify to:

$$\begin{aligned}
\mathbf{V}_{DV,a}\left[\widetilde{\mathbf{e}}_{x,T+h}\right] &= \textstyle\sum_{s=0}^{h-1} \mathbf{\Upsilon}^s \mathbf{\Omega} \mathbf{\Upsilon}^{s\prime} + \boldsymbol{\alpha}\mathbf{V}\boldsymbol{\alpha}' \frac{\left(1-\lambda^h\right)^2}{\left(1-\lambda\right)^2} \\
\mathbf{V}_{DV,p}\left[\widetilde{\mathbf{e}}_{x,T+h}\right] &= h\mathbf{\Omega}_\xi \\
\mathbf{V}_{DV,c}\left[\widetilde{\mathbf{e}}_{x,T+h}\right] &= \begin{array}{l} h\mathbf{\Omega}_\xi + \frac{1}{1-\lambda}\left[h - \frac{1-\lambda^h}{1-\lambda}\right] \\ \times \left(2\lambda\boldsymbol{\alpha}\mathbf{V}\boldsymbol{\alpha}' + \boldsymbol{\alpha}\boldsymbol{\beta}'\mathbf{\Omega} + \mathbf{\Omega}\boldsymbol{\beta}\boldsymbol{\alpha}'\right). \end{array}
\end{aligned}$$

Similar expressions hold for the DDV.

Table 5.4 records the results of numerically evaluating the forecast-error variance formulae for DV and DDV models for the parameter

Table 5.4
Illustrative forecast-error variances.

h	V_{VEqCM}	$V_{DV,a}$	$V_{DV,p}$	$V_{DV,c}$	$V_{DDV,a}$	$V_{DDV,p}$	$V_{DDV,c}$
1	1.00	1.16	1.16	1.16	2.49	2.49	2.49
2	1.68	2.13	2.31	2.53	7.37	12.47	7.47
3	2.23	2.98	3.47	4.06	14.58	34.92	14.98
4	2.74	3.75	4.63	5.70	24.08	74.82	25.09
5	3.24	4.45	5.78	7.41	35.87	137.18	37.88
6	3.74	5.10	6.94	9.18	49.93	226.96	53.46
7	4.26	5.73	8.10	10.98	66.28	349.18	71.92
8	4.79	6.33	9.25	12.81	84.91	508.80	93.37
9	5.32	6.92	10.41	14.66	105.82	710.82	117.92
10	5.86	7.50	11.57	16.52	129.03	960.24	145.66
11	6.40	8.08	12.73	18.39	154.54	1262.02	176.72
12	6.95	8.64	13.88	20.26	182.35	1621.18	211.18

values $\{\boldsymbol{\Omega}= \mathbf{I}_2, \boldsymbol{\alpha}' = (-0.2, 0.1), \boldsymbol{\beta}' = (1, -1)\}$. We report figures for predicting levels of the first variable at horizons up to 12: qualitatively similar results hold for the second variable.

DV results. Forecast confidence intervals calculated on the basis of $\mathbf{V}_p$ are far too wide, particularly at longer horizons, and overstate the true ($\mathbf{V}_a$) uncertainty attached to the DV model forecasts. Correcting for the serial correlation in the DV model residuals (as in $\mathbf{V}_c$) tends to inflate the bands further, since the omission of the equilibrium-correction term induces positive autocorrelation in the DV equations' errors. The first column records the DGP baseline forecast-error variance, as an aid to comparison. The degree to which $\mathbf{V}_p$ (and $\mathbf{V}_c$) overstate the uncertainty depends on λ. As $\lambda \to 1$, so that there is no cointegration and the DV is correctly specified, then all the measures converge.

DDV results. The actual forecast uncertainty associated with the DDV model increases much more quickly, but this is greatly exacerbated by the $\mathbf{V}_p$ measure. Now, the correction for autocorrelation ($\mathbf{V}_c$) largely undoes the inflation in the $\mathbf{V}_p$ measure, by accounting for the substantial negative moving average induced in the DDV model errors.

These results should be kept in mind when interpreting the empirical application in chapter 8.

5.8 Post-transition Forecast Errors

The above formulae can be simplified considerably if we approximate changing post-break expectations by stationary post-break expectations. The resulting reduction in complexity allows us to consider a DGP with a higher-order deterministic term, and to illustrate the impact on both VEqCM and DV forecasts.

5.8.1 *The data generation process*

Relative to (1.12), we allow a linear deterministic trend in addition to the constant term:

$$\mathbf{x}_t = \boldsymbol{\tau}_0 + \boldsymbol{\tau}_1 t + \boldsymbol{\Upsilon}\mathbf{x}_{t-1} + \boldsymbol{\nu}_t \tag{5.40}$$

where $\boldsymbol{\nu}_t \sim \mathsf{IN}_n\left[\mathbf{0}, \boldsymbol{\Omega}_\nu\right]$. As before:

$$\boldsymbol{\Upsilon} = \mathbf{I}_n + \boldsymbol{\alpha}\boldsymbol{\beta}',$$

where $\boldsymbol{\alpha}$ and $\boldsymbol{\beta}$ are $n \times r$ matrices of rank r. Then (5.40) can be reparameterized as the VEqCM:

$$\Delta\mathbf{x}_t = \boldsymbol{\tau}_0 + \boldsymbol{\tau}_1 t + \boldsymbol{\alpha}\boldsymbol{\beta}'\mathbf{x}_{t-1} + \boldsymbol{\nu}_t. \tag{5.41}$$

The impact of the deterministic components on the series depends on the relationship between $\boldsymbol{\alpha}$ and $\boldsymbol{\tau}_0$, $\boldsymbol{\tau}_1$. Following Johansen (1994), decompose the $2n$ parameters in $\boldsymbol{\tau}_0 + \boldsymbol{\tau}_1 t$ as:

$$\boldsymbol{\tau}_0 + \boldsymbol{\tau}_1 t = \boldsymbol{\alpha}_\perp \boldsymbol{\zeta}_0 - \boldsymbol{\alpha}\boldsymbol{\lambda}_0 - \boldsymbol{\alpha}\boldsymbol{\lambda}_1 t + \boldsymbol{\alpha}_\perp \boldsymbol{\zeta}_1 t \tag{5.42}$$

where $\boldsymbol{\lambda}_i = -\left(\boldsymbol{\alpha}'\boldsymbol{\alpha}\right)^{-1}\boldsymbol{\alpha}'\boldsymbol{\tau}_i$ ($2r$ free parameters) and $\boldsymbol{\zeta}_i = \left(\boldsymbol{\alpha}_\perp'\boldsymbol{\alpha}_\perp\right)^{-1}\boldsymbol{\alpha}_\perp'\boldsymbol{\tau}_i$ ($2\left(n-r\right)$ free parameters) when $\boldsymbol{\alpha}'\boldsymbol{\alpha}_\perp = \mathbf{0}$. Then $\boldsymbol{\alpha}\boldsymbol{\lambda}_i$ and $\boldsymbol{\alpha}_\perp\boldsymbol{\zeta}_i$ are orthogonal by construction. When the $\mathbf{x}_t$ process does not contain a quadratic trend, $\boldsymbol{\alpha}_\perp\boldsymbol{\zeta}_1 = \mathbf{0}$, and $\boldsymbol{\lambda}_0$, $\boldsymbol{\zeta}_0$ and $\boldsymbol{\lambda}_1$ can all be varied freely. The $\mathbf{x}_t$ process may still contain linear trends, which will also be a feature of the cointegrating vectors, as seems to be the case in the empirical example. Then $\boldsymbol{\alpha}\boldsymbol{\lambda}_0 + \boldsymbol{\alpha}\boldsymbol{\lambda}_1 t$ lies in the cointegration space, and (5.41) can be written as:

$$\Delta \mathbf{x}_t = \boldsymbol{\alpha}_{\perp}\zeta_0 + \boldsymbol{\alpha}\left(\boldsymbol{\beta}'\mathbf{x}_{t-1} - \boldsymbol{\lambda}_0 - \boldsymbol{\lambda}_1 t\right) + \boldsymbol{\nu}_t. \tag{5.43}$$

When the system grows at the (vector) rate:

$$\mathsf{E}\left[\Delta \mathbf{x}_t\right] = \boldsymbol{\gamma} \tag{5.44}$$

from (5.43), we obtain:

$$\boldsymbol{\alpha}\mathsf{E}\left[\boldsymbol{\beta}'\mathbf{x}_{t-1}\right] = \boldsymbol{\gamma} - \boldsymbol{\alpha}_{\perp}\zeta_0 + \boldsymbol{\alpha}\left(\boldsymbol{\lambda}_0 + \boldsymbol{\lambda}_1 t\right). \tag{5.45}$$

When $\boldsymbol{\beta}'\boldsymbol{\alpha}$ is non-singular, as assumed throughout:

$$\mathsf{E}\left[\boldsymbol{\beta}'\mathbf{x}_{t-1}\right] = \left(\boldsymbol{\beta}'\boldsymbol{\alpha}\right)^{-1}\boldsymbol{\beta}'\left(\boldsymbol{\gamma} - \boldsymbol{\alpha}_{\perp}\zeta_0\right) + \boldsymbol{\lambda}_0 + \boldsymbol{\lambda}_1 t = \boldsymbol{\psi} + \boldsymbol{\lambda}_0 + \boldsymbol{\lambda}_1 t. \tag{5.46}$$

Hence, in (5.43):

$$\Delta \mathbf{x}_t = \boldsymbol{\alpha}_{\perp}\zeta_0 + \boldsymbol{\alpha}\boldsymbol{\psi} + \boldsymbol{\alpha}\left(\boldsymbol{\beta}'\mathbf{x}_{t-1} - \boldsymbol{\psi} - \boldsymbol{\lambda}_0 - \boldsymbol{\lambda}_1 t\right) + \boldsymbol{\nu}_t.$$

It is useful for subsequent calculations to introduce the idempotent matrix $\mathbf{K} = (\mathbf{I}_n - \boldsymbol{\alpha}\left(\boldsymbol{\beta}'\boldsymbol{\alpha}\right)^{-1}\boldsymbol{\beta}')$ such that $\mathbf{K}\boldsymbol{\alpha} = \mathbf{0}$, $\boldsymbol{\beta}'\mathbf{K} = \mathbf{0}$, $\mathbf{K}^2 = \mathbf{K}$ and $\boldsymbol{\Upsilon}\mathbf{K} = \mathbf{K}$, implying that $\mathbf{K}\boldsymbol{\tau}_0 = \mathbf{K}\boldsymbol{\gamma} = \mathbf{K}\boldsymbol{\alpha}_{\perp}\zeta_0$ and $\mathbf{K}\boldsymbol{\tau}_1 = \mathbf{0}$. The cost of orthogonality in (5.43) is that the cointegrating vectors are no longer deviations about their means, so the "intercept" $\boldsymbol{\alpha}_{\perp}\zeta_0$ is not the growth rate $\boldsymbol{\gamma}$ which can be expressed as:[1]

$$\boldsymbol{\gamma} = \boldsymbol{\alpha}_{\perp}\zeta_0 + \boldsymbol{\alpha}\boldsymbol{\psi} = \mathbf{K}\boldsymbol{\alpha}_{\perp}\zeta_0 + \boldsymbol{\alpha}\left(\boldsymbol{\beta}'\boldsymbol{\alpha}\right)^{-1}\boldsymbol{\lambda}_1 \tag{5.47}$$

since from (5.46) and (5.44):

$$\Delta\mathsf{E}\left[\boldsymbol{\beta}'\mathbf{x}_t\right] = \boldsymbol{\beta}'\mathsf{E}\left[\Delta\mathbf{x}_t\right] = \boldsymbol{\lambda}_1 \quad \text{so that} \quad \boldsymbol{\beta}'\boldsymbol{\gamma} = \boldsymbol{\lambda}_1. \tag{5.48}$$

Consequently, we can rewrite the VEqCM as:

$$\Delta \mathbf{x}_t = \boldsymbol{\gamma} + \boldsymbol{\alpha}\left(\boldsymbol{\beta}'\mathbf{x}_{t-1} - \boldsymbol{\mu}_0 - \boldsymbol{\mu}_1 t\right) + \boldsymbol{\nu}_t \tag{5.49}$$

where $\boldsymbol{\mu}_0 = \boldsymbol{\psi} + \boldsymbol{\lambda}_0$ and $\boldsymbol{\mu}_1 = \boldsymbol{\lambda}_1$ with:

$$\boldsymbol{\psi} = \left(\boldsymbol{\beta}'\boldsymbol{\alpha}\right)^{-1}\boldsymbol{\beta}'\left(\boldsymbol{\gamma} - \boldsymbol{\alpha}_{\perp}\zeta_0\right) = \left(\boldsymbol{\beta}'\boldsymbol{\alpha}\right)^{-1}\left(\boldsymbol{\lambda}_1 - \boldsymbol{\beta}'\boldsymbol{\alpha}_{\perp}\zeta_0\right).$$

[1] In previous work (eg. Clements and Hendry, 1995b, p.1005) with $\boldsymbol{\tau}_1 = \mathbf{0}$, we have used a simpler, non-orthogonal decomposition of $\boldsymbol{\tau}_0$. We are grateful to Bent Nielsen for bringing to our attention the problems with such an approach in the presence of the linear trend term.

5.8.2 VEqCM forecast errors

We now consider dynamic forecasts and their errors when parameters are subject to change in the forecast period, focusing on the bias and variance components. We also consider the implications of the deterministic terms lying in the cointegrating space. For simplicity, we again abstract from all the potential sources of forecast error set out in table 2.1, other than non-constancy.

Under these assumptions, the h-step ahead forecasts for the levels of the process are given by $\widehat{\mathbf{x}}_{T+h} = \mathsf{E}[\mathbf{x}_{T+h}|\mathbf{x}_T]$ for $h = 1, \ldots, H$:

$$\widehat{\mathbf{x}}_{T+h} = \boldsymbol{\tau}_0 + \boldsymbol{\tau}_1 (T+h) + \boldsymbol{\Upsilon}\widehat{\mathbf{x}}_{T+h-1} = \sum_{i=0}^{h-1} \boldsymbol{\Upsilon}^i \boldsymbol{\tau}(i) + \boldsymbol{\Upsilon}^h \mathbf{x}_T \tag{5.50}$$

where we let $\boldsymbol{\tau}_0 + \boldsymbol{\tau}_1(T+h-i) = \boldsymbol{\tau}(i)$ for notational convenience. The associated forecast errors are:

$$\widehat{\boldsymbol{\nu}}_{T+h} = \mathbf{x}_{T+h} - \widehat{\mathbf{x}}_{T+h}.$$

We consider the situation where the system experiences a step change between the estimation and forecast periods, such that $(\boldsymbol{\tau}_0 : \boldsymbol{\tau}_1 : \boldsymbol{\Upsilon})$ changes to $(\boldsymbol{\tau}_0^* : \boldsymbol{\tau}_1^* : \boldsymbol{\Upsilon}^*)$ over $h = 1, \ldots, H$, but the variance, autocorrelation, and distribution of the disturbance term remain unaltered. Thus, the data generated by the process for the next H periods is given by:

$$\begin{aligned} \mathbf{x}_{T+h} &= \boldsymbol{\tau}_0^* + \boldsymbol{\tau}_1^* (T+h) + \boldsymbol{\Upsilon}^* \mathbf{x}_{T+h-1} + \boldsymbol{\nu}_{T+h} \\ &= \sum_{i=0}^{h-1} (\boldsymbol{\Upsilon}^*)^i \boldsymbol{\tau}^*(i) + \sum_{i=0}^{h-1} (\boldsymbol{\Upsilon}^*)^i \boldsymbol{\nu}_{T+h-i} + (\boldsymbol{\Upsilon}^*)^h \mathbf{x}_T. \end{aligned} \tag{5.51}$$

Then, the h-step ahead forecast error, $\hat{\boldsymbol{\nu}}_{T+h}$, can be written as:

$$\begin{aligned} &\sum_{i=0}^{h-1} (\boldsymbol{\Upsilon}^*)^i \boldsymbol{\tau}^*(i) + \sum_{i=0}^{h-1} (\boldsymbol{\Upsilon}^*)^i \boldsymbol{\nu}_{T+h-i} \\ &\quad + (\boldsymbol{\Upsilon}^*)^h \mathbf{x}_T - \sum_{i=0}^{h-1} \boldsymbol{\Upsilon}^i \boldsymbol{\tau}(i) - \boldsymbol{\Upsilon}^h \mathbf{x}_T \\ = &\left(\sum_{i=0}^{h-1} (\boldsymbol{\Upsilon}^*)^i \boldsymbol{\tau}^*(i) - \sum_{i=0}^{h-1} \boldsymbol{\Upsilon}^i \boldsymbol{\tau}(i) \right) \end{aligned}$$

$$+\sum_{i=0}^{h-1}(\boldsymbol{\Upsilon}^*)^i\boldsymbol{\nu}_{T+h-i}+\left((\boldsymbol{\Upsilon}^*)^h-\boldsymbol{\Upsilon}^h\right)\mathbf{x}_T. \tag{5.52}$$

The three components of forecast error are due to the changed intercepts and slope parameters; error accumulation; and an interaction term occasioned by the change in the slope parameter, which depends on the forecast origin.

The expectation of the h-step forecast error conditional on $\mathbf{x}_T$ is:

$$\begin{aligned}\mathsf{E}\left[\widehat{\boldsymbol{\nu}}_{T+h}\mid\mathbf{x}_T\right] &= \left(\sum_{i=0}^{h-1}(\boldsymbol{\Upsilon}^*)^i\boldsymbol{\tau}^*(i)-\sum_{i=0}^{h-1}\boldsymbol{\Upsilon}^i\boldsymbol{\tau}(i)\right)\\ &\quad+\left((\boldsymbol{\Upsilon}^*)^h-\boldsymbol{\Upsilon}^h\right)\mathbf{x}_T\end{aligned} \tag{5.53}$$

so that the conditional forecast-error variance is:

$$\mathsf{V}\left[\widehat{\boldsymbol{\nu}}_{T+h}\mid\mathbf{x}_T\right]=\sum_{i=0}^{h-1}(\boldsymbol{\Upsilon}^*)^i\boldsymbol{\Omega}(\boldsymbol{\Upsilon}^*)^{i\prime}.$$

We now consider a number of special cases where only the deterministic components changes. With the assumption that $\boldsymbol{\Upsilon}^*=\boldsymbol{\Upsilon}$, we obtain (noting the dependence of $\boldsymbol{\tau}^*(i)$ on $T+h$) the following expression for $\mathsf{E}[\widehat{\boldsymbol{\nu}_{T+h}}|\mathbf{x}_T]$:

$$\begin{aligned}&\sum_{i=0}^{h-1}\boldsymbol{\Upsilon}^i\left(\left[\boldsymbol{\tau}_0^*+\boldsymbol{\tau}_1^*(T+h-i)\right]-\left[\boldsymbol{\tau}_0+\boldsymbol{\tau}_1(T+h-i)\right]\right)\\ &=\sum_{i=0}^{h-1}\boldsymbol{\Upsilon}^i\left[(\boldsymbol{\gamma}^*-\boldsymbol{\gamma})+\boldsymbol{\alpha}(\boldsymbol{\mu}_0-\boldsymbol{\mu}_0^*)+\boldsymbol{\alpha}(\boldsymbol{\mu}_1-\boldsymbol{\mu}_1^*)(T+h-i)\right]\end{aligned} \tag{5.54}$$

The bias is increasing in h due to the first term in square brackets. The impacts of the second and third terms eventually level off because:

$$\lim_{i\to\infty}\boldsymbol{\Upsilon}^i=\mathbf{I}_n-\boldsymbol{\alpha}\left(\boldsymbol{\beta}'\boldsymbol{\alpha}\right)^{-1}\boldsymbol{\beta}'=\mathbf{K},$$

and $\mathbf{K}\boldsymbol{\alpha}=\mathbf{0}$. When the linear trend is absent, and the constant term can be restricted to the cointegrating space (i.e., $\boldsymbol{\tau}_1=\mathbf{0}$ and $\boldsymbol{\zeta}_0=\mathbf{0}$, which implies $\boldsymbol{\lambda}_1=\mathbf{0}$ and therefore $\boldsymbol{\mu}_1=\boldsymbol{\gamma}=\mathbf{0}$), then only the second term appears, and the bias is $O(1)$ in h. The formulation in (5.54) assumes that $\boldsymbol{\Upsilon}$, and therefore the cointegrating space, remains unaltered. Moreover, the coefficient on the linear trend alters but still lies in the cointegrating space. Otherwise, after the structural break, $\mathbf{x}_t$ would be propelled by quadratic trends.

The conditional forecast-error variance is:

$$\mathsf{V}\left[\widehat{\boldsymbol{\nu}}_{T+h} \mid \mathbf{x}_T\right] = \sum_{i=0}^{h-1} \boldsymbol{\Upsilon}^i \boldsymbol{\Omega} \boldsymbol{\Upsilon}^{i\prime} \tag{5.55}$$

which is $O(h)$.

5.8.3 DV forecast errors

Now, consider forecasts from a simplified DV for $\Delta\mathbf{x}_t$ defined by setting $\Delta\mathbf{x}_{T+h}$ equal to the population growth rate $\boldsymbol{\gamma}$:

$$\Delta\widetilde{\mathbf{x}}_{T+h} = \boldsymbol{\gamma} \tag{5.56}$$

so that h-step ahead forecasts of the level of the process are obtained by integrating (5.56) from the forecast origin $\mathbf{x}_T$:

$$\widetilde{\mathbf{x}}_{T+h} = \widetilde{\mathbf{x}}_{T+h-1} + \boldsymbol{\gamma} = \mathbf{x}_T + h\boldsymbol{\gamma}. \tag{5.57}$$

When $\boldsymbol{\Upsilon}$ is unchanged over the forecast period, the expected value of the conditional h-step ahead forecast error is:

$$\mathsf{E}\left[\widetilde{\boldsymbol{\nu}}_{T+h} \mid \mathbf{x}_T\right] = \sum_{i=0}^{h-1} \boldsymbol{\Upsilon}^i \left[\boldsymbol{\tau}_0^* + \boldsymbol{\tau}_1^* \left(T + h - i\right)\right] - h\boldsymbol{\gamma} + \left(\boldsymbol{\Upsilon}^h - \mathbf{I}_n\right)\mathbf{x}_T. \tag{5.58}$$

The occurrence of $\mathbf{x}_T$ in (5.58) is awkward for comparisons with the VEqCM in (5.54). Thus, we average over $\mathbf{x}_T$ to give the unconditional bias $\mathsf{E}_{\mathbf{x}_T}\left[\widetilde{\boldsymbol{\nu}}_{T+h}\right]$. Since $\boldsymbol{\Upsilon} = \mathbf{I}_n + \boldsymbol{\alpha}\boldsymbol{\beta}'$, for $h > 0$:

$$\boldsymbol{\Upsilon}^h = \boldsymbol{\Upsilon}^{h-1} + \boldsymbol{\Upsilon}^{h-1}\boldsymbol{\alpha}\boldsymbol{\beta}' = \cdots = \mathbf{I}_n + \sum_{i=0}^{h-1} \boldsymbol{\Upsilon}^i \boldsymbol{\alpha}\boldsymbol{\beta}', \tag{5.59}$$

so from (5.46) using:

$$\left(\boldsymbol{\Upsilon}^h - \mathbf{I}_n\right) = \sum_{i=0}^{h-1} \boldsymbol{\Upsilon}^i \boldsymbol{\alpha}\boldsymbol{\beta}' \doteq \mathbf{A}_h \boldsymbol{\alpha}\boldsymbol{\beta}' \tag{5.60}$$

we obtain:

$$\mathsf{E}_{\mathbf{x}_T}\left[\left(\boldsymbol{\Upsilon}^h - \mathbf{I}_n\right)\mathbf{x}_T\right] = \mathbf{A}_h \boldsymbol{\alpha} \mathsf{E}_{\mathbf{x}_T}\left[\boldsymbol{\beta}'\mathbf{x}_T\right] = \mathbf{A}_h \boldsymbol{\alpha} \mathbf{f}_T \tag{5.61}$$

where $\mathbf{f}_T = \mathsf{E}_{\mathbf{x}_T}\left[\boldsymbol{\beta}'\mathbf{x}_T\right] = \boldsymbol{\mu}_0^a + \boldsymbol{\beta}'\boldsymbol{\gamma}^a(T+1)$, say, where the values of $\boldsymbol{\mu}_0^a$ and $\boldsymbol{\gamma}^a$ depend on the regime. Substituting from (5.61) into (5.58):

$$\mathsf{E}_{\mathbf{x}_T}\left[\widetilde{\boldsymbol{\nu}}_{T+h}\right] = \sum_{i=0}^{h-1}\boldsymbol{\Upsilon}^i\left[\boldsymbol{\gamma}^* - \boldsymbol{\alpha}\boldsymbol{\mu}_0^* - \boldsymbol{\alpha}\boldsymbol{\mu}_1^*(T+h-i)\right] - h\boldsymbol{\gamma} + \mathbf{A}_h\boldsymbol{\alpha}\mathbf{f}_T. \quad (5.62)$$

From (5.59), as $\boldsymbol{\Upsilon}^i = \mathbf{I}_n + \mathbf{A}_i\boldsymbol{\alpha}\boldsymbol{\beta}'$:

$$\begin{aligned}\mathbf{A}_h &= \sum_{k=0}^{h-1}\boldsymbol{\Upsilon}^k = \sum_{k=0}^{h-1}\left(\mathbf{I}_n + \mathbf{A}_k\boldsymbol{\alpha}\boldsymbol{\beta}'\right)\\ &= h\mathbf{I}_n + \left(\sum_{k=0}^{h-1}\mathbf{A}_k\right)\boldsymbol{\alpha}\boldsymbol{\beta}' = h\mathbf{I}_n + \mathbf{B}_h\boldsymbol{\alpha}\boldsymbol{\beta}'. \qquad (5.63)\end{aligned}$$

Thus from (5.62), since $\boldsymbol{\beta}'\boldsymbol{\gamma} = \boldsymbol{\mu}_1$ and $\boldsymbol{\beta}'\boldsymbol{\gamma}^* = \boldsymbol{\mu}_1^*$, $\mathsf{E}[\widetilde{\boldsymbol{\nu}}_{T+h}]$ becomes:

$$\begin{aligned}&\mathbf{A}_h\left(\boldsymbol{\gamma}^* - \boldsymbol{\alpha}\boldsymbol{\mu}_0^*\right) - \mathbf{A}_h\boldsymbol{\alpha}\boldsymbol{\beta}'\boldsymbol{\gamma}^*(T+h)\\ &\quad + \sum_{i=1}^{h-1} i\boldsymbol{\Upsilon}^i\boldsymbol{\alpha}\boldsymbol{\beta}'\boldsymbol{\gamma}^* - h\boldsymbol{\gamma} + \mathbf{A}_h\boldsymbol{\alpha}\mathbf{f}_T\\ &= h\left(\boldsymbol{\gamma}^* - \boldsymbol{\gamma}\right) + \mathbf{A}_h\boldsymbol{\alpha}\mathbf{f}_T - \boldsymbol{\mu}_0^* - \boldsymbol{\beta}'\boldsymbol{\gamma}^*T\\ &\quad + \left(\sum_{i=1}^{h-1} i\boldsymbol{\Upsilon}^i - h\mathbf{A}_h + \mathbf{B}_h\right)\boldsymbol{\alpha}\boldsymbol{\beta}'\boldsymbol{\gamma}^*\\ &= h\left(\boldsymbol{\gamma}^* - \boldsymbol{\gamma}\right) + \mathbf{A}_h\boldsymbol{\alpha}\left(\boldsymbol{\mu}_0^a - \boldsymbol{\mu}_0^* - \boldsymbol{\beta}'\left[\boldsymbol{\gamma}^* - \boldsymbol{\gamma}^a\right](T+1)\right)\\ &\quad + \mathbf{C}_h\boldsymbol{\alpha}\boldsymbol{\beta}'\boldsymbol{\gamma}^* \qquad (5.64)\end{aligned}$$

where $\mathbf{C}_h = (\mathbf{D}_h + \mathbf{B}_h - (h-1)\mathbf{A}_h)$ when $\mathbf{D}_h = \sum_{i=1}^{h-1} i\boldsymbol{\Upsilon}^i$. However, $\mathbf{C}_h\boldsymbol{\alpha}\boldsymbol{\beta}' = \mathbf{0}$ as follows. Since $\boldsymbol{\Upsilon}^h = \mathbf{I}_n + \mathbf{A}_h\boldsymbol{\alpha}\boldsymbol{\beta}'$ from (5.60), then:

$$h\mathbf{A}_h\boldsymbol{\alpha}\boldsymbol{\beta}' = h\boldsymbol{\Upsilon}^h - h\mathbf{I}_n,$$

and so eliminating $h\mathbf{I}_n$ using (5.63):

$$\left(\mathbf{B}_h - h\mathbf{A}_h\right)\boldsymbol{\alpha}\boldsymbol{\beta}' = \mathbf{A}_h - h\boldsymbol{\Upsilon}^h.$$

Also:

$$\begin{aligned}\mathbf{D}_h &= \sum_{i=1}^{h} i\boldsymbol{\Upsilon}^i - h\boldsymbol{\Upsilon}^h = \sum_{i=1}^{h}\boldsymbol{\Upsilon}^i - h\boldsymbol{\Upsilon}^h + \left(\sum_{i=1}^{h-1} i\boldsymbol{\Upsilon}^i\right)\boldsymbol{\Upsilon}\\ &= \mathbf{A}_h\boldsymbol{\Upsilon} - h\boldsymbol{\Upsilon}^h + \mathbf{D}_h\boldsymbol{\Upsilon}.\end{aligned}$$

Since $\boldsymbol{\Upsilon} = \mathbf{I}_n + \boldsymbol{\alpha\beta}'$:

$$\mathbf{D}_h\boldsymbol{\alpha\beta}' = h\boldsymbol{\Upsilon}^h - \mathbf{A}_h - \mathbf{A}_h\boldsymbol{\alpha\beta}'.$$

Combining these results:

$$\begin{aligned} \mathbf{C}_h\boldsymbol{\alpha\beta}' &= (\mathbf{D}_h + \mathbf{B}_h - (h-1)\,\mathbf{A}_h)\,\boldsymbol{\alpha\beta}' \\ &= h\boldsymbol{\Upsilon}^h - \mathbf{A}_h - \mathbf{A}_h\boldsymbol{\alpha\beta}' + \mathbf{A}_h - h\boldsymbol{\Upsilon}^h + \mathbf{A}_h\boldsymbol{\alpha\beta}' = \mathbf{0}. \end{aligned} \quad (5.65)$$

Thus:

$$\mathsf{E}\left[\widetilde{\boldsymbol{\nu}}_{T+h}\right] = h\left(\boldsymbol{\gamma}^* - \boldsymbol{\gamma}\right) + \mathbf{A}_h\boldsymbol{\alpha}\left(\left[\boldsymbol{\mu}_0^a - \boldsymbol{\mu}_0^*\right] - \boldsymbol{\beta}'\left[\boldsymbol{\gamma}^* - \boldsymbol{\gamma}^a\right](T+1)\right). \quad (5.66)$$

In the same notation, the VEqCM results from (5.54) are:

$$\mathsf{E}\left[\widehat{\boldsymbol{\nu}}_{T+h}\right] = h\left(\boldsymbol{\gamma}^* - \boldsymbol{\gamma}\right) + \mathbf{A}_h\boldsymbol{\alpha}\left(\left[\boldsymbol{\mu}_0 - \boldsymbol{\mu}_0^*\right] - \boldsymbol{\beta}'\left[\boldsymbol{\gamma}^* - \boldsymbol{\gamma}\right](T+1)\right). \quad (5.67)$$

Thus, (5.67) and (5.66) coincide when $\boldsymbol{\mu}_0^a = \boldsymbol{\mu}_0$, and $\boldsymbol{\gamma}^a = \boldsymbol{\gamma}$, as will occur if either there is no regime shift, or the shift occurs after the start of the forecast period.

5.8.4 *Forecast biases under deterministic shifts*

We now consider a number of interesting special cases of (5.66) and (5.67) which highlight the different behavior of the DV and VEqCM under regime changes. When $\boldsymbol{\gamma}^* = \boldsymbol{\gamma}$, then $\boldsymbol{\beta}'\boldsymbol{\gamma}^* = \boldsymbol{\beta}'\boldsymbol{\gamma}$, whereas $\boldsymbol{\gamma}^* \neq \boldsymbol{\gamma}$ does not necessarily entail that $\boldsymbol{\beta}'\boldsymbol{\gamma}^* \neq \boldsymbol{\beta}'\boldsymbol{\gamma}$. If we view $(\boldsymbol{\tau}_0, \boldsymbol{\tau}_1)$ as the primary parameters, then it is informative to map changes in these parameters, via the orthogonal decomposition into $(\boldsymbol{\zeta}_0, \boldsymbol{\lambda}_0, \boldsymbol{\lambda}_1)$, to the parameterization in terms of $(\boldsymbol{\gamma}, \boldsymbol{\mu}_0, \boldsymbol{\mu}_1)$ that underpins (5.66) and (5.67). We can summarize the interdependencies as follows: $\boldsymbol{\gamma}(\boldsymbol{\zeta}_0, \boldsymbol{\lambda}_1)$, $\boldsymbol{\mu}_0(\boldsymbol{\zeta}_0, \boldsymbol{\lambda}_0, \boldsymbol{\lambda}_1)$, $\boldsymbol{\mu}_1(\boldsymbol{\lambda}_1)$.

Case I $\boldsymbol{\tau}_0^* = \boldsymbol{\tau}_0$, $\boldsymbol{\tau}_1^* = \boldsymbol{\tau}_1$. Here, there is no structural change, $\boldsymbol{\mu}_0^a = \boldsymbol{\mu}_0$ and $\boldsymbol{\gamma}^a = \boldsymbol{\gamma}$ and so:

$$\mathsf{E}\left[\widehat{\boldsymbol{\nu}}_{T+h}\right] = \mathsf{E}\left[\widetilde{\boldsymbol{\nu}}_{T+h}\right] = \mathbf{0}. \quad (5.68)$$

Thus, the forecast error biases in the DV and VEqCM coincide when there is no regime change, even when the DV omits an EqCM which includes a non-zero trend, generalizing the earlier finding without trend.

Case II $\tau_0^* \neq \tau_0, \tau_1^* = \tau_1$, but $\zeta_0^* = \zeta_0$. Then $\gamma^* = \gamma; \mu_0^* \neq \mu_0$.

$$\mathsf{E}\left[\widehat{\boldsymbol{\nu}}_{T+h}\right] = \mathbf{A}_h \boldsymbol{\alpha}\left(\boldsymbol{\mu}_0 - \boldsymbol{\mu}_0^*\right) \tag{5.69}$$

$$\mathsf{E}\left[\widetilde{\boldsymbol{\nu}}_{T+h}\right] = \mathbf{A}_h \boldsymbol{\alpha}\left(\boldsymbol{\mu}_0^a - \boldsymbol{\mu}_0^*\right). \tag{5.70}$$

The biases are equal if $\boldsymbol{\mu}_0^a = \boldsymbol{\mu}_0$, so the shock is after the forecast origin. However, $\mathsf{E}\left[\widetilde{\boldsymbol{\nu}}_{T+h}\right] = \mathbf{0}$ when $\boldsymbol{\mu}_0^a = \boldsymbol{\mu}_0^*$, and hence the DV wins uniformly if the shock has occurred prior to the commencement of forecasting.[2] In this example, the component of the constant term orthogonal to $\boldsymbol{\alpha}$ is unchanged, so that the growth rate is unchanged.

Case III $\tau_0^* \neq \tau_0$, $\tau_1^* = \tau_1$ (as in Case II), but now $\boldsymbol{\lambda}_0^* = \boldsymbol{\lambda}_0$ which implies $\zeta_0^* \neq \zeta_0$ and therefore $\boldsymbol{\mu}_0^* \neq \boldsymbol{\mu}_0$ and $\boldsymbol{\gamma}^* \neq \boldsymbol{\gamma}$. However, $\boldsymbol{\beta}'\boldsymbol{\gamma}^* = \boldsymbol{\beta}'\boldsymbol{\gamma}$ holds so that:

$$\mathsf{E}\left[\widehat{\boldsymbol{\nu}}_{T+h}\right] = h\left(\boldsymbol{\gamma}^* - \boldsymbol{\gamma}\right) + \mathbf{A}_h \boldsymbol{\alpha}\left(\boldsymbol{\mu}_0 - \boldsymbol{\mu}_0^*\right) \tag{5.71}$$

$$\mathsf{E}\left[\widetilde{\boldsymbol{\nu}}_{T+h}\right] = h\left(\boldsymbol{\gamma}^* - \boldsymbol{\gamma}\right) + \mathbf{A}_h \boldsymbol{\alpha}\left(\boldsymbol{\mu}_0^a - \boldsymbol{\mu}_0^*\right), \tag{5.72}$$

since $\boldsymbol{\mu}_1$ depends only on τ_1. Consequently, the errors coincide when $\boldsymbol{\mu}_0^a = \boldsymbol{\mu}_0$, but differ when $\boldsymbol{\mu}_0^a = \boldsymbol{\mu}_0^*$, though it is unclear whether the terms augment or attenuate each other.

Case IV $\tau_0^* = \tau_0, \tau_1^* \neq \tau_1$. All of $\boldsymbol{\mu}_0$, $\boldsymbol{\mu}_1$ and $\boldsymbol{\gamma}$ change. If $\boldsymbol{\beta}'\boldsymbol{\gamma}^* \neq \boldsymbol{\beta}'\boldsymbol{\gamma}$ then we have (5.66) and (5.67), and otherwise the biases of Case III.

Alternatively, the difference in the forecast bias between the DV and the VEqCM is given by:

$$\mathsf{E}\left[\widetilde{\boldsymbol{\nu}}_{T+h}\right] - \mathsf{E}\left[\widehat{\boldsymbol{\nu}}_{T+h}\right] = \mathbf{A}_h \boldsymbol{\alpha}\left(\left[\boldsymbol{\mu}_0 - \boldsymbol{\mu}_0^a\right] + \boldsymbol{\beta}'\left[\boldsymbol{\gamma} - \boldsymbol{\gamma}^a\right](T+1)\right). \tag{5.73}$$

This is zero when $\boldsymbol{\mu}_0^a = \boldsymbol{\mu}_0$ and $\boldsymbol{\gamma}^a = \boldsymbol{\gamma}$, but otherwise enhances or attenuates the existing biases, generally inducing a smaller forecast error bias in the DV when there are unmodeled regime shifts.

An alternative representation is in terms of the changes between successive forecast errors. For the VEqCM, from (5.66) and that equation lagged, for $\mathsf{E}[\widehat{\boldsymbol{\nu}}_{T+h}] - \mathsf{E}[\widehat{\boldsymbol{\nu}}_{T+h-1}]$ we have:

$$\left(\boldsymbol{\gamma}^* - \boldsymbol{\gamma}\right) + \boldsymbol{\Upsilon}^{h-1}\boldsymbol{\alpha}\left(\left[\boldsymbol{\mu}_0 - \boldsymbol{\mu}_0^*\right] + \boldsymbol{\beta}'\left[\boldsymbol{\gamma} - \boldsymbol{\gamma}^*\right](T+1)\right) \tag{5.74}$$

[2]The formula here is consistent with table 5.1, "Forecasting after break". There, the DV model bias for a change in μ goes to zero as the time lapse between the break and forecast origin increases.

since $\mathbf{A}_h - \mathbf{A}_{h-1} = \boldsymbol{\Upsilon}^{h-1}$. The first term is constant, and hence can be removed by an intercept correction once the regime shift has occurred; the second tends to zero as h increases since:

$$\boldsymbol{\Upsilon}^{h-1}\boldsymbol{\alpha} \to \mathbf{K}\boldsymbol{\alpha} = \mathbf{0}.$$

The results for the DV are similar – $\mathsf{E}[\widetilde{\boldsymbol{\nu}}_{T+h}] - \mathsf{E}[\widetilde{\boldsymbol{\nu}}_{T+h-1}]$ is given by:

$$(\boldsymbol{\gamma}^* - \boldsymbol{\gamma}) + \boldsymbol{\Upsilon}^{h-1}\boldsymbol{\alpha}\left([\boldsymbol{\mu}_0^a - \boldsymbol{\mu}_0^*] + \boldsymbol{\beta}'\left[\boldsymbol{\gamma}^a - \boldsymbol{\gamma}^*\right](T+1)\right). \tag{5.75}$$

When $\boldsymbol{\mu}_0^a = \boldsymbol{\mu}_0^*$ and $\boldsymbol{\beta}'\boldsymbol{\gamma}^a = \boldsymbol{\beta}'\boldsymbol{\gamma}^*$, then only a constant error ensues; when $\boldsymbol{\mu}_0^a = \boldsymbol{\mu}_0$ and $\boldsymbol{\beta}'\boldsymbol{\gamma}^a = \boldsymbol{\beta}'\boldsymbol{\gamma}$, the outcome coincides with the VEqCM; and otherwise, it lies in between.

5.9 Conclusion

We have shown that VEqCM and DV models of cointegrated processes have identical forecast-error biases when a forecast is made before a break occurs for a horizon that includes the break. This is so despite the former including, and the latter excluding, all the cointegration information, although their forecast-error variances will differ. The biases for the VEqCM do not depend on whether the forecast starts pre or post the break: thus, there is no error correction after the break. However, the DV and DDV have different biases pre and post for breaks in the equilibrium means, and these are usually smaller than the corresponding biases from the VEqCM. Consequently, for short-term forecasting, the DV and DDV may be sufficiently more robust to structural breaks to offset their variance losses. However, as the horizon increases, their advantages fall. Moreover, if breaks do not occur, then the VEqCM will dominate.

5.10 Appendix I: A Dynamic DV

Here we derive the population parameters of a DV for $\Delta\mathbf{x}_t$ regressed on $\Delta\mathbf{x}_{t-1}$ and an intercept. First, from (5.49):

$$\boldsymbol{\alpha}_\perp'\Delta\mathbf{x}_t = \boldsymbol{\alpha}_\perp'\boldsymbol{\gamma} + \boldsymbol{\alpha}_\perp'\boldsymbol{\nu}_t \tag{5.76}$$

is a white-noise innovation process, accounting for $n - r$ of the equations in the DV. Next:

$$\boldsymbol{\beta}'\mathbf{x}_t - (\boldsymbol{\mu}_0 + \boldsymbol{\mu}_1 (t+1)) = (\mathbf{I}_r + \boldsymbol{\beta}'\boldsymbol{\alpha}) \left[\boldsymbol{\beta}'\mathbf{x}_{t-1} - (\boldsymbol{\mu}_0 + \boldsymbol{\mu}_1 t)\right] + \boldsymbol{\beta}'\boldsymbol{\nu}_t.$$

Also:

$$\Delta\boldsymbol{\beta}'\mathbf{x}_t = \boldsymbol{\mu}_1 + \boldsymbol{\beta}'\boldsymbol{\alpha} (\boldsymbol{\beta}'\mathbf{x}_{t-1} - \boldsymbol{\mu}_0 - \boldsymbol{\mu}_1 t) + \boldsymbol{\beta}'\boldsymbol{\nu}_t$$

Let:

$$\mathbf{w}_t \doteq \boldsymbol{\beta}'\mathbf{x}_t - \boldsymbol{\mu}_0 - \boldsymbol{\mu}_1 (t+1)$$

be the remaining r variables in the DV. Then:

$$\mathbf{w}_t = \boldsymbol{\Lambda}\mathbf{w}_{t-1} + \mathbf{u}_t$$

where:

$$\boldsymbol{\Lambda} = \mathbf{I}_r + \boldsymbol{\beta}'\boldsymbol{\alpha}$$

has all its eigenvalues inside the unit circle. So:

$$\begin{aligned}
\mathsf{E}\left[\Delta\mathbf{w}_t \Delta\mathbf{w}'_{t-1}\right] &= 2\mathsf{E}\left[\mathbf{w}_t\mathbf{w}'_{t-1}\right] - \mathsf{E}\left[\mathbf{w}_t\mathbf{w}'_{t-2}\right] - \mathsf{E}\left[\mathbf{w}_{t-1}\mathbf{w}'_{t-1}\right] \\
&= 2\boldsymbol{\Lambda}\mathsf{E}\left[\mathbf{w}_{t-1}\mathbf{w}'_{t-1}\right] - \boldsymbol{\Lambda}^2\mathsf{E}\left[\mathbf{w}_{t-2}\mathbf{w}'_{t-2}\right] \\
&\quad -\mathsf{E}\left[\mathbf{w}_{t-1}\mathbf{w}'_{t-1}\right] \\
&= (\mathbf{I}_r - 2\boldsymbol{\Lambda} + \boldsymbol{\Lambda}^2)\mathbf{M} = (\mathbf{I}_r - \boldsymbol{\Lambda})^2\mathbf{M} = -(\boldsymbol{\beta}'\boldsymbol{\alpha})^2\mathbf{M}
\end{aligned}$$

and:

$$\begin{aligned}
\mathsf{E}\left[\Delta\mathbf{w}_{t-1}\Delta\mathbf{w}'_{t-1}\right] &= 2\mathsf{E}\left[\mathbf{w}_{t-1}\mathbf{w}'_{t-1}\right] - \mathsf{E}\left[\mathbf{w}_{t-1}\mathbf{w}'_{t-2}\right] - \mathsf{E}\left[\mathbf{w}_{t-2}\mathbf{w}'_{t-1}\right] \\
&= (\mathbf{I}_r - \boldsymbol{\Lambda})\mathbf{M} + \mathbf{M}(\mathbf{I}_r - \boldsymbol{\Lambda}') = -\boldsymbol{\beta}'\boldsymbol{\alpha}\mathbf{M} - \mathbf{M}\boldsymbol{\alpha}'\boldsymbol{\beta}.
\end{aligned}$$

Finally:

$$\mathsf{E}\left[\mathbf{w}_t\mathbf{w}'_t\right] = \mathbf{M} = \boldsymbol{\Lambda}\mathbf{M}\boldsymbol{\Lambda}' + \boldsymbol{\beta}'\boldsymbol{\Omega}\boldsymbol{\beta}.$$

Noting that $\Delta\mathbf{w}_t = \boldsymbol{\beta}'\Delta\mathbf{x}_t - \boldsymbol{\mu}_1$ and letting:

$$\Delta\boldsymbol{\beta}'\mathbf{x}_t = -\boldsymbol{\beta}'\boldsymbol{\alpha}\boldsymbol{\mu}_1 + \boldsymbol{\Lambda}\Delta\boldsymbol{\beta}'\mathbf{x}_{t^{\cdot}} + \mathbf{e}_t \tag{5.77}$$

then:

$$\boldsymbol{\Lambda} = (\boldsymbol{\beta}'\boldsymbol{\alpha})^2\mathbf{M}(\boldsymbol{\beta}'\boldsymbol{\alpha}\mathbf{M} + \mathbf{M}\boldsymbol{\alpha}'\boldsymbol{\beta})^{-1}.$$

Thus, we stack the $n-r$ equations from (5.76) with the r from (5.77) to yield:

$$\Delta \mathbf{x}_t = \begin{pmatrix} \boldsymbol{\alpha}'_{\perp} \\ \boldsymbol{\beta}' \end{pmatrix}^{-1} \left[\begin{pmatrix} \boldsymbol{\alpha}'_{\perp}\boldsymbol{\gamma} \\ -\boldsymbol{\beta}'\boldsymbol{\alpha}\boldsymbol{\mu}_1 \end{pmatrix} + \begin{pmatrix} \mathbf{0} \\ \boldsymbol{\Lambda}\boldsymbol{\beta}' \end{pmatrix} \Delta \mathbf{x}_t + \begin{pmatrix} \boldsymbol{\alpha}'_{\perp}\boldsymbol{\nu}_t \\ \mathbf{e}_t \end{pmatrix} \right].$$

5.11 Appendix II: DV and DDV Forecast-error Derivations

From T to $T+1$

From (5.6) and (5.7) respectively:

$$\widetilde{\mathbf{e}}_{T+1|T} = \mathbf{x}_{T+1} - \widetilde{\mathbf{x}}_{T+1|T} = \boldsymbol{\gamma}^* - \boldsymbol{\gamma} + \boldsymbol{\alpha}^* \left(\boldsymbol{\beta}'\mathbf{x}_T - \boldsymbol{\mu}^*\right) + \boldsymbol{\nu}_{T+1}, \quad (5.78)$$

and:

$$\overline{\mathbf{e}}_{T+1|T} = \mathbf{x}_{T+1} - \overline{\mathbf{x}}_{T+1|T} = \boldsymbol{\gamma}^* + \boldsymbol{\alpha}^* \left(\boldsymbol{\beta}'\mathbf{x}_T - \boldsymbol{\mu}^*\right) + \boldsymbol{\nu}_{T+1} - \Delta\mathbf{x}_T. \quad (5.79)$$

Let $\boldsymbol{\beta}'\mathbf{x}_T - \boldsymbol{\mu} = \boldsymbol{\kappa}_T$, then the *conditional* biases are:

$$\mathsf{E}\left[\widetilde{\mathbf{e}}_{T+1|T} \mid I_T\right] = (\boldsymbol{\gamma}^* - \boldsymbol{\gamma}) - \boldsymbol{\alpha}^* \left(\boldsymbol{\mu}^* - \boldsymbol{\mu}\right) + \boldsymbol{\alpha}^*\boldsymbol{\kappa}_T, \quad (5.80)$$

and:

$$\mathsf{E}\left[\overline{\mathbf{e}}_{T+1|T} \mid I_T\right] = (\boldsymbol{\gamma}^* - \Delta\mathbf{x}_T) - \boldsymbol{\alpha}^* \left(\boldsymbol{\mu}^* - \boldsymbol{\mu}\right) + \boldsymbol{\alpha}^*\boldsymbol{\kappa}_T. \quad (5.81)$$

From $T+1$ to $T+2$

The three 1-step forecasts become:

$$\Delta\widetilde{\mathbf{x}}_{T+2|T+1} = \boldsymbol{\gamma}, \quad (5.82)$$

and:

$$\Delta\overline{\mathbf{x}}_{T+2|T+1} = \Delta\mathbf{x}_{T+1}, \quad (5.83)$$

with corresponding 1-step forecast errors:

$$\widetilde{\mathbf{e}}_{T+2|T+1} = \boldsymbol{\gamma}^* - \boldsymbol{\gamma} + \boldsymbol{\alpha}^* \left(\boldsymbol{\beta}'\mathbf{x}_{T+1} - \boldsymbol{\mu}^*\right) + \boldsymbol{\nu}_{T+2} \quad (5.84)$$

and:

$$\overline{\mathbf{e}}_{T+2|T+1} = \boldsymbol{\gamma}^* + \boldsymbol{\alpha}^* \left(\boldsymbol{\beta}'\mathbf{x}_{T+1} - \boldsymbol{\mu}^*\right) + \boldsymbol{\nu}_{T+2} - \Delta\mathbf{x}_{T+1}, \quad (5.85)$$

from which the conditional biases follow as cited in the text.

From T to $T+2$

Since $\mathbf{x}_{T+1} = \boldsymbol{\Upsilon}^*\mathbf{x}_T + (\boldsymbol{\gamma}^* - \boldsymbol{\alpha}^*\boldsymbol{\mu}^*) + \boldsymbol{\nu}_{T+1}$, the data are generated by:

$$\mathbf{x}_{T+2} = (\boldsymbol{\Upsilon}^*)^2 \mathbf{x}_T + (\mathbf{I}_n + \boldsymbol{\Upsilon}^*)(\boldsymbol{\gamma}^* - \boldsymbol{\alpha}^*\boldsymbol{\mu}^*) + \boldsymbol{\Upsilon}^*\boldsymbol{\nu}_{T+1} + \boldsymbol{\nu}_{T+2}. \quad (5.86)$$

Also:

$$\widetilde{\mathbf{x}}_{T+2|T} = \mathbf{x}_T + 2\boldsymbol{\gamma}; \quad (5.87)$$

and:

$$\overline{\mathbf{x}}_{T+2|T} = \overline{\mathbf{x}}_{T+1|T} + \Delta\overline{\mathbf{x}}_{T+1|T} = \mathbf{x}_T + 2\Delta\mathbf{x}_T. \quad (5.88)$$

After some simplification, using $\boldsymbol{\Upsilon}\boldsymbol{\gamma} = \boldsymbol{\gamma}$ and $\boldsymbol{\Upsilon}^*\boldsymbol{\gamma}^* = \boldsymbol{\gamma}^*$, and:

$$\begin{aligned}(\boldsymbol{\Upsilon}^*)^2 - \boldsymbol{\Upsilon}^2 &= ((\mathbf{I}_n + \boldsymbol{\Upsilon}^*)\boldsymbol{\alpha}^* - (\mathbf{I}_n + \boldsymbol{\Upsilon})\boldsymbol{\alpha})\boldsymbol{\beta}' \\ &= [\boldsymbol{\alpha}^*(\mathbf{I}_r + \boldsymbol{\Lambda}^*) - \boldsymbol{\alpha}(\mathbf{I}_r + \boldsymbol{\Lambda})]\boldsymbol{\beta}' \quad (5.89)\end{aligned}$$

and as $(\boldsymbol{\Upsilon}^*)^2 \mathbf{x}_T - \mathbf{x}_T = \boldsymbol{\alpha}^*(2\mathbf{I}_r + \boldsymbol{\beta}'\boldsymbol{\alpha}^*)\boldsymbol{\beta}'\mathbf{x}_T = \boldsymbol{\alpha}^*(\mathbf{I}_r + \boldsymbol{\Lambda}^*)\boldsymbol{\beta}'\mathbf{x}_T$ then the corresponding 2-step ahead forecast errors are:

$$\begin{aligned}\widetilde{\mathbf{e}}_{T+2|T} &= \boldsymbol{\alpha}^*(2\mathbf{I}_r + \boldsymbol{\beta}'\boldsymbol{\alpha}^*)\boldsymbol{\kappa}_T + 2(\boldsymbol{\gamma}^* - \boldsymbol{\gamma}) - \boldsymbol{\alpha}^*(\mathbf{I}_r + \boldsymbol{\Lambda}^*)(\boldsymbol{\mu}^* - \boldsymbol{\mu}) \\ &\quad + \boldsymbol{\Upsilon}^*\boldsymbol{\nu}_{T+1} + \boldsymbol{\nu}_{T+2} \\ &= \mathsf{E}\left[\widetilde{\mathbf{e}}_{T+2|T}\right] + \boldsymbol{\alpha}^*(\mathbf{I}_r + \boldsymbol{\Lambda}^*)\boldsymbol{\kappa}_T + \boldsymbol{\Upsilon}^*\boldsymbol{\nu}_{T+1} + \boldsymbol{\nu}_{T+2}, \quad (5.90)\end{aligned}$$

and as $\Delta\mathbf{x}_T - \boldsymbol{\gamma} = \boldsymbol{\alpha}\boldsymbol{\kappa}_{T-1} + \boldsymbol{\nu}_T$:

$$\begin{aligned}\overline{\mathbf{e}}_{T+2|T} &= \boldsymbol{\alpha}^*(2\mathbf{I}_r + \boldsymbol{\beta}'\boldsymbol{\alpha}^*)\boldsymbol{\kappa}_T + 2(\boldsymbol{\gamma}^* - \boldsymbol{\gamma}) - \boldsymbol{\alpha}^*(\mathbf{I}_r + \boldsymbol{\Lambda}^*)(\boldsymbol{\mu}^* - \boldsymbol{\mu}) \\ &\quad + \boldsymbol{\Upsilon}^*\boldsymbol{\nu}_{T+1} + \boldsymbol{\nu}_{T+2} - 2(\Delta\mathbf{x}_T - \boldsymbol{\gamma}) \\ &= \mathsf{E}\left[\overline{\mathbf{e}}_{T+2|T}\right] + \boldsymbol{\alpha}^*(\mathbf{I}_r + \boldsymbol{\Lambda}^*)\boldsymbol{\kappa}_T - 2\boldsymbol{\alpha}\boldsymbol{\kappa}_{T-1} \\ &\quad - 2\boldsymbol{\nu}_T + \boldsymbol{\Upsilon}^*\boldsymbol{\nu}_{T+1} + \boldsymbol{\nu}_{T+2}. \quad (5.91)\end{aligned}$$

From $T+1$ to $T+3$

First, the two-step derivations closely match those from T to $T+2$ shifted forward one period:

$$\mathbf{x}_{T+3} = (\boldsymbol{\Upsilon}^*)^2 \mathbf{x}_{T+1} + (\mathbf{I}_n + \boldsymbol{\Upsilon}^*)(\boldsymbol{\gamma}^* - \boldsymbol{\alpha}^*\boldsymbol{\mu}^*) + \boldsymbol{\Upsilon}^*\boldsymbol{\nu}_{T+2} + \boldsymbol{\nu}_{T+3} \quad (5.92)$$

so that:

$$\boldsymbol{\beta}'\mathbf{x}_{T+3} = (\mathbf{I}_r + 2\boldsymbol{\beta}'\boldsymbol{\alpha}^* + \boldsymbol{\beta}'\boldsymbol{\alpha}^*\boldsymbol{\beta}'\boldsymbol{\alpha}^*)\boldsymbol{\beta}'\mathbf{x}_{T+1} \quad (5.93)$$

$$+\boldsymbol{\beta}'\left(\mathbf{I}_n+\boldsymbol{\Upsilon}^*\right)\left(\boldsymbol{\gamma}^*-\boldsymbol{\alpha}^*\boldsymbol{\mu}^*\right)$$

with:

$$\begin{aligned}\boldsymbol{\beta}'\mathbf{x}_{T+2} &= \left(\mathbf{I}_r+2\boldsymbol{\beta}'\boldsymbol{\alpha}^*+\boldsymbol{\beta}'\boldsymbol{\alpha}^*\boldsymbol{\beta}'\boldsymbol{\alpha}^*\right)\boldsymbol{\beta}'\mathbf{x}_T \\ &\quad +\boldsymbol{\beta}'\left(\mathbf{I}_n+\boldsymbol{\Upsilon}^*\right)\left(\boldsymbol{\gamma}^*-\boldsymbol{\alpha}^*\boldsymbol{\mu}^*\right).\end{aligned} \tag{5.94}$$

Also:

$$\widetilde{\mathbf{x}}_{T+3}=\mathbf{x}_{T+1}+2\boldsymbol{\gamma}, \tag{5.95}$$

and:

$$\overline{\mathbf{x}}_{T+3}=\mathbf{x}_{T+1}+2\Delta\mathbf{x}_{T+1}. \tag{5.96}$$

Using (5.89) and:

$$\mathsf{E}\left[\boldsymbol{\kappa}^*_{T+1}\right]=-\boldsymbol{\Lambda}^*\left(\boldsymbol{\mu}^*-\boldsymbol{\mu}\right),$$

then $\widetilde{\mathbf{e}}_{T+3|T+1}$ equals:

$$\begin{aligned}&\left[\left(\boldsymbol{\Upsilon}^*\right)^2-\mathbf{I}_n\right]\mathbf{x}_{T+1}+\left(\mathbf{I}_n+\boldsymbol{\Upsilon}^*\right)\left(\boldsymbol{\gamma}^*-\boldsymbol{\alpha}^*\boldsymbol{\mu}^*\right) \\ &\quad +\boldsymbol{\Upsilon}^*\boldsymbol{\nu}_{T+2}+\boldsymbol{\nu}_{T+3}-2\boldsymbol{\gamma} \\ &= \boldsymbol{\alpha}^*\left(\mathbf{I}_r+\boldsymbol{\Lambda}^*\right)\boldsymbol{\beta}'\mathbf{x}_{T+1}+2\left(\boldsymbol{\gamma}^*-\boldsymbol{\gamma}\right)-\boldsymbol{\alpha}^*\left(\mathbf{I}_r+\boldsymbol{\Lambda}^*\right)\boldsymbol{\mu}^* \\ &\quad +\boldsymbol{\Upsilon}^*\boldsymbol{\nu}_{T+2}+\boldsymbol{\nu}_{T+3} \\ &= 2\left(\boldsymbol{\gamma}^*-\boldsymbol{\gamma}\right)+\boldsymbol{\alpha}^*\left(\mathbf{I}_r+\boldsymbol{\Lambda}^*\right)\boldsymbol{\kappa}^*_{T+1}+\boldsymbol{\Upsilon}^*\boldsymbol{\nu}_{T+2}+\boldsymbol{\nu}_{T+3} \\ &= \mathsf{E}\left[\widetilde{\mathbf{e}}_{T+3|T+1}\right]+\boldsymbol{\alpha}^*\left(\mathbf{I}_r+\boldsymbol{\Lambda}^*\right)\left(\boldsymbol{\kappa}^*_{T+1}-\mathsf{E}\left[\boldsymbol{\kappa}^*_{T+1}\right]\right) \\ &\quad +\boldsymbol{\Upsilon}^*\boldsymbol{\nu}_{T+2}+\boldsymbol{\nu}_{T+3},\end{aligned}$$

as:

$$\mathsf{E}\left[\widetilde{\mathbf{e}}_{T+3|T+1}\right]=2\left(\boldsymbol{\gamma}^*-\boldsymbol{\gamma}\right)-\boldsymbol{\alpha}^*\boldsymbol{\Lambda}^*\left(\mathbf{I}_r+\boldsymbol{\Lambda}^*\right)\left(\boldsymbol{\mu}^*-\boldsymbol{\mu}\right).$$

Finally, the DDV forecast-error, $\overline{\mathbf{e}}_{T+3|T+1}$, is:

$$\begin{aligned}&\left[\left(\boldsymbol{\Upsilon}^*\right)^2-\mathbf{I}_n\right]\mathbf{x}_{T+1}+\left(\mathbf{I}_n+\boldsymbol{\Upsilon}^*\right)\left(\boldsymbol{\gamma}^*-\boldsymbol{\alpha}^*\boldsymbol{\mu}^*\right) \\ &\quad +\boldsymbol{\Upsilon}^*\boldsymbol{\nu}_{T+2}+\boldsymbol{\nu}_{T+3}-2\Delta\mathbf{x}_{T+1} \\ &= 2\left(\boldsymbol{\gamma}^*-\Delta\mathbf{x}_{T+1}\right)+\boldsymbol{\alpha}^*\left(\mathbf{I}_r+\boldsymbol{\Lambda}^*\right)\boldsymbol{\kappa}^*_{T+1}+\boldsymbol{\Upsilon}^*\boldsymbol{\nu}_{T+2}+\boldsymbol{\nu}_{T+3} \\ &= \mathsf{E}\left[\overline{\mathbf{e}}_{T+3|T+1}\right]+2\left(\mathsf{E}\left[\Delta\mathbf{x}_{T+1}\right]-\Delta\mathbf{x}_{T+1}\right) \\ &\quad +\boldsymbol{\alpha}^*\left(\mathbf{I}_r+\boldsymbol{\Lambda}^*\right)\left(\boldsymbol{\kappa}^*_{T+1}-\mathsf{E}\left[\boldsymbol{\kappa}^*_{T+1}\right]\right)+\boldsymbol{\Upsilon}^*\boldsymbol{\nu}_{T+2}+\boldsymbol{\nu}_{T+3},\end{aligned}$$

where:

$$\mathsf{E}\left[\overline{\mathbf{e}}_{T+3|T+1}\right] = -\boldsymbol{\alpha}^{*}\left(2\mathbf{I}_{r}+\boldsymbol{\Lambda}^{*}\right)\boldsymbol{\beta}'\boldsymbol{\alpha}^{*}\left(\boldsymbol{\mu}^{*}-\boldsymbol{\mu}\right).$$

6 Intercept Corrections

Summary

This chapter now considers a well-known trick to robustify forecasts against change, namely intercept corrections. Appropriate intercept corrections can enhance the performance of vector equilibrium-correction mechanisms, albeit that reductions in forecast bias may be achieved at the cost of inflated forecast-error variances. We also consider whether the differential susceptibility of differenced-data models to breaks – established in the previous chapter – can be exploited to correct the VEqCM.

6.1 Introduction

Chapter 3 showed that shifts in equilibrium means are a key cause of mis-prediction in vector equilibrium-correction mechanisms. Chapter 5 established the impact of such shifts on the forecasting performance of vector autoregressions in first and second differences (denoted DVs and DDVs), and showed that DVs and DDVs were more robust than VEqCMs in the face of deterministic shifts. This chapter evaluates the role of adjustments, or "intercept corrections", to purely model-based forecasts.[1] We show that intercept corrections may help VEqCMs

[1] Recognition of the potential for intercept adjustments has a long lineage: see, for example, Theil (1961) and Klein (1971).

match the performance of differenced representations in terms of reduction in bias. However, this may be achieved at the cost of inflated forecast-error variances.

Our previous book (see Clements and Hendry, 1998b, ch. 8) provided an extensive treatment of the general theory of intercept corrections (ICs), including their application to correcting structural breaks. In this chapter, we investigate their usefulness for offsetting deterministic shifts, assuming post-break stationarity. We derive expressions for the forecast biases and error variances, allowing an assessment of intercept-correcting strategies in terms of squared-error loss. We then consider whether the approximate unbiasedness established in chapter 5 for DV and DDV forecasts, despite equilibrium-mean shifts, can be exploited to derive more efficient ICs for the VEqCM. To investigate the usefulness in practice of IC strategies as compared to differencing, empirical illustrations follow in chapters 7 and 11, the latter reporting the results of applying some of these correction strategies to econometric models based on Mizon (1995), where wider classes of breaks than those we examine analytically may be important.

Section 6.2 describes the main principles of intercept corrections in the simplest setting, and offers four alternative explanations for their ability to offset deterministic shifts. In §6.3, the impact of intercept correcting the VEqCM is analyzed, in terms of its bias and variance effects. Then in §6.4, we consider corrections that exploit information contained in DV forecasts. Section 6.5 concludes.

6.2 The Basics of Intercept Corrections

It is widely recognized that published macroeconomic forecasts are rarely purely model-based, and adjustments are often made to arrive at a final forecast (see, e.g., Turner, 1990, for case studies of the impacts of such adjustments on the final forecasts). Thus, published economic forecasts reflect in varying degrees the properties of the models and the skills of the models' proprietors. These adjustments are sometimes known as intercept corrections, a term we shall use to refer to the practice of specifying non-zero values for a model's error terms over the forecast period. Hendry and Clements (1994b) provide a general theory of intercept corrections in macro-econometric forecasting, but here we shall focus on their role in offsetting regime shifts. When the model's in-sample error is an innovation on the information set, in the absence of anticipated structural breaks over the future, or of other extraneous factors, it is natural to set the future values of the equations' error terms to zero.

However, if past systematic forecast errors have occurred, or a recent deterministic shift has happened, it may pay to set a new value for the intercept to offset such errors. We first consider a simple example, where y_t is assumed to be generated around an unconditional mean μ by:

$$y_t = \mu + u_t \text{ where } u_t \sim \mathsf{IN}\left[0, \sigma_u^2\right]. \tag{6.1}$$

Then μ is estimated from a sample of size T by least squares, and used to forecast:

$$\widehat{y}_{T+1} = \widehat{\mu} = T^{-1}\sum_{t=1}^{T} y_t. \tag{6.2}$$

When (6.1) coincides with the DGP, (6.2) is the estimated conditional expectation:

$$\mathsf{E}\left[y_{T+1} \mid y_T\right] = \mu,$$

and as $\mathsf{E}\left[\widehat{\mu}\right] = \mu$, is the minimum-variance unbiased forecast. Nevertheless, many factors could induce a departure of (6.1) from the DGP, including error autocorrelation and past shifts in $\mathsf{E}\left[y_t\right]$.

Let the DGP actually be:

$$y_t = \mu + \delta 1_{\{t \geq T_1\}} + \rho y_{t-1} + \epsilon_t \text{ where } \epsilon_t \sim \mathsf{IN}\left[0, \sigma_\epsilon^2\right], \tag{6.3}$$

$|\rho| < 1$ and $1_{\{t \geq T_1\}}$ is an indicator with the value zero till time $T_1 < T$, after which it is unity. Now, $\mathsf{E}\left[y_{T+1}\right] = (\mu + \delta) / (1 - \rho)$ and:

$$\mathsf{E}\left[y_{T+1} \mid y_T\right] = \mu + \delta + \rho y_T,$$

for both of which (6.2) is a poor estimate since:

$$\mathsf{E}\left[\widehat{\mu}\right] = T^{-1}\left(\sum_{t=1}^{T_1} \mathsf{E}\left[y_t\right] + \sum_{t=T_1+1}^{T} \mathsf{E}\left[y_t\right]\right) = \frac{\mu + \delta}{1 - \rho} - \kappa\frac{\delta}{1 - \rho},$$

where $\kappa = T^{-1}T_1$.

At T, there was a residual of $\widehat{u}_T = y_T - \widehat{\mu}$, so to set the model "back on track" (i.e., fit the last observation perfectly), the intercept correction $\widehat{u}_T$ is often added to (6.2) to yield:

$$\widehat{y}_{\iota,T+1} = \widehat{\mu} + \widehat{u}_T = y_T. \tag{6.4}$$

Thus, the IC forecast changes the forecasting model to a random walk, thereby losing all the information about the equilibrium mean. However, one consequence is that:

$$\mathsf{E}\left[\widehat{y}_{\iota,T+1}\right] = \mathsf{E}\left[y_T\right] = \frac{\mu+\delta}{1-\rho},$$

which is unconditionally unbiased, despite the mis-specification of (6.1) for (6.3). Further:

$$\begin{aligned} y_{T+1} - \widehat{y}_{\iota,T+1} &= \mu + \delta + (\rho - 1)\, y_T + \epsilon_{T+1} \\ &= (\rho - 1)\left(y_T - \frac{\mu+\delta}{1-\rho}\right) + \epsilon_{T+1}, \end{aligned}$$

so that the unconditional MSFE is:

$$\mathsf{E}\left[\left(y_{T+1} - \widehat{y}_{\iota,T+1}\right)^2\right] = \sigma_\epsilon^2 + (1-\rho)^2\,\mathsf{V}\left[y_T\right] = \frac{2\sigma_\epsilon^2}{1+\rho}, \tag{6.5}$$

as against the minimum obtainable (for known parameters) of σ_ϵ^2. Clearly, such ICs as $\widehat{u}_T$ have excellent properties in this setting.

There are eight distinct, but obviously closely-related, ways to interpret this IC, depending partly on the postulated underlying source of the problem to be fixed. The first is that just presented, simply adding back the most recent error, $\widehat{u}_T$. That sets the model back on track, in that the forecasts commence from the last observed outcome, rather than the last fitted value.

The second notices that $\widehat{u}_T$ is identical to the coefficient on the indicator variable $1_{\{t\geq T\}}$ which is an excellent proxy at T for the omission of $\delta 1_{\{t\geq T_1\}} + \rho y_T$. When this IC dummy is not included, letting $w = \mathsf{E}\left[\widehat{\mu}\right] - \widehat{\mu}$ and $\widehat{u}_{T+1} = y_{T+1} - \widehat{\mu}$, then:

$$\widehat{u}_{T+1} = \rho\left(y_T - \frac{\mu+\delta}{1-\rho}\right) + \epsilon_{T+1} + \kappa\frac{\delta}{1-\rho} + w,$$

so:

$$\mathsf{V}\left[\widehat{u}_{T+1}\right] = \sigma_{\epsilon}^{2} + \rho^{2}\frac{\sigma_{\epsilon}^{2}}{1-\rho^{2}} + \mathsf{V}\left[w\right] \simeq \frac{\sigma_{\epsilon}^{2}}{1-\rho^{2}}, \tag{6.6}$$

as $\mathsf{V}[w]$ is $O\left(T^{-1}\right)$. Comparing (6.5) and (6.6), when $\rho = 0$, the dummy doubles the forecast-error variance, but for $\rho > 0.5$, it even lowers the variance. When $\delta \neq 0$, the IC offsets that bias, whereas $\widehat{\mu}$ does not: in particular, if the break has just happened, $\kappa = 1$, and the bias could be large. The generalizations of this view of intercept correcting are to: (a) set the indicator to non-zero values for several pre-sample observations; and (b) use weights on future observations that differ from that on $\widehat{u}_T$.

A third interpretation is to focus on the fact that (6.4) could have been obtained by differencing (6.1), and ignoring the resulting (negative) moving-average error:

$$\Delta y_t = e_t \text{ with } \overline{y}_{T+1} = y_T,$$

where $e_t = \Delta u_t$. This view explains the loss of information about the equilibrium mean, and relates the IC approach to the results in the previous chapter about the efficacy of differencing in removing the forecast-error biases resulting from deterministic shifts, thereby accounting directly for the forecasting success of $\widehat{y}_{\iota,T+1}$. However, the DDV in chapter 5 differenced all the data, sample and forecast period, whereas the IC only differences the forecast-period data. Section 7.5 provides an empirical illustration.

That last comment leads directly to the fourth interpretation, namely that the IC approach forecasts the next error, u_{T+1} using $\widetilde{u}_{T+1} = \widetilde{u}_T$ $(= \widehat{u}_T)$. Such a forecast imposes a common factor of unity on the dynamics of the process over the forecast period (on common factors in dynamic models, see Sargan, 1964b, Sargan, 1980, Hendry and Mizon, 1978, and Hendry, 1995a, ch. 7). To see this, extend (6.1) to:

$$y_t = \mu + u_t \text{ where } u_t = u_{t-1} + \varsigma_t,$$

then:

$$(1-L)\,y_t = (1-L)\,\mu + \varsigma_t. \tag{6.7}$$

Thus, the factor $(1-L)$ of the polynomial in L in (6.7) has a coefficient of unity and is common to both sides (although here $(1-L)\,\mu$ happens to be zero). Consequently, we can reinterpret (6.4) as:

$$\widehat{y}_{\iota,T+1} = \widehat{y}_{T+1} + \widetilde{u}_{T+1} \text{ where } \widetilde{u}_{T+1} = \widetilde{u}_{T},$$

so:

$$(1-L)\,\widetilde{u}_{T+1} = 0. \tag{6.8}$$

Thus, (6.8) implements the common-factor representation in (6.7). For generalizations to systems, or to sequential 1-step forecasting, the unit-common-factor interpretation is the most convenient.

The fifth interpretation is in terms of time-varying coefficients which follow a random walk, so this time we extend (6.1) to:

$$y_t = \mu_t + u_t \text{ where } \mu_t = \mu_{t-1} + \omega_t \tag{6.9}$$

with $\mu_0 = \mu$ and $\omega_t \sim \mathsf{IN}\left[0, \sigma^2_\omega\right]$ independently of u_t so:

$$y_t = \mu_0 + \sum_{i=0}^{t} \omega_{t-i} + u_t = \mu_0 + \eta_t \tag{6.10}$$

where:

$$(1-L)\,\eta_t = \omega_t + (1-L)\,u_t.$$

As before, a common factor of unity is introduced, and can be offset by the corresponding IC. From (6.10), $\{\eta_t\}$ is very heteroscedastic, and a good estimate of the local state will heavily discount past observations: the IC does so by only using the last observation.

Next, denote the random-walk forecast by $\widetilde{y}_{T+1} = y_T$, then as $\widehat{y}_{T+1} = \widehat{\mu}$ and $\widehat{u}_T = y_T - \widehat{\mu} = \widetilde{y}_{T+1} - \widehat{y}_{T+1}$:

$$\widehat{y}_{\iota,T+1} = \theta\widehat{y}_{T+1} + (1-\theta)\,\widetilde{y}_{T+1}, \tag{6.11}$$

provides a "combination of forecasts" interpretation, although the actual choice of $\theta = 0$ in (6.4) eliminates $\widehat{y}_{T+1}$ (negative weights may be needed to eliminate breaks). Indeed, (6.11) suggests a potential role for using time-series forecasts to intercept-correct econometric model-based ones, a theme we return to in §6.4.

Clements and Hendry (1998b, chapter 8) note that ICs can have "shrinkage" interpretations, namely, placing a weight of less than unity on a short-term forecast to move it closer to an equilibrium mean. This can best be illustrated in a constant-parameter AR(1) DGP with a zero mean, and assuming the model coincides with the DGP. Consider two predictors: $\widehat{y}_{T+1}$, from the estimated model, which incorporates parameter-estimation uncertainty, and $\overline{y}$, the unconditional mean of the process, which is assumed known. A composite predictor is given by:

$$\widetilde{y}_{s,T+1} = \theta \overline{y} + (1-\theta)\, \widehat{y}_{T+1} = (1-\theta)\, \widehat{y}_{T+1}, \tag{6.12}$$

which, with $0 \leq \theta \leq 1$, "shrinks" the model predictor toward the equilibrium mean of zero. Here, the IC is $-\theta \widehat{y}_{T+1} = -\theta \widehat{\rho} y_T$.

Finally, intercept corrections can sometimes be given a "pooling" interpretation in multivariate or systems contexts. This interpretation does not follow immediately from the above examples, but will be developed briefly below to show just how general the notion of intercept correcting is. The illustration is based on Hoogstrate, Palm and Pfann (1996), who wish to forecast output growth rates for a number of countries. To that end, forecasts are calculated from autoregressive-distributed lag (ADL) models estimated for each country separately, and from models estimated by pooling data across a number of countries. Simplifying by assuming AR(p) models, forecasts based on the country-specific parameter estimates are:

$$\widehat{y}_{j,T+1} = \widehat{\boldsymbol{\beta}}_j' \mathbf{Y}_{j,T} \tag{6.13}$$

for country $j \in J$, where $\mathbf{Y}_{j,T} = (y_{j,T}, y_{j,T-1}, \ldots, y_{j,T-p-1})'$, where $\widehat{\boldsymbol{\beta}}_j = (\mathbf{Y}_j^{*\prime}\mathbf{Y}_j^*)^{-1}\mathbf{Y}_j^{*\prime}\mathbf{Y}_j$, with $\mathbf{Y}_j^* = (\mathbf{Y}_{j-1}, \ldots, \mathbf{Y}_{j-p})$, $\mathbf{Y}_{j-s} = (y_{j,p+1-s}, \ldots, y_{j,T-s})'$ and $\mathbf{Y}_j \equiv \mathbf{Y}_{j-0}$. Thus $\mathbf{Y}_{j-s}$ denotes the vector of $(T-p)$ observations for country j lagged s periods relative to T, and $\mathbf{Y}_j^*$ denotes the matrix of regressors.

Pooled forecasts for country j may take the form:

$$\widetilde{y}_{j,T+1} = \widetilde{\boldsymbol{\beta}}' \mathbf{Y}_{j,T} \tag{6.14}$$

where:

$$\widetilde{\boldsymbol{\beta}} = (\mathbf{Y}'\mathbf{Y})^{-1}\mathbf{Y}'\mathbf{y},$$

with $\mathbf{Y} = (\mathbf{Y}_1^{*\prime}, \ldots, \mathbf{Y}_j^{*\prime}, \ldots, \mathbf{Y}_J^{*\prime})'$ and $\mathbf{y} = (\mathbf{Y}_1', \ldots, \mathbf{Y}_j', \ldots, , \mathbf{Y}_J')'$. $\widetilde{\boldsymbol{\beta}}$ is the same for all countries and is calculated by OLS on the stacked data vectors.

A linear combination of the non-pooled and pooled forecasts is the "θ-shrinkage" forecast, defined by:

$$y^{\theta_j}_{j,T+1} = (1 - \theta_j)\,\widehat{y}_{j,T+1} + \theta_j \widetilde{y}_{j,T+1}.$$

which shrinks the forecast based on $\widehat{\beta}_j$ to that based on the pooled estimate, $\widetilde{\beta}$. This practice can be interpreted as an intercept-correcting strategy, because:

$$\begin{aligned} y^{\theta_j}_{j,T+1} &= \widehat{y}_{j,T+1} + \theta_j \left(\widetilde{y}_{j,T+1} - \widehat{y}_{j,T+1}\right) \\ &= \widehat{y}_{j,T+1} + \theta_j \left(\widetilde{\beta} - \widehat{\beta}\right)' \mathbf{Y}_{j,T}, \end{aligned}$$

so the IC is $(\widetilde{\beta} - \widehat{\beta}_j)'\mathbf{Y}_{j,T}$, with weight θ_j. The IC-interpretation of pooling is unchanged if $\widetilde{\beta}$ is estimated by systems estimators to allow for contemporaneous correlations in the equations' disturbance terms.

Several of these interpretations will recur below and in the empirical applications.

6.3 Intercept Corrections to VEqCMs

As in §5.8, we consider post-transition forecast errors when the DGP is (5.40), reproduced as:

$$\mathbf{x}_t = \boldsymbol{\tau}_0 + \boldsymbol{\tau}_1 t + \boldsymbol{\Upsilon}\mathbf{x}_{t-1} + \boldsymbol{\nu}_t \tag{6.15}$$

where $\boldsymbol{\nu}_t \sim \mathsf{IN}_n\left[\mathbf{0}, \boldsymbol{\Omega}_\nu\right]$ and we can write the VEqCM as in (5.49):

$$\Delta\mathbf{x}_t = \boldsymbol{\gamma} + \boldsymbol{\alpha}\left(\boldsymbol{\beta}'\mathbf{x}_{t-1} - \boldsymbol{\mu}_0 - \boldsymbol{\mu}_1 t\right) + \boldsymbol{\nu}_t. \tag{6.16}$$

We can show that if there is a one-off change in the value of the deterministic parameters $\boldsymbol{\tau}_0$ in the DGP, which has occurred prior to the period on which the forecasts are conditioned, then the optimal (in the sense of yielding unbiased forecasts) intercept correction for the VEqCM is simply to add in the period T residual each step ahead. Below we denote forecasts generated by this method by $\dot{\mathbf{x}}_{T+h}$. We also consider some other general strategies for intercept correcting, which are applied in the empirical work. In practice, the circumstances under which the $\dot{\mathbf{x}}_{T+h}$ strategy is optimal are unlikely to hold exactly: the $\boldsymbol{\tau}_1$ parameters may shift as well; $\boldsymbol{\tau}_0$ may change a number of times over the forecast period; the slope parameters may also alter, etc. Thus it may be of interest empirically to compare the performance of other adjustment schemes, so in this section we consider what can be deduced analytically about their properties.

We may also wish to base the adjustment on some average of recent errors rather than simply the observed model error at the forecast origin. Again, this occurs commonly in practice. The forecast origin value is assumed to be correctly measured, though empirically, only preliminary data may be available.

Below, we assume that the period T residual embodies the change in the process, and the discussion is in terms of the VEqCM, even though there may also be scope for adjustments to the DV. Assuming $\boldsymbol{\Upsilon}$ does not change, the period T residual is given by:

$$\hat{\boldsymbol{\nu}}_T = \mathbf{x}_T - \hat{\mathbf{x}}_T = (\boldsymbol{\tau}_0^* - \boldsymbol{\tau}_0) + (\boldsymbol{\tau}_1^* - \boldsymbol{\tau}_1)T + \boldsymbol{\nu}_T. \tag{6.17}$$

We now consider a number of options for forecasting h-steps ahead. The IC can be held constant over the forecast period, so that the period T error is added at each step ahead. This is perhaps the most commonly-used form of IC, where the adjustment over the future is held constant at an average of the most recent errors (in our example, just the period T error). This amounts to solving:

$$\dot{\mathbf{x}}_{T+h} = \boldsymbol{\tau}_0 + \boldsymbol{\tau}_1 (T+h) + \boldsymbol{\Upsilon}\dot{\mathbf{x}}_{T+h-1} + \hat{\boldsymbol{\nu}}_T \tag{6.18}$$

where $\dot{\mathbf{x}}_T = \mathbf{x}_T$, so that:

$$\dot{\mathbf{x}}_{T+h} = \hat{\mathbf{x}}_{T+h} + \sum_{i=0}^{h-1} \boldsymbol{\Upsilon}^i \hat{\boldsymbol{\nu}}_T = \hat{\mathbf{x}}_{T+h} + \mathbf{A}_h \hat{\boldsymbol{\nu}}_T. \tag{6.19}$$

Secondly, only adjust the 1-step forecast:

$$\begin{aligned} \overrightarrow{\mathbf{x}}_{T+1} &= \dot{\mathbf{x}}_{T+1} \\ &\vdots \\ \overrightarrow{\mathbf{x}}_{T+h} &= \boldsymbol{\tau}_0 + \boldsymbol{\tau}_1 (T+h) + \boldsymbol{\Upsilon}\overrightarrow{\mathbf{x}}_{T+h-1} \end{aligned} \tag{6.20}$$

which implies that:

$$\overrightarrow{\mathbf{x}}_{T+h} = \hat{\mathbf{x}}_{T+h} + \boldsymbol{\Upsilon}^{h-1}\hat{\boldsymbol{\nu}}_T. \tag{6.21}$$

Thirdly, one may adjust the h-step forecast by the full amount of the period T error:

$$\overleftrightarrow{\mathbf{x}}_{T+h} = \hat{\mathbf{x}}_{T+h} + \hat{\boldsymbol{\nu}}_T. \tag{6.22}$$

Finally, tailing-off the adjustment induces:

$$\begin{aligned} \overline{\mathbf{x}}_{T+h} &= \boldsymbol{\tau} + \boldsymbol{\Upsilon}\overline{\mathbf{x}}_{T+h-1} + \mathbf{H}^{h-1}\hat{\boldsymbol{\nu}}_T \\ &= \hat{\mathbf{x}}_{T+h} + \sum_{i=0}^{h-1} \boldsymbol{\Upsilon}^i \mathbf{H}^{h-1-i}\hat{\boldsymbol{\nu}}_T \end{aligned} \tag{6.23}$$

where $\mathbf{H}$ may be diagonal, say, with typical element $|h_{ii}| < 1$.

6.3.1 *Biases*

It is straightforward to derive expressions for the biases associated with the above forecasts, since in each case the forecasts are written as the conditional expectation ($\hat{\mathbf{x}}_{T+h}$) plus another term, and the conditional expectation forecast biases are given by (5.54) or (5.67). For the first strategy, from (6.17):

$$\mathsf{E}\left[\hat{\boldsymbol{\nu}}_T\right] = \left(\boldsymbol{\tau}_0^* - \boldsymbol{\tau}_0\right) + \left(\boldsymbol{\tau}_1^* - \boldsymbol{\tau}_1\right)T,$$

and noting that the conditional and unconditional (over $\mathbf{x}_T$) expectations coincide here, then in the $(\boldsymbol{\tau}_0, \boldsymbol{\tau}_1)$ notation:

$$\mathsf{E}\left[\dot{\boldsymbol{\nu}}_{T+h} \mid \mathbf{x}_T\right] = \mathsf{E}\left[\hat{\boldsymbol{\nu}}_{T+h} - \mathbf{A}_h\hat{\boldsymbol{\nu}}_T\right] = \left[h\mathbf{A}_h - \mathbf{D}_h\right]\left(\boldsymbol{\tau}_1^* - \boldsymbol{\tau}_1\right). \tag{6.24}$$

Thus, the constant-adjustment strategy yields unbiased forecasts when $\boldsymbol{\tau}_1^* = \boldsymbol{\tau}_1$.

In terms of the notation of §5.8.2:

$$\mathbf{A}_h\hat{\boldsymbol{\nu}}_T = \mathbf{A}_h\left(\gamma^* - \gamma\right) - \mathbf{A}_h\boldsymbol{\alpha}\left(\boldsymbol{\mu}_0^* - \boldsymbol{\mu}_0\right) - \mathbf{A}_h\boldsymbol{\alpha}\boldsymbol{\beta}'\left(\gamma^* - \gamma\right)T,$$

and taking $\mathsf{E}\left[\hat{\boldsymbol{\nu}}_{T+h}\right]$ from (5.67) we obtain:

$$\begin{aligned} \mathsf{E}\left[\dot{\boldsymbol{\nu}}_{T+h} \mid \mathbf{x}_T\right] &= \left(h - \mathbf{A}_h - \mathbf{A}_h\boldsymbol{\alpha}\boldsymbol{\beta}'\right)\left(\gamma^* - \gamma\right) \\ &= -\left(\mathbf{A}_h + \mathbf{B}_h\right)\boldsymbol{\alpha}\boldsymbol{\beta}'\left(\gamma^* - \gamma\right). \end{aligned}$$

In fact, this expression is zero when the time trend is absent, since then $\boldsymbol{\beta}'\left(\gamma^* - \gamma\right) = \boldsymbol{\mu}_1^* - \boldsymbol{\mu}_1 = \mathbf{0}$.

Expressions for the conditional biases resulting from the other adjustment schemes are:

$$\mathsf{E}\left[\overrightarrow{\boldsymbol{\nu}}_{T+h} \mid \mathbf{x}_T\right] = \mathsf{E}\left[\widehat{\boldsymbol{\nu}}_{T+h} - (\mathbf{A}_h - \mathbf{A}_{h-1})\,\widehat{\boldsymbol{\nu}}_T\right],$$

so $\mathsf{E}[\overrightarrow{\boldsymbol{\nu}}_{T+h} \mid \mathbf{x}_T]$ is given by:

$$h(\gamma^* - \gamma) - (\mathbf{A}_h - \mathbf{A}_{h-1})\left(\mathbf{I}_n + \boldsymbol{\alpha\beta}'\right)(\gamma^* - \gamma) \\ -\mathbf{A}_{h-1}\left(\boldsymbol{\alpha}\left(\boldsymbol{\mu}_0^* - \boldsymbol{\mu}_0\right) + \boldsymbol{\alpha\beta}'(\gamma^* - \gamma)[T+1]\right) \tag{6.25}$$

and $\mathsf{E}[\overleftrightarrow{\boldsymbol{\nu}}_{T+h} \mid \mathbf{x}_T]$ by:

$$h(\gamma^* - \gamma) - \left(\mathbf{I}_n + \boldsymbol{\alpha\beta}'\right)(\gamma^* - \gamma) \\ -(\mathbf{A}_h - \mathbf{I}_n)\left(\boldsymbol{\alpha}\left(\boldsymbol{\mu}_0^* - \boldsymbol{\mu}_0\right) + \boldsymbol{\alpha\beta}'(\gamma^* - \gamma)[T+1]\right). \tag{6.26}$$

Finally, $\mathsf{E}\left[\overline{\boldsymbol{\nu}}_{T+h}|\mathbf{x}_T\right]$ is:

$$h(\gamma^* - \gamma) - \sum_{i=0}^{h-1} \boldsymbol{\Upsilon}^i \mathbf{H}^{h-1-i}\left(\mathbf{I}_n + \boldsymbol{\alpha\beta}'\right)(\gamma^* - \gamma) \\ -\left(\sum_{i=0}^{h-1} \boldsymbol{\Upsilon}^i\left(\mathbf{I}_n - \mathbf{H}^{h-1-i}\right)\right) \\ \times\left(\boldsymbol{\alpha}\left(\boldsymbol{\mu}_0^* - \boldsymbol{\mu}_0\right) + \boldsymbol{\alpha\beta}'(\gamma^* - \gamma)[T+1]\right). \tag{6.27}$$

When the time trend is absent, the biases with ICs become:

$$\begin{aligned} \mathsf{E}\left[\overrightarrow{\boldsymbol{\nu}}_{T+h} \mid \mathbf{x}_T\right] &= h(\gamma^* - \gamma) - \mathbf{A}_{h-1}\boldsymbol{\alpha}\left(\boldsymbol{\mu}_0^* - \boldsymbol{\mu}_0\right) \\ &\quad -(\mathbf{A}_h - \mathbf{A}_{h-1})(\gamma^* - \gamma) \\ &= (h - \mathbf{A}_h + \mathbf{A}_{h-1})(\gamma^* - \gamma) \\ &\quad -\mathbf{A}_{h-1}\boldsymbol{\alpha}\left(\boldsymbol{\mu}_0^* - \boldsymbol{\mu}_0\right). \end{aligned} \tag{6.28}$$

$$\begin{aligned} \mathsf{E}\left[\overleftrightarrow{\boldsymbol{\nu}}_{T+h} \mid \mathbf{x}_T\right] &= h(\gamma^* - \gamma) - (\gamma^* - \gamma) \\ &\quad -(\mathbf{A}_h - \mathbf{I}_n)\,\boldsymbol{\alpha}\left(\boldsymbol{\mu}_0^* - \boldsymbol{\mu}_0\right) \\ &= (h-1)(\gamma^* - \gamma) \\ &\quad -\boldsymbol{\alpha}\sum_{i=1}^{h-1}\left(\mathbf{I} + \boldsymbol{\beta}'\boldsymbol{\alpha}\right)^i\left(\boldsymbol{\mu}_0^* - \boldsymbol{\mu}_0\right) \end{aligned} \tag{6.29}$$

$$
\begin{aligned}
\mathsf{E}\left[\overline{\boldsymbol{\nu}}_{T+h} \mid \mathbf{x}_T\right] &= h\left(\gamma^* - \gamma\right) \\
&\quad - \left(\sum_{i=0}^{h-1} \boldsymbol{\Upsilon}^i \left(\mathbf{I}_n - \mathbf{H}^{h-1-i}\right)\right) \boldsymbol{\alpha}\left(\boldsymbol{\mu}_0^* - \boldsymbol{\mu}_0\right) \\
&\quad - \sum_{i=0}^{h-1} \boldsymbol{\Upsilon}^i \mathbf{H}^{h-1-i} \left(\gamma^* - \gamma\right)
\end{aligned} \tag{6.30}
$$

Thus, when $\gamma^* = \gamma$ but $\boldsymbol{\mu}_0^* \neq \boldsymbol{\mu}_0$, just adjusting the h-step forecast (that is, $\overleftrightarrow{\mathbf{x}}_{T+h}$, in (6.29)) will yield a larger bias than adjusting only the 1-step forecast (see (6.28). Even if the process remains unchanged, there is no penalty in terms of bias from intercept correcting.

6.3.2 *Variances*

The penalty to intercept correcting when the process is unchanged is in terms of increased uncertainty. The conditional forecast-error variances for strategies (6.19) to (6.23) are given by (6.31) to (6.34) below, and all exceed the conditional expectation forecast-error variance $\mathsf{V}\left[\widehat{\boldsymbol{\nu}}_{T+h}|\mathbf{x}_T\right]$ in (5.55) by a positive semi-definite matrix:

$$
\mathsf{V}\left[\dot{\boldsymbol{\nu}}_{T+h} \mid \mathbf{x}_T\right] = 2\mathsf{V}\left[\widehat{\boldsymbol{\nu}}_{T+h} \mid \mathbf{x}_T\right] + \sum_{j=0}^{h-1}\sum_{i=0}^{h-1} \boldsymbol{\Upsilon}^j \boldsymbol{\Omega} \boldsymbol{\Upsilon}^{i\prime} \quad j \neq i \tag{6.31}
$$

$$
\mathsf{V}\left[\overrightarrow{\boldsymbol{\nu}}_{T+h} \mid \mathbf{x}_T\right] = \mathsf{V}\left[\widehat{\boldsymbol{\nu}}_{T+h} \mid \mathbf{x}_T\right] + \boldsymbol{\Upsilon}^{h-1} \boldsymbol{\Omega} \boldsymbol{\Upsilon}^{h-1\prime} \tag{6.32}
$$

$$
\mathsf{V}\left[\overleftrightarrow{\boldsymbol{\nu}}_{T+h} \mid \mathbf{x}_T\right] = \mathsf{V}\left[\widehat{\boldsymbol{\nu}}_{T+h} \mid \mathbf{x}_T\right] + \boldsymbol{\Omega} \tag{6.33}
$$

$$
\begin{aligned}
\mathsf{V}\left[\overline{\boldsymbol{\nu}}_{T+h} \mid \mathbf{x}_T\right] &= \mathsf{V}\left[\widehat{\boldsymbol{\nu}}_{T+h} \mid \mathbf{x}_T\right] \\
&\quad + \sum_{j=0}^{h-1}\sum_{i=0}^{h-1} \boldsymbol{\Upsilon}^i \left(\mathbf{I} - \mathbf{H}^{h-1-i}\right) \boldsymbol{\Omega} \left(\mathbf{I} - \mathbf{H}^{h-1-i\prime}\right) \boldsymbol{\Upsilon}^{i\prime}.
\end{aligned} \tag{6.34}
$$

For example, the error variance more than doubles for the constant-adjustment strategy. The problem is apparent from (6.17), since the intercept correction comprises terms reflecting the change in the intercept and trend parameter plus the full value of the period T disturbance, which has an (unconditional) variance of $\boldsymbol{\Omega}$. A more precise estimate of the change-in-parameter component could be obtained by averaging a number of recent errors, provided the break occurred sufficiently far back.

Nevertheless, summing the (squared) bias and variance components, for a sufficiently large change in $\boldsymbol{\tau}_0$, holding the adjustment constant over the forecast period will result in the smallest MSFE (since the bias components of the other adjustment schemes can be made arbitrarily large).

6.4 Time-series Intercept Corrections

While intercept corrections can reduce the bias of forecasts from VEqCMs when there are shifts in deterministic factors, provided the change has occurred prior to the forecast origin, this is typically only achieved at the cost of an increase in the forecast error variance, so that in an unchanged world, for example, the indiscriminate use of ICs may adversely affect accuracy measured by squared-error loss. This suggests either a more judicious use of ICs – repeated pre-testing or monitoring for structural change (see, e.g., Chu, Stinchcombe and White, 1996) – so that the correction is conditional, or devising forms of correction that have a smaller variance effect.

We consider corrections that exploit the greater adaptability of unit-root models in the face of structural change. We revert to the statistical framework of (1.12), and again assume stationary post-break expectations.

6.4.1 VEqCM and DV forecast errors

We briefly sketch the VEqCM and DV forecast errors when there are changes in the deterministic components. These are simplified versions of the formulae presented in §5.8 since the linear trend is excluded from the analysis.

The h-step ahead VEqCM forecasts for the levels of the process are given by $\widehat{\mathbf{x}}_{T+h} = \mathsf{E}[\mathbf{x}_{T+h}|\mathbf{x}_T]$:

$$\widehat{\mathbf{x}}_{T+h} = \boldsymbol{\tau} + \boldsymbol{\Upsilon}\widehat{\mathbf{x}}_{T+h-1} = \sum_{i=0}^{h-1} \boldsymbol{\Upsilon}^i \boldsymbol{\tau} + \boldsymbol{\Upsilon}^h \mathbf{x}_T \tag{6.35}$$

with associated forecast errors of:

$$\widehat{\boldsymbol{\nu}}_{T+h} = \mathbf{x}_{T+h} - \widehat{\mathbf{x}}_{T+h}.$$

Consider the situation where the system experiences a step change between the estimation and forecast periods, such that $\boldsymbol{\tau}$ changes to $\boldsymbol{\tau}^*$. The data generated by the process is then:

$$\begin{aligned}\mathbf{x}_{T+h} &= \boldsymbol{\tau}^* + \boldsymbol{\Upsilon}\mathbf{x}_{T+h-1} + \boldsymbol{\nu}_{T+h} \\ &= \sum_{i=0}^{h-1} \boldsymbol{\Upsilon}^i \boldsymbol{\tau}^* + \sum_{i=0}^{h-1} \boldsymbol{\Upsilon}^i \boldsymbol{\nu}_{T+h-i} + \boldsymbol{\Upsilon}^h \mathbf{x}_T.\end{aligned} \tag{6.36}$$

Then, the h-step ahead forecast error can be written as:

$$\begin{aligned}\widehat{\boldsymbol{\nu}}_{T+h} &= \sum_{i=0}^{h-1} \boldsymbol{\Upsilon}^i \boldsymbol{\tau}^* + \sum_{i=0}^{h-1} \boldsymbol{\Upsilon}^i \boldsymbol{\nu}_{T+h-i} \\ &\quad + \boldsymbol{\Upsilon}^h \mathbf{x}_T - \sum_{i=0}^{h-1} \boldsymbol{\Upsilon}^i \boldsymbol{\tau} - \boldsymbol{\Upsilon}^h \mathbf{x}_T \\ &= \sum_{i=0}^{h-1} \boldsymbol{\Upsilon}^i (\boldsymbol{\tau}^* - \boldsymbol{\tau}) + \sum_{i=0}^{h-1} \boldsymbol{\Upsilon}^i \boldsymbol{\nu}_{T+h-i}.\end{aligned} \tag{6.37}$$

Conditional and unconditional forecast-error expectations coincide:

$$\begin{aligned}\mathsf{E}[\widehat{\boldsymbol{\nu}}_{T+h} \mid \mathbf{x}_T] = \mathsf{E}[\widehat{\boldsymbol{\nu}}_{T+h}] &= \sum_{i=0}^{h-1} \boldsymbol{\Upsilon}^i (\boldsymbol{\tau}^* - \boldsymbol{\tau}) \\ &= \sum_{i=0}^{h-1} \boldsymbol{\Upsilon}^i [(\boldsymbol{\gamma}^* - \boldsymbol{\gamma}) + \boldsymbol{\alpha}(\boldsymbol{\mu} - \boldsymbol{\mu}^*)]\end{aligned} \tag{6.38}$$

and the forecast-error variance is:

$$\mathsf{V}[\widehat{\boldsymbol{\nu}}_{T+h}] = \sum_{i=0}^{h-1} \boldsymbol{\Upsilon}^i \boldsymbol{\Omega} \boldsymbol{\Upsilon}^{i\prime}.$$

The bias is increasing in h due to the first term in square brackets. The impact of the second term eventually levels off because:

$$\lim_{i\to\infty} \boldsymbol{\Upsilon}^i = \mathbf{I}_n - \boldsymbol{\alpha}(\boldsymbol{\beta}'\boldsymbol{\alpha})^{-1}\boldsymbol{\beta}' = \mathbf{K}$$

and $\mathbf{K}\boldsymbol{\alpha} = \mathbf{0}$.

Now, consider forecasts from the DV, defined by setting $\Delta\mathbf{x}_{T+h}$ equal to the population growth rate $\boldsymbol{\gamma}$:

$$\Delta\widetilde{\mathbf{x}}_{T+h} = \boldsymbol{\gamma} \tag{6.39}$$

so that h-step ahead forecasts of the level of the process are obtained by integrating (6.39) from the initial condition $\mathbf{x}_T$:

$$\widetilde{\mathbf{x}}_{T+h} = \widetilde{\mathbf{x}}_{T+h-1} + \boldsymbol{\gamma} = \mathbf{x}_T + h\boldsymbol{\gamma}. \tag{6.40}$$

The expected value of the conditional h-step ahead forecast error is:

$$\begin{aligned} \mathsf{E}\left[\widetilde{\boldsymbol{\nu}}_{T+h} \mid \mathbf{x}_T\right] &= \sum_{i=0}^{h-1} \boldsymbol{\Upsilon}^i \boldsymbol{\tau}^* - h\boldsymbol{\gamma} + \left(\boldsymbol{\Upsilon}^h - \mathbf{I}_n\right)\mathbf{x}_T \\ &= \sum_{i=0}^{h-1} \boldsymbol{\Upsilon}^i \boldsymbol{\tau}^* - h\boldsymbol{\gamma} + \mathbf{A}_h \boldsymbol{\alpha}\boldsymbol{\beta}'\mathbf{x}_T \end{aligned} \tag{6.41}$$

using:

$$\left(\boldsymbol{\Upsilon}^h - \mathbf{I}_n\right) = \sum_{i=0}^{h-1} \boldsymbol{\Upsilon}^i \boldsymbol{\alpha}\boldsymbol{\beta}' = \mathbf{A}_h \boldsymbol{\alpha}\boldsymbol{\beta}' \tag{6.42}$$

as in Clements and Hendry (1996b). Let:

$$\mathsf{E}\left[\boldsymbol{\beta}'\mathbf{x}_T\right] = \mathbf{f}_T = \boldsymbol{\mu}^* \tag{6.43}$$

which is a justifiable approximation if the break happened long enough before T.

Substituting from (6.43) into (6.41):

$$\begin{aligned} \mathsf{E}\left[\widetilde{\boldsymbol{\nu}}_{T+h}\right] &= \sum_{i=0}^{h-1} \left(\mathbf{I}_n + \mathbf{A}_i \boldsymbol{\alpha}\boldsymbol{\beta}'\right)\left[\boldsymbol{\gamma}^* - \boldsymbol{\alpha}\boldsymbol{\mu}^*\right] - h\boldsymbol{\gamma} + \mathbf{A}_h \boldsymbol{\alpha}\boldsymbol{\mu}^* \\ &= h\left(\boldsymbol{\gamma}^* - \boldsymbol{\gamma}\right) - \sum_{i=0}^{h-1} \left(\mathbf{I}_n + \mathbf{A}_i \boldsymbol{\alpha}\boldsymbol{\beta}'\right)\boldsymbol{\alpha}\boldsymbol{\mu}^* + \mathbf{A}_h \boldsymbol{\alpha}\boldsymbol{\mu}^* \\ &= h\left(\boldsymbol{\gamma}^* - \boldsymbol{\gamma}\right) \end{aligned} \tag{6.44}$$

assuming $\boldsymbol{\beta}'\boldsymbol{\gamma}^* = \mathbf{0}$, and using:

$$\mathbf{A}_h = \sum_{k=0}^{h-1} \boldsymbol{\Upsilon}^k = \sum_{k=0}^{h-1} \left(\mathbf{I}_n + \mathbf{A}_k \boldsymbol{\alpha}\boldsymbol{\beta}'\right) = h\mathbf{I}_n + \left(\sum_{k=0}^{h-1} \mathbf{A}_k\right)\boldsymbol{\alpha}\boldsymbol{\beta}'. \tag{6.45}$$

Thus:

$$\mathsf{E}\left[\widetilde{\boldsymbol{\nu}}_{T+h}\right] = h\left(\boldsymbol{\gamma}^* - \boldsymbol{\gamma}\right). \tag{6.46}$$

while for the VEqCM:

$$\mathsf{E}\left[\widehat{\boldsymbol{\nu}}_{T+h}\right] = h\left(\boldsymbol{\gamma}^{*} - \boldsymbol{\gamma}\right) + \mathbf{A}_{h}\boldsymbol{\alpha}\left(\boldsymbol{\mu} - \boldsymbol{\mu}^{*}\right) \tag{6.47}$$

so that the DV eliminates the equilibrium mean shift, and is unbiased when the growth rate is unchanged.

6.4.2 *Residual-based intercept corrections*

Consider a correction formed as an average of the last l 1-step errors up to (and including) period T:

$$\widehat{\boldsymbol{\nu}}_{T,l} = l^{-1}\sum_{i=0}^{l-1}\left(\mathbf{x}_{T-i} - \widehat{\mathbf{x}}_{T-i}\right) = \left(\boldsymbol{\tau}^{*} - \boldsymbol{\tau}\right) + l^{-1}\sum_{i=0}^{l-1}\boldsymbol{\nu}_{T} \tag{6.48}$$

where we again assume that the break occurred more than l periods ago.

When this correction is added in at each step ahead:

$$\dot{\mathbf{w}}_{T+h} = \boldsymbol{\tau} + \boldsymbol{\Upsilon}\dot{\mathbf{w}}_{T+h-1} + \widehat{\boldsymbol{\nu}}_{T,l} \tag{6.49}$$

where $\dot{\mathbf{w}}_{T} = \mathbf{x}_{T}$, so that:

$$\dot{\mathbf{w}}_{T+h} = \hat{\mathbf{x}}_{T+h} + \sum_{i=0}^{h-1}\boldsymbol{\Upsilon}^{i}\widehat{\boldsymbol{\nu}}_{T,l} = \hat{\mathbf{x}}_{T+h} + \mathbf{A}_{h}\widehat{\boldsymbol{\nu}}_{T,l}. \tag{6.50}$$

Then the h-step forecast error is:

$$\dot{\boldsymbol{\nu}}_{T+h} = \sum_{i=0}^{l-1}\boldsymbol{\Upsilon}^{i}\boldsymbol{\nu}_{T+h-i} + \mathbf{A}_{h}l^{-1}\sum_{i=0}^{l-1}\boldsymbol{\nu}_{T}.$$

The bias of the forecast is given by:

$$\begin{aligned}\mathsf{E}\left[\dot{\boldsymbol{\nu}}_{T+h}\right] &= \mathsf{E}\left[\widehat{\boldsymbol{\nu}}_{T+h} - \mathbf{A}_{h}\widehat{\boldsymbol{\nu}}_{T,l}\right] \\ &= h\left(\boldsymbol{\gamma}^{*} - \boldsymbol{\gamma}\right) + \mathbf{A}_{h}\boldsymbol{\alpha}\left(\boldsymbol{\mu} - \boldsymbol{\mu}^{*}\right) - \mathbf{A}_{h}\left(\boldsymbol{\tau}^{*} - \boldsymbol{\tau}\right) = \mathbf{0},\end{aligned}$$

since:

$$\mathsf{E}\left[\widehat{\boldsymbol{\nu}}_{T,l}\right] = \boldsymbol{\tau}^{*} - \boldsymbol{\tau},$$

so the constant-adjustment strategy yields unbiased forecasts, independently of l for $l > 0$.

However, the forecast-error variance cost is reduced:

$$\begin{aligned}
\mathsf{V}\left[\dot{\boldsymbol{\nu}}_{T+h}\right] &= \mathsf{V}\left[\widehat{\boldsymbol{\nu}}_{T+h}\right] + l^{-1}\mathbf{A}_h\boldsymbol{\Omega}\mathbf{A}_h' \\
&= \left(\frac{1+l}{l}\right)\mathsf{V}\left[\widehat{\boldsymbol{\nu}}_{T+h}\right] + l^{-1}\sum_{j=0}^{h-1}\sum_{i=0}^{h-1}\boldsymbol{\Upsilon}^j\boldsymbol{\Omega}\boldsymbol{\Upsilon}^{i\prime} \quad j \neq i \qquad (6.51)
\end{aligned}$$

which approximately doubles only for $l = 1$, and is declining in l. A more precise estimate of the change-in-parameter component results as l increases only if the break occurred sufficiently far back. Nevertheless, summing the (squared) bias and variance components, for a sufficiently large change in $\boldsymbol{\tau}$, the adjustment outlined will result in a smaller MSFE than that of the VEqCM, since the bias components can be made arbitrarily large.

6.4.3 Time-series based intercept corrections

Since the DV is less biased in the face of equilibrium-mean shifts, an alternative to the residual-based intercept-correcting strategy is to use the DV to intercept correct the VEqCM. One possibility is to adjust the VEqCM by the difference between VEqCM and DV forecasts (or, equivalently, *ex post* forecast errors) of the periods immediately prior to the forecast origin, T. Thus, if the recent errors from the DV are less than those from the VEqCM, an adjustment to the VEqCM forecasts, based on the amount of the difference, may be called for. Compared to the residual-based ICs, the difference between the two sets of forecasts (or, equivalently, forecast errors) will give a cleaner estimate of the structural change, since both models' errors will contain the underlying disturbance terms. Reconsider a correction based on the latest l errors:

$$\begin{aligned}
\overline{\boldsymbol{\nu}}_{T,l} &= l^{-1}\sum_{i=0}^{l-1}\left(\hat{\boldsymbol{\nu}}_{T-i} - \widetilde{\boldsymbol{\nu}}_{T-i}\right) = l^{-1}\sum_{i=0}^{l-1}\left(\widetilde{\mathbf{x}}_T - \hat{\mathbf{x}}_T\right) \\
&= -l^{-1}\boldsymbol{\alpha}\sum_{i=1}^{l}\left(\boldsymbol{\beta}'\mathbf{x}_{T-i} - \boldsymbol{\mu}\right). \qquad (6.52)
\end{aligned}$$

When this correction is added in at each step ahead:

$$\overline{\mathbf{x}}_{T+h} = \boldsymbol{\tau} + \boldsymbol{\Upsilon}\overline{\mathbf{x}}_{T+h-1} + \overline{\boldsymbol{\nu}}_{T,l} \qquad (6.53)$$

where $\overline{\mathbf{x}}_T = \mathbf{x}_T$, so that:

$$\overline{\mathbf{x}}_{T+h} = \hat{\mathbf{x}}_{T+h} + \sum_{i=0}^{h-1} \mathbf{\Upsilon}^i \overline{\boldsymbol{\nu}}_{T,l} = \hat{\mathbf{x}}_{T+h} + \mathbf{A}_h \overline{\boldsymbol{\nu}}_{T,l} \tag{6.54}$$

the forecast error becomes:

$$\begin{aligned}\overline{\boldsymbol{\nu}}_{T+h} &= \mathbf{A}_h (\boldsymbol{\tau}^* - \boldsymbol{\tau}) + \sum_{i=0}^{h-1} \mathbf{\Upsilon}^i \boldsymbol{\nu}_{T+h-i} + l^{-1} \mathbf{A}_h \boldsymbol{\alpha} \sum_{i=1}^{l} (\boldsymbol{\beta}' \mathbf{x}_{T-i} - \boldsymbol{\mu}) \\ &= h(\boldsymbol{\gamma}^* - \boldsymbol{\gamma}) + l^{-1} \mathbf{A}_h \boldsymbol{\alpha} \sum_{i=1}^{l} (\boldsymbol{\beta}' \mathbf{x}_{T-i} - \boldsymbol{\mu}^*) .\end{aligned}$$

Now the bias is given by:

$$\mathsf{E}[\overline{\boldsymbol{\nu}}_{T+h}] = h(\boldsymbol{\gamma}^* - \boldsymbol{\gamma}) \tag{6.55}$$

again independently of l for $l > 0$, so unbiased forecasts result when the underlying growth rate is unchanged.

The unconditional variance is given by:

$$\mathsf{V}[\overline{\boldsymbol{\nu}}_{T+h}] = \mathsf{V}[\widehat{\boldsymbol{\nu}}_{T+h}] + l^{-2} \mathbf{A}_h \boldsymbol{\alpha} \mathbf{C}_{\beta,l} \boldsymbol{\alpha}' \mathbf{A}_h' \tag{6.56}$$

where:

$$\mathbf{C}_{\beta,l} = \mathsf{E}\left[\sum_{i=1}^{l} \sum_{j=1}^{l} (\boldsymbol{\beta}' \mathbf{x}_{T-i} - \boldsymbol{\mu}^*) (\boldsymbol{\beta}' \mathbf{x}_{T-j} - \boldsymbol{\mu}^*)' \right] .$$

While this coincides with the DV forecast-error variance for $l = 1$, for $l > 1$ it is smaller, and is smaller than the residual-based IC for a given l – see table 6.1 which summarizes the bias and variance formulae, and table 6.2 which further aids comparison by evaluating the formulae for a given set of parameter values.

Thus, the DV and time-series IC strategy coincide for $l = 1$, but for $l > 1$ the latter dominates. The time-series IC has a smaller forecast-error variance than the residual-based correction, but will not remove the bias for growth-rate changes. A straightforward extension of the analysis to mitigate against growth rate changes would be to use the DDV to intercept correct the VEqCM.

In the empirical work, however, the time-series IC strategy is applied in a discretionary fashion. It is applied at a given forecast origin if

Table 6.1
Summary of bias and variance formulae.

	Bias		Variance
	$\gamma = \gamma^*$	$\mu = \mu^*$	
VEqCM	$\mathbf{A}_h\boldsymbol{\alpha}(\boldsymbol{\mu} - \boldsymbol{\mu}^*)$	$h(\gamma^* - \gamma)$	$\sum_{i=0}^{h-1} \boldsymbol{\Upsilon}^i\boldsymbol{\Omega}\boldsymbol{\Upsilon}^{i\prime}$
DV	0	$h(\gamma^* - \gamma)$	$\sum_{i=0}^{h-1} \boldsymbol{\Upsilon}^i\boldsymbol{\Omega}\boldsymbol{\Upsilon}^{i\prime} + \mathbf{A}_h\boldsymbol{\alpha}\mathbf{V}_\beta\boldsymbol{\alpha}'\mathbf{A}_h'$
IC	0	0	$\sum_{i=0}^{h-1} \boldsymbol{\Upsilon}^i\boldsymbol{\Omega}\boldsymbol{\Upsilon}^{i\prime} + l^{-1}\mathbf{A}_h\boldsymbol{\Omega}\mathbf{A}_h'$
TS-IC	0	$h(\gamma^* - \gamma)$	$\sum_{i=0}^{h-1} \boldsymbol{\Upsilon}^i\boldsymbol{\Omega}\boldsymbol{\Upsilon}^{i\prime} + l^{-2}\mathbf{A}_h\boldsymbol{\alpha}\mathbf{C}_{\beta,l}\boldsymbol{\alpha}'\mathbf{A}_h'$

the absolute value of the average of the last l DV errors is less than that of the VEqCM. This strategy is referred to as $\mathrm{TS}_p[l]$. Since the quantities involved are vectors, the above is to be understood to apply element-by-element.

A number of cautions are warranted. The formulae for the "corrected" forecasts suggest that l should be made large. In practice, the break will not have occurred infinitely long ago, and forming the correction by averaging pre- with post-break errors will dilute the corrections and hence the bias reduction. These corrections are not necessarily optimal, in the sense that if we knew the form of the DGP, when the break occurred, etc., then they would be unlikely to minimize our loss function (say MSFE). For example, for a given l, the residual IC strategy eliminates bias but will not be optimal for any loss function which penalizes forecast-error variance, where one would wish to trade bias against variance. The corrections are rule-of-thumb, but without knowledge of the DGP or structural breaks, appear to be worth consideration.

In order to simplify the analyses and sharpen the findings, many simplifications have been, and it is reasonable to wonder whether the conclusions can be expected to hold in practice. In chapter 11, we calculate the effects of intercept correcting the VEqCM in the three-variable system of wages, prices, and unemployment of Mizon (1995), using both the residual-based and time-series varieties. While this system

Table 6.2
Numerical evaluation of variance formulae.

l	Forecast horizon							
	1	2	3	4	5	6	7	8
VEqCM								
	1.00	1.68	2.23	2.74	3.24	3.74	4.26	4.79
DV								
	1.16	2.13	2.98	3.75	4.45	5.10	5.73	6.33
IC-residual								
1	2.00	4.96	8.57	12.83	17.80	23.59	30.28	37.94
2	1.50	3.32	5.40	7.78	10.52	13.67	17.27	21.36
3	1.33	2.77	4.35	6.10	8.09	10.36	12.93	15.84
4	1.25	2.50	3.82	5.26	6.88	8.71	10.77	13.07
IC-time-series								
1	1.16	2.13	2.98	3.75	4.45	5.10	5.73	6.33
2	1.13	2.07	2.87	3.59	4.26	4.90	5.51	6.10
3	1.12	2.02	2.80	3.50	4.15	4.77	5.37	5.95
4	1.11	1.99	2.74	3.42	4.06	4.66	5.26	5.83

The values are the forecast-error variances of the first variable in a bivariate cointegrated system with $\mathbf{\Omega}_\nu = \mathbf{I}_2$, $\boldsymbol{\alpha} = (-0.2 : 0.1)'$ and $\boldsymbol{\beta}' = (1 : -1)$.

is a good deal simpler than the models routinely used for forecasting by the large-scale macro-econometric modeling groups, it allows us to generate a reasonable sample of intercept-corrected forecasts, so that the properties of the strategy can be analyzed statistically.

6.4.4 Updating

For a correct specification, updating increases estimation precision. As an antidote to structural breaks, the relative benefits of updating versus differencing depend upon the type of change. If the economy is evolving slowly over time in a smooth manner (as conjectured by Granger and Swanson, 1996), then allowing $\hat{\theta}$ to change over time may work reasonably well, particularly using a fixed "window", so that earlier, and now less relevant, observations are dropped. As seen in §4.3.6, when an incorrectly-included irrelevant variable suddenly changes, updating can rapidly remove its pernicious effect on forecasts.

However, if structural change due to deterministic shifts is sudden and discrete, then differencing may be preferable.

A task that awaits completion is formally deriving the general effects of estimation updating when the forecast-error taxonomy in table 2.1 applies sequentially through time as the forecast origin advances. However, a simple illustration with a sample-mean predictor indicates the likely orders of the impacts of updating on forecast-error biases and variances.

Consider a DGP given by:

$$y_t = \mu + \epsilon_t \text{ where } \epsilon_t \sim \mathsf{IN}\left[0, \sigma_\epsilon^2\right], \tag{6.57}$$

when a sample $t = 1, \ldots, T$ is available for estimation. At time T, prior to forecasting, there is a shift in the value of μ to $\mu + \delta$ where $\delta \neq 0$. To illustrate the benefits of updating, we will derive the mean and variance of the forecast errors for a sequence of 1-step ahead forecasts for $y_{T+1} \ldots y_{T+H}$ with updating (i.e., using $\widetilde{y}_{T+h|T+h-1} = \widehat{\mu}_{T+h-1}$), where:

$$\begin{aligned} \widehat{\mu}_{T+h} &= (T+h)^{-1} \textstyle\sum_{t=1}^{T+h} y_t \\ &= \mu + \delta h (T+h)^{-1} + (T+h)^{-1} \textstyle\sum_{t=1}^{T+h} \epsilon_t \\ &= \mu + \delta h (T+h)^{-1} + \overline{\epsilon}_{T+h}. \end{aligned} \tag{6.58}$$

We will then compare these to the corresponding expressions in the absence of updating (i.e., using the predictor $\widehat{y}_{T+h|T} = \widehat{\mu}_T$). The forecast error after updating, denoted $\widetilde{e}_{T+h|T+h-1} = y_{T+h} - \widetilde{y}_{T+h|T+h-1}$, is:

$$\begin{aligned} \widetilde{e}_{T+h|T+h-1} &= \mu + \delta + \epsilon_{T+h} - \widehat{\mu}_{T+h-1} \\ &= \delta \left(\frac{T}{T+h-1} \right) + \epsilon_{T+h} - \overline{\epsilon}_{T+h-1}, \end{aligned}$$

with:

$$\mathsf{E}\left[\widetilde{e}_{T+h|T+h-1}\right] = \delta \frac{T}{T+h-1}, \tag{6.59}$$

and since ϵ_{T+h} and $\overline{\epsilon}_{T+h-1}$ are independent, then:

$$\mathsf{V}\left[\widetilde{e}_{T+h|T+h-1}\right] = \mathsf{V}\left[\epsilon_{T+h}\right] + \mathsf{V}\left[\overline{\epsilon}_{T+h-1}\right] = \sigma_\epsilon^2 \frac{T+h}{T+h-1}.$$

The MSFE is:

$$\mathsf{E}\left[\widetilde{e}^2_{T+h|T+h-1}\right] = \frac{\delta^2 T^2 + \sigma^2_\epsilon (T+h)(T+h-1)}{(T+h-1)^2}.$$

When there is no updating:

$$\begin{aligned}\widehat{e}_{T+h|T+h-1} &= y_{T+h} - \widehat{y}_{T+h|T+h-1} \\ &= \mu + \delta + \epsilon_{T+h} - \widehat{\mu}_T \\ &= \delta + \epsilon_{T+h} - \overline{\epsilon}_T,\end{aligned}$$

so:

$$\mathsf{E}\left[\widehat{e}_{T+h|T+h-1}\right] = \delta \tag{6.60}$$

and:

$$\mathsf{V}\left[\widehat{e}_{T+h|T+h-1}\right] = \mathsf{V}\left[\epsilon_{T+h}\right] + \mathsf{V}\left[\overline{\epsilon}_T\right] = \sigma^2_\epsilon \frac{T+1}{T},$$

with MSFE given by:

$$\mathsf{E}\left[\widehat{e}^2_{T+h|T+h-1}\right] = \frac{\delta^2 T^2 + \sigma^2_\epsilon T (T+1)}{T^2}.$$

Hence, comparing (6.59) with (6.60), updating reduces the bias by:

$$\delta \frac{(h-1)}{T+h-1},$$

which is $O(T^{-1})$, whereas the forecast-error variance reduction is only:

$$\sigma^2_\epsilon \frac{(h-1)}{T(T+h-1)},$$

which is $O(T^{-2})$. In terms of comparisons based on MSFE, however, the reduction in the squared bias is given by:

$$\left(\mathsf{E}\left[\widehat{e}_{T+h|T+h-1}\right]\right)^2 - \left(\mathsf{E}\left[\widetilde{e}_{T+h|T+h-1}\right]\right)^2 = \frac{\delta^2 (h-1)(2T+h-1)}{(T+h-1)^2},$$

which is again $O(T^{-1})$, so that for large breaks ($|\delta| \gg 0$), the main benefits from updating seem likely to come from reducing biases.

Chapter 11 provides an empirical illustration where updating a VEqCM enhances its performance noticeably, with larger percentage reductions in biases than variances (see table 11.4).

6.5 Conclusion

The chapter has provided a range of interpretations for a commonly-used intercept correction. It then showed that intercept corrections can improve forecast accuracy on bias measures, although at some cost in forecast-error variance. From the differential impact of breaks on the VEqCMs and DV, we argued that it may be possible to do better still, and corrections based on DVs were analyzed. Nonetheless, although the intercept-corrected, or differenced-data, forecast may be more accurate, this does not entail choosing the "robustified" model for policy, or later modeling exercises. Chapter 8 empirically illustrates the advantages of intercept corrections after a deterministic shift, and compares the effectiveness of ICs with differenced-data representations, while chapter 11 contrasts ICs and updating.

7 Modeling Consumers' Expenditure

Summary

When the assumption of constant parameters fails, the in-sample fit of a model may be a poor guide to *ex-ante* forecast performance. In chapters 3 and 4, we showed that deterministic non-constancy was one of the most important sources of forecast failure, and in chapters 5 and 6 analyzed a number of potential solutions. In this chapter, we illustrate the impacts of structural breaks on forecast accuracy, and evaluate some of the suggested solutions using a univariate empirical example and Monte Carlo simulations. Although the forecasting models we consider are exceptionally simple, they show that a theory of economic forecasting which allows for model mis-specification and structural breaks is feasible, and may provide a useful basis for interpreting and circumventing systematic forecast failure in macroeconomics. Multivariate illustrations are provided in chapters 8 and 11: the outcomes there will also transpire to match the theory.

7.1 Introduction

We now illustrate both empirically and by a Monte Carlo simulation study some of the theoretical results established above about the properties of macroeconomic forecasting in the presence of structural breaks. If the data-generating process really was stationary (perhaps after differencing or cointegration transforms) with time-invariant parameters, and if we were equipped with a forecasting model which coincided with that process, then there would be little scope for the practices of differencing and intercept corrections discussed in chapters 5 and 6, and some of the predictive failures (or systematic forecast errors) that have occurred in recent economic forecasting would not have occurred – or would remain largely inexplicable.

We consider approximating a process with a break by a variety of types of simple model, ranging from predicting the sample mean of the process, to "no change" forecasts, and include members of the autoregressive, integrated moving-average (ARIMA) class of the Box and Jenkins (1976) time-series modeling tradition. The estimators considered include least squares and instrumental variables, using 1-step and multi-step (also called "adaptive forecasting" or dynamic estimation) criteria; and the forecasting procedures include both unmodified models as well as intercept corrections.

The plan of the chapter is as follows. In §7.2, we describe the DGP. This is an autoregressive process with a one-off change in the mean only, at an exogenously determined point of time. Section 7.3 describes the forecasting methods used to analyze this DGP, and §7.4 introduces the empirical example which illustrates the performance of these methods on an actual data series. Sections 7.5–7.11 present analytical results for the various forecasting methods, as well as their results for the artificial (simulated) data and the actual empirical data, demonstrating in most cases an acceptable concordance with the earlier theory. Finally, §7.12 concludes and summarizes.

7.2 The Data Generation Process

The DGP is given by the following scalar first-order autoregressive process:

$$y_t = \rho y_{t-1} + \mu_1 + \delta_\mu 1_{\{t>T_1\}} + \epsilon_t \qquad (7.1)$$

where, for most of the discussion, we set $\rho = 0$, and assume that $\epsilon_t \sim \mathsf{IN}\left[0, \sigma_\epsilon^2\right]$. In (7.1), $1_{\{t>T_1\}}$ is an indicator with the value zero till time $T_1 < T$, after which it is unity. This allows the intercept (μ) to take on two values: μ_1 when $t \leq T_1$, and $\mu_2 = \mu_1 + \delta_\mu$ when $t > T_1$. Thus, the baseline DGP is simply white noise ($\rho = 0$) with a shift in mean at time $t = T_1 + 1$. Letting $y_t = \Delta z_t$ where $z_t = \log Z_t$ is a natural interpretation, so that μ is the growth rate, and the underlying levels process X_t is integrated (after a log transform). When we consider the small-sample properties of estimators and moments of the forecast-error distributions, we shall use Monte Carlo, and set $\mu_1 = 1$, $\mu_2 = 10$, $T_1 = T/2, T = 100$, $\sigma_\epsilon^2 = 1$, replicating the process $10,000$ times.

7.3 Forecasting Methods

In this chapter, we are primarily concerned with short-term forecasts of y_t, so consider horizons h of 1 to 4-steps ahead, where the forecast origin is taken to

Table 7.1
Forecasting Models.

Label	ARIMA description	Constant	Comment
M_1	-	constant	Sample mean predictor
M_2	ARIMA$(1, 0, 0)$	yes	1-step minimization
M_3	ARIMA$(1, 0, 0)$	yes	Dynamic estimation
M_4	ARIMA$(0, 1, 0)$	yes	Unit root imposed.
M_5	ARIMA$(0, 1, 0)$	no	Unit root imposed.
M_6	ARIMA$(0, 1, 1)$	yes	IMA
M_7	ARIMA$(0, 1, 1)$	no	IMA
M_8	ARIMA$(1, 0, 1)$	yes	ARMA

be T. The process in (7.1) is invariant to specifying the dependent variable as y_t or Δy_t so long as y_{t-1} enters unrestrictedly. But, beyond 1-step, most conventional evaluation criteria are not invariant, and it matters for which transforms of the dependent variable forecast errors are evaluated (see Clements and Hendry, 1993).

The models of y_t we consider are summarized in table 7.1, and we take each in turn in subsequent sections. Section 7.11 allows for $\rho \neq 0$, in which case, following the impact of the break at period T_1, the process will undergo a period of adjustment to the new equilibrium, in contrast to instantaneous adjustment when $\rho = 0$. The results of the Monte Carlo using Gauss for the models/methods described in table 7.1 are presented in table 7.2, which reports the MSFEs, the squared forecast biases, and the forecast-error variances, for horizons $1 - 4$. The Monte Carlo distributions of the parameter estimates of the various models are shown in table 7.4. We refer to these as required below.

7.4 An Empirical Example

The empirical illustration uses aggregate real consumers' expenditure on non-durables and services in the United Kingdom (denoted C_t), quarterly (not seasonally adjusted) from 1961:1 to 1992:4. There is a long history of predictive failure of this variable using econometric models, as witnessed by the results in Hendry (1974), Davidson, Hendry, Srba and Yeo (1978), Muellbauer and Murphy (1989), Carruth and Henley (1990), and Hendry (1994) *inter alia*. Figure 7.1a–d shows the time series of the level (C_t), log level (c_t), first difference (denoted $Dc_t = c_t - c_{t-1}$), and fourth difference or annual growth (denoted $D4c_t$ for $\Delta_4 c_t = c_t - c_{t-4}$).

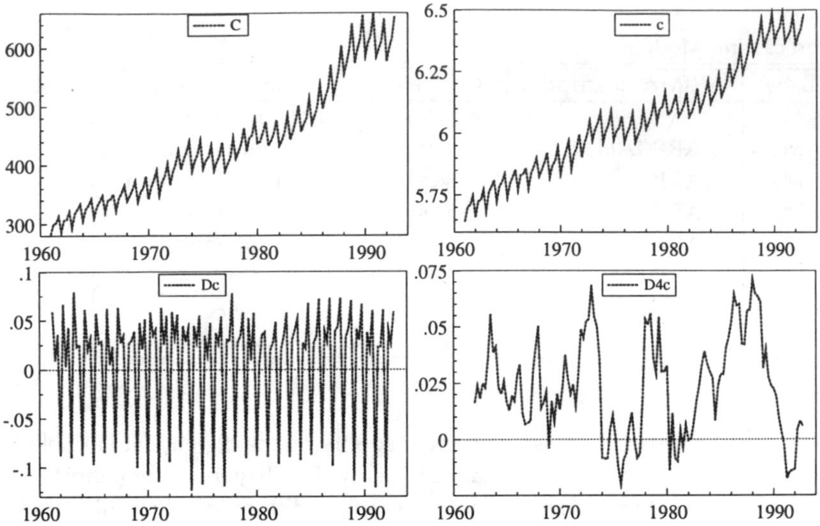

Figure 7.1
Time series of real consumers' expenditure in the UK.

The original series C_t is highly seasonal, around a strong trend, with a growing seasonal movement.[1] The log transform is both variance stabilizing and induces a more constant seasonal pattern, so is used below. In economics, it is unsurprising that movements are closer to proportional than absolute: even the UK economy has grown about 12-fold over the last 150 years so absolute errors would by now be trivially small proportionally. The quarterly growth series in panel c is dominated by the movements between seasons, which are of the order of 15% switches, and may reflect seasonal unit roots. The annual growth, measured by $\Delta_4 c_t$, has usually been positive, with only a few falls, notably in the mid-1970s and early 1990s; even so, the sustained large growth through most of the 1980s is distinctive. We focus on $\Delta_4 c_t$ as the variable y_t (for $\rho \neq 0$) in (7.1), and presume that a change in the underlying growth rate occurred around 1980. Over the whole sample, the mean and standard deviation of $\Delta_4 c_t$ are almost equal at 2.3% and 2.2% respectively.

To show the nature of the predictive failure, we consider 1-step *ex post* forecasts for the equation in Davidson *et al.* (1978) (known as DHSY), which is close to the equation in the Treasury model during the early 1980s. Let i_t denote

[1] All empirical estimates and graphs are based on GiveWin and PcGive for Windows: see Doornik and Hendry (1996) and Hendry and Doornik (1996).

real personal disposable income and p_t its implicit deflator. Their equation relates the annual changes of the variables current and lagged, together with an equilibrium-correction mechanism (EqCM) from the previous year's differential between consumption and income such that, on a steady-state growth path for income, consumption is proportional to income. The estimates over the sample 1962:2–1982:4 are (these differ from the original estimates mainly due to problems with the data revisions implemented in the early 1990s for the mid-1970s data: see Hendry (1994) for a discussion):

$$\begin{aligned}
\widehat{\Delta_4 c_t} &= \underset{(0.04)}{0.37}\ \Delta_4 i_t + \underset{(0.04)}{0.15}\ \Delta_4 i_{t-1} - \underset{(0.02)}{0.11}\ (c-i)_{t-4} - \underset{(0.02)}{0.13}\ \Delta_4 p_t \\
\mathsf{R}^2 &= 0.89\ \ \widehat{\sigma}_e = 0.96\%\ \ \mathsf{F}_{\mathsf{ar}}(5,74) = 0.96\ \ \mathsf{F}_{\mathsf{arch}}(4,71) = 1.19 \qquad (7.2) \\
\chi^2_{\mathsf{nd}}(2) &= 3.23\ \ \mathsf{F}_{\mathsf{het}}(8,70) = 1.29\ \ \mathsf{F}_{\mathsf{res}}(1,78) = 3.67\ \ \mathsf{J} = 0.55\ \ \mathsf{SC} = -9.12
\end{aligned}$$

R^2 is the squared multiple-correlation coefficient, $\widehat{\sigma}_e$ is the residual standard deviation expressed as a percentage of C_t, SC is the Schwarz criterion; and the diagnostic tests are of the form $\mathsf{F_j}(k, T-l)$ which denotes an F-test against the alternative hypothesis j for: 5th-order residual serial correlation ($\mathsf{F_{ar}}$: see Godfrey, 1978), 4th-order residual autoregressive conditional heteroscedasticity ($\mathsf{F_{arch}}$: see Engle, 1982), heteroscedasticity ($\mathsf{F_{het}}$: see White, 1980); the RESET test ($\mathsf{F_{res}}$: see Ramsey, 1969); the joint parameter constancy tests in Hansen (1992b) (J), and a chi-square test for normality ($\chi^2_{\mathsf{nd}}(2)$: see Doornik and Hansen, 1994): * and ** denote significance at the 5% and 1% levels respectively. All these in-sample tests are acceptable, and suggest the model is congruent with the evidence even though the period 1962:2–1982:4 included considerable turbulence around the mid-1970s oil crises.

Figure 7.2 panels a–d respectively show the fitted, actual and forecast values; their cross plot with separate regression lines pre and post 1982; the residuals and forecast errors scaled by the equation standard error; and the forecasts with 1-step 95% confidence bands around the forecasts. From panel a, it is visible that the forecast-period performance is very poor compared to the in-sample: the high growth is seriously under-predicted, and the fall is over-predicted. Panel b confirms that the forecast and sample regressions have distinctly different slopes, and c shows that the post-sample residuals greatly exceed the in-sample ones. Finally, in panel d, many forecasts lie outside their one-off confidence intervals, and the Chow (1960) constancy test over 1983:1–1992:3 yields $\mathsf{F}(40,79) = 2.90^{**}$ which rejects at the 1% level, consistent with the low correlation between outturns and forecasts over the later period in fig. 7.2a.

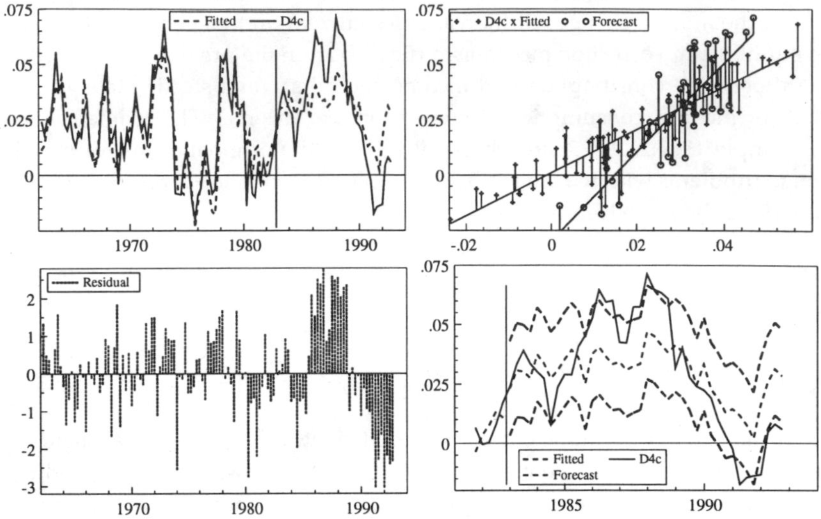

Figure 7.2
Graphical statistics for the DHSY model.

Considerable effort has been devoted to understanding the causes of this predictive failure, and there are many potential explanations ranging from inaccurate data, inappropriate economic analysis, an invalid model class, bad methodology, structural change (particularly the financial deregulation of the mid-1980s, and possibly demographic change), and omitted variables (mainly wealth-related measures): see the excellent review in Muellbauer (1994). Our own view is that financial deregulation allowed a substantial reduction in credit rationing for many consumers, who were thereby able to finance purchase growth in excess of income growth. As (7.2) ensures proportionality between c_t and i_t, and does not include de-rationing measures, it cannot account for that increased expenditure – indeed, the forecast series more closely tracks i_t than c_t. In the marginal process for c_t, such a shift is equivalent to a change in the growth rate, at least until the end of credit rationing (around the point where c_t collapses). The falls in c_t derive from the need to pay the interest on the hugely increased debt stock, at the same time as income falls and interest rates rise sharply as the late 1980s boom is terminated by policy to avoid increased inflation. The main point of the above illustration is to demonstrate that a change of some form did occur in the underlying DGP, and that previously-successful equations did not forecast through that change; partial statistical explanations will emerge as we proceed. Deterministic shifts appear to play an important role here as well, so the example seems suitable to test the theoretical results obtained in earlier chapters.

7.5 The Sample Mean as a Predictor

The forecast function for M_1 is simply the sample mean. In the Monte Carlo, for $\rho = 0$ and $T_1 = T/2$, the population value of the sample mean is $\mu_p = \frac{1}{2}(\mu_1 + \mu_2)$. The form of this predictor is that forecasts are not conditional on the value(s) of the process around the forecast origin, and forecasts are badly biased when the recent behavior of the process is very different from the history on which μ_p is based. Ignoring the imprecision in estimating μ, the forecast-error variance is only σ_ϵ^2, the minimum obtainable using $y_{T+h} = \mu_2$. But on MSFE comparisons (the sum of the squared bias and forecast-error variance), this strategy fares poorly (compare ch. 6):

$$bias = \mathsf{E}\left[y_{T+h} - \mu_p\right] = \mu_2 - \frac{1}{2}\left(\mu_1 + \mu_2\right) = \frac{\delta_\mu}{2}$$

where $\delta_\mu = \mu_2 - \mu_1$ can be made arbitrarily large relative to σ_ϵ. When $\rho \neq 0$, the bias is scaled up by $(1-\rho)^{-1}$ and the forecast-error standard deviation by $1/\surd\left(1-\rho^2\right)$, since:

$$y_t = \frac{\mu_1 + \delta_\mu 1_{\{t \geq T_1\}}}{(1-\rho)} + u_t \text{ where } u_t = \rho u_{t-1} + \epsilon_t$$

so that $\sigma_u^2 = \sigma_\epsilon^2 / \left(1-\rho^2\right)$, yielding:

$$\mathsf{E}\left[\left(y_{T+h} - \mu_p\right)^2\right] = \frac{\sigma_\epsilon^2}{1-\rho^2} + \frac{\delta_\mu^2}{4\left(1-\rho\right)^2}.$$

The empirical performance is much as might be anticipated, and is shown in fig. 7.3. Systematic errors are made throughout the forecast period, albeit not dramatically worse than the econometric model (panels a, c and d, which provides 95% confidence bands). The more interesting aspect is illustrating §6.2, shown in panels b and d, where we apply the common-factor implementation of intercept correction to the sample mean predictor.[2] The in-sample and forecast-period regressions of fitted on actual are close, and the forecasts are fairly good. Thus, intercept correcting works almost precisely as analyzed, and greatly reduces both the MSFE and the systematic nature of the forecast errors.

[2]These are the same as the corresponding panels in fig. 7.4, although in general intercept correcting and differencing will yield different results.

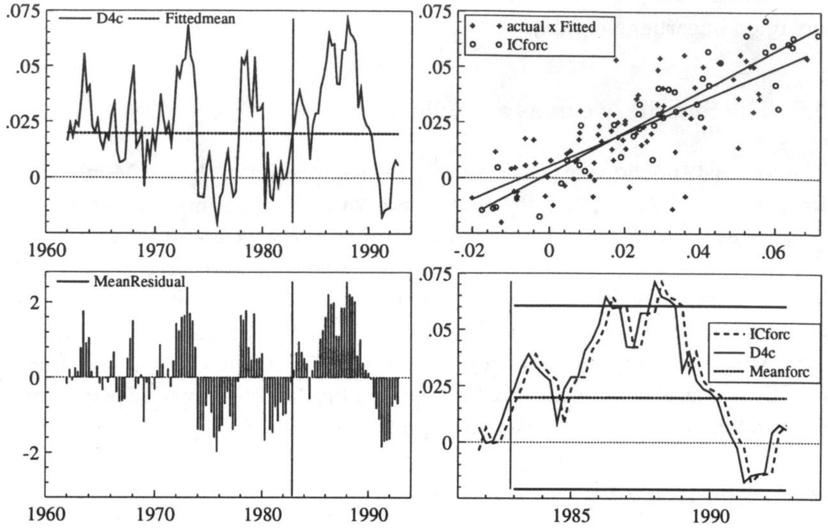

Figure 7.3
Graphical statistics for the constant-mean model, and intercept correction.

7.6 Differencing

As a polar case, consider M_5. Let $y_{T+h|T}$ denote the forecast function for the model under consideration, where T is the forecast origin (on which the forecast is conditioned), and h is the period ahead being forecast. Here $y_{T+h|T} = y_T$, so that the history of the process, other than the value at the forecast origin, is irrelevant. "Complete" conditioning on the origin would appear to be a good idea when the future is exactly like the present, but will be costly if the present is atypical, and if in the future the process returns to its long-run average. Hence, differencing offers potential advantages for short-term forecasting when the present pattern persists for a number of quarters, but may yield unreliable forecasts over longer horizons. As an extreme example, suppose the shift in mean to μ_2 at period $T_1 + 1$ is reversed in period $T_1 + 2$. Multi-step forecasts conditional on period $T_1 + 1$ will fare badly compared to using the sample mean. The sample mean is robust to irregular or outlier observations at the forecast origin, whereas differencing quickly incorporates change, and gains if that change persists. These are extremely simple examples of forecasting methods but serve to illustrate that when constancy fails to hold, quite different approaches to forecasting may be called for, depending upon the expected nature of the non-constancy. Fildes and Makridakis (1995), p.302, remark upon more elaborate models, and changes in trend rather than mean, but the upshot of their argument is similar.[3]

While differencing may reduce bias, since the process is stochastic, it will not repeat the previous period (barring an event with probability zero), which has implications for the forecast-error variance attached to this type of predictor. Since the structural break (mean shift) has occurred prior to the forecast origin (at period $T/2$ compared to period T), differencing results in largely unbiased forecasts when the constant is not estimated. This is because:

$$\mathsf{E}\left[y_{T+h|T}\right] = \mathsf{E}\left[y_T\right] = \mu_2,$$

and:

$$\mathsf{E}\left[y_{T+h}\right] = \mu_2.$$

However, the cost in forecast-error variance arises because the predictor projects y_T, which is $\mu_2 + \epsilon_T$, so there is an "error" in the present. Because the future value of the process is $\mu_2 + \epsilon_{T+h}$, and since ϵ_T and ϵ_{T+h} are independent for all h, the forecast-error variance is twice the minimum. Formally, when $\rho = 0$ the unconditional variance component is:

$$\mathsf{E}\left[\left(\mu_2 + \epsilon_{T+h} - y_T\right)^2\right] = \sigma_\epsilon^2 + \mu_2^2 + \mathsf{E}\left[y_T^2\right] - 2\mu_2 \mathsf{E}\left[y_T\right] = 2\sigma_\epsilon^2.$$

When a constant is included (M_4), then ignoring parameter estimation uncertainty, the forecast function is:

$$y_{T+h|T} = y_T + hT^{-1}\delta_\mu,$$

with forecast bias:

$$bias = \mathsf{E}\left[y_{T+h} - y_{T+h|T}\right] = -hT^{-1}\delta_\mu,$$

so that the bias is small but increases with the forecast horizon. Again, in large samples, the forecast error variance is $2\sigma_\epsilon^2$ (ignoring the impact of estimating the constant term).

The empirical illustration of these two cases is a revealing confirmation of the analysis: differencing corresponds to estimating:

$$\Delta_4 c_t = \alpha + \Delta_4 c_{t-1} + u_t \tag{7.3}$$

where $\alpha = 0$ for M_5. Since $\widehat{\alpha}$ is tiny (10^{-5}), we report the results where it is unrestricted. The graphical statistics are shown in fig. 7.4a–d, where the last

[3]For example, they suggest that single exponential smoothing or damped trend smoothing may be more robust to a range of changes in trend than ARIMA models.

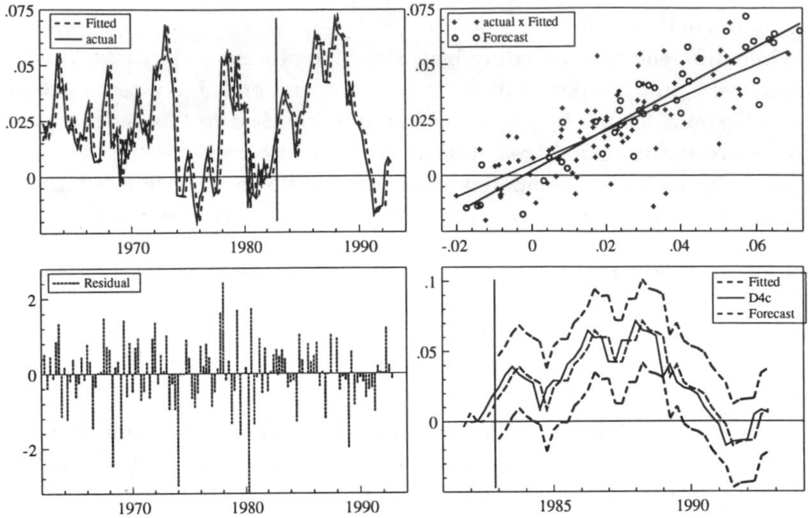

Figure 7.4
Graphical statistics for the differenced model.

panel reports 1-step forecasts.[4] There is no evidence of predictive failure, the two regressions (in and out of sample) have nearly equal slopes and the post-sample residuals are smaller than the in-sample. Now $\widehat{\sigma}_u = 1.47\%$, so the residual variance exceeds that based on $\widehat{\sigma}_e$ by more than 100% (although the latter model has the advantage of unmodeled regressors). However, there is evidence of residual autocorrelation at 4 lags, as $\mathsf{F}_{\mathsf{ar}}(5, 74) = 5.04$, and non-normality, as $\chi^2_{\mathsf{nd}}(2) = 6.57$. To the extent that the predictive failure in (7.2) is due to a shift in the equilibrium mean, differencing offsets that and allows nearly unbiased forecasts, as anticipated from the analysis for M_5.

7.7 AR(1) Model: 1-step Estimation

Consider now M_2, the AR(1) with a constant term, estimated by OLS. Thus the model is:

$$y_t = \alpha + \beta y_{t-1} + v_t \tag{7.4}$$

[4]We estimated this equation in terms of $\Delta_1\Delta_4 c_t$ on a constant with $\Delta_4 c_t$ determined by an identity (using FIML) to maintain $\Delta_4 c_t$ as the dependent variable, imposing the coefficient of $\Delta_4 c_{t-1}$ at unity, yet allowing the calculation of prediction intervals (based on the error variance component only).

and for the break outlined above, $0 < \beta < 1$ with $\mu_1 < \alpha/(1-\beta) < \mu_2$. Also, $\beta \to 1$ as $\delta_\mu \to \infty$ where α and β are the plims of the intercept and slope estimates of an AR(1) model when the DGP is given by (7.1). The forecast function (ignoring parameter-estimation uncertainty) is:

$$y_{T+h|T} = \alpha \sum_{i=0}^{h-1} \beta^i + \beta^h y_T \to \frac{\alpha}{1-\beta} \quad \text{as } h \to \infty.$$

Let $\mu^+ = \alpha/(1-\beta)$. Then μ^+ is the long-run mean of the process from the historical data, which incorporates the two regimes. The long-run mean of the process after $t = T_1$ is μ_2, and $\mu^+ < \mu_2$, so the forecasts are biased for large h. Incorporating historical information on the long-run mean of the process leads to biased predictions as the earlier information is outdated.

Write (7.4) as:

$$\Delta y_t = (\beta - 1)\left(y_{t-1} - \frac{\alpha}{1-\beta}\right) + v_t \tag{7.5}$$

and consider forecasting without the term $(y_{t-1} - \mu^+)$: this delivers the differenced model M_5. Thus, the comparison between M_2 and M_5 is the scalar analogue of the comparison in chapter 5 between the vector equilibrium-correction model (VEqCM) and the vector autoregression in the differences of the variables (DV), which neglects the long-run means of the cointegrated processes.

In terms of the scalar Monte Carlo, α, β are estimated as:

$$\widehat{y}_t = \underset{[0.0034]}{0.452} + \underset{[0.0001]}{0.934}\, y_{t-1}, \tag{7.6}$$

where the coefficients are the Monte Carlo estimates (averages over replications), and the figures in brackets are the standard deviations of the estimates across replications. Thus, for large h, from (7.6), $\mathsf{E}[\widehat{\mu^+}] = 0.452/0.066 = 6.85$, so for $\widehat{v}_{T+h} = y_{T+h} - y_{T+h|T}$:

$$bias = \mathsf{E}\left[\widehat{v}_{T+h}\right] = \mu_2 - \mathsf{E}\left[\widehat{\mu^+}\right] = 10 - 6.85 = 3.15.$$

The Monte Carlo estimates of the (squared) biases for $h = 1, \ldots, 4$, are shown in table 7.2, confirming that the forecasts are biased, while those from M_5 are unbiased.

Table 7.2
Measures of Forecast Accuracy.

	M_2	M_2^{IC}	M_3	M_3^{IC}	M_4	M_5	M_6	M_7	M_8
					MSFEs				
1	1.93	5.56	1.93	5.56	2.01	1.98	1.45	1.42	1.44
2	1.95	12.02	1.88	5.38	2.02	1.95	1.47	1.39	1.46
3	2.07	20.75	1.84	5.20	2.06	1.94	1.51	1.39	1.51
4	2.31	31.47	1.86	5.26	2.20	1.99	1.64	1.43	1.62
					Squared biases				
1	0.04	0.00	0.04	0.00	0.01	0.00	0.03	0.00	0.02
2	0.16	0.00	0.04	0.00	0.03	0.00	0.06	0.00	0.06
3	0.36	0.00	0.05	0.00	0.06	0.00	0.11	0.00	0.13
4	0.59	0.00	0.05	0.00	0.12	0.00	0.18	0.00	0.20
					Forecast Error Variances				
1	1.89	5.56	1.89	5.56	2.00	1.98	1.42	1.42	1.42
2	1.79	12.02	1.83	5.38	1.99	1.95	1.40	1.39	1.39
3	1.71	20.75	1.79	5.20	2.00	1.94	1.41	1.39	1.38
4	1.72	31.47	1.81	5.26	2.08	1.99	1.46	1.43	1.41

The forecast-error variances (asymptotically, ignoring the contributions from parameter estimation) are given by $\mathsf{E}[(\widehat{v}_{T+h} - \mathsf{E}[\widehat{v}_{T+h}])^2]$ which equals:

$$\mathsf{E}\left[\left\{\epsilon_{T+h} - \left(\alpha\sum_{i=0}^{h-1}\beta^i + \beta^h y_T - \mathsf{E}\left[\alpha\sum_{i=0}^{h-1}\beta^i + \beta^h y_T\right]\right)\right\}^2\right]$$
$$= \mathsf{E}\left[\left(\epsilon_{T+h} - \beta^h \epsilon_T\right)^2\right] = \sigma_\epsilon^2\left(1+\beta^{2h}\right).$$

The forecast-error variance is always less than from differencing (since $\beta < 1$) and declines towards the minimum attainable as h increases (σ_ϵ^2): that this does not happen in the Monte Carlo is due to parameter estimation effects.

Empirically, for UK consumption, we obtain:

$$\begin{aligned}
\widehat{\Delta_4 c_t} &= \underset{(0.0017)}{0.0052} + \underset{(0.07)}{0.74}\ \Delta_4 c_{t-1} \\
\mathsf{R}^2 &= 0.54\ \widehat{\sigma}_v = 1.38\%\ \mathsf{F_{ar}}(4,77) = 3.44^{**}\ \mathsf{F_{arch}}(4,73) = 0.40 \qquad (7.7)\\
\chi^2_{\mathsf{nd}}(2) &= 5.60\ \mathsf{F_{het}}(2,78) = 1.77\ \mathsf{F_{res}}(1,80) = 0.06\ \mathsf{J} = 0.50\ \mathsf{SC} = -8.48
\end{aligned}$$

The fit is little better than (7.3), as fig. 7.5a–d confirms, whereas the forecasts are poorer in terms of tracking, though never significantly bad.

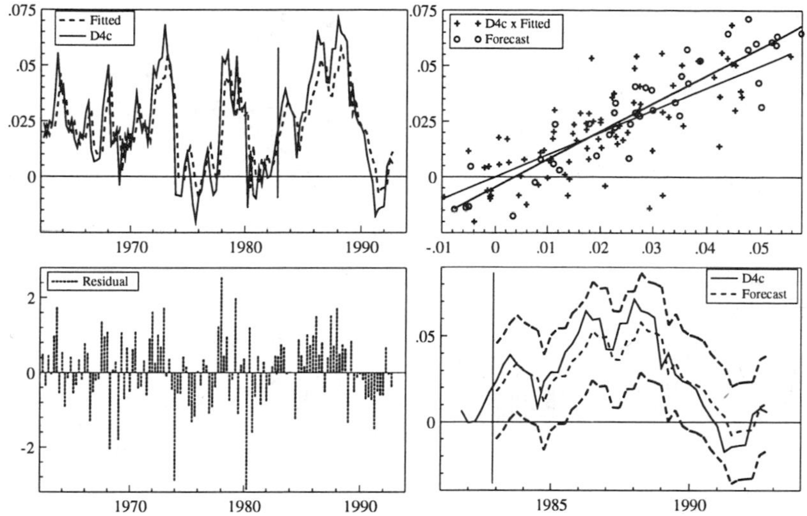

Figure 7.5
Graphical statistics for the AR(1) model, M_2.

7.8 Intercept Corrections

Here, we consider the simplest form of intercept correction for the AR(1) model, whereby the forecaster reacts to perceived recent predictive failure by adding in the equation error in predicting T, the forecast origin. For M_2, the AR(1) model, the period T model error is, ignoring estimation uncertainty:

$$\xi_T = y_T - y_{T|T-1} = \mu_2 + \epsilon_T - (\alpha + \beta y_{T-1}) = \mu_2 (1 - \beta) - \alpha + (1 - \beta L) \epsilon_T, \tag{7.8}$$

where L is the lag operator (i.e., $L\epsilon_t = \epsilon_{t-1}$). We saw in §6.2 that a sequentially-updated IC is equivalent to differencing the forecast errors, so here we consider the case when the IC adjustment is held constant over the forecast period, so ξ_T is added in at each step ahead:

$$\overline{y}_{T+h|T} = \alpha + \beta \overline{y}_{T+h-1|T} + \xi_T \tag{7.9}$$

where $\overline{y}_{T|T} = y_T$, so that:

$$\overline{y}_{T+h|T} = y_{T+h|T} + \xi_T \sum_{i=0}^{h-1} \beta^i = (\alpha + \xi_T) \sum_{i=0}^{h-1} \beta^i + \beta^h y_T, \tag{7.10}$$

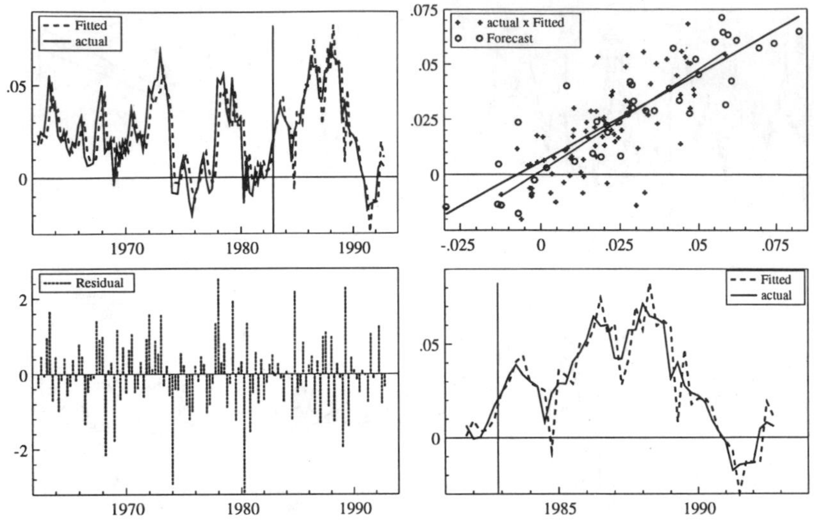

Figure 7.6
Graphical statistics for the intercept-corrected AR(1) model.

The bias from using (7.10) as a predictor is:

$$\mathsf{E}\left[y_{T+h} - \overline{y}_{T+h|T}\right] = \mu_2 - \frac{\alpha + \mathsf{E}\left[\xi_T\right]}{1-\beta} = 0, \quad \text{for large } h$$

as $\mathsf{E}\left[\xi_T\right] = \mu_2\,(1-\beta) - \alpha$ from (7.8). When there is no structural break, $\mu_2 = \mu_1$ and $\alpha = \mu_2$, $\beta = 0$, so that $\mathsf{E}\left[\xi_T\right] = \mathsf{E}\left[\epsilon_T\right] = 0$, and hence intercept correcting does not induce a bias.

However, ICs usually result in an inflated forecast-error variance. In our example, for large h:

$$\begin{aligned} \mathsf{V}\left[y_{T+h} - \overline{y}_{T+h|T}\right] &= \mathsf{E}\left[\left(\epsilon_{T+h} - \frac{\epsilon_T\,(1-\beta L)}{1-\beta}\right)^2\right] \\ &= \sigma_\epsilon^2 \frac{2\,(1-\beta+\beta^2)}{(1-\beta)^2} \end{aligned} \qquad (7.11)$$

constituting a doubling when there is no mean shift and $\rho = 0$. Moreover, for β close to unity, $\mathsf{V}\left[\cdot\right]$ gets very large. Intuitively, as $\beta \to 1$, the stochastic component of ξ_T, namely $\xi_T - \mathsf{E}\left[\xi_T\right] \to \Delta\epsilon_T$, and this is being multiplied by an

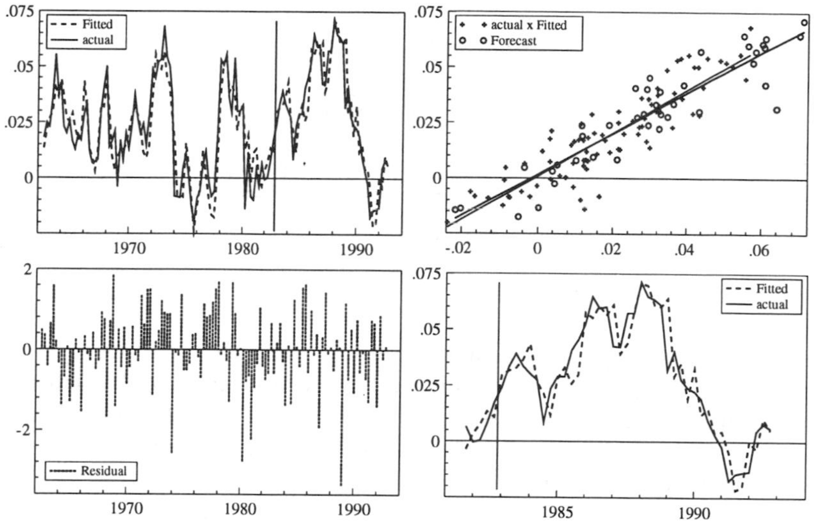

Figure 7.7
Graphical statistics for the intercept-corrected DHSY model.

only-just convergent sum $\sum_{i=0}^{h-1} \beta^i$. Evaluating (7.11) for 1-step forecasts gives:

$$\mathsf{V}\left[y_{T+1} - \overline{y}_{T+1|T}\right] = 2\left(1 + \beta + \beta^2\right);$$

see the Monte Carlo estimates in table 7.2 where the error variance for M_2^{IC} (the IC model M_2) is 5.56 compared to 1.89 for M_2, or 1.98 for M_5, the differenced model.

In summary, in the absence of a structural break, the differenced model and IC strategies both yield unbiased forecasts and doubled forecast error variances (relative to $y_{T+h|T} = \mu_2$). However, these two forecasting methods are differentially susceptible to structural breaks. For the DGP we consider here, the IC strategy is worse in terms of forecast-error variance, but this is not necessarily the case generally (see the empirical example in ch. 11).

For consumers' expenditure, the common-factor intercept correction for 1-step forecasts yields the outcomes shown in fig. 7.6: the in-sample behavior is identical by construction, but the forecasts track the outcomes, albeit with a larger variance. Of course, the more pertinent issue is the effect of intercept correcting on (7.2), and as fig. 7.7 shows, the effect is dramatic: unbiased forecasts do indeed result, again with considerable volatility due to incorporating the whole of the previous error as well as the impact of any shift.

Table 7.3
Empirical distribution of DW from OLS for M_2.

		Percentiles								
Mean	Std. Dev.	1	5	10	25	50	75	90	95	99
2.5980	0.0200	2.25	2.36	2.41	2.50	2.60	2.70	2.78	2.83	2.90

7.9 ARMA Predictors

The mean shift induces negative autocorrelation in the estimated residual of M_2 (as shown in the distribution of the Durbin and Watson, 1950, *DW* statistic in the Monte Carlo, table 7.3). To see why this occurs, recall that for a large enough value of δ_μ, the optimal value of the AR(1) parameter is unity when $\rho = 0$, so that differencing (7.1) yields:

$$\Delta y_t = \delta_\mu 1_{\{t=T_1+1\}} + \Delta \epsilon_t \tag{7.12}$$

where $1_{\{t=T_1+1\}}$ is an impulse indicator which is unity when $t = T_1 + 1$, and zero otherwise. If the break is not modeled, then we have the IMA(1,1) representation of the process:

$$\Delta y_t = \kappa + \xi_t + \theta \xi_{t-1} \tag{7.13}$$

As $\delta_\mu \to 0$, $\theta \to -1$, so the limit is an over-differenced process, with a strictly non-invertible MA component. For $\delta_\mu > 0$, the role of differencing is to convert the step-change in the mean of the white-noise process y_t into a blip in the estimated residual of the IMA representation. Figure 7.8 shows time series plots for a single realization of y_t from the Monte Carlo and the estimated residual $(\widehat{\xi}_t)$ from M_7.

For the size of break in the Monte Carlo, the AR root in M_8 close to unity. In M_6 and M_7 (IMA(1,1) models with and without constant terms), the MA coefficient is estimated at -0.42 and -0.40, respectively, and in M_8 (ARMA(1,1)) at -0.39. A neglected negative MA and near-unit root are conditions under which the results in Clements and Hendry (1996c) suggest that multi-step estimation of purely autoregressive models, such as M_2, should yield gains. We elaborate on this line of reasoning in §7.10.

The optimal forecast function for the IMA(1,1) is:

$$y_{T+h|T} = y_T + \widehat{\theta \xi_T}$$

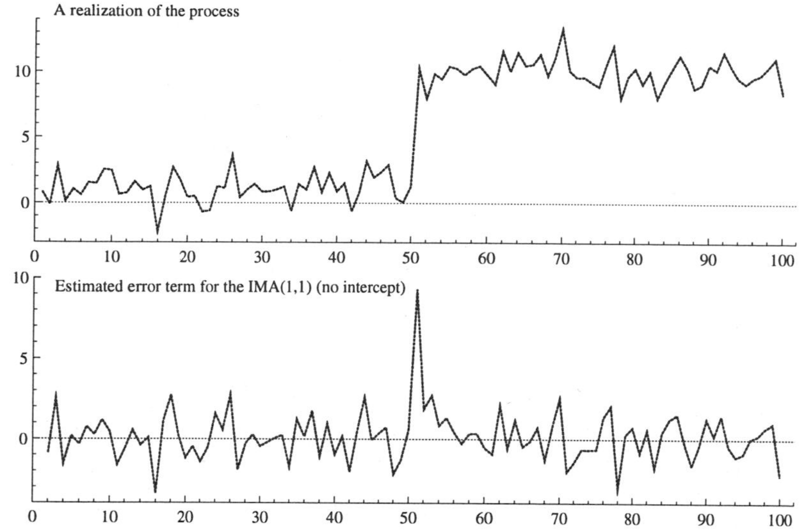

Figure 7.8
Time series of a single realization of y_t with the estimated errors from M_7.

where $\widehat{\theta}$ and $\widehat{\xi}_T$ denote estimates. The bias of this predictor is zero:

$$\mathsf{E}\left[y_{T+h} - y_{T+h|T}\right] = \mu_2 - \mu_2 - \widehat{\theta}\mathsf{E}\left[\widehat{\xi}_T\right] = 0.$$

since $\mathsf{E}[\widehat{\xi}_t] = 0$ except at $t = T_1 + 1$, where it picks up the effect of the mean shift. The forecast-error variance is approximately (ignoring the fact that $\widehat{\theta}$ is a random variable):

$$\begin{aligned}\mathsf{E}\left[\left(y_{T+h} - y_{T+h|T}\right)^2\right] &= \mathsf{E}\left[\left(\epsilon_{T+h} - \epsilon_T - \widehat{\theta\xi_T}\right)^2\right] \\ &\simeq 2\sigma_\epsilon^2 + \widehat{\theta}^2\mathsf{E}\left[\widehat{\xi_T^2}\right] + 2\widehat{\theta}\mathsf{E}\left[\widehat{\xi}_T\epsilon_T\right].\end{aligned}$$

We have:

$$\widehat{\xi}_T = y_T - y_{T-1} - \widehat{\theta\xi}_{T-1} = \Delta\epsilon_T - \widehat{\theta\xi}_{T-1} = \Delta\epsilon_T - \widehat{\theta}\left(\Delta\epsilon_{T-1} - \widehat{\theta\xi}_{T-2}\right) \quad (7.14)$$

so that $\mathsf{E}\left[\widehat{\xi}_T\epsilon_T\right] \simeq \sigma_\epsilon^2$. Also, from (7.14):

$$\widehat{\xi}_T = \epsilon_T - \left(1 + \widehat{\theta}\right)\epsilon_{T-1} + \widehat{\theta}\left(1 + \widehat{\theta}\right)\epsilon_{T-2} - \cdots$$

so:

$$\mathsf{E}\left[\widehat{\xi}_T^2\right] = \sigma_\epsilon^2 \left[1 + \left(1+\widehat{\theta}\right)^2 \sum_{i=0}^{\infty} \widehat{\theta}^{2i}\right] \simeq \sigma_\epsilon^2 \frac{2\left(\widehat{\theta}+1\right)}{1-\widehat{\theta}^2},$$

effectively assuming that the structural break occurred sufficiently far back to be ignored. Then:

$$\mathsf{E}\left[\left(y_{T+h} - y_{T+h|T}\right)^2\right] = \sigma_\epsilon^2 \left(2 + 2\widehat{\theta} + \frac{2\widehat{\theta}^2\left(\widehat{\theta}+1\right)}{1-\widehat{\theta}^2}\right) = \frac{2\sigma_\epsilon^2}{1-\widehat{\theta}},$$

yielding a forecast error variance less than that for the differenced-model (for $\theta < 0$). This result is unsurprising since the IMA model fits the data better than the ARIMA(0, 1, 0) (due to its negative serial correlation). In terms of bias, the IMA (M_7) forecasts are similar to the differenced-model (M_5) forecasts since the expected value of the MA term in the forecast function is zero.

As before, the empirical results conform to these analytic predictions. However, as there is no first-order residual autocorrelation in (7.7), but there is fourth, we estimated an ARMA(1,4) where only the lag-four error is included. This yielded the estimates in (7.15), and the graphical outcomes in fig. 7.9. small

$$\begin{aligned}
\widehat{\Delta_4 c_t} &= \underset{(0.0014)}{0.0029} + \underset{(0.06)}{0.83}\ \Delta_4 c_{t-1} - \underset{(0.09)}{0.58}\ \widehat{\xi}_{t-4} \\
\mathsf{R}^2 &= 0.66\ \ \widehat{\sigma}_\xi = 1.22\%\ \ \mathsf{F_{ar}}(4,73) = 0.53\ \ \mathsf{F_{arch}}(4,69) = 0.44 \qquad (7.15) \\
\chi^2_{\mathsf{nd}}(2) &= 0.93\ \ \mathsf{F_{het}}(4,72) = 3.20^{**}\ \ \mathsf{SC} = -8.69
\end{aligned}$$

The forecasts remain poor, although the residual autocorrelation has vanished. This is in line with our result in §5.2 that the double differencing that buys forecast-shift robustness will be lost if the residual autocorrelation is "removed", and here delivers an outcome that is noticeably worse than imposing both a zero intercept and a unit root on $\Delta_4 c_{t-1}$ (when $\widehat{\sigma} = 1.26\%$ and $\mathsf{SC} = -8.71$): see fig. 7.10.

7.10 AR(1) Model – Multi-step Estimation

Multi-step (adaptive, or dynamic) estimation may improve forecast accuracy whenever the parameter defined by projection of y_{T+h} on to y_T is not h times the parameter defined by the 1-step projection, that is, when $\mathsf{E}[y_{T+1}|y_T] = \psi y_T$

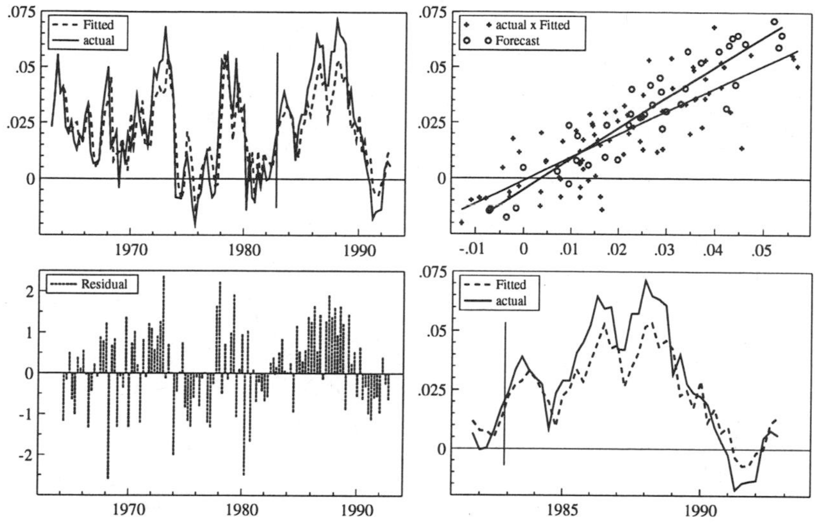

Figure 7.9
Graphical statistics for the ARMA(1,4) model.

(say), but $\mathsf{E}[y_{T+h}|y_T] = \psi_h y_T \neq \psi^h y_T$. Then, no matter how accurately $\widehat{\psi}$ estimates ψ, $(\widehat{\psi})^h$ need not be close to ψ_h. In the case we consider, this discrepancy arises because of the mean shift inducing a negative MA term, which is omitted from M_2. Thus, when $\kappa = 0$ in (7.13), and no intercept is estimated:

$$\mathsf{E}\left[y_{T+h} \mid y_T\right] = \rho^h y_T + \rho^{h-1}\theta \mathsf{E}\left[\xi_T \mid y_T\right] = \rho^{h-1}\left(\rho + \theta\lambda\right) y_T = \rho^{h-1}\phi y_T,$$

where $\mathsf{E}[\xi_T|y_T] = \lambda y_T$. Consequently, $\psi = (\rho + \theta\lambda)$, but $\psi_h = \rho^{h-1}\psi \neq \psi^h$ unless $\theta = 0$. We can handle $\kappa \neq 0$ with a change of notation, and for models of arbitrary lag order, this analysis is applicable to their first-order companion forms. For example, when $\kappa \neq 0$ write $\mathbf{y}_t = (y_t : 1)'$ with $\mathbf{v}_t = \boldsymbol{\xi}_t + \boldsymbol{\theta}\boldsymbol{\xi}_{t-1}$ where $\boldsymbol{\xi}_t = (\xi_t : 0)'$, so that:

$$\boldsymbol{\rho} = \begin{pmatrix} \rho & \kappa \\ 0 & 1 \end{pmatrix} \text{ and } \boldsymbol{\theta} = \begin{pmatrix} \theta & 0 \\ 0 & 1 \end{pmatrix},$$

then:

$$\mathbf{y}_t = \boldsymbol{\rho}\mathbf{y}_{t-1} + \boldsymbol{\xi}_t + \boldsymbol{\theta}\boldsymbol{\xi}_{t-1}.$$

Clements and Hendry (1996c) consider the role of multi-step estimation in such a model both when $\rho = 1$ and $|\rho| < 1$. For the stationary case with $\kappa = 0$, they

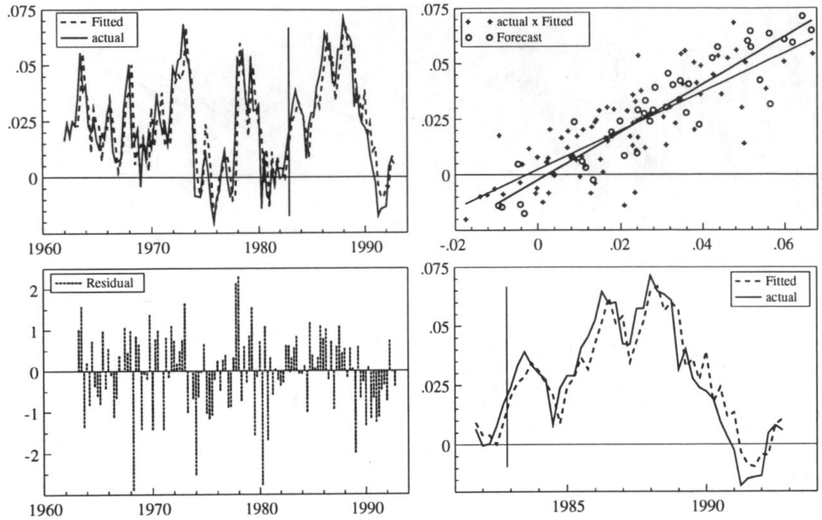

Figure 7.10
Graphical statistics for the IMA(1,4) model.

show that the optimal value of ψ_h in the AR(1) model h-step forecast function (in the sense of minimizing h-step ahead MSFE) is:

$$y_{T+h|T} = \psi_h y_T,$$

when ψ_h is given by:

$$\psi_h \equiv \rho_{\{h\}} = \rho^{(h-1)} \times \rho_{\{1\}}$$

where $\rho_{\{1\}}$ is optimal for 1-step ahead forecast errors, and is given by:

$$\rho_{\{1\}} = \rho + \frac{\theta\left(1-\rho^2\right)}{1+\theta^2+2\rho\theta}.$$

Thus, $\psi_h = \psi^h \equiv \left(\rho_{\{1\}}\right)^h$ requires that $\theta = 0$. When $\rho = 1$:

$$\rho_{\{h\}} = \left(\rho_{\{1\}}\right)^{1/h}$$

so that $\rho_{\{h\}} \to 1$ as h increases (when $\theta > -1$). Notice that $\psi^h \equiv \left(\rho_{\{1\}}\right)^h \to 0$ in h when $|\rho_{\{1\}}| < 1$.

In the Monte Carlo, multi-step estimation inflates the forecast-error variances over 1-step estimation, but generates smaller biases and an overall gain in terms of MSFE (compare the column headed M_3 with M_2 in table 7.2).

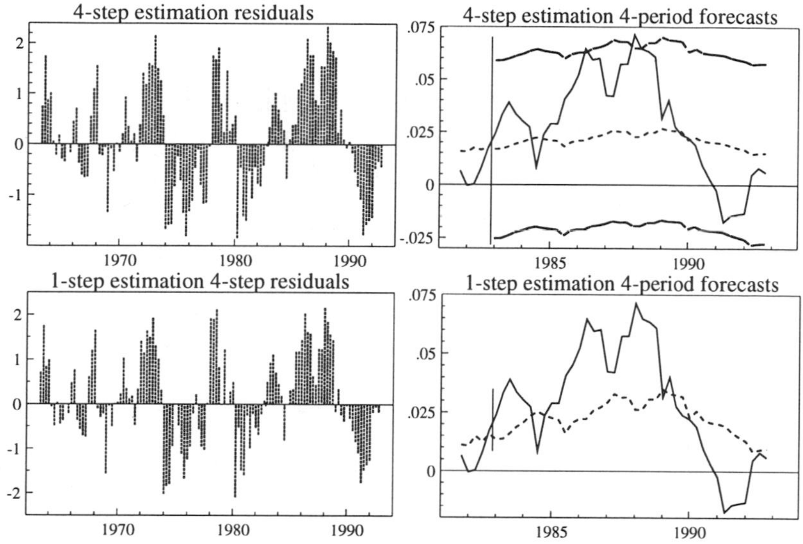

Figure 7.11
Graphical statistics for 4-step ahead forecasts of annual growth.

For $\rho = 1$, the limiting distribution of $\widehat{\psi_h}$ is closely related to that of $\widehat{\psi}$ (see Clements and Hendry, 1996c), and predicts that biases remain and do not change much with h. However, different estimators are required for each linear transform of the dependent variable (e.g., $\Delta_4 c_t$ versus $\Delta_1\Delta_4 c_t$ even though $\Delta_1\Delta_4 c_t \equiv \Delta_1 c_t - \Delta_1 c_{t-4}$).

Here we compare 4-step estimation for 4-period ahead forecasts with fourth powering of the 1-step form. The AR(1) given by (7.7) provides 4-step ahead forecasts of $\Delta_4 c_t$ by powering up. Direct estimation of the 4-step representation yields:

$$\widehat{\Delta_4 c_t} = \underset{(0.0033)}{0.017} + \underset{(0.11)}{0.14}\ \Delta_4 c_{t-4} \tag{7.16}$$

$$\mathsf{R}^2 = 0.02\ \ \widehat{\sigma}_\varsigma = 2.08\%\ \ \mathsf{J} = 1.82\ \ \mathsf{SC} = -7.66$$

This is for the annual growth in c_t one year ahead, and reveals almost no forecastability from the previous year's annual growth. Few tests are valid due to the residual autocorrelation, which also biases the conventional standard errors. The fourth power of 0.74 (the slope coefficient in (7.7)) is 0.30 and imposing that yields $\widetilde{\sigma}_\varsigma = 2.09\%$: fig. 7.11 shows the comparison of their residuals and forecasts. There is little to choose between the two estimators, but the

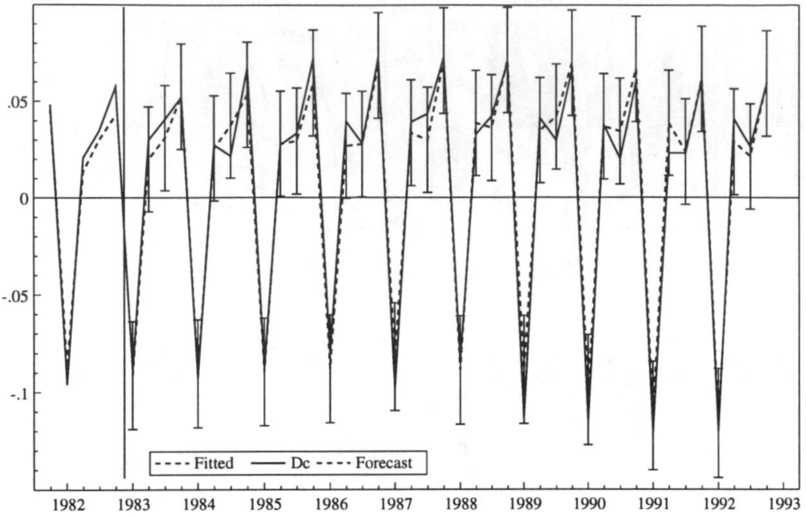

Figure 7.12
4-step ahead forecasts of quarterly growth.

powered-up forecasts are somewhat better here with MSFE s of 2.4% versus 2.75%. In absolute terms, neither would be of use for economic policy, with forecast errors of 4% occurring regularly.

The situation is more sanguine for quarterly growth one-year ahead. Using the identity noted above, $\Delta_1 c_t \equiv \Delta_1\Delta_4 c_t + \Delta_1 c_{t-4}$ and as $\Delta_1\Delta_4 c_t$ can be explained in part as $-\frac{1}{2}\Delta_1\Delta_4 c_{t-4}$ we have (unrestricted estimates are 0.98 (0.03) and −0.43 (0.10)):

$$\widehat{\Delta_1 c_{T+4}} = \Delta_1 c_T - \tfrac{1}{2}\,\Delta_1\Delta_4 c_T$$

$$\mathsf{R}^2 = 0.95 \;\; \widehat{\sigma}_\zeta = 1.36\% \;\; \mathsf{SC} = -8.55$$

Figure 7.12 shows the forecasts with conventionally-calculated 95% confidence bars.

This overestimates the uncertainty from the policy-makers perspective, since tax changes are known to them, so to establish a "minimum" innovation variance, we added indicator variables for the main changes in consumers' taxes (purchase tax in 1968(1)/(2); VAT in 1973(1)/(2) and 1979(2)/(3)), and interventions in 1974(1), 1977(4)/1978(1) and 1980(1) for the remaining outliers. Then $\widetilde{\sigma}_\zeta = 0.93\%$ and fig. 7.13 shows the graphical statistics in terms of $\Delta_1\Delta_4 c_t$, with 95% confidence bands rather than bars.

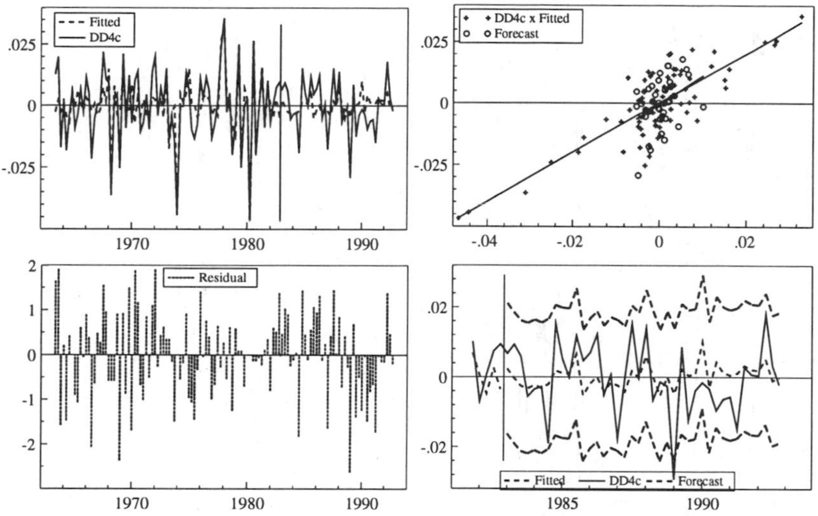

Figure 7.13
Graphical statistics for 4-step ahead forecasts of quarterly changes in annual growth.

There is only one significant forecast error, and the MSFE is just under 0.9%. However, it is hard to decide what the 1-step comparative method would be, since models of $\Delta_1\Delta_4 c_t$ primarily depend on $\Delta_1\Delta_4 c_{t-4}$. Finally, fig. 7.14 shows the forecasts from 4–7 steps ahead for $\Delta_1 c_t$ based on the "models":

$$\begin{aligned}
\widehat{\Delta_1 c}_{t|t-4} &= \widehat{\alpha}_4 + \Delta_1 c_{t-4} - 0.5\Delta_1\Delta_4 c_{t-4} \\
\widehat{\Delta_1 c}_{t|t-5} &= \widehat{\alpha}_5 + \Delta_1 c_{t-8} - 0.25(\Delta_4 c_{t-5}) \\
\widehat{\Delta_1 c}_{t|t-6} &= \widehat{\alpha}_6 + \Delta_1 c_{t-8} - 0.33(\Delta_4 c_{t-6}) \\
\widehat{\Delta_1 c}_{t|t-7} &= \widehat{\alpha}_7 + \Delta_1 c_{t-8} - 0.33(\Delta_4 c_{t-7})
\end{aligned}$$

where only the α_i are estimated. There is not a great deal of deterioration as the horizon increases, the sample and forecast statistics being:

i	$100\widehat{\alpha}_i$	100SE	$100\widehat{\sigma}_i$	$\chi^2_i(40)$
4	−0.01	0.15	1.36	17.9
5	0.50	0.17	1.52	20.2
6	0.64	0.17	1.47	23.9
7	0.64	0.17	1.47	22.6

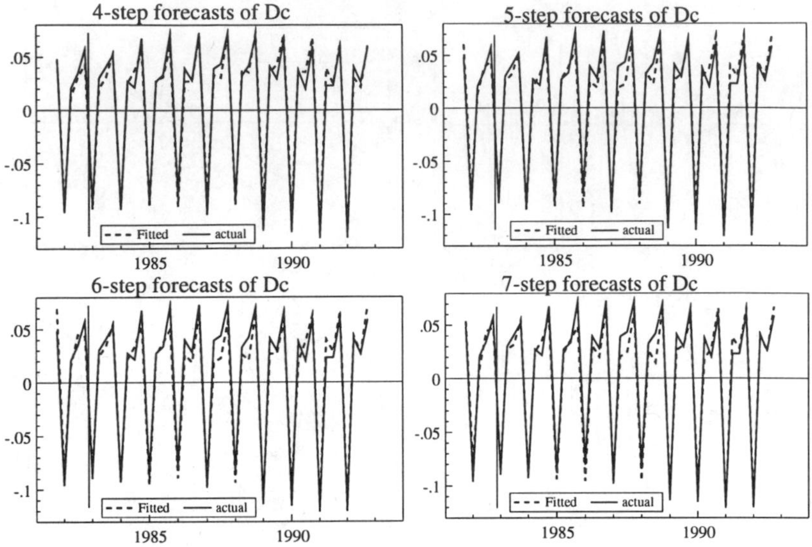

Figure 7.14
4-step to 7-step ahead forecasts of quarterly growth.

where:

$$\chi_i^2(40) = \frac{1}{\widehat{\sigma_i^2}} \sum_{t=T+1}^{T+40} \left(\Delta_1 c_t - \widehat{\Delta_1 c_t}\right)^2 = (40/\widehat{\sigma_i^2}) \times \mathsf{MSFE}.$$

Thus, in every case, the average squared forecast errors are about half the in-sample.

7.11 Disequilibrium Adjustment

When the process is (7.1) but with $\rho \neq 0$, that is:

$$y_t = \rho y_{t-1} + \mu_1 + \delta_\mu 1_{\{t>T_1\}} + \epsilon_t \tag{7.17}$$

then there will be a period of adjustment when the mean of y alters from $\mu_1/(1-\rho)$ to $\mu_2/(1-\rho)$, since:

$$y_t = \mu_2 \sum_{s=0}^{t-T_1-1} \rho^s + \mu_1 \sum_{s=t-T_1}^{t-1} \rho^s + \sum_{s=0}^{t-1} \rho^s \epsilon_{t-s} + \rho^t y_0$$

for $t > T_1 + 1$. When $y_0 \sim \mathsf{N}[\mu_1/(1-\rho), \sigma_\epsilon^2/(1-\rho^2)]$, then for $t \leq T_1$, $\mathsf{E}[y_t] = \mu_1/(1-\rho)$. For $t > T_1$, $\mathsf{E}[y_t] \to \mu_2/(1-\rho)$ as $t \to \infty$. The speed of adjustment depends on how close ρ is to zero: at $\rho = 0$ the adjustment is instantaneous. If, as in the Monte Carlo, $T_1 = T/2$ and T is relatively large, then forecasting from an origin of T will yield similar results to when $\rho = 0$. Since $\mathsf{E}[y_T] \simeq \mu_2$, the latest observation (nearly) fully embodies the new equilibrium mean, so the differenced-model M_5 forecasts will be approximately unbiased.

Reconsider (7.1) pre-break, written as:

$$\Delta y_t = (\rho - 1)\left(y_{t-1} - \frac{\mu_1}{1-\rho}\right) + \epsilon_t. \tag{7.18}$$

Within the first regime, the disequilibrium:

$$y_{t-1} - \frac{\mu_1}{1-\rho} = y_{t-1} - \mathsf{E}[y_{t-1}]$$

helps correct the current growth Δy_t, and ensures a stationary outcome. However, when the long-run mean changes to $\mu_2/(1-\rho)$, the DGP becomes:

$$\Delta y_t = (\rho - 1)\left(y_{t-1} - \frac{\mu_2}{1-\rho}\right) + \epsilon_t. \tag{7.19}$$

whereas the model in use remains:

$$\begin{aligned}\Delta y_t &= (\rho - 1)\left(y_{t-1} - \frac{\mu_1}{1-\rho}\right) + v_t \\ &= (\rho - 1)\left(y_{t-1} - \frac{\mu_2}{1-\rho}\right) + v_t - \delta_\mu. \end{aligned} \tag{7.20}$$

When $\delta_\mu > 0$, as in fig. 7.8, the EqCM computed in (7.18) will be persistently positive, so will continually predict negative Δy_{t+j}. Thus, as noted in §7.4, this is the opposite of error correction, and corrects only within equilibria and not between. We suspect that this underlies the failure of DHSY, namely a shift in the desired long-run propensity to spend following financial deregulation that lifted the rationing constraint on borrowing for many consumers, enabling them to finance a higher ratio of expenditure to income. Rationing ceased to bite around 1989, and the rise in interest rates, exacerbated by a reduction in the tax deductibility of interest payments, and a fall in house prices (the main collateral for the debt) together forced a rapid return to previous levels of expenditure to income, undershooting en route. Such mean shifts are consistent with the success of the intercept-correction strategy above.

7.12 Conclusion

The aim of this chapter has been to exposit some of the results in chapters 3–6 (and elsewhere) on forecasting after a shift in the mean of a stochastic process. When economic systems are subject to structural breaks, conventional models need not forecast satisfactorily. The empirical example of consumers' expenditure reveals that some shift in the econometric relation occurred, and that the various strategies considered helped circumvent the implicit shift. Analysis suggests that differencing can mitigate the effects of changes in equilibrium means, and this was shown above empirically, and in a Monte Carlo. Alternatively, intercept corrections can offset the mean shift, albeit at the cost of an increased variance. However, models that do neither performed badly analytically and empirically. There was little benefit to multi-step estimation over repeated backward solution of 1-step estimates.

Thus, in-sample fit may be a poor guide to *ex-ante* forecast performance when the assumption of constancy fails, so alternative strategies may be called for. A theory of forecasting allowing for structural breaks when the model is not the mechanism is feasible. Moreover, on the limited evidence of the empirical example considered here, that theory provides a useful basis for interpreting and circumventing systematic predictive failure in economics.

The next chapter develops a multivariate empirical example to illustrate the theory, applied in a more realistic context. Again, we find considerable concordance, and an ability to interpret otherwise somewhat confusing evidence. Then we will consider two alternative approaches to avoiding systematic forecast failure, by seeking to model the changes that occur. The first, called co-breaking, eliminates deterministic shifts across linear combinations of variables, and is discussed in chapter 9. The second, considered in chapter 10 assumes that shifts are recurrent, and tries to model the regimes into which the economy systematically moves. Finally, we will discuss a second multivariate empirical example.

Table 7.4

Empirical distributions of model parameter estimates.

Model	Mean	Std. Dev. $\times 100$	Percentiles								
			1	5	10	25	50	75	90	95	99
M_2 β	0.934	0.01	0.91	0.92	0.92	0.93	0.93	0.94	0.95	0.95	0.95
M_2 α	0.452	0.34	0.33	0.36	0.38	0.41	0.45	0.49	0.53	0.55	0.61
M_2 β^2	0.872	0.04	0.82	0.84	0.85	0.86	0.87	0.89	0.90	0.90	0.91
M_2 β^3	0.815	0.07	0.74	0.77	0.78	0.80	0.82	0.83	0.85	0.86	0.87
M_2 β^4	0.761	0.11	0.68	0.70	0.72	0.74	0.76	0.78	0.80	0.81	0.83
M_3 ψ_2	0.915	0.01	0.88	0.89	0.90	0.91	0.92	0.92	0.93	0.93	0.94
M_3 const.	0.645	0.48	0.50	0.54	0.56	0.60	0.64	0.69	0.74	0.76	0.82
M_3 ψ_3	0.896	0.02	0.86	0.87	0.88	0.89	0.90	0.91	0.91	0.92	0.93
M_3 const.	0.838	0.61	0.67	0.71	0.74	0.78	0.83	0.89	0.94	0.97	1.03
M_3 ψ_4	0.877	0.02	0.84	0.85	0.86	0.87	0.88	0.89	0.90	0.90	0.91
M_3 const.	1.031	0.71	0.85	0.90	0.92	0.97	1.03	1.09	1.14	1.18	1.23
M_4 const.	0.091	0.02	0.06	0.07	0.07	0.08	0.09	0.10	0.11	0.11	0.12
M_6 θ	-0.420	0.42	-0.54	-0.51	-0.50	-0.46	-0.43	-0.38	-0.33	-0.31	-0.24
M_6 const.	0.092	0.01	0.07	0.08	0.08	0.09	0.09	0.10	0.10	0.11	0.11
M_7 θ	-0.404	0.39	-0.53	-0.50	-0.48	-0.45	-0.41	0.37	-0.32	-0.29	-0.23
M_8 ρ	0.978	0.00	0.97	0.97	0.97	0.98	0.98	0.98	0.98	0.98	0.99
M_8 θ	-0.388	0.43	-0.51	-0.48	-0.47	-0.43	-0.40	-0.35	-0.30	-0.27	-0.20
M_8 const.	5.499	5.47	4.95	5.11	5.20	5.34	5.50	5.65	5.80	5.88	6.04

8 A Small UK Money Model

Summary

This is the first of two multivariate illustrations of forecasting in the face of structural breaks. We focus on VEqCM, DV and DDV models. In chapters 3 and 5, we derived expressions for their unconditional and conditional forecast-error biases and unconditional variances. When the forecast evaluation sample includes sub-periods following breaks, we showed that non-causal models could outperform at short horizons. At longer horizons, variance costs may outweigh bias gains. This chapter analyzes a small monetary model of the UK to illustrate the theory. The empirical results closely support the theory predictions. There was a major financial innovation immediately prior to our first forecast period, and the uncorrected VEqCM performs poorly over that horizon, especially when formulated in levels. Differencing corrects the forecast biases, but the calculated variances increase rapidly, partly because the formulae do not reflect residual autocorrelation induced by differencing. In the second forecast period, believed to have no major breaks, the VEqCM performs well. Intercept corrections are able to offset some of the forecast-error biases in the VEqCM.

8.1 Introduction

Deterministic non-constancies seem responsible for many major episodes of empirical forecast failure, when model-based forecasts have systematically over- or under-predicted for substantial periods, and realized outcomes lay well outside any reasonable *ex ante* prediction intervals (i.e., computed from the uncertainties due to parameter estimation and lack of fit). Economies are high dimensional, dynamic, non-linear, and evolving over time as technology, production and financial possibilities alter, social behavior fluctuates, and institutional and legal changes affect the environment within which agents interact. Consequently, relationships observed to hold in the past between variables are not immutable, and mechanically-derived forecasts (i.e., forecasts made without human intervention) are often adjusted to capture perceived or expected changes. As a result, forecasting strategies that would appear bizarre in a constant-parameter world deserve consideration. Some of the properties of these strategies have been discussed in chapters 5 and 6: here, we illustrate by a small model of UK money demand. Our findings cohere with the scalar UK consumers' expenditure illustration in chapter 7, and offer some extensions, particularly pertaining to the possible efficacy of "over-differencing".

This study of UK M1 (using quarterly, seasonally-adjusted data) allows us to analyze forecast failure emanating from a major financial innovation. Specifically, Hendry and Ericsson (1991) show that the introduction of a non-zero own interest rate (learning adjusted) on checking accounts was tantamount to a deterministic shift in the equilibrium demand for M1, and failure to model that effect induced very poor forecasts. The model we investigate is a descendant of that first proposed in Hendry (1979b), and builds on Hendry and Mizon (1993) who embedded it in a 4-variable system. Hendry (1996) considered the forecast behavior of the single-equation model of UK M1 estimated over the sample 1963:3 to 1983:2, and showed that its forecasts failed badly when the data period was extended to 1989:2. This study extends his analysis to the multivariate context. Finally, Hendry and Doornik (1994) embedded the equation from Hendry and Ericsson (1991) in a 4-variable system. Relative to these studies, we return to the system in Hendry and Mizon (1993), to illustrate the impact of an unmodeled deterministic shift, but over an extended sample. We focus on the multi-period forecast performance of the alternative systems under analysis, to discuss which methods win in practice in this setting. When needed, we treat the model in Hendry and Doornik (1994) as if it were the DGP.

Let M denote nominal M1, I total final expenditure, P its deflator, and R the interest rate on three-month Local-Authority bills: $\Delta = (1 - L)$ is the first difference, when L is the lag operator. Lower case letters denote logs, with the key exception that r continues to denote the number of cointegrating relations, as $\log R$ is never used. We consider forecasting over two distinct historical periods. For the first, the sample period is 1964:3–1985:2, after initial values for lags, with the remaining observations for 1985:3–1989:2 retained for out-of-sample forecasting. Figure 8.1 shows four views designed to clarify our interpretation of the financial innovation as a deterministic shift, relative to any pre-existing model. Panel a plots R and $R_n = R - R_o$ where R_o is the own rate of interest, payment of which became legal in 1984:2. The sharp departure in the level of the actual opportunity cost of holding money (R_n) from the in-sample measure (R) is tantamount to a deterministic shift. Panel b plots the time series of real money $(m - p)$ and R_o, revealing that R_o acts as level shift for the demand for money. Panel c shows the velocity of circulation of M1 ($v = i + p - m$) and the two interest rates R_n and R to show the high whole-sample relation between v and R_n, and the end-of-sample departure from its relation with R, which rises while v continues to fall like R_n. The final panel reports the relation between $\Delta(m - p)$ and $-R_n$ with R_o also shown to reveal the departure that would occur if R were used.

The four variables ($m - p$, Δp, i, R) appear to be I(1), so we first develop a dynamic system in §8.2, undertake a cointegration analysis in §8.3, reduce the data to I(0) in §8.4, then simplify to a model in §8.5. As expected, the system's multi-step forecast performance is very poor. Adding a step-shift dummy to allow a separate intercept (autonomous growth) over the forecast period rescues the forecasts in §8.7, similar to those from the "correct" model: this is a form of intercept correction.

In §8.6, we develop "time-series" models which do not fail on forecasting, as the test period commences after the structural break. This choice of forecast period illustrates the efficacy of intercept corrections and time-series models when a major break has occurred prior to forecasting. In §8.8, a second exercise selects the immediately preceding

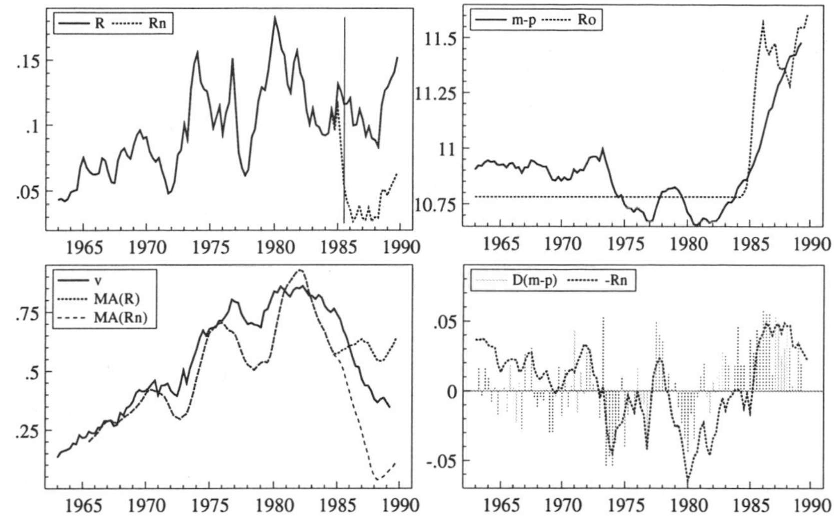

Figure 8.1
UK M1 and interest rates.

16 observations as the forecast period, i.e., 1981:3–1985:2, to assess the costs of the various strategies over a period when the dynamic system remained a reasonably good approximation to the DGP. The specifications of the models for the second exercise are carried over directly from those estimated on the longer sample – given its in-sample constancy, re-specifying the model would probably make little difference. Below we emphasize the "post-break" forecast period, where the hitherto well-specified simultaneous-equations model exhibits spectacular forecast failure, but full results are also reported using the "pre-break" forecast period for the empirical forecast comparisons of the various methods. Section 8.9 draws various conclusions from the study.

8.2 A Four-equation VAR

The variables $((m - p_t), \Delta p_t, i_t, R_t)$ were analyzed in a VAR with 2 lags, including a constant, linear deterministic trend, and two indicator variables for output (*dout* equal to zero, except for unity in 1972(4), 1973(1), and 1979(2)) and the oil crises (*doil*, unity in 1973(3), 1973(4), 1974(2) and 1979(3)). These indicators adjust for the largest residuals

Table 8.1
System goodness of fit and evaluation.

statistic	$m-p$	i	Δp	R	VAR
$\widehat{\sigma}$	1.76%	1.11%	0.62%	1.33	
$\mathsf{F}_{\mathsf{ar}}\,(5,67)$	3.15*	1.02	1.68	1.02	
$\mathsf{F}_{\mathsf{arch}}\,(4,64)$	0.40	0.24	0.58	2.32	
$\mathsf{F}_{\mathsf{het}}\,(18,53)$	0.82	1.17	0.74	1.32	
$\chi^2_{\mathsf{nd}}\,(2)$	3.08	1.62	3.76	1.99	
$\mathsf{F}^{\mathsf{v}}_{\mathsf{ar5}}\,(80,195)$					1.40*
$\mathsf{F}^{\mathsf{v}}_{\mathsf{het}}\,(180,407)$					0.94
$\chi^{2\,\mathsf{v}}_{\mathsf{nd}}\,(8)$					4.95

in the Hendry and Mizon (1993) system; the issues raised by how the dummies enter the system are discussed in Doornik, Hendry and Nielsen (1999). All computations and graphics were again produced by GiveWin and PcFiml (see Doornik and Hendry, 1996, 1997).

Table 8.1 shows the individual-equation, and system, goodness-of-fit and evaluation statistics: the individual-equation statistics are the same as chapter 7; vector diagnostic tests are of the form $\mathsf{F}^{\mathsf{v}}_{\mathsf{jk}}(n^2k, T-l)$ which denotes an F-test against the alternative hypothesis j for: k^{th}-order vector serial correlation ($\mathsf{F}^{\mathsf{v}}_{\mathsf{ar}}$: see Hendry, 1971, Guilkey, 1974, and Doornik, 1995); system residual heteroscedasticity ($\mathsf{F}^{\mathsf{v}}_{\mathsf{het}}$: see White, 1980); and a chi-square test for multivariate normality ($\chi^{2\,\mathsf{v}}_{\mathsf{nd}}(8)$: see Doornik and Hansen, 1994): * and ** again denote significance at the 5% and 1% levels respectively.

The money-demand equation reveals some residual autocorrelation, but otherwise the outcomes are consistent with a congruent system. Table 8.2 records the correlations of fitted and actual (on the diagonal), and the residual inter-correlations: those between $m-p$ and (Δp, R) are much the largest.

The eigenvalues of the long-run matrix are -0.41, -0.05, and $-0.11 \pm 0.19\iota$ (using ι to denote $\sqrt{-1}$ to avoid confusion with income, i), so the rank seems non-zero, and is likely to be one or perhaps two. The eigenvalues of the companion matrix (denoted λ) are shown in table 8.3. Only one root is very close to unity, two have moduli near 0.9, and the remainder are small.

Table 8.2
System correlations and residual cross correlations.

	$m-p$	i	Δp	R
$m-p$	0.986			
i	0.01	0.998		
Δp	−0.47	−0.15	0.911	
R	−0.48	0.04	0.29	0.924

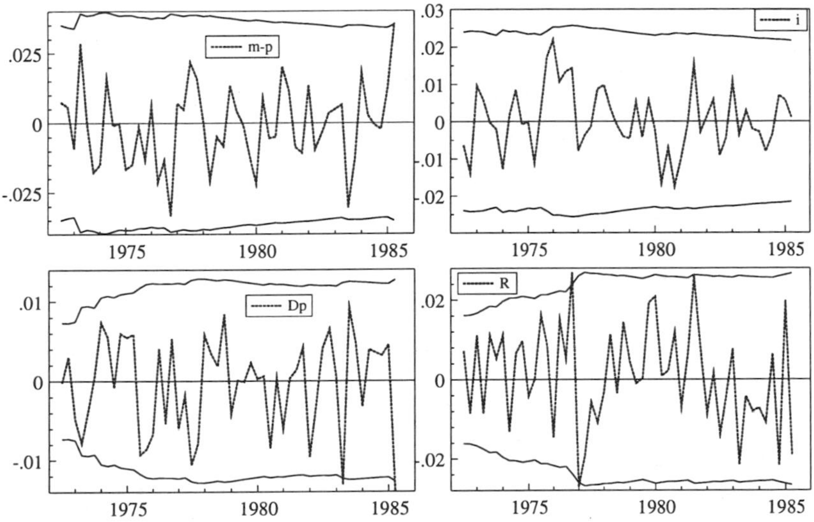

Figure 8.2
System recursive 1-step residuals.

Table 8.3
System dynamics.

λ	0.97	$0.86 \pm 0.17\iota$	0.64	−0.32	$-0.22 \pm 0.12\iota$	0.19
$\|\lambda\|$	0.97	0.87,0.87	0.64	0.32	0.25,0.25	0.19

First lags were significant, but the second lags and the trend were insignificant (on F(4, 72), at 5% or less). Figure 8.2 shows the in-sample recursively-computed system 1-step residuals with 95% confidence bands: those for Δp and R increase initially, although the system

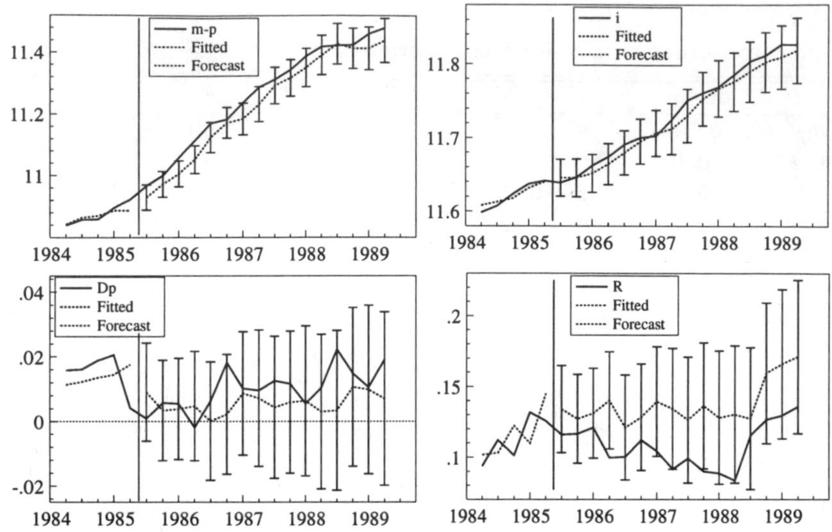

Figure 8.3
System1-step ahead forecasts.

break-point Chow (1960) test did not exceed any (one-off) 1% critical value within sample.

Figure 8.3 reports the 1-step ahead out-of-sample forecasts with approximate 95% prediction intervals: there is some evidence of mis-forecasting in the money and interest-rate equations, but overall, the performance is respectable, consistent with the constancy-test outcome of $\mathsf{F}(64, 72) = 0.87$. This outcome can be interpreted as a sequence of the form in §3.5.1 and §3.5.2, etc.

Finally, fig. 8.4 records the fitted and actual values for each variable together with the 16-steps ahead forecasts and their approximate 95% error bars: the excellent fit but awful multi-step forecast performance of this unrestricted system is manifest. This outcome can be interpreted as a sequence of the form in §3.5.1 and §3.5.3, etc., so is the combination of the non-modeled deterministic shift due to financial innovation, interacting with the I(1) formulation and the over-parameterization. We address these last two issues in turn.

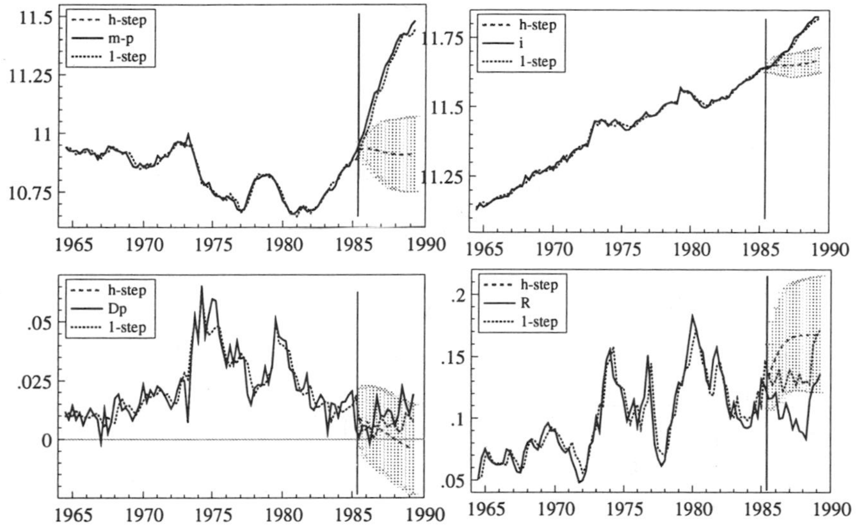

Figure 8.4
System graphical statistics with 1 to 16-step ahead forecasts .

8.3 Cointegration

To minimize its dependence on nuisance parameters, the cointegration analysis restricted the trend to the cointegration space, but let the constant and dummies enter unrestrictedly (see Johansen, 1995a, and Doornik and Hendry, 1997; Doornik *et al.*, 1999, discuss the general issue of rank determination for this model). For each value of the rank$r \geq 1$ of the long-run matrix in the Johansen (1988) procedure, table 8.4 reports the log-likelihood values (ℓ), eigenvalues (λ) and associated maximum eigenvalue (*Max*) and trace (*Tr*) statistics together with the estimated cointegrating vectors ($\widehat{\beta}$) and feedback coefficients ($\widehat{\alpha}$). The null of no cointegration is strongly rejected at conventional I(1) critical values, but $r > 1$ is not formally rejected. Although the second cointegrating vector is not very significant, we retain it given the interpretability of its coefficients after restrictions.

To uniquely determine and interpret the two possible cointegration vectors, we removed the trend from the first, and $m-p$ from the second. Then we restricted the income coefficient to -1 in the first vector, and the trend coefficient in the second to the mean value of Δi (namely,

Table 8.4
Cointegration analysis.

r	1	2	3	4
ℓ	1541	1548	1553	1556
λ	0.52	0.16	0.11	0.06
Max	61.4**	14.8	9.9	5.3
Tr	91.4**	30.0	15.2	5.3

$\widehat{\alpha}$	1	2	3	4
$m-p$	−0.03	−0.01	−0.16	−0.02
i	−0.01	0.00	0.37	−0.00
Δp	−0.00	0.02	−0.06	0.01
R	−0.01	−0.03	0.00	0.01

$\widehat{\beta}'$	$m-p$	i	Δp	R	t
1	1	−0.74	13.4	16.6	−0.0125
2	−1.12	1	−10.1	2.56	−0.0108
3	0.07	−0.46	1	−0.11	0.0026
4	1.37	4.43	−6.54	1	−0.0271

0.0062, approximately 2.5% p.a.), also eliminating inflation. Finally, we set the feedbacks to zero for the second vector on the first equation, and the first on the last three equations (related to long-run weak exogeneity: see Engle, Hendry and Richard, 1983), which yielded the results shown in table 8.5, with the test of these restrictions jointly being $\chi^2(7) = 9.58$.

The first cointegration vector relates the ratio of money to expenditure (inverse velocity: $m-p-i$) negatively to inflation and interest rates, so it has the interpretation of an excess demand for transactions money. The second cointegration vector is interpretable as the excess demand for goods and services (the deviation of expenditure from trend, negatively related to interest rates), and its main influence is onto the i equation, so we retain these two long-run relations.

Figure 8.5 records the time series of the two unrestricted and restricted cointegration vectors, and the associated recursively-computed eigenvalues. The two cointegrated time-series for money are very similar, whereas the restrictions have noticeably altered that for income; however, both eigenvalues seem constantly estimated (see Hansen and

Table 8.5
Restricted Cointegration analysis.

$\widehat{\alpha}$	1	2
$m-p$	-0.098 (0.014)	0 (–)
i	0 (–)	-0.124 (0.030)
Δp	0 (–)	-0.019 (0.016)
R	0 (–)	-0.007 (0.035)

$\widehat{\beta}'$	$m-p$	i	Δp	R	t
1	1 (–)	-1 (–)	6.67 (1.61)	6.53 (0.67)	0 (–)
2	0 (–)	1 (–)	0 (–)	1.22 (0.31)	-0.0062 (–)

Johansen, 1992). The two, zero-mean, I (0) linear combinations defining the equilibrium-correction mechanisms (EqCMs) are given by:

$$c_{1,t} = m_t - p_t - i_t + 6.67\Delta p_t + 6.53R_t - 0.223 \tag{8.1}$$

and:

$$c_{2,t} = i_t - 0.0062t + 1.22R_t - 11.125. \tag{8.2}$$

The definitions in (8.1) and (8.2) are required for multi-step forecasts when formulating the model in terms of the differences ($\Delta(m-p)_t$, Δi_t, $\Delta^2 p_t$, ΔR_t) of the original variables.

8.4 The I(0) system

Going from the second-order VAR in the levels of the variables ($(m-p_t)$, Δp_t, i_t, R_t) to a simultaneous-equations model involves a number of steps (see, e.g., Hendry and Mizon, 1993, Clements and Mizon, 1991), any of which might potentially affect forecast performance. We first considered the impact of imposing cointegration. The initial system in the levels of the variables is given an equivalent representation

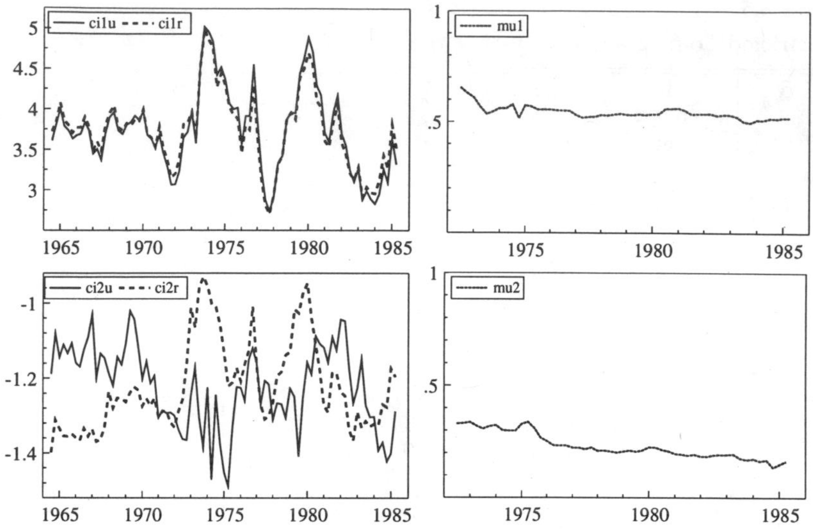

Figure 8.5
Cointegration vectors, and recursively-computed eigenvalues.

in terms of differences, cointegrating combinations, and (two) lagged level terms. The I (1) level terms are then deleted from all four equations to assess the impact of imposing unit roots and cointegration (as studied by Clements and Hendry, 1995a, via Monte Carlo, and empirically in a simplified monetary model), as distinct from parsimony *per se*, so insignificant I(0) terms are retained. Imposing cointegration made little difference to forecasting performance relative to the unrestricted VAR. Full results are shown in the empirical forecast comparisons.

8.5 A Simultaneous-equations Model

A model of the I(0) system was developed by sequential simplification, based on earlier findings, and delivered the estimates shown in table 8.6, augmented by the definitions in (8.1) and (8.2). This resulted in only 13 estimated I(0) parameters with the three I(1) parameters from table 8.5 (so should avoid any over-parameterization problems that may have affected the initial system), but was an acceptable reduction as the likelihood-ratio test of all the restrictions yielded $\chi^2_{\text{or}}(23) = 14.1$

Table 8.6
FIML model estimates.

$$
\begin{aligned}
\Delta(m-p)_t &= -\underset{(0.06)}{0.16}\ \Delta(m-p-i)_{t-1} - \underset{(0.16)}{0.68}\ (\Delta^2 p_t + \Delta R_t) \\
&\quad - \underset{(0.009)}{0.098}\ c_{1,t-1} \\
\Delta i_t &= \underset{(0.006)}{0.050}\ \mathit{Dout} - \underset{(0.022)}{0.11}\ c_{2,t-1} + \underset{(0.07)}{0.20}\ \Delta i_{t-1} + \underset{(-)}{0.0062} \\
\Delta^2 p_t &= -\underset{(0.08)}{0.34}\ \Delta^2 p_{t-1} + \underset{(0.004)}{0.028}\ \mathit{Doil} - \underset{(0.0007)}{0.0015} - \underset{(0.015)}{0.029}\ c_{2,t-1} \\
\Delta R_t &= \underset{(0.10)}{0.14}\ \Delta R_{t-1} + \underset{(0.007)}{0.014}\ \mathit{Doil} + \underset{(0.06)}{0.14}\ \Delta(m-p)_{t-1}
\end{aligned}
$$

Table 8.7
Model evaluation statistics.

Residual correlations				
	$\Delta(m-p)_t$	Δi_t	$\Delta^2 p_t$	ΔR_t
$\Delta(m-p)_t$	1.40%	0.03	−0.47	−0.45
Δi_t	0.02	1.06%	−0.19	0.06
$\Delta^2 p_t$	−0.09	−0.17	0.65%	0.24
ΔR_t	0.18	0.07	0.27	1.35

Model diagnostic tests	
$\mathsf{F}^{\mathsf{v}}_{\mathsf{ar}}(80, 231)$	1.25
$\mathsf{F}^{\mathsf{v}}_{\mathsf{het}}(160, 488)$	0.84
$\chi^{2\mathsf{v}}_{\mathsf{nd}}(8)$	6.97

($p > 0.92$), which does not reject. Table 8.7 records the model evaluation statistics (entries above the first diagonal are for the I(0)-VAR; the diagonal shows $\widehat{\sigma}$ values, and the lower triangle, the model outcomes).

Thus, the model is a valid reduction of the initial system. However, $\mathsf{F}_{\mathsf{Ch}}(64, 80) = 3.99^{**}$, so parameter constancy out-of-sample is strongly rejected, and the 1-step forecast performance is poor relative to the in-sample fit, as fig. 8.6 shows, especially for $\Delta(m-p)$.

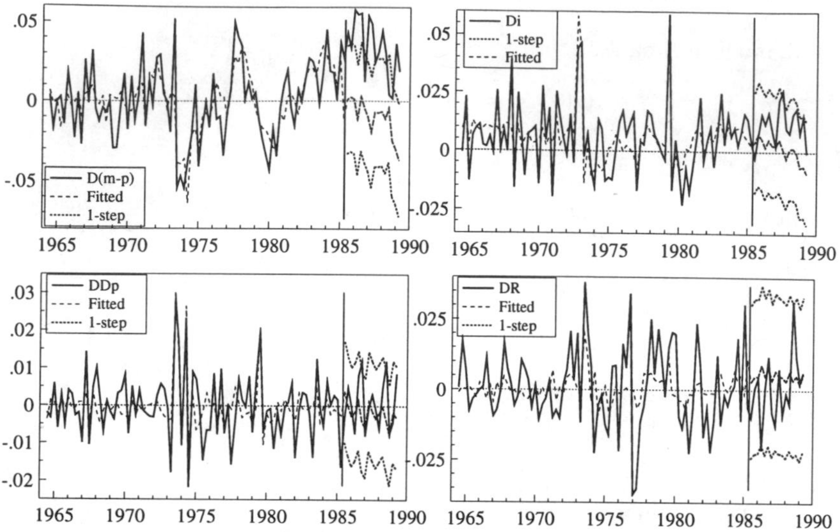

Figure 8.6
Fitted and actual values with 1-step forecasts, from the VEqCM.

8.5.1 *Multi-step forecasts*

The model's multi-step forecast performance is not nearly as poor as that of the system, suggesting some benefit from the I(0) reduction and parsimony, perhaps because the explanatory variables in table 8.6 have small mean values, a feature the taxonomy in table 2.1 suggested was valuable. Figure 8.7 shows both the multi-step and the 1-step forecasts for comparison, over the forecast horizon. For the last three variables, the forecast bands for the multi-step forecasts hardly increase as the horizon increases, consistent with their nearly non-dynamic nature, so the forecasts quickly become the unconditional means of their respective growth rates. Further, the bands are not much larger than the corresponding 1-step bars. The bands increase at first for $m - p$, where the EqCM plays a key role, but again the forecasts converge to the mean growth, although now the 1-step bars are distinctly narrower. Nevertheless, despite the structural break revealed by the parameter constancy test, multi-step predictive failure is not nearly so manifest. This phenomenon was predicted by the theory in §3.6.

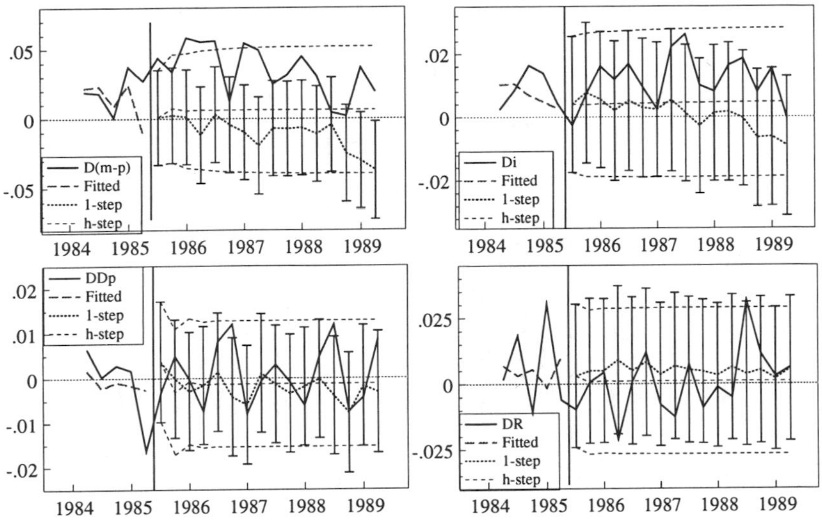

Figure 8.7
1-step and multi-step VEqCM forecasts.

8.6 Forecast Comparisons

The earlier theory predicts that the DV and DDV should be less susceptible to a deterministic structural break in the equilibrium mean than the VEqCM, but have larger forecast standard errors. The former model corresponds to dropping the EqCMs from the VEqCM, replacing the $\Delta(m-p)$ equation by its "reduced form", and eliminating insignificant variables in the resulting model. Figure 8.8 shows the combined 1-step and multi-step forecasts. By eliminating the equilibrium-correction terms, the DV suffers from residual autocorrelation ($\mathsf{F}_{\mathsf{ar}}(80,231) = 1.51^{**}$), so its confidence intervals calculated by the usual formulae are incorrect, probably understating the uncertainty relative to calculations that allow for the error autocorrelation (see section 5.7). Nevertheless, the absence of bias in the forecasts conforms to the earlier theory, when forecasting after a break.

Figure 8.9 shows the same set of forecasts for the DDV. By double differencing, there is substantial negative residual autocorrelation ($\mathsf{F}_{\mathsf{ar}}(80,211) = 2.01^{**}$), so the calculated confidence intervals are again

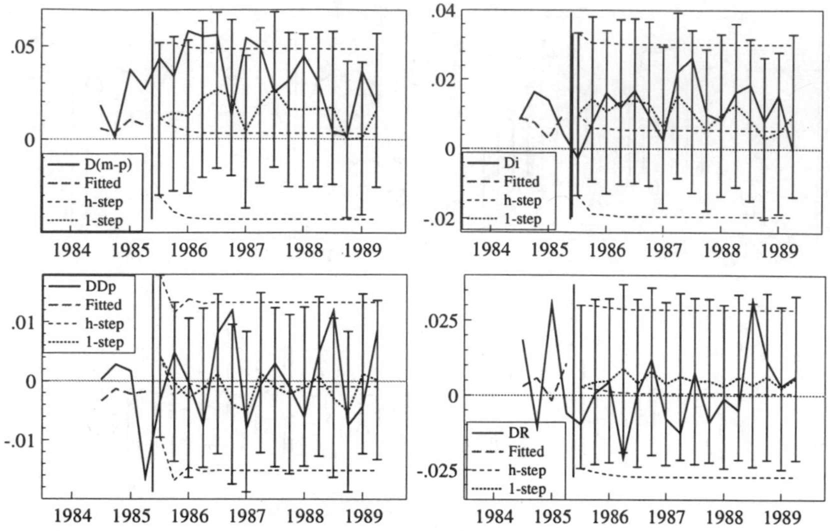

Figure 8.8
1-step and multi-step DV forecasts.

incorrect, this time seriously overstating the uncertainty. Nevertheless, the bias performance seems good visually.

Next, fig. 8.10 compares all three multi-step forecasts, in the space of $(\Delta(m-p), \Delta i, \Delta R, \Delta^2 p)$. The actual multi-step forecasts are very similar for all three forecasting devices, namely zero $(\Delta R, \Delta^2 p)$ or the unconditional growth rate $(\Delta(m-p), \Delta i)$. In this representation, the DDV has easily the largest confidence intervals, and they increase rapidly in the horizon, matching the theoretical calculations in §5.7. Between the VEqCM and the DV, the VEqCM has the wider intervals for money demand where the EqCM is strongest, but they are closely similar for the other three variables.

Finally, we compare the VEqCM and the DDV in levels in fig. 8.11, which exemplifies the main theory predictions: the robustness to the break of the DDV; its large and rapidly-increasing prediction intervals as conventionally computed (drawn at one standard deviation to avoid distorting the figure – see §5.7); and the forecast failure of the VEqCM after the break.

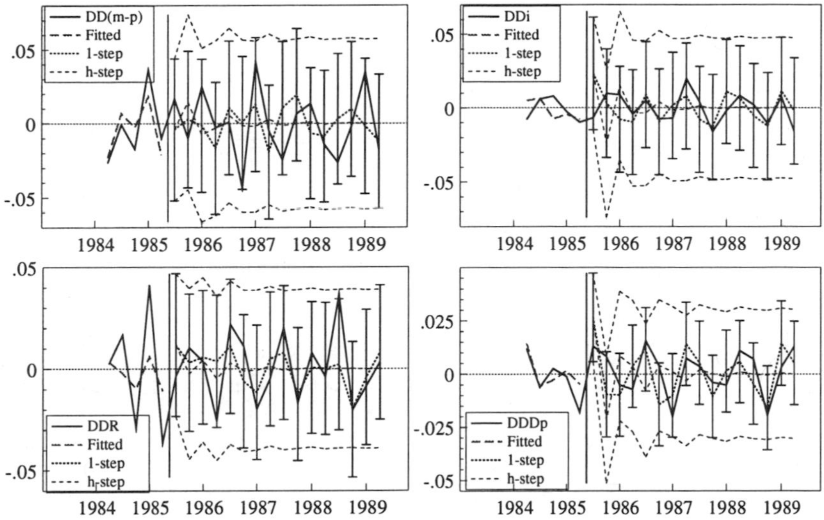

Figure 8.9
1-step and multi-step DDVEqCM forecasts.

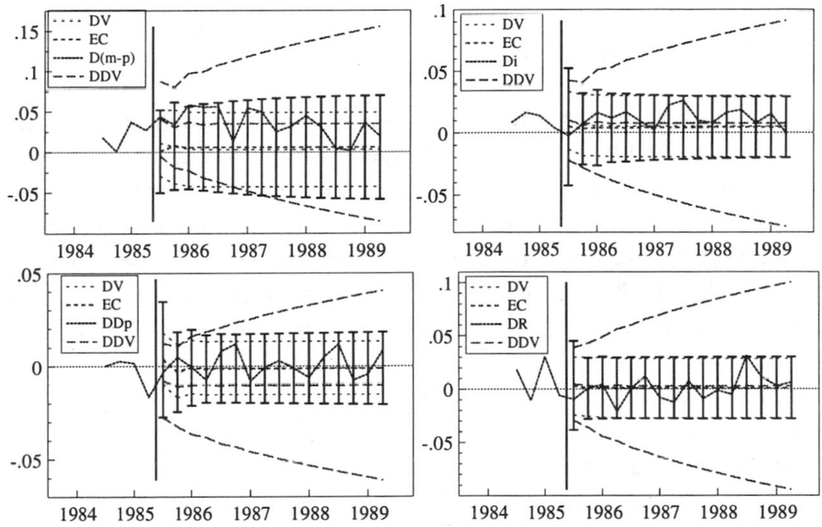

Figure 8.10
Multi-step forecasts in differences from the three forecasting devices.

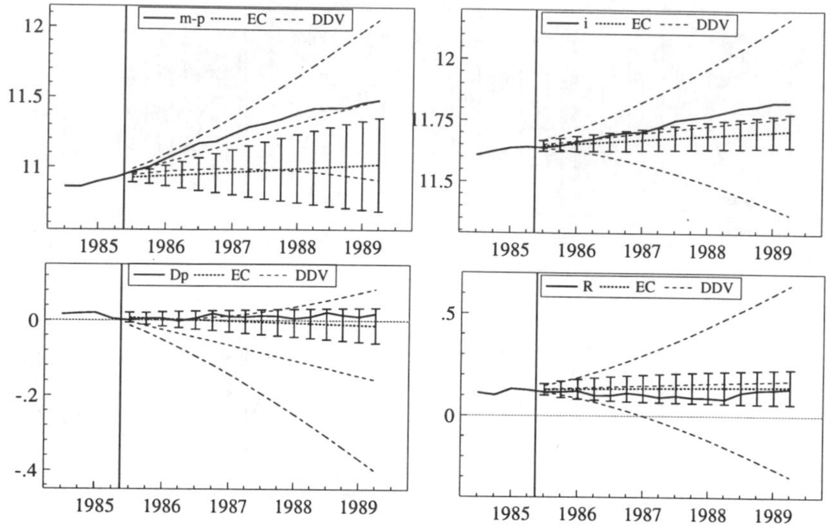

Figure 8.11
VEqCM and DDV multi-step levels forecasts.

8.7 Intercept Corrections

When the source of a model's mis-specification is known, it is usually corrected, but in many settings, mis-specifications are unknown, so are difficult to correct. One trick is intercept correction (denoted IC), which sets the model "back on track" to start from the actual forecast origin $\mathbf{x}_T$. In §6.2 and §6.3, we showed that such corrections can also robustify forecasts against breaks, provided that such breaks have already occurred by the time the forecast is made, but typically only at the cost of an increased forecast-error variance. The form of correction envisaged in that analysis is such that the correction alters as the forecast origin moves through the sample – the correction is always based on the error(s) made at, or immediately prior to, the origin. However, those forms of correction require a steadily expanding information set, and to treat the intercept-correcting strategy on a par with the other forecasting models, in this section we consider a simpler correction. This form of intercept correction can be implemented by adding an indicator variable equal to unity from the last sample observation onwards, so that

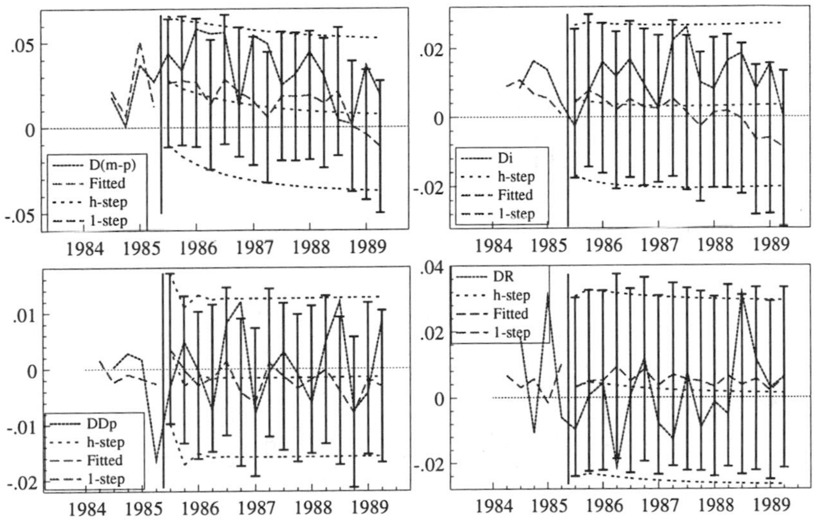

Figure 8.12
I(0) forecasts from the VEqCM with IC.

the same correction is applied at all forecast origins. Figure 8.7a shows why such an IC will work here: immediately prior to forecasting, the model is under-fitting by a substantial amount, and "shifting" the forecast origin to the data will offset much of the later mis-forecasting. To reduce the forecast-error variance, the IC can be set to unity for the last few sample observations: here we chose two (namely 1985:1–2). Further, to highlight the effects, we only entered the IC in the first equation (where it was significant at the 5% level: it was insignificant if added to the remaining equations). Figure 8.12 shows the impact in the I(0) representation, and fig. 8.13 in the I(1). The IC shifts upward the sequence of forecasts of $\Delta(m-p)$, but still underestimates the resulting growth, and hence the level. Equally, the improvement in the UK's rate of output growth from 0.62% per quarter over the estimation sample to 1.17% over the forecast period leads to substantial under-prediction of the final level for the i equation with c_2.

Thus, these outcomes are all in line with the theory.

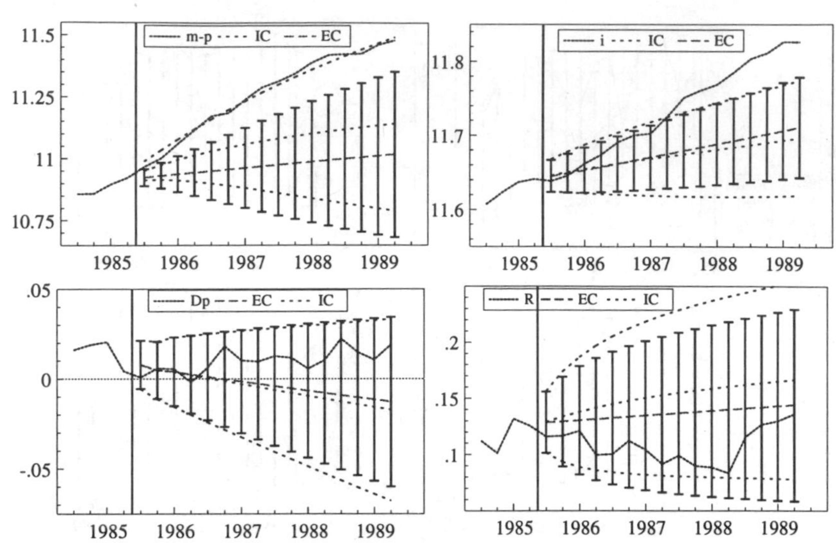

Figure 8.13
I(1) multi-step forecasts from the VEqCM with IC.

8.8 Empirical Forecast-accuracy Comparison

The bias and variance formulae developed in chapters 3, 5 and 6 for the various forecasting models in the presence of structural breaks suggest a number of implications that can be confronted with data. In the preceding section, several of these have already been borne out by the empirical example, and depicted graphically. In this section, we undertake an empirical forecast-accuracy comparison. We consider the pre- and post-break forecast periods for six forecasting methods – the unrestricted system (denoted SYS), the I(0)-VAR (SYSI(0)), the simultaneous-equations model (SEM), the VAR in differences (DV), the VAR in second differences (DDV), and the intercept-corrected model (IC) – computing forecast biases, error variances and MSFE s for 1- and 4-step ahead forecasts.[1] The IC strategy is that described in the previous section, but we also consider a strategy that more closely reflects the analysis in, e.g., Clements and Hendry (1996b) and §6.3. This is denoted IC*. It is

[1]Notwithstanding that MSFEs can be problematic for evaluating multi-step forecasts from systems.

implemented by estimating the SEM on data up to each forecast origin, with an indicator variable equal to unity from the immediately prior period onwards. Thus the model estimates are updated as the origin moves through the sample, and for each origin the correction is an average of the error made at the origin and of the previous error. The model specification was held constant over time, and the parameter constraints of the SEM were imposed except for the forecast origins of 88(2) to 89(1), when the model failed to solve with the constraints imposed. Alternatively, the correction could have been allowed to depend on the forecast origin, but with the parameter estimates held fixed at their sample period values. This would have disentangled the effects of parameter updating and changing the correction. Since the correction is being tuned to set the forecasts back on track as we move through the sample, the IC* strategy should result in greater bias reduction than the IC, but at the cost of inflated forecast-error variances, for the reasons described in ch. 6. The IC* results were only calculated for the post-break forecast period, and then only for $m - p$, since the other equations were not intercept-corrected, so the first-round effects apply only to $m - p$. The results are shown in tables 8.8–8.10.

A number of features are worthy of comment.

(1) In the absence of structural change, the SEM is generally at least as good as the other forecasting models on MSFE at 1- and 4-steps ahead. Moreover, on MSFE, imposing unit roots and cointegration also appears to pay dividends, particularly at 4-steps (compare SYS and SYSI(0)).

(2) As expected in the absence of structural change, the "time-series" models (DV and DDV) lose out relative to the SEM. Their forecast-error variances are larger, particularly that of the DDV, especially at 4-steps ahead.

(3) On the post-break sample, however, many of these findings are reversed. In terms of forecasting $m - p$, the SEM is clearly dominated on MSFE by the DV, the DDV, and the IC*-strategy, at both horizons.

(4) The DDV and IC* have the smallest biases for $m - p$.

(5) However, the DDV and IC* have the largest error variances for forecasting $m - p$, again at both horizons.

(6) The IC has a small impact on variance compared to the IC*, but fails to reduce the SEM bias to the same degree as the IC* strategy.

Table 8.8
Empirical forecast-bias comparisons (×100).

Model	m-p		i		Δp		R	
	1-step	4-step	1-step	4-step	1-step	4-step	1-step	4-step
Post-break forecast period								
SYS	3.288	17.395	0.740	5.097	0.417	1.178	−2.974	−8.621
SYSI(0)	4.749	14.255	1.294	3.927	0.126	0.809	−0.360	−0.139
SEM	4.522	14.010	1.069	3.696	0.296	0.941	−0.445	−0.369
DV	1.995	10.889	0.149	2.312	0.197	0.766	−0.425	−0.857
DDV	−0.091	−2.141	−0.022	0.715	0.134	0.735	0.013	1.383
IC	1.973	7.221	1.070	3.832	0.300	0.983	−0.461	−1.335
IC*	0.259	2.057						
Pre-break forecast period								
SYS	−0.079	3.538	0.642	2.990	0.240	0.469	−1.353	−5.213
SYSI(0)	0.274	3.052	0.165	0.784	−0.109	−0.208	−0.549	−2.886
SEM	−0.043	1.105	0.165	0.539	−0.018	0.108	−0.260	−1.952
DV	0.724	4.573	0.241	1.173	0.048	0.289	−0.249	−1.312
DDV	0.194	1.195	0.069	0.317	−0.096	0.130	0.050	0.516
IC	−0.989	−1.194	0.164	0.595	−0.017	0.124	−0.261	−2.396

Table 8.9
Empirical forecast standard-error comparisons (×100).

Model	m-p		i		Δp		R	
	1-step	4-step	1-step	4-step	1-step	4-step	1-step	4-step
Post-break forecast period								
SYS	1.826	2.243	0.695	1.334	0.685	0.778	1.261	2.070
SYSI(0)	1.728	3.990	0.874	1.074	0.661	0.655	1.218	2.657
SEM	1.794	3.957	0.805	0.970	0.686	0.681	1.248	2.585
DV	1.877	4.645	0.753	0.933	0.690	0.680	1.245	2.537
DDV	1.921	5.099	1.035	2.617	0.995	2.001	1.561	3.704
IC	1.791	3.967	0.806	0.971	0.686	0.682	1.250	2.588
IC*	2.093	5.386						
Pre-break forecast period								
SYS	1.783	3.502	0.719	1.014	0.815	0.580	1.711	2.175
SYSI(0)	1.781	2.431	0.742	0.627	0.873	0.612	1.526	1.802
SEM	1.660	2.747	0.714	0.675	0.700	0.631	1.541	2.063
DV	1.499	3.043	0.777	0.970	0.725	0.674	1.542	2.431
DDV	1.810	5.270	1.222	3.051	1.106	2.042	1.951	5.064
IC	1.666	2.745	0.714	0.675	0.700	0.631	1.540	2.064

8.9 Conclusion

In chapter 1, we presented a taxonomy of forecast errors which suggested that deterministic shifts were a primary determinant of serious

Table 8.10
Empirical MSFE comparisons (×1000).

Model	m-p		i		Δp		R	
	1-step	4-step	1-step	4-step	1-step	4-step	1-step	4-step
				Post-break forecast period				
SYS	1.415	30.763	0.103	2.776	0.064	0.199	1.043	7.860
SYSI(0)	2.553	21.914	0.244	1.657	0.045	0.108	0.161	0.708
SEM	2.367	21.194	0.179	1.460	0.056	0.135	0.176	0.682
DV	0.750	14.014	0.059	0.621	0.052	0.105	0.173	0.717
DDV	0.370	3.058	0.107	0.736	0.101	0.454	0.244	1.563
IC	0.710	6.788	0.179	1.562	0.056	0.143	0.178	0.848
IC*	0.445	3.324						
				Pre-break forecast period				
SYS	0.318	2.478	0.093	0.997	0.072	0.056	0.476	3.190
SYSI(0)	0.325	1.522	0.058	0.101	0.077	0.042	0.263	1.158
SEM	0.276	0.877	0.054	0.075	0.049	0.041	0.244	0.807
DV	0.277	3.017	0.066	0.232	0.053	0.054	0.244	0.763
DDV	0.331	2.920	0.150	0.941	0.123	0.419	0.381	2.591
IC	0.375	0.896	0.054	0.081	0.049	0.041	0.244	1.000

forecast failure. Chapter 3 discussed the biases that arise from shifts in a VEqCM, and chapter 5 extended those derivations to DVs and DDVs. Finally, chapters 5 and 6 considered potential remedies for breaks: the empirical illustration in chapter 7 was consistent with that theory.

The present chapter applies that analysis in a multivariate empirical context. We developed a four-variable empirical example of forecasting using a small monetary model of the UK, when there was a known major financial innovation. Taking the data generation process as a vector equilibrium-correction mechanism subject to deterministic shifts, the earlier theoretical results matched the outcomes over both pre- and post-break forecast periods for the three methods considered, and were supported by the effectiveness of the two intercept-correction strategies investigated. These findings are also consistent with the results of using the large Norges Bank macro-econometric system as reported in Eitrheim, Husebø and Nymoen (1997). Thus, although other forms of structural break, model mis-specification, a lack of parsimony, including failing to impose restrictions such as unit roots and cointegration, inaccurate forecast-origin data, and inefficient estimation may all exacerbate forecast failure, we believe they play supporting roles.

One consequence of these findings is to caution against automatic adoption of a method that happens to win a particular forecasting competition: careful analysis as to why it did so is strongly recommended. If a deterministic shift is suspected, or confirmed, then methods that are not robust to such a shift are likely to have performed poorly. That would not necessarily preclude the continued use of a model that suffered forecast failure, subject to appropriate intercept corrections being used. In the policy context of forecasting after a structural break, where policy is then altered, Hendry and Mizon (1998c) show the benefits of using a "time-series" model (such as the DDV) to intercept correct the econometric system, when the latter is retained for policy analysis despite forecast failure. Here, for some policy analyses, such as a change in money demand resulting from an increase in income taxes, the outcome could be accurately determined from the VEqCM, despite the forecast failure. Other policy analyses might be badly wrong, such as the impact of raising the level of R: after the break, only the differential $R - R_o$ in fact matters, and that need not change when R does. Indeed, an attempt to lower the rapid increase in money demand after 1984:2 by raising R would have been near disastrous, as its effectiveness would have relied on lowering income thereby needlessly causing unemployment since, being a portfolio effect, the increase in real money had no inflationary implications.

We conjectured that a major factor determining the outcome of forecasting competitions on economic time series is the occurrence of deterministic shifts immediately prior to some of the forecast-evaluation periods. Thus, the length of the forecast horizon also should matter. Our theory predicts that differencing several times would be most effective, when multiple breaks have occurred, for evaluation based on many short horizons.

As suggested in §5.7, some care is required in interpreting the PcFiml generated prediction intervals in any of the figures. The formulae are predicated upon the model being correctly specified for the DGP, which is manifestly untrue for the DDV, at least. The forecast confidence intervals we present understate the true uncertainty attached to the DV model forecasts. For the DDV, the failure to account for the substantial negative moving average induced in its errors leads to an over-estimate of the actual uncertainty.

Finally, other potential remedies need considered. Chapter 9 discusses co-breaking, and evaluates its interpretation in the context of UK money demand, and chapter 10 considers modeling systematic switches in regimes, perhaps defined by different equilibrium means or growth rates.

9 Co-breaking

Summary

We consider the removal of deterministic shifts in systems of equations using linear combinations of variables. The general formulation establishes a reduced-rank condition, analogous to cointegration. The properties of co-breaking are explored, and both common trends and cointegration vectors are shown to be co-breaking vectors for equilibrium-mean and growth-rate shifts respectively. The concept is then applied to multiple breaks and conditional models. The analysis is illustrated by evaluating whether co-breaking removes the forecast failure in UK M1 using a larger information set.

9.1 Introduction

When deterministic shifts occur in several variables, these may or may not be related. Structural breaks are "permanent large shifts" that occur intermittently, as against "permanent small shifts" occurring frequently and so generating I(1) effects. Nevertheless, these two forms of non-stationarity are closely related (see Rappoport and Reichlin, 1989), can be hard to discriminate empirically (see Perron, 1989, and Hendry and Neale, 1991), and have similar solutions (for example, both unit roots and mean shifts can be "removed" by differencing: see ch. 5 above). Cointegration also removes unit roots in I(1) systems, but by taking linear combinations of variables (see Engle and Granger, 1987).

A similar notion, called co-breaking, applies to systems with structural breaks. We define co-breaking as the removal of deterministic shifts using linear combinations of variables. The interdependence of economic phenomena suggests co-breaking may occur as often as cointegration, so this chapter explores its properties.

The case most analogous to cointegration from I(1) to I(0) is called contemporaneous mean co-breaking, whereby linear combinations of variables at the same point in time do not depend on the breaks, even though the system is subject to them. Since the impacts of breaks can be delayed, intertemporal co-breaking must also be considered. This is more analogous to seeking cointegration from I(2) to I(0), where timing matters, and either lagged combinations of variables are needed, or relatedly, I(1) differences of I(2) variables may be required to obtain I(0) combinations (see Johansen, 1992).

Just as unit roots can induce "nonsense regressions", where relationships are apparently significant, but in fact no causal links exist, so regime shifts can cancel spuriously. It is shown below that the existence of few breaks, or of a sample size smaller than the number of variables, both lead to "spurious" co-breaking. Dynamics can also matter in practice in establishing spurious co-breaking, exploiting apparent latencies in break effects manifesting themselves. However, when a sufficiently large number of regime shifts has occurred in a small set of variables which nevertheless co-break, so some combinations do not depend on the breaks, then the equivalent of a "natural experiment" has occurred which comes close to establishing "causal" linkages. Leading indicators are often not causally related to the variables they lead, and if subject to breaks, their relationships are unlikely to co-break so will manifest predictive failure. Hendry and Mizon (1998a) discuss the implications of co-breaking for the Lucas (1976) critique.

The general formulation in §9.2 establishes a reduced-rank condition for the existence of contemporaneous mean co-breaking (abbreviated by its acronym to CMC). The properties of co-breaking are explored, and conditions for mean co-breaking shown for several cases of interest. Section 9.3 extends the results to intertemporal mean co-breaking, where breaks may occur using lags of different relations. The effects of shifts in levels and growth rates in a VEqCM are considered in §9.4 and co-breaking conditions obtained. Then, in §9.5 both common trends and cointegration vectors are shown to be examples of contemporaneous mean co-breaking for specific structural breaks. The analysis is generalized to multiple breaks in §9.6 and applied to conditional models in §9.7. Section 9.8 shows how co-breaking between the own rate R_o and real money demand removes the forecast failure discussed in the previous chapter, without needing any changes to the number of parameters or their values. This is an example of the phenomenon discussed in §2.7 of "extended model constancy". Section 9.9 concludes.

9.2 Contemporaneous Co-breaking

Consider an n-dimensional vector stochastic process $\{\mathbf{y}_t\}$ over $\mathcal{T} = (1, \ldots, T)$, which has well-defined unconditional expectations around an initial parameter ψ at $t = 0$:

$$\mathsf{E}\left[\mathbf{y}_t - \boldsymbol{\psi}\right] = \boldsymbol{\mu}_t \in \mathbb{R}^n \tag{9.1}$$

where $|\boldsymbol{\mu}_t| < \infty$, but otherwise are unrestricted. When any $\boldsymbol{\mu}_t \neq \mathbf{0}$, a deterministic shift occurs.

Co-breaking is defined as the cancellation of deterministic breaks in time series across linear combinations of variables.

Definition 1. *The $n \times s$ matrix $\boldsymbol{\Phi}$ of rank s ($n > s > 0$) is said to be contemporaneous mean co-breaking of order s for $\{\mathbf{y}_t\}$ in (9.1) if $\boldsymbol{\Phi}'\boldsymbol{\mu}_t = \mathbf{0}$ $\forall t \in \mathcal{T}$.*

Contemporaneous mean co-breaking of order s (denoted CMC(s)) could be defined for sub-vectors by appropriate partitioning, and for higher moments by direct extension (e.g., variance co-breaking). Similarly, the concept can be extended to functions of non-stationary processes where some combinations of variables have well-defined expectations, such as $\mathbf{y}_{1,t} = \Delta\mathbf{x}_t$ (differences in I(1) processes) or $\mathbf{y}_{2,t} = \boldsymbol{\beta}'\mathbf{x}_t$ (cointegrated combinations). The class of processes $\{\mathbf{y}_t\}$ in (9.1) may be extended to conditional functions of past variables, so that:

$$\mathsf{E}\left[(\mathbf{y}_t - \boldsymbol{\psi}) \mid \mathbf{Y}_{t-1}^1\right] = \sum_{k=1}^{K} \boldsymbol{\pi}_k \mathbf{y}_{t-k} + \boldsymbol{\mu}_t$$

where $\mathbf{Y}_{t-1}^1$ denotes the σ-field generated by past $\{\mathbf{y}_t\}$. While changes in the $\{\boldsymbol{\pi}_k\}$ are also possible, the main impacts on forecast biases seem to derive from entailed changes in deterministic factors (see ch. 3), so the focus here is on the removal of mean breaks.

It follows from definition 1 in (9.1) that:

$$\mathsf{E}\left[\boldsymbol{\Phi}'\mathbf{y}_t - \boldsymbol{\Phi}'\boldsymbol{\psi}\right] = \boldsymbol{\Phi}'\boldsymbol{\mu}_t = \mathbf{0} \tag{9.2}$$

so that the parameterization of the reduced set of s linear transforms $\boldsymbol{\Phi}'\mathbf{y}_t$ is independent of the deterministic shifts. Thus, that subset should not experience forecast failure even though the system as a whole will.

At first sight, mean co-breaking seems unlikely when the $\{\boldsymbol{\mu}_t\}$ can change in any possible way from period to period, since a single matrix $\boldsymbol{\Phi}$ is required to annihilate all deterministic changes. Nevertheless, there are many cases where co-breaking can occur in principle even though no μ_{it} stays constant. To see this possibility, we next link CMC to a reduced rank condition.

Consider the $n \times T$ matrix $\mathbf{M}_T^1 = (\boldsymbol{\mu}_1\ \boldsymbol{\mu}_2\ \cdots\ \boldsymbol{\mu}_T)$ where $T > n$. The condition that $\boldsymbol{\phi}'\boldsymbol{\mu}_t = 0\ \forall t \in \mathcal{T}$ when $\boldsymbol{\phi} \neq \mathbf{0}$ is $n \times 1$ can be written as $\boldsymbol{\phi}'\mathbf{M}_T^1 = \mathbf{0}'$, then we have:

Theorem 1. *A necessary and sufficient condition for $\boldsymbol{\phi}'\boldsymbol{\mu}_t = 0\ \forall t \in \mathcal{T}$ when $\boldsymbol{\phi} \neq \mathbf{0}$ is $n \times 1$ (CMC of order 1) is that rank $\left[\mathbf{M}_T^1\right] < n$.*

The theorem follows immediately from the equivalence of reduced rank and linear dependence.

Corollary 2. *CMC is at least of order r if there exist r linearly independent vectors satisfying $\boldsymbol{\phi}_i'\boldsymbol{\mu}_t = \mathbf{0}$ such that the $n \times r$ matrix $\boldsymbol{\Phi} = (\boldsymbol{\phi}_1 : \cdots : \boldsymbol{\phi}_r)$ has rank $r < n$. Then $\boldsymbol{\Phi}'\mathbf{M}_T^1 = \mathbf{0}_{r,T}$ so rank$(\mathbf{M}_T^1) \leq n - r$, so the nullity of $\mathbf{M}_T^1$, denoted nul$(\mathbf{M}_T^1) \geq r$, determines the order of CMC.*

Since CMC(s) implies CMC($s-1$), and unmodeled remaining breaks entail model mis-specification, it seems natural to seek the maximum degree of CMC. Note that the matrix $\boldsymbol{\Phi}$ in corollary 2 is not unique without suitable normalization, since if $\mathbf{H}$ is any $s \times s$ non-singular matrix, then $\boldsymbol{\Phi}'\mathbf{M}_T^1 = \mathbf{0}$ implies that $\mathbf{H}\boldsymbol{\Phi}'\mathbf{M}_T^1 = \mathbf{0}$ as well.

Corollary 3. *CMC cannot exceed order $n-1$ if breaks occur (i.e. $\boldsymbol{\mu}_s \neq \mathbf{0}$ for some s) since when $\boldsymbol{\Phi}$ is $n \times n$ and non-singular, the equations $\boldsymbol{\Phi}'\mathbf{M}_T^1 = \mathbf{0}$ would entail $\mathbf{M}_T^1 = \mathbf{0}$.*

Alternatively, reformulate the breaks in terms of row vectors $\boldsymbol{\mu}^{(i)\prime} = (\mu_{i,1}\ \mu_{i,2}\ \cdots\ \mu_{i,T})$ affecting each variable $y_{i,t}$ so that:

$$\mathbf{M}_T^1 = \left(\ \boldsymbol{\mu}^{(1)} \quad \boldsymbol{\mu}^{(2)} \quad \cdots \quad \boldsymbol{\mu}^{(n)}\ \right)'.$$

Corollary 4. *CMC cannot occur when the $\boldsymbol{\mu}^{(i)}$ are linearly independent, since then for all $\boldsymbol{\phi} \neq \mathbf{0}$:*

$$\mathbf{M}_T^{1\prime}\boldsymbol{\phi} = \sum_{i=1}^{n} \phi_i \boldsymbol{\mu}^{(i)} \neq \mathbf{0}.$$

An obvious case inducing reduced rank is when there are fewer than n breaks.

Theorem 5. *Let there be only $k < n$ distinct values of $\boldsymbol{\mu}_t$, then CMC of at least order $s = n - k$ must occur.*

Proof. The matrix $\mathbf{M}_T^1$ contains only k distinct values of $\{\boldsymbol{\mu}_t\}$ and hence $\text{rank}(\mathbf{M}_T^1) \leq k = n - s$. ■

A sub-case is an undersized sample:

Corollary 6. *When $T < n$, rank($\mathbf{M}_T^1$) $\leq T < n$ so there must be CMC of (at least) order $n - T$.*

Consequently, CMC($n - T$) must occur when $T < n$, although this may be "spurious" (i.e., even if there are T unrelated breaks).

If any unconditional means are constant, then CMC clearly occurs:

Corollary 7. *When any $m \times 1$ subvector ($m < n$) $\boldsymbol{\mu}_{1,t}$ of $\boldsymbol{\mu}_t$ is zero $\forall t \in \mathcal{T}$, then CMC of at least order m occurs.*

An important practical case is where breaks are related across variables:

Theorem 8. *If $\boldsymbol{\mu}_t = \boldsymbol{\alpha}\mathbf{l}_t\ \forall t$ where $\boldsymbol{\alpha}$ is $n \times k$ of rank $k < n$ and $\mathbf{l}_t$ is $k \times 1$, then CMC occurs for at least order $s = n - k$.*

Proof. Let $\mathbf{L}_T^1 = (\mathbf{l}_1\ \mathbf{l}_2\ \cdots\ \mathbf{l}_T)$ then:

$$\text{rank}\left(\mathbf{M}_T^1\right) = \text{rank}\left(\boldsymbol{\alpha}\mathbf{l}_1\ \boldsymbol{\alpha}\mathbf{l}_2\ \cdots\ \boldsymbol{\alpha}\mathbf{l}_T\right) = \text{rank}\left(\boldsymbol{\alpha}\mathbf{L}_T^1\right) \leq k.$$

■

Alternatively, consider the $n \times (n-k)$ matrix $\boldsymbol{\alpha}_{\perp}$ of rank $n-k$ such that $(\boldsymbol{\alpha} : \boldsymbol{\alpha}_{\perp})$ is rank n and $\boldsymbol{\alpha}'_{\perp}\boldsymbol{\alpha} = \mathbf{0}$. Then for $\boldsymbol{\Phi} = \boldsymbol{\alpha}_{\perp}$:

$$\boldsymbol{\alpha}'_{\perp}\boldsymbol{\mu}_t = \boldsymbol{\alpha}'_{\perp}\boldsymbol{\alpha}\mathbf{l}_t = \mathbf{0}\ \forall t.$$

Theorem 8 links co-breaking to cointegration and common trends, and leads to two further special cases (conditioning co-breaking and simultaneous co-breaking).

As an example, consider the application of CMC to deterministic seasonal dummies. Consider a set of $N < n < T$ dummy variables $d_{i,t}$ each of which is zero except for unity at times $t \in \mathcal{T}_i$, so that "breaks" are written as $\mu_{j,t} = \sum_{i=1}^{N} \gamma_{j,i} d_{i,t}$, or $\boldsymbol{\mu}_t = \boldsymbol{\Gamma}\mathbf{d}_t$, where $\boldsymbol{\Gamma}$ is $n \times N$ and $\mathbf{d}_t$ is $N \times 1$. Then:

$$\mathbf{M}_T^1 = (\boldsymbol{\Gamma}\mathbf{d}_1 : \boldsymbol{\Gamma}\mathbf{d}_2 : \cdots : \boldsymbol{\Gamma}\mathbf{d}_T) = \boldsymbol{\Gamma}\mathbf{D}$$

which has maximum rank N, so CMC$(n - N)$ will occur. As with Theorem 8, take $\boldsymbol{\Phi} = \boldsymbol{\Gamma}_{\perp}$. This example covers such deterministic shifts as trends and seasonal dummies with constant coefficients. These can be eliminated by analyzing $\boldsymbol{\Gamma}_{\perp}\mathbf{y}_t$, but may not deliver minimal models on doing so. This result is implicitly used in Hendry and Doornik (1994) to eliminate the trend from one of two cointegrating vectors.

9.3 Intertemporal Co-breaking

Intertemporal mean co-breaking seeks the elimination of breaks which occur at different points of time, such as:

$$\sum_{i=1}^{n}\sum_{j=0}^{p} \phi_{i,j}\mu_{i,t-j} = 0$$

where the latency j may differ with i. Thus, breaks may vanish between combinations of current and lagged values of variables. Since most time-series models are dynamic, and breaks to a system of n variables could be related in time in almost any conceivable way, intertemporal co-breaking merits consideration.

Let L denote the lag operator such that $L^m\mathbf{y}_t = \mathbf{y}_{t-m}$, and let $\boldsymbol{\Phi}(L)$ be an $n \times s$ polynomial matrix of degree $p > 0$:

$$\boldsymbol{\Phi}(L) = \sum_{i=0}^{p} \boldsymbol{\Phi}_i L^i.$$

Associate with $\mathbf{\Phi}(L)$ the $n(p+1) \times s$ matrix $\mathbf{\Phi}^*$:

$$\mathbf{\Phi}^{*\prime} = \begin{pmatrix} \mathbf{\Phi}_0' & \mathbf{\Phi}_1' & \cdots & \mathbf{\Phi}_{p-1}' & \mathbf{\Phi}_p' \end{pmatrix},$$

then:

Definition 2. *The $n \times s$ polynomial matrix $\mathbf{\Phi}(L)$ of degree $p > 0$ where the rank of $\mathbf{\Phi}^*$ is s ($n \geq s > 0$), is said to be intertemporal mean co-breaking of order s for $\{\mathbf{x}_t\}$ in (9.1) if $\mathbf{\Phi}'(L)\boldsymbol{\mu}_t = \mathbf{0}\ \forall t \in \mathcal{T}$, and no $n \times s$ matrix polynomial of degree $p-1$ and rank s annihilates $\boldsymbol{\mu}_t\ \forall t \in \mathcal{T}$.*

Intertemporal mean co-breaking as in (2) is denoted by IMC(p, s). The requirement that IMC($p-1$, s) does not occur is to ensure a unique choice of $\mathbf{\Phi}(L)$ up to an $s \times s$ non-singular linear transformation.

In this extended notation, definition 1 requires that $\mathbf{\Phi}'(1)\mathbf{y}_t$ does not depend on the deterministic shifts, so CMC(s) entails IMC(1, s) and IMC($p-1$, s) entails IMC(p, s). Thus, the condition $\mathbf{\Phi}'(L)\boldsymbol{\mu}_t = \mathbf{0}$ is much weaker than $\mathbf{\Phi}'\boldsymbol{\mu}_t = \mathbf{0}$, and from definition 2 and (9.1):

$$\mathsf{E}\left[\mathbf{\Phi}'(L)\mathbf{y}_t - \mathbf{\Phi}'(1)\boldsymbol{\psi}\right] = \mathbf{\Phi}'(L)\boldsymbol{\mu}_t = \mathbf{0} \tag{9.3}$$

only requires that the reduced s-dimensional dynamic system of p lags in n variables $\mathbf{\Phi}'(L)\mathbf{y}_t$ does not depend on the deterministic shifts.

However, CMC(0) is consistent with IMC(1, n), since complete removal of the breaks is possible once lags are allowed. For example, when $\boldsymbol{\mu}_1 \neq \mathbf{0}$ and CMC is of order zero, let:

$$\boldsymbol{\mu}_t = \mathbf{R}\boldsymbol{\mu}_{t-1} \text{ for } t = 2, \ldots, T, \tag{9.4}$$

where $\mathbf{R}$ is full rank n. Then $\boldsymbol{\mu}_t - \mathbf{R}\boldsymbol{\mu}_{t-1} = \mathbf{0}$ so that IMC(1, n) occurs over $t = 2, \ldots, T$. However, by requiring intertemporal transformations of $\mathbf{y}_t$ to eliminate all effects from lagged $\boldsymbol{\mu}_{t-i}$, IMC will usually alter the serial correlation properties of the errors on stochastic systems.

Inter-temporal mean co-breaking may capture a genuine delay in the causes of breaks affecting different relationships, or also may be a form of "spurious" co-breaking when only a few breaks have happened and lagged values of variables chance to match. The issue of "spurious" co-breaking is perhaps most important when the actual lag length of the dynamic system under analysis is $q < p$ (the lag length of $\mathbf{\Phi}(L)$).

As presaged in the definition, the simplest formulation of IMC(p, s) stacks the lagged breaks, reducing the problem to a variant of CMC in the extended vector, denoted CMC^e. In general, one might have a maximum of CMC(s_1) given by $\mathbf{\Phi}'_{00}\boldsymbol{\mu}_t = \mathbf{0}_{r_1}\ \forall t$, then a maximum of IMC(1, $s_1 + s_2$) such that:

$$\begin{pmatrix} \mathbf{\Phi}'_{00} & \mathbf{0} \\ \mathbf{\Phi}'_{10} & \mathbf{\Phi}'_{11} \end{pmatrix} \begin{pmatrix} \boldsymbol{\mu}_t \\ \boldsymbol{\mu}_{t-1} \end{pmatrix} = \begin{pmatrix} \mathbf{0}_{s_1} \\ \mathbf{0}_{s_2} \end{pmatrix} \ \forall t \tag{9.5}$$

where for $j = 1, 2$, $\mathbf{\Phi}_{1j}$ is $n \times s_2$ such that $\mathbf{\Phi}'_{1j}\boldsymbol{\mu}_t \neq \mathbf{0}\ \forall t$ and:

$$\text{rank}\begin{pmatrix} \mathbf{\Phi}'_{10} & \mathbf{\Phi}'_{11} \end{pmatrix} = s_2$$

and so on (the 1,2 sub-matrix in (9.5) could also be $\mathbf{\Phi}'_{00}$, but we choose the lower triangular form for simplicity). Continuing:

$$\begin{pmatrix} \mathbf{\Phi}'_{00} & \mathbf{0} & \cdots & \mathbf{0} & \mathbf{0} \\ \mathbf{\Phi}'_{10} & \mathbf{\Phi}'_{11} & \cdots & \mathbf{0} & \mathbf{0} \\ \vdots & \vdots & \ddots & \vdots & \vdots \\ \mathbf{\Phi}'_{p-1,0} & \mathbf{\Phi}'_{p-1,1} & \cdots & \mathbf{\Phi}'_{p-1,p-1} & \mathbf{0} \\ \mathbf{\Phi}'_{p0} & \mathbf{\Phi}'_{p1} & \cdots & \mathbf{\Phi}'_{p,p-1} & \mathbf{\Phi}'_{pp} \end{pmatrix} \begin{pmatrix} \boldsymbol{\mu}_t \\ \boldsymbol{\mu}_{t-1} \\ \vdots \\ \boldsymbol{\mu}_{t-p+1} \\ \boldsymbol{\mu}_{t-p} \end{pmatrix} = \mathbf{0} \tag{9.6}$$

for $t = p + 1, \ldots, T$, or in a compact notation:

$$\mathbf{\Phi}^{*\,\prime}\boldsymbol{\mu}_t^* = \mathbf{0} \tag{9.7}$$

where $s = \sum_{i=0}^{p} s_i$, $\mathbf{\Phi}^*$ is $n(p+1) \times s$ and $\boldsymbol{\mu}_t^*$ is $n(p+1) \times 1$. Now CMC^e in (9.7) is IMC(s) in the original formulation and involves a reduced-rank condition on the $n(p + 1) \times (T - p)$ matrix $(\mathbf{M}_T^{p+1})^*$: the nullity of $(\mathbf{M}_T^{p+1})^*$ determines the order of co-breaking, and the earlier theorems apply to it, noting that IMC($p - 1$, s) does not occur. Since $\mathbf{\Phi}^*$ is not square when $p > 0$, CMC^e(n) is possible in the extended formulation, even though all $\boldsymbol{\mu}_t$ are non-zero. The number of breaks and the sample size would have to be very large to preclude the possibility of spurious co-breaking given theorem 5 and its corollary 6. As an example, extend (9.4) to a pth-order process:

$$\boldsymbol{\mu}_t = \sum_{i-1}^{p} \mathbf{R}_i \boldsymbol{\mu}_{t-i} \ \text{ for } \ t = p + 1, \ldots, T, \tag{9.8}$$

then $\mathbf{\Phi}'(L) = -\sum_{i=0}^{p} \mathbf{R}_i L^i$ (where $\mathbf{R}_0 = -\mathbf{I}_n$) is IMC($p$, n).

Delays in regime shifts affecting different variables may, but need not, preclude CMC. As an example, consider extending theorem 8:

$$\boldsymbol{\mu}_t = \sum_{j=0}^{q} \boldsymbol{\alpha}_j \mathbf{l}_{t-j} \tag{9.9}$$

where each $\boldsymbol{\alpha}_j$ is $n \times k$ with rank$(\boldsymbol{\alpha}_j) = k_j < k$. Thus, there exist T vectors of k-dimensional "basic" regime shift factors $\{\mathbf{l}_t\}$, such that rank$(\mathbf{L}_T^1) = k$, but only k_j equations respond to the shock $\mathbf{l}_{t-j}$ with a delay of $j < p$ periods. There are two ways of formulating the model: either with all $\mathbf{l}_{t-j}$ of length k, or introducing vectors $\mathbf{l}_{j,t-j}$ of length k_j only having the k_j relevant sub-elements. The former leads to a direct rank calculation, and the latter to an orthogonal formalization which we consider first. Let $\boldsymbol{\alpha}_{i,i}$ be the $n \times k_i$ matrix with rank$(\boldsymbol{\alpha}_i) = k_i$ which drops zero columns from $\boldsymbol{\alpha}_i$ and let:

$$\mathbf{l}_{i,t-i} = \mathbf{S}_i \mathbf{l}_{t-i}$$

where $\mathbf{S}_i$ is a $k_i \times k$ selection matrix comprising zeros except for unity in positions corresponding to non-zero elements in $\boldsymbol{\alpha}_i$, then:

$$\boldsymbol{\alpha}_{i,i}\mathbf{l}_{i,t-i} = \boldsymbol{\alpha}_{i,i}\mathbf{S}_i\mathbf{l}_{t-i} = \boldsymbol{\alpha}_i\mathbf{l}_{t-i}$$

so from (9.9):

$$\boldsymbol{\mu}_t = \boldsymbol{\alpha}^*\mathbf{l}_t^* = \boldsymbol{\alpha}^+\mathbf{l}_t^+$$

where

$$\boldsymbol{\alpha}^*\mathbf{l}_t^* = \begin{pmatrix} \boldsymbol{\alpha}_0 & \boldsymbol{\alpha}_1 & \cdots & \boldsymbol{\alpha}_q \end{pmatrix} \begin{pmatrix} \mathbf{l}_t \\ \mathbf{l}_{t-1} \\ \vdots \\ \mathbf{l}_{t-q} \end{pmatrix}$$

and:

$$\boldsymbol{\alpha}^+\mathbf{l}_t^+ = \begin{pmatrix} \boldsymbol{\alpha}_{0,0} & \boldsymbol{\alpha}_{1,1} & \cdots & \boldsymbol{\alpha}_{q,q} \end{pmatrix} \begin{pmatrix} \mathbf{l}_{0,t} \\ \mathbf{l}_{1,t-1} \\ \vdots \\ \mathbf{l}_{q,t-q} \end{pmatrix}$$

so $\boldsymbol{\alpha}^{+}$ is $n \times \sum_{i=0}^{q} k_i$. When $n > k^{+} = \sum_{i=0}^{q} k_i$, choose $\boldsymbol{\alpha}_{\perp}^{+}$ $(n \times (n - k^{+}))$ which now induces CMC(s) for $s = n - k^{+}$:

$$\boldsymbol{\alpha}_{\perp}^{+\prime}\boldsymbol{\mu}_t = \boldsymbol{\alpha}_{\perp}^{+\prime}\boldsymbol{\alpha}^{+}\mathbf{l}_t^{+} = \mathbf{0}.$$

Otherwise, the condition for CMC(s) with $s = n - k^{+}$ is that rank$(\boldsymbol{\alpha}^{*}) = k^{+} < n$.

Assume that there is no CMC in (9.9) as $k^{+} \geq n$: then IMC cannot occur either for any finite lag as there is always one longer lag of $\mathbf{l}$ due to the moving-average form. Consider $k_i = k\ \forall i$ and $q = 1$ where $\boldsymbol{\alpha}^{*}$ is $n \times 2k$ and $2k > n$, then:

$$\boldsymbol{\mu}_t = \boldsymbol{\alpha}_0\mathbf{l}_t + \boldsymbol{\alpha}_1\mathbf{l}_{t-1} = \boldsymbol{\alpha}^{*}\mathbf{l}_t^{*} \tag{9.10}$$

where rank$(\boldsymbol{\alpha}^{*}) = n$. Since $\boldsymbol{\alpha}^{*}$ has full row rank, there is no vector $\boldsymbol{\phi}'$ such that $\boldsymbol{\phi}'\boldsymbol{\alpha}^{*} = \mathbf{0}$. Stacking $\boldsymbol{\mu}_t$ and $\boldsymbol{\mu}_{t-1}$ just induces an enlarged full row rank form:

$$\begin{pmatrix} \boldsymbol{\mu}_t \\ \boldsymbol{\mu}_{t-1} \end{pmatrix} = \begin{pmatrix} \boldsymbol{\alpha}^{*} & \mathbf{0} \\ \mathbf{0} & \boldsymbol{\alpha}^{*} \end{pmatrix} \begin{pmatrix} \mathbf{l}_t^{*} \\ \mathbf{l}_{t-1}^{*} \end{pmatrix},$$

replicating the problem on a larger scale. Thus, (9.9) either allows CMC or no co-breaking, whereas (9.8) has no CMC but sustains IMC(p, n). While neither form is a realistic model for breaks, they are useful illustrations of the concepts.

We now embed the general formulation of CMC in the integrated-cointegrated DGP described in section 1.5.1, and reproduced here for convenience as:

$$(\Delta\mathbf{x}_t - \boldsymbol{\gamma}) = \boldsymbol{\alpha}\left(\boldsymbol{\beta}'\mathbf{x}_{t-1} - \boldsymbol{\mu}\right) + \boldsymbol{\nu}_t. \tag{9.11}$$

where $\mathbf{x}_t$ is a vector of n I(1) variables, and $\Delta\mathbf{x}_t$ and $\boldsymbol{\beta}'\mathbf{x}_t$ are I(0) by virtue of differencing and cointegration, respectively. Each are expressed as deviations about their means, so that for r cointegrating vectors, $\boldsymbol{\mu}$ is $r \times 1$.

9.4 Co-breaking in a VEqCM

The parameterization in (9.11) holds within sample, and is an example of the "meta-parameters" defining $\boldsymbol{\gamma}$ in (9.1) in §9.2. However, the system is then subject to a regime shift at time T. There could be changes in any or all of $\boldsymbol{\alpha}, \boldsymbol{\beta}, \boldsymbol{\gamma}$, or $\boldsymbol{\mu}$, but here, we only consider one-off shifts in the last two parameters, so that $\boldsymbol{\Upsilon}$ stays constant. Attention is focussed on the VEqCM for 1-step ahead forecasts.

Denote a deterministic shift by $\boldsymbol{\mu}^* = \boldsymbol{\mu}+\nabla\boldsymbol{\mu}$ and $\boldsymbol{\gamma}^* = \boldsymbol{\gamma}+\nabla\boldsymbol{\gamma}$. Given that shift in the parameters:

$$\Delta\mathbf{x}_{T+1} = \boldsymbol{\gamma}^* + \boldsymbol{\alpha}\left(\boldsymbol{\beta}'\mathbf{x}_T - \boldsymbol{\mu}^*\right) + \boldsymbol{\nu}_{T+1}. \tag{9.12}$$

When a break occurs, the timing of its start matters when calculating conditional expectations, as shown in chapter 5, so let:

$$\mathsf{E}\left[\boldsymbol{\beta}'\mathbf{x}_T\right] = \boldsymbol{\mu}^a \text{ and } \mathsf{E}\left[\Delta\mathbf{x}_t\right] = \boldsymbol{\gamma}^a,$$

where the values of $\boldsymbol{\mu}^a, \boldsymbol{\gamma}^a$ depend on the regime. Then from (9.12):

$$\begin{aligned}\Delta\mathbf{x}_{T+1} &= \boldsymbol{\gamma}+\nabla\boldsymbol{\gamma} + \boldsymbol{\alpha}\left(\boldsymbol{\beta}'\mathbf{x}_T - (\boldsymbol{\mu}+\nabla\boldsymbol{\mu})\right) + \boldsymbol{\nu}_{T+1} \\ &= \left[\boldsymbol{\gamma} + \boldsymbol{\alpha}\left(\boldsymbol{\beta}'\mathbf{x}_T - \boldsymbol{\mu}\right) + \boldsymbol{\nu}_{T+1}\right] + \left[\nabla\boldsymbol{\gamma} - \boldsymbol{\alpha}\nabla\boldsymbol{\mu}\right] \\ &= \widetilde{\Delta\mathbf{x}_{T+1}} + \left[\nabla\boldsymbol{\gamma} - \boldsymbol{\alpha}\nabla\boldsymbol{\mu}\right]. \end{aligned} \tag{9.13}$$

The first bracketed term, denoted by $\widetilde{\Delta\mathbf{x}_{T+1}}$, is the constant-parameter value of $\Delta\mathbf{x}_{T+1}$. The second term in brackets is the composite shift.

When $\boldsymbol{\gamma}$ changes, one could enforce (a) $\boldsymbol{\beta}'\nabla\boldsymbol{\gamma} = \mathbf{0}$ which corresponds to the absence of a trend in the cointegrating vectors both before and after the break; or (b) $\boldsymbol{\beta}'\nabla\boldsymbol{\gamma} \neq \mathbf{0}$. The latter is problematic, as then the cointegration vectors trend.

In terms of the system (9.13), consider the $n \times s$ matrix $\boldsymbol{\Phi}$, and form the s linear combinations $\boldsymbol{\Phi}'\Delta\mathbf{x}_{T+1}$, then we have:

$$\boldsymbol{\Phi}'\Delta\mathbf{x}_{T+1} = \boldsymbol{\Phi}'\widetilde{\Delta\mathbf{x}_{T+1}} + \boldsymbol{\Phi}'\left[\nabla\boldsymbol{\gamma} - \boldsymbol{\alpha}\nabla\boldsymbol{\mu}\right]. \tag{9.14}$$

Then s-dimensional equilibrium-mean co-breaking requires that $\boldsymbol{\Phi}'\boldsymbol{\alpha}\nabla\boldsymbol{\mu} = \mathbf{0}$, and s-dimensional drift co-breaking requires $\boldsymbol{\Phi}'\nabla\boldsymbol{\gamma} = \mathbf{0}$.

When $\boldsymbol{\beta}'\boldsymbol{\gamma} = \boldsymbol{\beta}'\nabla\boldsymbol{\gamma} = \mathbf{0}$, and hence the cointegrating vectors are trend free both before and after the shift, then equilibrium-mean co-breaking requires:

$$\boldsymbol{\Phi}'\Delta\mathbf{x}_{T+1} = \boldsymbol{\Phi}'\widetilde{\Delta\mathbf{x}_{T+1}} + \boldsymbol{\Phi}'\nabla\boldsymbol{\gamma}, \tag{9.15}$$

whereas for drift co-breaking, we need:

$$\boldsymbol{\Phi}'\Delta\mathbf{x}_{T+1} = \boldsymbol{\Phi}'\widetilde{\Delta\mathbf{x}_{T+1}} - \boldsymbol{\Phi}'\boldsymbol{\alpha}\nabla\boldsymbol{\mu}. \tag{9.16}$$

Complete co-breaking requires both conditions to hold, but there is little chance of achieving equilibrium-mean and drift co-breaking simultaneously, should both deterministic shifts occur. While the practical likelihood of co-breaking is not obvious, there are some interesting cases, closely related to cointegration, as shown in the next section.

9.5 Cointegration Co-breaking

This section shows the existence of at least some co-breaking combinations. We assume that $\boldsymbol{\alpha}_{\perp} \neq \boldsymbol{\beta}$.

Theorem 9. *"Common trends" are equilibrium-mean co-breaking.*

Proof. Since $\boldsymbol{\alpha}'_{\perp}\boldsymbol{\alpha} = \mathbf{0}$, the choice $\boldsymbol{\Phi} = \boldsymbol{\alpha}_{\perp}$ automatically eliminates equilibrium-mean shifts. Premultiply (9.13) by $\boldsymbol{\alpha}'_{\perp}$:

$$\boldsymbol{\alpha}'_{\perp}\Delta\mathbf{x}_{T+1} = \boldsymbol{\alpha}'_{\perp}\boldsymbol{\gamma} + \boldsymbol{\alpha}'_{\perp}\boldsymbol{\nu}_{T+1} + \boldsymbol{\alpha}'_{\perp}\nabla\boldsymbol{\gamma}. \tag{9.17}$$

■

Since $\boldsymbol{\alpha}_{\perp}$ is the "selector" of the equations which are not dependent on EqCMs, this result is close to explaining the effectiveness of differencing as a "solution" to equilibrium-mean shifts: second differencing, or further co-breaking, would be required to remove the shift in the drift coefficient. Since $\boldsymbol{\alpha}_{\perp}$ is $n \times (n-p)$ such that $\boldsymbol{\alpha}'\boldsymbol{\alpha}_{\perp} = \mathbf{0}$, take:

$$\boldsymbol{\alpha}'_{\perp} = (\mathbf{0}_p : \mathbf{I}_{n-p}) \quad \text{when} \quad \boldsymbol{\alpha} = \begin{pmatrix} \mathbf{a}_p \\ \mathbf{0}_{n,p} \end{pmatrix}$$

then for the lower block of $(n-p)$ equations, denoted by $\mathbf{x}_{b,t}$:

$$\Delta\mathbf{x}_{b,T+1} = \boldsymbol{\gamma}_b + \boldsymbol{\nu}_{b,T+1} + \nabla\boldsymbol{\gamma}_b. \tag{9.18}$$

For a one-off change $\nabla\boldsymbol{\gamma}_b \neq \mathbf{0}$, when $n - p > 1$, there will always exist some linear combinations $\boldsymbol{\Phi}'\Delta\mathbf{x}_{b,T+1}$ that are break free.

Theorem 10. *When the cointegrating vectors are trend free ($\boldsymbol{\beta}'\boldsymbol{\gamma} = \mathbf{0}$) and $\boldsymbol{\beta}'\boldsymbol{\alpha} \neq \mathbf{0}$, then the cointegration vector is drift co-breaking.*

Proof. Premultiply (9.13) by $\boldsymbol{\beta}$, which yields:

$$\boldsymbol{\beta}'\Delta\mathbf{x}_{T+1} = \boldsymbol{\beta}'\boldsymbol{\alpha}\left(\boldsymbol{\beta}'\mathbf{x}_T - \boldsymbol{\mu}\right) + \boldsymbol{\beta}'\boldsymbol{\nu}_{T+1} - \boldsymbol{\beta}'\boldsymbol{\alpha}\nabla\boldsymbol{\mu}, \tag{9.19}$$

which has eliminated the shift in the drift parameter. ■

Thus, there are close relationships between cointegration and co-breaking for some parameter changes. Conversely, from (9.19) the elimination of the drift break makes the further elimination of an equilibrium-mean shift seem unlikely without destroying the system. Letting $\mathbf{y}_{2,t} = \boldsymbol{\beta}'\mathbf{x}_t$ denote the r cointegrating combinations with errors $\mathbf{u}_t = \boldsymbol{\beta}'\boldsymbol{\nu}_t$, dynamic parameters $\boldsymbol{\Lambda} = \mathbf{I}_r + \boldsymbol{\beta}'\boldsymbol{\alpha}$ and intercepts $\boldsymbol{\rho} = \boldsymbol{\beta}'\boldsymbol{\alpha}\boldsymbol{\mu}$, then:

$$\mathbf{y}_{2,T+1} = \boldsymbol{\rho} + \boldsymbol{\Lambda}\mathbf{y}_{2,T} + \mathbf{u}_{T+1} - \boldsymbol{\beta}'\boldsymbol{\alpha}\nabla\boldsymbol{\mu}. \tag{9.20}$$

Some combinations may seem to yield to co-breaking: for example, consider the $r \times s$ matrix $\boldsymbol{\Gamma}$, such that $\boldsymbol{\Gamma}'\boldsymbol{\beta}'\boldsymbol{\alpha}\nabla\boldsymbol{\mu} = \mathbf{0}$. However, $\boldsymbol{\Gamma}'\boldsymbol{\beta}' \neq \mathbf{0}$ is needed to avoid eliminating the $\mathbf{y}_{2,t}$. Nevertheless, one cannot preclude other ways of eliminating one of the two forms of break, allowing both growth and equilibrium-mean co-breaking to be achieved (e.g., adding a previously omitted variable which was the source of the apparent shift).

Generalizations to more shifts at different times in the system, dynamics shifting, shifts carried forward to other equations in a model etc. all merit study. Of these, we briefly consider multiple shifts in the next section: Bai, Lumsdaine and Stock (1998) develop methods for dating such breaks in cointegrated systems.

9.6 Multiple Shifts

When multiple breaks occur, their timing relative to the calculation of expectations matters. Consider the cointegrated representation written as:

$$\Delta\mathbf{x}_t = \boldsymbol{\gamma}_t + \boldsymbol{\alpha}\left(\boldsymbol{\beta}'\mathbf{x}_{t-1} - \boldsymbol{\mu}_{t-1}\right) + \boldsymbol{\nu}_t, \tag{9.21}$$

for an arbitrary number of shifts. Let $\mathsf{E}\left[\boldsymbol{\beta}'\mathbf{x}_t\right] = \boldsymbol{\mu}_t$ so that

$$\mathsf{E}\left[\Delta\mathbf{x}_t\right] = \boldsymbol{\gamma}_t.$$

Pre-multiplying (9.21) by $\boldsymbol{\beta}'$ and taking expectations:

$$\boldsymbol{\beta}'\mathsf{E}\left[\Delta\mathbf{x}_t\right] = \boldsymbol{\beta}'\boldsymbol{\gamma}_t = \mathsf{E}\left[\Delta\boldsymbol{\beta}'\mathbf{x}_t\right] = \boldsymbol{\beta}'\Delta\boldsymbol{\mu}_t.$$

Thus, cointegration vectors do not trend at any time only if $\boldsymbol{\beta}'\Delta\boldsymbol{\mu}_t = \mathbf{0}$, which requires that no equilibrium-mean shifts occur. If so, then cointegration vectors are co-breaking for drift shifts when:

$$\begin{aligned}\boldsymbol{\beta}'\mathbf{x}_t &= \boldsymbol{\beta}'\boldsymbol{\gamma}_t + (\mathbf{I}_r + \boldsymbol{\beta}'\boldsymbol{\alpha})\,\boldsymbol{\beta}'\mathbf{x}_{t-1} - \boldsymbol{\beta}'\boldsymbol{\alpha}\boldsymbol{\mu} + \boldsymbol{\beta}'\boldsymbol{\nu}_t \\ &= \boldsymbol{\mu} + \boldsymbol{\Lambda}\left(\boldsymbol{\beta}'\mathbf{x}_{t-1} - \boldsymbol{\mu}\right) + \boldsymbol{\beta}'\boldsymbol{\nu}_t.\end{aligned}$$

This is independent of drift shifts, but fully constant only because the equilibrium mean does not alter.

When $\boldsymbol{\mu}$ shifts, and $\boldsymbol{\beta}'\boldsymbol{\gamma}_t = \mathbf{0}$, then:

$$\boldsymbol{\beta}'\mathbf{x}_t - \boldsymbol{\mu}_t = \boldsymbol{\Lambda}\left(\boldsymbol{\beta}'\mathbf{x}_{t-1} - \boldsymbol{\mu}_{t-1}\right) - \Delta\boldsymbol{\mu}_t + \boldsymbol{\beta}'\boldsymbol{\nu}_t,$$

so complete co-breaking does not occur. Then (9.20) applies, with time-dated equilibrium-means.

Common trends remain co-breaking for equilibrium-mean changes:

$$\boldsymbol{\alpha}'_\perp\Delta\mathbf{x}_t = \boldsymbol{\alpha}'_\perp\boldsymbol{\gamma}_t + \boldsymbol{\alpha}'_\perp\boldsymbol{\alpha}\left(\boldsymbol{\beta}'\mathbf{x}_{t-1} - \boldsymbol{\mu}_{t-1}\right) + \boldsymbol{\alpha}'_\perp\boldsymbol{\nu}_t = \boldsymbol{\alpha}'_\perp\boldsymbol{\gamma}_t + \boldsymbol{\alpha}'_\perp\boldsymbol{\nu}_t.$$

However, while $\boldsymbol{\alpha}'_\perp$ eliminates all the equilibrium-mean shifts, the resulting equations do not depend on the cointegration vectors either, and are still affected by growth-rate changes.

9.7 Conditional Models

An alternative explanation for co-breaking in a VEqCM is that the underlying behavioral equations are constant, but policy or legislation alters the behavior of their conditioning variables. Constant conditional models with changing marginals "generate" co-breaking in the solved form for both growth rate and equilibrium-mean changes. Thus, super exogenous conditioning variables (see Engle, Hendry and Richard, 1983, and Engle and Hendry, 1993) ensure conditional co-breaking.

Formally, we allow r_1 cointegration vectors in the first n_1 block and r_2 in the second n_2 block where $r = r_1 + r_2$ and $n = n_1 + n_2$, and partition all vectors and matrices accordingly. Then for general shifts in the $\{\mathbf{x}_{2t}\}$ process, the conditional form of the VEqCM is:

$$\begin{aligned}\begin{pmatrix}\Delta\mathbf{x}_{1t}\\ \Delta\mathbf{x}_{2t}\end{pmatrix} &= \begin{pmatrix}\boldsymbol{\Gamma}\Delta\mathbf{x}_{2t}\\ \mathbf{0}\end{pmatrix} + \begin{pmatrix}\boldsymbol{\varphi}_1\\ \boldsymbol{\gamma}_{2t}\end{pmatrix} \\ &\quad + \begin{pmatrix}\boldsymbol{\delta}_{11} & \boldsymbol{\delta}_{12}\\ \boldsymbol{\delta}_{21} & \boldsymbol{\delta}_{22}\end{pmatrix}\begin{pmatrix}\boldsymbol{\beta}'_1\mathbf{x}_{t-1} - \boldsymbol{\mu}_1\\ \boldsymbol{\beta}'_2\mathbf{x}_{t-1} - \boldsymbol{\mu}_{2t}\end{pmatrix} + \begin{pmatrix}\mathbf{e}_{1t}\\ \boldsymbol{\nu}_{2t}\end{pmatrix}\end{aligned}$$

where $\mathsf{E}\left[\mathbf{e}_{1t}\boldsymbol{\nu}'_{2t}\right] = \mathbf{0}$, so that $\boldsymbol{\Gamma} = \boldsymbol{\Omega}_{12}\boldsymbol{\Omega}_{22}^{-1}$, with the weak-exogeneity requirements that $\boldsymbol{\delta}_{21} = \mathbf{0}$ and $\boldsymbol{\delta}_{12} = \mathbf{0}$, or:

$$\Delta\mathbf{x}_t = \begin{pmatrix} \boldsymbol{\varphi}_1 \\ \mathbf{0} \end{pmatrix} + \begin{pmatrix} \boldsymbol{\Gamma} \\ \mathbf{I}_{n_2} \end{pmatrix} \boldsymbol{\gamma}_{2t} + \boldsymbol{\alpha}\left(\boldsymbol{\beta}'\mathbf{x}_{t-1} - \boldsymbol{\mu}_t\right) + \boldsymbol{\nu}_t$$

for $\boldsymbol{\beta} = (\boldsymbol{\beta}_1 : \boldsymbol{\beta}_2)$ with:

$$\boldsymbol{\alpha} = \begin{pmatrix} \boldsymbol{\alpha}_{11} & \boldsymbol{\alpha}_{12} \\ \mathbf{0} & \boldsymbol{\alpha}_{22} \end{pmatrix}, \quad \boldsymbol{\mu}_t = \begin{pmatrix} \boldsymbol{\mu}_1 \\ \boldsymbol{\mu}_{2t} \end{pmatrix}$$

and:

$$\boldsymbol{\gamma}_t = \begin{pmatrix} \boldsymbol{\gamma}_{1t} \\ \boldsymbol{\gamma}_{2t} \end{pmatrix} = \begin{pmatrix} \boldsymbol{\varphi}_1 + \boldsymbol{\Gamma}\boldsymbol{\gamma}_{2t} \\ \boldsymbol{\gamma}_{2t} \end{pmatrix},$$

where $\boldsymbol{\nu}_{1t} = \mathbf{e}_{1t} + \boldsymbol{\Gamma}\boldsymbol{\nu}_{2t}$, $\boldsymbol{\alpha}_{11} = \boldsymbol{\delta}_{11}$, $\boldsymbol{\alpha}_{22} = \boldsymbol{\delta}_{22}$, and $\boldsymbol{\alpha}_{12} = \boldsymbol{\Gamma}\boldsymbol{\delta}_{22}$. Then $(\mathbf{I}_{n_1} : -\boldsymbol{\Gamma})$ is co-breaking for both drift and mean shifts, as is clear from the form of the conditional model. If weak exogeneity fails by $\boldsymbol{\delta}_{21} \neq \mathbf{0}$, then:

$$\begin{aligned} \begin{pmatrix} \Delta\mathbf{x}_{1t} \\ \Delta\mathbf{x}_{2t} \end{pmatrix} &= \begin{pmatrix} \boldsymbol{\gamma}_{1t} \\ \boldsymbol{\gamma}_{2t} \end{pmatrix} + \begin{pmatrix} \boldsymbol{\delta}_{11} + \boldsymbol{\Gamma}\boldsymbol{\delta}_{21} & \boldsymbol{\Gamma}\boldsymbol{\delta}_{22} \\ \boldsymbol{\delta}_{21} & \boldsymbol{\delta}_{22} \end{pmatrix} \\ &\quad \times \begin{pmatrix} \boldsymbol{\beta}'_1\mathbf{x}_{t-1} - \boldsymbol{\mu}_1 \\ \boldsymbol{\beta}'_2\mathbf{x}_{t-1} - \boldsymbol{\mu}_{2t} \end{pmatrix} + \begin{pmatrix} \boldsymbol{\nu}_{1t} \\ \boldsymbol{\nu}_{2t} \end{pmatrix} \end{aligned}$$

so that $(\mathbf{I}_{n_1} : -\boldsymbol{\Gamma})$ is still co-breaking, but conditioning is not valid. If instead, $\boldsymbol{\delta}_{12} \neq \mathbf{0}$, then:

$$\begin{aligned} \begin{pmatrix} \Delta\mathbf{x}_{1t} \\ \Delta\mathbf{x}_{2t} \end{pmatrix} &= \begin{pmatrix} \boldsymbol{\gamma}_{1t} \\ \boldsymbol{\gamma}_{2t} \end{pmatrix} + \begin{pmatrix} \boldsymbol{\delta}_{11} & \boldsymbol{\delta}_{12} + \boldsymbol{\Gamma}\boldsymbol{\delta}_{22} \\ \mathbf{0} & \boldsymbol{\delta}_{22} \end{pmatrix} \\ &\quad \times \begin{pmatrix} \boldsymbol{\beta}'_1\mathbf{x}_{t-1} - \boldsymbol{\mu}_1 \\ \boldsymbol{\beta}'_2\mathbf{x}_{t-1} - \boldsymbol{\mu}_{2t} \end{pmatrix} + \begin{pmatrix} \boldsymbol{\nu}_{1t} \\ \boldsymbol{\nu}_{2t} \end{pmatrix} \end{aligned}$$

so $(\mathbf{I}_{n_1} : -\boldsymbol{\Gamma})$ is co-breaking for growth shifts only.

Simultaneous equations co-breaking is closely similar. Slope, or adjustment, parameter co-breaking could also be defined, but now effects depend on variation freeness with the intercept, namely whether the long-run mean or the intercept (if either) is fixed under the parameter shift: see chapter 3.

9.8 Empirical Co-breaking in UK Money Demand

To illustrate co-breaking empirically, we reconsider the UK M1 quarterly data, but this time, study the impact of the omitted variable. The M1 demand model in chapter 8 from Hendry and Mizon (1993), estimated over the sample $T = 1963{:}4 - 1983{:}2$, forecasted badly for the period to 1989:2. Rebuilding that model over the whole sample on the same set of variables shows a failure of cointegration, and delivers little improvement in forecasting. However, the own interest rate (learning adjusted) was added by Hendry and Ericsson (1991), who thereby recovered the earlier model's parameter estimates, found cointegration again, and avoided predictive failure.

Hendry and Mizon (1993) find that the regressors are weakly exogenous for the parameters of the conditional equation, which can therefore be modeled in isolation, and simplify it to a more parsimonious form. We therefore consider their single equation for real money demand, which differs slightly from that used in the previous chapter. As in chapter 8, let M denote nominal M1, I total final expenditure, P its deflator, and R the Local-Authority interest rate on three-month bills: lower case denotes logs. The long-run solution (cointegrating vector) from a 2-lag conditional unrestricted equation in $m - p - i$ is:

$$\begin{aligned} c_1 &= m - p - i - 0.25 + 6.7\Delta p + 6.9R \qquad (9.22) \\ \mathsf{t}_{ur} &= -6.8^{**} \end{aligned}$$

where t_{ur} tests for a unit root in the dependent-variable lag polynomial (see Doornik and Hendry, 1994), and strongly rejects. Reduction led to the dynamic model:

$$\begin{aligned} \Delta(m-p)_t = &- \underset{(0.06)}{0.28}\ \Delta(m-p-i)_{t-1} - \underset{(0.16)}{0.76}\ \Delta_2\Delta p_t - \underset{(0.08)}{0.62}\ \Delta_2 R_t \\ &- \underset{(0.009)}{0.097}\ c_{1,t-2} \qquad (9.23) \end{aligned}$$

$$\begin{aligned} \mathsf{R}^2 &= 0.70\ \ \hat{\sigma} = 1.30\%\ \ \mathsf{F}_{\mathsf{ar}}(5,70) = 1.3\ \ \mathsf{F}_{\mathsf{arch}}(4,67) = 0.8 \\ \chi^2_{\mathsf{nd}}(2) &= 2.5\ \ \mathsf{F}_{\mathsf{het}}(8,66) = 0.64\ \ \mathsf{F}_{\mathsf{res}}(1,74) = 0.1\ \ V = 0.27\ \ \mathsf{J} = 0.75 \end{aligned}$$

Equation (9.23) satisfies all the reported diagnostics, defined as before (see §7.4), with V denoting the variance-change test in Hansen

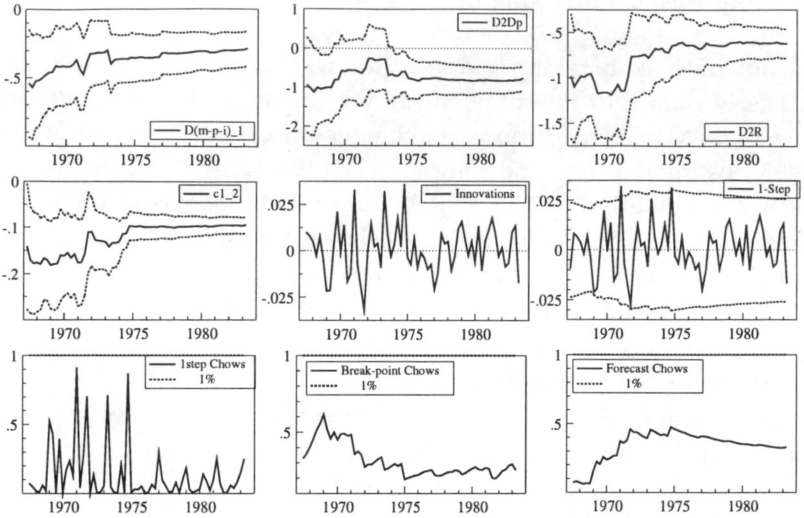

Figure 9.1
Short-sample recursive estimates and tests.

(1992b). It has interpretable parameters in a parsimonious model, and as fig. 9.1 shows, the recursive estimates are constant.

Nevertheless, updating to 1989:2 yields a Chow (1960) statistic of $\mathsf{F_{Ch}}(24, 75) = 7.71^{**}$: this is massive predictive failure, as seen in fig. 9.2. The fitted and actual values are far apart, the regressions of actual on fitted are completely different in-sample and over the forecast period, the residuals explode for the forecasts, and the 95% prediction intervals include few of the outcomes. Further, a recursively computed t-test for a zero forecast innovation mean yields $\mathsf{t}(23) = 5.84^{**}$, consistent with a mean shift. Note that panel d is close to the corresponding graph for the $\Delta(m-p)_t$ equation in the system, so most of the forecast failure is internal to the money-demand equation.

Re-estimation over the extended sample $T = 1963{:}4 - 1989{:}2$ produces:

$$\Delta(m-p)_t = -\underset{(0.09)}{0.06}\ \Delta(m-p-i)_{t-1} - \underset{(0.23)}{0.73}\ \Delta_2\Delta p_t - \underset{(0.12)}{0.42}\ \Delta_2 R_t - \underset{(0.012)}{0.064}\ c_{1,t-2} \tag{9.24}$$

$$\mathsf{R}^2 = 0.39 \;\; \hat{\sigma} = 2.10\% \;\; \mathsf{F}_{\mathsf{ar}}(5,94) = 13.7^{**} \;\; \mathsf{F}_{\mathsf{arch}}(4,91) = 11.4^{**}$$
$$\chi^2_{\mathsf{nd}}(2) = 5.1 \;\; \mathsf{F}_{\mathsf{het}}(8,90) = 1.92 \;\; \mathsf{F}_{\mathsf{res}}(1,98) = 2.3 \;\; V = 1.74^{**} \;\; \mathsf{J} = 3.95^{**}$$

These full-sample recursive estimates show the predictive failure starkly. The residual standard deviation has almost doubled, and all the instability tests reveal non-constancy. Figure 9.3 reports the full-sample recursive estimates and shows the large increase in residual variance. In fact, returning to the unrestricted model highlights the disintegration of cointegration: the long-run outcome is badly determined with uninterpretable coefficient magnitudes, and the unit-root t-test does not reject the null of no cointegration. Such problems often seem to occur in empirical research, and may appear to cast doubt on empirical modeling strategies, such as that advocated in (e.g.) Hendry (1995a). As will be shown below, this disaster could not be predicted *ex ante* by any in-sample statistical test, and does not reveal a failure of methodology, nor a failure of rigorous testing. With hindsight – as ever – it is clear that the measure of opportunity cost needed changed when interest-bearing accounts became legal, although initially, no data existed by which to do so.

In terms of the preceding analysis (e.g., ch. 3), there is a clear structural break. The interesting issue here is whether there is a co-breaking vector that re-creates a constant-parameter money-demand equation in which the original parameters are closely reproduced. We have just shown that does not occur within the information set of linear functions of $m - p$, i, R, and Δp, but it may on an extended set.

The solution proposed by Hendry and Ericsson (1991) is to add a measure of the own interest rate on M1, a variable that was zero until 1984 (other than implicit interest payments used to offset transactions costs for which commercial banks did not charge), when a change in the law allowed interest payments on retail sight deposits (interest-bearing checking accounts), which induced a large change in the opportunity cost of holding M1. Let $R_{o,t}$ denote the own rate on M1. This is shown in fig. 8.1b with the real money stock $m-p$. Then, co-breaking is sought in the five-dimensional system $m - p$, i, R, R_o, and Δp.

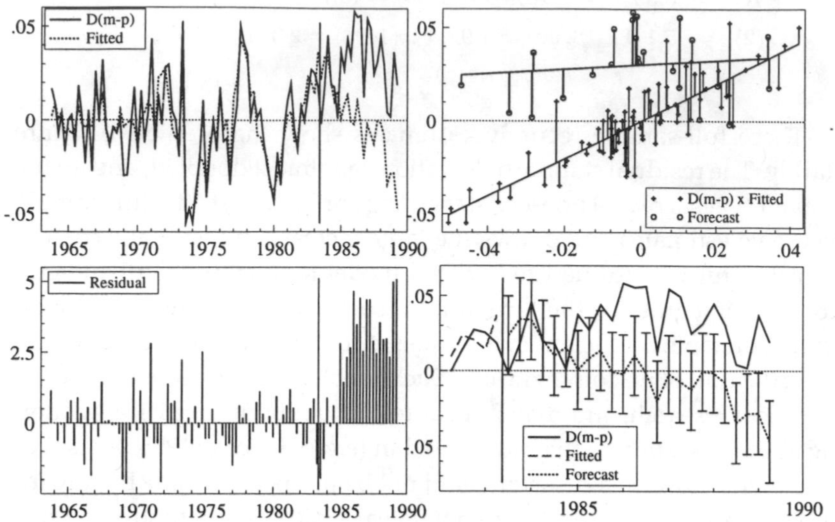

Figure 9.2
Short-sample estimation with forecast statistics.

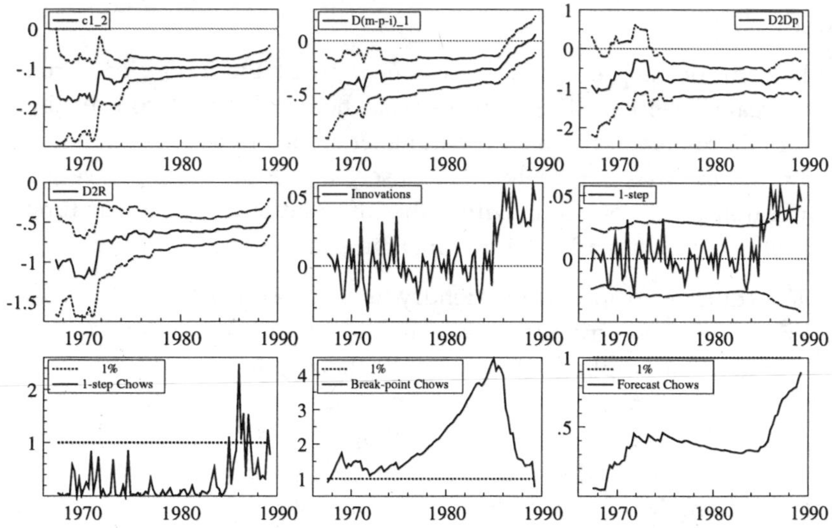

Figure 9.3
Full-sample recursive estimates and tests.

We have not yet developed system procedures analogous to Johansen (1988) for multivariate cointegration, so we continue with a single-equation analysis. There are several ways to demonstrate conditional co-breaking in that context. The simplest is to extend the model by adding $R_{o,t}$ and checking for constancy. The sharp rise in $m - p$ coincides with the jump from zero in R_o, which is necessary, but insufficient, for contemporaneous co-breaking to occur. Thus, adding $R_{o,t}$ and $\Delta_2 R_{o,t}$ to (9.23) over $T = 1963{:}4 - 1989{:}2$ delivers equation (9.25):

$$\begin{aligned}\Delta(m-p)_t &= -\underset{(0.06)}{0.27}\,\Delta(m-p-i)_{t-1} - \underset{(0.14)}{0.84}\,\Delta_2\Delta p_t - \underset{(0.07)}{0.59}\,\Delta_2 R_t \\ &\quad - \underset{(0.008)}{0.092}\,c_{1,t-2} + \underset{(0.06)}{0.67}\,R_{o,t} + \underset{(0.17)}{0.43}\,\Delta_2 R_{o,t} \qquad (9.25)\end{aligned}$$

$$\begin{aligned}\mathsf{R}^2 &= 0.78 \;\; \hat{\sigma} = 1.29\% \;\; \mathsf{F}_{\mathsf{ar}}(5,92) = 1.8 \;\; \mathsf{F}_{\mathsf{arch}}(4,89) = 0.6 \\ \chi^2_{\mathsf{nd}}(2) &= 1.7 \;\; \mathsf{F}_{\mathsf{het}}(12,84) = 0.71 \;\; \mathsf{F}_{\mathsf{res}}(1,96) = 0.1 \;\; V = 0.26 \;\; \mathsf{J} = 0.77\end{aligned}$$

The coefficient estimates on the variables in common are almost identical; and the added regressors are highly significant. Moreover, $\hat{\sigma}$ and all the diagnostic tests for the full sample closely match those in (9.23) for the early sample.

The most interesting aspect is that when opportunity cost of holding M1 is now measured by the net rate: $R_{n,t} = R_t - R_{o,t}$, then re-estimating (9.24) just replacing R_t by $R_{n,t}$ yields ($R_{n,t}$ is also used in $c_{1,t-2}$):

$$\begin{aligned}\Delta(m-p)_t &= -\underset{(0.06)}{0.26}\,\Delta(m-p-i)_{t-1} - \underset{(0.14)}{0.84}\,\Delta_2\Delta p_t - \underset{(0.07)}{0.58}\,\Delta_2 R_{n,t} \\ &\quad - \underset{(0.006)}{0.093}\,c_{1,t-2} \qquad (9.26)\end{aligned}$$

$$\begin{aligned}\mathsf{R}^2 &= 0.77 \;\; \hat{\sigma} = 1.28\% \;\; \mathsf{F}_{\mathsf{ar}}(5,94) = 1.78 \;\; \mathsf{F}_{\mathsf{arch}}(4,91) = 0.81 \\ \chi^2_{\mathsf{nd}}(2) &= 1.3 \;\; \mathsf{F}_{\mathsf{het}}(8,90) = 0.88 \;\; \mathsf{F}_{\mathsf{res}}(1,98) = 0.1 \;\; V = 0.23 \;\; \mathsf{J} = 0.67\end{aligned}$$

The final parameter estimates, imposing the restriction that the outside and own rates have equal magnitude, opposite-sign effects (so only their net differential $R_{n,t}$ affects money demand), are reported in equation (9.26), and are very close to those in (9.23). Figure 9.4 shows the forecast statistics for this model, estimated on the short sample, and forecasting the previously difficult period. As can be seen, the forecast failure has been removed, confirming co-breaking in the extended set of variables. The test of parameter constancy over 1983:3–1989:2 yields

$\mathsf{F_{Ch}}(24, 75) = 0.91$ and the t-test for a zero forecast innovation mean delivers $t(23) = -0.14$, confirming the constancy of the revised model. The close similarity of new and old parameter estimates suggests that the co-breaking is not spurious.

There are five implications to be drawn from this example. First, it is an example of co-breaking across the variables m, i, p, R_t, $R_{o,t}$. Secondly, it illustrates the concept of "extended constancy": when $R_{o,t}$ is used as an unrestricted regressor, the model is enlarged, but the crucial index of its constancy is that all the previous parameters retain their original values. This is an essential attribute of co-breaking, since a constant vector must eliminate all the breaks. Thirdly, updating models requires the use of sensible measurements which adapt to changing environments (see Ericsson, Hendry and Prestwich, 1998b): retaining R_t is a bad proxy for opportunity cost after 1984. Further, as noted, there is no possible within-sample test of later behavior: whether or not predictive failure is manifested depends on how the model is updated, not on the in-sample behavior since $R_{n,t} \equiv R_t$ till 1984:3. Since, the pre-1984 model was appropriate, the methodology by which it was developed empirically did not fail, even though that model later did.

Finally, if the shift is in the intercept of the original model, then a step-shift dummy should also remove the predictive failure, being one implementation of an intercept correction. The problem is how to date the break point at which the dummy commences, and *ex post* empirical experimentation suggested 1985:1, leading to a dummy denoted D851 (zero before, unity thereafter). The dummy mimics the effect of R_o remarkably well, inducing almost the same residual variance and long-run outcome. Indeed, even using only three non-zero in-sample values for estimation allows respectable forecasts: fig. 9.5 records the estimation and forecast statistics for the model with a shift dummy, expressed for the level of real money, to illustrate how dramatically that variable increased, yet the IC allows reasonable tracking. Formally: $\mathsf{F_{Ch}}(16, 81) = 1.03$, which is far from significant, even though the IC increased the forecast-error variance.

A related view of testing conditional co-breaking follows from Salkever (1976), who suggested adding zero-one indicators $1_{\{t=T+h\}}$ $(h = 1, \ldots, H)$ over the forecast period to calculate forecast errors. If the indicators are jointly insignificant, then co-breaking occurs. Each

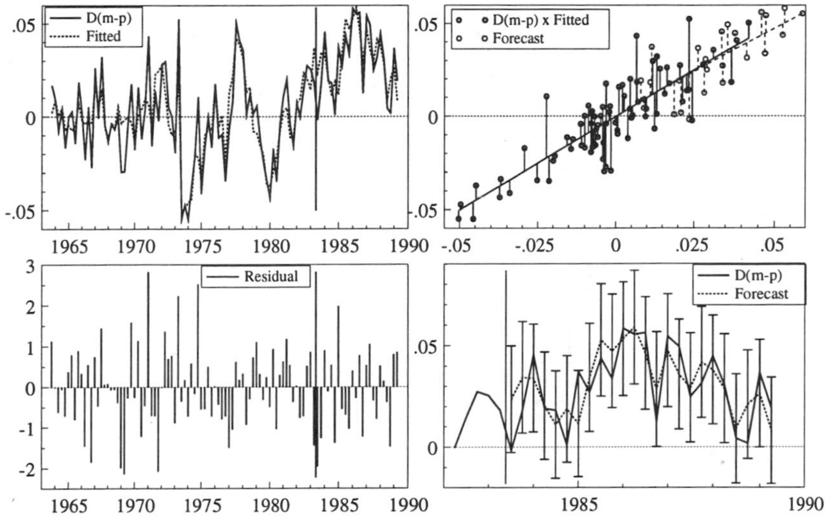

Figure 9.4
Estimation of extended model with forecast statistics.

indicator estimates the mean shift μ_{T+h} plus the error ϵ_{T+h}. The latter has a known in-sample distribution, so significant indicators reveal breaks (or blip outliers). If the conditional model is constant, then variables co-break with that combination. When a step shift is anticipated, the indicators can be reparameterized as $1_{\{t>T\}}$ and $H-1$ blips: the outcome is isomorphic, but may be easier to interpret. and later simplify.

For (9.23), none of the seventeen blip indicators was individually significant when $1_{\{t>T\}}$ (i.e., D851) was included, and a reduction test yielded $\mathsf{F}(17,81) = 1.03$, which is an alternative method for calculating that test-period's Chow test. When eighteen blip indicators were used, all but one had a t-statistic in excess of 2. When only $1_{\{t>T\}}$ was included, t = 12.5.

For (9.26), only the indicator for 1985:1 had a t of 2; all the others were insignificant, and the reduction $\mathsf{F}(18,81) = 0.75$; adding only $1_{\{t>T\}}$ produced t = 0.6. Thus, the very significant mean shift in the mis-specified relation vanishes in the model based on the five-variable information set. This strategy extends to systems.

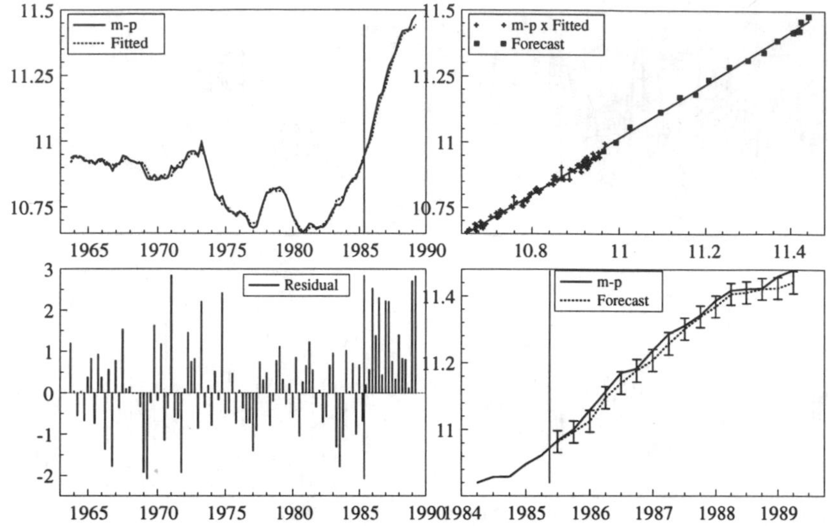

Figure 9.5
Estimation and forecast statistics with a shift dummy.

9.9 Conclusion

The main points of the chapter were to establish the characterization of co-breaking, namely the removal of deterministic shifts by linear combinations of variables, its potential existence in a cointegrated VAR, and the relationship between co-breaking and cointegration. These were developed in the first three sections. As the limit of persistent breaks in every period is essentially an I(1) process (see Rappoport and Reichlin, 1989), the close connections of co-breaking and cointegration are unsurprising. Nevertheless, that cointegration vectors also co-break for shifts in the growth rate when there is no trend in the cointegration space is encouraging, since at first sight there may be thought to be an apparent contradiction between long-run constancy and breaks in trends.

Since cointegration implies Granger causality in at least one direction, it is not a property of series that just happen to be correlated (which is sufficient in stationary processes for an explanation), but entails a more fundamental link (albeit that Granger causality in a limited information set is insufficient for "genuine causality": see Hendry and Mizon, 1999). The situation seems even more stark with co-breaking:

for a regime shift to vanish across a linear combination of variables entails either a coincidentally equal effect, or a genuine relationship. In particular, it highlights the key distinction between, say, a leading indicator which is non-causal of, and non-caused by, the target variable, and a causally-related variable. The former seems unlikely to experience the same shift as the target in a systematic way. Thus, although leading indicators and econometric models face similar problems for *ex ante* forecasting in a world of deterministic shifts, the cards seem heavily stacked against the former when the mappings of the indicators to the outcomes are not causal relations: the repeated failure to lead consistently may be a consequence of the absence of co-breaking between variables which in fact are causally unrelated (see Emerson and Hendry, 1996).

In retrospect, it can be seen that many model types already exhibit co-breaking, and examples include: constant conditional models faced by changing marginal processes must co-break in the joint distribution (see e.g. Campos, Ericsson and Hendry, 1996); models that are resilient to the Lucas (1976) critique and so embody super exogeneity (see Favero and Hendry, 1992, and Engle and Hendry, 1993); etc. Although the theorems in §9.2 suggest that the empirical power may be low when only a few breaks, or many variables, are involved within sample, the continuation of constant conditional equations out of sample despite changing marginal processes suggests a deeper link. Equally, the significance of "peculiar" effects in dynamic models may be a symptom of spurious intertemporal co-breaking, where sufficient flexibility in the lag length allows matching of shifts despite the absence of a causal link.

Multivariate estimation, testing, and modeling of co-breaking are not resolved at this stage, although many possibilities seem promising avenues for future research currently in progress. For example, the regime-switching ideas discussed in the next chapter could be used for deterministic breaks that recur.

Since failure in forecasting was shown above to be closely associated with deterministic shifts, and is part of the explanation for the "success" of forecasts based on differenced relations, the need for co-breaking in econometric relations if they are to forecast successfully is clear. Nevertheless, as even co-breaking relations can change in a social science, continual monitoring of forecasting models will remain essential.

10 Modeling Shifts

Summary

Regime-switching autoregressive models seek to characterize shifts between two or more regimes, or distinct patterns of behavior. By explicitly incorporating the possibility of regime changes in the probabilistic structure of the model, a more realistic assessment of the uncertainty surrounding model predictions can often be obtained. These models have proved popular in contemporary empirical macroeconomic research on business cycles, and in this chapter, we consider whether some of the models in the literature are capable of yielding improved forecasts relative to linear autoregressive alternatives.

10.1 Introduction

As an alternative to updating, differencing, and intercept corrections, it may be possible to model intercept shifts. The idea behind the residual-based method of intercept corrections is that the structural change occurs close to the end of the sample but is unknown to the forecaster. Consequently the variability of the last-period dummy variable is of the same order as the equation standard error, which causes the forecast-error variance to rise. More precise estimates of the required correction result if the structural change occurred several periods before the forecast origin, or if evidence can be brought to bear from other sources, such as the performance of time-series models.

However, in some instances a time series may have exhibited a sudden change in mean over the sample period. For example, consider the time series depicted by Hamilton (1993), figures 2–4, pp.232–234. Then a number of possibilities arise, one of which is to include appropriate dummy variables (impulse or shift, depending on whether the change is immediately reversed) to capture the effects of outliers or "one-off" factors, without which the model may not be constant over the past. This strategy is popular in econometric modeling: see, for example, Clements and Mizon (1991) . However, to the extent that these "one-off" factors could not have been foreseen *ex ante* and may occur again, the model standard error is an under-estimate of the true uncertainty inherent in explaining the dependent variable (1-step ahead), and prediction intervals derived from the model may be similarly misleading.

A more accurate picture of the uncertainty surrounding the model predictions may be obtained by explicitly building into the probabilistic structure of the model the possibility that further regime changes may occur. For example, if one regime change of a particular type was observed historically in the last 30 years, then the model could be set up in such a way that a typical sample of 30 years generated by the model would include one such episode of that type. Hamilton (1989) suggested using Markov switching regression (MS–R) models in these circumstances, where the temporal dependence in time series suggested the use of autoregressions (hence, MS–AR), building on the work of, e.g., Goldfeld and Quandt (1973).[1]

Models of this type have also been used to characterize processes that switch regularly between two or more regimes. Both the MS–AR model, and self-exciting threshold autoregressive (SETAR) models have been extensively applied, and in contemporary empirical macroeconomics, are used to characterize asymmetries between the expansionary and contractionary phases of business cycles: see §10.2.[2]

[1]See *inter alia* Albert and Chib (1993), Diebold, Lee and Weinbach (1994), Ghysels (1994), Goodwin (1993), Hamilton (1994), Kähler and Marnet (1994), Kim (1994), Krolzig and Lütkepohl (1995), Krolzig (1997), Lam (1990), McCulloch and Tsay (1994), and Phillips (1991).

[2]See Tong (1978, 1983, 1995) and Tong and Lim (1980). A switching regression model with an observable switching variable appears in Goldfeld and Quandt (1972). SETAR has been used to model exchange rates, output variables and unemployment rates: see, for example, Tiao and Tsay (1994), Potter (1995), Hansen (1996b), Montgomery, Zarnowitz, Tsay and Tiao (1998) and Rothman (1998).

However, from a forecasting perspective, there appears to be no clear consensus as to whether allowing for non-linearities of these types leads to an improved forecast performance (see, e.g., De Gooijer and Kumar, 1992), so in §10.3–§10.5 we report on research in Clements and Krolzig (1998) that attempts a systematic evaluation, and seeks to isolate some of the key factors. Since it has often been argued (e.g., Granger and Teräsvirta, 1993, ch. 9, and Teräsvirta and Anderson, 1992) that the superior in-sample performance of non-linear models will only be matched out-of-sample if the "non-linear features" also characterize the later period, we report on a Monte Carlo that ensures the future bears the same non-linear imprint as the past. Thus, each of the empirical non-linear models is taken in turn as the data generating process, to ensure that the non-linearities captured in the model on the past data do indeed persist into the future, and we assess the gains relative to a linear model, as well as the costs to using the "wrong" non-linear model: that is, how much less accurate our forecasts would be if we used a SETAR model when the process generating the data is an MS-AR, and vice versa. Put bluntly, does the choice of non-linearity matter in this instance? In §10.5, we provide analytical results which help illuminate some of the key findings of the simulation study. Finally, §10.6 summarizes and concludes.

10.2 Regime-switching Models

10.2.1 MS-AR models

In MS-AR processes, contractions and expansions are modeled as switching regimes of the stochastic process generating the growth rate of GNP. The regimes are associated with different conditional distributions of the growth rate of real GNP, where, for example,the mean is positive in the first regime ("expansion") and negative in the second regime ("contraction").

The Hamilton (1989) model of the US business cycle fits a fourth-order autoregression to the quarterly percentage change in US real GNP from 1953 to 1984:

$$\Delta y_t - \mu(s_t) = \alpha_1 \left(\Delta y_{t-1} - \mu(s_{t-1})\right) + \cdots + \alpha_4 \left(\Delta y_{t-4} - \mu(s_{t-4})\right) + u_t \quad (10.1)$$

where $u_t \sim \mathsf{IN}[0, \sigma_u^2]$. The conditional mean $\mu(s_t)$ switches between two states ($M = 2$):

$$\mu(s_t) = \begin{cases} \mu_1 > 0 & \text{if } s_t = 1 \text{ ("expansion" or "boom")}, \\ \mu_2 < 0 & \text{if } s_t = 2 \text{ ("contraction" or "recession")}, \end{cases} \tag{10.2}$$

The description of a MS-AR model is completed by the specification of a model for the stochastic and unobservable regimes on which the parameters of the conditional process depend. Once a law has been specified for the states s_t, the evolution of regimes can be inferred from the data. The regime-generating process is assumed to be an ergodic Markov chain with a finite number of states $s_t = 1, 2$ (for a two-regime model), defined by the transition probabilities:

$$\mathsf{p}_{ij} = \Pr(s_{t+1} = j \mid s_t = i), \quad \sum_{j=1}^{2} \mathsf{p}_{ij} = 1 \quad \forall i, j \in \{1, 2\}. \tag{10.3}$$

The assumption of fixed transition probabilities p_{ij} can be relaxed (see, e.g., Diebold, Rudebusch and Sichel, 1993, Diebold *et al.*, 1994, Filardo, 1994, Lahiri and Wang, 1994, and Durland and McCurdy, 1994).

Maximum likelihood estimation of the MS-AR model entails an iterative technique, based on an implementation of the expectation maximization (EM) algorithm proposed in Hamilton (1990) – an overview of alternative numerical techniques for the maximum likelihood estimation of MS(M)-AR(p) models is given in Krolzig (1997). The EM algorithm of Dempster, Laird and Rubin (1977) is used because the observable time series depends on the s_t, which are unobservable stochastic variables.

Forecasting is straightforward. While the minimum MSFE predictor is not linear, it can be derived analytically, unlike the situation for many non-linear models. For the Hamilton model, we solve the recursion:

$$\widehat{\Delta y}_{T+h|T} = \hat{\mu}_{T+h|T} + \sum_{k=1}^{4} \alpha_k \left(\widehat{\Delta y}_{T+h-k|T} - \hat{\mu}_{T+h-k|T} \right) \tag{10.4}$$

with initial values $\widehat{\Delta y}_{T+h|T} = \Delta y_{T+h}$ for $h \leq 0$ and where the predicted mean is given by:

$$\hat{\mu}_{T+h|T} = \sum_{j=1}^{2} \mu_j \Pr(s_{T+h} = j \mid Y_T).$$

The predicted regime probabilities:

$$\Pr(s_{T+h} = j \mid Y_T) = \sum_{i=1}^{2} \Pr(s_{T+h} = j \mid s_T = i)\Pr(s_T = i \mid Y_T),$$

only depend on the transition probabilities $\Pr(s_{T+h} = j|s_{T+h-1} = i) = \mathsf{p}_{ij}$, $i, j = 1, 2$, and the filtered regime probability $\Pr(s_T = i|Y_T)$.

The optimal predictor of the MS-AR model is linear in the last p observations and the last regime inference, but there exists no purely linear representation of the optimal predictor in the information set (this is discussed in more detail in Krolzig, 1997, ch. 4). However, the optimal forecasting rule becomes linear in the limit as the regimes become completely unpredictable, defined by, $\Pr(s_t|s_{t-1}) = \Pr(s_t)$ for $s_t, s_{t-1} = 1, 2$, since then $\hat{\mu}_{T+h} = \bar{\mu}$, the unconditional mean of y_t. Taking a first-order model for simplicity, we have:

$$\widehat{\Delta y}_{T+h|T} = \hat{\mu}_{T+h|T} + \alpha \left(\widehat{\Delta y}_{T+h-1|T} - \hat{\mu}_{T+h-1|T} \right) \tag{10.5}$$

with:

$$\hat{\mu}_{T+h|T} = \bar{\mu}$$

so:

$$\begin{aligned} \widehat{\Delta y}_{T+h|T} &= \bar{\mu} + \alpha \left(\widehat{\Delta y}_{T+h-1|T} - \bar{\mu} \right) \\ &= \bar{\mu} \left(1 - \alpha^h\right) + \alpha^h \Delta y_T \end{aligned}$$

hence, to a first approximation, apart from differences arising from parameter estimation, forecasts will be similar to those from linear autoregressive models.

10.2.2 SETAR models

Contrary to the MS–AR model, in a SETAR model, the linear autoregression that generates the values of the time series at any instant depends upon the value taken by the process d periods earlier, where d is known as the length of the delay. Formally, y_{t-d} is continuous on $\mathbb{R}$, so that partitioning the real line defines the number of distinct regimes, say N_r, where the process is in the ith regime when $r_{i-1} \leq y_{t-d} < r_i$.

In that case, the pth order linear AR is defined by:

$$y_t = \phi_0^{\{i\}} + \phi_1^{\{i\}} y_{t-1} + \ldots + \phi_p^{\{i\}} y_{t-p} + \epsilon_t^{\{i\}}, \quad i = 1, 2, \ldots, N_r \qquad (10.6)$$

where $\epsilon_t^{\{i\}} \sim \mathsf{IID}\left[0, \sigma^{2\{i\}}\right]$, and the parameters super-scripted by $\{i\}$ may vary across regimes. This model is sometimes written as a SETAR($N_r; p, \ldots, p$). A lag order that varies over regimes can be accommodated within this framework by defining p as the maximum lag order across the regimes, and noting that some of the $\phi_j^{\{i\}}$ may be zero.

Conditional on the number of regimes, the regime r (assuming $N_r = 2$), and the delay, d, the sample can simply be split in two, and an OLS regression can be estimated from the observations belonging to each regime separately. In practice, r is unknown, and the model is estimated by searching over r and d: r is allowed to take on each of the sample period values of y_{t-d} in turn, and d typically takes on the values $0, 1, 2, \ldots$ up to the maximum lag length allowed.[3] The choice of p will also typically be data-based.

Exact analytical solutions are not available for multi-period forecasts. Exact numerical solutions require sequences of numerical integrations (see, e.g., Tong, 1995, §4.2.4 and §6.2) based on the Chapman–Kolmogorov relation. As an alternative, one might use a Monte Carlo method (e.g., Tiao and Tsay, 1994, and Clements and Smith, 1999), particularly for high-order autoregressions, or the normal forecast-error method (NFE) suggested by Al-Qassam and Lane (1989) for the exponential-autoregressive model, and adapted by De Gooijer and De Bruin (1997) to forecasting with SETAR models. Clements and Smith (1997) compare a number of alternative methods of obtaining multi-step forecasts from SETAR models, and conclude that the Monte Carlo method performs reasonably well.

To see the difficulty, suppose $y_t = g(y_{t-1}) + \epsilon_t$, where $g(\cdot)$ is a non-linear function. For a 2-regime SETAR model, an example is:

$$g(y_{t-1}) = \left[\phi^{\{1\}} + 1_{\{y_{t-1}>r\}}\left(\phi^{\{2\}} - \phi^{\{1\}}\right)\right] y_{t-1}$$

where $1_{\{\cdot\}}$ is the usual indicator function, equal to unity when the argument is true, and zero when false. Also, ϵ_t is IID with mean zero and

[3]In practice the range of values of y_{t-d} is restricted to those between the 15th and 85th percentile of the empirical distribution, following Andrews (1993) and Hansen (1996b).

distribution function $\mathsf{D}_{\epsilon}(\cdot)$. The exact 1-step ahead forecast defined by $\widehat{y}_{T+1} \equiv \mathsf{E}[y_{T+1}|\mathcal{I}_T]$, where $\mathcal{I}_T = y_T, y_{T-1}, \ldots \equiv Y_T$, is given by:

$$\widehat{y}_{T+1} = \mathsf{E}\left[\left(g\left(y_T\right) + \epsilon_{T+1}\right) \mid \mathcal{I}_T\right] = g\left(y_T\right).$$

However, for 2-steps ahead:

$$\begin{aligned} \widehat{y}_{T+2} &\equiv \mathsf{E}[y_{T+2} \mid \mathcal{I}_T] = \mathsf{E}\left[\left(g\left(y_{T+1}\right) + \epsilon_{T+2}\right) \mid \mathcal{I}_T\right] \\ &= \mathsf{E}\left[g\left(y_{T+1}\right) \mid \mathcal{I}_T\right] = \mathsf{E}\left[g\left(\widehat{y}_{T+1} + \epsilon_{T+1}\right) \mid \mathcal{I}_T\right]. \end{aligned} \tag{10.7}$$

Complications arise, relative to the linear case, because when $g(\cdot)$ is a non-linear function:

$$\mathsf{E}\left[g\left(y_{t+1}\right)\right] \neq g\left(\mathsf{E}\left[y_{t+1}\right]\right) = g(\widehat{y}_{t+1}).$$

The exact method in this case is:

$$\widehat{y}_{e,T+2} = \int_{-\infty}^{\infty} g\left(\widehat{y}_{T+1} + z\right) \mathrm{d}\Phi\left(z\right),$$

where $\Phi(z)$ is the distribution function of ϵ_t. Finally, the Monte Carlo method is:

$$\widehat{y}_{m,T+2} = \frac{1}{N}\sum_{j=1}^{N} g\left(\widehat{y}_{T+1} + z_j\right)$$

where z_j are random numbers, drawn from $\Phi(z)$. Implicit in the above is that the distribution of the errors may be regime dependent. Granger and Teräsvirta (1993) also mention the bootstrap method, which is of course closely related to the Monte Carlo method.

10.3 Empirical Models

Clements and Krolzig (1998) estimate MS-AR and SETAR models for (one hundred times) the difference in the logarithm of seasonally-adjusted, quarterly US GNP ("GNP growth"), and test these models against single-regime (linear) models. They also report an empirical forecast-accuracy comparison of the models, but we focus on their Monte Carlo study, to better isolate those features which affect the relative performance of the non-linear versus linear models.

10.3.1 SETAR models of US GNP

The results of estimating SETAR models on two vintages on data, 1947–90 and 1959–96, and sub-periods of each, are reported in table 10.1. The model on the earlier vintage is similar to those of Potter (1995) and Tiao and Tsay (1994). The latter find that the empirical performance of the SETAR model relative to a linear AR model is markedly improved when the comparison is made in terms of how well the models forecast when the economy is in recession. The reason is easily understood. Since a majority of the sample data points (approximately 78%) fall in the upper regime, the linear AR(2) model will be largely determined by these points, and will closely match the upper-regime SETAR model. Thus the forecast performance of the two models will be broadly similar when the economy is in the expansionary phase of the business cycle. However, to the extent that the data points in the lower regime are characterized by a different process, there will be gains to the SETAR model during the contractionary phase. Clements and Smith (1999, 1997) find evidence for this effect in empirical and Monte Carlo analyses of the forecast performance of SETAR and linear models. If we do not evaluate forecasts conditional upon regimes, then the gains in the minority regime need to be sufficiently large for the SETAR to perform well on average.

The estimates for the sub- and full-sample periods are similar for a given data vintage, indicating parameter constancy, but differ markedly between vintages. The models for the more recent vintage indicate a threshold at a quarterly growth rate of 0.32%, so that there is a distinction between low growth and high growth rather than between absolute declines and increases in the level of GNP.

10.3.1.1 Testing for several regimes: the SETAR model

Hansen (1996b) presents a general framework for testing the null of linearity against the alternative of threshold autoregression, that delivers valid inference when the threshold value r and delay d are unknown *a priori*, in the sense that they have to be learned from the data (either by a formal estimation procedure, or by casual inspection, as in Potter, 1995). Since r and d are nuisance parameters that are unidentified under the null hypothesis, the testing procedure is non-standard. Hansen

Table 10.1
SETAR Models.

Sample	47:2–84:4	47:2–90:4	59:2–90:4	59:2–96:2
Lower regime				
α_{0L}	−0.4996	−0.4693	0.2099	0.2528
α_{1L}	0.3976	0.3936	0.1374	0.1687
α_{2L}	−0.8676	−0.8520	−0.2345	−0.1482
σ_L	1.2844	1.2684	1.2393	1.1027
Upper regime				
α_{0U}	0.4573	0.4016	0.5530	0.5405
α_{1U}	0.3223	0.3160	0.3337	0.3338
α_{2U}	0.1541	0.1863	0.0225	0.0234
σ_U	0.9333	0.8775	0.6408	0.6126
Threshold	−0.0580	−0.0580	0.3189	0.3189
Delay	2	2	2	2
N_L	34	35	30	39
N_U	115	138	95	108
AIC	0.0882	−0.0429	−0.4773	−0.5867

$_L$ and $_U$ refer to the "contractionary" and "expansionary" regimes.

finds only weak evidence for rejecting the linear model in favor of the Potter (1995) SETAR model of US GNP.

Table 10.2 records the p-values for the Hansen (1996b) supT_T, aveT_T and expT_T tests of the null of linearity, for the fifth-order Potter (1995) model, and the second-order models. The former appears to obtain more support from the data. Nonetheless, the evidence for the SETAR model is weak – on any test and for either sample period, the null of linearity is not rejected at the 5% level. The results for the fifth-order model and the earlier sample period are similar to those reported by Potter (1995), table IV, p.115. However, Potter (1995) (same table) also records Monte Carlo evidence indicating that the tests are too conservative, particularly the heteroscedasticity-robust versions, and that the powers at the nominal 5% level are low. Correcting for size, he finds evidence in favor of non-linearity at the 10% level. The supT_T and expT_T tests of the fifth-order model on the later sample have p-values only just over 10%, so a size correction here might suggest a similar outcome.

Table 10.2
Asymptotic p-values of linear null versus SETAR.

SETAR model	(2; 2, 2)	(2; 5, 5)	(2; 2, 2)	(2; 5, 5)
	1947–90		1959–96	
	Robust LM Statistics			
SupT_T	0.653	0.191	0.263	0.473
ExpT_T	0.529	0.182	0.556	0.305
AveT_T	0.477	0.265	0.698	0.208
	Standard LM Statistics			
SupT_T	0.094	0.054	0.860	0.125
ExpT_T	0.183	0.100	0.860	0.113
AveT_T	0.322	0.278	0.855	0.176

The results were obtained using Bruce Hansen's Gauss code `tar.prg`.

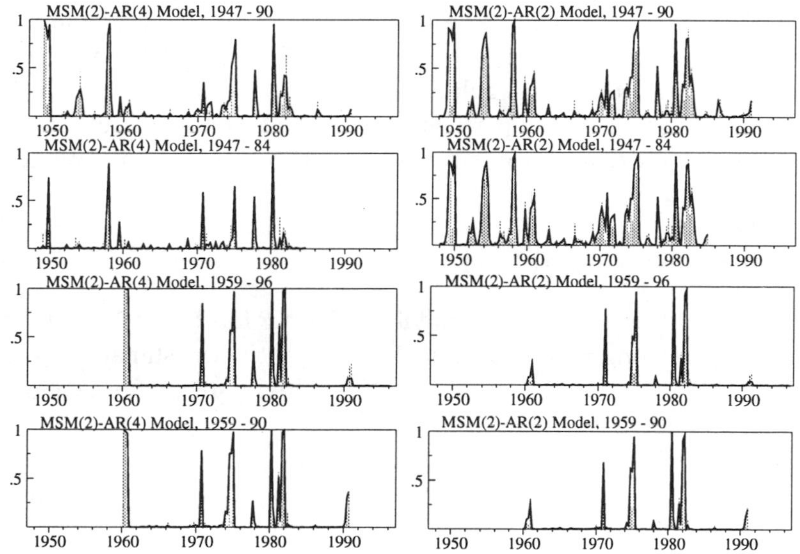

Figure 10.1
MSM(2)-AR smoothed and filtered probabilities of the lower regime, L.

10.3.2 MS-AR models of US GNP

10.3.2.1 Hamilton's MSM(2)-AR(4) Model

Figure 10.1 (left panels) presents the time paths of smoothed full-sample probabilities (line) and filtered probabilities (bars) for the contractionary regime (L) for the MSM(2)-AR(4) model, for the two data vintages we consider. The right panels are for second-order models, considered below, and are markedly similar. The reported probabilities are of being in a recession at time t.[4] Figure 10.1 along with table 10.3 suggests that the statistical characterization of the US business cycle afforded by the MSM(2)-AR(4) model is inadequate. The MSM(2)-AR(4) model estimated over both sample periods (1947–90 and 1959–96, and sub-samples thereof) does not exhibit business cycle features, in contrast to the findings of Hamilton (1989) for the 1953–84 period, because the average duration of regime L is only a little over unity for the sub-sample of the earlier data vintage, with a probability of staying in regime L (p_{LL}) of only 15%. Thus, for this period at least, the MSM(2)-AR(4) model often attributes single, isolated observations to regime L, and is more a "model of outliers" than a business-cycle model. For the other three sub-samples, the duration of regime L is never much longer than 2 periods. Boldin (1996) raises doubts about the contraction-expansion interpretation even on Hamilton's original sample period.

10.3.2.2 MSIH(3)-AR(4) Model

An adequate "business-cycle" model of US GNP for this period (in the sense of generating regime durations consonant with estimates based on the NBER chronology, for example) required a third regime and a regime-dependent error variance:

$$y_t = \mu(s_t) + \sum_{k=1}^{4} \alpha_k y_{t-k} + \epsilon_t, \tag{10.8}$$

[4]The filtered regime probabilities $\Pr(s_t = m|Y_t) = \Pr(s_t = m|y_t, y_{t-1}, \ldots, y_0)$ are based on information up to time t, while the smoothed probabilities $\Pr(s_t = m|Y_T) = \Pr(s_t = m|y_T, \ldots, y_{t+1}, y_t, y_{t-1}, \ldots, y_0)$ are calculated from full-sample information, employing observations known only after period t. Each constitutes optimal inference on the state of nature given the information set.

Table 10.3
MSM(2)-AR(4) Models.

Sample	47:2–84:4	47:2–90:4	59:2–90:4	59:2–96:2
Mean μ_L	−1.2297	−0.9919	−1.0268	−1.1467
Mean μ_H	0.9014	0.9607	0.8924	0.8369
α_1	0.3712	0.3210	0.3109	0.3541
α_2	0.2355	0.2629	0.1087	0.1372
α_3	−0.0958	−0.0458	−0.1063	−0.0846
α_4	−0.1930	−0.0975	0.0415	0.0176
σ^2	0.8198	0.7307	0.4143	0.3728
Trans.prob p_{LL}	0.1543	0.6163	0.4905	0.4359
Trans.prob p_{HH}	0.9569	0.9616	0.9537	0.9626
Uncond.prob.L	0.0485	0.0909	0.0832	0.0622
Uncond.prob.H	0.9515	0.9091	0.9168	0.9378
Duration L	1.18	2.61	1.96	1.77
Duration H	23.21	26.07	21.62	26.74
Observations	147	168	123	145
LogLikelihood	−210.31	−232.52	−142.76	−158.48

where $\epsilon_t \sim \mathsf{IN}[0, \sigma^2(s_t)]$ and $s_t \in \{1, 2, 3\}$ is generated by a Markov chain. The specification has a shifting intercept term (MSI*ntercept*, rather than MSM*ean-adjusted*) and in the following, will be denoted by MSIH(3)-AR(4) (where the H flags the heteroscedastic error term). The lag order is 4.

Figure 10.2 and table 10.4 summarize the business-cycle characteristics of this model. The figure depicts the filtered and smoothed probabilities of the "high growth" regime H and the contractionary regime L (the middle regime M probabilities are not shown). The expansion and contraction episodes produced by the three-regime model correspond fairly closely to the NBER classifications of business-cycle turning points. In contrast to the two-regime model, all three regimes are reasonably persistent.

10.3.3 *Testing for several regimes: the MS-AR model*

Results of formal tests of the MS-AR model against AR models have been at best mixed. Hansen (1992a, 1996a) is unable to reject an AR(4)

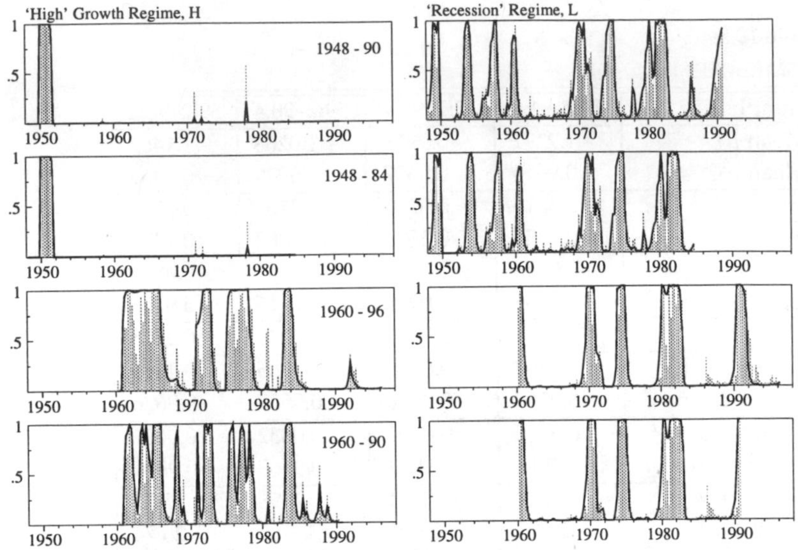

Figure 10.2
MSIH(3)-AR(4) model smoothed and filtered probabilities of the "extreme" regimes, H, L.

in favor of Hamilton's model (on the Hamilton data) using a standardized LR test designed to deliver (asymptotically) valid inference. Conventional testing approaches are not applicable due to the presence of unidentified nuisance parameters under the null of linearity (that is, the transition probabilities), and because the scores associated with parameters of interest under the alternative may be identically zero under the null. Since Hansen's approach delivers only a bound on the asymptotic distribution of the standardized LR test, the test may be conservative, tending to be under-sized in practice, and of low power.[5]

Table 10.5 reports the p-values of the standardized LR test of a linear AR model against the MS-AR model for our two sample sizes, and for second-order models as well as the more popular fourth-order model. The lower order model tended to be selected by AIC. For comparison, the first two rows of the table record the tests of the Hamilton model for 1952–84, for $p = 2$ as well as $p = 4$ (the latter approximately reproduces

[5]Hansen argues that this is not in fact the case, based on Monte Carlo calculations of the finite-sample size and power of the standardized LR test.

Table 10.4
MSIH(3)-AR(4) Models.

Sample	47:2–84:4	47:2–90:4	59:2–90:4	59:2–96:2
Mean μ_H	3.0677	2.9844	1.6230	1.4435
Mean μ_M	1.2833	1.1911	0.8171	0.8659
Mean μ_L	−0.0894	−-0.0251	−0.0953	−0.0625
α_1	0.0455	0.0680	−0.0467	0.0130
α_2	0.0762	0.0877	−0.0198	−0.0228
α_3	−0.1463	−0.1522	−-0.0955	−0.1283
α_4	−0.1627	−0.1456	−0.0153	−0.0559
σ^2_H	0.1149	0.1478	0.3245	0.4050
σ^2_M	0.5117	0.4683	0.1013	0.1175
σ^2_L	0.9429	0.9123	0.8055	0.7724
Trans.prob p_{HH}	0.8388	0.8164	0.7434	0.9096
Trans.prob p_{HM}	0.1612	0.1836	0.2566	0.0904
Trans.prob p_{HL}	0.0000	0.0000	0.0000	0.0000
Trans.prob p_{MH}	0.0000	0.0000	0.1320	0.0000
Trans.prob p_{MM}	0.8955	0.8981	0.7754	0.9245
Trans.prob p_{ML}	0.1045	0.1019	0.0926	0.0755
Trans.prob p_{LH}	0.0255	0.0261	0.1472	0.1305
Trans.prob p_{LM}	0.1937	0.1800	0.0000	0.0216
Trans.prob p_{LL}	0.7808	0.7938	0.8528	0.8479
Uncond.prob.H	0.0486	0.0450	0.3495	0.3240
Uncond.prob.M	0.6442	0.6392	0.3993	0.4517
Uncond.prob.L	0.3072	0.3158	0.2512	0.2243
Duration H	6.2041	5.4477	3.8968	11.0656
Duration M	9.5659	9.8162	4.4524	13.2391
Duration L	4.5612	4.8502	6.7918	6.5751
Observations	147	171	123	145
LogLikelihood	−201.06	−226.10	−132.38	−145.65

part of Hansen, 1996a, table III, p.196). In no case do we reject the null of one state at even the 20% level.

The evidence for non-linearities in US GNP from the formal testing procedures reviewed here, and in §10.3.1.1 for the SETAR model, is mixed. Nonetheless, since the Hansen bounds test is likely to be conservative, an over-reliance on formal testing procedures appears unwarranted. We wish to see whether the success of the non-linear models

Table 10.5
Standardized LR statistic p-values for MS-AR model.

	Lags	LR test	M					
			0	1	2	3	4	5
1952–84	4	1.546	0.713	0.713	0.622	0.658	0.650	0.652
1952–84	2	2.305	0.311	0.311	0.295	0.295	0.259	0.243
1947–90	4	1.255	0.856	0.817	0.803	0.795	0.768	0.745
1947–90	2	2.153	0.368	0.362	0.352	0.337	0.336	0.327
1959–96	4	2.410	0.254	0.237	0.264	0.260	0.244	0.246
1959–96	2	2.152	0.364	0.386	0.370	0.388	0.371	0.375

See Hansen (1996a) for details of the test statistic, such as the definition of M. The results were obtained using Bruce Hansen's Gauss code `markovm.prg` with the "Grid 3" option of Hansen (1996a).

in characterizing important aspects of the business cycle translates in to an improved forecast performance, and the following section reports on a systematic appraisal of their forecast performance.

10.4 A Monte Carlo Study

The Monte Carlo study allows an evaluation of the costs (in terms of forecast performance, as measured by RMSE) to using the "wrong" non-linear model (or a linear model as an approximation to a non-linear model) when we abstract from the vagaries of the models only poorly representing the DGP, or of the non-linearities present in the past not persisting in the future. By simulating the future to mimic the past, the "non-linear features" occur in the forecast period, even if the non-linear structure captured in the empirical model was primarily due to "outliers" and unhelpful for improving empirical forecasts.

Since the DGP is taken in turn to be each of the non-linear empirical models estimated over the full-sample of the earlier data vintage (1947–90), any general conclusions are tempered by the possible specificity of the results to the particular design. While fully exploring the parameter space that might be of interest would require a very extensive set of simulations, with computational requirements that might be prohibitive given some of the necessary calculations (such as estimating the MS-AR, and forecasting the SETAR model), a few interesting

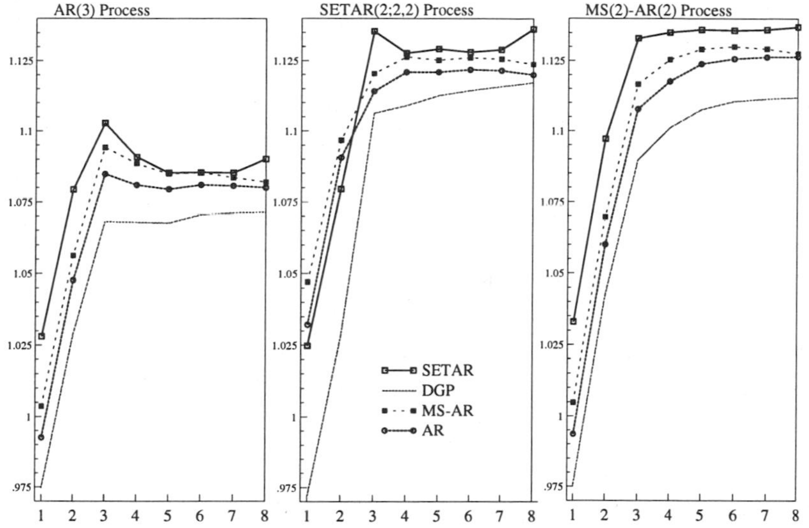

Figure 10.3
Monte Carlo comparison of the models on RMSE.

departures from the estimated non-linear models are explored, and the Monte Carlo results are in line with the analytical results in §10.5. It seems preferable to use empirical models as the DGP, rather than an artificial DGP whose relevance for actual economic data may be questionable.

Results are presented for three DGPs: AR(3), SETAR(2; 2, 2), and MSM(2)-AR(2). The last yielded similar results to the MSM(2)-AR(4) of Hamilton, and was chosen by AIC for the sample period in question. While the MSI(3)-AR(2) was more appealing from a business-cycle viewpoint, it was no better than the simpler two-regime models in empirical forecast-accuracy comparisons, and computationally more demanding for a Monte Carlo study. The MS-AR and SETAR forecasting models are restricted to be two-regime models, but are otherwise unrestricted, so that p (and d, r for the SETAR) are chosen on each iteration of the Monte Carlo to minimize AIC. The SETAR forecasts are calculated by Monte Carlo using 500 iterations.

The results are summarized in fig.10.3. Consider first the AR DGP. There appears to be little additional cost in terms of forecast accuracy to using one of the non-linear models, while the height of the circled line above the solid line reflects AR model specification and estimation uncertainty. Next, consider the SETAR DGP. The SETAR model is only better than the AR model at 1- and 2-step horizons on RMSE . The maximum cost to using the wrong non-linear model (the MS-AR model) occurs at these horizons, and is less than 2%. Thereafter, the AR outperforms both non-linear models. Surprisingly, when the MS-AR is the DGP, the AR is best at short horizons on RMSE. The cost to using the SETAR is generally greater than when the roles are reversed.

Thus, the failure to improve on the forecast performance of linear models is the finding that warrants further investigation, and we take this up in §10.5, where we isolate the factors which determine the performance of the MS-AR model.

10.5 Analysis of the MS-AR Model Forecast Performance

The Monte Carlo results employing empirical business-cycle models for the DGP have shown that linear models are relatively robust forecasting devices even when the DGP is non-linear. In this section, some theoretical explanations for this surprising outcome are advanced, and the Monte Carlo is modified to illustrate. The focus is on the MS-AR model, since it allows an explicit analytical expression for the optimal predictor.

For the sake of simplicity, consider an MSM(2)-AR(1):

$$\Delta y_t - \mu(s_t) = \alpha\left(\Delta y_{t-1} - \mu(s_{t-1})\right) + \epsilon_t, \qquad (10.9)$$

which can be rewritten as the sum of two independent processes:

$$\Delta y_t - \mu_y = \mu_t + z_t,$$

where μ_y is the unconditional mean of Δy_t, such that $\mathsf{E}[\mu_t] = \mathsf{E}[z_t] = 0$. While the process z_t is Gaussian:

$$z_t = \alpha z_{t-1} + \epsilon_t, \quad \epsilon_t \sim \mathsf{IN}\left[0, \sigma_\epsilon^2\right],$$

the other component, μ_t, represents the contribution of the Markov chain:

$$\mu_t = (\mu_2 - \mu_1)\zeta_t,$$

where $\zeta_t = 1 - \Pr(s_t = 2)$ if $s_t = 2$ and $-\Pr(s_t = 2)$ otherwise. $\Pr(s_t = 2) = \mathsf{p}_{12}/(\mathsf{p}_{12} + \mathsf{p}_{21})$ is the unconditional probability of regime 2. Invoking the unrestricted VAR(1) representation of a Markov chain (see Krolzig, 1997, p.40):

$$\zeta_t = (\mathsf{p}_{11} + \mathsf{p}_{22} - 1)\zeta_{t-1} + v_t,$$

then predictions of the hidden Markov chain are given by:

$$\widehat{\zeta}_{T+h|T} = (\mathsf{p}_{11} + \mathsf{p}_{22} - 1)^h \widehat{\zeta}_{T|T}$$

where $\widehat{\zeta}_{T|T} = \mathsf{E}[\zeta_T|Y_T] = \Pr(s_T = 2|Y_T) - \Pr(s_T = 2)$ is the filtered probability $\Pr(s_T = 2|Y_T)$ of being in regime 2 corrected for the unconditional probability. Thus, the conditional mean of Δy_{T+h} is given by $\widehat{\Delta y}_{T+h|T} - \mu_y$ which equals:

$$\begin{aligned} &\widehat{\mu}_{T+h|T} + \widehat{z}_{T+hT} \\ &= (\mu_2 - \mu_1)(\mathsf{p}_{11} + \mathsf{p}_{22} - 1)^h \widehat{\zeta}_{T|T} + \alpha^h \left[\Delta y_T - \mu_y - (\mu_2 - \mu_1)\widehat{\zeta}_{T|T}\right] \\ &= \alpha^h (\Delta y_T - \mu_y) + (\mu_2 - \mu_1)\left[(\mathsf{p}_{11} + \mathsf{p}_{22} - 1)^h - \alpha^h\right] \widehat{\zeta}_{T|T}. \qquad (10.10) \end{aligned}$$

The first term in (10.10) is the optimal prediction rule for a linear model, and the contribution of the Markov regime-switching structure is given by the term multiplied by $\widehat{\zeta}_{T|T}$, where $\widehat{\zeta}_{T|T}$ contains the information about the most recent regime at the time the forecast is made. Thus, the contribution of the non-linear part of (10.10) to the overall forecast depends on both the magnitude of the regime shifts, $|\mu_2 - \mu_1|$, and on the persistence of regime shifts $\mathsf{p}_{11} + \mathsf{p}_{22} - 1$ relative to the persistence of the Gaussian process, given by α.

In the empirical DGP, $\mathsf{p}_{11} + \mathsf{p}_{22} - 1 = 0.65$, and the largest root of the AR polynomial is 0.64, so that the second reason explains the success of the linear AR model in forecasting the MS-AR process. Since the predictive power of detected regime shifts is extremely small, $\mathsf{p}_{11} + \mathsf{p}_{22} - 1 \simeq \alpha$ in (10.10), the conditional expectation collapses to a linear prediction rule.

In figs. 10.4 and 10.5 the potential for outperforming linear forecasts is explored by simulating variants of the empirical MS-AR process, where the directions of change are motivated by the discussion surrounding (10.10). Figure 10.4 records the results for an increased persistence of recessions (p_{LL}). The left graph replicates the RMSEs for

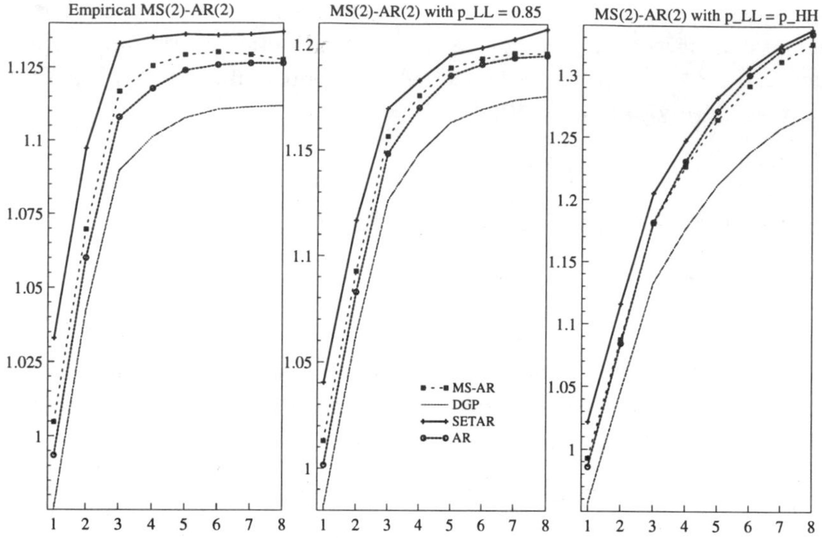

Figure 10.4
Post-simulation analysis I. RMSE when the DGP is an MS(2)-AR(2).

the empirical MS-AR process, for ease of comparison, and the middle and right graphs report results for increasing values of p_{LL}. Figure 10.5 depicts a 50% increase in the difference of the regime-dependent means $\mu_H - \mu_L$ (middle graph), and the right graph couples this with a higher persistence of recessions ($p_{LL} = p_{HH} = 0.9568$). Compared to the results for the empirical DGP given in the left graphs, we see improvements in the relative forecasting performance of MS-AR model (the effects are more dramatic if the lag length is constrained to 2 as in the DGP). The performance of the SETAR improves relative to the linear AR model, but is still dominated by it at all horizons.

10.6 Conclusion

The forecast performance of two popular non-linear extensions of the Box and Jenkins (1976) time-series modeling tradition, applied to modeling the growth rate of US GNP, has been analyzed. By allowing for changes in regime in the process generating the time series, the models are proposed as contenders to the constant-parameter, linear time

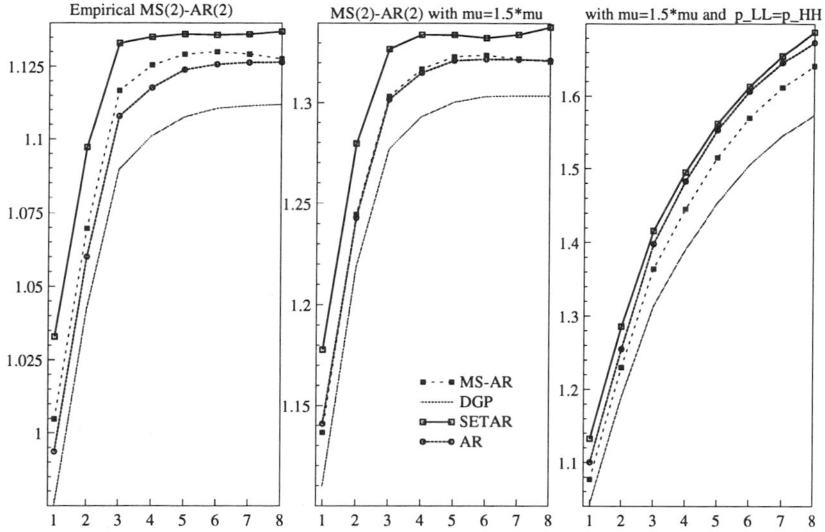

Figure 10.5
Post-simulation analysis II. RMSE when the DGP is an MS(2)-AR(2).

series models of the earlier tradition, and as a way of modeling structural change. The SETAR and MS-AR models differ as to how they model the movement between regimes, and thus the changes in the parameter values of the difference equations that govern the series. The SETAR model moves between regimes depending on the past realizations of the process. For the MS-AR model, the movements between regimes are unrelated to the past realizations of the process, and result from the unfolding of an unobserved stochastic process, modeled as a Markov chain.

While both the MS-AR and SETAR models are superior to linear models in capturing certain features of the business cycle, their superiority from a forecasting perspective is less convincing. In an empirical forecast-accuracy comparison (not reported), Clements and Krolzig (1998) find that allowing for non-linearity appears to be beneficial for forecasting US GNP over one sample period, but not on another, highlighting the sensitivity of the outcome to the extent to which the future is characterized by "non-linear features". Stock and Watson (1998) undertake an empirical comparison of smooth-transition AR models, neural nets, and linear AR models for 215 US macro time series and arrive at a broadly similar conclusion, namely, that the non-linear models are not clearly better. Specifically, the non-linear models sometimes record small gains at short horizons, but at longer horizons the linear models are preferred.

Rather than carrying out extensive empirical forecast accuracy comparisons of linear and non-linear models, we report the Clements and Krolzig (1998) simulation-based comparison approach which controls for some of the factors that might detract from the performance of the non-linear models, and present their analysis which explores characteristics of the models that contribute to a more favorable forecast performance. Nevertheless, the linear AR model is a relatively robust forecasting device, even when the data are generated by a non-linear model.

Clements and Smith (1999) investigate the multi-period forecast performance of some empirical SETAR models, again by Monte Carlo, but using both quantitative and qualitative measures of forecast accuracy, and focusing on the importance of the regime at the time the forecast was made. They find that the ability to exploit non-linearities for forecasting may turn on whether forecasts are evaluated conditional upon the regime, reflecting the ability of non-linear models to forecast well in certain states of nature, but not always sufficiently well to score better than linear models on average (across all states of nature). Moreover, non-linear models appear to be favored by qualitative measures of forecast performance.

Finally, Clements and Smith (1998a) compare the forecast performance of linear and non-linear, univariate and systems, models of the change in the US unemployment rate, and the US GNP growth rate, using quarterly data over the period 1948–94. On an MSFE evaluation of conditional mean predictions, the non-linear models yield no improvement over the linear models. However, using the forecast density evaluation methods of Diebold, Gunther and Tay (1998), the non-linear multivariate model does appear to provide a better characterization of the density of future realizations of the variables over this period than does the VAR. They find that an evaluation of the joint and conditional densities of the multivariate models appears to have greater discriminatory power than a consideration of the marginal forecast densities of the two variables in isolation. Their results suggest a narrow focus on MSFE criteria may be misleading, and evaluation techniques which consider the entire forecast density may discriminate between models which would otherwise appear very similar. Such an avenue of investigation may be particularly fruitful when comparing forecasts from linear and non-linear models.

11 A Wage-Price Model

Summary

We now investigate a second multivariate empirical illustration of techniques to counter the non-constancies responsible for serious predictive failures in VEqCMs. The approaches considered include differencing, intercept corrections, updating, and univariate models. In the first multivariate illustration in chapter 8 of a small UK money-demand model, we contrasted VEqCM, DV and DDV model forecasts, and brought out the dependence of forecast accuracy comparisons on, *inter alia*, the forecast horizon. The focus now is on updating relative to intercept-correcting strategies, as discussed in chapter 5.

11.1 Introduction

Our second multivariate illustration is the three-variable system of wages, prices and unemployment in Mizon (1995). Whilst simpler than might be countenanced by some applied macro-modelers, his model allows many rolling sequences of multi-step forecasts for a variety of forecasting techniques. This sustains a "statistical analysis" of intercept corrections and other strategies, rather than relying on comparing a small number of forecasts, as in many previous studies (e.g., Turner, 1990).

The plan of the chapter is as follows. In §11.2, we briefly describe the UK wage-price model that will form the basis for the comparison of forecasting methods. Just as limited-information methods may be better than full-information methods in model estimation when the axiom of correct specification is violated, so in forecasting, univariate models may then yield superior forecasts to multivariate models or systems of equations. This issue is briefly discussed in §11.3. Section 11.4 considers direction-of-change measures of forecast accuracy, as a prelude to their use in the empirical analysis. Sections 11.5 and 11.6 record the results of the quantitative and qualitative evaluation of the VEqCM, DV, and intercept-corrected VEqCM, to assess the efficacy of intercept-correcting versus updating the parameter estimates in the empirical example where many changes may have been occurring over the forecast period as labor-market reform gathered pace. We also assess the forecast performances of VARs in levels (LV) and scalar AR models as alternatives to the VEqCM. Then, in §11.7, we address the question of how much better the time-series model (the DV) does intercept correcting the VEqCM, compared to the usual (VEqCM) residual-based corrections, and the extent to which ICs remain useful when the VEqCM is continually updated. We also provide a more detailed breakdown of the trace MSFEs into bias and variance components, for both types of correction, since the formulae in §6.3 predict what we should find. Finally, §11.8 concludes.

11.2 Modeling Wages, Prices, and Unemployment

Mizon (1995) estimated a simultaneous model of the determination of wages, prices, and unemployment over the period 1965:1 to 1993:1. More precisely, the inter-relationships between e_t, the natural logarithm of earnings per person-hour (loosely referred to as "wages"), the log of the retail price index, r_t, and the log of the unemployment rate u_t, were modeled. The logs of all the variables were multiplied by 100 to aid interpretation. Precise definitions and sources are given in Mizon (1995). A single cointegrating vector was found that entered only the wage and price equations (see his table 10). If the full-sample estimates of the cointegrating vector are retained, with the model otherwise being estimated up to 1979:2, and used to forecast (the 55 observations) 1979:3–1993:1, the model's 1-step ahead forecast performance is satisfactory, as is that of a DV estimated, and used to forecast, over the same period. However, if the cointegrating vector is also determined from the sub-sample estimation period (as would necessarily be the case in *ex ante* forecasting), the model fails to provide reliable forecasts.

Clements and Hendry (1996b) show that this finding is not peculiar to the model specification found on the full-sample. A "general-to-simple" model selection strategy applied to the sub-sample led to a model which differed somewhat from the full-sample specification, but nevertheless possessed the feature that the equilibrium-correction terms caused the 1-step forecasts to go awry.[1] Thus, models that incorporated long-run information, estimated on the period up to 1979:4, forecast less well than models that eschewed the long-run constraints on the levels of the variables implied by cointegration. A possible reason is that the equilibrium-correction terms were non-constant over the 1980s, and their inclusion tended to drag the model forecasts off course. Various residual-based intercept-correcting strategies (as discussed in §6.3) were shown to improve the overall MSFEs due to a reduction in forecast bias, notwithstanding the inflation of the forecast-error variance components.

11.3 Univariate versus Multivariate Methods

Forecasts from single-equation models with explanatory variables, such as autoregressive-distributed (ADL) lag models, invariably require that either the future values of the explanatory variables are known, or that the explanatory variables themselves are modeled. We rule out the first possibility for non-deterministic time series. Once the second is adopted, then given the interdependent nature of many economic time series, we cannot preclude models for the explanatory variables depending on lagged values of the models' regressands. This route leads back to the vector autoregression framework of Sims (1980). Otherwise, imposing strong exogeneity invalidly may distort multi-step forecasts, as well as model evaluation (see Chong and Hendry, 1986). Howsoever the single-equation model is completed for forecasting purposes, it is apparent that the quality of forecasts of the variable of interest will depend on how well we can forecast the "explanatory"

[1] We use the sub-sample 1965:1–1979:4 rather than 1965:1–1979:2, which makes little difference to the results.

variables, and on the constancy of the relationship between the variable of interest and these variables. If either link is suspect, then univariate models that obviate the need to model and forecast other variables may yield superior forecasts.

An implicit example of this phenomenon was presented in chapter 7, where univariate models of UK aggregate real consumers' expenditure on non-durables and services exhibited less forecast failure than the DHSY model, even when its regressors were treated as known. Since real personal disposable income is approximately as hard to forecast as consumers' expenditure, univariate models are not easily beaten in that context despite their more restrictive information sets.

11.4 Direction-of-change Measures of Forecast Accuracy

Since most forecasts are quantitative in nature, it is not surprising that measures based on the distance between the forecast and realization (i.e., the magnitude of the forecast error) have dominated the forecast-evaluation literature. However, we can also evaluate models in terms of how well they forecast the direction of change in a variable. Examples include predicting rates of return on market investments by Henriksson and Merton (1981), and in macroeconomic forecasting, the papers by Schnader and Stekler (1990) and Stekler (1994), as well as Pesaran and Timmermann (1992). The former show that the test of market timing is asymptotically equivalent to the standard χ^2 test of independence in the standard 2×2 contingency table (see below), and while exact analogues are available (in the references just given: also see Granger and Swanson, 1996, for a detailed empirical study reporting such measures) our implementation of direction-of-change tests will use this idea.

Evaluating a model in terms of how well it forecasts the direction of change of a variable would appear to be particularly relevant for business-cycle models of output growth, such as the Hamilton (1989) MS-AR model, or for regime-switching models more generally (see ch. 10). An obvious limitation to the use of such an evaluation criterion is that a forecast of a very small increase when a small decline occurred, will be counted one-for-one with a forecast of a large increase when a large decline occurred. However, as noted by Schnader and Stekler (1990) and Stekler (1994), we could evaluate forecasts of the direction of change in terms of high ($> 2\%$) versus low ($\leq 2\%$) growth, although in the limit, such decompositions return us to quantitative measures.

The confusion-rate (CR) measure of qualitative accuracy is based on the number of times the forecasts correctly predict the direction of change. For example, a confusion matrix might be:

$$\begin{array}{lll} & & \text{outcome} \\ & & \begin{array}{cc}\text{up} & \text{down}\end{array} \\ \text{forecast} & \begin{array}{c}\text{up}\\ \text{down}\end{array} & \left[\begin{array}{cc} n_{uu} & n_{ud} \\ n_{du} & n_{dd} \end{array}\right] \end{array}$$

when n_{ud} is the number of time $\widehat{y} > 0$ and $y < 0$, where $\widehat{y}$ denotes a forecasts (for a given step ahead), and y the outcome (both expressed as rates of change). Thus, the diagonal cells correspond to correct directional forecasts. The confusion rate is:

$$\text{CR} = \frac{n_{ud} + n_{du}}{n} \quad \text{where } n = \sum\nolimits_{i,j \in u,d} n_{ij}.$$

A model with a lower CR is "less confused". A χ^2 test of independence between the actual and predicted directions is calculated as:

$$\sum_{i=1}^{4} \frac{\left(f_{o,i} - f_{e,i}\right)^2}{f_{e,i}}$$

where $f_{o,i}$ is the observed number in cell i, and $f_{e,i}$ is the expected number. For example, for the cell $i = 1$ (actual = up and predicted = up), the probability of actual up is $\left(n_{uu} + n_{du}\right)/n$. The probability of forecast up is $\left(n_{uu} + n_{ud}\right)/n$. Under the null of independence, the product of these probabilities times n is $f_{e,i}$. We present the p-values of the null that the model is not useful as a predictor of the sign of change.

It is also possible to derive tests for equal forecast accuracy of rival forecasts based on the quantitative evaluation of forecast accuracy. Diebold and Mariano (1995) present a test of equal forecast accuracy that allows an arbitrary loss function (rather than just squared-error loss), and Harvey, Leybourne and Newbold (1997) propose a modification with better size properties.

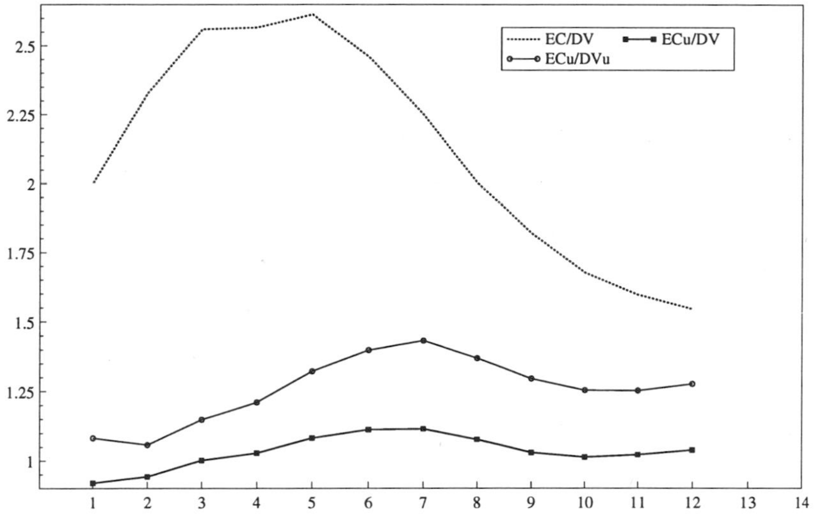

Figure 11.1
Effects of updating VEqCM and DV models on TMSFEs of e, r.

11.5 Quantitative Evaluation of System Forecasts

The line denoted EC_DV in fig. 11.1 is the ratio of the trace MSFE (TMSFE) for the VEqCM (EC) to the DV for 1 to 12-steps ahead (along the x-axis).[2] The precise way in which the TMSFEs are calculated is as follows. The models are estimated only once on data up to 1979:4. Then, 1979:4 is taken as the first forecast origin from which we calculate forecasts for 1 through to 12 steps ahead. The exercise is repeated with 1980:1 as the forecast origin, and so on, subject to the constraint that we have data on the period being forecast (the sample ends in 1993:1). This gives fifty-three 1-step forecasts, where the last forecast is made in 1992:4 for 1993:1, fifty-two 2 step forecasts (a forecast made in 1979:4 for 1980:2 through to a forecast made in 1992:3 for 1993:1), and so on to forty-two 12 steps. From the forecasts and actual values, the forecast errors are calculated. The TMSFE for horizon h is the sum of the squared h-step forecast errors for e (divided by the number of forecasts), plus

[2]The TMSFEs are of e and r only, given that the MSFE of u is large relative to that of e and r (notwithstanding that all variables are in logs) and may dominate the comparisons.

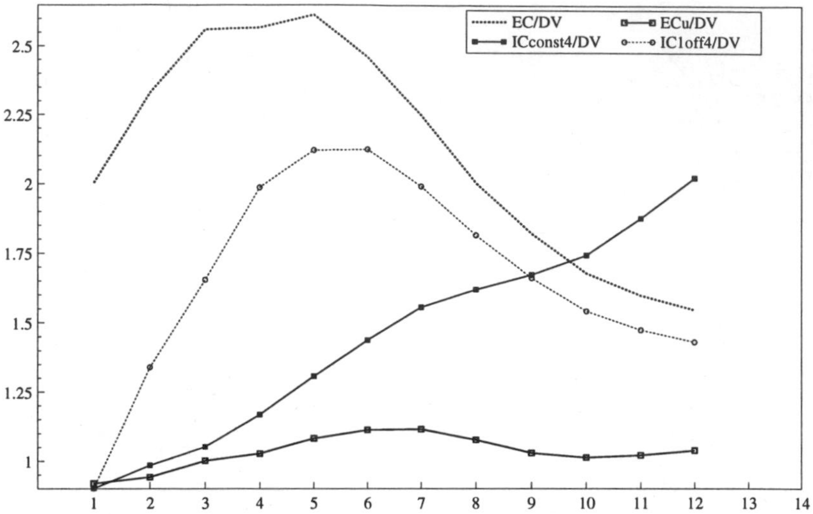

Figure 11.2
Effects of updating versus intercept correcting on TMSFE of e, r.

the same quantity for r. Thus, fig. 11.1 indicates that for the VEqCM, TMSFE is approximately double that of the DV at 1-step ahead, and higher still for longer horizons, before declining. These results are consistent with the theoretical calculations in chapters 3 and 5, particularly table 5.1 (showing larger VEqCM than DV forecast-error biases when forecasting after breaks) and tables 5.2 and 5.3 (showing relatively larger DV forecast-error variances as the horizon grows). Again, this evidence is consistent with a deterministic shift explaining forecast failure.

We also calculate the TMSFEs when both models are updated at each point as we move the forecast origin through the sample. ECu_DV is the ratio of VEqCM TMSFEs to those of the DV when only the former is updated, whereas ECu_DVu results when both models are continually updated. Here, updating the VEqCM results in a dramatic improvement in relative accuracy (compare ECu_DV and EC_DV), while updating DV (DVu) restores some of its advantage, but still leaves the VEqCM relatively much better placed.

Figure 11.2 allows the gains to updating VEqCM to be compared with those from intercept correcting. ICconst4-DV is the ratio to the

DV model of intercept-correcting the VEqCM model with a constant adjustment throughout the period based on an average of the latest four equation errors at the forecast origin. IC1off4_DV is the ratio to the DV model of intercept-correcting the VEqCM model with a one-off adjustment (so that the adjustment is used in calculating the 1-step ahead forecast, but not subsequent step ahead forecasts) based on an average of the latest 4 equation errors at the forecast origin. The constant adjustment yields dramatic improvements at short horizons, but rapidly deteriorates, and is less useful than updating in this example. The constant-adjustment IC performs better than the 1-off till about 8-steps ahead, then is worse than no adjustment.

11.6 Qualitative Evaluation of System Forecasts

Table 11.1 shows the confusion rates for the three models VEqCM, DV and LV, for the VEqCM updated (EC_u), and for the VEqCM with intercept corrections. Since Δe and Δr (first or fourth differences) are positive for most observations, it makes more sense to look at how well the models predict the second difference of these variables. The elements of the confusion matrix (see §11.4) relate to whether the actual and forecast values of $\Delta_1\Delta_4 x$ are positive or not (for $x = e, r$). Thus, the confusion rate for updating the VEqCM model (EC_u) for r is lower than for differencing (DV) and for intercept-correcting. In terms of confusion rates, the VEqCM model is similar to the DV for short horizons, except perhaps for forecasting e.

Table 11.2 records the results of a standard χ^2 test of whether the models are useful as a predictor of the sign of $\Delta_1\Delta_4$ for e and r. p-values less than 0.05% are evidence against the null of "no value"' at the 5% level. Generally, the models appear to have predictive ability for horizons up to 4 steps ahead.

11.6.1 Scalar model forecasts

The MSFEs for Δe and Δr for the AR models relative to the MSFEs from the VAR in differences are shown in table 11.3, allowing a comparison of the multivariate and univariate models in terms of forecast performance.

Table 11.1
Confusion rates for systems forecasts.

	EC	DV	LV	EC_u	ICconst4	IC1off4
				e		
1	0.36	0.28	0.49	0.28	0.23	0.23
2	0.33	0.27	0.46	0.27	0.23	0.35
3	0.39	0.27	0.47	0.29	0.27	0.33
4	0.36	0.28	0.46	0.30	0.22	0.38
5	0.37	0.37	0.35	0.39	0.41	0.47
6	0.42	0.44	0.38	0.40	0.46	0.42
7	0.49	0.49	0.43	0.49	0.51	0.36
8	0.50	0.57	0.37	0.54	0.48	0.48
9	0.53	0.60	0.36	0.58	0.56	0.56
10	0.55	0.59	0.61	0.66	0.61	0.57
11	0.53	0.44	0.63	0.60	0.63	0.51
12	0.52	0.50	0.60	0.60	0.52	0.55
				r		
1	0.28	0.26	0.38	0.17	0.32	0.32
2	0.33	0.33	0.46	0.17	0.37	0.27
3	0.29	0.31	0.51	0.20	0.35	0.27
4	0.32	0.28	0.54	0.24	0.36	0.32
5	0.45	0.45	0.55	0.37	0.47	0.45
6	0.50	0.44	0.44	0.44	0.56	0.52
7	0.53	0.43	0.36	0.38	0.55	0.51
8	0.52	0.41	0.41	0.43	0.54	0.52
9	0.51	0.33	0.40	0.49	0.51	0.51
10	0.50	0.32	0.43	0.48	0.50	0.50
11	0.49	0.33	0.42	0.51	0.58	0.49
12	0.50	0.43	0.43	0.52	0.64	0.45

Except for forecasting Δe at 1-step ahead, the multivariate model clearly dominates, whether the AR model parameters are fixed, updated each period, or whether the AR order is picked optimally (minimizing AIC) each period. Such results do not support general claims about the value of parsimony *per se*.

Table 11.2
p-values for tests of independence of predictions.

	EC	DV	LV	EC_u	ICconst4	IC1off4
				e		
1	0.05	0.00	-	0.00	0.00	0.00
2	0.01	0.00	-	0.00	0.00	0.03
3	-	0.00	-	0.00	0.00	0.01
4	-	0.00	-	0.00	0.00	-
5	0.10	0.08	0.03	0.11	0.22	-
6	0.38	0.53	0.08	0.16	0.76	0.38
7	0.84	0.89	-	0.85	0.93	0.10
8	0.76	0.55	0.11	0.76	1.00	1.00
9	0.92	0.30	0.09	-	-	0.67
10	0.85	0.38	-	-	-	0.60
11	0.92	0.57	-	-	-	0.83
12	1.00	0.73	-	-	-	0.73
				r		
1	0.01	0.00	-	0.00	0.04	0.04
2	0.02	0.01	-	0.00	0.19	0.00
3	0.01	0.00	-	0.00	0.17	0.00
4	0.01	0.00	-	0.00	0.19	0.02
5	-	0.23	-	0.05	0.79	0.45
6	0.92	0.27	-	0.46	0.27	0.96
7	0.85	0.23	0.03	0.12	0.61	0.94
8	0.78	0.20	-	0.36	0.89	0.78
9	0.92	0.03	0.12	0.70	0.99	0.92
10	0.99	0.02	0.31	-	-	0.99
11	0.93	0.05	0.32	-	-	0.93
12	0.96	0.61	-	-	-	0.58

Blank cells indicate that at least one of the expected values f_{ei} was less than five, implying the test may be misleading. The p-values were calculated with Yates' correction.

11.7 Time-series Intercept Corrections

Table 11.4 contrasts the performance of the time-series and residual-based corrections, and details the effects on biases and variances. With

Table 11.3
Ratio of MSFEs for a univariate AR to a DV.

h	AR(2)	AR(2)u	Changing Spec.
		e	
1	0.92	0.86	0.87
2	1.14	1.10	1.10
3	1.39	1.28	1.29
4	1.65	1.51	1.53
5	1.78	1.54	1.55
6	1.78	1.51	1.53
7	1.88	1.53	1.56
8	1.88	1.53	1.55
9	1.91	1.53	1.54
10	1.97	1.58	1.59
11	2.01	1.62	1.63
12	2.03	1.66	1.66
		r	
1	1.92	1.90	2.00
2	2.36	2.14	2.45
3	2.13	1.84	1.88
4	1.89	1.54	1.64
5	2.88	2.55	2.64
6	2.87	2.34	2.49
7	2.90	2.25	2.33
8	2.58	2.01	2.13
9	2.83	2.49	2.58
10	2.74	2.35	2.43
11	2.88	2.34	2.40
12	2.80	2.23	2.30

Each column is the MSFE of a scalar AR model in the difference of the variable to that of the DV model. AR(2) denotes a second-order scalar autoregression, AR(2)u the same model with updating, and "Changing Spec." indicates that the lag order is chosen optimally by AIC each period.

no updating (left-hand side of the table), the approximate doubling of the TMSFE of the VEqCM relative to that of the DV noted earlier is primarily due to greater biases of the VEqCM forecasts of e (nearly

1%-point at 1-step ahead, compared to around 1/3% for the DV), and larger forecast standard errors for both variables. Consider now the constant-adjustment residual-based ICs, also depicted graphically in fig. 11.1.[3] Corrections based on the latest error (const[1]) generally dramatically reduce the biases in forecasting e and r, but at the cost of inflated forecast-error variances, which increase in the horizon. Thus, by 4-steps ahead, the intercept-corrected forecasts are no better than the VEqCM on TMSFE. Averaging four residuals to form the constant-adjustment IC (const[4]) is generally less successful in reducing biases, but has a smaller inflationary effect on the variances. One-off adjustments or tailed adjustments (not shown) only reduce biases for short horizons, with a minimal impact on the variance component.

In summary, as seen earlier, residual-based ICs can improve the performance of the VEqCM at short to medium horizons (i.e., up to two years ahead) but the DV remains dominant on TMSFE.

Re-estimating the models for each origin, but with a fixed specification or form, (the right-hand side of the table) clearly benefits the VEqCM more than the DV, but the DV is still preferred at all horizons on TMSFE, and its comparative advantage increases in the horizon.[4] Generally, updating results in larger percentage reductions in the VEqCM forecast-error biases than the variances.

The two time-series corrections we consider are denoted by $\mathrm{TS}_p[l]$ and $\mathrm{TS}_a[l]$, and we focus on the "updating" results. Both "corrections" are applied on a discretionary basis, in that they are only implemented if the absolute value of the average of the last l VEqCM errors up to that origin exceeds that of the DV. The $\mathrm{TS}_p[l]$ strategy is the correction outlined in §6.4, and uses a correction based on the last l forecasts, whilst the $\mathrm{TS}_a[l]$ strategy chooses either the VEqCM or DV to generate forecasts for all horizons for a given origin, based on a comparison of the last l VEqCM and DV forecasts. The results are unambiguous – $\mathrm{TS}_p[4]$ is the dominant strategy on TMSFE . "Time-series intercept-correcting" the VEqCM, and so exploiting both models (the TS_p strategy), is better than simply choosing between the VEqCM and DV at each origin, based on past performance (the TS_a strategy). The $\mathrm{TS}_p[4]$ strategy is

[3]These adjustments are made to the e and r equations only.

[4]Granger and Swanson (1996) assess the benefits of re-specifying the model as the origin is moved through the sample.

generally less successful at bias reduction than VEqCM residual-based adjustment, such as const[4], but wins on TMSFE by controlling the variance explosion.

11.8 Conclusion

Well-constructed (in-sample) models may yield inferior forecasts relative to models which omit long-run relations, or compared to models subjected to various corrections. The empirical findings generally bear out our expectations based on the analytical results, notwithstanding that the latter were derived for highly stylized DGPs and models that of necessity abstract from many factors that may be important in practice. For example, there may be a number of breaks of differing degrees of severity, which are gradual rather than abrupt, all of the relevant parameters may alter at the same time, the VEqCM may not be correctly specified "pre break", and in reality is likely to be mis-specified in unknown ways pre and post break, with changing correlations between included and omitted variables. The simplifying assumption that expectations taken around the time of the forecast origin will take on their "post-break stationary values" will at best hold only loosely in the presence of multiple breaks.

To summarize: vector autoregressions in the differences of the variables (which eschew long-run information) forecast well compared to VEqCMs in the face of apparent structural change. While updating the estimates of the model parameters, as the forecast origin moves through the sample, brings a greater relative improvement to the VEqCM forecasts, the DV remains dominant on MSFE . Residual-based intercept corrections of the VEqCM resulted in significant reductions in forecast bias, but came with a variance cost. Time-series corrections were less successful at reducing bias, but had a smaller variance cost and fared better on MSFE.

Table 11.4
Effect of ICs on means and SDs of forecast errors.

	No updating					Updating				
	Mean		Std. dev.		TMSFE	Mean		Std. dev.		TMSFE
Model	e	r	e	r		e	r	e	r	
1-step forecast										
DV	−0.37	−0.17	1.19	0.77	2.16	−0.21	−0.15	1.12	0.71	1.84
VEqCM	−0.90	0.36	1.44	1.16	4.34	−0.33	−0.09	1.16	0.73	1.99
const[1]	−0.08	0.03	1.21	1.05	2.57	−0.06	0.01	1.26	0.99	2.56
const[4]	−0.19	0.09	1.10	0.84	1.95	−0.11	0.02	1.10	0.78	1.82
$TS_p[1]$	−0.41	−0.13	1.26	0.84	2.46	−0.22	−0.11	1.15	0.77	1.97
$TS_p[4]$	−0.41	−0.03	1.13	0.80	2.07	−0.19	−0.06	1.11	0.73	1.81
$TS_a[1]$	−0.42	−0.14	1.33	0.84	2.67	−0.19	−0.11	1.21	0.76	2.09
$TS_a[4]$	−0.29	−0.14	1.21	0.81	2.23	−0.15	−0.10	1.20	0.75	2.04
4-step forecast errors										
DV	−1.93	−1.25	2.56	1.82	15.18	−1.41	−0.98	2.48	1.93	12.85
VEqCM	−3.64	0.01	3.76	3.39	38.86	−1.85	−0.82	2.81	1.90	15.55
const[1]	−0.88	0.14	4.43	4.29	38.81	−0.74	−0.02	4.60	4.07	38.25
const[4]	−1.26	0.28	2.94	2.72	17.69	−0.92	−0.02	2.85	2.38	14.64
$TS_p[1]$	−2.22	−1.21	3.22	2.43	22.68	−1.45	−0.79	2.87	2.16	15.62
$TS_p[4]$	−2.16	−0.67	2.51	2.26	16.51	−1.36	−0.51	2.53	1.86	11.98
$TS_a[1]$	−2.06	−1.29	3.12	2.05	19.82	−1.29	−0.82	2.66	2.01	13.45
$TS_a[4]$	−1.76	−1.25	2.54	1.96	14.92	−1.38	−0.80	2.65	1.95	13.37
8-step forecast errors										
DV	−4.58	−3.37	2.53	2.70	45.99	−3.72	−2.68	2.61	2.90	36.17
VEqCM	−6.80	−2.38	4.36	4.61	92.08	−4.44	−2.39	3.51	4.61	49.53
const[1]	−2.52	0.18	8.38	9.27	162.4	−2.22	−0.29	8.71	8.83	158.9
const[4]	−3.03	0.24	4.87	6.44	74.43	−2.24	−0.23	4.65	5.43	56.19
$TS_p[1]$	−5.06	−2.89	3.93	4.38	68.59	−4.05	−2.27	3.90	4.30	55.21
$TS_p[4]$	−4.92	−1.88	2.92	4.09	52.95	−3.32	−1.41	2.96	3.39	33.27
$TS_a[1]$	−4.66	−3.57	3.33	3.25	56.18	−3.55	−2.38	2.90	3.38	38.05
$TS_a[4]$	−4.41	−3.52	2.46	3.28	48.58	−3.68	−2.36	2.94	3.22	38.08
12-step forecast errors										
DV	−6.89	−5.38	2.80	3.26	96.20	−5.75	−4.40	3.37	3.82	78.27
VEqCM	−8.90	−5.49	3.75	5.03	147.8	−6.82	−4.52	3.59	4.48	99.91
const[1]	−3.19	0.52	12.20	15.17	389.5	−2.67	−0.22	12.04	14.49	362.1
const[4]	−4.09	0.06	8.02	10.65	194.4	−3.04	−0.47	7.29	8.79	139.9
$TS_p[1]$	−7.34	−5.17	4.83	7.16	155.2	−6.06	−4.06	4.93	6.70	122.3
$TS_p[4]$	−6.68	−3.25	3.39	5.08	92.51	−4.95	−2.64	3.60	4.64	65.94
$TS_a[1]$	−6.96	−5.90	2.89	4.12	108.4	−5.72	−4.32	3.40	4.36	81.92
$TS_a[4]$	−6.88	−5.78	2.80	3.94	104.1	−5.70	−4.40	3.56	4.16	81.83

12 Postscript

Summary

The book has discussed economic forecasting in processes that are not reducible to stationarity after differencing or cointegration transforms. The analytical framework allowed the forecasting model to be a mis-specified representation, estimated from data on an integrated-cointegrated data generation process subject to intermittent structural breaks. All these aspects had some impact on forecast accuracy. The main finding, however, is that deterministic shifts over the forecast horizon are a primary cause of forecast failure: this result followed from the forecast-error taxonomy, the Monte Carlo studies, and the empirical modeling exercises. Other possible sources – such as model mis-specification and estimation uncertainty – were less central, except to the extent that they concerned deterministic terms. Many results changed radically when parameter non-constancy was introduced: examples above included the role of causal variables in forecasting relative to non-causal, and the value added from intercept corrections or differencing when models were differentially susceptible to structural breaks. These sources and implications of forecast failure suggested possible solutions: in addition to differencing and intercept corrections, co-breaking and regime-shift modeling were considered, and their empirical performance evaluated for a range of macro-economic variables.

12.1 Overview

The repeated occurrence of forecast failure in macro-economics is manifest evidence that economic data that are not reducible to stationarity just by differencing and cointegration transforms. Economies evolve and are subject to sudden shifts, sometimes precipitated by changes in legislation, major discoveries, and political turmoil. We have proposed an analytical framework which explicitly allows the forecasting model to be a mis-specified representation of the economic mechanism, to be estimated from (possibly inaccurate) data, which was generated by an integrated-cointegrated process that is subject to intermittent structural breaks. The extent of mis-specification in the model for the DGP was unknown. Since such assumptions mimic the empirical setting, we explored their implications for economic forecasting.

The fundamental concepts needed to develop a theory of economic forecasting relevant to empirical economic data were discussed. Predictability (a property of random variables relative to information) and forecastability (an ability to make statements with value-added about future events) were distinguished. The former is necessary but not sufficient for the latter. Moreover, predictability must decrease as the forecast horizon grows, but forecast accuracy need not, and we presented both theoretical and empirical examples where multi-step forecasts were more accurate than a sequence of 1-step. We also reconsidered the role of causal variables in forecasting relative to non-causal, and demonstrated by a counter example that causal could not be shown to always dominate non-causal in our framework. While causally-based econometric systems are hardly supported by such a result, it opens the possibility to rationally explaining many empirical practices in macroeconomic forecasting, such as intercept corrections, and potentially could account for the efficacy of differencing strategies.

We applied these notions to explain forecast failure in previously congruent models, whereas non-congruent models need not have failed from the same events. This outcome emphasized the need to distinguish between equilibrium-correction models (embodying cointegration relations) and error-correction models (that automatically offset past mistakes). Indeed, the concept of a constant model needed to be revised, and we suggested extended constancy as an empirically-useful construct. Nevertheless, in the forecasting context for the class of cointegrated I(1) DGPs subject to deterministic shifts , causally-based, congruent vector equilibrium-correction models (VEqCMs) with extended parameter constancy could well be dominated by non-causal, non-congruent, error-correction formulations. The next three chapters investigated this issue in detail.

First, taxonomies of sources of multi-step forecast errors were developed for both non-integrated (I(0)) and I(1) processes. These clarified which sources were likely to induce systematic errors (forecast-error biases), and which had variance consequences. Perhaps the main finding is that deterministic shifts over the forecast horizon are the primary cause of systematic forecast failure. This finding applied to both taxonomies, and suggested a range of potential results, that we then turned to explore, theoretically, by Monte Carlo studies, and in empirical modeling exercises. All three forms of investigation produced results consistent with the basic theoretical framework.

One implication concerned the difficulty of determining the occurrence of breaks in mean-zero processes relative to those with large means. In the former, the equilibrium mean remains unaltered, whereas in the latter, it shifts when any parameter changes, and hence induces systematic biases. The Monte Carlo experiments corroborated this result, particularly in the case where both intercepts and dynamic reactions were altered, but the equilibrium mean remained constant, where rejection of the null of constancy rarely occurred. Moreover, differencing was found to be much more effective in I(1) processes with breaks, than in the equivalent I(0) case; as differencing seems effective empirically, this suggests unit roots do occur. The detailed derivation of multi-step forecast-error biases when forecasts are made both before and after breaks showed that VEqCMs made the same systematic mistakes in these two states. Corresponding derivations for VARs in first and second differences (denoted DVs and DDVs) revealed very different biases pre and post breaks: in particular, both models "error corrected" for equilibrium-mean shifts that had already occurred. While little can be done to offset unanticipated breaks that occur after forecasts are announced, this result shows it is possible to partially circumvent breaks that have happened.

We found that multi-step forecasts of growth rates from VEqCMs of I(1) systems could be more accurate than the sequence of 1-step forecasts based on fixed parameter estimates; such a result can even not hold for the entailed forecasts of levels. Finding such an outcome empirically suggests testing whether a deterministic shift has recently happened. As noted above, it also confirms the need to distinguish predictability properties from forecasting ones.

Other potential sources of forecast failure from the taxonomy were then studied in detail. Mis-specification of zero-mean stochastic components did not by itself seem a major source, but interacting with breaks elsewhere in the economy might precipitate failure. However, deterministic mis-specification – such as omitting an intercept or trend – could easily precipitate failure. Similarly, estimation uncertainty seemed a secondary problem for stochastic variables, but again, mis-estimation of deterministic terms could be deleterious to forecast accuracy. Neither collinearity nor a lack of parsimony *per se* were key culprits, but interacting with breaks occurring elsewhere in the economic system they could induce serious problems. Even when the parameters of a forecasting model remained constant, a break in the correlation structure of the regressors could induce poor forecasts due to variance effects from the least significant variables retained, consistent with the need to eliminate non-systematic effects. Nevertheless, *ex post*, such problems would not be apparent (e.g., collinearity would vanish, and precise coefficient estimates appear), so a clear demarcation from deterministic shifts is feasible in practice, albeit after the event. The importance of "overfitting" was less clear, and remains on our research agenda, albeit that the results just discussed suggest it should not be a primary cause of failure. Unless sample sizes are small relative to the number of parameters, parameter-selection effects seem unlikely to so downwards bias equation standard errors as to induce forecast failure. Finally, forecast-origin mis-measurement could be dangerous, particularly if intercept corrections are used.

We then turned to investigate potential remedies to deterministic shifts such as differencing. Such forecasting models need have no causal basis, but from our earlier result, this is unproblematic. By detailed derivations of the comparable multi-step forecast-error biases and variances from DVs and DDVs, when forecasts are made both before and after breaks, the effectiveness of differencing was established, particularly for the DDV. However, the forecast-error variances exceeded those for the VEqCM, so at longer horizons, the dominance could reverse, as found in the study by Eitrheim, Husebø and Nymoen (1997) for the Norges Bank model competing with DVs and DDVs. Over a 12-quarter evaluation horizon, the Bank's model performed best, and the equivalent of the DDV did worst, whereas the DDV did best in two out of the three 4-period divisions of the same data. Consequently, when deterministic breaks occur, the outcomes of "forecasting competitions" will not only depend on the size, sign, and frequency of breaks, but also on their timing relative to the forecast origin, and hence on the lengths of the forecast-evaluation horizons used.

It was important not to correct the DDV for the residual autocorrelation resulting from over-differencing if robustness to breaks was to be maintained. Thus, mis-specification testing for residual serial correlation followed by any attempt to correct that problem would defeat the point of using a DDV for forecasting in the face of structural breaks. Since residual autocorrelation entailed the invalidity of the conventional calculations of forecast-error variances, we compared the correct forecast-error variances for the DV and DDV with those which a computer program would produce, as well as rough approximations to autocorrelation-corrected formulae. Post-transition forecast errors were also studied, for a DGP with a linear deterministic trend. Overall, the DDV provided an example of a non-causal, non-congruent, predictor that could be demonstrated theoretically (and in later chapters, empirically) to dominate the pre-break causal DGP in forecasting, albeit that robustness could be obtained against recent deterministic shifts by over-differencing only over fairly short horizons.

Allen and Fildes (1998) overview the empirical evidence on "what works" in econometric forecasting. They argue in favor of simple models, estimated by least squares, simplified from VARs with relatively generous lag specifications, and tested for constant parameters. In their summary, they also note a number of important questions that remain unresolved. These comprise:

(1) what role causal variables should play, particularly if they need to be forecast by auxiliary models;
(2) whether or not congruent models outperform non-congruent, and consequentially:
(3) what importance to attach to rigorous mis-specification testing in

selecting forecasting models;
(4) while cointegration seems to help in modeling, it has ambiguous effects in improving forecasting.

We believe all these issues are potentially explicable by the results discussed above.

Because intercept corrections (ICs) can eliminate recent deterministic shifts, we also considered their role as a potential remedy for breaks. The various interpretations of why they worked suggested many approaches, several of which were investigated both theoretically and empirically. The dominant approach in this book was to view ICs as imposing common factors of unity on the forecast-period errors. The resulting forecast-error bias reductions were again offset by variance increases, so their efficacy depended on the size of the deterministic shift relative to the horizon to be forecast. Estimation updating seemed sensible, and could complement or substitute for ICs, depending on the source of the problem, but more analysis is required to establish if there are cases where updating is detrimental to forecast accuracy.

Co-breaking – the removal of deterministic shifts by linear combinations of variables – was proposed as a solution for deterministic shifts in sub-systems. We showed that cointegration vectors also co-break for shifts in the growth rate when there is no trend in the cointegration space, and common trends co-break for equilibrium-mean shifts. For a regime shift to vanish by co-breaking across a linear combination of variables entails either a coincidentally equal effect, or a genuine relationship, re-introducing a potential role for causal explanations. For example, although composite leading indicators and econometric models face similar problems in the face of deterministic shifts, the former seem less likely to fare well if based on non-causal relations that do not co-break. Many model were shown that potentially can exhibit co-breaking, including conditional models under super exogeneity (Hendry and Mizon, 1998a, investigate the implications of co-breaking for the Lucas critique).

The forecast performance of two non-linear models (namely, SETAR and MS-AR) was analyzed. These seek to model changes in regime by including stochastic and deterministic shifts in their probability structure, albeit in different ways. While they seem superior to linear models in describing the business cycle, by separately modeling expansionary and contractionary phases, their forecasting superiority is more controversial. When forecast performance is evaluated conditional on being in a particular regime (at the time the forecast is made) such models can offer clear gains (see, e.g., Tiao and Tsay, 1994), but unconditionally there is often little improvement over linear models on MSFE. However, they may be favored on qualitative measures of forecast performance, or approaches that evaluate the whole forecast density. Given the prominence of deterministic shifts as an explanation for forecast failure suggested by our research, efforts to model such shifts may yield rewards.

Three detailed empirical studies sought to test the practical value of the various implications derived from our theoretical framework. All three conformed closely to the theory predictions. In the scalar illustration of UK aggregate real consumers' expenditure on non-durables and services, the predictive failure of DHSY revealed that some shift had occurred. Differencing helped mitigate the effects of the changed equilibrium mean, and intercept corrections also offset the shift, albeit at the cost of an increased variance. There was little benefit to multi-step estimation over 1-step, matching Clements and Hendry (1996c).

The first multivariate empirical illustration was a four-variable monetary model of the UK, when there was a known major financial innovation just prior to the forecast origin. The earlier theoretical results on the impacts of deterministic shifts matched the outcomes over both pre- and post-break forecast periods for the three methods considered (VEqCM, DV and DDV), and were also supported by the effectiveness of the two IC strategies evaluated. Although other forms of structural break, model mis-specification, a lack of parsimony, inaccurate forecast-origin data, and inefficient estimation may all exacerbate forecast failure, this outcome confirms that these factors played supporting roles in the present empirical setting.

In the second multivariate empirical example, a well-constructed (in-sample) model yielded inferior forecasts to both a DV and an IC-corrected VEqCM. This set of empirical findings generally bore out the analytical results, even though the theory was derived for a highly stylized DGP using simple models that abstracted from many factors which may be important in practice. Here, updating the estimates of the parameters produced a greater relative improvement to the VEqCM forecasts, although the DV remained dominant. Again, conventional intercept corrections of the VEqCM reduced forecast-error bias, and while time-series corrections were less successful at reducing bias, they had a smaller variance cost. This close concordance of theory and empirical outcomes across three studies, and often in surprising ways, both confirms the feasibility of a theory of forecasting that allows for structural breaks in an economic mechanism for which the econometric model is mis-specified, and shows that the resulting theory can provide a useful basis for interpreting and potentially circumventing systematic forecast failure in economics.

12.2 Methodological Implications

A number of important methodological implications of the analysis were noted throughout the text. We concluded that forecast performance in a world of deterministic shifts is not a good guide to model choice unless the sole objective is short-term forecasting. Thus, there are no grounds for selecting the best forecasting model for other purposes, such as economic policy analysis, or testing economic theories. For example, despite the 4-equation monetary VEqCM of the UK failing grievously in forecasting, its policy implications for (say) income increases would have been correct, although those for the effects of raising the level of interest rates would have been badly wrong once the differential between own and competitive rates became the determining variable. The same parameter estimates delivered excellent forecasts using only a different measure of the opportunity cost of holding money, illustrating extended parameter constancy. Similarly, tests of economic theories by whole-sample goodness of fit could be seriously misled by breaks. For example, a DV could well outperform, suggesting the irrelevance of lagged information from other variables, and the absence of cointegration (see, e.g., tests of the implications of the Hall, 1978, consumption theory).

Further, if forecast failure is primarily due to forecast-period deterministic shifts, then there are no possible within-sample tests of later failure. Our theoretical and empirical examples of extended parameter constancy illustrated the difficulty: whether failure was manifested depended on how a model was updated, not on its in-sample behavior or properties. On one update, the model failed, and on another did not: tests that correctly detected the former are seen to be wrong when the latter is discovered; and if they did not anticipate failure, would be wrong if the latter was never discovered. Equally, we have shown that non-congruent models may not fail, and congruent fail, so conventional diagnostic tests do not suffice either as indicators of potential failure. Consequently, the methodology by which a model is developed empirically may have little to do with its later forecasting success or failure, in stark contrast to the claims in Hess, Jones and Porter (1997).

Conversely, as a usable knowledge base, theory-related, congruent, encompassing models remain undominated, and for empirical understanding seem likely to remain an integral component of any progressive research strategy. Even the "best available model" could be caught out when forecasting by the sudden and unanticipated outbreak of (say) a major war or other crisis for which no effect was included in the forecast. We suggested an astronomical analogy in which a spacecraft was hit by a meteor, resulting in dramatic forecast failure, yet there were no implications for Newton's laws or for the forecasting algorithms used. Forecast failure does not, though it might, entail an invalid theoretical model; it does reveal forecast data that are different from the in-sample observations, and hence an incomplete empirical model for the whole period. It is a *non sequitur* to reject the theory on which a model is based simply because of forecast failure: thus, any decision about the invalidity of the so-called Keynesian macro-models after the oil-crises of the mid-1970s was not justifiable on that basis alone. The same models, first expanded to incorporate the effects that changed, then re-parameterized, might reduce to the originals, thereby manifesting extended parameter constancy. Equally, they may have remained rejected, with the deterministic shifts simply revealing their mis-specifications. Careful evaluation was – and still is – needed to check which case applied.

Overfitting by itself seems likely to be a transient problem in a progressive research strategy for cointegrated-stationary processes: extended data samples should reduce the significance of irrelevant effects. By modeling past breaks, however, equations may be "overfitted" relative to their likely forecast performance if future unanticipated breaks continue to occur. Since forecast success or failure depends primarily on what happens over the forecast horizon relative to the in-sample period, and the degree of congruence or non-congruence of a model is neither necessary nor sufficient for forecasting success or failure, few general results seem likely on the implications for forecasting of having "data mined".

Finally, our results have important implications for theories of expectations-generating mechanisms. We have presented a range of theoretical and empirical situations in which the forecast performance of the VEqCM – which represents the DGP in-sample – was dominated by DV and DDV models. Consider, then, the plight of economic agents in such an economy: without precognition or prescience, they too would mis-forecast badly if they used the in-sample "rational expectation", namely the conditional expectation given the DGP. After a few such mistakes, many agents would have discovered, like some British Chancellors of the Exchequer, that "same change" or perhaps "random-walk" predictors are better indicators of short-term developments. If they did so, then an appropriate econometric specification would be that postulated on rather different grounds by Favero and Hendry (1992), namely, the use of second-differenced predictors in agents' decision rules (also see Flemming, 1976, for a similar view). These constitute model-free forecasting rules that help deliver the "least-biased forecasts" feasible under deterministic shifts, and are immune to the type of argument advanced by Lucas (1976). In turn, conditional models expressed after cointegration transforms in double differences with EqCMs (as in the first equation in table 8.6, say) would embody such expectations. That outcome is consistent with the detailed study of empirical evidence in Ericsson and Irons (1995), both on the Lucas critique, and on the prevalence of super exogeneity in conditional models.

Thus, the study of forecasting not only has considerable interest in its own right, it has wide-reaching methodological implications for both empirical economic and econometric research. Many other consequences almost certainly await elucidation.

12.3 The Way Ahead

One of the main results to come out of the analysis is that deterministic shifts over the forecast horizon are a primary cause of forecast failure in macro-econometrics, and this in turn points to many new inter-related issues requiring further analysis.

12.3.1 What influences deterministic terms?

Many economic variables are inherently positive, including land area, labor inputs, the capital stock, inventories, and time itself on the production side; all prices, especially the two key ones of interest rates and exchange rates; all expenditures by both value and volume; and all income and wealth measures, including financial assets. Thus, non-zero means are certain for levels of many economic variables. The units of measurement of most of these variables are arbitrary, but this may not matter as both means and shifts therein are likely to be proportional to the units used, and most econometric systems take log transforms of inherently-positive variables. Of course, net variables such as assets minus debt, balancing items such as deficits, and the like can take either sign, so such combinations have near-zero means.

The deterministic terms of relevance to an integrated-cointegrated system are growth rates, and equilibrium means of cointegrating relations, both of which depend on economic agents' decision rules. Here, logic and theory offer little guidance on likely ranges of values. For example, savings rates can vary from 50% to zero, or even be negative for time spans that are long relative to forecast horizons, and they differ greatly across countries; the velocity of circulation of various money measures also varies widely across countries and time periods, etc. Of course, in both these examples, other causal variables help explain some of the variation, and hence part of the equilibrium mean values; but then their means need explaining in turn.

Growth rates are best viewed as being endogenous to economies, rather than being deterministic, depending on such factors as R&D, technical progress, discoveries and innovations, as well as investment in human and physical capital. The VEqCM model class is not well suited to this problem, since the growth in the system comes about from the term γ, which is itself left unexplained. Variables could be added in an attempt to model γ, but this would occasion new γs in their equations, and so on. Although a non-zero value of γ in a VEqCM leads to linear deterministic trends in the moving-average representation, the use of t as a regressor in a model can only be a local approximation to the slow evolution of the endogenous determinants of growth. If the data really were stationary around an "exogenous" deterministic trend, even with autonomous breaks therein (see e.g., Perron, 1989), we should all stop working (and researching), and enjoy limitless leisure while the economy continues to grow at γt. We suspect that doing so would cause a trend break, suggesting that γ is endogenous; and being a permanent growth change if we all stopped working permanently, seems much better modeled as a unit-root process. Deterministic changes in γ (as with μ), while treated as "autonomous" in our analysis, are viewed as deriving from shifts in unmodeled variables that are ultimately open to empirical testing: the key feature was the non-zero value of the derived equilibrium mean.

In deference to Occam's razor, the analysis is built around the two concepts of a DGP and a model thereof, and attributes the major problems of forecasting to structural breaks in the model relative to the DGP. However, an additional layer arguably allows a better conceptualization of the problem, and of the issues raised in the previous paragraph: see Bontemps and Mizon (1996). Between the actual DGP of the economy and the forecasting model, lies the local DGP of the variables being modeled – the LDGP. Using a VEqCM as the DGP in the two-tier system, entails that the VEqCM is the LDGP in the three-tier stratification, and changes in its autonomous growth rates and equilibrium means proxy the unmodeled influences in the DGP. The correspondence between the LDGP and DGP is assumed to be close enough to allow an analysis of the forecasting model by assuming that the LDGP holds (the analytical content of this book), checked by its relation to what happens in practice (the empirical illustrations, where the outcomes rest on the mapping between the forecasting model and the economy). In terms of the discussion of stochastic and deterministic trends, the economy-wide DGP has endogenously generated stochastic trends, but the LDGP might be taken as either a trend, or difference, stationary process for short- term horizons, even though different behavior results for long horizons: see fig. 1.1.

12.3.2 What causes deterministic terms to change?

The growth rate γ probably changes little over time for real variables in many countries, although exceptions occur, such as China over the last half century, or the so-called "productivity slowdown" in OECD economies during the first half of the 1980s. However, for nominal variables, the many actual and near hyperinflations suggest that substantive changes do occur. Explanations may exist for such phenomena, so that models with more constant meta-parameters may be found: for example, while switching models provide more flexible ways of capturing regular changes, the driving forces are generally left unspecified.

Changes to equilibrium means may reflect shifts in unmodeled determinants, as seemed to be the case in the consumers' expenditure and money-demand empirical examples. That hardly resolves the problem, since it entails changes in the means of those variables, which therefore need explained. Legislation can matter, as can various innovations in technology and finance. Much more research is merited on this issue.

Variation freeness between γ and μ is also unlikely, and changes in one almost surely alter the other. For example, the savings rate varies empirically with economic growth, and many theories suggest it should (see, e.g., Ando and Modigliani, 1963). Such dependence could be incorporated in the taxonomy, and may matter for interpreting forecast failure. As we note in §12.3.5, the relation between deterministic terms becomes even more crucial in open systems, where changes in means and shocks may have very different effects in theory (perhaps due to inadvertent "variation independence" assumptions) and practice: see, for example, Hendry and Mizon (1998c).

12.3.3 How to detect changes in deterministic terms?

If changes other than in equilibrium means and growth rates do not induce forecast failure, and are not easily detected in-sample, then directed tests for those deterministic shifts are merited. Many tests of parameter non-constancy check all the parameters of a model, usually in the original parameterization. Greater power might result by focusing a test on shifts in γ and μ, which is potentially very different from testing for shifts in the intercepts of (say) a VAR (see e.g., Hendry, Krolzig and Sensier, 1997). Recent research on monitoring for breaks (see e.g., Chu, Stinchcombe and White, 1996, and Banerjee, Clements and Hendry, 1997) holds promise, and could be adapted to focus on the equilibrium mean shifting. Tests for shifts near the forecast origin also seem valuable, and current macro-econometric model practice –

carefully scrutinizing the latest errors – probably reflects such an idea, albeit informally. Forecasting procedures that rapidly adapt to shifts, as in Pole, West and Harrison (1994), do so more formally. We have sought to apply the formal theory of h-step parsimony in Clements and Hendry (1998b, ch. 12) to the selection of end-of-sample indicators, but as yet without success, although we believe a formal decision-theoretic approach merits continued study.

12.3.4 *How to offset changes in deterministic terms?*

That is manifestly a most important issue. To allow for *ex ante* breaks need foresight from some non-model source (perhaps judgement, or early-warning signals in other domains): we do not yet know how to predict when economic volcanoes will erupt, and can but advise on what to do after they have exploded. The book has considered a range of methods for ameliorating biases when forecasting after breaks, and more detailed study is needed to select definitively between these, and other contenders that may be proposed. Genuine error-correction devices could repay handsome dividends, but need considerable adaptibility in a non-stationary environment; and even then are unlikely to anticipate problems. Given the cumulative multi-step errors found in chapters 3 and 4, we have considered extending the theory of integral-correction mechanisms (ICMs) to forecast-error correction (see, *inter alia*, Phillips, 1954, 1957, Hendry and von Ungern-Sternberg, 1981, and Hendry and Mizon, 1998b). For example, recent past errors could be cumulated, and that term used to correct forecasts. Two problems occur: first, the resulting term is usually I(1) even for forecasting I(0) variables; and second, if the ICM has an equilibrium mean, then that too could shift, recreating the original problem at a higher level of integration. A possible solution is to reset the ICM to zero at regular intervals, perhaps when a new congruent in-sample representation has been developed. Again, many approaches merit study.

12.3.5 *Open systems*

Almost all the analyses above were for closed systems, and most of the findings need to be generalized to open cointegrated models, particularly if economic policy is to be discussed (see e.g., Banerjee, Hendry and Mizon, 1996). We have made considerable progress in doing so, including developing an extended forecast-error taxonomy, and deriving forecast-error biases and variances generalizing those reported above. Weak and strong exogeneity must be addressed, the former to sustain conditional estimation, the latter if conditional forecasts are to be computed (see e.g., Ericsson, Hendry and Mizon, 1998a). Co-breaking and Granger causality both play important, but very different, roles in economic policy analyses and their implementation: see Hendry and Mizon (1998a). In open systems, the cross-dependence of the deterministic terms between endogenous and non-modeled variables is central to making sense of deterministic shifts, and highlights a lacuna in existing economic theories. The forecasting–policy dilemma is marked when breaks occur, and hints that different models may be needed for these two purposes. Preliminary results are reported in Hendry and Mizon (1998c); in due course, we intend to complete our trilogy on forecasting with a book on the *Econometrics of Economic Forecasting*, devoted to the open-model case.

12.4 Conclusion

Despite the relatively weak assumptions that the economy under analysis is non-stationary and subject to unanticipated structural breaks, that the model may differ from the mechanism in unknown ways, and that it requires estimation from available data, many useful insights were derived. The resulting implications often differed considerably from those obtained when the model was assumed to coincide with a constant mechanism. The fundamental concepts of predictability and forecastability pointed towards many of the general problems confronting successful forecasting: for example, causal information cannot be shown to uniformly dominate non-causal in such a setting, and there are no unique measures of forecast accuracy, although some measures are not even invariant across isomorphic model representations. Also, intercept corrections have a theoretical justification in a world subject to structural breaks of unknown form, size, and timing by robustifying forecasts against deterministic shifts that have occurred. Such ICs reveal that the best forecasting model is not necessarily the best policy model.

The taxonomy of sources of forecast error clarified the roles of model mis-specification, sampling variability, error accumulation, forecast origin mis-measurement, intercept shifts, and slope-parameter changes. While structural breaks reduce forecastability, the consequences of many forms of break can be derived analytically. Further, models may be differentially susceptible to structural breaks, as shown analytically for VEqCMs and DVs. Intercept-correction solutions based on using this susceptibility to eliminate the impact of breaks were noted.

Co-breaking suggests the possibility of eliminating structural breaks by taking linear combinations of variables, which may help produce more robust sub-systems. Multivariate estimation, testing, and modeling of co-breaking are not resolved at this stage, although promising research avenues are currently under study. Also, regime-switching models could be used for deterministic breaks that recur. Equally, while leading indicators based on *ex post* correlations should forecast well in constant-parameter processes, they seem unlikely to provide a reliable forecasting approach under structural breaks, as their intercepts are not likely to co-break when variables are genuine indicators that are not linked causally to the target. Thus, causal information retains a central role.

In many ways, this research aims to discover why methods such as Box–Jenkins or DVs succeed when econometric systems fail. Some potential answers have been proposed, namely, that they impose (so do not estimate) unit roots; that their formulation therefore retains the full values of the previous levels of the transformed variables which ensures a form of error correction; they restrict the information used by appealing to parsimony claims, and thereby happen to exclude non-systematic effects that might otherwise swamp forecastability; and overdifferencing removes permanent breaks in deterministic factors (perhaps at the cost of inducing negative moving-average residuals), demonstrated above to be useful in avoiding systematic forecast error biases. Their very advantages as forecasting devices that are somewhat robust against deterministic shifts mitigate against their use in a policy setting.

The case for continuing to use econometric systems seems to depend in practice on their competing successfully in the forecasting arena. Cointegration, co-breaking, model selection procedures and rigorous testing help, but none of these ensures immunity to forecast failure from new forms of break. Thus, there is a powerful case for adopting more robust forecasting approaches than intercept corrections: a key development must be error-correction methods that do not eliminate other sources of information such as cointegration. An approach that incorporates causal information in the econometric system for co-breaking and policy, but operates with robustified forecasts, obviously merits development. This may require non-standard methods of pooling, involving several predictors, some entering with negative weights.

We end by echoing the sentiments we expressed in the Preface to Clements and Hendry (1998b):

Many of the conclusions entail positive prescriptions for action; many are at first sight counter-intuitive, but become obvious in retrospect; and many of the difficulties have possible remedies. In particular, we have only just begun to explore the implications of forecasting across structural breaks with mis-specified models, and many surprises undoubtedly await future researchers.

Exercises

1. Consider the following stochastic process:

$$y_t = \mu + \epsilon_t \text{ where } \epsilon_t \sim \mathsf{IN}\left[0, \sigma_\epsilon^2\right]. \tag{12.1}$$

A sample $t = 1, \ldots, T$ is available for estimation prior to forecasting.
(a) Using the maximum likelihood estimator $\widehat{\mu}$ of μ, obtain the mean, variance, and mean square of the forecast errors for the sequence of 1-step ahead forecasts for $y_{T+1} \ldots y_{T+h}$ holding $\widehat{\mu}$ fixed.

(b) At time T, prior to forecasting but unknown to the forecaster, there is a shift in the value of μ to $\mu + \delta$ where $\delta \neq 0$. Derive the resulting mean square forecast errors (MSFEs).

(c) To robustify the forecasts against such breaks, an intercept correction is used to "set the model back on track" by adding an indicator $d_t = 1_{\{t \geq T\}}$ equal to unity for $t \geq T$, and zero otherwise. Obtain the coefficient of d_t, and show that the forecast-error variance is doubled at $h = 1$ when $\delta = 0$. Also derive its impact on the MSFEs, both when $\delta = 0$ and $\delta \neq 0$ for $h = 2$.

(d) To what is the forecasting model equivalent after the intercept correction? Hence explain why intercept correction provides robustness to structural breaks. Discuss whether the outcome in this simple case generalizes.

(e) In the light of your answer to (d) suggest four other interpretations of intercept corrections, and show how each would be implemented for (12.1).

2. Consider the bivariate I(0) DGP:

$$\begin{pmatrix} y_{1,t} \\ y_{2,t} \end{pmatrix} = \begin{pmatrix} \mu_1 \\ \mu_2 \end{pmatrix} + \begin{pmatrix} \rho \\ 0 \end{pmatrix} y_{2,t-1} + \begin{pmatrix} \epsilon_{1,t} \\ \epsilon_{2,t} \end{pmatrix}, \tag{12.2}$$

where $|\rho| < 1$, and:

$$\begin{pmatrix} \epsilon_{1,t} \\ \epsilon_{2,t} \end{pmatrix} \sim \mathsf{IN}_2 \left[\begin{pmatrix} 0 \\ 0 \end{pmatrix}, \begin{pmatrix} \sigma^2_{\epsilon_1} & 0 \\ 0 & \sigma^2_{\epsilon_2} \end{pmatrix} \right].$$

The generating mechanism in (12.2) holds till time $\tau = T - 1$, then changes to:

$$\begin{pmatrix} y_{1,\tau+i} \\ y_{2,\tau+i} \end{pmatrix} = \begin{pmatrix} \mu_1 \\ \mu_2^* \end{pmatrix} + \begin{pmatrix} \rho^* \\ 0 \end{pmatrix} y_{2,\tau+i-1} + \begin{pmatrix} \epsilon_{1,\tau+i} \\ \epsilon_{2,\tau+i} \end{pmatrix}, \tag{12.3}$$

where $|\rho^*| < 1$. An investigator wishes to forecast $\{y_{1,T+h}\}$ for $h = 1, \ldots, H$. Only the first block in (12.2) is modeled, with 1-step forecasts generated by the in-sample system:

$$\widehat{y}_{1,T+h} = \mu_1 + \rho y_{2,T+h-1}. \tag{12.4}$$

(a) Derive the forecast-error bias and variance of $\widehat{y}_{1,T+h}$, treating the DGP (12.3) as in its new stochastic equilibrium from T onwards.

(b) Compare the "non-causal" predictor:

$$\widetilde{y}_{1,T+h} = y_{1,T+h-1}, \tag{12.5}$$

prove it is unbiased, and derive its forecast-error variance.

(c) Compare the MSFEs of $\widehat{y}_{1,T+h}$ and $\widetilde{y}_{1,T+h}$, and prove that (12.5) can outperform (12.4) for some parameter values. In particular, derive the outcome when $\rho^* = 0$.

(d) How well would an intercept correction to (12.4) work here?

(e) Hence, discuss the role of causal information in forecasting.

3. Consider the I(0) DGP:

$$\Delta y_t = -\rho (y_{t-1} - \mu) + \epsilon_t, \tag{12.6}$$

where $0 < \rho < 1$ and $\epsilon_t \sim \mathsf{IN}[0, \sigma^2_\epsilon]$.

The process in (12.6) holds till time T, then changes to:

$$\Delta y_{T+h} = -\rho\left(y_{T+h-1} - \mu^{*}\right) + \epsilon_{T+h}, \tag{12.7}$$

for $h = 1, \ldots, H$. An investigator forecasts the h-step ahead sequence $\{\Delta y_{T+h}\}$ using:

$$\Delta \widehat{y}_{T+h|T} = -\rho\left(\widehat{y}_{T+h-1|T} - \mu\right). \tag{12.8}$$

(a) Derive the forecast-error bias of $\Delta \widehat{y}_{T+h|T}$, and of the derived levels forecast $\widehat{y}_{T+h|T}$, when the DGP (12.7) generated the outcomes from T onwards.

(b) Compare the sequence of 1-step forecasts:

$$\Delta \widehat{y}_{T+h|T+h-1} = -\rho\left(y_{T+h-1} - \mu\right), \tag{12.9}$$

and derive its forecast-error bias and variance.

(c) Compare the forecast-error biases of $\Delta \widehat{y}_{T+h|T}$ and $\Delta \widehat{y}_{T+h|T+h-1}$, and establish that there are parameter values such that (12.7) is less biased than (12.9). Also, show parameter values such that the outcome favors (12.9).

(d) Could these outcomes ever hold for MSFE comparisons between (12.7) and (12.9)? If so, does such a finding contradict the result that predictability cannot increase as the forecast horizon grows?

(e) How well would an intercept correction to (12.8) work here?

(f) Are there values of ρ in (12.6) for which it remains stationary and invertible, yet multi-step forecasts of levels $\widehat{y}_{T+h|T}$ are more accurate than 1-step $\widehat{y}_{T+h|T+h-1}$?

4. Obtain the 2-step ahead forecast error for the data generation process:

$$x_t = x_{t-1} + u_t \quad \text{where} \quad u_t = \epsilon_t + \theta\epsilon_{t-1},$$

and $\epsilon_t \sim \mathsf{IN}\left[0, \sigma_\epsilon^2\right]$ for the assumed model:

$$x_t = \rho x_{t-1} + v_t,$$

when the investigator incorrectly assumes that $v_t \sim \mathsf{IN}[0, \sigma_v^2]$, and ρ is estimated from a large sample of T observations.

(a) Since the limiting distribution of the least-squares estimator of $\hat{\rho}$ is:

$$T(\hat{\rho}-1) = \frac{\frac{1}{T}\sum_{t=1}^{T} u_t x_{t-1}}{\frac{1}{T^2}\sum_{t=1}^{T} x_{t-1}^2} \Rightarrow \left(\int_0^1 W(r)^2 \mathrm{d}r\right)^{-1}\left[\frac{1}{2}\left(W(1)^2-1\right)+\frac{\theta}{(1+\theta)^2}\right] \tag{12.10}$$

where $W(r) \sim \mathsf{N}[0,r]\ \forall r \in [0,1]$ is a standard Wiener process, obtain the limiting distribution of $\hat{\rho}^2$. You may use without proof that:

$$T^{-2}\sum_{t=1}^{T} x_{t-1}x_{t-2} \Rightarrow (1+\theta)^2\sigma_\epsilon^2 \int_0^1 W(r)^2 \mathrm{d}r \tag{12.11}$$

and:

$$T^{-1}\sum_{t=1}^{T} x_{t-1}u_t \Rightarrow \frac{(1+\theta)^2\sigma_\epsilon^2}{2}\left[W(1)^2-1\right]+\frac{\theta\sigma_\epsilon^2}{2} \tag{12.12}$$

whereas:

$$T^{-1}\sum_{t=1}^{T} x_{t-2}u_t \Rightarrow \frac{(1+\theta)^2\sigma_\epsilon^2}{2}\left(W(1)^2-1\right). \tag{12.13}$$

(b) Compare your result to the limiting distribution of the estimator delivered by minimizing the sum of squares of two-period errors:

$$x_t = \gamma x_{t-2} + e_t$$

where $\delta = \rho^2$, namely:

$$\widetilde{\delta} = \frac{\sum_{t=1}^{T} x_t x_{t-2}}{\sum_{t=1}^{T} x_{t-2}^2}.$$

(c) Explain how instrumental variables estimation of ρ, using x_{t-2} as an instrument, offers a solution to the problem of the non-central limiting distribution following from (12.10):

$$\overline{\rho} = \frac{\sum_{t=1}^{T} x_t x_{t-2}}{\sum_{t=1}^{T} x_{t-1}x_{t-2}}.$$

(d) Discuss the implications of your results for multi-step forecasting.

(e) Suggest other sources of mis-specification that might favor multi-step estimation.

5. When models are mis-specified for the underlying mechanism, multi-step estimation criteria have been proposed as preferable to 1-step for multi-step forecasting. That is, when:

$$\mathsf{E}\left[x_{T+1} \mid x_T\right] = \rho x_T \text{ whereas } \mathsf{E}\left[x_{T+h} \mid x_T\right] = \rho_h x_T \neq \rho^h x_T,$$

then minimizing an in-sample criterion such as $\sum_{t=h+1}^{T}(x_t - x_{t-h})^2$ is suggested when desiring to forecast x_{T+h}.

(a) How sustainable is such a claim when the process to be forecast is weakly stationary, and h is large (e.g., $h > 10$)? Under what conditions would it be sensible to consider a multi-step estimator for forecasting?

(b) If the underlying process is:

$$x_t = \rho x_{t-1} + v_t \text{ where } \epsilon_t \sim \mathsf{IN}\left[0, \sigma_v^2\right],$$

and $\rho = 1$, derive the distribution of the OLS estimator $\widehat{\rho}$ of ρ.

(c) Obtain the distribution of $\widehat{\rho^h}$ as a function of the 1-step distribution in (b).

(d) Derive the distribution of the h-step minimizing estimator $\widetilde{\rho}_h$ as a function of the same Wiener integrals.

(e) What happens in (c) and (d) when the assumption that $v_t \sim \mathsf{IN}[0, \sigma_v^2]$ is false, and in fact, v_t is a first-order negative moving average?

(f) Comment on the relative forecast errors of the two estimators in case (e).

Letting $W(r)$ be the standardized Wiener process associated with v_t (so $W(r) \sim \mathsf{N}[0, r]$), you may assume without proof that:

$$(\sigma_\epsilon T)^{-2} \sum_{t=1}^{T} x_t^2 \Rightarrow \int_0^1 W(r)^2 \,\mathrm{d}r,$$

and:

$$(\sigma_\epsilon T)^{-1}\sum_{t=1}^{T} x_{t-1}\epsilon_t \Rightarrow \frac{1}{2}\left(W(1)^2-1\right).$$

6. Consider the stochastic process:

$$x_t = x_{t-1} + \mu + v_t \qquad \text{where } v_t \sim \mathsf{ID}\left[0, \sigma_v^2\right].$$

(a) Derive the h-step ahead conditional forecast error variance when the form of this difference stationary (DS) model and its parameter values are known.

(b) Suppose the investigator estimates the model:

$$x_t = \mu + \rho x_{t-1} + e_t,$$

on the sample $1, \ldots, T$, when the DGP is as above. Now calculate the h-step ahead conditional forecast error variance.

(c) The DGP is instead given by the trend stationary (TS) process:

$$x_t = \phi + \gamma t + u_t, \quad \text{where } u_t \sim \mathsf{ID}\left[0, \sigma_u^2\right] \tag{12.14}$$

Calculate the conditional h-step forecast error variances when the parameters are known, and when they have to be estimated. **Hint:** in the second case:

$$\begin{aligned}\mathsf{V}\begin{bmatrix}\widehat{\phi}\\ \widehat{\gamma}\end{bmatrix} &= \sigma_u^2\begin{pmatrix}T & \frac{1}{2}T(T+1)\\ \frac{1}{2}T(T+1) & \frac{1}{6}T(T+1)(2T+1)\end{pmatrix}^{-1}\\ &= \sigma_u^2 T^{-1}(T-1)^{-1}\begin{pmatrix}2(2T+1) & -6\\ -6 & 12(T+1)^{-1}\end{pmatrix}.\end{aligned} \tag{12.15}$$

(d) Finally, assess the claim in Sampson (1991) that allowing for parameter uncertainty leads to forecast-error variances which grow with the square of the forecast horizon for both the DS and TS models, so that asymptotically the two are indistinguishable in terms of their implications for forecastability.

7. Suppose that the scalar process $\{x_t\}$ we wish to forecast can be written as an ARIMA (p,d,q) model:

$$\phi(L)\,\Delta^d x_t = \mu + \theta(L)\,v_t, \tag{12.16}$$

where $v_t \sim \mathsf{IN}[0, \sigma_v^2]$. $\phi(L)$ and $\theta(L)$ are the AR and MA polynomials, respectively, with orders p and q, so that:

$$\phi(L) = 1 - \phi_1 L - \cdots - \phi_p L^p, \qquad \theta(L) = 1 + \theta_1 L + \cdots + \theta_q L^q,$$

setting $\phi_0 = 1$ and $\theta_0 = 1$. Let $\varphi(L) = \phi(L)\Delta^d$ so we have an ARMA$(p+d, q)$.

(a) Write down an expression for the level of the process in period $T+h$ conditional on period T information.

(b) Show how this specializes for an AR(1) model, and for an ARIMA(0,1,1).

(c) Show that the conditional expectation is the MMSFE predictor for a general ARMA process.

(d) Derive 1-step and 2-step ahead forecasts for an ARIMA(1,1,1) for both levels and differences (i.e., $y_t = \Delta x_t$), and their forecast-error variances.

(e) When:

$$x_t = \mu + \delta 1_{\{t \geq T\}} + \epsilon_t \text{ where } \epsilon_t \sim \mathsf{IN}\left[0, \sigma_\epsilon^2\right].$$

where $1_{\{t \geq T\}}$ is an indicator variables, derive an approximating ARIMA(1,1,1) representation. Comment on the altered interpretation of your results in (d).

8. Reconsider the DGP in (12.1):

$$y_t = \mu + \epsilon_t \text{ where } \epsilon_t \sim \mathsf{IN}\left[0, \sigma_\epsilon^2\right], \tag{12.17}$$

and, as before, a sample $t = 1, \ldots, T$ is available for estimation prior to forecasting.

(a) Obtain a recursive updating expression for the maximum likelihood estimator $\widehat{\mu}_{T+h}$ of μ, as a function of the previous value $\widehat{\mu}_{T+h-1}$, where for $h = 0, \ldots, H$:

$$\widehat{\mu}_{T+h} = (T+h)^{-1} \sum_{t=1}^{T+h} y_t.$$

Obtain the means and variances of the $\widehat{\mu}_{T+h}$ when the model coincides with the DGP in (12.1).

(b) Derive the mean, variance, and mean square of the forecast errors (MSFEs) for the sequence of 1-step ahead forecasts for $y_{T+1} \cdots y_{T+H}$, where each forecast $\widetilde{y}_{T+h}$ is based on $\widehat{\mu}_{T+h-1}$. Compare these to the corresponding expressions when all the forecasts $\widehat{y}_{T+h}$ are based on $\widehat{\mu}_T$. Comment on the benefits of updating.

(c) At time T, prior to forecasting – but unknown to the forecaster – there is a shift in the value of μ to $\mu+\delta$ where $\delta \neq 0$. Derive the resulting means and variances of the $\widehat{\mu}_{T+h}$ when the model remains as in (12.17).

(d) Derive the MSFEs for $\widetilde{y}_{T+h}$ and $\widehat{y}_{T+h}$ in case (c) where the former updates $\widehat{\mu}_{T+h}$ and the latter does not. Again, comment on the benefits of updating.

9. In modeling economic time series, structural breaks and unit roots both seem to occur. Discuss the following issues, proposing the solutions you would adopt empirically:

(a) discriminating between the effects of structural breaks and unit roots;

(b) testing for unit roots when breaks occur; and for breaks when there are unit roots;

(c) the role of dummy variables in approximating the impacts of breaks;

(d) selecting econometric models by forecast-accuracy criteria; and:

(e) the impact of breaks on Engle–Granger tests for cointegration.

10. Why has economic forecasting suffered so many episodes of large forecast errors? Detail the various hypotheses that may account for this phenomenon, carefully explaining in each case whether the hypothesis in question is likely to have played a major role in practice.

11. What factors determine which methods will win forecasting competitions in economics?

12. How should forecast accuracy, or "success" in forecasting, be assessed?

13. If a model performs as well out of sample as we would expect on the basis of in-sample fit, but is clearly inferior out of sample to a rival model, what should we conclude? What about the situation where a model is dominated by a rival in-sample, but fares better out of sample?

14. What seem to be the main causes of predictive failure in macroeconomic forecasting? Describe methods for ameliorating at least two important forecasting problems.

References

Al-Qassam, M. S. and Lane, J. A. (1989). Forecasting exponential autoregressive models of order 1. *Journal of Time Series Analysis*, **10**, 95–113.

Albert, J. and Chib, S. (1993). Bayes inference via Gibbs sampling of autoregressive time series subject to Markov mean and variance shifts. *Journal of Business and Economic Statistics*, **11**, 1–16.

Allen, P. G. and Fildes, R. A. (1998). Econometric forecasting strategies and techniques. Mimeo, University of Massachussets, USA. Forthcoming, J. S. Armstrong, (ed.) Principles of Forecasting, Kluwer Academic Press.

Ando, A. and Modigliani, F. (1963). The 'life cycle' hypothesis of saving: Aggregate implications and tests. *American Economic Review*, **53**, 55–84.

Andrews, D. W. K. (1993). Tests for parameter instability and structural change with unknown change point. *Econometrica*, **61**, 821–856.

Attfield, C. L. F., Demery, D. and Duck, N. W. (1995). Estimating the UK demand for money function: A test of two approaches. Mimeo, Economics department, University of Bristol.

Bai, J., Lumsdaine, R. L. and Stock, J. H. (1998). Testing for and dating common breaks in multivariate time series. *Review of Economics and Statistics*, **63**, 395–432.

Baillie, R. T. (1979a). The asymptotic mean squared error of multistep prediction from the regression model with autoregressive errors. *Journal of the American Statistical Association*, **74**, 175–184.

Baillie, R. T. (1979b). Asymptotic prediction mean squared error for vector autoregressive models. *Biometrika*, **66**, 675–678.

Banerjee, A., Clements, M. P. and Hendry, D. F. (1997). Monitoring for structural change in forecasting. Mimeo, Oxford Institute of Economics and Statistics, Oxford.

Banerjee, A., Hendry, D. F. and Mizon, G. E. (1996). The econometric analysis of economic policy. *Oxford Bulletin of Economics and Statistics*, **58**, 573–600.

Bjørnstad, J. F. (1990). Predictive likelihood: A review. *Statistical Science*, **5**, 242–265.

Boldin, M. D. (1996). A check on the robustness of Hamilton's Markov switching model approach to the economic analysis of the Business Cycle. *Studies in Nonlinear Dynamics and Econometrics*, **1**, 35–46.

Bollerslev, T., Chou, R. S. and Kroner, K. F. (1992). ARCH modelling in finance – A review of the theory and empirical evidence. *Journal of Econometrics*, **52**, 5–59.

Bollerslev, T., Engle, R. F. and Nelson, D. B. (1994). ARCH models. In Engle, R. F. and McFadden, D. (eds.), *The Handbook of Econometrics, Volume 4*, pp. 2959–3038: North-Holland.

Bontemps, C. and Mizon, G. E. (1996). Congruence and encompassing. Economics department, mimeo, European University Institute.

Boucelham, J. and Teräsvirta, T. (1990). Use of preliminary values in forecasting industrial production. *International Journal of Forecasting*, **6**, 463–8.

Box, G. E. P. and Jenkins, G. M. (1976). *Time Series Analysis, Forecasting and Control*. San Francisco: Holden-Day. First published, 1970.

Breusch, T. S. (1978). Testing for autocorrelation in dynamic linear models. *Australian Economic Papers*, **17**, 334–355.

Burns, T. (1986). The interpretation and use of economic predictions. In *Proceedings of the Royal Society*, No. A407, pp. 103–125.

Campos, J. (1992). Confidence intervals for linear combinations of forecasts from dynamic econometric models. *Journal of Policy Modeling*, **14**, 535–560.

Campos, J., Ericsson, N. R. and Hendry, D. F. (1996). Cointegration tests in the presence of structural breaks. *Journal of Econometrics*, **70**, 187–220.

Carruth, A. and Henley, A. (1990). Can existing consumption functions forecast consumer spending in the late 1980s?. *Oxford Bulletin of Economics and Statistics*, **52**, 211–222.

Chatfield, C. (1993). Calculating interval forecasts. *Journal of Business and Economic Statistics*, **11**, 121–135.

Chong, Y. Y. and Hendry, D. F. (1986). Econometric evaluation of linear macroeconomic models. *Review of Economic Studies*, **53**, 671–690. Reprinted in Granger, C. W. J. (ed.) (1990), *op cit*.

Chow, G. C. (1960). Tests of equality between sets of coefficients in two linear regressions. *Econometrica*, **28**, 591–605.

Chu, C.-S., Stinchcombe, M. and White, H. (1996). Monitoring structural change. *Econometrica*, **64**, 1045–1065.

Clements, M. P. and Hendry, D. F. (1993). On the limitations of comparing mean squared forecast errors. *Journal of Forecasting*, **12**, 617–637. With discussion.

Clements, M. P. and Hendry, D. F. (1994). Towards a theory of economic forecasting. In Hargreaves, C. (ed.) (1994), 9–52, *op cit*.

Clements, M. P. and Hendry, D. F. (1995a). Forecasting in cointegrated systems. *Journal of Applied Econometrics*, **10**, 127–146.

Clements, M. P. and Hendry, D. F. (1995b). Macro-economic forecasting and modelling. *Economic Journal*, **105**, 1001–1013.

Clements, M. P. and Hendry, D. F. (1996a). Forecasting in macro-economics. In Cox, D. R., Hinkley, D. V. and Barndorff-Nielsen, O. E. (eds.), (1996), 101–141, *op cit*.

Clements, M. P. and Hendry, D. F. (1996b). Intercept corrections and structural change. *Journal of Applied Econometrics*, **11**, 475–494.

Clements, M. P. and Hendry, D. F. (1996c). Multi-step estimation for forecasting. *Oxford Bulletin of Economics and Statistics*, **58**, 657–684.

Clements, M. P. and Hendry, D. F. (1997). An empirical study of seasonal unit roots in forecasting. *International Journal of Forecasting*, **13**, 341–356.

Clements, M. P. and Hendry, D. F. (1998a). Forecasting economic processes. *International Journal of Forecasting*, **14**, 111–131.

Clements, M. P. and Hendry, D. F. (1998b). *Forecasting Economic Time Series*. Cambridge: Cambridge University Press. The Marshall Lectures on Economic Forecasting.

Clements, M. P. and Hendry, D. F. (1998c). Forecasting with difference stationary and trend stationary models. Mimeo, Department of Economics, University of Warwick.

Clements, M. P. and Hendry, D. F. (1998d). On winning forecasting competitions in economics. *Spanish Economic Review*. Forthcoming.

Clements, M. P. and Krolzig, H.-M. (1998). A comparison of the forecast performance of Markov-switching and threshold autoregressive models of US GNP. *Econometrics Journal*, **1**, C47–75.

Clements, M. P. and Mizon, G. E. (1991). Empirical analysis of macroeconomic time series: VAR and structural models. *European Economic Review*, **35**, 887–932.

Clements, M. P. and Smith, J. (1997). The performance of alternative forecasting methods for SETAR models. *International Journal of Forecasting*, **13**, 463–475.

Clements, M. P. and Smith, J. (1998a). Evaluating the forecast densities of linear and non-linear models: Applications to output growth and unemployment. mimeo, Department of Economics, University of Warwick.

Clements, M. P. and Smith, J. (1999). A Monte Carlo study of the forecasting performance of empirical SETAR models. *Journal of Applied Econometrics*, **14**, 123–141.

Cook, S. (1995). Treasury economic forecasting. mimeo, Institute of Economics and Statistics, University of Oxford.

Cooper, J. P. and Nelson, C. R. (1975). The ex ante prediction performance of the St. Louis and FRB-MIT-PENN econometric models and some results on composite predictors. *Journal of Money, Credit, and Banking*, **7**, 1–32.

Corsi, P., Pollock, R. E. and Prakken, J. C. (1982). The Chow test in the presence of serially correlated errors. In Chow, G. C. and Corsi, P. (eds.), *Evaluating the Reliability of Macro-Economic Models*. New York: John Wiley.

Cox, D. R. and Miller, H. D. (1965). *The Theory of Stochastic Processes*: Chapman and Hall.

Cox, D. R., Hinkley, D. V. and Barndorff-Nielsen, O. E. (eds.)(1996). *Time Series Models: In econometrics, finance and other fields*. London: Chapman and Hall.

Davidson, J. E. H., Hendry, D. F., Srba, F. and Yeo, J. S. (1978). Econometric modelling of the aggregate time-series relationship between consumers' expenditure and income in the United Kingdom. *Economic Journal*, **88**, 661–692.

Reprinted in Hendry, D. F. (1993), *op. cit.*

De Gooijer, J. G. and De Bruin, P. (1997). On SETAR forecasting. *Statistics and Probability Letters*, **37**, 7–14.

De Gooijer, J. G. and Kumar, K. (1992). Some recent developments in non-linear time series modelling, testing and forecasting. *International Journal of Forecasting*, **8**, 135–156.

Dempster, A. P., Laird, N. M. and Rubin, D. B. (1977). Maximum likelihood estimation from incomplete data via the EM algorithm. *Journal of the Royal Statistical Society*, **39**, 1–38. Series B.

Diebold, F. X., Gunther, T. A. and Tay, A. S. (1998). Evaluating density forecasts: With applications to financial risk management. *International Economic Review*, **39**, 863–883.

Diebold, F. X., Lee, J. H. and Weinbach, G. C. (1994). Regime switching with time-varying transition probabilities. In Hargreaves, C. (ed.)(1994), 283–302, *op cit*.

Diebold, F. X. and Mariano, R. S. (1995). Comparing predictive accuracy. *Journal of Business and Economic Statistics*, **13**, 253–263.

Diebold, F. X., Rudebusch, G. D. and Sichel, D. E. (1993). Further evidence on business cycle duration dependence. In Stock, J. and Watson, M. (eds.), *Business Cycles, Indicators, and Forecasting*, pp. 255–280: Chicago: University of Chicago Press and NBER.

Doan, T., Litterman, R. and Sims, C. A. (1984). Forecasting and conditional projection using realistic prior distributions. *Econometric Reviews*, **3**, 1–100.

Doornik, J. A. (1995). Testing vector autocorrelation and heteroscedasticity in dynamic models. Mimeo, Nuffield College.

Doornik, J. A. (1996). *Object-Oriented Matrix Programming using Ox*. London: International Thomson Business Press and Oxford: http://www.nuff.ox.ac.uk/Users/Doornik/.

Doornik, J. A. and Hansen, H. (1994). A practical test for univariate and multivariate normality. Discussion paper, Nuffield College.

Doornik, J. A. and Hendry, D. F. (1994). *PcGive 8: An Interactive Econometric Modelling System*. London: International Thomson Publishing, and Belmont, CA: Duxbury Press.

Doornik, J. A. and Hendry, D. F. (1996). *GiveWin: An Interactive Empirical Modelling Program.* London: Timberlake Consultants Press.

Doornik, J. A. and Hendry, D. F. (1997). *Modelling Dynamic Systems using PcFiml 9 for Windows.* London: Timberlake Consultants Press.

Doornik, J. A. and Hendry, D. F. (1998). Monte Carlo simulation using PcNaive for Windows. Unpublished typescript, Nuffield College, University of Oxford.

Doornik, J. A., Hendry, D. F. and Nielsen, B. (1999). Inference in cointegrated models: UK M1 revisited. *Journal of Economic Surveys,* **12**, 533–572.

Duesenberry, J. S. (1949). *Income, Saving and the Theory of Consumer Behaviour.* Cambridge: Harvard University Press.

Durbin, J. and Watson, G. S. (1950). Testing for serial correlation in least squares regression I. *Biometrika,* **37**, 409–428.

Durland, J. M. and McCurdy, T. H. (1994). Duration dependent transitions in a Markov model of U.S. GNP growth. *Journal of Business and Economic Statistics,* **12**, 279–288.

Eitrheim, Ø., Husebø, T. A. and Nymoen, R. (1997). Error-correction versus differencing in macroeconometric forecasting. Mimeo, Department of Economics, University of Oslo.

Emerson, R. A. and Hendry, D. F. (1996). An evaluation of forecasting using leading indicators. *Journal of Forecasting,* **15**, 271–91.

Engle, R. F. (1982). Autoregressive conditional heteroscedasticity, with estimates of the variance of United Kingdom inflations. *Econometrica,* **50**, 987–1007.

Engle, R. F. and Granger, C. W. J. (1987). Cointegration and error correction: Representation, estimation and testing. *Econometrica,* **55**, 251–276.

Engle, R. F. and Hendry, D. F. (1993). Testing super exogeneity and invariance in regression models. *Journal of Econometrics,* **56**, 119–139. Reprinted in Ericsson, N. R. and Irons, J. S. (eds.) *Testing Exogeneity,* Oxford: Oxford University Press, 1994.

Engle, R. F., Hendry, D. F. and Richard, J.-F. (1983). Exogeneity. *Econometrica,* **51**, 277–304. Reprinted in Hendry, D. F., *op. cit.*; and in Ericsson, N. R. and Irons, J. S. *op. cit.*

Ericsson, N. R., Hendry, D. F. and Mizon, G. E. (1998a). Exogeneity, cointegration and economic policy analysis. *Journal of Business and Economic Statistics*, **16**, 370–387.

Ericsson, N. R., Hendry, D. F. and Prestwich, K. M. (1998b). The demand for broad money in the United Kingdom, 1878–1993. *Scandinavian Journal of Economics*, **100**, 289–324.

Ericsson, N. R. and Irons, J. S. (1995). The Lucas critique in practice: Theory without measurement. In Hoover, K. D. (ed.), *Macroeconometrics: Developments, Tensions and Prospects*. Dordrecht: Kluwer Academic Press.

Ericsson, N. R. and Marquez, J. R. (1989). Exact and approximate multi-period mean-square forecast errors for dynamic econometric models. International finance discussion paper 348, Federal Reserve Board.

Ericsson, N. R. and Marquez, J. R. (1996). A framework for simulated and analytical properties of economic forecasts. In Mariano, R., Weeks, M. and Schuermann, T. (eds.), *Simulation-based Inference in Econometrics: Methods and Applications*: Cambridge: Cambridge University Press. Forthcoming.

Fair, R. C. (1980). Estimating the expected predictive accuracy of econometric models. *International Economic Review*, **21**, 355–378.

Fair, R. C. (1984). *Specification, Estimation, and Analysis of Macroeconometric Models*. Cambridge, MA: Harvard University Press.

Favero, C. and Hendry, D. F. (1992). Testing the Lucas critique: A review. *Econometric Reviews*, **11**, 265–306.

Filardo, A. J. (1994). Business–cycle phases and their transitional dynamics. *Journal of Business and Economic Statistics*, **12**, 299–308.

Fildes, R. A. and Makridakis, S. (1995). The impact of empirical accuracy studies on time series analysis and forecasting. *International Statistical Review*, **63**, 289–308.

Findley, D. F. (1983). On the use of multiple models for multi-period forecasting. *ASA Proc. Bus. Econ. Sec.*, 528–531.

Flemming, J. S. (1976). *Inflation*. Oxford: Oxford University Press.

Friedman, M. and Schwartz, A. J. (1982). *Monetary Trends in the United States and the United Kingdom: Their Relation to Income, Prices, and Interest Rates, 1867–1975*. Chicago: University of Chicago Press.

Frisch, R. (1934). *Statistical Confluence Analysis by means of Complete Regression Systems.* Oslo: University Institute of Economics.

Gallo, G. M. (1996). Forecast uncertainty reduction in nonlinear models. *Journal of Italian Statistical Society,* **5**, 73–98.

Ghysels, E. (1994). On the periodic structure of the business cycle. *Journal of Business and Economic Statistics,* **12**, 289–298.

Gilbert, C. L. (1986). Professor Hendry's econometric methodology. *Oxford Bulletin of Economics and Statistics,* **48**, 283–307. Reprinted in Granger, C. W. J. (ed.) (1990), *op. cit.*

Godfrey, L. G. (1978). Testing for higher order serial correlation in regression equations when the regressors include lagged dependent variables. *Econometrica,* **46**, 1303–1313.

Goldfeld, S. M. and Quandt, R. E. (1972). *Non-linear Methods in Econometrics.* Amsterdam: North-Holland.

Goldfeld, S. M. and Quandt, R. E. (1973). A Markov model for switching regressions. *Journal of Econometrics,* **1**, 3–16.

Goodwin, T. H. (1993). Business-cycle analysis with a Markov-switching model. *Journal of Business and Economic Statistics,* **11**, 331–339.

Granger, C. W. J. (1969). Investigating causal relations by econometric models and cross-spectral methods. *Econometrica,* **37**, 424–438.

Granger, C. W. J. (ed.)(1990). *Modelling Economic Series.* Oxford: Clarendon Press.

Granger, C. W. J. and Newbold, P. (1986). *Forecasting Economic Time Series,* 2nd edn. New York: Academic Press.

Granger, C. W. J. and Swanson, N. (1996). Further developments in the study of cointegrated variables. *Oxford Bulletin of Economics and Statistics,* **58**, 537–554.

Granger, C. W. J. and Teräsvirta, T. (1993). *Modelling Nonlinear Economic Relationships.* Oxford: Oxford University Press.

Guilkey, D. K. (1974). Alternative tests for a first order vector autoregressive error specification. *Journal of Econometrics,* **2**, 95–104.

Haavelmo, T. (1944). The probability approach in econometrics. *Econometrica,* **12**, 1–118. Supplement.

Hall, R. E. (1978). Stochastic implications of the life cycle-permanent income hypothesis: Evidence. *Journal of Political Economy*, **86**, 971–987.

Hamilton, J. D. (1989). A new approach to the economic analysis of nonstationary time series and the business cycle. *Econometrica*, **57**, 357–384.

Hamilton, J. D. (1993). Estimation, inference, and forecasting of time series subject to changes in regime. In Maddala, G. S., Rao, C. R. and Vinod, H. D. (eds.), *Handbook of Statistics*, Vol. 11: Amsterdam: North–Holland.

Hamilton, J. D. (1994). *Time Series Analysis.* Princeton: Princeton University Press.

Hamilton, J. D. (1990). Analysis of time series subject to changes in regime. *Journal of Econometrics*, **45**, 39–70.

Hansen, B. E. (1992a). The likelihood ratio test under nonstandard conditions: testing the Markov switching model of GNP. *Journal of Applied Econometrics*, **7**, S61–S82.

Hansen, B. E. (1992b). Testing for parameter instability in linear models. *Journal of Policy Modeling*, **14**, 517–533.

Hansen, B. E. (1996a). Erratum: The likelihood ratio test under nonstandard conditions: testing the Markov switching model of GNP. *Journal of Applied Econometrics*, **11**, 195–198.

Hansen, B. E. (1996b). Inference when a nuisance parameter is not identified under the null hypothesis. *Econometrica*, **64**, 413–430.

Hansen, H. and Johansen, S. (1992). Recursive estimation in cointegrated VAR-models. Discussion paper, Institute of Mathematical Statistics, University of Copenhagen.

Hargreaves, C. (ed.)(1994). *Non-stationary Time-series Analysis and Cointegration.* Oxford: Oxford University Press.

Harvey, A. C. (1989). *Forecasting, Structural Time Series Models and the Kalman Filter.* Cambridge: Cambridge University Press.

Harvey, A. C., McKenzie, C. R., Blake, D. P. C. and Desai, M. J. (1983). Irregular data revisions. In Zellner, A. (ed.), *Applied Time Series Analysis of Economic Data.* Washington, DC: Bureau of the Census.

Harvey, A. C. and Scott, A. (1994). Seasonality in dynamic regression models. *Economic Journal*, **104**, 1324–1345.

Harvey, A. C. and Shephard, N. G. (1992). Structural time series models. In Maddala, G. S., Rao, C. R. and Vinod, H. D. (eds.), *Handbook of Statistics*, Vol. 11. Amsterdam: North-Holland.

Harvey, D., Leybourne, S. and Newbold, P. (1997). Testing the equality of prediction mean squared errors. *International Journal of Forecasting*, **13**, 281–291.

Hendry, D. F. (1971). Maximum likelihood estimation of systems of simultaneous regression equations with errors generated by a vector autoregressive process. *International Economic Review*, **12**, 257–272. Correction in **15**, p.260.

Hendry, D. F. (1974). Stochastic specification in an aggregate demand model of the United Kingdom. *Econometrica*, **42**, 559–578. Reprinted in Hendry, D. F. (1993), *op. cit.*

Hendry, D. F. (1979a). The behaviour of inconsistent instrumental variables estimators in dynamic systems with autocorrelated errors. *Journal of Econometrics*, **9**, 295–314.

Hendry, D. F. (1979b). Predictive failure and econometric modelling in macroeconomics: The transactions demand for money. In Ormerod, P. (ed.), *Economic Modelling*, pp. 217–242. London: Heinemann. Reprinted in Hendry, D. F. (1993), *op. cit.*

Hendry, D. F. (1984). Econometric modelling of house prices in the United Kingdom. in Hendry and Wallis (1984), pp. 135–172.

Hendry, D. F. (1988). The encompassing implications of feedback versus feedforward mechanisms in econometrics. *Oxford Economic Papers*, **40**, 132–149.

Hendry, D. F. (1993). *Econometrics: Alchemy or Science?*. Oxford: Blackwell Publishers.

Hendry, D. F. (1994). HUS revisited. *Oxford Review of Economic Policy*, **10**, 86–106.

Hendry, D. F. (1995a). *Dynamic Econometrics*. Oxford: Oxford University Press.

Hendry, D. F. (1995b). Econometrics and business cycle empirics. *Economic Journal*, **105**, 1622–1636.

Hendry, D. F. (1996). On the constancy of time-series econometric equations. *Economic and Social Review*, **27**, 401–422.

Hendry, D. F. (1997). The econometrics of macro-economic forecasting. *Economic Journal*, **107**, 1330–1357.

Hendry, D. F. and Clements, M. P. (1994a). Can econometrics improve economic forecasting?. *Swiss Journal of Economics and Statistics*, **130**, 267–298.

Hendry, D. F. and Clements, M. P. (1994b). On a theory of intercept corrections in macro-economic forecasting. In Holly, S. (ed.), *Money, Inflation and Employment: Essays in Honour of James Ball*, pp. 160–182. Aldershot: Edward Elgar.

Hendry, D. F. and Clements, M. P. (1998). Economic forecasting in the face of structural breaks. In Holly, S. and Weale, M. (eds.), *Econometric Modelling: Techniques and Applications*. Cambridge: Cambridge University Press. Forthcoming.

Hendry, D. F. and Doornik, J. A. (1994). Modelling linear dynamic econometric systems. *Scottish Journal of Political Economy*, **41**, 1–33.

Hendry, D. F. and Doornik, J. A. (1996). *Empirical Econometric Modelling using PcGive for Windows*. London: Timberlake Consultants Press.

Hendry, D. F. and Doornik, J. A. (1997). The implications for econometric modelling of forecast failure. *Scottish Journal of Political Economy*, **44**, 437–461.

Hendry, D. F. and Ericsson, N. R. (1991). Modeling the demand for narrow money in the United Kingdom and the United States. *European Economic Review*, **35**, 833–886.

Hendry, D. F., Krolzig, H.-M. and Sensier, M. (1997). Testing for shifts in equilibrium means. Mimeo, Oxford Institute of Economics and Statistics, Oxford.

Hendry, D. F. and Mizon, G. E. (1978). Serial correlation as a convenient simplification, not a nuisance: A comment on a study of the demand for money by the Bank of England. *Economic Journal*, **88**, 549–563. Reprinted in Hendry, D. F. (1993), *op. cit.*

Hendry, D. F. and Mizon, G. E. (1993). Evaluating dynamic econometric models by encompassing the VAR. In Phillips, P. C. B. (ed.), *Models, Methods and Applications of Econometrics*, pp. 272–300. Oxford: Basil Blackwell.

Hendry, D. F. and Mizon, G. E. (1998a). Exogeneity, causality, and co-breaking in economic policy analysis of a small econometric model of money in the UK. *Empirical Economics*, **23**, 267–294.

Hendry, D. F. and Mizon, G. E. (1998b). The influence of A. W. H. Phillips on econometrics. In Leeson, R. (ed.), *A. W. H. Phillips: Collected Works in Contemporary Perspective*. Cambridge: Cambridge University Press. Forthcoming.

Hendry, D. F. and Mizon, G. E. (1998c). On selecting policy analysis models by forecast accuracy. In Atkinson, A. B. and Stern, N. H. (eds.), *Festschrift in Honour of Michio Morishima*. STICERD, London School of Economics. Forthcoming.

Hendry, D. F. and Mizon, G. E. (1999). The pervasiveness of Granger causality in econometrics. In Engle, R. F. and White, H. (eds.), *Festschrift for C.W.J. Granger*. Oxford: Oxford University Press. Forthcoming.

Hendry, D. F. and Morgan, M. S. (1995). *The Foundations of Econometric Analysis*. Cambridge: Cambridge University Press.

Hendry, D. F. and Neale, A. J. (1991). A Monte Carlo study of the effects of structural breaks on tests for unit roots. In Hackl, P. and Westlund, A. H. (eds.), *Economic Structural Change, Analysis and Forecasting*, pp. 95–119. Berlin: Springer-Verlag.

Hendry, D. F. and Trivedi, P. K. (1972). Maximum likelihood estimation of difference equations with moving-average errors: A simulation study. *Review of Economic Studies*, **32**, 117–145.

Hendry, D. F. and von Ungern-Sternberg, T. (1981). Liquidity and inflation effects on consumers' expenditure. In Deaton, A. S. (ed.), *Essays in the Theory and Measurement of Consumers' Behaviour*, pp. 237–261. Cambridge: Cambridge University Press. Reprinted in Hendry, D. F. (1993), *op. cit.*

Hendry, D. F. and Wallis, K. F. (eds.)(1984). *Econometrics and Quantitative Economics*. Oxford: Basil Blackwell.

Henriksson, R. D. and Merton, R. C. (1981). On market timing and investment performance. II Statistical procedures for evaluating forecast skills. *Journal of Business*, **54**, 513–533.

Hess, G. D., Jones, C. S. and Porter, R. D. (1997). The predictive failure of the Baba, Hendry and Starr model of M1. forthcoming, Journal of Economics and Business.

Hoogstrate, A. J., Palm, F. C. and Pfann, G. A. (1996). To pool or not to pool: Forecasting international output growth rates. Research Memorandum 96/025, Meteor, University of Limburg, Maastricht.

Hoover, K. D. and Perez, S. J. (1996). Data mining reconsidered: Encompassing and the general-to-specific approach to specification search. Mimeo, Economics department, University of California, Davis.

Hoque, A., Magnus, J. R. and Pesaran, B. (1988). The exact multi-period mean-square forecast error for the first-order autoregressive model. *Journal of Econometrics*, **39**, 327–346.

Howrey, E. P. (1978). The use of preliminary data in econometric forecasting. *Review of Economics and Statistics*, **60**, 193–200.

Hylleberg, S. and Mizon, G. E. (1989). Cointegration and error correction mechanisms. *Economic Journal*, **99**, 113–125. Supplement.

Johansen, S. (1988). Statistical analysis of cointegration vectors. *Journal of Economic Dynamics and Control*, **12**, 231–254.

Johansen, S. (1992). A representation of vector autoregressive processes integrated of order 2. *Econometric Theory*, **8**, 188–202.

Johansen, S. (1994). The role of the constant and linear terms in cointegration analysis of nonstationary variables. *Econometric Reviews*, **13**, 205–229.

Johansen, S. (1995a). *Likelihood-based Inference in Cointegrated Vector Autoregressive Models*. Oxford: Oxford University Press.

Johansen, S. (1995b). *Likelihood based Inference on Cointegration in the Vector Autoregressive Model*. Oxford: Oxford University Press.

Johansen, S. and Juselius, K. (1990). Maximum likelihood estimation and inference on cointegration – With application to the demand for money. *Oxford Bulletin of Economics and Statistics*, **52**, 169–210.

Kähler, J. and Marnet, V. (1994). Markov-switching models for exchange rate dynamics and the pricing of foreign-currency options. In Kähler, J. and Kugler, P. (eds.), *Econometric Analysis of Financial Markets*: Heidelberg: Physica Verlag.

Kalman, R. E. (1960). A new approach to linear filtering and prediction problems. *Journal of Basic Engineering*, **82**, 35–45.

Kennedy, P. (1985). *A Guide to Econometrics*. Oxford: Basil Blackwell. Second Edition.

Keynes, J. M. (1939). Professor Tinbergen's method. *Economic Journal*, **44**, 558–568.

Kim, C. J. (1994). Dynamic linear models with Markov-switching. *Journal of Econometrics*, **60**, 1–22.

Kiviet, J. F. (1986). On the rigor of some mis-specification tests for modelling dynamic relationships. *Review of Economic Studies*, **53**, 241–261.

Klein, L. R. (1971). *An Essay on the Theory of Economic Prediction.* Chicago: Markham Publishing Company.

Krolzig, H.-M. (1997). *Markov Switching Vector Autoregressions: Modelling, Statistical Inference and Application to Business Cycle Analysis*: Lecture Notes in Economics and Mathematical Systems, 454. Springer-Verlag, Berlin.

Krolzig, H.-M. and Lütkepohl, H. (1995). Konjunkturanalyse mit Markov–Regimewechselmodellen. In Oppenländer, K. H. (ed.), *Konjunkturindikatoren. Fakten, Analysen, Verwendung*, pp. 177–196: Oldenbourg: München Wien.

Kuhn, T. (1962). *The Structure of Scientific Revolutions.* Chicago: University of Chicago Press.

Lahiri, K. and Wang, J. G. (1994). Predicting cyclical turning points with leading index in a Markov switching model. *Journal of Forecasting*, **13**, 245–263.

Lam, P.-S. (1990). The Hamilton model with a general autoregressive component. Estimation and comparison with other models of economic time series. *Journal of Monetary Economics*, **26**, 409–432.

Leamer, E. E. (1978). *Specification Searches. Ad-Hoc Inference with Non-Experimental Data.* New York: John Wiley.

Lucas, R. E. (1976). Econometric policy evaluation: A critique. In Brunner, K. and Meltzer, A. (eds.), *The Phillips Curve and Labor Markets*, Vol. 1 of *Carnegie-Rochester Conferences on Public Policy*, pp. 19–46. Amsterdam: North-Holland Publishing Company.

Maasoumi, E. (1978). A modified Stein-like estimator for the reduced form coefficients of simultaneous equations. *Econometrica*, **46**, 695–704.

Marget, A. W. (1929). Morgenstern on the methodology of economic forecasting. *Journal of Political Economy*, **37**, 312–339.

Marquez, J. R. and Ericsson, N. R. (1993). Evaluating the predictive performance of trade-account models. In Bryant, R., Hooper, P. and Mann, C. L. (eds.), *Evaluating Policy Regimes: New Research in Empirical Macroeconomics*. Washington, DC: Brookings Institution.

McCabe, B. and Tremayne, A. R. (1993). *Elements of Modern Asymptotic Theory with Statistical Applications*. Manchester: Manchester University Press.

McCulloch, R. E. and Tsay, R. S. (1994). Bayesian analysis of autoregressive time series via the Gibbs sampler. *Journal of Time Series Analysis*, **15**, 235–250.

Miller, P. J. (1978). Forecasting with econometric methods: A comment. *Journal of Business*, **51**, 579–586.

Mizon, G. E. (1995). Progressive modelling of macroeconomic time series: the LSE methodology. In Hoover, K. D. (ed.), *Macroeconometrics: Developments, Tensions and Prospects*, pp. 107–169. Dordrecht: Kluwer Academic Press.

Montgomery, A. L., Zarnowitz, V., Tsay, R. S. and Tiao, G. C. (1998). Forecasting the U.S. unemployment rate. *Journal of the American Statistical Association*. Forthcoming.

Morgenstern, O. (1928). *Wirtschaftsprognose: eine Untersuchung ihrer Voraussetzungen und Möglichkeiten*. Vienna: Julius Springer.

Muellbauer, J. N. J. (1994). The assessment: Consumer expenditure. *Oxford Review of Economic Policy*, **10**, 1–41.

Muellbauer, J. N. J. and Murphy, A. (1989). *Why has UK Personal Saving Collapsed?* London: Credit Suisse First Boston.

Muth, J. F. (1961). Rational expectations and the theory of price movements. *Econometrica*, **29**, 315–335.

Pain, N. and Britton, A. (1992). The recent experience of economic forecasting in Britain: some lessons from National Institute forecasts. Discussion paper (new series) 20, National Institute.

Perron, P. (1989). The Great Crash, the oil price shock and the unit root hypothesis. *Econometrica*, **57**, 1361–1401.

Persons, W. M. (1924). *The Problem of Business Forecasting*. No. 6 in Pollak Foundation for Economic Research Publications. London: Pitman.

Pesaran, M. H. and Timmermann, A. (1992). A simple nonparametric test of predictive performance. *Journal of Business and Econometic Statistics*, **10**, 461–465.

Phillips, A. W. H. (1954). Stabilization policy in a closed economy. *Economic Journal*, **64**, 290–333.

Phillips, A. W. H. (1957). Stabilization policy and the time form of lagged response. *Economic Journal*, **67**, 265–277.

Phillips, P. C. B. (1994). Bayes models and forecasts of Australian macroeconomic time series. In Hargreaves, C. (ed.), (1994), 52–87, *op cit*.

Phillips, K. (1991). A two-country model of stochastic output with changes in regime. *Journal of International Economics*, **31**, 121–142.

Pole, A., West, M. and Harrison, P. J. (1994). *Applied Bayesian Forecasting and Time Series Analysis*. London: Chapman and Hall.

Potter, S. (1995). A nonlinear approach to U.S. GNP. *Journal of Applied Econometrics*, **10**, 109–125.

Rahiala, M. and Teräsvirta, T. (1993). Business survey data in forecasting the output of Swedish and Finnish metal and engineering industries. *Journal of Forecasting*, **12**, 255–71.

Ramsey, J. B. (1969). Tests for specification errors in classical linear least squares regression analysis. *Journal of the Royal Statistical Society B*, **31**, 350–371.

Rappoport, P. and Reichlin, L. (1989). Segmented trends and non-stationary time series. *Economic Journal*, **99**, 168–177.

Richard, J.-F. and Zhang, W. (1996). Econometric modelling of UK house prices using accelerated importance sampling. *Oxford Bulletin of Economics and Statistics*, **58**, 601–613.

Rothman, P. (1998). Forecasting asymmetric unemployment rates. *The Review of Economics and Statistics*, **80**, 164–168.

Salkever, D. S. (1976). The use of dummy variables to compute predictions, prediction errors and confidence intervals. *Journal of Econometrics*, **4**, 393–397.

Sampson, M. (1991). The effect of parameter uncertainty on forecast variances and confidence intervals for unit root and trend stationary time-series models. *Journal of Applied Econometrics*, **6**, 67–76.

Sargan, J. D. (1964a). Three-stage least-squares and full maximum likelihood estimates. *Econometrica*, **32**, 77–81. Reprinted in Sargan J. D. (1988), 118–123, *op cit*.

Sargan, J. D. (1964b). Wages and prices in the United Kingdom: A study in econometric methodology (with discussion). In Hart, P. E., Mills, G. and Whitaker, J. K. (eds.), *Econometric Analysis for National Economic Planning*, Vol. 16 of *Colston Papers*, pp. 25–63. London: Butterworth Co. Reprinted in Hendry D. F. and Wallis K. F. (eds.) (1984), 275–314, *op cit*, and in Sargan J. D. (1988), 124–169, *op cit*.

Sargan, J. D. (1980). Some tests of dynamic specification for a single equation. *Econometrica*, **48**, 879–897. Reprinted in Sargan J. D. (1988), 191–212, *op cit*.

Sargan, J. D. (1982). On Monte Carlo estimates of moments that are infinite. In Basmann, R. L. and Rhodes, G. F. (eds.), *Advances in Econometrics: A Research Annual*, Vol. 1, pp. 267–299. Greenwich, Connecticut: Jai Press Inc.

Sargan, J. D. (1988). *Contributions to Econometrics*, Vol. 1–2. Cambridge: Cambridge University Press. Edited by E. Maasoumi.

Schmidt, P. (1974). The asymptotic distribution of forecasts in the dynamic simulation of an econometric model. *Econometrica*, **42**, 303–309.

Schmidt, P. (1977). Some small sample evidence on the distribution of dynamic simulation forecasts. *Econometrica*, **45**, 97–105.

Schnader, M. H. and Stekler, H. O. (1990). Evaluating predictions of change. *Journal of Business*, **63**, 99–107.

Shephard, N. G. (1996). Statistical aspects of ARCH and stochastic volatility. In Cox, D. R., Hinkley, D. V. and Barndorff-Nielsen, O. E. (eds.), (1996), 1–67, *op cit*.

Sims, C. A. (1980). Macroeconomics and reality. *Econometrica*, **48**, 1–48. Reprinted in Granger, C. W. J. (ed.), (1990), *op cit*.

Spanos, A. (1986). *Statistical Foundations of Econometric Modelling*. Cambridge: Cambridge University Press.

Stekler, H. O. (1994). Are economic forecasts valuable?. *Journal of Forecasting*, **13**, 495–505.

Stock, J. H. (1996). VAR, error correction and pre-test forecasts at long horizons. *Oxford Bulletin of Economics and Statistics*, **58**, 685–701.

Stock, J. H. and Watson, M. W. (1996). Evidence on structural instability in macroeconomic time series relations. *Journal of Business and Economic Statistics*, **14**, 11–30.

Stock, J. H. and Watson, M. W. (1998). A comparison of linear and nonlinear univariate models for forecasting macroeconomic time series. Nber working paper no. 6607, NBER.

Teräsvirta, T. and Anderson, H. M. (1992). Characterizing nonlinearities in business cycles using smooth transition autoregressive models. *Journal of Applied Econometrics*, **7**, 119–139.

Theil, H. (1961). *Economic Forecasts and Policy*, 2nd edn. Amsterdam: North-Holland Publishing Company.

Tiao, G. C. and Tsay, R. S. (1994). Some advances in non-linear and adaptive modelling in time-series. *Journal of Forecasting*, **13**, 109–131.

Todd, R. M. (1990). Improving economic forecasts with Bayesian vector autoregression. In Granger, C. W. J. (ed.), *Modelling Economic Series*, Ch. 10. Oxford: Clarendon Press.

Tong, H. (1978). On a threshold model. In Chen, C. H. (ed.), *Pattern Recognition and Signal Processing*, pp. 101–141. Amsterdam: Sijhoff and Noordoff.

Tong, H. (1983). *Threshold Models in Non-Linear Time Series Analysis*: Springer-Verlag, New York.

Tong, H. (1995). *Non-linear Time Series. A Dynamical System Approach*. Oxford: Clarendon Press. First published 1990.

Tong, H. and Lim, K. S. (1980). Threshold autoregression, limit cycles and cyclical data. *Journal of The Royal Statistical Society*, **B 42**, 245–292.

Turner, D. S. (1990). The role of judgement in macroeconomic forecasting. *Journal of Forecasting*, **9**, 315–345.

Wallis, K. F. (1989). Macroeconomic forecasting: A survey. *Economic Journal*, **99**, 28–61.

Wallis, K. F., Andrews, M. J., Bell, D. N. F., Fisher, P. G. and Whitley, J. D. (1984). *Models of the UK Economy, A Review by the ESRC Macroeconomic Modelling Bureau*. Oxford: Oxford University Press.

Wallis, K. F., Andrews, M. J., Bell, D. N. F., Fisher, P. G. and Whitley, J. D. (1985). *Models of the UK Economy, A Second Review by the ESRC Macroeconomic Modelling Bureau*. Oxford: Oxford University Press.

Wallis, K. F., Andrews, M. J., Fisher, P. G., Longbottom, J. and Whitley, J. D. (1986). *Models of the UK Economy: A Third Review by the ESRC Macroeconomic Modelling Bureau*. Oxford: Oxford University Press.

Wallis, K. F., Fisher, P. G., Longbottom, J., Turner, D. S. and Whitley, J. D. (1987). *Models of the UK Economy: A Fourth Review by the ESRC Macroeconomic Modelling Bureau*. Oxford: Oxford University Press.

Wallis, K. F. and Whitley, J. D. (1991). Sources of error in forecasts and expectations: U.K. economic models 1984–8. *Journal of Forecasting*, **10**, 231–253.

Weiss, A. A. (1991). Multi-step estimation and forecasting in dynamic models. *Journal of Econometrics*, **48**, 135–149.

West, K. D. (1988). Asymptotic normality when regressors have a unit root. *Econometrica*, **56**, 1397–1417.

West, M. and Harrison, P. J. (1989). *Bayesian Forecasting and Dynamic Models*. New York: Springer Verlag.

White, H. (1980). A heteroskedastic-consistent covariance matrix estimator and a direct test for heteroskedasticity. *Econometrica*, **48**, 817–838.

Wold, H. O. A. (1938). *A Study in The Analysis of Stationary Time Series*. Stockholm: Almqvist and Wicksell.

Wold, H. O. A. and Juréen, L. (1953). *Demand Analysis: A Study in Econometrics*, 2nd edn. New York: John Wiley.

Glossary

$\boldsymbol{\alpha}$	$n \times r$ feedback matrix in VEqCM
$\boldsymbol{\beta}$	$n \times r$ cointegration matrix
$\boldsymbol{\gamma}$	$n \times 1$ vector of growth parameters $(\gamma_1 \dots \gamma_n)$
$\Delta_q \mathbf{x}_t$	q-period time difference of $\mathbf{x}_t$, $\mathbf{x}_t - \mathbf{x}_{t-q}$
$\Delta^d \mathbf{x}_t$	d^{th}-order time difference of $\mathbf{x}_t$
ϵ_t	stochastic error (usually white noise)
λ_i	i^{th} eigenvalue
$\boldsymbol{\Lambda}$	$r \times r$ dynamic matrix of cointegration relations
$\boldsymbol{\mu}$	$r \times 1$ equilibrium mean
ν_t	innovation, error
$\boldsymbol{\theta} \in \Theta$	parameter vector $(\theta_1 \dots \theta_k)'$, an element in a parameter space Θ
$\boldsymbol{\theta}_p$	population parameter vector
π	ratio of circumference to diameter in a circle
$\boldsymbol{\pi}$	$n \times n$ long-run matrix
$\boldsymbol{\Pi}$	system reduced-form matrix
σ_u^2	variance of $\{u_t\}$
$\widehat{\sigma}$	estimated standard deviation
$\sigma(\mathbf{X}_{t-1})$	sigma field generated by $\mathbf{X}_{t-1}$
$\sum$	summation over implicit range (text)
$\sum_{t=1}^{T}$	sum over range shown
$\boldsymbol{\Sigma}$	error variance matrix with elements $\{\sigma_{ij}\}$
χ_k^2	chi-square distribution with k degrees of freedom
$\chi_k^2(\psi^2)$	$\chi^2(k)$ with non-centrality ψ^2
$\boldsymbol{\Omega}$	error variance matrix with elements (ω_{ij})
$\{\cdot\}$	stochastic process

$\forall t$	for all admissible values of t
$\in$	element of a set
$\notin$	not an element of the set
$\subset$	strict subset of
$\subseteq$	subset of
$\times$	product of two spaces or numbers
$\otimes$	Kronecker product $\mathbf{A} \otimes \mathbf{B} = (b_{ij}\mathbf{A})$ $((m \cdot n) \times (q \cdot s)$ yielding an $mq \cdot ns$ matrix)
$(\cdot)^v$	vectoring operator, stacks columns of a matrix in a vector
$\boldsymbol{\Upsilon}$	lagged variable matrix
$\lvert \cdot \rvert$	absolute value
$\lvert \mathbf{A} \rvert$	determinant of a matrix (depending on context)
$'$	transpose of a matrix
$\int_0^1$	integral over range shown
$\simeq$	approximately equal to
$\Rightarrow$	weak convergence in probability measure
$\rightarrow$	tends to
$\sim$	is distributed as
$\widetilde{a}$	is asymptotically distributed as
$\widetilde{app}$	is approximately distributed as
$\widehat{\ }$	an estimator or forecast depending on context
$\widetilde{\ }$	an alternative estimator or forecast
$\bar{\ }$	sample mean or average forecast
$\mathsf{C}[y, z]$	covariance of y with z
$\mathsf{D}_{\mathsf{X}}(\mathbf{X}; \boldsymbol{\theta})$	joint distribution of $\mathbf{X}$ with parameter $\boldsymbol{\theta} \in \Theta$
$\mathsf{D}_{\mathsf{x}}(\mathbf{x}_t; \boldsymbol{\theta})$	distribution of $\mathbf{x}_t$ with parameter $\boldsymbol{\theta}$
$\mathsf{D}_{\mathsf{y}\lvert\mathsf{z}}(y_t \lvert z_t, \cdot)$	conditional distribution of y_t given z_t
$\mathsf{D}_{\mathsf{x}}(\mathbf{x}_t \lvert \mathcal{I}_{t-1}, \cdot)$	sequential distribution of $\mathbf{x}_t$ given $\mathcal{I}_{t-1}$
$\mathsf{E}[Y]$	expectation of the random variable Y
$\mathsf{E}[y_t \lvert \mathbf{z}_t]$	conditional expectation of the random variable y_t given $\mathbf{z}_t$
$\mathsf{F}^k_m)$	F-distribution with k, m degrees of freedom
H	number of observations in the forecast period
H_0	null hypothesis
$\mathbf{I}_k$	unit matrix of dimension k
$\mathsf{I}(d)$	integrated of order d
$\mathcal{I}_{t-1}$	previous information
$\mathsf{IID}[\mu, \sigma^2_\epsilon]$	independent, identically distributed with mean μ and variance σ^2_ϵ

$\mathsf{IN}[\mu, \sigma^2]$
: independent normal distribution with mean μ and variance σ^2

$\mathsf{IN}_\mathsf{k}[\boldsymbol{\mu}, \boldsymbol{\Sigma}]$
: k-dimensional multivariate independent normal distribution with mean $\boldsymbol{\mu}$ and variance matrix $\boldsymbol{\Sigma}$

L — lag operator $L^k x_t = x_{t-k}$

$\lim_{T\to\infty}$
: limit as T tends to infinity

$\mathsf{N}[0,1]$ — normal density function with zero mean and unit variance

$O(1)$ — at most of order unity

p — probability value

$\Pr$ — probability function

$\operatorname{plim}_{T\to\infty} Z_T$
: probability limit of the random variable Z_T

$\operatorname{rank}(\mathbf{A})$
: rank of $\mathbf{A}$

R^2 — squared multiple correlation

$\mathbb{R}^k$ — k-dimensional real space

$\mathsf{t}_k(\psi)$ — Student's t-distribution with k degrees of freedom and non-centrality parameter ψ

T — number of observations in a time series

$\operatorname{tr}(\mathbf{A})$ — trace of $\mathbf{A}$

$\mathcal{T}$ — the time sequence $\{\ldots, -2, -1, 0, 1, 2, \ldots\}$

$\mathsf{V}[\mathbf{x}]$ — variance matrix of $\mathbf{x}$

$W(j)$ — continuous Wiener process for $j \in [0,1]$

$\mathbf{x}_t$ — vector random variable $(x_{1,t} \ldots x_{n,t})'$

$\mathbf{X}$ — sample observation matrix $(T \times n)$ $(\mathbf{x}_1 \ldots \mathbf{x}_n)$

$\mathbf{X}_{t-1}^1$ — $(\mathbf{x}_1 \ldots \mathbf{x}_{t-1})$

$\mathbf{X}_{t-1}$ — $(\mathbf{X}_0, \mathbf{x}_1, \ldots, \mathbf{x}_{t-2}, \mathbf{x}_{t-1}) = (\mathbf{X}_0, \mathbf{X}_{t-1}^1)$

Author Index

Subject Index